Governors State University
Library
Hours:
Monday thru Thursday 8:30 to 10:30
Friday and Saturday 8:30 to 5:00
Sunday 1:00 to 5:00 (Fall and Winter Trimester Only)

DEMCO

BOTTOM LINE MEDICINE

BOTTOM LINE MEDICINE:

A LAYMAN'S GUIDE TO EVIDENCE-BASED MEDICINE

Richard K. Stanzak

Algora Publishing
New York

© 2006 by Algora Publishing
All Rights Reserved
www.algora.com

ISBN-10: 0-87586-455-4 (soft cover)
ISBN-10: 0-87586-456-2 (hardcover)
ISBN-10: 0-87586-457-0 (ebook)

Library of Congress Cataloging-in-Publication Data —

Stanzak, Richard K.
Bottom line medicine : a layman's guide to evidence-based medicine
  / by Richard K. Stanzak.
    p. ; cm.
Includes bibliographical references and index.
ISBN 0-87586-455-4 (trade paper : alk. paper) — ISBN 0-87586-456-2
(hard cover : alk. paper)
    1. Evidence-based medicine. I. Stanzak, Richard K. II. Title. [DNLM: 1.
Evidence-Based Medicine—United States. 2. Delivery of Health Care—trends--
United States. 3. Iatrogenic Disease—United States. 4. Medical Errors—United
States. WB 102 S792b 2006]
    RA427.S73 2006
    616—dc22

                          2006010297

Cover Image: Patient laying in bed while doctor administers money in an IV
Creator: Brian Jensen

Printed in the United States

To Emily, the wife of my youth

TABLE OF CONTENTS

Foreword

This book is not written as an indictment against physicians. Its purpose is to recognize that practitioners of medicine are human and therefore prone to the same weaknesses and foibles which plague the rest of humanity. They are no more or less caring than ministers, social workers, teachers or any other profession. Yet each of these fields has had their fair share of scandals and is held accountable for their mistakes and failures while medicine, until recently, has been immune from this scrutiny.

The specialized knowledge base of medicine and the fear we each have of our own mortality elevates the practitioners of medicine to near sainthood status. Physicians often appear to hold our destinies in their hands, pronouncing who will live or die, by near miraculous methods. To their credit, they are more often right than wrong. However, they are not infallible. The failure of many physicians to openly acknowledge their shortcomings or inability to offer meaningful "cures" establishes the foundations for much of what is wrong in western medicine.

Many physicians believe they rely almost exclusively on the scientific method, this reliance is frequently without merit and physicians are often practitioners of "faith based medicine" more than they would probably care to acknowledge. Most physicians would strongly reject this accusation; they vehemently assert that all they do is backed by scientific study and has been validated in the scientific literature. The purpose of this book is to evaluate this assertion; it is my belief that the literature does not support most of the contentions of western medicine. The same peer review journals which physicians rely so heavily to support their practice of medicine more often than not repudiate these claims. My intent is to present, in a hopefully unbiased manner, the actual findings published in these journals to the layman. Knowledge of the limits and benefits of medicine should help all those in need to make choices more congruent to their belief system while facilitating dialogue between the physician and patient and/or family.

1

CHAPTER 1. THE BEST MEDICINE FOR WHOM?

IS MEDICAL SCIENCE AN OXYMORON?

> *He's the best physician that knows the worthlessness of the most medicines.*
> *Benjamin Franklin. American scientist, publisher, diplomat (1706-1790)*

"Evidence-based medicine" (EBM) is the term used to describe a recent method in the practice of medicine. Its basic assumption is that optimum patient care is possible by the use of the best current available evidence. Researchers at McMaster University in Ontario developed EBM during the early 1980s and defined EBM as "the conscientious, explicit and judicious use of current best evidence in making decisions about the care of individual patients."[1] EBM relies heavily upon randomized controlled trials; however it also utilizes statistical methods to assess study results focusing on the strength of the evidence that effects clinical decisions. Literature is reevaluated from peer review medical journals with the most notable being the *American College of Physicians Journal Club* and *Evidence-Based Medicine*. An international group of more than 10,000 scientists and epidemiologists calling themselves "The Cochrane Collaboration" are dedicated to "preparing, maintaining and disseminating systematic reviews of health care. Their basic premise is "scientifically conducted review articles (systematic overviews) represent the most efficient means by which clinicians can quickly access relevant information."[2]

EBM's goal is to improve patient care, relying only on the use of proven therapies and diagnostic tests where a substantial amount of data exists to support their use. It discourages the use of unproven therapies, and advises for

---

1. Sackett, D.L., Rosenberg, W.M. Muir Gray, J. A., Haynes, R.B., Richardson, W.S.. "Evidence based medicine: what it is and what it isn't.." British Medical Journal vol 312 1996. p. 71-72.
2. Moynihan, Ray. "Cochrane at crossroads over drug company sponsorship." BMJ vol 327 2003. p. 924-926.

further studies on therapies where the evidence is less clear. Its goal is to minimize waste while optimizing the use of limited medical funds. This should provide more effective and efficient patient care. Many western nations' medical budgets are being drained by payment for overpriced technologies of dubious benefit, the choice of which are often the result of aggressive promotional campaigns by the healthcare industry and fear of litigation. Skepticism should be advised towards many newer products and technologies whose chief appeal is that they are "newer", because newer does not necessarily equate to better.

PHYSICIAN PRESCRIBING PATTERNS

> *Doctors are men who prescribe medicines of which they know little, to cure diseases of which they know less, in human beings of whom they know nothing.*
> *Voltaire. French historian, writer (1694-1778)*

The practice of Evidence Based Medicine becomes pertinent when you consider the manner in how much of current medicine is prescribed. Most physicians are very caring and well meaning, wanting nothing but the best for their patients and rely heavily upon modern science and the pharmaceutical industry to provide them with the most current standards of practice. The burdens of an ever increasing workload combined with the constraints of managed care provides little free time for most physicians to keep current with the most recent findings in health and medicine. A tremendous amount of new literature is published weekly in medical and scientific journals describing the most recent findings in the treatment of medical conditions. The pharmaceutical industries both directly or indirectly sponsor the majority of this research. They have vast numbers of scientist and non-medical professionals who make a living by reviewing this data in the hope of finding potentially new and marketable technologies. Therefore, it would seem both prudent and efficient for physicians to rely on the sponsors of this research to provide them with a concise summary of these findings. Unfortunately, the pharmaceutical firms are not unbiased in their presentation of these findings. They invest billions of dollars each year in research and obviously wish to regain their investment and increase their profits so they can again sponsor more research, because on average, it takes 12 to 15 years and more than $500 million to bring a new medicine to the marketplace.

BETTER LIVING THROUGH CHEMISTRY?

> *When will they realize that there are too many drugs? No fewer than 150,000 preparations are now in use. About 15,000 new mixtures and dosages hit the market each year; while about 12,000 die off...We simply don't have enough diseases to go around. At the moment the most helpful contribution is the new drug to counteract the untoward effect of other new drugs.*
>
> *Dr. Walter Modell, Chairman Advisory Committee on Investigational New Drugs, Time, May 26, 1961*

Typically, drug companies test 5,000 to 10,000 new compounds for every one that is ultimately marketable.[1] Less than a third of those that reach the market generate enough profit to offset their research and development costs. Pharmaceutical firms believe maximal profits are required from marketable agents in order to offset the enormous financial drain of research and development. Unfortunately, they fail to mention that much of the profit from newly developed drugs is actually used to disseminate information to physicians. Historically, they have been very friendly to hospital medical staff and medical students by providing substantial giveaways to practitioners. Their goal is to improve patient care while nurturing a friendly relationship with the physician. This relationship may have a negative impact on the clinician's judgment and result in over prescription of newer, less tested and more expensive agents. The time constrained physician may accept the information provided by pharmaceutical firms as being objective and unbiased. It seems reasonable that the very sponsors of the research should certainly know the benefits and hazards of the research they have sponsored. This logic is seriously undermined by the fact that the sponsors of this research are not objective, in fact they are significantly influenced by the need to show profit to stock holders. Profit by itself is not bad; capitalism is the very basis for the growth and development of our nation. However, profit and science is nearly an oxymoron. Science is supposed to be objective, it seeks to discover truth and present these findings in a manner to others so they may use this information as a building block to discover additional truths. Profit is the financial or monitory gain obtained by the investment in services, technologies or products. Validity has little to do with profit. All that really matters is whether there is a market for these products or services and that it is willing to pay more for their use than it costs to develop and distribute them. Pharmaceutical firms are not primarily driven by altruism, they are in fact primarily motivated by the need to show a profit, and this motivation significantly taints all they sponsor and present because they are essentially self-serving. The need for profit to fund additional profit generating

---

1. Bandow, Doug. "Demonizing Drug makers: The Political Assault on the Pharmaceutical Industry." Cato Institute Policy Analysis vol 475 2003. p. 8-10.

research motivates these firms to utilize whatever means they are able to disseminate information they deem to be favorable in helping them reach these goals. They breach this bond of trust with health care workers and the result is the physician is now practicing medicine whose primary purpose is no longer altruism but profit. It would be wrong to say that the healthcare industry is only concerned with profits. It would however, be accurate to conclude that concerns for your health are secondary to concerns for maximizing their profits.

ORPHAN DRUGS

> *Research is subordinated (not to a long-term social benefit) but to an immediate commercial profit. Currently, disease (not health) is one of the major sources of profit for the pharmaceutical industry, and the doctors are willing agents of those profits.*
> Dr. Pierre Bosquet, *Nouvelle Critique*, 1961

Profit motives are clearly evident by their failure to treat rare diseases without considerable financial support from the government. There are many rare diseases that have been virtually abandoned by the pharmaceutical companies because research for treatments is deemed as too expensive. Drugs developed to treat these rare disorders have been appropriately referred to as orphan drugs. In 1983 Congress passed the Orphan Drug Act to entice the pharmaceutical firms into conducting research for these rare disorders. It stated that an orphan drug is one that is used to treat a disease which affects fewer than 200,000 people in the United States. Congressional legislation provided tax incentives and a seven-year monopoly on drug sales in an effort to spur the development and manufacturing of drugs to treat these rare disorders.[1] Pharmaceutical firms were unwilling to develop treatments for these rare diseases unless they received financial remuneration clearly showing that their primary concern was for profit. Although it may be too much to expect these firms to be totally altruistic, it certainly isn't unreasonable to expect them to curtail their greed to a morally acceptable level. Not only did they profit from the development of drugs to treat these rare disorders, they are nearly extorting those who are afflicted by this diseases charging fees far in the excess of the already bloated costs for the treatment of the more mundane variety of diseases and illnesses. The law has led to the introduction of valuable new drugs for the treatment of rare diseases, but some drug companies have been accused of abusing the law's provisions by making inordinately high profits on orphan drugs under monopoly. The Orphan Drug Act rests upon a Congressional finding that "because so few individuals are affected by any one rare disease or

---

1. "The Orphan Drug Act." U.S. Food and Drug Administration. 08/02/2001 ‹http://www.fda.gov/orphan/oda.htm›.

condition, a pharmaceutical company which develops an orphan drug may reasonably expect the drug to generate relatively small sales in comparison to the cost of developing the drug and consequently to incur a financial loss."[1] Congress therefore provided marketing exclusivity as an incentive for drug manufacturers to develop drugs that otherwise would be unprofitable. Genentech certainly has a reasonable expectation of recovering the costs of developing and manufacturing Protropin (a human growth hormone). The actual size of the market may be as high as 15,000 patients. Both Eli Lilly and Genentech sell "orphan" human growth hormone drugs at prices as high as $30,000 per year per patient. According to a June 16, 1991 story in the *New York Times Magazine*, 1990 U.S. sales for Genentech's Protropin "orphan" drug were $157 million.[2]

WHY DO YOU THINK THEY CALL IT A CHECK UP?

> *Restore a man to his health; his purse lies open to thee.*
> Robert Burton. *English clergyman and scholar (1577–1640)*

Pharmaceutical firms are unwilling to settle for increasing profits through new drug development alone. They also actively promote their existing products by "educating" physicians on new or novel uses of already developed drugs. This "education" is merely an attempt to cause physicians to increase their prescription writing for their products.[3] This persuasion is clearly seen in recent studies on how pharmaceutical firms affect the prescribing practice of physicians by sponsoring "free lunch" symposia.[4] The authors of other studies also found significant increases in the prescribing pattern of drugs occurred following the drug symposia.[5] An approximately three-fold increase in prescribing patterns occurred even though the majority of physicians attending the symposia believed such enticements would not alter their prescribing patterns. Another study suggested peer pressure was responsible for most

---

1. Mirza, Naureen. Public Health Management & Policy. Neuhauser, Duncan. Treating Rare Diseases: The Orphan Drug Act 05/05 ‹http://www.cwru.edu/med/epidbio/mphp439/Orphan_Drug.htm›.
2. Love, James. "Comments on the Orphan Drug Act and Government Sponsored Monopolies for Marketing Pharmaceutical Drugs." Committee on the Judiciary, Subcommittee on Antitrust, Monopolies and Business Rights, Anticompetitive Abuse of the Orphan Drug Act: Invitation to High Prices. United States Senate. US Senate, Washington, DC. 21 January, 1992.
3. Krassner, D. "Gifts from physicians to patients: an ethical dilemma." Psychiatr Serv. May; 55(5) 2004. p. 505-6.
4. Brett, A.S. Burr, W., Moloo, J. "Are gifts from pharmaceutical companies ethically problematic? A survey of physicians." Arch Intern Med. Oct 13; 163(18) 2003. p. 2213-8. Rogers, W.A., Mansfield, P.R., Braunack-Mayer, A.J., Jureidini, J.N. "The ethics of pharmaceutical industry relationships with medical students." Med J Aust. Apr Watkins, R.S., Kimberly, J. Jr. "What residents don't know about physician-pharmaceutical industry interactions." Acad Med. May; 79(5) 2004. p. 432-7.19; 180(8) 2004. p. 411-4.
5. Keim, S.M., Mays, M.Z., Grant, D. "Interactions between emergency medicine programs and the pharmaceutical industry." Acad Emerg Med. Jan; 11(1) 2004. p. 19-26.

physicians taking gifts and meals the majority of their patients themselves would be unable to afford. A survey of 31 family physicians (FP) and 47 general internal medicine (GIM) doctors found FPs received more information from pharmaceutical representatives than their GIM counterparts.[1] The following table lists their stated preferences for medical information:

Main Source of Information

(physicians may have made more than one choice)

	Family Doctors	General Internal Medicine Doctors
Journal articles	61%	49%
Lectures	51%	49%
1993 5th Joint National Comm.	23%	38%
Colleagues	42%	34%
Drug reps	23%	9%

Their stated preferences for information contrast greatly to what these same doctors prescribed as the initial treatment of choice for a 44 year old with newly-diagnosed essential hypertension unresponsive to non-pharmacological interventions:

	ACE inhibitor and/or calcium antagonist	Beta-blocker and/or diuretic
Family doctor	48%	77%
General internist	13%	96%

The medical literature strongly supports the use of low cost beta-blockers and diuretics as the first line of treatment in uncomplicated hypertension. Yet, in this study, family doctors were less likely to use the accepted medical standard. This suggests they were highly influenced by pharmaceutical promotional campaigns for the use of more recent and costly agents. Family doctors prescribing patterns were more consistent to what a drug rep would recommend

---

1. Wysong, P. "Time with drug reps affects prescribing." The Medical Post Sept. 8 1998. Wysong, Pippa. "Time with drug reps affects prescribing: study." Healthy Skepticism: Countering Misleading Drug Promotion. 2005. www.healthyskepticism.org. 09 Jan 2006 ‹http://www.healthyskepticism.org/library/ref.php?id=235›.

than to guidelines established by the journal *Hypertension* or the American Heart Association. The study concluded doctors who spend more time with drug reps were more likely to prescribe newer, more costly drugs. A recent study of physicians in northwest England found 70% of the doctors believed that drug company representatives were the preferred source for obtaining information on new drugs.[1] They expressed skepticism as to the objectivity of information from drug representatives, but, still thought the information represented was an accurate synopsis of new agents. They mistakenly believed they could detect deceptive and misleading statements; however, the study found only 17% actually researched new agents from peer-reviewed journals before prescribing these drugs. Many reasons were cited for their failure to do follow-up research including; lack of time, difficulty in interpretation, irrelevance and lack of attention to clinical experience. The authors concluded physicians "were largely reactive and opportunistic recipients of new drug information, rarely reporting an active information search." The decision to initiate a new drug is heavily influenced by 'who says what', in particular the pharmaceutical industry, hospital consultants and patients. This lackadaisical attitude is especially frightening because a 2004 German study concluded 94% of the information found in advertising material and marketing brochures mailed to GPs in Germany had virtually no scientific basis.[2] These "educational" materials routinely misquoted medical guidelines from scientific societies, minimized drug side effects and risks, suppressed non-supportive studies, exaggerated treatment benefits, misrepresented beneficial effects from animal studies as representing positive effects in human studies.

Study[3] after study[4] has confirmed that more frequent contact by a physician with a pharmaceutical representative generally results in increased prescription of newer, more costly drugs.[5] The pervasiveness of this problem becomes apparent when you consider that at one time eighty-five% of U.S. residency-training programs permitted "free lunches" sponsored by pharmaceutical representatives. These findings prompted the Senate Labor and Human

1. Prosser, Hellen. "Influences on GPs' decision to prescribe new drugs-the importance of who says what." Family Practice vol 20 2003. p. 61-68.
2. Tuffs, A. "Only 6% of drug advertising material is supported by evidence.." British Medical Journal vol 328 2004. p. 4
3. Caudill T.S., Johnson M.S., Rich E.C., McKinney W.P. "Physicians, pharmaceutical sales representatives, and the cost of prescribing." Arch Fam Med Apr 5:4 1996. p. 201-6. Spurgeon, D. "Doctors accept $50 a time to listen to drug representatives." BMJ May 11; 324(7346) 2002. p. 1113.
4. Zoorob R., Larzelere M. "Gifts to physicians from the pharmaceutical and medical manufacturing industry: what every physician should know." J La State Med Soc Jan-Feb; 156(1) 2004. p. 28-32. Ziegler, M.G., Lew, P. and Singer, B.C. "The Accuracy of Drug Information From Pharmaceutical Sales Representatives." JAMA vol 273 1995. p. 1296-1298.
5. Bergeron L. "Psychological aspects of gifts from drug companies." JAMA Nov 12; 290(18) 2003. p. 2406. Breen K.J. "The medical profession and the pharmaceutical industry: when will we open our eyes?" Med J Aust Apr 19; 180(8) 2004. p. 409-10. Monaghan M.S., Galt K.A., Turner P.D., Houghton B.L., Rich E.C., Markert R.J., Bergman-Evans B. "Student understanding of the relationship between the health professions and the pharmaceutical industry." Med J Aust Winter; 15(1) 2003. p. 14-20.

Resources committee to hold hearings about pharmaceutical company marketing practices. They found instances such as, "Offering a physician $100 to simply read a company's literature that encourages the prescribing of a highly toxic drug for a use that was not approved by the Food and Drug Administration."[1] A 2002 publication reveals the practice of paying physicians for listening to drug promotions continues, one must conclude the Senate hearings of 1991 were nothing more than political rhetoric.[2]

These hearings infuriated editors of the journal *JAMA* to such an extent they wrote "Something is wrong with a system that allows large amounts of money to induce physicians to use a certain healthcare product, while many who may need that very product cannot afford it."[3] Unfortunately, after more than a decade since the hearings, the practice continues to be well documented.[4] A skeptic may very well conclude that their words were nothing more than political posturing.[5]

THERE IS NO SUCH THING AS A FREE LUNCH

It is said that gifts persuade even the gods.
Euripides. Greek playwright (480-406 BC)

Many studies have confirmed pharmaceutical companies significantly affect physicians' professional prescribing patterns by the offering of gifts, free meals, sponsored travels, teachings and symposia.[6] This "investment" amounts to over 12 billion dollars annually with an expenditure of $8,000 to $13,000 on each US physician. One study found 85% of medical students believed it was unethical for politicians to accept gifts. However, the authors of this study report only 46% of respondents believed it improper to accept similarly valued gifts

1. Greger, Michael. "Drug Promotion." Heart Failure — Diary of a Third Year Medical Student. 1999. United Progressive Alumni. ‹http://upalumni.org/medschool/appendices/appendix-72a.html#fn848›.
2. Chin, T. "Drug firms score by paying doctors for time." AMA American Medical News. 2002. AMA. May 6 ‹https://ssl3.ama-assn.org/apps/ldap/login.cgi/id/amnews?URL=http://www.ama-assn.org/amednews/2002/05/06/bil20506.htm›.
3. Randall, T. "Kennedy Hearings Say No More Free Lunch — Or Much Else — From Drug Firms." JAMA vol 265 1991. p. 440-41.
4. Hamaty, D., Villarreal, A., Murphy, T. "Continuing education or bribe?" Pain Med Sep; 4(3) 2003. p. 295. Wager, E. "How to dance with porcupines: rules and guidelines on doctors' relations with drug companies." BMJ vol 326 2003. p. 1196-98.
5. Gianelli, D.M. "Revisiting the Ethics of Industry Gifts." American Medical News August 24-31:(9) 1998. p. 12-14. Steinman M.A., Shlipak M.G., McPhee S.J. "Of principles and pens: attitudes and practices of medicine housestaff toward pharmaceutical industry promotions." Am J Med May; 110(7) 2001. p. 551-57.
6. Krimsky, S. "Small gifts, conflicts of interest, and the zero-tolerance threshold in medicine." Am J Bioeth Summer; 3(3) 2003. p. 50-52; Moynihan, R. "Who pays for the pizza? Redefining the relationships between doctors and drug companies. 1: entanglement." BMJ May 31; 326(7400) 2003. p. 1189-92. Strong, C. "Lunch with Lilly: who pays?" Am J Bioeth Summer; 3(3) 2003. p. 62-63; Fitzpatrick, C. "No more free lunches: it is time to own up." BMJ Aug 9; 327(7410) 2003. p. 342.

themselves from a pharmaceutical company.[1] The indoctrination of physicians begins very early in their careers. This study reported pharmaceutical industry gift giving was initiated during medical school and continued at a frequency of about four times per month.

Most physicians believed information presented by pharmaceutical representatives was accurate, and acceptance of gifts did not alter their prescription practices. However, the researchers of this study concluded interaction with pharmaceutical representatives had a very negative impact on physicians prescribing practices. These practices lead to an increase in irrational prescribing, preference for newer and therefore costlier drugs and reduced prescribing of generic drugs. The net result is a large increase in the prescription of newer, more expensive drugs which provide no benefits over cheaper generic drugs. They also result in the addition of these more expensive agents to hospital formularies even though they provide no obvious advantages over preexisting generics. Physicians requesting the addition of a new drug to the hospital formulary were five times more likely to have received money from drug companies to attend meetings, give speeches and performing research for pharmaceutical firms. They were also 13 times more likely to have met with drug company representatives, and 19 times more likely to have accepted money from drug companies compared to physicians who did not request a formulary addition.[2]

Although many physicians are unconcerned by these interactions[3], the general public does not seem to share their opinion.[4] A study of 268 physicians from two large medical centers (one military and the other private) rated the appropriateness of ten pharmaceutical gifts and if they were likely to influence prescribing. Patients found gifts less appropriate and more influential than their physicians. Approximately half of the patients stated they were unaware of such gifts. Of those unaware, 24% responded this knowledge altered their perception of the medical profession. They stated such gifts were more influential and less appropriate than their physicians. The *New England Journal of Medicine* and *Journal of General Internal Medicine* surveys showed 35% of patients believe these gifts obligate a doctor to prescribe a certain product.

If these findings aren't bad enough, other studies have found some researchers who test the efficacy and safety of new drugs are actually paid by the

1. Hakansson, J. "[Others are influenced, not me!" Physicians are often not aware how manipulated they are by drug industry]." Lakartidningen Dec 11; 100(50) 2003. p. 4158-59.
2. Chren, M.M., Landefeld, C.S. "Physicians' behavior and their interactions with drug companies: A controlled study of physicians who requested additions to a hospital drug formulary." JAMA Mar 2; 271(9) 1994. p. 684-689.
3. Gibbons, R.V., Landry, F.J., Blouch, D.L., Jones, D.L., Williams, F.K., Lucey, C.R., Kroenke, K. "A comparison of physicians' and patients' attitudes toward pharmaceutical industry gifts." J Gen Intern Med Mar; 13(3) 1998. p. 151-54.
4. Mainous, A.G. 3rd, Hueston, W.J., Rich, E.C. "Patient perceptions of physician acceptance of gifts from the pharmaceutical industry." Arch Fam Med vol 4 1995. p. 335-39. Wazana, A. "Physicians and the Pharmaceutical Industry Is a Gift Ever Just a Gift?" JAMA vol 283 2000. p. 373-380.

drug manufacturer to test these new agents on patients.[1] Patients who are enrolled in these trials are usually unaware of this potential conflict of interest by their physician and may actually be billed for these services.[2]

The ties to the pharmaceutical industry go far beyond the simple prescription of drugs. Many studies have shown pharmaceutical company sponsorship greatly influences the findings of these supposedly impartial scientists. They are more likely to publish data presenting these pharmacological agents in a positive manner, while minimizing many of the adverse properties associated with their sponsors' products. In fact, it is very difficult to find an objective researcher who does not have close financial ties with the pharmaceutical industry. Articles sponsored by pharmaceutical companies[3] nearly always present these agents in a favorable manner.[4] Even the very journals in which these findings are published are suspect,[5] since they receive millions of dollars in advertising from drug companies.[6] One study showed over 10% of the income of five medical organizations came from drug advertisements published in a single journal. It also reported that four major organizations profited as much or more from drug advertisement as from its members. Another study found some medical journals receive half of their income from pharmaceutical company advertising. The conflict of interest in drug testing of special concern[7] because human lives are routinely endangered by poorly-tested agents.[8]

A study of 167 researchers from the top research universities in the U.S. found 43% of researchers reported having received significant financial gifts from the pharmaceutical firms in the previous three years. Two-thirds of those receiving these gifts classified them as important or very important to their research. Over half of the recipients reported drug companies placed restrictions or other conditions on this "investment." A very recent survey of 105 residents,

---

1. Chin, T. "Drug firms score by paying doctors for time." AMA American Medical News. 2002. AMA. May 6 ⟨https://ssl3.ama-assn.org/apps/ldap/login.cgi/id/amnews?URL=http://www.ama-assn.org/amednews/2002/05/06/bil20506.htm⟩. Resnik, D.B. "Research participation and financial inducements." Am J Bioeth Spring; 1(2) 2001. p. 54-56. Shimm, D.S., Spece, R.G. Jr. "Industry reimbursement for entering patients into clinical trials: legal and ethical issues." Ann Intern Med Jul 15; 115(2) 1991. p. 148-51.
2. Helft, P.R., Ratain, M.J., Epstein, R.A., Siegler, M. "Inside information: Financial conflicts of interest for research subjects in early phase clinical trials." J Natl Cancer Inst May 5; 96(9) 2004. p. 656-61. Lemmens, T., Miller, P.B. "The human subjects trade: ethical and legal issues surrounding recruitment incentives." J Law Med Ethics Fall; 31(3) 2003. p. 398-418.
3. Amsden, G.W. "Industry sponsorship in research and publishing: who is really to blame for perceived bias?" Ann Pharmacother Apr; 38(4) 2004. p. 714-16.
4. Norris, J.W. "Industry and academic medicine: a dangerous liaison?" Can J Neurol Sci Feb; 31(1) 2004. p. 5-6. Wahlbeck, K et al. "Sponsored drug trials show more-favourable outcomes." BMJ vol 318 1999. p. 464.
5. Knight, J. "Journals wrestle with definition of 'competing' interest." Nature Jun 26; 423(6943) 2003. p. 908.
6. Olivieri, N.F. "Patients' health or company profits? The commercialisation of academic research." Sci Eng Ethics Jan; 9(1) 2003. p. 29-41. Steinbrook, R. "Financial conflicts of interest and the NIH." N Engl J Med Jan 22; 350(4) 2004. p. 327-30.
7. Angell, M. "Is Academic Medicine for Sale?" N Engl J Med vol 342 2000. p. 1516-1518.
8. Gottlieb, S. "Medical societies accused of being beholden to the drugs industry." BMJ vol 319 199. p. 1321. Smith, R. "Journals fail to adhere to guidelines on conflicts of interest." BMJ Sep 22; 323(7314) 2001. p. 651.

published in *The American Journal of Medicine*, indicated 60% of respondents stated pharmaceutical gifts do not influence their prescription patterns. However, only 16% felt other physicians had a similar attitude about receiving these gifts.

The survey also found 42% of residents believed it was appropriate to accept free travel to an educational seminar and 15% believed it was acceptable to receive free expensive luggage from pharmaceutical representatives. According to guidelines established by the AMA in 1990, neither of these gifts would be deemed appropriate. Concerns about physician ethics do little to curb this unseemly conduct in the field of medicine. There are hundreds of studies documenting ethical problems with physician and pharmaceutical representative interactions. Unfortunately, neither the government[1] nor the AMA appears to be willing to enforce these voluntary regulations.[2]

THE HIGH COST OF HEALTH

> *If you think health care is expensive now, wait until you see what it costs when it's free.*
> P. J. O'Rourke, US humorist

Although the majority of gifts offered to physicians would not be considered major items,[3] the universality of this practice adds billions to healthcare spending each year.[4] This shameless hawking of drugs is not confined to "free lunches"[5] and personal gifts.[6] The industry also promotes their products by direct advertising to consumers in the form of "public service" ads and sponsorship of peer review medical journals. The *Associated Press* reported major pharmaceutical firms spend nearly twice the amount for advertising as for research. *Family USA*, an outspoken critic of the pharmaceutical industry, recently reported drug manufacturers spend two and a half times more for advertisements and compensation to executives than for research or development.[7] They reached these conclusions after reviewing revenues from sales and net profits, then comparing this to what is spent on marketing,

1. Appleby, Julie. "Drugmakers bankroll ethics guidelines on 'freebies'." USA Today. 2001. 04/27/2001 ⟨http://www.usatoday.com/news/health/2001-04-27-drugs-ethics.htm⟩.
2. Campbell, E.G., Louis, K.S., Blumenthal, D. "Looking a gift horse in the mouth: corporate gifts supporting life sciences research." JAMA Apr 1; 279(13) 1998. p. 995-99 Relman, A.S., Angell, M. "America's other drug problem: how the drug industry distorts medicine and politics." New Repub Dec 16; 227(25) 2002. p. 27-41.
3. Brett, A.S. "Cheap trinkets, effective marketing: small gifts from drug companies to physicians." Am J Bioeth Summer; 3(3) 2003. p. 52-54; Brody H. "Pens and other pharmaceutical industry gifts." Am J Bioeth Summer; 3(3) 2003. p. 58-60. Paris, J.J. "Large or small, a gift is a gift is a gift." Am J Bioeth Summer; 3(3) 2003. p. W30.
4. Katz, D., Caplan, A.L., Merz, J.F. "All gifts large and small: toward an understanding of the ethics of pharmaceutical industry gift-giving." Am J Bioeth Summer; 3(3) 2003. p. 39-46.
5. Williams, S.C. "Food for thought: Why physicians should reconsider gifts from pharmaceutical companies." Curr Surg Mar-Apr; 60(2) 2003. p. 152-5.
6. Grady, D. "Ambiguous gifts: when patients give and doctors take." NY Times Jan 11 2004, Natl ed.: WK2.

administration, research and development. According to their findings, the nine major drug companies profits were 60% higher than their expenditures on R&D. Merck's profits, for example, were nearly three times the amount it spent on R&D in 2001. Pharmaceutical companies actually spend more on their drug representatives than they do on raw materials for the manufacturing of these drugs.

This aggressive campaigning of newer agents by the pharmaceutical firms is responsible for escalating drug costs. A study published in May 2001 found a nearly 19% increase in spending for pharmaceuticals over the previous year with the four best selling drugs being among the ten most heavily marketed to physicians.

The pharmaceutical industry has long believed sales of these newer agents directly correlates with their intensive promotion by drug representatives during office visits.[1] These millions of office visits to physicians require a veritable army of drug sales representatives. The pharmaceutical industry has met this challenge by doubling the number of drug reps since 1996 from 41,800 to 83,000 for 2000 and increasing the number of office visits by 10%.[2] They also increased spending in medical journals for advertising to a record high of $5.3 billion for the year 2000 and doubled the number of drug company sponsored events to more than 314,000 during the year 2000, at a cost of nearly $2 billion. These accusations rile the pharmaceutical industry; they emphatically refute charges that research spending is far less than that of promotion and marketing. A recent Tufts University study estimated the average cost for new drug development to be $802 million in 2004 dollars.[3] However, a Public Citizen report refutes this value and claims expenditures are intentionally being inflated to justify the exorbitant costs for newer agents.[4] They argue many of the costs associated with drug development are tax deductible and believe the actual average cost for new drug development is only $150 million.

A 2004 analysis of pharmaceutical spending shows actual research and development require a mere 14% of their revenues.[5] Peddling of these agents by

7. "New 2001 Data Show Big Drug Companies Spent Almost Two-and-a-Half Times as Much on Marketing, Advertising and Administration as They Spent on Research and Development." Family USA: The Voice for Health Care Consumers. 2005. Family USA. 13 Sep 2005 ‹http://www.familiesusa.org/search.jsp?query=research+development›.
1. Mallard, C. "Smarter Selling." Beyond 2005: The Future of Pharmaceutical Marketing and Sales. 2002. Cap Gemini Ernst & Young Group. 10/01/2002 ‹http://www.e-detailing.info/pdf/capgemini1.pdf›.
2. Clayton, E. "'Tis Always the Seaon for Giving: A White Paper on the Practice and Problems of Pharmaceutical Detailing." CALPRIG: The Consumer Advocate. 2004. CALIFORNIA PUBLIC INTEREST RESEARCH GROUP. 16 Sep 2004 ‹http://calpirg.org/reports/TistheSeasonForGiving04.pdf›.
3. DiMasi, J.A. "The Price of Innovation: New Estimates of Drug Development Costs." Journal of Health Economics vol 22 2003. p. 151-185.
4. "Tufts Drug Study Sample Is Skewed; True Figure of R&D Costs Likely Is 75 Percent Lower." Public Citizen Press Room. 2001. 04 Dec 2001 ‹http://www.citizen.org/pressroom/release.cfm?ID=954›.
5. Reinhardt, U.E. "An Information Infrastructure For The Pharmaceutical Market." Health Affairs vol 23 Issue 1 2004. p. 107-112.

representatives and bureaucrats consumes one-third of all pharmaceutical spending. Pharmaceutical executives will nearly sell their souls to maintain their hefty 20.6% corporate profits.

Allocation Of Revenue Dollars In Thirteen Large Research-Based Pharmaceutical Companies, 2002

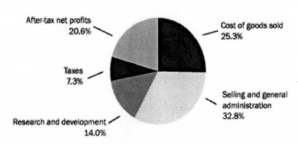

SOURCE: Banc of America Securities Equity Research, personal communication, 3 November 2003.

Source: Uwe E. Reinhardt An Information Infrastructure For The Pharmaceutical Market Health Affairs, Vol. 23, Issue 1, 107-112

Many would argue the public is still receiving considerable benefit by this 14% investment in research and development. Unfortunately, drug companies disgrace themselves even further by squandering this investment to fund research for "me too" agents instead of original and innovative products. According to the National Institutes of Health, the top ten drugs were responsible for 46.8% of total prescription drug costs for the year 2000 ($61.7 billion in sales).[1] One report found total prescription drug expenditures at retail outlets nearly doubled from $78.9 billion in 1997 to $154.5 billion in 2001. This same report states National spending for drugs increased 8.5% from $131.9 billion in 2000 to $154.5 billion in 2001. Another report, concluded prescription drug spending increased 14.5% a year between 1997 and 2001. Drug spending is expected to double by 2010 to nearly 10% ($366 billion) of all health care expenditures.[2] This contrasts to the 5% ($12 billion) for drug spending during 1980. This is demonstrated in graphs from Public Citizen's web site.

---

1. The National Institute for Health Care. U.S. Bureau of Labor Statistics. Prescription Drug Expenditures in 2001: Another Year of Escalating Costs. May 2002. 02/12/06 ‹http://www.nihcm.org/spending2001.pdf›.
2. Strunk, B.C, Ginsburg, P.B, Gabel, J.R. "Tracking Health Care Costs: Growth Accelerates Again In 2001." Health Affairs. 2002. 25 Sep 2002 ‹http://content.healthaffairs.org/cgi/content/abstract/hlthaff.w2.299v1›. Health Care Financing Administration, Office of the Actuary. National Health Expenditure Projections 2000-2010. Mar 2001. ‹http://www.hcfa.gov/stats›. Congressional Budget Office. Projections of Medicare and Prescription Drug Spending. By Crippen, D.L. 07 Mar 2002. ‹http://cbo.gov/showdoc.cfm?index=3304&sequence=0›.

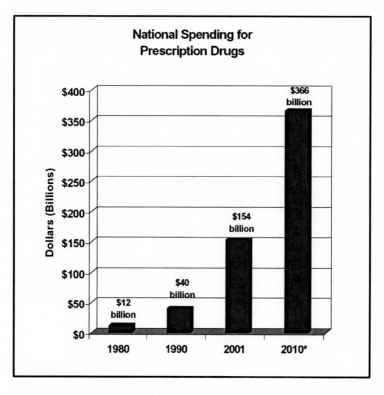

National Spending for Prescription Drugs

Source: National Institute for Health Care Management, "Prescription Drug Expenditures in 2001: Another Year of Escalating Costs," April 2002.
*Projected

Annual Medicare payments are expected to increase from $2,440 in 2003 to $5,820 by 2012. Increases in drug spending are attributable to increased prescription writing (an increase of 39% just for the year 2001), a trend toward increased prescribing of more expensive agents (resulted in a 24% increase prescription spending for 2001) and a 37% increase in the prices of individual medicines. However, the primary reason for increased prescription spending is to pay for the 34 most heavily promoted drugs. Of 9,882 available medicines, these agents are responsible for 50.7% of the increase to national drug spending for the year 2001. Prescription costs increased more than six times the rate of inflation in 2001. Average prescription prices increased 10% from 2000 to 2001, which contrasts to the 1.6% inflation rate for 2001.

For the year 2001, prescriptions for the 50 best-selling drugs increased by more than 25%. The remaining 9,482 drugs on the market only experienced a 1.7% increase in prescription writing. A *Families USA* study anticipates the

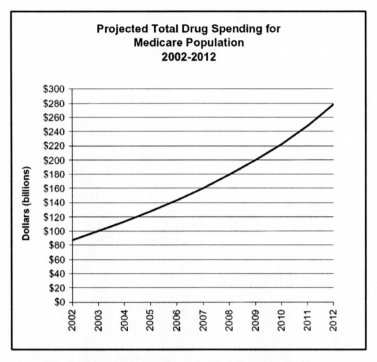

**Projected Total Drug Spending for
Medicare Population
2002-2012**

Source: Dan Crippen, Director of the Congressional Budget Office, "Projections of Medicare and Prescription Drug Spending," Testimony before the United States Senate Committee on Finance, March 7, 2002.

average cost of a prescription to double by 2010.[1] Although brand-name drugs account for only 58% of all drugs prescribed, they are responsible for 92% ($129.7 billion) of the retail cost for prescription drugs. This price gouging is primarily restricted to the US market. A Canadian survey of all patentable drugs found foreign drug prices are 36% to 50% less than what is charged for the same drug in the US. Many foreign nations have price restraints to limit the cost of prescription drugs. Drug company lobbyists block legislation to control pharmaceutical prices because they believe most Americans are willing to pay these inflated costs.

1. "Seniors' Prescription Drug Bills Projected to More Than Double in the Next 10 Years." Families USA. Lemmon, D. 2000. 15 Jul 2000 ‹http://www.familiesusa.org/resources/newsroom/press-releases/press-release-seniors-prescription-drug-bills-projected-to-more-than-double-in-the-next-lo-year.html›.

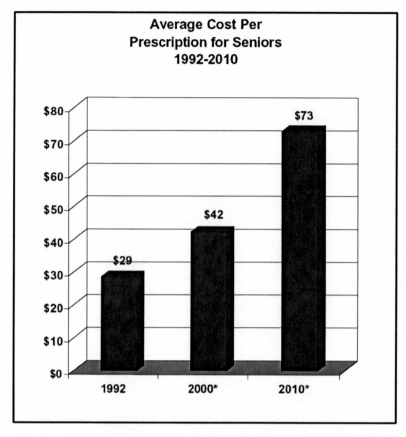

Source: Families USA/PRIME Institute, University of Minnesota, "Cost Overdose: Growth in Spending for the Elderly, 1992-2010," July 2000.
* Projected

The following graph compares the cost of health care from 1970 to 2000 to other expenditures related to personal consumption. Personal health care costs consumers a greater percentage of their budget than even food or housing. Free market and economic restraints control prices for most household expenses; medical expenses appear to be immune from these controls. The government's "hands off" policies on regulating health care pricing coupled with the subsidization of unhealthy lifestyle choices has resulted in Americans' spending more of their personal income for fewer services.

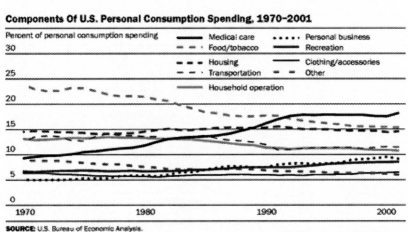

Components Of U.S. Personal Consumption Spending, 1970–2001

SOURCE: U.S. Bureau of Economic Analysis.
NOTES: "Other" includes religious activities, education and research, personal care, and foreign travel. Components add to 100 percent.

What do you get for this increased expenditure on health care, fewer health care benefits and more spending on bureaucrats! One author states only 50% of health care spending is actually used for health care. The remaining 50% is squandered maintaining governmental bureaucracies, regulatory bodies, defending itself against litigation and paying for iatrogenic induced events (doctors' mistakes"). The following graph shows the percentage of healthcare spending for non-health related services. Their data suggest health care spending could be reduced in half[1] simply by implementing tort reform (legislation to reduce the number of frivolous lawsuits) and abolishing governmental regulatory agencies.[2]

A pie chart from a Center for Medicare and Medicaid Services study shows a breakdown of health care spending for 2002. Hospital care and physicians services account for the majority of health care services.

1. Reinhardt, U.E., Hussey, P.S, Anderson , G.F. "U.S. Health Care Spending In An International Context." Health Affairs vol 23 Issue 3 2004. p. 10-25
2. Woolhandler, S., Campbell, T., Himmelstein, D.U. "Costs of Health Care Administration in the United States and Canada." NEJM vol 349 2003. p. 768-75 "AAHP Unveils New Pricewaterhouse-Coopers Report." American Association of Health Plans Press Release. 2002. American Association of Health Plans. Apr 24 2002 ‹http://www.aahp.org/ DocTemplate.cfm?Section=Access_Cost&template=/ContentManagement/ContentDisplay.cfm&ContentID=4804›.

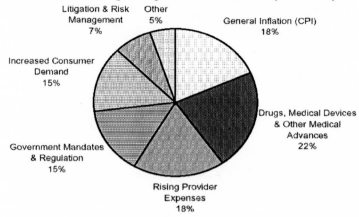

The Factors Driving Rising Costs in Healthcare (2001-2002)

Litigation & Risk Management 7%
Other 5%
General Inflation (CPI) 18%
Increased Consumer Demand 15%
Drugs, Medical Devices & Other Medical Advances 22%
Government Mandates & Regulation 15%
Rising Provider Expenses 18%

Source: PricewaterhouseCoopers, April 2002.

In 2001, payments for managed care siphoned off 18% of Medicare spending thereby significantly reducing payments for hospital and physicians services.

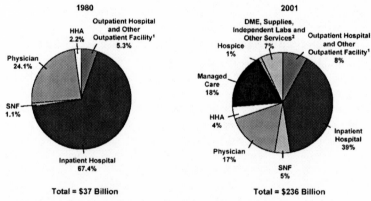

Where the Medicare Dollar Went: 1980 and 2001

Medicare spending has moved from inpatient hospital services to outpatient settings.

1980
Outpatient Hospital and Other Outpatient Facility¹ 5.3%
HHA 2.2%
Physician 24.1%
SNF 1.1%
Inpatient Hospital 67.4%
Total = $37 Billion

2001
DME, Supplies, Independent Labs and Other Services² 7%
Outpatient Hospital and Other Outpatient Facility¹ 8%
Hospice 1%
Managed Care 18%
HHA 4%
Inpatient Hospital 39%
Physician 17%
SNF 5%
Total = $236 Billion

¹ Other outpatient facilities include ESRD freestanding dialysis facilities, RHCs, outpatient rehabilitation facilities, and federally qualified health centers.
² Other services include ambulatory surgical center facility costs and ambulance services.
Note: Data do not sum due to rounding. Spending includes benefit dollars only.
Source: CMS, Office of the Actuary

An article in *Public Citizen* criticizes the US for health care bureaucratic waste. They report administrative expenses consume at least $399.4 billion out of total health expenditures of $1,660.5 billion in 2003.[1] The authors of this article suggest streamlining administrative overhead to Canadian levels.

Decreasing administrative costs could save approximately $286.0 billion in 2003, $6,940 for each of the 41.2 million Americans who were uninsured as of 2001. *Reductions in bureaucracy would liberate sufficient funds to adequately insure all uninsured Americans!*

Spending on hospital services is still the largest component of quickly growing pie, as seen below.

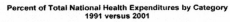

Percent of Total National Health Expenditures by Category
1991 versus 2001

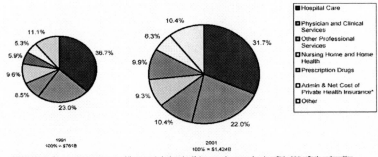

* Administration for government programs and the net cost of private health insurance (premiums less benefits) which reflects underwriting gains/losses.
Source: Centers for Medicare and Medicaid Services (CMS). Office of the Actuary, National Health Statistics Group, National Health Accounts.

A closer examination of hospital expenses is shown in the next pie chart.

Physicians routinely complain they are receiving less reimbursement for services. Revenue from Medicaid and Medicare payments has been reduced by over 7% since 1980 and studies have shown physician salaries are 6% less than they were in 1999.[1] However, many fail to mention they are still receiving nearly six times more than the average worker (see next bar graph).[2]

A 2002 survey of physician salaries showed a relatively low paid family practitioner still averaged $128,000 with just 1-2 years of experience.[3] The maximum average for a FP was $299,000 per year.[4] These salaries included base salaries, net income or hospital guarantees minus expenses.

1. Himmelstein, D.U, Woolhandler, S., Wolfe, S.M. "Administrative Waste in the U.S. Health Care System in 2003: The Cost to the Nation, the States and the District of Columbia, with State-Specific Estimates of Potential Savings." Public Citizen. 2003. 20 Aug 2003 ‹//www.citizen.org/documents/AdminWaste.pdf›.
1. "An Overview of the U.S. Healthcare System:Two Decades of Change, 1980-2000." Centers for Medicare & Medicaid Services. ‹http://new.cms.hhs.gov/TheChartSeries/downloads/us_health_chap1_p.pdf.
2. Guglielmo, W.J. "Physicians' earnings. As demand for primary care doctors plateaus, so does income." Medical Economics. 2003. 19 Sep 2003 ‹http://www.memag.com/memag/article/articleDetail.jsp?id=112482›. Weiss, G.G. " How do your staff salaries stack up?" Medical Economics. 2003. 11 Apr 2003 ‹http://www.medicaleconomics.com/memag/article/articleDetail.jsp?id=111341›.
3. Reed, M.C., Ginsburg, P.B. "Behind the Times: Physician Income, 1995-99." Center for Studying Health System Change. 2003. Mar 2003 ‹http://www.hschange.com/CONTENT/544/›.
4. "Physician Salaries and Salary Surveys." Allied Physicians. 2006. Jan 2004 ‹http://www.allied-physicians.com/salary_surveys/physician-salaries.htm›.

Percent of Total Hospital Costs by Type of Expense*

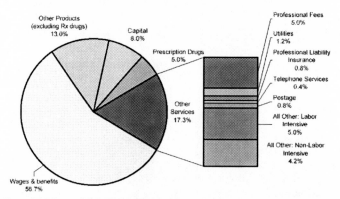

* Based on CMS Medicare hospital Market Basket Index weights from 1997.
Source: Centers for Medicare and Medicaid Services (CMS), Office of the Actuary: Data from the National Health Statistics Group; Federal Register, Medicare Program. Changes to the Hospital Inpatient Prospective Payment Systems and FY2003 Rates, 67(148), August 1, 2002.

Physician Income Compared to All Workers, Selected Years

Physician income continues to be much higher than that of all full-time workers.

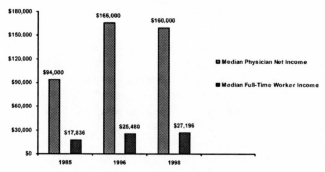

Notes: Median Full-Time Worker Income reflects median weekly earnings of full-time workers multiplied by 52.

Source: 1998 Median Physician Net Income from *Modern Healthcare*, "Follow the Money, AMA's Long-Delayed Annual Report Offers Unsettling News on Physicians' Incomes" (January 1, 2001), p. 12.

Wage & salary information for full-time workers from U.S. Census Bureau, *Statistical Abstract of the United States*, 1995-2000. Census web site at www.census.gov/prod/www/statistical-abstract-us.html.

1985 and 1996 physician salary data from Kaiser Family Foundation analysis of data published by the American Medical Association, *Physician Marketplace Statistics*, and U.S. Census Bureau, *Statistical Abstract of the United States* as shown in *Trends and Indicators in the Changing Health Care Marketplace Chartbook*. Kaiser Family Foundation (August 1998). Exhibit 6.10, p.65.

Trends and Indicators in the Changing Health Care Marketplace, 2002 – Chartbook.

A 2003 report states, "Despite the decline in inflation-adjusted net income, medicine remains one of the highest paid professions in America. More than half of all physicians earned more than $150,000 in 1999, while average physician net income was about $187,000." This study found primary care physicians spent

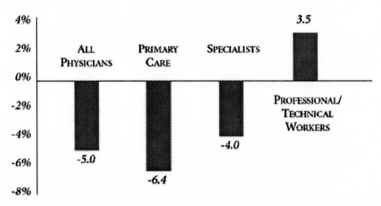

Percent Change in Average Physician Income, Adjusted for Inflation, 1995-99

Source: HSC Community Tracking Study Physician Survey

more than half of their 2002 practice revenue on operating expenses.[1] The largest expenses were for office payroll, rent and malpractice insurance premiums.[2]

A five year analysis of physician payments found an overall increase of about 5.2% from 1995-2000. A later analysis of group payments to physicians seems to confirm these trends.[3]

Some physicians offset reductions in Medicaid and Medicare reimbursements by simply increasing the number of patients seen and providing more for fee services.[4] Many physicians would believe their position of responsibility, leadership, training and education entitles them to large incomes. American physicians are grossly overpaid by world standards and far more than the majority of governmental leaders. Canadian physicians average only $76,010 annually (US dollars).[5] The Office of Personnel Management lists the following salaries for governmental leaders.

1. Guglielmo, W.J. "Physicians' earnings. As demand for primary care doctors plateaus, so does income." Medical Economics. 2003. 19 Sep 2003
2. "Adequacy of Payments Relative to Costs and Implications for Maryland Health Care Providers." Maryland Health Care Commission. 2002. 16 Jan 2004 ‹http://mhcc.maryland.gov/legislative/hb805/ch1.pdf›.
3. "Earning By Occupation and Education." Earnings By Detailed Occupation: 1999. U.S. Census Bureau. 13 May 2004 ‹http://www.census.gov/hhes/income/earnings/call2mdboth.html›.
4. Cunningham, P.J. "Mounting Pressures: Physicians Serving Medicaid Patients and the Uninsured, 1997-2001." Center for Studying Health System Change. 2002. Dec 2002 ‹http://hschange.com/CONTENT/505/›.
5. Reinhardt, U.E., Hussey, P.S, Anderson , G.F. "U.S. Health Care Spending In An International Context." Health Affairs vol 23 Issue 3 2004. p. 10-25

Figure 10. MGMA Median Physician Income, 1998-2002

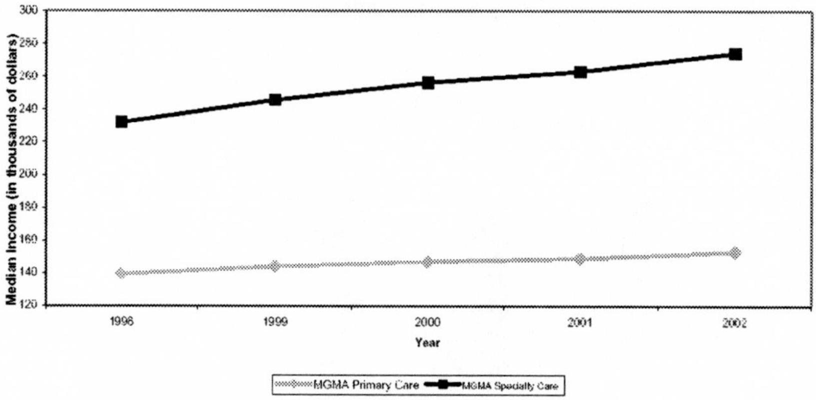

Source: HSC Community Tracking Study Physician Survey

Salaries of the President, Vice President, and Other U.S. Officials, 2004[1]

Position	Salary
President	$400,000[1]
Vice President	$202,900[2]
Senator	$158,000
Representative	$158,000
Majority and Minority Leaders	$175,600
Speaker of the House	$202,900
Chief Justice, U.S. Supreme Court	$202,900
Assoc. Justice, U.S. Supreme Court	$194,200

1. Plus $50,000 expense allowance to assist in defraying expenses relating to or resulting from the discharge of his official duties.
2. Plus $10,000 expense allowance.

I find it incredible that a physician believes their services are more valuable than a Supreme Court justice. One would hope these officials are into public service for the right to serve and influence government policy. Cynicism by some may suggest these public servants are motivated primarily by power and perks from special interests groups. Physicians should be the last professionals to point out the hypocrisy of governmental leaders.

Insurance companies offset these increased health care expenditures by simply raising insurance premiums. One analysis shows insurance premiums have increased by 12% since 1996, far in excess of workers wages and inflation.[2]

1. "Salaries of the President, Vice President, and Other U.S. Officials, 2005." Infoplease. 2005 ‹http://www.infoplease.com/ipa/A0875856.html›.
2. "2003 Employer Health Benefits Survey Charts." Kaiser Family Foundation. 2003. 2003 ‹http://www.kff.org/insurance/ehbs2003-charts-set.cfm›.

FIGURE 3:   **National Data on the Changes in the Cost of Health Insurance**

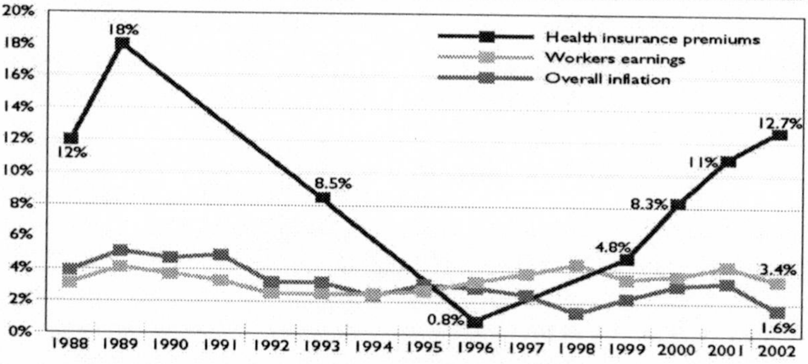

Note: Data on premium increases reflect the cost of health insurance premiums for a family of four.

Source: KFF/HRET *Survey of Employer-Sponsored Health Benefits: 1999, 2000, 2001, 2002;* KPMG *Survey of Employer-Sponsored Health Benefits: 1988, 1993, 1996*

A survey by the Kaiser Family Foundation and Health Research and Educational Trust determined the total premium for a typical employment-based health insurance policy for a family in 2003 was $8,800. Premiums have continued to increase at rates much in the excess of ten percent annually. If rates continue to grow at "only" ten percent each year for the next decade, a typical family coverage would cost about $21,000 per year. This would be 42% of a family's projected wages for 2013 ($50,000).

The escalating costs for medical spending will far exceed the average worker's usable income. Increases in medical spending[1] coupled with probable increases in social security taxes may make our next generation the poorest since the great depression.[2] Advocates of health care reform often cite other measures for reducing medical expenditures such as limiting tort liability to help reduce the extent to which physicians practice "defensive medicine." Advocates of tort reform claim limiting medical liability will reduce the number of excessive procedures. These conjectures will be discussed more thoroughly in later chapters. The average payment for a malpractice claim has risen fairly steadily since 1986, from about $95,000 in that year to $320,000 in 2002. This increase represents an annual

---

1. The National Institute for Health Care. U.S. Bureau of Labor Statistics. Prescription Drug Expenditures in 2001: Another Year of Escalating Costs. May 2002. 02/12/06 ‹http://www.nihcm.org/ spending2001.pdf›. "Cost Overdose: Growth in Spending for the Elderly." Impossible Choices: Food and Housing or Prescription Drugs? 2000. Fiscal Policy Institute for USAction. Jul 2000 ‹http://www.fiscalpolicy.org/ImpossibleChoicesSummary.htm›.
2. Tanouye, E. "Drug Dependency: U.S. Has Developed An Expensive Habit; Now, How to Pay for It?" The Wall Street Journal 16 Nov 1998. "Report to the President." Office of Health Policy. 2000. Department of Health & Human Services. Apr 2000 ‹http://aspe.hhs.gov/health/reports/drug-study/›.

growth rate of nearly 8% — more than twice the general rate of inflation. Those figures are based on data collected by the Physician Insurers Association of America. Malpractice claims typically include a component to compensate plaintiffs for additional medical costs they incur because of their injuries, so one factor contributing to the growth in the average value of claims since 1986 has been increases in health care spending — which, on a per-person basis, has risen at an average rate of 6.9% a year during that period.

Although the cost per successful claim has increased, the *number* of such claims has remained relatively constant. Each year, about 15 malpractice claims are filed for every 100 physicians, and about 30% of those claims result in an insurance payment.[1] A 2003 study that examined state data from 1993 to 2002 found two restrictions — a cap on non-economic damages and a ban on punitive damages — would together reduce premiums by more than one-third (all other things being equal). Based on its own research on the effects of tort restrictions, the Congressional Budget Office (CBO) estimated the provisions of the Help Efficient, Accessible, Low-cost, Timely Healthcare (HEALTH) Act of 2003 (H.R. 5) would lower premiums nationwide by an average of 25 to 30% from the levels likely to occur under current law. Even these savings would not have a significant impact on total health care costs. Malpractice costs amounted to only approximately $24 billion for 2002. According to data from the Office of the Actuary at the Centers for Medicare and Medicaid Services, this figure represents less than 2% of the $1.4 trillion spent overall for health care spending in 2002 (excluding spending on public health and capital improvements). A reduction of 25 to 30% in malpractice costs would lower health care costs by only about 0.4% to 0.5%. This would probably have little if any effect on reducing health insurance premiums.

Proponents of limiting malpractice liability have argued much greater savings in health care costs would be possible through reductions in the practice of defensive medicine. However, some "defensive medicine" spending may be motivated less by liability concerns than by the income it generates. On the basis of existing studies and its own research, CBO believes savings from reducing defensive medicine would be very small. A comprehensive study using 1984 data from the state of New York did not find a strong relationship between the threat of litigation and medical costs, even though physicians reported that their practices had been affected by the threat of lawsuits.[2] However, when the CBO evaluated Medicare patients hospitalized for heart disease and a broader set of ailments, it found no evidence that restrictions on tort liability reduce medical spending.

---

1. Thorpe, K.E. "The Medical Malpractice 'Crisis': Recent Trends and the Impact of State Tort Reforms." Health Affairs. 2004. 21 Jan 2004.
2. Harvard Medical Practice Study, Patients, Doctors, and Lawyers: Medical Injury, Malpractice Litigation, and Patient Compensation in New York. Boston: Harvard University School Of Public Health, 1990.

Furthermore, the CBO found no statistically significant difference in per capita health care spending between states with and without limits on malpractice torts.[1] The General Accounting office did confirm some cases of reduced access to emergency services and newborn delivery "in scattered, often rural areas where providers identified other long-standing factors that affect the availability of services." However, it found many reported reductions in supply by health care providers could not be substantiated or "did not widely affect access to health care."

Very few medical injuries actually result in a claim being filed. A 1984 New York study estimated 27,179 cases of medical negligence occurred in hospitals throughout the state that year, but only 415 — or 1.5%—actually led to claims.[2] The few claims actually being filed as a result of medical injury suggests that restricting malpractice liability would have little effect on health care spending.[3] Physicians are more concerned about premium rates for insurance companies and contingency fees for lawyers than they are the actually number of medical malpractice claims.

DRUG MISREPRESENTATIVES

If fifty million people say a foolish thing, it is still a foolish thing.
Anatole France. French author (1844-1924)

Even though drug seminars are significantly biased[4], they may still offer the potential of providing concise accurate synopses of new agents. Unfortunately, the information presented during luncheon seminars is highly suspect.[5] Several studies that evaluated the information provided by pharmaceutical representatives to physicians found drug representatives nearly always provided the indications for the use of the drug along with its brand and generic name.[6]

However, they consistently failed to mention safety information such as side effects or contraindications. They instead focused their presentations primarily

1. "Medical Malpractice: Implications of Rising Premiums on Access to Health Care." United States General Accounting Office Report to Congressional Requesters. 2003. General Accounting Office. Aug 2003 ‹http://www.gao.gov/new.items/d03836.pdf›.
2. see reference 90
3. "The Economics of U.S. Tort Liability: A Primer." The Economics of U.S. Tort Liability: A Primer. Congressional Budget Office. Oct 2003 ‹http://www.cbo.gov/showdoc.cfm?index=4641&sequence=0›. Localio, A.R, et al. "Relation between malpractice claims and adverse events due to negligence. Results of the Harvard Medical Practice Study III." NEJM vol 325 1991. p. 245-251.
4. Lexchin, J. "What information do physicians receive from pharmaceutical representatives?" Can Fam Phys vol 43 1997. p. 941-45.
5. Als-Nielsen, B., Chen, W., Gluud, C., Kjaergard, L.L. "Association of funding and conclusions in randomized drug trials: a reflection of treatment effect or adverse events?" JAMA Aug 20; 290 2003. p. 921-28. Bekelman, J.E,, Li, Y., Gross, C.P. "Scope and impact of financial conflicts of interest in biomedical research: a systematic review." JAMA Jan 22-29; 289(4) 2003. p. 454-65.
6. Villanueva, P., Peiro, S., Librero, J., Pereiro, I. "Accuracy of pharmaceutical advertisements in medical journals." Lancet vol 361 2003. p. 27-32.

upon on the drugs' benefits while side stepping questions associated with risks or costs. A recent study done by UCSD analyzed tape recordings of thirteen presentations by pharmaceutical representatives during luncheon seminars to residents, found most contained inaccurate statements and 11% of all statements were blatantly false.[1] All the inaccurate statements tended to be favorable to the drug being promoted and only 26% of residents in attendance were able to detect these inaccuracies. A 2003 study concluded 44.1% of all promotional statements were not supported by their references.[2] Multiple studies indicate pharmaceutical representatives greatly distort the benefit of their products[3] while minimizing their risks and side effects. Favorable research is 3.60 times more likely to be published[4] than non-favorable studies.[5]

The exorbitant spending on drug promotions is a primary reason why pharmaceuticals are so expensive. Many ethicists believe these gifts, even those benefiting patients, do little to bolster the public's trust in physicians. They cite the obvious conflict of interest between a doctor prescribing drugs and a company providing the physician "gifts" to write prescriptions for these same drugs. We would not tolerate this behavior in any other profession.

However, pharmaceutical firms brush these concerns aside by saying they are just trying to help both the patient and the physician. If a politician directly received money from a tobacco firm asking them to support legislation favorable to their industry, the media would be screaming "quid pro quo", yet this problem generally remains under-reported. Although the AMA expresses concern over the magnitude of this wide spread practice, they offer only a "voluntary code of ethics" to restrict this behavior.[6] The true irony is that in June, 2001 the American Medical Association accepted a $645,000 "gift" from major pharmaceutical companies to fund an educational effort to help curtail the increasing financial influence of drug companies. The "Gifts to Physicians Campaign" contributors include Eli Lilly, Bayer Corp., Glaxo Wellcome, Johnson & Johnson, Merck & Co., Pfizer and Procter & Gamble. These firms provided unrestricted grants ranging from $50,000 to $100,000 and included $50,000 from a coalition of drug manufacturers called the "Industry Round

1. Ziegler, M.G., Lew, P., Singer, B.C. "The Accuracy of Drug Information from Pharmaceutical Sales Representatives." JAMA vol 273 1995. p. 1298-1298.
2. Waldorff, S. "Results of clinical trials sponsored by for-profit vs nonprofit entities." JAMA vol 290 2003. p. 3071.
3. Buchkowsky, S.S., Jewesson, P.J. "Industry sponsorship and authorship of clinical trials over 20 years." Ann Pharmacother Apr; 38(4) 2002. p. 579-85.
4. Bhandari, M., et al. "Association between industry funding and statistically significant pro-industry findings in medical and surgical randomized trials." CMAJ Feb 17; 170(4) 2004. p. 477-80.
5. Clifford, T.J., Barrowman, N.J., Moher, D. "Funding source, trial outcome and reporting quality: are they related? Results of a pilot study." BMC Health Serv Res Sep 4; 2(1) 2002. p. 18. Lexchin, J., Bero, L.A., Djulbegovic, B., Clark, O. "Pharmaceutical industry sponsorship and research outcome and quality: systematic review." BMJ vol 326 2003. p. 1167-1170.
6. "Ethics Manual, 5th Edition." Ethics Manual 5th Edition. American College of Physicians. 2005 <http://www.acponline.org/ethics/index.html#manual>.

Table."[1] The AMA states this campaign is designed to remind physicians of their voluntary code of ethics which restricts the gifts they may receive from pharmaceutical firms.[2]

A recent AMA sponsored survey found nearly half of all physicians in the US denied knowledge of this voluntary code that permits only "modest" meals for educational events and gifts of no more than $100. The code further restricts such gifts to those providing benefit to patients care. Unfortunately, this voluntary code is routinely ignored and the practice of accepting expensive meals, gifts and trips is still wide spread.[3]

In 2000, these same firms spent about $15 billion on promotional marketing. During 1990 over 180,000 physicians participated in "dinner meeting" lectures sponsored by the pharmaceutical industry. Besides the customarily expensive meal, those in attendance also received a $100-$200 "honoraria" as payment for their time. An AMA committee reported, "[drug-company sponsored] conferences are typically held at attractive locations, and some physicians are flown in with their spouses for a weekend of presentations, recreation, and entertainment, all at the company's expense."[4]

Recognizing their industry is under scrutiny for these overt practices, the pharmaceutical firms are attempting to switch to "stealth technology." Physicians, who would not be enticed by these "personal gifts", may not be so hesitant to accept promotional gifts designed to improve patient care without marketing a specific drug. However, those accepting these gifts fail to consider acceptance of these gifts further inflates the cost of medicine and alters their prescribing patterns. A recent ploy now being utilized is the offering of hand-held computers and software to assist the physician in reducing medication and prescribing errors.[5] Although this may seem a worthwhile goal, it seems incredible that a physician would whine they are unable to afford these $400 devices from the enormous revenues they generate in their practices. The pharmaceutical firms are capitalizing on recent findings that computerization can decrease errors and enhance evidence-based practices. They choose to refer to these promotional gifts as "health promotion services" or "value-added programs" in an effort to avoid the obvious conflict of interest.

---

1. Harrison, B.J. "Tainted money?" Fund Raising Manage Sep; 32(7) 2001. p. 34-37. Romano, M. "Prescription for conflict: AMA accepts funding from drug firms for campaign." Modern Healthcare vol 18 Jun 2001. p. 14.
2. McCarthy, M. "Drug firm support of American Medical Association ethics effort draws fire." Lancet Sep 8; 358(9284) 2001. p. 821.
3. Beverley, D., Rowley, B.D., Harrison, R.V., Thomas, A.M. "Professionalism and Gifts to Physicians from Industry." Module 3: Professionalism and Gifts to Physicians from Industry. 2005. AMA. 14 Jan 2005 ‹http://www.ama-assn.org/ama/pub/category/8688.html›.
4. "Gifts to Physicians From Industry." CEJA Report G 1-90 Gifts to Physicians From Industry. 1990. AMA. 14 Jan 2005 ‹http://www.ama-assn.org/amal/pub/upload/mm/369/ceja_gi90.pdf›.
5. Maguire, P. "New breed of gifts from drug makers: Good for care or crossing the line?" ACP Observer. 2001. American College of Physicians. January 2001 ‹https://www.acponline.org/journals/news/jan01/gifts.htm›.

However, according to IMS Health (a health care research company) the industries promotional budget was $3.6 billion in 1999. These costs further inflate the price of drugs.[1] It is ludicrous to believe a physician is unable to afford a hand-held computer yet finds it acceptable to charge the uninsured poor hundreds of dollars for an antibiotic. If drug firms are so concerned with the general health of the public, then why are their "gifts" almost always exclusively related to products they manufacture? Why do they restrict most of these promotional gifts and grants to large medical groups instead of small general practices? Physicians should surely realize not only is the acceptance of these gifts questionable at best, but they are also designed to facilitate the process of tracking a physicians or groups prescribing practices. This is merely a refinement of a previous tactic of the "Physicians' Computer Network." This system was an office computer used for handling many routine office tasks while making the users' prescribing patterns accessible to the drug companies.[2] In this "Network", the physicians received the computer system, worth over $35,000, free of charge provided they reviewed 32 electronic-mail drug promotional messages via the Network each month and answered brief quizzes related to this material. It seems incredible that people with so much education and intelligence could be so naïve and easily manipulated. They are no more immune from the allure of "something for nothing" than the general public in whom they are supposed to serve.

Many physicians weary of visits from an average of four to five drug reps each week are now delegating this task to non-physician personnel. A survey conducted by the pharmaceutical tracking firm, Scott-Levin Associates, found physician assistants and nurse practitioners are increasingly becoming the focus of many drug representatives.[3] Their survey found 52% of physician assistants and 41% of nurse practitioners polled stated they received more drug representative visits than their supervising physicians. Physician assistants averaged 4.4 visits per week and nurse practitioners averaged 5.2 drug representative visits per week. This is comparable to the four to five drug reps each week that most physicians generally endure. Obviously, the pharmaceutical industry views these health care extenders as the "weakest link" and wishes to further capitalize on the potential market generated by these professions. The study found, on average, a physician assistant saw an average of 92 patients each week and wrote 75 prescriptions for these visits. Nurse practitioners saw an average of 63 patients each week and wrote 54 prescriptions for these patients. Scott-Levin Associates found there were

---

1. Darves, B. "Too close for comfort? How some physicians are re-examining their dealings with drug detailers." ACP Observer. 2003. American College of Physicians. Jul 2003 ⟨http://www.acponline.org/journals/news/jul-aug03/drug.htm⟩.
2. Atkinson, C., Geiger, J. "Just Say No? When Drug Companies Make Offers Doctors Can't Refuse." Lycaeum. 1991. Public Citizen Magazine. Mar 1991 ⟨http://paranoia.lycaeum.org/war.on.drugs/misc/private.greed⟩.
3. Williamson, J. "Make nurses your advocates." The Insider. 2003. Pharmaceutical Representative. 01 Aug 2003 ⟨http://www.pharmrep.com/pharmrep/article/articleDetail.jsp?id=118994⟩.

approximately 38,000 PAs and 60,000 NPs in 1999 and their numbers are expected to increase by an additional 10% each year.[1]

The potential for revenue is enormous considering the number of prescriptions generated by PAs and NPs and the fact that 80% of PAs and 69% of NPs say they make recommendations to physicians on new drugs.[2] This market has not been overlooked by the drug industry; the number of drug reps increased 61% to nearly 80,000 in 1999 from 50,000 in 1995 to meet this additional "demand."

A review of 538 studies published in the January, 2001 issue of *Journal of the American Medical Association* further reinforced the belief physician prescription patterns are negatively affected by interactions with pharmaceutical firms.[3] One critic of the field succinctly states "the manufacturers wouldn't do it if it didn't work."[4]

DIRECT TO CONSUMER ADS

> *You can fool all the people all the time if the advertising is right and the budget is big enough.*
> *Joseph E. Levine, movie mogul (1905-1987)*

This increased promotional activity and direct to consumer ads has greatly increased the costs of pharmaceuticals. According to a fact sheet by the Kaiser Family Foundation, spending on prescription drugs in 2003 had more than quadrupled since 1990.[5] The study determined prescription drug prices had increasing at double digit rates since 1993. It attributed these increases to a 68% increase in total prescriptions between 1994 and 2004, an 8.3% increase in prescription prices and increased utilization of newer more costly agents. A 2001 Kaiser chart book reported 10% of those receiving Medicare were responsible for 39% of all Medicare drug expenditures.[6] Prescription drug costs have risen by $43 billion over a five years period to a record $93 billion in sales, mainly due to increased advertising and cost of designer medications such as Claritin and Prilosec. These promotional activities have been estimated to add nearly $12 billion each year to the total costs of prescriptions.

A recent JAMA article summarizes these influences best and is quoted in its entirety as "physician-industry interaction has a mainly negative impact on

1. "Nurse Practitioners Writing More Prescriptions." Nurse Practitioners Writing More Prescriptions. 1999. 29 Jul 1999 〈http://www.nurses.com/content/news/article.asp?DocID=%7BD7E5B2CF-42CE-11D3-9A54-00A0C9C83AFB&VNETCOOKIE=NO〉.
2. Greene, J. "Nurse practitioners and physician assistants with prescribing rights are the new audience when drug company sales representatives visit doctors' offices." AMNews vol 43 no. 12 2000.
3. Wazana, A. "Physicians and the Pharmaceutical Industry Is a Gift Ever Just a Gift?" JAMA vol 283 2000. p. 373-380.
4. Appleby, J. "Sales pitch: Drug firms use perks to push pills." USA Today 16 May 2001.
5. "Prescription Drug Trends." Kaiser Family Foundation. 2005. Nov 2005 〈http://www.kff.org/insurance/upload/3057-04.pdf〉.
6. "Medicare Statistics." Medicare Statistics. Medicare Rights Center. 2001 〈http://www.medicarerights.org/maincontentstatssupplemental.html〉.

physician knowledge of the appropriateness and the effectiveness of specific drugs, on physicians attitude towards drug representatives and their products with preferential prescribing of sponsored drug and rapid prescriptions of new drugs, and on physician behavior resulting in inaccurate prescribing, increased prescribing, prescribing of new, more expensive drugs with no benefits over cheaper generic drugs, and requests of adding sponsored drugs to the hospital formulary with no obvious advantages over pre-existing ones."[1]

The net results of these findings are that most physicians are practicing medicine that has been heavily influenced by the need for profit and is not necessarily the most beneficial or economical. Dependence on profit instead of proven worth is a prescription for even greater health care spending with increased risk to the public while discrediting the medical profession. The close ties to the pharmaceutical firms greatly influence the reporting of their findings in peer-review journals which are heavily financed by contributions from drug companies. These findings make it very difficult to obtain truly objective data that has not been adulterated by financial incentives. Patients trust their physicians to provide them the best medical care currently available, how disheartening is it to find that many lack both the ethical and moral backbone to place their patient's health concerns over their own economic interests.

According to a recent article published in the Boston Globe, Federal investigators have issued subpoenas to medical centers throughout the nation to obtain records related to their interactions with pharmaceutical firms.[2] This investigation is to evaluate whether grants and free lunches were used to educate or simply to influence physician prescribing practices. Federal guidelines state this behavior is illegal under federal anti-kickback laws and may contribute to the high cost of drugs.[3] The article states prosecutors are especially interested in probing teaching hospitals because they have tremendous influence over the behavior of new and future physicians. The *Boston Globe* article reports one spokesperson for the university systems acknowledging, "There's been a general sense among physicians that industry money doesn't affect their judgment . . . [but] we're learning through more studies it does affect judgment, and people are seeing the amount of money being spent by companies is more than they believed."

These issues of pharmaceutical greed were discussed by the Nobel Prize winning scientist, Sir John Sulston, at the Edinburgh International Science Festival. In comments critical to the industry, he accused the pharmaceutical firms of having a "hidden agenda" in placing profit over treating diseases.[4] He noted 90% of the world's diseases receive only a 10% investment by drug

1. Wazana, A. "Physicians and the Pharmaceutical Industry Is a Gift Ever Just a Gift?" JAMA vol 283 2000. p. 373-380.
2. Kowalczyk, L. "Hospital, drug firm relations probed." The Boston Globe 29 2003, natl ed.: 1.
3. Barclay, L. "BMJ: Pharmaceutical Industry-Physician "Entanglement" Affects Research, Care." Medscape Medical News. Medscape from WebMD. 03 Jun 2003 ⟨http://www.medscape.com/viewarticle/456554?src=searchcol⟩.

companies. He accused them of spending three times more for marketing than for research. He also criticized the industry as being too concerned about diseases of the affluent and being more interested in making "me too" drugs than developing treatments for the poor. The article quotes him as saying, "So, if you are a typical rich person — are depressed, have high cholesterol, are ulcerated, arthritic, hypertense and allergic — then you have many products available to you. If you are in a developing country suffering from tuberculosis or malaria, then just 10% of the research will go on your 90% problem."

4. Templeton, S. "Drug Firms Cure the Rich." Sunday Herald. 2003. 20 Apr 2003 ‹http://www.sundayherald.com/33196›.

CHAPTER 2. A PILL FOR ALL ILLS AND AN ILL FOR ALL PILLS

DRUGS — THE FOURTH LEADING CAUSE OF DEATH

> *To live by medicine is to live horribly.*
> *Carolus Linnaeus, Swedish botanist (1707-1778)*

Although the above findings may initially seem of concern only for economic reasons, they also reflect a more serious consequence of physician prescription by indoctrination. According to researchers at the University of Toronto, PROPERLY prescribed prescription medications and over-the-counter remedies kill more than 106,000 Americans each year and seriously injure an additional 2.1 million.[1] These statistics do not include deaths and injury from drug abuse or medical errors. Their report estimated the number of deaths in 1994 from adverse reactions at between 137,000 and 76,000 with an average of 106,000. Recently there has been considerable media coverage over medication errors, although they are certainly a serious problem, they pale in comparison to the toll adverse drug reactions exact upon human lives.[2]

Medication errors are a systems problem;[3] they exist because the pace of modern medicine exceeds the average person's ability to provide 100% accuracy all the time.[4] However, the system may be reorganized to minimize the likelihood of human error, thereby greatly reducing the number of deaths

1. Bates, D.W. et al. "Incidence of adverse drug events and potential adverse drug events. Implications for prevention. ADE Prevention Study Group." JAMA. 1995. American Medical Association. 05 Jul 1995 ‹http://jama.ama-assn.org/cgi/content/abstract/274/1/29›.
2. Lazarou, J., Pomeranz, B., Corey, P. " Incidence of Adverse Drug Reactions in Hospitalized Patients." JAMA. 1998. American Medical Association. 15 Apr 1998 ‹http://jama.ama-assn.org/cgi/content/abstract/279/15/1200›.
3. Maulik, J., et.al. "A Systems Approach to Improving Error Reporting." Journal of Health Care Information Management vol 16 No. 1 2002. p. 40-45.
4. Gurwitz, J.H., et al. "Incidence and preventability of adverse drug events among older persons in the ambulatory setting." JAMA Mar 5; 289(9) 2003. p. 1107-16.

attributable to medical errors. Unfortunately, adverse drug reactions (ADRs) are not preventable; they are inherent to the use of a drug. In fact, one study suggests that they are actually increasing.[1]

Hospitals traditionally rely upon voluntary reporting of adverse drug reactions to determine their incidence within the hospital setting. This is notoriously unreliable because hospitals have strong incentives not to report too many of these adverse events. High rates of adverse events within a hospital system may lead to increased scrutiny from regulators and the public. According to one study, spontaneous reporting identifies only about 1 in 20 adverse reactions[2] which greatly underestimate their actual frequency of occurrence.[3] The authors of this study estimated over 770,000 people are either injured or die each year in hospitals from adverse drug events. Recent studies report under-reporting of mistakes remains commonplace,[4] especially when the error is committed by a physician.[5]

THE POISON IS IN THE DOSE

> *[Medicine is] a collection of uncertain prescriptions the results of which, taken collectively, are more fatal than useful to mankind.*
> *Napoleon Bonaparte, Emperor of France (1769-1821)*

Every drug has the potential for side effects and some of these may actually be fatal. The use of drugs with known side effects is a guarantee that some portion of its users will suffer from deleterious side effects. The range of effects may be from mild nausea to sudden death.[6] Widespread use of agents with serious inherent side effects virtually assures there will be a substantial number of deaths attributable to the use of that agent. The authors of one study concluded ADRs may be the fourth to sixth leading cause of death. They also found drug-related injuries occur in 6.7% of hospitalized patients.[7] The FDA's annual Adverse Drug Reaction report of 1995 concludes ADRs are a significant

1. Phillips, D.P, Christenfeld, N., Glynn, L.M. "Increase in US medication-error deaths between 1983 and 1993." Lancet vol 351 1998. p. 663-44.
2. Cullen, D.J., Bates, D.W, Small, S.D., Cooper, J.B., Nemeskal, A.R., Leape, L.L. "The incident reporting system does not detect adverse drug events: a problem for quality improvement." Jt Comm J Qual Improv vol 21 1995. p. 541-48.
3. Bates, D.W. "Drugs and Adverse Drug Reactions How Worried Should We Be?" JAMA vol 279 No. 15 1998. p. 1216-17. Classen, D.C., Pestotnik, S.L., Evans, R.S., Lloyd, J.F., Burke, J.P. "Adverse drug events in hospitalized patients. Excess length of stay, extra costs, and attributable mortality.." JAMA vol 277 1997. p. 301-06.
4. Jeffe, D.B et al. "Using focus groups to understand physicians' and nurses' perspectives on error reporting in hospitals." Jt Comm J Qual Saf Sep; 30(9) 2004. p. 471-79.
5. Forster, A.J., van Walraven, C.. "Adverse events: past and future." CMAJ. 2004. CMAJ. 14 Sep 2004 ‹http://www.cmaj.ca/cgi/content/full/171/6/550›. Lawton, R., Parker, D. "Barriers to incident reporting in a healthcare system." Qual Saf Health Care. Mar; 11(1) 2002. p. 15-18.
6. Woos, A.J.J., Stein, C.M., Woosley, R. "Making Medicines Safer." NEJM vol 339 1998. p. 1851-54.
7. Lazarou, J., Pomeranz, B.H., Corey, P.N. "Incidence of adverse drug reactions in hospitalized patients: a meta-analysis of prospective studies." JAMA vol 279 1998. p. 1200-05.

ongoing problem.[1] In an examination of 130,950 post-marketing ADR reports for 1995, hospitalization occurred in about 16% of all reported cases.[2] It is shocking to note 4% of all ADRs were considered life threatening and 5% were actually fatal.[3] These findings were initially disputed by some[4] but other studies concluded medical errors may actually be increasing.[5]

This report does not reflect the additional increase in mortality observed by the CDC. They concluded approximately 90,000 people are killed annually in the US by hospital acquired infections. A separate study by the Institute of Medicine titled "To Err is Human," estimated 44,000-98,000 deaths each year are attributable to medical errors.[6] They also assert millions more suffer serious injuries, such as heart irregularities and internal bleeding, as a result of allergic reactions or other complications from physician prescribed drugs. The problem has gone largely undetected because the Food and Drug Administration relies on voluntary compliance by hospitals, doctors and drug companies to report such cases. These complications increase the length of hospital stay and medical costs by $1.5 billion to $4 billion, with even conservative estimates suggesting about 50,000 deaths are caused by adverse reactions to properly prescribed medication each year in the US.

It has been repeatedly shown that 3-4% of patients in the developed world suffer some kind of harm related to hospitalization (nosocomial injury). For 70%, this injury is temporary; however, 14% of these injuries result in death. These findings were reaffirmed by a British report produced by the Kellogg Foundation. It examined the records of 30,195 patients and found a 3.7% error rate which resulted in death in 14% of those injured. The researchers of this study concluded 70% of all errors, and 155,000 deaths, were avoidable. According to the initial report by the IOM "These horrific cases are just the tip of the iceberg"; they express outrage at the reaction of the medical community to these findings by stating "Yet silence surrounds this issue. . .The status quo is not acceptable and cannot be tolerated any longer." They reminded physicians of

1. Knapp, D.E., Robinson, J.I., Britt, A.L. "Annual Adverse Drug Experience Report: 1995." Annual Adverse Drug Experience Report: 1995. 1995. 1995 ‹http://www.fda.gov/medwatch/safety/ar95.pdf›.
2. Lazarou, J., Pomeranz, B., Corey, P. " Incidence of Adverse Drug Reactions in Hospitalized Patients." JAMA. 1998. American Medical Association. 15 Apr 1998 ‹http://jama.ama-assn.org/cgi/content/abstract/279/15/1200›.
3. Youngson, R.E., Robinson, I.S, et al. Medical Blunders. Amazing True Stories Of Mad, Bad And Dangerous Doctors. New York: New York University Press, 1999.
4. Hayward, R.A., Hofer, T.P. "Estimating Hospital Deaths Due to Medical Errors: Preventability Is in the Eye of the Reviewer." JAMA vol 286 2001. p. 415-20. Sox, H.C. Jr., Woloshin, S. "How Many Deaths Are Due to Medical Error? Getting the Number Right." American College of Physicians. 2000. Nov 2000 ‹http://www.acponline.org/journals/ecp/novdec00/sox.htm›.
5. Phillips, D.P., Christenfeld, N. Glynn, L.M. "Increase in US Medication-Error Deaths Between 1983 and 1993." Lancet vol 351 1998. p. 643-44. Thomas, E.J., Brennan, T.A. "Incidence and types of preventable adverse events in elderly patients: population based review of medical records." BMJ. 2000. British Medical Journal. 18 Mar 2000 ‹http://bmj.bmjjournals.com/cgi/content/full/320/7237/741›.
6. To err is human: building a safer health system. Kohn, L.T., Corrigan, J.M., Donaldson, M.S. The National Acadamies Press. 2000 ‹http://fermat.nap.edu/books/0309068371/html/›.

their promise to "do no harm" and emphasized that eliminating errors were the most important thing a physician could do for their patients.

Their initial estimate that physicians were responsible for approximately 44,000 to 98,000 deaths per year caused such brouhaha that it prompted a presidential commission to determine the impact medical errors has on in-hospital mortality. The initial study evaluated patient outcomes in only three states. A 2004 study examined 37 million patient records from Medicare hospital admissions nationwide from 2000 to 2002. This study by *HealthGrades* represented approximately 45% of all hospital admissions (excluding obstetric patients) from 2000 to 2002.[1] They concluded that the initial IOM study was a tad off in its findings. The 1998 IOM study reported 98,000 Medicare patients died as the result of medical errors. The 2004 *HealthGrades* study found 195,000 Medicare patients die each year as a result of medical errors. This translates into a 25% death rate for all hospitalized Medicare patients from a patient-safety incident. The authors of this study concluded most of these deaths were in fact preventable. These findings nearly double the death rates of the original IOM study and another study published in *JAMA* by Drs. Zhan and Miller in October of 2003. The Zhan and Miller study supported the Institute of Medicine's (IOM) 1999 report conclusion, which found that medical errors caused up to 98,000 deaths annually and should be considered a national epidemic. *HealthGrades'* vice president of medical affairs stated the new death rate is "The equivalent of 390 jumbo jets full of people are dying each year due to likely preventable, in-hospital medical errors, making this one of the leading killers in the U.S."

The *HealthGrades* study evaluated 16 of 20 patient-safety indicators defined by the Agency for Healthcare Research and Quality (AHRQ) — from bedsores to post-operative sepsis — and concluded most deaths were the result of failure to rescue and death in low risk hospital admissions. One investigator concluded prevention of bed sores, postoperative sepsis, and postoperative pulmonary embolism and failure to rescue could reduce the preventable deaths by 20% possibly saving 39,000 premature deaths each year. During the study period of 2000-2002, about 1.14 million patient-safety incidents occurred among the 37 million hospitalized Medicare patients. Eighty-one percent or 263,864 deaths from a total 323,993 were considered directly attributable to these incidents. These lapses in patient safety were also responsible for adding an additional $8.54 billion to in-patient costs during the three years studied. If these results are extrapolated to the entire U.S., they add an extra $19 billion for wasted medical spending and may be responsible for an additional 575,000 preventable deaths from 2000 to 2002.

---

1. "In-Hospital Deaths from Medical Errors at 195,000 per Year, HealthGrades Study Finds." Health-Grades Press Release. 2004. HealthGrades. 27 Jul 2004 ‹javascript:openWin('index.cfm?fuseaction=log&modtype=DMS&modact=/media/DMS/doc/InhosptialDeathsPatientSafetyPressRelease072704.doc')›.

James Reason, a psychologist who wrote a book called *Human Error,*[1] and Charles Perrow, a sociologist who published a book called *Normal Accidents* both believe complex technological systems produce conditions which allow errors to occur.[2] They believe improvements will result only when we quit blaming individuals and focus upon redesigning the system that promotes these errors. The field of medicine is still entrenched in a blame game, ever fearful of lawsuits, health care workers frequently cover-up their mistakes instead of acknowledging them. Admission of errors is discouraged by the punitive system so prevalent in medicine.

Failure to willingly admit medical errors for fear of litigation creates an environment that increases their likelihood. Medication errors and other failings in patient safety are surprisingly common, often preventable, and exert an enormous toll on health care spending. The Institute of Medicine estimated medication errors in hospitals alone incur a total cost between $17 billion and $29 billion annually.[3] Although they have the potential to affect the quality of health care provided to all Americans, medication errors and other patient safety lapses disproportionately affect the sickest patients, both in terms of their incidence and in severity of consequences.[4]

Some within the medical community refused to believe the findings of the initial IOM study. They conjectured that those who died as the result of medical therapy probably would have died anyway, therefore their deaths don't really count.[5] The deaths of the weak and inflicted at the hands of those trusted with their care are an outrage. The trivializing of their deaths shows how reluctant many healthcare workers are to admit their mistakes. Stating that a sick person was going to die despite medical therapy raises a very serious moral question; if they truly had a fatal non-treatable illness, then why is the medical profession wasting limited resources that merely prolong the act of dying? Our culture's failure to effectively cope with dying combined with the advent of for profit medicine may explain many deaths within the medical system, but it is no excuse for callous indifference.

The Food and Drug Administration (FDA)is supposed to be our federal watchdog to help protect the public from dangerous products.[6] Unfortunately, they seem more interested in attacking the defenders of public safety than

---

1. Reason, J.T. Human Error. New York: Cambridge Univ Press, 1990. Reason, J.T. "Human error: models and management." BMJ: Education and Debate. 2000. BMJ. 18 Mar 2000 ⟨http://bmj.bmjjournals.com/cgi/content/full/320/7237/768⟩.
2. Perrow, C. Normal accidents living with high-risk technologies. Princeton, NJ: Princeton University Press, 1999.
3. To err is human: building a safer health system. Kohn, L.T., Corrigan, J.M., Donaldson, M.S. The National Acadamies Press. 2000 ⟨http://fermat.nap.edu/books/0309068371/html/⟩.
4. Shelton P.S., Fritsch, M.A. "Assessing medication appropriateness in the elderly: a review of available measures." Drugs and Aging vol 16 2000. p. 437-50.
5. McDonald, C.J., Weiner, M., Hui, S.L. "Deaths due to medical errors are exaggerated in Institute of Medicine report." JAMA vol 284 2000. p. 93-95.
6. Topol, E.J., Falk, G.W. "A coxib a day won't keep the doctor away." Lancet vol 364 2004. p. 639-40.

enforcing regulations concerning public safety.[1] There has recently been an epidemic of drugs being removed from the market place because of the severity of these adverse events.[2] The Food and Drug Administration (FDA) reports on their web site many of these deaths and injuries occur because physicians ignore posted safety warnings.[3] The FDA has also contributed to this problem by their new policy of accelerated drug approval.[4] The time needed for review of an agent has been decreased to a third of the time it was in 1993 with average review times now being 14.6 months in 2000 compared to 34.3 months during 1993. In special circumstances, this review process may occur in as little as 6 months. This short duration of testing, coupled with the small numbers actually being tested (a typical study usually consists of less than 5,000 patients) affords little opportunity for the magnitude of side effects to be measured.[5]

Determination of adverse events requires a longer duration and larger population before these rare events become statistically significant. Unfortunately, these longer testing periods and greater population sizes do not occur until the agent reaches the market.[6] The first five years after an agent is released to the market is when the vast majority of adverse events and corresponding relabeling occur! As of the year 2001, the FDA had only 82 employees responsible for tracking side effects once drugs reach the market and only twelve actually review not only the hundreds of drug advertisements in print but all the rest of the industry's promotional activities.[7] Usually, misleading advertisements are identified only after they have actually been printed and disseminated. Both physicians and the general public are responsible for voluntarily reporting the majority of post-market adverse

1. Abbassi, K. "Is drug regulation failing?" BMJ 2004. 27 Nov 2004 ‹http://bmj.bmjjournals.com/cgi/content/full/329/7477/0-g›. Lenzer, J. "Public interest group accuses FDA of trying to discredit whistleblower." BMJ. 204. 27 Nov 2004 ‹http://bmj.bmjjournals.com/cgi/content/full/329/7477/1255-a›.
2. Lenzer, J. "FDA is incapable of protecting US "against another Vioxx."" BMJ. 2004. 27 Nov 2004 ‹http://bmj.bmjjournals.com/cgi/content/full/329/7477/1253›. Wood, A.J., Stein, C.M., Woosley, R. "Making Medicines Safer — The Need for an Independent Drug Safety Board." NEJM vol 339 1999. p. 1851-54.
3. Fontanarosa, P.B., Drummond, R., DeAngelis, C.D. "Postmarketing Surveillance—Lack of Vigilance, Lack of Trust." JAMA. 2004. 01 Dec 2004 ‹http://jama.ama-assn.org/cgi/content/full/292/21/2647?eaf›. Griffin MR, Stein CM, Ray WA. "Postmarketing suveillance for drug safety: surely we can do better." Clin Pharmacol Ther vol 2004 75. p. 491-94.
4. Ross, S.D. "Drug-Related Adverse Events: A Readers' Guide to Assessing Literature Reviews and Meta-analyses." Arch Intern Med vol 161 2001. p. 1041-46.
5. Nebeker, J.R., Barach, P., Samore, M.H. "Clarifying Adverse Drug Events: A Clinician's Guide to Terminology, Documentation, and Reporting." Annals of Internal Medicine. 2004. 18 May 2004 ‹http://www.annals.org/cgi/reprint/140/10/795›. Roden, D.M. "An Underrecognized Challenge in Evaluating Postmarketing Drug Safety." Circulation. 2005. American Heart Association. 25 Jan 2005 ‹http://circ.ahajournals.org/cgi/content/full/111/3/246›.
6. Carpenter, D., Chernew, M., Smith, D.G, Fendrick, A.M. "Approval times for new drugs: does the source of funding for FDA staff matter?" Health Affairs. 17 Dec 2003 ‹http://content.healthaffairs.org/cgi/content/full/hlthaff.w3.618vl/DCl›.
7. Ahmad, S.R. "Adverse drug event monitoring at the Food and Drug Administration." LookSmart. 2001. AORN Journal. Feb 2001 ‹http://www.findarticles.com/p/articles/mi_m0FSL/is_2_73/ai_70871451›.

events.[1] The public may report any suspected drug side effect or adverse event using the FDA's MedWatch site. If a potential problem is identified, the FDA will issue clinical warning to physicians. However, they complain most physicians pay little heed to these warnings once a drug is released to the market.

A study was conducted by a group of independent specialist physicians at UCLA. They reviewed 109 randomly selected drug advertisements from major medical journals for drugs in their field of expertise.[2] The consensus from these researchers was for 28% of the advertisements outright rejection should be recommended; major revisions should be required in 34% and 92% of advertisements were considered to be in violation of the FDA regulations. The content of medical journals has become so biased, the editor Lancet complained, "Journals have devolved into information laundering operations for the pharmaceutical industry."[3] The former editor of the *New England Journal of Medicine* accused the industry for becoming "primarily a marketing machine" and co-opting "every institution that might stand in its way."[4] The Public Library of Science internet site has an excellent essay that discusses in detail the dependency of medical journals on pharmaceutical monies.[5]

BITTER PILLS

> *There are some remedies worse than the disease.*
> *Publilius Syrus, Latin writer of mimes (1st c. BC)*

Occasionally side effects are so serious, warnings are insufficient. In extreme cases, the FDA may recommend that the drug manufacturer withdraw the agent from the market. The graph on page 43 is from the FDA site and illustrates the number of drug withdrawals in recent years. If they do not voluntarily comply, the FDA has the authority to remove the offending drug. Although infrequent, these drug withdrawals are by no means rare. Thalidomide is probably the most notorious of all drugs withdrawn.[6] It was first introduced for use as a sedative in 1956 and was specifically marketed for use during pregnancy. It was withdrawn

1. Fontanarosa, P.B., Drummond, R., DeAngelis, C.D. "Postmarketing Surveillance—Lack of Vigilance, Lack of Trust." JAMA. 2004. 01 Dec 2004 ⟨http://jama.ama-assn.org/cgi/content/full/292/21/2647?eaf⟩.
2. Wilkes, M., B.H. Doblin, and M.F. Shapiro, 1992. Pharmaceutical Advertisements in Leading Medical Journals: experts' assessments. Annals of Internal Medicine 116:912-919.
3. Horton, R. The dawn of McScience. New York: New York Rev Books, 2004.
4. Angell, M. The truth about drug companies: How they deceive us and what to do about it. New York: Random House, 2005.
5. Smith, R. "Medical Journals Are an Extension of the Marketing Arm of Pharmaceutical Companies." Public Library of Science. 2005. May 2005 ⟨http://medicine.plosjournals.org/perlserv/?request=get-document&doi=10.1371/journal.pmed.0020138⟩.
6. Knightley, P., Evans, H., Potter, E. Wallace, M , et al. Suffer The Children. The Story Of Thalidomide. London: Andre Deutsch, 1979.

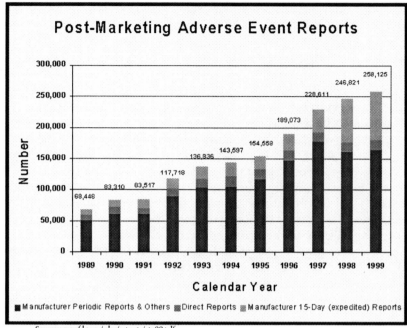

Post-Marketing Adverse Event Reports

Source: www.fda.gov/cder/reports/rtn99.pdf

from the market in 1961 after researchers found that it was responsible for severe birth defects. Unfortunately, the withdrawal of Thalidomide was just the tip of the iceberg. The list of pharmaceuticals withdrawn from the market is extensive and growing at an alarming rate. The FDA maintains a site on the Internet that allows easy access to a listing of drugs either recalled (temporarily withdrawn from the market, relabeled (a change of labeling to reflect newer findings of serious side effects or contraindications) or withdrawn (permanently removed) from the market.[1] Recent examples of drug withdrawals are listed below:

The drug's manufacturer, Merrell Dow, withdrew Bendectin, a drug used for the treatment morning sickness, in 1983 due to a barrage of lawsuits claiming that it caused birth defects.[2]

The once-popular antihistamine Seldane was discontinued from marketing in the United States because it can cause abnormal heart rhythms when taken with the antibiotic erythromycin, or with ketaconozole, an antifungal drug sold as Nizoral.[3]

---

1. "Medical Product Safety Information." Medwatch. U.S. Food and Drug Administration. 14 Feb 2006 <http://www.fda.gov/medwatch/>.
2. Koren, G., Pastuszak, A., Ito, S. "Drugs in Pregnancy." NEJM vol 338 No. 16 1998. p. 1128-37.
3. "Seldane and Generic Terfenadine Withdrawn From Market." FDA Talk Paper. 1998. 27 Feb 1998 <http://www.fda.gov/bbs/topics/ANSWERS/ANS00853.html>.

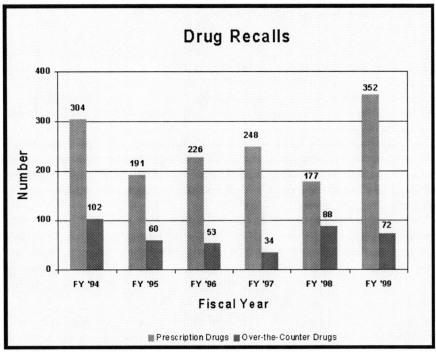

Drug Recalls

Source: www.fda.gov/cder/reports/rtn99.pdf

Rosiglitazone (Rezulin), a drug that lowers blood sugar in diabetics, was linked to 63 deaths and 90 confirmed cases of liver failure. It had been on the US market since mid-1997 but was withdrawn in 2001.[1]

Lotronex received approval by the FDA on February 9, 2000 for the treatment of Irritable Bowel Syndrome (IBS). It generated about $29 million in the first half of the year 2000 and was used in over 300,000 patients. The manufacturer voluntarily withdrew it from the market on November 28, 2000 after determining it was responsible for causing serious bowel dysfunction in many patients.[2]

Phenylpropanolamine (PPA) was a drug used in many over-the-counter products, such as cough and cold syrup and diet pills. Recent research showed it greatly increases the risk of strokes due to hypertension; it was voluntarily withdrawn from the market in 2001.[3]

---

1. "FDA Opts For Safer Diabetes Drugs." CBS News. 2000. 22 Mar 2000 ‹http://www.cbsnews.com/stories/2000/03/21/national/main174732.shtml›.
2. "Lotronex withdrawn from market." Harv Womens Health Watch Feb; 8(6) 2001. p. 6.
3. "Novartis Consumer Health US Announces Voluntary Withdrawal and Reformulation of Phenyl-propanolamine-Containing Cold and Allergy Products." Risk World. 2000. 07 Nov 2000 ‹http://www.riskworld.com/PressRel/2000/00q4/PR00a069.htm›.

Baycol was a cholesterol lowering drug recalled in August 2001 because of 31 deaths from muscle destruction (rhabdomyolysis), and liver failure.[1]

Posicor, a drug used to treat high blood pressure and angina, was voluntarily withdrawn from the market after it was found to have potentially dangerous interactions with more than 25 other medications.[2]

Propulsid, used for the treatment of nausea and heartburn, was linked to potentially fatal irregular heartbeats. After 341 reports of heart-rhythm abnormalities, including 80 reports of deaths, it was withdrawn from the market on March 24, 2000.[3]

Frequently, withdrawal of a drug from the market is preceded by acknowledgement its side effects exceed any therapeutic benefit. Recognition of these adverse effects is often accompanied by a flurry of litigation and label changes. Revelations of serious side effects has endangered the status of several currently popular agents.

Ultram is a synthetic opiate manufactured by Ortho-McNeil and marketed as a pain reliever. It has the potential for severe adverse side effects including seizures, convulsions and anaphylactoid reactions. These warnings were not contained in the original monograph. Ortho was required to revise its warning statement to include these serious adverse reactions. There have been reports concerning Ortho's claim that Ultram[4] is non-addicting.[5]

A study of 9,067 patients found those receiving Cardura had an increased incidence of congestive heart failure. Researchers investigating Cardura were so convinced of its health threat, the trial was terminated two years earlier than planned. Unfortunately, neither the manufacturer (Pfizer) nor the FDA was as convinced. They chose not to alert either physicians or patients of this possible serious side effect. Two former Cardura users filed suit against Pfizer in January 2000 after analysis of data from the Antihypertensive and Lipid-Lowering Treatment to Prevent Heart Attack Trial (ALLHAT) found patients on Cardura were twice as likely to be hospitalized for congestive heart failure as those on a cheaper diuretic. In their petition, they claimed Pfizer had aggressively tried to minimize the study findings in an effort to protect their annual worldwide sales of $800 million.[6] The *American College of Cardiology* has issued a rare "clinical alert" admonishing physicians to "carefully reassess" their use of Cardura.[7]

1. Sorelle, R. "Baycol withdrawn from market.." Circulation Aug 21; 104(8) 2001. p. E9015-6.
2. SoRelle, R. "Withdrawal of Posicor From Market." Circulation. 1998. American Heart Association. 1998 ⟨http://circ.ahajournals.org/cgi/content/full/98/9/83⟩.
3. Twersky, O. "Heartburn Drug Withdrawn." WebMD. 2000. 23 Mar 2000 ⟨http://www.webmd.com/content/article/22/1728_55973⟩.
4. Liu, Z.M. et al. "Drug dependence and abuse potential of tramadol." Zhongguo Yao Li Xue Bao. Jan; 20(1) 1999. p. 52-54.
5. Naslund, S., Dahlqvist, R. "Treatment with tramadol can give rise to dependence and abuse." Lakartidningen Feb 27; 100(9) 2003. p. 712-14. Skipper, G.E., Fletcher, C., Rocha-Judd, R., Brase, D.. "Tramadol abuse and dependence among physicians." JAMA vol 20; 292(15) 2004. p. 1818-19.
6. Rubin, R. "Effectiveness of Cardura being questioned." USA Today. 2001. 24 May 2001 ⟨http://www.usatoday.com/news/health/2001-05-25-cardura-usat.htm⟩.
7. "ACC Issues Clinical Alert On Use Of Cardura (Doxazosin) For Hypertension." Doctor's Guide. 16 Mar 2000 ⟨http://www.pslgroup.com/dg/19097a.htm⟩.

A nationwide class action suit for "fraud" and "conspiracy" in over-promoting the stimulant Ritalin was filed against Novartis, a parents' organization (CHADD: Children and Adults with Attention Deficit/Hyperactivity Disorder), and the American Psychiatric Association.[1] The suit alleged that Novartis, CHADD, and the American Psychiatric Association committed fraud by over-promoting the diagnosis of Attention Deficit Hyperactivity Disorder (ADHD) and its ensuing treatment with Ritalin. These allegations stated that Novartis "deliberately, intentionally, and negligently promoted the diagnosis of ADD/ADHD and sales of Ritalin through its promotional literature and through its training of sales representatives."

Use of Celebrex and Vioxx (agents used to treat arthritis) have been found to be associated with serious side effects including heart attacks, severe intestinal damage, including ulcerations and bleeding, and a fatal skin disease. New research found Vioxx patients had four times the risk of heart attacks as those taking aspirin or ibuprofen. The manufacturer of Vioxx, Merck, had voluntarily withdrawn it from the marketing in 2004.[2] The FDA is currently considering relabeling of Celebrex to include warnings related to these possible risks.[3] On December 17, 2004, the National Cancer Institute stopped the Adenoma Prevention with Celecoxib study after finding it increases the risk of heart attack or other serious cardiovascular problems in a dose dependent manner. A 400 mg. twice daily dose increased risks by 3.4 times compared to placebo. The 200 mg. twice daily dose increased heart attack risk by 2.5 times.[4] Clinical trials initially suggested these drugs were safer on the stomach. However, additional studies were unable to demonstrate a decreased incidence of serious ulcers in Celebrex patients when compared to those on ibuprofen or diclofenac.[5] Worse yet, Celebrex patients on low dose aspirin therapy for secondary prevention of a heart attack actually had a significantly higher rate of serious ulcers than those on aspirin alone.[6] The FDA grudgingly admitted Vioxx may have caused 27,785 deaths.[7] However, the associate director of the FDA's Office of Drug Safety, called the FDA's approval of arthritis drug Vioxx, "The single greatest drug safety catastrophe in the history of this country or the

1. "Ritalin Class Action Suit Filed." Dr. Breggin Testifies Before US Congress. 29 Sep 2000 ‹http://www.breggin.com/congress.html›.
2. "Merck Announces Voluntary Worldwide Withdrawal of VIOXX." Vioxx Press Release. 2004. 30 Sep 2004 ‹http://www.vioxx.com/vioxx/documents/english/vioxx_press_release.pdf›.
3. Pierson, R. "US Regulators Likely to Scrutinize Vioxx Adverse Events." Cox 2. Reuters. 01 May 2000 ‹http://stillswebsite.tripod.com/new_page_48.htm›.
4. Solomon, S.D. "Cardiovascular Risk Associated with Celecoxib in a Clinical Trial for Colorectal Adenoma Prevention." NEJM. 2005. 17 Mar 2005 ‹http://content.nejm.org/cgi/content/abstract/352/11/1071›. ‹http://www.fda.gov/cder/drug/infopage/celebrex/celebrex-hcp.htm›.
5. "FDA panel rejects Celebrex's marketing request." USA Today. 2001. 08 Feb 2001 ‹http://www.usatoday.com/news/health/2001-02-08-celebrex.htm›.
6. A study raises concerns about Vioxx and Celebrex, the nation's top-selling arthritis drugs. What's a patient to do? May 25, 2001 NEWSWEEK WEB EXCLUSIVE.
7. "FDA Estimates Vioxx Caused 27,785 Deaths." Consumer Affairs. 2004. 04 Nov 2004 ‹http://www.consumeraffairs.com/news04/vioxx_estimates.html›.

history of this world." His report claims up to 139,000 Americans have died or been seriously injured from its use.[1] On February 18, 2005, after 3 days of hearings, a 32 member FDA advisory panel decided in a 17 to 15 vote to allow Vioxx to return to the market. They also voted 31-1 to keep Pfizer's Celebrex on the market and 17-13 with 2 abstentions in favor of Pfizer's Bextra.[2] A study published by the Center for Science in the Public Interest states 10 of the 32 panel members had financial ties to either Pfizer or Merck. They suggest these conflicts of interest tainted the approval process for the recommendations on Cox 2 inhibitors.[3] *Vioxx had been Merck's second best selling drug, generating about $2.5 billion in annual revenues.*[4] Currently, the Vioxx debacle continues with jury awards being rescinded, witnesses recanting their testimonies and lawyers using every legal shenanigan available to stop the bleeding of an estimated $50 billion dollars in awards.[5]

The FDA issued an alert in October 1996 about the potential for tendon injuries related to the use of antimicrobial agents known as ciprofloxacin, enoxacin, lomefloxacin, norfloxacin, and ofloxacin. Studies demonstrated they significantly increased the risk of tendonitis and rupture of the shoulder, hand and Achilles tendons to such an extent that surgery may be required.

The injectable anesthesia drug RAPLON (rapacuronium bromide) was voluntarily withdrawn from the market in March 2001 after its manufacturer received reports of five deaths related to its use. The reports indicated it may cause bronchospasm, a mild to severe inability to breathe normally, that can lead to permanent injury or death.

In 1997 the FDA issued a warning about the potential risk for damage to heart valves from the use of the weight loss agents Redux and Pondimin. The warning was followed by a report in the *New England Journal of Medicine* that finally resulted in their withdrawal from the market in September 1997.

Three pending lawsuits filed in June, 2001 in Virginia and West Virginia accuses Purdue Pharma L.P. sales representatives of inappropriately influencing physicians to prescribe oxycontin. The three lawsuits allege Purdue Pharma L.P. sales representatives used "coercive and inappropriate practices" to promote OxyContin to physicians and encouraged doctors to prescribe the drug for short-term pain.[6] These complaints prompted the FDA to issue a warning letter

---

1. Graham, D.J. "Risk of acute myocardial infarction and sudden cardiac death in patients treated with cyclo-oxygenase 2 selective and non-selective non-steroidal anti-inflammatory drugs: nested case-control study." Lancet Feb 5; 365(9458) 2005. p. 475-81.
2. Zwillich, T. "Panel Says Vioxx Can Come Back, Celebrex, Bextra Should Stay." WebMD. 2005. 18 Feb 2005 ‹http://my.webmd.com/content/article/101/105995.htm›.
3. "Conflicts cited for 10 voters on FDA panel." Chicago Tribune [Chicago] 2005, Final ed. sec. News: 14.
4. Gold, J. "Federal Judge in N.J. to Handle Vioxx Suits." ABC News. 2005. 24 Feb 2005 ‹http://abcnews.go.com/Business/wireStory?id=528395›.
5. Pizzo, S. "Shielding Big Pharma." Tom Paine. 2006. 25 Jan 2006 ‹http://www.tompaine.com/articles/2006/01/25/shielding_big_pharma.php›.
6. "Oxycontin Maker, Others Sued by Kentucky Plaintiffs." Common Sense for Drug Policy. 2001. Lexington Herald-Leader. 22 Jun 2001 ‹http://www.mapinc.org/newscsdp/v01/n1150/a04.html›.

to Purdue Pharma demanding they cease using deceptive advertising to increase the sales of this potentially addictive drug.[1]

Warner-Lambert admitted guilt to and agreed to pay more than $430 million in criminal and civil charges for the illegal and fraudulent promotion of unapproved uses of the drug Neurontin.[2] The promotion paid physicians to attend lush dinners, conferences or events to "educate" them in the non-authorized use of Neurontin. These events included expensive trips to Florida, the 1996 Atlanta Olympics and Hawaii. They had been charged with promoting the off label (non FDA approved) use of Neurontin even when scientific studies had shown it was not effective. Neurontin sales approached $2.3 billion in 2003, with 78% of all prescriptions being for unapproved uses.

The average number of drugs recalled over a 5-year period is generally about 2%. This is graphically represented in the illustration below that was obtained from the FDA's web site.

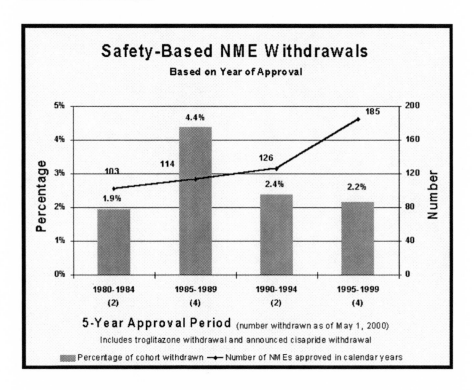

Safety-Based NME Withdrawals

Based on Year of Approval

5-Year Approval Period (number withdrawn as of May 1, 2000)

Includes troglitazone withdrawal and announced cisapride withdrawal

▓ Percentage of cohort withdrawn ◆ Number of NMEs approved in calendar years

---

1. "Warning Letter: RE Oxycontin." FDA Warning Letter. Department of Health and Human Services. 17 Jan 2003 ⟨http://www.fda.gov/foi/warning_letters/g3797d.htm⟩.
2. "Warner-Lambert to Pay $430 Million to Resolve Criminal & Civil Health Care Liability Relating to Off-Label Promotion." Department of Justice. 2004. 13 May 2004 ⟨http://www.usdoj.gov/opa/pr/2004/May/04_civ_322.htm⟩.

CHAPTER 3. PROFITS WITHOUT HONOR

THE BEST HEALTH MONEY CAN BUY

> *Research into illness has progressed so much that it is almost impossible to find someone who is completely healthy.*
> *Aldous Huxley. English novelist and critic (1894-1963)*

The pharmaceutical industry deals with this bad press in a very simple, yet effective manner; they shamelessly promote their products directly to the consumer, bypassing the physician entirely. These direct promotions "inform" the consumer of the newest and most expensive drugs currently available. The "informed" consumer is then more likely to ask his physician for therapies. Given the indoctrination many physicians receive by pharmaceutical representatives, they are probably guaranteed of taking home a bag full of the best modern medicine has to offer. One survey of 5,000 physicians from 14 specialties and 5,000 consumers found one-third of the doctors indicating their patient's requests for specific drugs alter their prescription practice to favor newer agents. Nearly one-half of all physicians surveyed indicated they had a negative attitude concerning direct to consumer ads. The *American Academy of Family Physicians* found 71% of family physicians believed advertising pressures them to use drugs they wouldn't ordinarily prescribe.[1] They frequently complied with their patients request just to keep them happy and prevent them from "doctor shopping." Many physicians believe these ads have made the public suspicious of physician prescribing practices. They may believe the doctor is withholding better drugs from them in order to maximize their HMOs profits. These ads may

---

1. "Direct to Consumer Advertising For Prescription Drugs." American College of Physicians. 1998. 9 Oct 1998 ‹http://www.acponline.org/hpp/pospaper/dtcads.htm›.

create an adversarial relationship between the patient and the doctor. Some HMOs are so enraged over these ads they have countered them with a position paper which is available to both the consumer and physician on their web site.

PROFITS OF DOOM

> *The Greatest Sales Strategy in the world: Don't tell me how good you make it; tell me how good it makes me when I use it.*
> Leo Burnett. *Advertising executive (1891-1971)*

According to a 2000 survey, their concerns about being pressured into prescribing newer agents seem to be legitimate. This survey found in 1999, the 25 top-selling direct to consumer drugs accounted for 40.7% or $7.2 billion of total drug sales.[1] This represented a 19% increase over 1998 sales. Prescriptions for these drugs has increased by 34.2% since 1998. However, prescriptions for drugs not directly being advertised to the public increased by only 5.1%. Direct advertising to consumers has obviously altered the prescribing patterns of most physicians into favoring newer, more expensive agents instead of older, safer and considerably cheaper generics. Scott-Levin, a drug marketing research firm in Newtown, Pa., reported all office visits to physicians increased by only 2% during the first nine months of 1998.[2] However, there was a huge increase in the number of office visits for conditions targeted by consumer ads. They quoted several examples of this explosive growth including increases in office visits of:[3]

- 263% related to smoking cessation
- 113% related to impotence
- 30% for hair loss
- 22% for osteoporosis
- 19% for high cholesterol
- 11% for allergies

The *American College of Physicians-American Society of Internal Medicine* reports consumer advertising totaled $1.3 billion during 1998 and was expected to increase an additional 30% during 1999. These dramatic increases caused some analysts to project drug-advertising budgets may reach $7 billion a year by 2005. The increased costs associated with the use of newer drugs often conflicts with

1. Fintor, L. "Direct-to-consumer marketing: how has it fared?" JNCI. 2002. Journal of the National Cancer Institute. 06 Mar 2002 ‹http://jncicancerspectrum.oxfordjournals.org/cgi/content/full/jnci; 94/5/329?ijkey=a5lda2ad459637c7a3ece2abb488afc8593a9bfc&keytype2=tf_ipsecsha›.
2. Macguire, P. "How direct-to-consumer advertising is putting the squeeze on physicians." ACP. 1999. American College of Physicians. Mar 1999 ‹http://www.acponline.org/journals/news/mar99/squeeze.htm›.
3. "Direct To Consumer Advertising: Finasteride for male pattern hair loss." Therapeutics Letter. Mar/Apr 2001 ‹http://www.ti.ubc.ca/pages/letter40.htm›. "Prescription Drugs and Mass Media Advertising." National Institutes for Health Care Management. Sep 2000 ‹http://www.nihcm.org/DTCbrief.pdf›.

the demands of HMOs and administrators who are attempting to curtail escalating prescription spending. Many of these analysts also agree with the public advocacy group, *Public Citizen*, which states "the primary purpose of advertising is to sell drugs and the history of drug advertising indicates that ads are designed to be as misleading, and sometimes, as false as they can get away with." *Public Citizen* strongly opposes the FDA's policy on TV advertising of prescription drugs.[1] They believe these new guidelines are only a front for increasing the pharmaceutical firms' profits on newer, more expensive patent protected drugs. They complain the FDA is being irresponsible by allowing pharmaceutical companies to advertise misinformation with the intent of increasing their profits. They also state their distrust of the pharmaceutical industry's motives in "educating the public and treating undiagnosed ailments." *Public Citizen* concludes direct to consumer advertising may actually increase the cost of prescription medicines while increasing the potential for serious injury from adverse drug reactions. The American Medical Association (AMA) basically supports *Public Citizen's* efforts to force the FDA increase their regulation over the practice of radio and TV commercials directed toward the public.

The increased targeting of consumers by pharmaceutical firms is in direct response to a FDA decision in August 1997 which permitted TV and radio commercials to extol a drug's benefits while only mentioning its major side effects.[2] Drug firms are required only to provide a Web address and toll-free phone number for those wishing to obtain additional information about common side effects and contraindications. These consumer oriented drug ads have the tendency to "dumb down" the drug information allowing the general public to understand only the basics of this agent. They neglect the subtler facts like: prescription drugs may not work equally well, if at all, across all populations, side effects may be severe or even fatal, or the same benefit may be obtained by cheaper and better tested generics. *Consumer Reports* magazine had medical experts evaluate 28 consumer directed ads in 1995 and concluded nearly a third of all ads were factually inaccurate or made scientifically unfounded assertions.[3] They also concluded only 40% of consumer drug ads honestly reported a drug's effectiveness and described potential benefits and risks accurately in the main text. These findings reiterated those of an earlier 1992 study which also evaluated claims drug ads made to physicians. The authors of this study concluded 30% of ads made dubious claims and 40% did not give an accurate assessment of a drug's potential benefits versus its risks. Critics to direct consumer ads say they encourage the use of newer, patent-protected,

1. "Direct to Consumer Advertising For Prescription Drugs." ACP. 1998. American College of Physicians. 09 Oct 1998 ‹http://www.acponline.org/hpp/pospaper/dtcads.htm›.
2. "Guidance for Industry: Consumer-Directed Broadcast Advertisements." Center for Drug Evaluation and Research: Guidance Document. Center for Drug Evaluation and Research. Aug 1999 ‹http://www.fda.gov/cder/guidance/1804fnl.htm›.
3. "Drug advertising: is this good medicine?" Consum Rep Jun; 61(6) 1996. p. 62-63.

brand name drugs in the place of older, better tested, cheaper and safer agents. Rare side effects require large populations before than can be accurately documented, worse they may not be noted at all until the agent is released to the market with possibly devastating consequences. The first five years after release of an agent to market constitutes a period of drug testing for side effects, where the patient is essentially acting as a guinea pig, while paying premium prices for the least tested therapies.[1]

This self-promotion by the drug industry does not come cheap. According to a recently published paper, drug companies increased their advertising budget to $2.1 billion in 2000 which represents a 17% increase over 1999 spending for direct consumer marketing. *IMS Health and Competitive Media Reporting* found increased advertisement spending resulted in a 6% increase in the number of written prescriptions and a 15% increase in net sales (from $126 billion to $145 billion) for industry wide US sales.[2] This increased advertisement spending does not include the hundreds of millions of dollars also being spent each year in medical journals. The IMS reported drug firms paid for the increased advertising by raising the cost of prescription drugs by 3.9% for the year 2000.[3]

Top advertised drugs were:

Drug	Total
Vioxx	$145 million
Claritin	$111 million
Prilosec	$60 million
Viagra	$93 million
Paxil	$82 million
Flonase	$63 million
Celebrex	$61 million
Zyrtec	$60 million
Prempro	$60 million
Allegra	$60 million

Two of the biggest sellers were Vioxx and Celebrex. For the year 2000, Merck spent more than $318 million on advertising with $145 million of that being used to promote Vioxx which resulted in a 308% sales increase or $1.5 billion annual sales. Pfizer successfully promoted Celebrex, an alternative to Vioxx, and realized a 52% increase over 1999 sales with a value of $2.2 billion. These increases are seen for all major non-generic drugs and are a preview of things to come, exorbitant spending on drug advertisements and escalating drug prices for the consumer.

The revenue to support this increased spending on newer pharmaceuticals has to come from somewhere.[4] Many HMOs have simply opted to raise health

1. Lasser, K.E. "Timing of New Black Box Warnings and Withdrawals for Prescription Medications." JAMA May 1; 287(17) 2002. p. 2215-20. Temple, R.J., Himmel, M. H. "Safety of Newly Approved Drugs." JAMA vol 287 2002. p. 2273-75.
2. Appleby, J. "Prescriptions increase as drugmakers spend more on ads Critics: Ads drive up costs and lead people to pop pills they don't need." USA Today 21 Feb 2001.
3. Appleby, J. "Prescriptions up as drugmakers spend more on ads." USA Today. 2001. 21 Feb 2001 ‹http://www.usatoday.com/news/health/2001-02-21-drugads.htm›.

insurance premiums to cover the increase in prescription spending. Others have refused to allow coverage for certain high cost drugs or raised co-payments by the consumer. Some have even offered different priced HMO packages which offer coverage by generics at a lower cost than treatment with newer agents. This trend has resulted in one expert before the Senate concluding many of the most effective drugs are underused, rather than overused.

HMOs would rather pocket the additional profit than provide more effective therapies to their patients.[1]

However, don't think the physician is being ignored by direct to consumer ads. Even though the pharmaceutical industry spent nearly half a billion dollars on television commercials during the first nine months of 1998, they spent more than five times that ($2.7 billion) for promotion to office-based physicians. This is nearly a 23% increase from the first three-quarters of 1997. The health care consulting firm Scott-Levin found pharmaceutical companies spent an additional $1 billion during 1998 to sponsor events promoting drug sales to the physician.

The naturalist Lewis Thomas was quite prophetic about trends in modern medicine when he wrote; "If people are educated to believe they are fundamentally fragile, always on the verge of mortal disease, perpetually in need of healthcare professionals at every side, always dependent on an imagined discipline of 'preventive' medicine, there can be no limit to the numbers of doctors' offices, clinics, and hospitals required to meet the demand."[2]

Over one-quarter of all hospitalizations are directly attributed to the very drugs the physician has prescribed. Even though these drugs may be taken exactly as directed, the side effects attributable to these drugs add hundreds of billions of dollars to the annual national budget. Even worse, they cause the death of as many as a 100,000 each year. These numbers do not reflect improperly prescribed drugs, drug overdoses, or illicit drug use. The pharmaceutical firms offset these findings by saturating the market with embellished claims in direct to consumer ads. The purpose of these ads is simply to encourage the consumer to pressure their physician in prescribing these newer; more expensive and least tested agents. An adverse outcome of direct to consumer ads may take five years or more to evaluate, since typically it requires at least five years of post-marketing release to obtain sufficient information on the side effects and drug interaction with most medications.

---

4. Macguire, P. "How direct-to-consumer advertising is putting the squeeze on physicians." ACP. 1999. American College of Physicians. Mar 1999 ‹http://www.acponline.org/journals/news/mar99/squeeze.htm›.

1. Calfee, J.E. "Public Hearings on Direct-to-Consumer Advertising of Prescription Drugs Written testimony before the Senate Subcommittee on Consumer Affairs, Foreign Commerce, and Tourism Committee on Commerce, Science, and Transportation for Public Hearings on Direct-to-Consumer Advertising of Prescription Drugs." U.S. Senate Committee on Commerce, Science & Transportation. 2001. 24 Jul 2001 ‹http://commerce.senate.gov/hearings/072401Calfee.pdf›.

2. Thomas, L. The Medusa and the Snail. New York: Bantam Books, 1980.

A 2002 survey of 500 physicians showed 75% believed television ads caused patients to believe drugs were more effective than supported by data. Twenty-five percent stated they felt pressured by patients to write prescriptions for advertised drugs.[1] A recent analysis from the Kaiser Family Foundation concluded each additional $1 spent on drug advertising resulted in $4.20 of new drug sales for the year 2000[2].

Pharmaceutical promotional spending has increased an average of 16% a year since 1996 approaching $3 billion for the year 2000. Instead of developing newer agents, the authors of the Kaiser study state most "investment" is on only a few new drugs that have experienced significant sales growth.

Although these "investments" have slowed, they are still expected to average 9% to 12% for most of the next decade. The prices of the 50 most-prescribed drugs for the elderly climbed an average of three times the rate of inflation for the year 2002.[3]

MEDIOCRE MEDICINE

> *America's health care system is second only to Japan... Canada, Sweden, Great Britain... well, all of Europe. But you can thank your lucky stars we don't live in Paraguay!*
>
> *Homer Simpson. American animated TV icon and folk philosopher*

The assumption exists in the US that our expensive medicine corresponds to superior medicine. This assumption is blatantly wrong. Recent comparisons of health indicators[4] between the US and 13 other industrialized nations showed the US ranks an average of 12th for 16 available health indicators.[5] More specifically, the ranking of the US on several indicators was:

- 13th (last) for low-birth-weight percentages
- 13th for neonatal mortality and infant mortality overall
- 11th for post neonatal mortality
- 13th for years of potential life lost (excluding external causes)
- 11th for life expectancy at 1 year for females, 12th for males
- 10th for life expectancy at 15 years for females, 12th for males

1. "Drug Ads Pressuring Doctors To Prescribe Certain Medications, AMA Official Says." Daily Reports: The Comprehensive Source. 2003. Kaiser Network. 23 Jul 2003 ‹http://www.kaisernetwork.org/daily_reports/rep_index.cfm?DR_ID=18971›.
2. Rosenthal, M.B., Berndt, E.R., Donohue, J.M., Epstein, A.M., Frank, R.G. "Demand Effects of Recent Changes in Prescription Drug Promotion." Kaiser Family Foundation. 2003. 25 Jun 2003 ‹http://www.kff.org/rxdrugs/6085-index.cfm›.
3. Hallam, K. "Seniors' Drug Prices Outpace Inflation, Report Says." Bloomberg News 09 Jul 2003.
4. Starfield, B. "Is US Health Really the Best in the World?" JAMA vol 284 2000. p. 483-85.
5. Starfield, B. Primary Care: Balancing Health Needs, Services, and Technology. New York: Oxford University Press, 1998.

- 10th for life expectancy at 40 years for females, 9th for males
- 7th for life expectancy at 65 years for females, 7th for males
- 3rd for life expectancy at 80 years for females, 3rd for males
- 10th for age-adjusted mortality

The World Health Organization using different criteria, ranked the United States as 15th among 25 industrialized countries and 37th of 191 countries in terms of the overall performance of its health system.[1] It may be assumed our poor lifestyle choices are contributory to these dismal findings; however, this is not supported by factual data. In comparison to other countries, we may be considered as moderate in the abuse of our bodies.[2] For example: In the US, 24% of all females are smokers as compared to 14% of females in Japan and 41% in Denmark; ranking us as fifth highest among industrial nations. For males, the range is from 26% in Sweden to 61% in Japan; and 28% in the United States making us third highest. We rank only fifth highest for alcoholic beverage consumption. The US has relatively low consumption of animal fats (fifth lowest in animal fat consumption for men aged 55-64 years and the third lowest mean cholesterol concentrations among men aged 50 to 70 years among 13 industrialized countries.

Technologically, we lead all nations except Japan in the availability of MRI units and CT scanners per million populations; yet the Japanese rank highest in health while we rank near the bottom of all industrialized nations.

The Japanese are less prone to provide medical treatment once diagnoses have been made, whereas in the US diagnostic technology most frequently precedes aggressive management and treatment even if this treatment is not supported by literature. Is it any wonder that many people feel that the first law of the Hippocratic oath — *Primum non nocere* (First, do no harm) — is a farce[3] and cynically suggest that the Hippocratic oath should be renamed the "Hypocritic oath"?[4]

IATROGENESIS: THE THIRD LEADING CAUSE OF DEATH IN THE US

Doctors will have more lives to answer for in the next world than even we generals.

1. "The world health report 2000 — Health systems: improving performance." The World Health Report. 2000. WHO. Jan 2001 ‹http://www.who.int/whr/2000/en/›.
2. Anderson, G., Poullier, J.P, et al. Health Spending, Access, And Outcomes: Trends In Industrialized Countries. New York: The Commonwealth Fund, 1999.
3. Gordon, D.T. "Hippocrates or Hypocrisy?" Northeastern University Magazine On Line. Jan 2000 ‹http://www.numag.neu.edu/0001/health.html›.
4. Bernhardt, M.J. "Hippocratic Oath (Or Is It the Hypocritic Oath?)." Duval County Medical Society On Line. 1997. Feb 1997.

Napoleon Bonaparte

In a recent study, Dr. Barbara Starfield of the Johns Hopkins School of Hygiene and Public Health states our medical system is responsible for increased mortality and decreased health with the following reported per year[1]:

- 12,000 Unnecessary surgery[2]
- 7,000 Medication errors in hospitals[3]
- 20,000 Other errors in hospitals[4]
- 80,000 Infections in hospitals[5]
- 106,000 Non-error, negative effects of drugs[6]

This means physicians and hospitals are responsible for approximately 225,000 deaths per year! Worse, these data are inferred from studies in hospitalized patients only and do not include adverse effects causing disablement or pain. A large 2004 study found projected medical error rates may be greater than 250,000 deaths annually. If this study is correct, medical therapy may actually be the third leading cause of death in America. These numbers bolster the findings of another report which evaluates the quality of health care in the US. It concludes the care delivered in the United States often does not meet professional standards.[7]

A previous study reported in November 1999 by the Institute of Medicine (IOM) evaluated the extent of medical errors in US hospitals based on an analysis of two previous studies, one in New York (1984) and the other in Colorado and Utah (1992).[8] Called the Harvard Medical Practice Study,[9] it appraised 30,000 randomly selected discharges from 51 randomly selected hospitals in New York and concluded that adverse events occurred in 3.7% of all hospitalizations, of which 58% could be attributable to preventable errors and 27.6% to negligence. Although most resulted in only short-term disability, 13.6%

1. Starfield, B.. "Is US health really the best in the world?" JAMA. 2000. American Medical Association. 26 Jul 200 ⟨http://jama.ama-assn.org/cgi/content/extract/284/4/483⟩.
2. Leape, L.L. "Unnecessary Surgery." Annual Reviews. 1992. May 1992 ⟨http://arjournals.annualreviews.org/doi/abs/10.1146/annurev.pu.13.050192.002051?journalCode=publhealth⟩.
3. Phillips, D.P., Christenfeld, N., Glynn, L.M. "Increase in US medication-error deaths between 1983 and 1993." Lancet Feb 28; 351(9103) 1998. p. 643-44.
4. Lazarou, J., Pomeranz, B.H., Corey, P.N. "Incidence of adverse drug reactions in hospitalized patients: a meta-analysis of prospective studies." JAMA Apr 15; 279(15) 1998. p. 1200-05.
5. Ibid. p. 1200-05.
6. National Academy Press. To Err Is Human: Building a Safer Health System. By Kohn, L., Corrigan, J., Donaldson, M. 1999. 29 Nov 1999 ⟨http://fermat.nap.edu/books/0309068371/html/⟩.
7. Schuster, M., McGlynn, E., Brook, R. "How good is the quality of health care in the United States?" Milbank Q vol 76 1999. p. 517-63.
8. Brennan, T. et al. "Incidence of Adverse Events and Negligence in Hospitalized Patients. Results of the Harvard Medical Practice Study I." NEJM vol 324 No. 6 1991. p. 370-76.
9. Leape, L. et al. "The Nature of Adverse Events in Hospitalized Patients: Results of the Harvard Medical Practice Study II." NEJM vol 324 No. 6 1991. p. 377-84.

resulted in death and 2.6% resulted in permanent disability. The authors concluded between 44,000 and 98,000 Americans die each year as a result of preventable medical errors. At 225,000 deaths per year, iatrogenic related deaths would be the third leading cause of death in the United States, surpassed only by deaths from heart disease and cancer.

Causes of Deaths according to the Centers for Disease Control[1]

1.	696,947	Heart Disease
2.	557,271	Malignant Neoplasms
3.	225,000	Medical system
4.	162,672	Stroke
5.	124,816	Bronchitis Emphysema Asthma
6.	106,742	Accidents & Adv. Effects
7.	73,249	Diabetes
8.	65,681	Pneumonia & Influenza
9.	58,866	Alzheimer's disease
10.	40,974	Nephritis
11.	33,865	Septicemia

These data for iatrogenic deaths does not include the 4% to 18% of those treated as outpatient who experience adverse effects, resulting in:[2]

- 116 million extra physician visits
- 77 million extra prescriptions
- 17 million emergency department visits
- 8 million hospitalizations
- 3 million long-term admissions
- 199,000 additional deaths
- $77 billion in extra costs

According to recent studies, the number of medically related deaths is inflated even further. A Dartmouth-Hitchcock Medical Center study[3] suggests 11,200 lives could be saved each year if rural physicians were more prompt in referring patients to high volume hospitals[4] that utilize evidence based medical standards.[5]

More than four million patients are admitted to US intensive care units (ICUs) each year, approximately 500,000 or 10-20% die within this setting.[6] A 2002 study concluded hospital ICUs not using intensivists (physicians

1. "Deaths-Leading Causes." National Center for Health Statistics. 2005. CDC. 14 Nov 2005 ‹http://www.cdc.gov/nchs/fastats/lcod.htm›.
2. Weingart, S.N., McL Wilson, R., Gibberd, R.W., Harrison, B. "Epidemiology of medical error." West J Med Jun; 172(6) 2000. p. 390-93.
3. Birkmeyer JD, Dimick JB. Leapfrog safety standards: potential benefits of universal adoption. The Leapfrog Group. Washington, DC: 2004. http://www.leapfroggroup.org/media/file/Leapfrog-Evidence-based_Hospital_Referral_Fact_Sheet.pdf
4. Birkmeyer, J.D. et al. "Hospital Volume and Surgical Mortality in the United States." NEJM. 2002. 11 Apr 2002 ‹http://content.nejm.org/cgi/content/short/346/15/1128›.
5. Begg, C.B., Cramer, L.D., Hoskins, W.J., Brennan, M.F. "Impact of hospital volume on operative mortality for major cancer surgery." JAMA vol 280 1998. p. 1747-51. Comarow, A. "Higher volume, fewer deaths.." U.S. News & World Report 2000.
6. Zimmerman, J.E., Wagner, D.P, Draper, E.A., Wright, L., Alzola, C., Knaus, W.A. "Evaluation of acute physiology and chronic health evaluation III predictions of hospital mortality in an independent database." Crit Care Med vol 26 1998. p. 1317-26.

specializing in the treatment of the critically ill) were responsible for over 54,000 deaths annually.[1]

These two studies add another 65,200 deaths attributable to our medical system. Combining the Dartmouth Leapfrog Group's estimates of deaths attributable to inefficient medical practices to the 1998 Johns Hopkins group's estimates means the US health care system may be responsible for over 290,000 deaths annually. More recent studies suggesting nurse work overload increases the risk of dying to a greater extent than the possible benefit from surgery. These findings may further inflate these numbers.

The 2002 study concluded that mortality increases by 7% for every patient added to the average nurse's workload. In surgical patients, mortality is 30% higher for nurses with an average patient load of 8 patients than it is for those with four. Adverse outcomes from falls, medical errors, failure to rescue[2] and neglect[3] may increase mortality rates above those who never sought medical treatment. Poor nurse staffing[4] may neutralize or reverse any benefit obtained by medical therapy.[5]

The implementation of managed care and for profit medicine has coincided with a mass exodus by many nurses from the medical profession. The resulting nursing shortages exacerbate the problem of understaffing and increased mortality associated with medical care. Understaffed hospitals have poorer outcomes than those with better nurse to patient ratios. The 2004 study which concluded that poor in-hospital care is responsible for 195,000 preventable deaths each year indirectly confirmed the findings of studies the effects of nurse workload on patient mortality.

The authors of this study state that most of these deaths were in fact preventable and occurred in low risk patients. The HealthGrades study examined 45% of all hospital admissions in the United States from 2000-2002. After evaluating 37 million hospital records, the study determined the initial mortality rates published in the "To Err is Human" report of 1998 by the Institutes of Medicine was only half the actual number of deaths associated with medical errors. They projected in addition to human lives lost; medical errors added an additional $6 billion per year to health care spending. Unlike the IOM study, which extrapolated national findings from data based on three states or the Zhan and Miller study of 7.5 million patient records from 28 states over one

---

1. Pronovost, P.J., Angus, D.C., Dorman, T., Robinson, K.A., Dremsizov, T.T., Young, T.L. "Physician staffing patterns and clinical outcomes in critically ill patients: a systematic review." JAMA vol 288 2002. p. 2151-62.
2. Clarke SP, Aiken LH. Failure to rescue: measuring nurses' contributions to hospital performance. Am J Nursing. 2003; 103:42-47.
3. Needleman, J., Buerhaus, P.I., Mattke, S., Stewart, M., Zelevinsky, K. "Nurse-staffing levels and the quality of care in hospitals." NEJM. 2002. 30 May 2002. ‹http://content.nejm.org/cgi/content/abstract/346/22/1715›.
4. Cho SH, Ketefian S, Barkauskas VH, Smith DG. The effects of nurse staffing on adverse events, morbidity, mortality, and medical costs. Nurs Res. 2003; 52:71-79.
5. Aiken, L.H., Clarke, S.P., Sloane, D.M., Sochalski, J., Silber, J.H. "Hospital nurse staffing and patient mortality, nurse burnout, and job dissatisfaction." JAMA vol 288 2002. p. 1987-93.

year, the HealthGrades study examined three years of Medicare data throughout the entire United States. One author quotes the vice president of medical affairs for the HealthGrades study as saying "The HealthGrades study shows that the IOM report may have underestimated the number of deaths due to medical errors, and, moreover, that there is little evidence that patient safety has improved in the last five years," and this is "The equivalent of 390 jumbo jets full of people are dying each year due to likely preventable, in-hospital medical errors, making this one of the leading killers in the U.S." The highest levels of mortality, failure to rescue and death in low risk hospital admissions, were not evaluated in the earlier studies. The authors suggest major reductions from medical errors may be obtained by reducing the incidence of failure to rescue, bed sores, postoperative infections, and postoperative blood clots. The HealthGrades study may be found at www.healthgrades.com. The studies major findings were:

- About 1.14 million patient-safety incidents occurred among the 37 million hospitalizations in the Medicare population over the years 2000-2002.
- Eighty-one percent of the total 323,993 deaths were directly attributable to lapses in patient-safety.
- Twenty-five percent of those who experienced a patient-safety incident died.
- These patient-safety incidents increased patient care costs by $8.54 billion during the three years studied.
- If extrapolated to the entire U.S. these incidents would result in $19 billion additional medical costs and more than 575,000 preventable deaths during the study period between the years 2000-2002.
- Sixty percent of patient-safety incidents were associated with failure to rescue, bedsores and postoperative infections.

THE MONEY MACHINE

> *As long as men are liable to die and are desirous to live, a physician will be*
> *made fun of, but he will be well paid.*
> Jean De La Bruyère 1645-1696, French Classical Writer

Although western medicine has always had to contend with a bad public image because of the perceived greed of many of its practitioners, it wasn't until the mid-nineties that the drive for profit clearly superseded any altruistic motive by many medical establishments. This is not meant to condemn the individual practitioner; many remain in medicine primarily because of a desire to fulfill a perceived social obligation. However, with the advent of managed care medicine and health maintenance organizations, the need for profit resulted in few physicians remaining in medicine, "just to help the poor." Socialized medicine was actually slandered within the US. References to countries whose primary care consisted of socialized medicine were replete with horrible examples of how many are neglected and left to die because socialized medicine lacks both the resources and will to treat all the poor.[1] Canadian medicine was vilified as being backward and ill prepared to meet the medical needs of the sick in the new millennium.[2] How ironic that much of the new practice of "Evidence Based Medicine" was actually conceived within the Canadian medical system.[3] Researchers at McMasters University are in the forefront of this emerging practice of medicine.[4] Their basic premise is a country's limited financial resources are better utilized on therapies of proven benefit than being squandered willy-nilly for therapies of unproven worth. Traditional therapies are evaluated to determine their efficacy, often their use is dictated more by profit and tradition than actual benefit.

Unfortunately, within the US the attitude has been "more is better" and "newer is always better than older." This attitude has resulted in obscene increases for the costs of medicines and medical or surgical therapies. Hospitals have rejected their traditional role of offering community services for the sick and the poor. Instead the focus is now to view the patient as a potential source of profit.[5] The profit obtained is used to expand services, not to the poor, but instead for those who are better insured.[6] Many hospitals have become nearly malignant in their growth, having saturated their growth potential in the local market; they acquire small community hospitals that still maintain these traditional services.[7] This produces "chain hospitals" where a single larger corporation dictates what each community hospital will offer.[8] Obviously, like any corporation, profits are the number one determinant of what constitutes a successful hospital.

If these statements seem like exaggerations, consider the following quotes from prominent hospital CEOs: "Do we have an obligation to provide healthcare to everybody? Where do we draw the line? Is any fast-food restaurant obligated to feed everyone who shows up"?[9] No wonder former president Jimmy Carter

1. Cihak, R.J. 'Canada's Medical Nightmare.' Health Care News Sept 2004 2004. Lemieux, P. 'Socialized Medicine: The Canadian Experience.' The Freeman. Mar 1989 ⟨http://www.theadvocates.org/freeman/8903lemi.html⟩.
2. Mercer, I. 'Failure Defined As Success in Socialized Medicine.' The Vancouver Sun 26 Oct 2000. Reed, L.W. 'Socialized Medicine Leaves a Bad Taste in Patients' Mouths.' Mackinac Center for Public Policy. 2003. 23 Feb 2003 ⟨http://www.mackinac.org/article.asp?ID=2748⟩.
3. Evidence-based Medicine Working Group. 'A new approach to the teaching of medicine.' JAMA vol 268 1992. p. 2420-25.
4. 'Definition of Evidence-based medicine.' MedicineNet. 2006. 20 Feb 2006 ⟨http://www.medterms.com/script/main/art.asp?articlekey=33300⟩.
5. Hasan, M.M. 'Let's end the nonprofit charade.' NEJM vol 334 1996. p. 1055-57. Salmon, J.W. 'A perspective on the corporate transformation of health care.' Int J Health Serv vol 25 1995. p. 11-42.
6. Appleby, J. 'Hospitals fight for turf in medical arms race.' USA Today 19 Feb 2002.
7. Himmelstein, D.U., Woolhandler, S. 'The High Price of Health.' Frontline. 1998. ⟨http://www.pbs.org/wgbh/pages/frontline/shows/hmo/etc/synopsis.html⟩.
8. Watt, J.M. 'The comparative economic performance of investor-owned chain and not-for-profit hospitals.' NEJM vol 314(2) 1986. p. 89-96.

expressed contempt for the medical field by stating: "The oil lobby, perhaps the most powerful lobby on earth, is almost matched by hospital owners and doctors"?[1]

In December 2000, Columbia HCA (the nation's largest for profit hospital organization) pled guilty to defrauding Medicare of hundreds of millions of dollars and was required to pay more than $840 million in criminal fines, civil penalties and damages.[2] Did these fines shame the company into honesty? A 2001 Justice Department statement accusing HCA of continuing to owe more than $400 million seems to indicate the answer is no.[3]

They have also been accused of:[4]

• Inflating the cost of treatment in order to larger reimbursements.

• Charging Medicare for unused hospital space that they said was being used for patient care.

• Covering up overcharges and auditing errors favorable to HCA.

• Refusal to obey Medicare auditors by the continued claiming of costs previously rejected.

• Moving lower cost expenditures to high cost home health care.

In June 2003, Columbia/HCA finally agreed to pay the government a total of $1.7 billion in criminal fines and civil penalties for systematically defrauding federal health care programs. This is the largest recovery ever reached by the government in a health care fraud investigation.[5]

One HMO executive was quoted in the Wall Street Journal: saying "We see people as numbers, not patients. It's easier to make a decision. Just like Ford, we're a mass production assembly line and there is no room for the human equation in the bottom line. Profits are king."[6]

According to an Internet site that tracks physicians' salaries, the average physician earned approximately $200,000 in 2004.[7] Many Americans have little

9. Court, J., Smith, F. Making a Killing: HMOs and the Threat to Your Health. Common Courage Press. 20 Feb 2006 ‹http://www.makingakilling.org/chapter3.html›. Ginsburg, C. 'The Patient As Profit Center; Hospital Inc. Comes To Town.' The Nation 18 Nov 1996, Natl ed.: 18.

1. 'The Drug Story.' The Pharmaceutical Drug Racket. 1993. Campaign Against Fraudulent Medical Research. 1995 ‹http://www.pnc.com.au/~cafmr/online/medical/druglb.html›. Greger, M. 'Appendix 59b - Club Med.' Heart Failure - Diary of a Third Year Medical Student. 1999. Jan 1999 ‹http://upalumni.org/medschool/appendices/appendix-59b.html›.

2. Appleby, J. "Columbia agrees to pay $745m penalty." USA Today 19 May 2000, Natl ed. "HCA agrees to pay U.S. $840 million to settle criminal, civil allegations." Health Care Fraud Report 01 Oct 2001.

3. Brubaker, B. "HCA faces new fraud charges", The Washington Post, 17 Mar 2001. Russell, R. "Justice Department says HCA owes 'hundreds of millions' in fraud case," Tennessean, 17 Mar 2001.

4. "Justice Department accuses hospital chain of fraud." USA Today 13 Aug 2001.

5. Statement of Peter D. Keisler Assistant Attorney General Civil Division Department of Justice Before the Subcommittee on Commercial and Administrative Law Committee on the Judiciary United States House of Representatives Concerning Budget and Resource Needs of the Justice Department Civil Division for Fiscal Year 2005 Presented on March 9, 2004

6. Beckham, J.D. "The Accountability Crisis in Health Care." The Health Forum Journal. 1998. 18 Feb 2006 ‹http://www.beckhamco.com/index_files/048_accountabilityinhealthcare.doc›. Greger, M. "Surgery — A Cut Below the Rest." Heart Failure — Diary of a Third Year Medical Student. 1999. Jan 1999 ‹http://upalumni.org/medschool/surgery.html›.

7. "Physician Salaries and Salary Surveys." Allied Physicians. 2004. Jan 2004 ‹http://www.allied-physicians.com/salary_surveys/physician-salaries.htm›.

faith in their physician's ability to exercise restraint concerning money.[1] One survey found two thirds of Americans believe physicians are "too interested in making money."[2] A random survey of 1000 households in the US found 82% believe, "Medical care has become a big business that puts profits ahead of people."[3] Physicians may routinely earn hundreds of dollars for procedures involving only minutes of their time. And yet the very ones requiring the greatest need are often denied access to basic medical services. HMOs define the cost of patient care as the "medical loss ratio"; [4] the monies used to treat the sick are viewed as a loss of profit. Their focus is clearly on profit margins and not on the healing of the sick and inflicted.[5] The impoverished and minorities are truly on the horns of a dilemma; having to choose between inadequate healthcare versus no healthcare.[6]

A recent study in *JAMA* states "Lower socioeconomic status is probably the most powerful single contributor to premature morbidity and mortality, not only in the United States but worldwide."[7] The care is so disparate, a recent study found the average life expectancy of an African-American is seven years less than their Caucasian counterparts.[8] If you still aren't convinced money and status affects your level of healthcare, consider the following; children of physicians are five times more likely to be treated by an attending than by a resident.[9]

In the two decades from 1970 to 1990, medical charges increased over three times the rate of inflation, while the services provided decreased.[10] The typical physician makes over five times the average workers salary in the US.[11] Even worse, the insurance premiums of the average patient would nearly make an extortionist blush. They charge you indefinitely at a rate far exceeding the costs they will incur from your treatment.

A new method of cost containment (or greed if you prefer) is capitation. Capitation is when a physician agrees to provide healthcare on a per patient

1. Bloche, M.G. "Cutting Waste and Keeping Faith." Annals of Internal Medicine vol 128 1998. p. 688-89. Feldman, D.S., Novack, D.H., E Gracely, E. "Effects of Managed Care on Physician-Patient Relationships, Quality of Care, and the Ethical Practice of Medicine." Archives of Internal Medicine vol 158 1998. p. 1626-32.
2. Nelson, A.R. "Humanism and the Art of Medicine." JAMA vol 262 1989. p. 1228-30.
3. "A Report on a National Survey." Journal of Health Care Finance vol 23 1997. p. 12-20.
4. "List of Health Insurance Definitions." Health Symphony. 2006. 20 Feb 2006 ‹http://www.health-symphony.com/insurancedefinitions.htm›.
5. Schiff, G. "Why For-Profit Managed Care Fails You and Your Patients." American College of Physicians' Observer. 1996. ‹http://www.acponline.org/journals/news/nov96/forprofi.htm›.
6. Gornick M.E., et al. "Effects of Race and Income on Mortality and Use of Services Among Medicare Beneficiaries." NEJM vol 335 1996. p. 791-99.
7. Smith et al. "Socioeconomic Factors and Determinants of Mortality." JAMA vol 280 1998. p. 1744-45. Williams, R.B. "Lower Socioeconomic Status and Increased Mortality." JAMA vol 279 1998. p. 1745-46.
8. "Life Tables." National Center for Health Statistics. 2005. 23 Aug 2005 ‹http://www.cdc.gov/nchs/data/hus/hus05.pdf#027›.
9. Diekema, D.S., Cummings, P., Quan, L. "Physician's Children are Treated Differently in the Emergency Department." American Journal of Emergency Medicine vol 14 1996. p. 6-9.
10. Massell, T.B. "Letter." The Pharos Summer 1994. p. 44.
11. Smith, J.M. Women and Doctors. New York: Atlantic Monthly Press, 1992.

basis. They receive a fixed payment each month for every member of the HMO.[1] With capitation, profits are directly proportional to the number of healthy HMO members. Greater numbers of the truly sick increases the frequency of medical intervention, thereby reducing the profits of the HMO. Furthermore, once a patient's medical treatment reaches a lifetime limit, additional payments are no longer available, no matter how sick they may become.

Don't think this is only a theoretical discussion; I personally had to discharge a quadriplegic from home health services after he had reached his capitation limit, and he died within a year of being discharged. Sadly, he would have remained a patient if it weren't for the company's policy of "maximizing visits." This is a euphemism for bilking Medicaid and/or Medicaid for all that is legally possible. Congressional investigations into home health care fraud[2] found it was not uncommon for the home health care agencies definition of "legally" to differ from their own.[3] The resulting scandals[4] only succeeded in making the agencies more circumspect with the claims they filed.[5] Capitation favors over-management of relatively healthy patients while encouraging physicians to withhold more expensive technologies from those in the most need.[6] The net result is physicians receive greater profits by allowing the sickest members of HMOs to die; the sickest patients actually become a financial liability to a HMO.

A national study of medical school students, residents, faculty members, and deans found there was a profoundly negative attitude against managed care.[7] This negative view was reiterated by a later study which found over half those surveyed stating "cost reduction takes priority over quality of patient care."[8] The ultimate goal of capitation is to control medical costs by under treating, delaying or discouraging treatment, and blocking access to care. It is hoped newly funded congressional investigations will agree that HMOs have gone too far in the search for profits. Unfortunately, the government legislation has had little impact regulating many HMO practices. One study reports in 1995, the least expensive half of all Medicare beneficiaries cost the system an average of less than $335 annually to treat.[9] By contrast, the most expensive 5% of beneficiaries

1. Korcopk, M. "Capitation Begins to Transform the Face of American Medicine." Canadian Medical Association Journal vol 154 1996. p. 688-91.
2. Limbacher, P.B. "Columbia probe widens. Federal raid in 7 states targets lab, home-care records." Mod Healthc. Jul 21; 27(29) 1997.p. 2-3.
3. Brent, N.J. "Healthcare reform: implications for home healthcare nursing and agencies." Home Healthc Nurse Jan-Feb; 12(1) 1994. p. 10-11. Brent, N.J. "Home healthcare fraud: implications for the home healthcare agency and nurse." Home Healthc Nurse. Jan; 15(1) 1997. p. 38-40.
4. . Weissenstein, E. "Government targets fraud in home infusion industry." Mod Healthcare Sep 13; 23(37) 1993. p. 14.
5. Brent, N.J. "Home care fraud & abuse: dishonest documentation." Home Healthc Nurse. Mar; 16(3) 1998. p. 196-8. Tahan, H.A. "Home healthcare under fire: fraud and abuse." JONAS Healthc Law Ethics Regul. Mar; 1(1) 1999. P. 16-24.
6. Danto, L.A. "The Tyranny of Capitation." Archives of Surgery vol 132 1997. p.579-585.
7. Simon, SR, et al. "Views of Managed Care." NEJM vol 340 1999. p. 928-36.
8. Feldman, D.S., Novack, D.H., Gracely, E. "Effects of Managed Care on Physician-Patient Relationships, Quality of Care, and the Ethical Practice of Medicine." Archives of Internal Medicine vol 158 1998. p. 1626-32.

cost an average of more than $45,000 annually each to treat.[1] The average cost of treatment for all beneficiaries in 1995 was $5,230. If an insurer receives the average payment and can enroll only clients from the lowest cost half of beneficiaries, it will earn an annual profit of nearly $5,000 per person. For each client from among the sickest 5%, it will lose $40,000. Many HMOs have unwritten policies encouraging enrollment of only healthy clients while rejecting or discouraging the enrollment of the sickest clients. HMOs may recruit patients at malls, restaurants or other places more frequented by healthy clients than by seniors. This practice is referred to as "cherry picking."[2] Although it is illegal, HMOs sidestep legal issues by promoting their businesses to populations of lowest risks (health clubs, dance halls for the elderly, etc.). Even if they are caught, they face maximum fines of only $100,000. There is little disincentive not to select coverage for healthy clients while dumping the unhealthiest on Medicare and Medicaid.[3]

Recently, activists promoting physician-assisted suicide have sought to advance the cause of euthanasia "in the public's interest." Claims of "death with dignity" are superficial, and appeal more to the emotions than the intellect. Physicians are the last group one should want to make decisions relating to the termination of a life. They may have a vested interest that greatly prejudices them, PROFIT![4] It is clearly a conflict of interest for physicians managing patients in HMOs because the incentive for "healthcare savings" may affect the physician's judgment about terminating care. The physician may be very caring and well meaning, however, societal norms may one day dictate it is the patient's moral duty to refuse all futile efforts and accept the reality of their pending death.[5] Concerns for the quality of life may actually reflect the physician's personal discomfort with their own mortality[6] and concerns about the legality of euthanasia.[7]

Just because a physician does not personally wish to live in a vegetative state or crippled by a degenerative neuromuscular disorder, does not mean they have the right to impose their personal beliefs[8] on others who believe

9. "U.S. Warns H.M.O.'s on Recruiting of Medicare Clients." Economic Reporting Review. 1999. 11 Jun 1999 ‹http://www.cepr.net/err/jun141999.htm›.
1. Ibid.
2. Grimaldi ,P.L. "New managed-care glossary." Nurs Manage Nov; 30(11) 1999. p. 16-20. Pear, R. "U.S. Warns H.M.O.'s on Recruiting of Medicare Clients." New York Times June 11 1999. p. 20.
3. Packer, S. "Capitated Care Is Unethical." Archives of Ophthalmology vol 115 1997. p. 1195-96. Sullivan, K. "On the 'Efficiency' of Managed Care Plans." Health Affairs July/August 2000. p. 139-48.
4. Dombeck, M.T., Olsan, T.H. "Ethics and managed care." J Interprof Care Aug; 16(3) 2002. p. 221-33.
5. Gill CJ. "Depression in the context of disability and the "right to die."." Theor Med Bioeth vol 25(3) 2004. p. 171-98.
6. Wenger, N.S., Carmel, S.. "Physicians' religiosity and end-of-life care attitudes and behaviors." Mt Sinai J Med Oct; 71(5) 2004. p. 335-43.
7. Hodges, M.O., Tolle, S.W., Stocking, C., Cassel, C.K. "Tube feeding. Internists' attitudes regarding ethical obligations." Arch Intern Med May 9; 154(9) 1994. p. 1013-20. Weber M., et al. "Ethical decision-making at the end of life—knowledge and attitudes of medical students]." Dtsch Med Wochenschr. 2004 Jul 9; 129(28-29) 2004. p. 1556-60.
8. Martyn, S.R, Bourguignon, H.J.. "Physicians' decisions about patient capacity: the Trojan horse of physician-assisted suicide." Psychol Public Policy Law Jun; 6(2) 2000. p. 388-401.

differently.[1] The eminent professor Dr. Stephen Hawkins is so crippled by Lou Gehrig's disease (amyotrophic lateral sclerosis) that he is reduced to communicating solely using a computer interface controlled by the use of only one finger. He is incontinent, wheelchair and bed ridden, and lacks the ability to do even the simplest of tasks necessary for daily living. However, he currently holds the esteemed position of Lucasian Professor of Mathematics in the Department of Applied Mathematics and Theoretical Physics at Cambridge University, a position held formerly by Sir Isaac Newton. He is the author of many scholarly papers in cosmology (he obtained his doctorate after he had been severely crippled by ALS) and is arguably the most intelligent human since Einstein.[2] Discussions of "quality of life" or "death with dignity" would surely provoke outrage from his peers and supporters.[3] They realize he is far more than a body; his mind is worth fighting for no matter how crippled he may become.[4]

Concerns about financial incentives to promote euthanasia may initially seem to be the exaggerations of an extremist. However, a recent paper in the most prestigious of all medical journals, the *New England Journal of Medicine*, poses this very question. In a 1998 paper, it cited a potential healthcare saving of $627 million annually by the implementation of physician-assisted suicide.[5] I personally find it very frightening researchers have actually assigned a financial value to the life of the terminally ill. Physicians are under ever increasing pressure to provide "cost efficient treatment." Care of the terminally ill is expensive; every dollar spent on the terminal patient detracts from the monies available to treat the "healthy." In this era of cost-containment, it is a matter of time before it becomes socially unacceptable to treat terminal conditions or illnesses that consume a disproportionate amount of the available healthcare dollars.[6]

The tragic case of Terri Schiavo has thrust these concerns from the hypothetical into reality. Public polls at the time of her death were generally supportive of the withdrawal of nutrition and hydration.[7] Most respondents expressed the opinion they would not want these measures for themselves or their loved ones. This event precipitated a strange alliance between political figures as dissimilar as Ralph Nader, Jesse Jackson, George Bush, and Pope John

1. Illingworth, P., Bursztajn, H. "Death with dignity or life with health care rationing.." Psychol Public Policy Law Jun; 6(2) 2000. p. 314-21.
2. Hawkins, S. "A brief history of mine." About Stephen. 2006. 20 Feb 2006 ‹http://www.hawking.org.uk/about/aindex.html›.
3. Fadem, P., et al. "Attitudes of people with disabilities toward physician-assisted suicide legislation: broadening the dialogue." J Health Polit Policy Law Dec; 28(6) 2003. p. 977-1001.
4. Avila, D. "Assisted suicide and the inalienable right to life.." Issues Law Med Fall; 16(2) 2000. p. 111-41.
5. Emanue, E.J., Battin, M.P. "What are the Potential Cost Savings from Legalizing Physician-Assisted Suicide." NEJM vol 339 1998. p. 167-71.
6. Hendlin, H. "Physician-assisted suicide: what next?" Responsive Community Fall; 7(4) 1997. p. 21-34. Sulmasy, D.P. "Managed Care and Managed Death." Archives of Internal Medicine vol 155 1995. p. 133-36.
7. "CNN/USA Today/Gallup Poll. March 22, 2005." Polling Report. 2005. 22 Mar 2005 ‹http://www.pollingreport.com/news.htm›.

Paul.[1] They expressed concerns that these measures supported by the medical and legal communities infringed upon the rights of the disabled. In an ironical twist, on the very day of her death, Pope John Paul was hospitalized for urosepsis and received the same heroic measures that were denied to Terri Schiavo. Pope John Paul had previously stated the Church's official position on artificial hydration and nutrition during a speech in 2004. He stated to an international conference on treatments for patients in a so-called persistent vegetative state that "I should like particularly to underline how the administration of water and food, even when provided by artificial means, always represents a natural means of preserving life, not a medical act. Its use, furthermore, should be considered, in principle, ordinary and proportionate, and as such MORALLY OBLIGATORY."[2]

These ethical and moral discrepancies are sure to plague both the medical and legal systems for years to come. Concerns for fiscal responsibility, an aging baby boomer population, soaring costs of medical therapy and ethical concerns about the right for life are on a collision course with managed medical care. The weak and disabled are clearly the first to suffer from shifts in societal attitudes and "for profit" medicine.[3] The businessmen and women of the new medicine will ultimately forsake those who jeopardize these profits.[4] Welcome to the realities of for profit medicine!

1. Dinan, S. "Case 'transcends politics' in coalition of right, left." The Washington Times March 30, 2005 30 Mar 2005.
2. D'Emilio, F. "Pope Has High Fever From Urinary Infection." SFGate. 2005. 31 Mar 2005 ‹http://www.sfgate.com/cgi-bin/article.cgi?f=/n/a/2005/03/31/international/i131049S18.DTL›.
3. Greger, M. "Appendix 55 — Money." Heart Failure — Diary of a Third Year Medical Student. 1999 ‹http://upalumni.org/medschool/appendices/appendix-55.html›. Landsberg, L. "Altruism in Medicine: Prescription for the Nineties." The Pharos vol Winter 1993. p. 9-10.
4. Owen, J.A. "Doctors and Dollars." The Pharos Winter 1994. p. 2-5.

CHAPTER 4. PILL PUSHING FOR NON-DISEASES

INVENTED DISEASES

> *When will they realize that there are too many drugs? No fewer than 150,000 preparations are now in use. About 15,000 new mixtures and dosages hit the market each year, while about 12,000 die off...We simply don't have enough diseases to go around. At the moment the most helpful contribution is the new drug to counteract the untoward effect of other new drugs.*
>
> Dr. Walter Modell, Cornell University Medical College, Time, May 26, 1961

Pharmaceutical firms are seldom content with current markets. They are in constant competition with other drug companies to sell newly developed drugs. A myriad of "me too" agents provide enormous revenues; off label (non-FDA approved) use of drugs further increases profits. Orphaned diseases add billions more to their already bloated revenues, and yet their greed is not satisfied.[1] A biotech analyst at AG Edwards in St Louis was quoted as saying, "We sometimes joke that when you're doing a clinical trial, there are two possible disasters. The first disaster is if you kill people. The second disaster is if you cure them. The truly good drugs are the ones you can use chronically for a long, long time."

Pharmaceutical firms' interests are best served by offering "treatments" for chronic conditions. This assures a long-term market for this new agent. Effective cures may be great for humanity, but they are lousy as marketable products. This is why tire manufacturers don't make tires that last a lifetime: the consumer only has to purchase your product one time. Drug companies are generally more

---

1. Cassel, A. "Peddling paranoia: selling cures for imaginary diseases is where the drug industry really rakes in the cash. Real need barely enters the picture — Skewing the Market." New International. 2003. Nov 2003 ‹http://www.findarticles.com/p/articles/mi_m0JQP/is_362/ai_111300635›.

concerned about the scarcity of "treatable" diseases than they are curing conditions. They have been accused of abandoning research on diseases of the third world because they are viewed as poor investments. The poor are unlikely to be able to pay enough to offset the costs of the drug's development. However, diseases of western nations are considered highly profitable because most consumers either have insurance or the government is willing to pick up the cost of therapy.[1] This was stated succinctly in 1971 by Julian Tudor-Hart.[2] His "inverse care law" states 'those who most need medical care are the least likely to get it.'

While the debilitating third world nation diseases such as malaria, tuberculosis and sleeping sickness have few or no treatments, drug companies are expanding the number of diseases for the rich and affluent. There are now drugs for toenail fungus,[3] pre-hypertension,[4] bedwetting,[5] compulsive shopping,[6] shoplifting[7] and gambling 'addiction'.[8]

THE MEDICALIZATION OF LIFE

> *Nothing is more fatal to health than an over care of it.*
> *Benjamin Franklin (1706-1790)*

Direct to consumer ads enable drug firms to "invent diseases" to further increase their sales of drugs. The journalist Lynn Payer authored a book titled *Disease Mongering*, which detailed how pharmaceutical firms created new diseases just to inflate the markets for their drugs.[9] Her book exposed how many doctors, drug companies and the media conspired to exaggerate the severity and magnitude of everyday symptoms or inconveniences so they could promote a drug as a "cure" for the newly created disease. Drug companies try to convince essentially healthy people they are sick and slightly sick people that they are very ill. Their goal is to market drugs to the widest possible audience by exploiting the elusiveness of the concepts of disease and health. Medical researchers have turned

---

1. Silverstein, K. "Millions for Viagra, Pennies for Diseases of the Poor." The Nation. 1999.)1 Jul 1999 ‹http://www.thenation.com/doc/19990719/silverstein›.
2. Hart, J.T. "The inverse care law." Lancet Feb 27; 1(7696) 1971. p. 405-12.
3. "Lamasil Tablet — Nail Fungus Treatment." Lamasil. 2006. Novartis. 16 Feb 2006 ‹http://www.lamisil.com/index.jsp›.
4. "NHLBI Issues New High Blood Pressure Clinical Practice Guidelines." NIH News. 2003. National Heart, Lung, and Blood Institute. 14 May 2003 ‹http://www.nhlbi.nih.gov/new/press/03-05-14.htm›.
5. Mikkelson, E.J. "Enuresis and encopresis: Ten years of progress." Journal of the American Academy of Child Adolescent Psychiatry vol 40 No. 10 2001. p. 1146-58.
6. Conger, K. "Drug offers promising lead in treating compulsive urge to shop." Stanford Report. 2000. 13 Dec 2000 ‹http://news-service.stanford.edu/news/2000/december13/shop-1213.html›.
7. Hall, L.E. "First-ever drug treatment study for kleptomania seeks volunteers for trials." Stanford Report. 09 Oct 2002 ‹http://news-service.stanford.edu/news/2002/october9/kleptomania.html›.
8. Grant, J.E, Kim, S.W. "Effectiveness of pharmacotherapy for pathological gambling: a chart review." Ann Clin Psychiatry Sep; 14(3) 2002. p. 155-61.
9. Moynihan, R., Heath, I., V, D. "Selling sickness: the pharmaceutical industry and disease mongering." BMJ: Education and debate. 2002. 13 Apr 2002 ‹http://bmj.bmjjournals.com/cgi/content/full/324/7342/886›.

everyday problems like baldness,[1] toenail fungus, urinary incontinence,[2] and a host of other annoyances into a disease needing a cure.[3] The definition of disease is often viewed as the absence of health and health may be seen as the absence of disease.[4] These cyclical definitions make it very easy for promoters of new therapies to claim mundane or irksome conditions qualify as diseases thereby creating a "demand" for their therapies. The limits of what constitutes a disease are frequently broadened which further increases the number of victims in need of therapy. Recent examples of redefined diseases are changes in the limits of hypertension,[5] LDL cholesterol[6] and diabetes.[7]

Imre Loeffler, surgeon, essayist, and wit, says that the World Health Organization's famous definition of health as "complete physical, psychological, and social wellbeing"[8] is achieved only at the point of simultaneous orgasm, leaving most of us diseased most of the time[9]. One marketer openly admitted these excesses by stating; "Once the need has been established and created, then the product can be introduced to satisfy that need/desire."[10]

INVENTING DISEASES

> *It is a most extraordinary thing, but I never read a patent medicine advertisement without being impelled to the conclusion that I am suffering from the particular disease therein dealt with in its most virulent form.*
>
> *Jerome K. Jerome. English humorist and playwright (1859–1927)*

This process of "disease mongering" begins by conducting surveys to identify potential diseases needing a therapy. If there are sufficient numbers of consumers expressing discontent about a condition, the drug company may then

1. Scow, D.T., Nolte, R.S., Shaughnessy, A.F. "Medical treatments for balding in men." American Family Physician. 1999. 15 Apr 1999 ⟨http://www.aafp.org/afp/990415ap/2189.html⟩.
2. "Stress Urinary Incontinence." Clinical Trial Opportunities. West Coast Clinical Research. 16 Feb 2006 ⟨http://www.clinicalresearch.org/SUI.html⟩.
3. "How medicine sells the media." BMJ: Press Release. 2002. 13 Apr 2002 ⟨http://bmj.bmjjournals.com/cgi/content/full/324/7342/924⟩. Bonaccorso, S.N., Sturchio, J.L. "Direct to consumer advertising is medicalising normal human experience." BMJ. 2002. 13 Apr 2002 ⟨http://bmj.bmjjournals.com/cgi/content/full/324/7342/910⟩.
4. Campbell, E.J.M., Scadding, J.G., Roberts. R.S. "The concept of disease." BMJ vol ii 1979. p. 757-62. Scully, J.L. "What is a disease?: Disease, disability and their definitions." EMBO Reports. 2004. 01 Jul 2004 ⟨http://www.nature.com/embor/journal/v5/n7/full/7400195.html⟩.
5. Chobanian, A.V. et al. "Seventh report of the Joint National Committee on Prevention, Detection, Evaluation, and Treatment of High Blood Pressure." Hypertension Dec; 42(6) 2003. p. 1206-52..
6. Grundy SM et al. "Implications of recent clinical trials for the National Cholesterol Education Program Adult Treatment Panel III guidelines." Circulation Jul 13; 110(2) 2004. p. 227-39.
7. Gavin, J.R. III,. "Report of the Expert Committee on the Diagnosis and Classification of Diabetes Mellitus." Diabetes Care vol 22(s01) 1999. p. s5-s19.
8. Wright, J., Rhys, W., Wilkinson, J.R. "Development and importance of health needs assessment." BMJ. 1998. 25 Apr 1998 ⟨http://bmj.bmjjournals.com/cgi/content/full/316/7140/1310⟩.
9. Gomes, P. "Disease and non-disease." Infosatellite. 2002. 19 Apr 2002 ⟨http://www.infosatellite.com/news/2002/04/p190402disease.html⟩.
10. Cook, H. "Practical Guide to Medical Education." Pharmaceutical Marketing. 2006. 07 Feb 2006 ⟨http://www.pmlive.com/pharm_market/prac_guides.cfm⟩.

partner with existing advocacy groups and intellectuals to do research to demonstrate the legitimacy of their concerns.[1] Funding by drug companies helps these not so impartial public advocates conduct "disease awareness campaigns" to educate the potential consumer of the seriousness of their condition.[2] The consumer is reassured when they discover they are not alone in their suffering.[3] Diffuse and difficult to characterize generalized symptoms may then be lumped together to show thousands or even millions suffer from this same infirmity.[4] Celebrities and other famous "opinion leaders" are paid enormous sums to further promote your cause and the "need" for something to be done to end the suffering of all those inflicted. Consumers are advised to ask their doctor for treatments to end their anguish. The harried physician is now overwhelmed by clients badgering them to do something to help them recover from their condition. Corporate sponsored academicians help "define" the problem by attaching a name or label to this emerging threat. Finally, drug company representatives arrive like shining white knights to educate the physician about the "newest" treatment options available for those inflicted by this newly recognized disease.[5] The not so unbiased "community leaders" receive considerable financial reward for the use of their names or face while promoting this new therapy.

Superficially, it appears everyone is a winner, the suffering now suffer less, "opinion leaders" receive more recognition in the community, researchers receive more research funds, the media feels good about itself for helping educate the public about these impediments to health and happiness, and the drug companies rake in a boatload of cash. How can any complain with this outcome?

Drug companies exercise care in selecting academic spokesmen supportive of their claims.[6] The opinion leader shills believe they are above reproach and are serving the publics best interest by educating the masses of the need for medical intervention.[7] Pharmaceutical firms avoid fronting the same experts too often fearing loss of credibility. A common ploy used by these firms is to hire "ghostwriters" to prepare articles for researchers to submit to respected journals.[8] Once published, these articles are quoted as authoritative and are used to help produce a market "by creating dissatisfaction with existing products and creating the need for something new."[9]

1. Anderson M, Karasz A, Lurie P. "The pharmaceutical industry and disease mongering. Deja vu all over again." BMJ Jul 27; 325(7357) 2002. p. 216. McKechnie, S.. "The pharmaceutical industry and disease mongering. Will industry's latest moves promote public health or private profit?" BMJ Jul 27; 325(7357) 2002. p. 216.
2. Reid, J.J. "Medicalisation of human conditions." N Z Med J Feb 26; 112(1082) 1999. p. 60-61.
3. Woodward, B.W. "Disease management: opportunity for pharmaceutical care?" Hosp Pharm Jul; 30(7) 1995. p. 596, 599-603, 606-8.
4. Hadler, N.M. "Fibromyalgia" and the medicalization of misery." J Rheumatol Aug; 30(8) 2003. p. 1668-70.
5. Branswell, H. "http://healtoronto.com/pillill.html." National Post Online. 2002. 12 Apr 2002 ‹http://healtoronto.com/pillill.html›.
6. Healy, D. "Is academic psychiatry for sale?" British Journal of Psychiatry. 2003. May 2003 ‹http://bjp.rcpsych.org/cgi/content/full/182/5/388?etoc›.
7. Taylor, M. "A look at what to do in a crisis apart from panic." Pharmaceutical Marketing. 2002. ‹http://www.pmlive.com/on_the_job/prac_guides.cfm?showArticle=1&ArticleID=884›.

Reprints of these articles are lauded as being "independent and authoritative."[1] These and other fronted titles are frequently cited as preliminary studies by drug representatives to extol the virtues of the drug du jour.[2] This scam was nearly perfect. Fortunately, recent requirements by many journals for authors to reveal their source of research funding and ties to pharmaceutical firms have exposed these compromised experts as frauds.[3]

This obfuscation makes it difficult for the honest doctor and consumer to obtain truly objective information. Public relation firms promote paid endorsements by key opinion leaders to help create a "buzz" about this new disease and its potential therapies.[4] The PR firm that launched Viagra and Celebrex declared "while buzz should always appear to be spontaneous, it should, in fact, be scientifically crafted and controlled as tightly as advertising in the *New England Journal of Medicine*."[5] Another PR firm states "key opinion leaders must maintain their credibility and integrity in order to have maximum market impact."

This charade was exposed and the process well documented in a January 2003 issue of the British Medical Journal.[6] An article by Moynihan disputed the use of exaggerated statistics by corporate-sponsored scientists seeking to create a new medical syndrome called "female sexual dysfunction."

PHARMACOTHERAPY FOR NON-DISEASES

> *I swallow it, therefore it is.*
>
> Florence King, American author

It is not uncommon for health risks to be promoted as actual diseases.[7] Many fear this elevation of unhealthy lifestyles[8] to the status of a disease excuses those

8. Flanagin, A. "Prevalence of Articles With Honorary Authors and Ghost Authors in Peer-Reviewed Medical Journals." JAMA. 1998. 15 Jul 1998 ‹http://jama.ama-assn.org/cgi/content/full/280/3/222›. Mowatt, G. "Prevalence of honorary and ghost authorship in Cochrane reviews." JAMA vol 287 2002. p. 2769-71.
9. Reed, C.R., Camargo, C.A.Jr. "Recent Trends and Controversies in Industry-sponsored Clinical Trials." Academic Emergency Medicine. 1999. Aug 1999 ‹http://www.aemj.org/cgi/content/abstract/6/8/833›.
1. Cook, H. "Practical guide to medical education." Pharmaceutical Marketing vol 16 2001. p. 5.
2. Burton, B., Rowell, A. "Unhealthy spin." BMJ. 2003. 31 May 2003 ‹http://bmj.bmjjournals.com/cgi/content/extract/326/7400/1205›. Grey, A. "Practical guide to medical publishingGrey, A." Pharmaceutical Marketing Nov 2000. p. 4.
3. "AAMC Announces Members of Task Force on Financial Conflicts of Interest in Clinical Research." AAMC. Association of American Medical Colleges. 29 Mar 2001 ‹http://www.aamc.org/newsroom/pressrel/2001/010329.htm›.
4. Elliott, C. "Not-So-Public Relations: How the drug industry is branding itself with bioethics.." Slate. 2003. 15 Dec 2003 ‹http://slate.msn.com/id/2092442›.
5. Burton, B., Rowell, A. "Disease Mongering." Center for Media and Democracy. 2003. Jan 2003 ‹http://www.prwatch.org/prwissues/2003Q1/monger.html›.
6. Moynihan, R. "The making of a disease: female sexual dysfunction." BMJ. 2003. 04 Jan 2003 ‹http://bmj.bmjjournals.com/cgi/content/full/326/7379/45›.
7. "Do we need lifestyle drugs?" BBC News. 2003.)3 Jan 2003 ‹http://news.bbc.co.uk/1/hi/health/2624547.stm›. Norton, A. "Are Everyday Problems Being Dubbed 'Disease'?" Rense. Reuters Health. 04 Dec 2002 ‹http://www.rense.com/general23/everydayproblems.htm›.
8. Mintzes, B. "Direct to consumer advertising is medicalising normal human experience." BMJ. 2002. 13 Apr 2002 ‹http://bmj.bmjjournals.com/cgi/content/full/324/7342/908›.

diagnosed from assuming any responsibility for their condition.[1] A poll of physicians in January 2003 issue of the British Medical Journal classified 174 conditions according to non-diseaseness. Ageing and work-related problems, followed by boredom, bags under the eyes, ignorance, baldness and freckles were the "non-diseases" most frequently cited by physicians. Other non-diseases that may be potential diseases included big ears, graying hair, ugliness, jet lag, cellulite and penis envy.[2]

Top 20 non-diseases voted by physicians in descending order of "non-diseaseness" are:[3]

1. Ageing

2. Work

3. Boredom

4. Bags under eyes

5. Ignorance

6. Baldness

7. Freckles

8. Big ears

9. Grey or white hair

10. Ugliness

11. Childbirth

12. Allergy to the 21st century

13. Jet lag

14. Unhappiness

15. Cellulite

16. Hangover

17. Anxiety about penis size/penis envy

18. Pregnancy

19. Road rage

20. Loneliness

The entire January, 2003 issue of the British Medical Journal explored the impact of "medicalization" on the consumer and health care. Pharmaceutical firms were accused of "disease-mongering" by promoting pills for shyness, baldness, urinary incontinence and more. The lead author of one study stated,

1. Bonaccorso, S.N., Sturchio, J.L. "Direct to consumer advertising is medicalising normal human experience." BMJ. 2002. 13 Apr 2002 ‹http://bmj.bmjjournals.com/cgi/content/full/324/7342/910›. Moynihan, R., Smith, R. "Too much medicine?" BMJ. 2002. 13 Apr 2002 ‹http://bmj.bmjjournals.com/cgi/content/full/324/7342/859›.
2. Moynihan, R., Smith, R. "Too much medicine?" BMJ. 2002. 13 Apr 2002 ‹http://bmj.bmjjournals.com/cgi/content/full/324/7342/859›.
3. Smith, R. "In search of 'non-disease'" BMJ. 2002. 13 Apr 2002 ‹http://bmj.bmjjournals.com/cgi/content/full/324/7342/883›.

"There is a lot of money to be made from telling healthy people they are sick" and "What for many people is a mild functional disorder requiring little more than reassurance about its benign natural course is currently being reframed as a serious disease attracting a label and a drug, with all the associated harms and costs."[1]

This disease mongering or promotion of pharmacotherapy to treat everyday problems adds billions of dollars to an already overpriced medical system.[2] It also increases the risk for adverse drug reactions and deadly drug interactions. The risk from use of a drug may far exceed any benefit obtained. Lifestyle changes or simply accepting that some conditions are a natural consequence of aging are not acceptable to many who desire "pills for all ills."[3] One of the fastest growing sectors within the drug industry is the search for drugs to abate the consequences of unhealthy living.[4]

Physicians routinely confuse conditions or risk factors with diseases (e.g. high cholesterol or hypertension).[5] Pharmaceutical firms are content not to correct these misconceptions. The authors of one article stated, "We wanted to prompt a debate on what is and what is not a disease and draw attention to the increasing tendency to classify people's problems as diseases. Worst of all, the diagnosis of a disease may lead you to regard yourself as forever flawed and incapable of 'rising above' your problem."[6] What was once considered a vice is now conveniently labeled a disease.[7] One large organization even expressed its uneasiness about labeling diabetes as a disease; they preferred the word "condition" to avoid any negative connotations.

The battle to label a condition as a disease opens the door to pharmacotherapy. Lifestyle changes are ignored and drugs are viewed as "the first line of defense." The medicalization of a condition for symptom improvement is the beginning a slippery slope towards using drugs to control unwanted social behavior. Physicians are frequently overwhelmed by patients and families to "do something" about untreatable conditions.[8] The physician author George Bernard Shaw wrote of this in his work entitled "The Doctor's

1. Hart, G., Wellings. K. "Sexual behaviour and its medicalisation: in sickness and in health." BMJ. 2003. 13 Apr 2002 ‹http://bmj.bmjjournals.com/cgi/content/full/324/7342/896›. Moynihan, R.,Heath, I., Henry, D. "Selling sickness: the pharmaceutical industry and disease mongering." BMJ. 2002. 13 Apr 2002 ‹http://bmj.bmjjournals.com/cgi/content/full/324/7342/886›.
2. Moynihan, R. "Drug firms hype disease as sales ploy, industry chief claims." BMJ. 2002. 13 Apr 2002 ‹http://bmj.bmjjournals.com/cgi/content/full/324/7342/867›.
3. Clark, D. "Between hope and acceptance: the medicalisation of dying." BMJ. 2002. 13 Apr 2002 ‹http://bmj.bmjjournals.com/cgi/content/full/324/7342/905›. Ebrahim, S. "The medicalisation of old age." BMJ. 2002. 13 Apr 2002 ‹http://bmj.bmjjournals.com/cgi/content/full/324/7342/861›.
4. Gotzsche, P.C. "The medicalisation of risk factors." BMJ vol 324 2002. p. 890-91.
5. Gilbert, D., Walley, T., New, B. "Lifestyle medicines." BMJ. 2000. 25 Nov 2000 ‹http://bmj.bmjjournals.com/cgi/content/full/321/7272/1341›.
6. Smith, R. "What is and what is not a disease?" BMJ vol 324 2002. p. 883-85.
7. Heath, I. "There must be limits to the medicalisation of human distress." BMJ Feb 13; 318(7181) 1999. p. 439-40.
8. Edwards, N., Kornacki, M.J., Silversin, J. "Unhappy doctors: what are the causes and what can be done?" BMJ. 2002. 06 Apr 2002 ‹http://bmj.bmjjournals.com/cgi/reprint/324/7341/835›.

Dilemma." He admonished those seeking "a cheap magic charm to prevent, and a cheap pill or potion to cure all diseases" to look elsewhere. He advised physicians to have a brass plate on their desks proclaiming "Remember that I too am mortal."[1]

YOU IS WHAT YOU THINK YOU IS

> *The only way to keep your health is to eat what you don't want, drink what you don't like and do what you'd druther not.*
>
> Mark Twain. *American humorist (1835-1910)*

The desire for a label to explain or excuse our behavior may even have a negative impact on health. Labeling a condition can legitimize an illness, but it also brands the labeled with all the negative connotations associated with that label.[2] The patient may feel vindicated by this "diagnosis" because they may now believe it is the first step toward recovery. Blame now becomes sympathy, expectations of productivity may now be lowered, you may be entitled to benefits such as sick pay, free prescriptions, insurance payments, and access to programs or services reserved only for the non-healthy.[3] Best of all, you finally have a reason to explain your suffering. But the diagnosis of a disease may also create many problems.[4] It may enable authorities to seek legal action against you or even perform tests against your will. You may be denied insurance, a mortgage, or employment. You are forever labeled as a victim of your disease. You are in danger of losing your identity to be seen only as a disease. The stigma associated with some diseases may create more problems than the condition itself. Is it helpful to blame your faults on genes or bad body chemistry?

Medical crutches may make one feel helpless and without hope but is a medical label better than a moral judgment? Does a disease relieve them of societal responsibilities? Illich questioned whether it was better to be seen as an "innocent victim of biological mechanisms rather than lazy, greedy, or envious deserter of a social struggle over the tools of production."[5] Medicalization can lead to hospitalization which has its own inherent risks like; infection, over-medication, iatrogenesis and medical errors.[6]

---

1. Shaw, G.B. The doctor's dilemma. Harmondsworth, Middlesex: Penguin Books, 1946.
2. Finestone, A.J. "Is a diagnosis disabling or enabling?" Arch Intern Med vol 157 1997. p. 491-92. Hadler, N.M. "If you have to prove you are ill, you can't get well. The object lesson of fibromyalgia." Spine vol 21 1996. p. 2397-400.
3. Hadler, N. The dangers of the diagnostic process. Iatrogenic labelling as in the fibrositis paralogism. New York: Raven Press, 1993.
4. Asbring, P., Narvanen ,A.L. "Women's experiences of stigma in relation to chronic fatigue syndrome and fibromyalgia." Qualitative Health Research. 2002. 12 Feb 2002 ‹http://qhr.sagepub.com/cgi/content/short/12/2/148›. Finestone, A.J. "Is a diagnosis disabling or enabling?" Arch Intern Med vol 157 1997. p. 491-92.
5. Illich, I. Limits to medicine. London: Marion Boyars, 1976.

SOMATIZATION AND MEDICALIZATION

Many ordinary illnesses are nothing but the expression of a serious dissat-
isfaction with life.
Paul Tournier 1898-1986, Physician and Author

Some think medical labels are better than no labels. Those with unlabeled ailments may receive the not so welcome label of somatosizer.[1] Somatic illnesses are viewed as "all in the head." Mental illnesses may manifest themselves with actual or perceived physical symptoms.[2] Somatosizers are frequently treated as hypochondriacs by the medical community.[3] The labeling of a vague syndrome or symptom helps to reassure the inflicted they are not just a "mental case."[4] A psychosomatic illness does not mean those inflicted do not suffer, people with asthma, migraines, irritable bowel syndrome, chronic fatigue or fibromyalgia have real physical symptoms. These symptoms may even be life threatening. However, it does not mean there is a causative agent other than the person's thoughts. These same thoughts may be mobilized to heal negative thought induced conditions responsible for actual pain and suffering. Suggesting to those inflicted that their suffering is self induced may anger them and their support groups. Challenging these labels may create near mass hysteria in like-minded believers. Newly created diseases legitimatize their suffering and increase their desire for recognition of this new disease and its associated therapies.

The trivializing of diseases by "symptom management" has resulted in the formation of large public advocacy groups supporting research for "cures" of their perceived disorder. Their desperate need for recognition and acceptance combined with their genuine suffering makes these groups easy prey for pharmaceutical companies. These groups are frequently manipulated for financial gain. One author believes somatization and medicalization are likely to increase in the era of managed care. Those suffering may resort to more urgent and exaggerated terms in order to gain access to the physician. This embellishment merely increases the "need" for new drugs or therapies while increasing the potential market margin.

6. Hadler, N.M. "If you have to prove you are ill, you can't get well. The object lesson of fibromyalgia." Spine vol 21 1996. p. 2397-400.
1. Soderberg, S,, Lundman, B., Norberg, A. "Struggling for Dignity: The meaning of women's experiences of living with fibromyalgia." Qualitative Health Research. 1999. 09 Sep 1999 ‹http://qhr.sagepub.com/cgi/content/abstract/9/5/575›.
2. Ebrahim, S. "The medicalisation of old age." BMJ. 2002. 13 Apr 2002 ‹http://bmj.bmjjournals.com/cgi/content/full/324/7342/861›. Green, J., Romei, J., Natelson, B.H. "Stigma and chronic fatigue syndrome." Journal of Chronic Fatigue Syndrome vol 5 1999. p. 63-75.
3. Barsky, A, Borus J. "Somatization and medicalization in the era of managed care." JAMA vol 274 1995. p. 1931-34.
4. Clark, D. "Between hope and acceptance: the medicalisation of dying." BMJ. 2002. 13 Apr 2002 ‹http://bmj.bmjjournals.com/cgi/content/full/324/7342/905›.

WHAT'S IN A NAME?

> *The difference between an itch and an allergy is about a hundred bucks.*
> Unknown

This potential market is expanding at an alarming rate.[1] "Cures" are being sought to treat "diseases" as diverse as: baldness, toe fungus, obesity, impotency,[2] Post Traumatic Stress Disorder, sexual dysfunction,[3] dysthymia, homosexuality,[4] bedwetting, menopause,[5] andropause, wrinkles, yellow teeth, shyness, hypertension, elevated cholesterol, nervous bladder, incontinence, enlarged prostate, osteoporosis,[6] premenstrual syndrome, precancer, dementia, and a host of other vague complaints or natural conditions.

Medicalization has even invaded the natural processes of birth, old age and death. Most pregnancies are uncomplicated, yet women are routinely scanned, probed, tested and evaluated just to make sure "everything is OK."[7] Breastfeeding, the most natural and loving act of a mother, has become so medicalized that many mothers are ignorant to the point of fear.[8] Many demur to breastfeed; they may instead opt for the commercialized, sanitized and desensitized bottle-feeding thrust upon them by medical authorities.

War is being waged against the natural declines associated with old age.[9] Despite the billions spent, death will still claim us all.[10] Many physicians are unwilling to let the terminally ill die in peace.[11] A major industry has been created[12] to "help" us have death with dignity.[13]

---

1. Kutchins, H., Kirk, S, et al. Making Us Crazy: Dsm The Psychiatric Bible And The Creation Of Mental Disorder. New York: Simon And Schuster, 1997.
2. Stulhofer, A. "The rise of essentialism and the medicalization of sexuality." Acta Med Croatica vol 54(4-5) 2000. p. 141-49.
3. Lauman, E., Paik, A., Rosen, R. "Sexual dysfunction in the US: prevalence and predictors." JAMA vol 281 1999. p. 537-44. Moynihan, R.. "The making of a disease: female sexual dysfunction." BMJ. 2003. 04 Jan 2003 ‹http://bmj.bmjjournals.com/cgi/content/full/326/7379/45›.
4. Conrad, P., Markens, S. "Constructing the "gay gene" in the news: optimism and scepticism in the US and British press." Health vol 5 2001. p. 373-90. Minton, H.L. "Community empowerment and the medicalization of homosexuality: constructing sexual identities in the 1930s." J Hist Sex Jan; 6(3) 1996. p. 435-58.
5. "The making of a disease: female sexual dysfunction." BMJ Letters. 2003. 22 Mar 2003 ‹http://bmj.bmjjournals.com/cgi/content/full/326/7390/658›.
6. Moynihan, R. "Claims by charity exaggerate dangers of osteoporosis." BMJ News. 2003. 16 Aug 2003 ‹http://bmj.bmjjournals.com/cgi/content/full/327/7411/358-a›.
7. Johanson, R., Newburn, M., Macfarlane, A. "Has the medicalisation of childbirth gone too far?" BMJ: Education and debate. 2002. 13 Apr 2002 ‹http://bmj.bmjjournals.com/cgi/content/full/324/7342/892›. McLean, M.T. "The medicalization of the second stage of labor." Midwifery Today Childbirth Educ Spring; (33) 1995. p. 36.
8. Apple, R.D. "The medicalization of infant feeding in the United States and New Zealand: two countries, one experience." J Hum Lact Mar; 10(1) 1994. p. 31-37; Auerbach KG. "The medicalization of breastfeeding." J Hum Lact Dec; 11(4) 1995. p. 259-60.
9. McCue, J.D. "The naturalness of dying." JAMA vol 273 1995. p. 1039-43.
10. Ebrahim, S. "The medicalisation of old age." BMJ Editorials. 2002. 13 Apr 2002 ‹http://bmj.bmjjournals.com/cgi/content/full/324/7342/861›. Van Weel, C., Michels, J. "Dying, not old age, to blame for costs of health care." Lancet vol 350 1997. p. 1159-60.
11. Hogan, C., Lunney, J., Gabel, J., Lynn, J. "Medicare beneficiaries' costs of care in the last year of life." Health Aff (Millwood) Jul-Aug; 20(4) 2001. p. 188-95. Scitovsky, A.A. "'The High Cost of Dying" Revisited." Milbank Q vol 72(4) 1994. p. 561-91.

Death, pain, and sickness are part of what makes us human. All cultures have developed customs to help them cope with all three. A good point can be made that real health can be defined as being successful in coping with these realities.[1] Modern medicine has minimized cultural and individual coping mechanisms. Instead, it has advanced a quixotic attempt to defeat death, pain, and sickness. It has merely succeeded in undermining our cultures mechanisms for coping with suffering. "People are conditioned to get things rather than to do them. . . . They want to be taught, moved, treated, or guided rather than to learn, to heal, and to find their own way."[2] One researcher concluded "the more a society spends on health care the more likely are its inhabitants to regard themselves as sick."[3]

GENETIC MARKERS OR MARKED FOR DEATH

> *Men worry over the great number of diseases, while doctors worry over the scarcity of effective remedies.*
> *Pien Ch'Iao, Chinese physician (600-500 BC)*

The "new genetics" is about to make the problem of medicalization even more problematic. There are very few genetic disorders associated with defects in single genes. Genetic screening is not predictive of a disease; it is just another risk factor. Genetic predisposition is not equivalent to a diagnosis, yet insurance companies are already seeking access to genetic profiles as a basis to reject claims of "pre-existing conditions." The authors of a recent article in BMJ conclude, "Genetic tests for markers that may not result in symptoms for half a century or more could be new examples of a process of premature medicalization — of attaching the 'disease' label before it has been established that prevention or treatment is clearly beneficial."[4] The advent of genetic screening could eventually mean apparently healthy people will be labeled "sick" decades before an actual diagnosis.

12. Field, D. "Palliative medicine and the medicalization of death." Eur J Cancer Care Jun; 3(2) 1994. p. 58-62.
13. Burgess, M.M. "The medicalization of dying." J Med Philos Jun; 18(3) 1993. p. 269-79. Connelly, R.J. "The medicalization of dying: a positive turn on a new path." Omega (Westport) vol 36(4) 1997. p. 331-41.
1. Moynihan, R., Smith, R. "Too much medicine?" BMJ. 2002. 13 Apr 2002 ⟨http://bmj.bmjjournals.com/cgi/content/full/324/7342/859⟩.
2. Ibid.
3. Sen, A. "Health: perception versus observation." BMJ Editorials. 2002. 13 Apr 2002 ⟨http://bmj.bmjjournals.com/cgi/content/full/324/7342/860⟩.
4. Melzer, D, Zimmern, R. "Genetics and medicalisation." BMJ Editorials. 2002. 13 Apr 2002 ⟨http://bmj.bmjjournals.com/cgi/content/full/324/7342/863⟩.

MISDIAGNOSES

> *Nurse: "Doctor, the man you just gave a clean bill of health to dropped*
> *dead right as he was leaving the office." Doctor: "Turn him around; make it*
> *look like he was walking in."*
> Henny Youngman 1906-1998, Comedian

Physicians are especially worried about missing a disease entirely. These "missed diagnoses" are frequently cited as major reasons for malpractice. The rates of these missed opportunities are difficult to determine because it is very difficult to get exact data on their rates. Whereas there are many studies of adverse drug events and nosocomial infections, there is a relative paucity of misdiagnosis studies. In a 1997 National Patient Safety Foundation (NPSF) phone survey 40% of 1,513 respondents reported a "misdiagnosis or treatment error."[1] The most frequently cited medical mistake (40%) by 639 respondents was misdiagnosis. Nearly half of all these mistakes occurred within the hospital setting. When asked, *"What was done about the mistake?"* 38% responded "nothing." Only 6% chose to file a lawsuit, even though 32% stated the mistake permanently affected their health. The following table lists the medical mistakes from a patient's perspective.

Causes of Medical Mistakes

Misdiagnosis / wrong treatment	40%
Medication error	28%
A mistake during a medical procedure	22%
Administrative error	4%
Communication error	2%
Inaccurate lab results	2%
Equipment malfunction	1%
Other	7%
Don't know	1%

Multiple studies report a range of misdiagnosis rates from 8% to 42%. Rates of misdiagnosis within the ICU or Emergency Department range from 20% to 40%. A 2000 study lists the top five misdiagnosed conditions in order of prevalence as myocardial infarction, breast cancer, appendicitis, lung cancer and colon cancer.[2] Another reliable source is the Physician Insurers Association of America, an organization that comprises professional liability insurers, owned or managed by physicians. According to their studies, the top five misdiagnosed conditions were breast cancer,[3] cancer of the bronchus and lung,[4] appendicitis,[5] acute myocardial infarction,[6] and ectopic pregnancy.[7]

1. "Public Opinion of Patient Safety Issues: Research Findings." National Patient Safety Foundation. 1997. Sep 1997 ‹http://www.npsf.org/download/1997survey.pdf›.
2. "How Common is Misdiagnosis?" Cure Research. 2005. 24 Mar 2005 ‹http://www.cureresearch.com/intro/common_printer.htm›.
3. Kern, K. "Causes of breast cancer malpractice litigation; a 20-year civil court review." Arch Surg vol 127 1992. p. 542. Spratt J., Spratt, S. "Medical and legal implications of screening and follow-up procedures for breast cancer." Cancer vol 66 1990. p. 1351.

Initial misdiagnosis rates of appendicitis in children are especially high, ranging from 28% to 57% for children under the age of 12 to nearly 100% in infants.[1] Up to as many as 30% of patients with proven appendicitis are misdiagnosed and discharged by a physician before being correctly identified.[2] Non-pregnant women of childbearing age with appendicitis are misdiagnosed in 33% of cases.[3]

An autopsy is frequently the last chance to confirm or reject a diagnosis.[4] Several studies have found discrepancy rates of clinical causes of death as high as 40% in the Medical ICU.[5] Unfortunately, rates of autopsy have been reduced from nearly 50% during the 1950s to the currently levels of only 12%.[6] The primary reasons for these reductions is family's are no longer requesting this procedure and insurance companies' reluctance to pay the additional $1500 it costs for a typical autopsy.[7] Despite concerns that relatives will be unwilling to give permission for a postmortem examination, a recent study has reported that if they are approached with sensitivity, up to 46% of relatives may agree.[8]

Previous studies of patients in ICUs have shown medical diagnoses are frequently incorrect and this misdiagnosis may have altered outcome in 27% of patients.[9] In one study of 636 deaths, fewer than half of the cases autopsied were

4. Kendrey, G., et al. "Misdiagnosis of lung cancer in a 2000 consecutive autopsy study in Budapest." Gen Diagn Pathol Mar; 141(3-4) 1996. p. 169-78. Lee, P.N. "Comparison of autopsy, clinical and death certificate diagnosis with particular reference to lung cancer. A review of the published data." APMIS vol 102 (Suppl 45) 1994. p. 1-42.

5. Flum, D.R., et al. "Has misdiagnosis of appendicitis decreased over time? A population-based analysis." JAMA Oct 10; 286(14) 2001. p. 1748-53. Rothrock, S.G., Pagane, J. "Acute appendicitis in children: emergency department diagnosis and management." Ann Emerg Med Jul; 36(1) 2000. p. 39-51.

6. Mehta, R.H., Eagle, K.A. "Missed diagnoses of acute coronary syndromes in the emergency room—continuing challenges." NEJM Apr 20; 342(16) 2000. p. 1207-10. Pope, J.H., et al. "Missed diagnoses of acute cardiac ischemia in the emergency department." NEJM Apr 20; 342(16): 2000. p. 1163-70.

7. Chan, L.Y., Fok, W.Y., Yuen, P.M. "Pitfalls in diagnosis of interstitial pregnancy." Acta Obstet Gynecol Scand Sep; 82(9): 2003. p. 867-70. DeWitt, C., Abbott, J. "Interstitial pregnancy: a potential for misdiagnosis of ectopic pregnancy with emergency department ultrasonography." Ann Emerg Med Jul; 40(1) 2002. p. 106-09.

1. Rothrock, S.G. Pagane, J. "Acute appendicitis in children: emergency department diagnosis and management." Ann Emerg Med Jul; 36(1) 2000. p. 39-51.

2. Rogers, J. "Abdominal pain: Foresight." American College of Emergency Physicians Dec Issue 3 1986.

3. Craig, S. "Appendicitis, Acute." emedicine. 2005. 26 May 2005 ‹http://www.emedicine.com/EMERG/topic41.htm›.

4. Podbregar, M., et al. "Should we confirm our clinical diagnostic certainty by autopsies?" Intensive Care Med Nov; 27(11) 2001. p. 1750-55.

5. Tai, D.Y., et al. "A study of consecutive autopsies in a medical ICU: a comparison of clinical cause of death and autopsy diagnosis." Chest Feb; 119(2) 2001. p. 530-36.

6. Anderson, R.E., Fox, R.E., Hill, R.B. "Medical uncertainty and the autopsy: occult benefits for students." Hum Pathol vol 21 1990. p. 128-35. Goldman. L., et al. "The value of the autopsy in three medical eras." NEJM vol 308 1983. p. 1000-05.

7. "Potential Benefits Of Autopsy Increase As Number Performed In U.S. Continues To Decline." Science Blog. 1998. 02 Dec 1998 ‹http://www.scienceblog.com/community/older/1998/A/199800909.html›.

8. Champ, C., et al. "Improve your hospital autopsy rate to 40-50 per cent, a tale of two towns." J Pathol vol 166 1992. p. 405-07. Osborn, M., Thompson,,E.M. "What have we learnt from the Alder Hey affair? Asking for consent would halt decline in voluntary necropsies." BMJ vol 322 2001. p. 1542-43.

9. Blosser, S.A., Zimmerman, H.E., Stauffer, J.L. "Do autopsies of critically ill patients reveal important findings that were clinically undetected?" Crit Care Med vol 26 1998. p. 1332-36.

in complete agreement with pre-death diagnoses. Major missed diagnoses were present in (39%) of the cases examined. Myocardial infarction, carcinoma and pulmonary embolism represented the most frequently missed diagnoses.[1] Many diagnoses are missed because the patient is either treating themselves or fail to provide essential information to the physician. Physicians may also contribute to these misdiagnoses by being unfamiliar with rare diseases, lack of skill, physician bias and avoiding more sensitive tests in an attempt to save the patient money. On the other hand, certain diseases are routinely over-diagnosed. The list includes many very common diseases, like:

- ADHD[2]
- Irritable Bowel Syndrome (IBS)[3]
- Middle ear infection in children[4]
- Sinusitis[5]
- Lyme disease[6]
- Alzheimer's disease[7]

Another reason for misdiagnosis is a lack of understanding by either the public or medical professionals.[8] Under-diagnosis can also occur for conditions that are rarer than other conditions and thus simply don't get considered by patients or their doctors.

Sometimes people are diagnosed with diseases even though they are perfectly healthy.[9] The opposite may also occur; occasionally people are diagnosed as healthy by their physician even though they have a disease. Side effects of medications are routinely overlooked and some symptoms of a diagnosed disease may mask a more serious underlying disease.[10]

1. Perkins, G.D., et al. "Discrepancies between clinical and postmortem diagnoses in critically ill patients: an observational study." Crit Care vol 7(6) 2003. p. R129-R132.
2. Jensen, P.S. "Current concepts and controversies in the diagnosis and treatment of attention deficit hyperactivity disorder." Curr Psychiatry Rep Apr; 2(2) 2000. p. 102-09. Thapar, A.K., Thapar, A. "Attention-deficit hyperactivity disorder." Br J Gen Pract Mar; 53(488) 2003. p. 225-30.
3. Longstreth, G.F. "Irritable bowel syndrome. Diagnosis in the managed care era." Dig Dis Sci Jun; 42(6) 1997. p. 1105-11. Sanders, D.S., et al. "Association of adult coeliac disease with irritable bowel syndrome: a case-control study in patients fulfilling ROME II criteria referred to secondary care." Lancet Nov 3; 358(9292) 2001. p. 1504-08.
4. Asher, E., et al. "Accuracy of acute otitis media diagnosis in community and hospital settings." Acta Paediatr Apr; 94(4) 2005. p. 423-28. Blomgren, K., Pitkaranta, A. "Is it possible to diagnose acute otitis media accurately in primary health care?" Fam Pract Oct; 20(5) 2003. p. 524-27.
5. Silberstein, S.D. "Headaches due to nasal and paranasal sinus disease." Neurol Clin Feb; 22(1) 2004. p. 1-19. Tepper, S.J. "New thoughts on sinus headache." Allergy Asthma Proc Mar-Apr; 25(2) 2004. p. 95-96.
6. Prasad, A., Sankar, D. "Overdiagnosis and overtreatment of Lyme neuroborreliosis are preventable." Postgrad Med J Nov; 75(889) 1999. p. 650-56. Qureshi, M.Z., et al. "Overdiagnosis and over-treatment of Lyme disease in children." Pediatr Infect Dis J Jan; 21(1) 2002. p. 12-14.
7. Larner, A.J. "Getting it wrong: the clinical misdiagnosis of Alzheimer's disease." Int J Clin Pract Nov; 58(11) 2004. p. 1092-94. Roman, G. "Diagnosis of vascular dementia and Alzheimer's disease." Int J Clin Pract Suppl May; (120) 2001. p. 9-13.
8. Leape, L.L., et al. "Systems analysis of adverse drug events." JAMA vol 274 1995. p. 35-43.
9. "Under-Diagnosed Diseases." Cure Search. 2005. 24 Mar 2005 <http://www.cureresearch.com/intro/underdiag_printer.htm>.

Patients within the ICU setting are particularly at high risk of being misdiagnosed.[1] A 2001 study concluded the reason for death was incorrect for 20% of all ICU deaths.[2] The authors of this study asserted these findings would have changed the treatment for half of those misdiagnosed. The authors stress the true extent of missed diagnoses remains unclear because very few autopsies are performed. The autopsy rate in the United States has dropped from about 50% of deaths in the 1950s to only about 10% today.[3]

These findings are reiterated by several other studies which compared actual causes of death as determined by autopsy to the physician's stated cause of death. A 1998 study of a 16 bed ICU evaluated the cause of death by autopsy over a one year period.[4] Additional diagnoses were made for 90% of all deaths. These findings would have changed treatment for 27% of those evaluated. A quality assurance study suggested nearly 25% of all cases had misdiagnoses that if properly managed would have affected patient outcome (Class I error).[5] A 1999 study of surgical deaths found 41% of all deaths had additional findings. The authors of this study also found nearly one quarter of all deaths may have been preventable (undiagnosed infections).[6] A more recent 2004 study found major discrepancy rates of 39% between stated and actual causes of death.[7] A very large study of 1492 deaths with 167 autopsies found 171 missed diagnoses. They also concluded 31.7% of all reported causes of death were not consistent with autopsy findings. Multiple studies concluded the actual cause of death was misdiagnosed approximately 25%[8] of the time within the ICU setting.[9] Recent advances in viewing technologies (computed tomography, ultrasound, nuclear scanning, etc,) have had virtually no impact[10] on decreasing the rates of misdiagnosis.[11]

10. "10 Diseases Doctors Miss." Reader's Digest Feb 2004: 120.
1. Gut, A.L., Ferreira, A.L., Montenegro, M.R. "Autopsy: quality assurance in the ICU." Intensive Care Med Apr; 25(4) 1999. p. 360-63. Pastores, S.M., Halpern, N.A. "Autopsies in the ICU: we still need them!." Crit Care Med vol 27 1999. p. 235-36.
2. Tai, D.Y., et al. "A study of consecutive autopsies in a medical ICU: a comparison of clinical cause of death and autopsy diagnosis." Chest Feb; 119(2) 2001. p. 530-36.
3. Hill, R.B., Anderson, R.E. "The recent history of the autopsy.." Arch Pathol Lab Med vol 120 1996. p. 702-12. Loughrey, M.B., McCluggage, W.G., Toner, P.G. "The declining autopsy rate and clinicians' attitudes." Ulst Med vol 69 2000. p. 83-89.
4. Blosser, S.A., Zimmerman, H.E., Stauffer, J.L. "Do autopsies of critically ill patients reveal important findings that were clinically undetected?" Crit Care Med vol 26 1998. p. 332-36.
5. Gut, A.L., Ferreira, A.L., Montenegro, M.R. "Autopsy: quality assurance in the ICU." Intensive Care Med Apr; 25(4) 1999. p. 360-63.
6. Mort, T.C., Yeston, N.S. "The relationship of pre mortem diagnoses and post mortem findings in a surgical intensive care unit." Crit Care Med vol 27 1999. p. 299-303.
7. Ferguson, R.P., et al. "Consecutive autopsies on an internal medicine service." South Med J Apr; 97(4) 2004. p. 335-37.
8. Perkins, G.D., McAuley, D.F., Davies, S., Gao, F. "Discrepancies between clinical and postmortem diagnoses in critically ill patients: an observational study." Crit Care Dec; 7(6) 2003. p. R129-32. Shojania, K.G., et al. "Changes in Rates of Autopsy-Detected Diagnostic Errors Over Time." JAMA vol 289 2003. p. 2849-56.
9. Nadrous, H.F., et al. "The role of autopsy in the intensive care unit." Mayo Clin Proc Aug; 78(8) 2003. p. 947-50. Shojania KG, Burton EC, McDonald KM, Goldman L.. "Changes in rates of autopsy-detected diagnostic errors over time: a systematic review." JAMA Jun 4; 289(21) 2003. p. 2849-56.
10. Sonderegger-Iseli K, et al. "Diagnostic errors in three medical eras: a necropsy study." Lancet Jun 10; 355(9220) 2000. p. 2027-31.

Emergency room diagnoses fair even worse. An emergency department study concluded misdiagnoses occurred in nearly 50% of all deaths evaluated.[1] The authors concluded correct diagnoses with accompanying treatment could have reduced the death rate by 7%. Even trauma patients are at risk, the authors of one study found 3% of all deaths studied would have been preventable if a proper diagnosis had been made.[2] Multiple recent studies all confirm significant error rates in diagnoses in a variety of patient populations. An estimated 20% of the money awarded in malpractice suits against emergency department physicians is related to the misdiagnosis and mistreatment of acute coronary syndromes.[3] Multiple studies[4] have shown 2-5% of patients with myocardial infarction[5] were sent home inappropriately from the emergency department.[6] Approximately 25% of these missed diagnoses resulted in either death or potentially lethal complications.[7] Despite their low frequency, missed heart attacks remain the third leading cause of malpractice claims, with an average award of $220,000. Emergency medicine doctors are the third most likely specialist to be sued for failing to diagnose AMI, and pay the most in damages per claim, the average award is $280,000 per case.[8]

VICTIMIZED BY DRUGS

> *Sunk deep in my TV*
> *Maybe sucked the soul from within me*
> *We need and we will always need*
> *Another invented disease*
> Manic Street Preachers, Lyrics to *"Another Invented Disease"*

Critics may argue that free market is the driving force behind the growing list of "diseases" needing medical treatments. They argue the consumer is not

11. Kirch, W., Schafii, C. "Misdiagnosis at a university hospital in 4 medical eras." Medicine vol 75 1996. p. 29-40.
1. O'Connor, A.E., et al. "A comparison of the antemortem clinical diagnosis and autopsy findings for patients who die in the emergency department." Acad Emerg Med Sep; 9(9) 2002. p. 957-59.
2. Ong, A.W., et al. "Unexpected findings in trauma patients dying in the intensive care unit: results of 153 consecutive autopsies." J Am Coll Surg Apr; 194(4) 2002. p. 401-06.
3. Mehta, R.H., Eagle, K.A. "Missed diagnoses of acute coronary syndromes in the emergency room—continuing challenges." NEJM Apr 20; 342(16) 2000. p. 1207-10.
4. McCarthy, B.D., et al. "Missed diagnosis of acute myocardial infarction in the emergency department: results from a multicenter study." Ann Emerg Med vol 22 1993. p. 579-82. Pope, J.H., Aufderheide, T.P., Ruthazer, R., et al.. "Missed diagnoses of acute cardiac ischemia in the emergency department." NEJM vol 342 2000. p. 1163-70.
5. Jesse, R.L., Kontos, M.C. "Evaluation of chest pain in the emergency department." Curr Probl Cardiol vol 22 1997. p. 149-236.
6. Morrow, D.A., et al. "The Search for a Biomarker of Cardiac Ischemia." Clinical Chemistry vol 49 2003. p. 537-39. Storrow, A.B., Gibler, W.B. "Chest pain centers: diagnosis of acute coronary syndromes." Ann Emerg Med vol 35 2000. p. 449-61.
7. McCarthy, B.D., et al. "Missed diagnosis of acute myocardial infarction in the emergency department: results from a multicenter study." Ann Emerg Med vol 22 1993. p. 579-582.
8. Brady, W.J. "Missing the Diagnosis of Acute MI: Challenging Presentations, Electrocardiographic Pearls, and Outcome-Effective Management Strategies." Emerg Med Rep 1997. p. 91-102.

forced to buy these therapies. It is their choice if they choose to opt for pharmacotherapy to treat irksome or distressful conditions. If their lives are made better by drug therapy then where is the harm? This argument may be more convincing if you were talking about M&Ms instead of drugs with side effects ranging from nausea to sudden death.[1]

Medicalized conditions are generally symptoms, these symptoms are seldom life threatening, too bad the same thing can't be said for the medical treatments of these non-diseases. Irritable bowel syndrome has long been considered a common functional disorder covering a range of symptom severity. It is by no means a fatal condition. The drug Lotronex was FDA approved for its treatment. It was withdrawn from the market after determining it was responsible for causing serious bowel dysfunction and fatal adverse reactions in some patients.[2]

Loss of hair is fairly common and so is the desire for luscious locks. Propecia is a drug being promoted as a treatment for baldness. It seems incredible that a consumer would want to take a medicine for life with known side effects so severe that women who are or who may become pregnant are warned not to even touch the tablets. Finasteride is known to cause birth defects in developing male babies.[3]

Lamisil is a drug frequently prescribed for the treatment of common nail fungus. Medline plus lists 42 separate drugs that may have bad drug interactions with terbinafine[4]. Liver failure and drug interactions are a poor exchange for relief from yellowed nails.

Obesity is certainly manageable by lifestyle changes, yet many seek medical therapy instead of increased exercise and dietary modification. Fen-phen was the common name for the drug combination of pondimin (fenfluramine), redux (dexfenfluramine) and phentermine. Several studies determined a large percentage of those taking this drug had abnormal echocardiograms with many suffering from a progressively disabling disease called pulmonary hypertension.[5] Drug management of obesity may actually result in death. These findings

1. Moynihan, R.,et al. "Coverage by the news media of the benefits and risks of medications." NEJM. 2001. 01 Jun 2000 ‹http://content.nejm.org/cgi/content/abstract/342/22/1645›.
2. "Glaxo Wellcome decides to withdraw Lotronex from the market." FDA Talk Paper. 2000. 28 Nov 2000 ‹http://www.fda.gov/bbs/topics/ANSWERS/ANS01058.html›. "Lotronex information." Center for Drug Evaluation and Research. 2002. 23 Jan 2002 ‹http://www.fda.gov/cder/drug/infopage/lotronex/dear_patient.htm›.
3. Bowman, C.J., Barlow, N.J., Turner, K.J., Wallace, D.G., Foster, P.M. "Effects of in utero exposure to finasteride on androgen-dependent reproductive development in the male rat." Toxicol Sci Aug; 74(2) 2003. p. 393-406. Prahalada S. et al. "Effects of finasteride, a type 2 5-alpha reductase inhibitor, on fetal development in the rhesus monkey (Macaca mulatta)." Teratology Feb; 55(2) 1997. p. 119-31.
4. "Terbinafine (Systemic)." Medline Plus. 2001. 27 Jun 2001 ‹http://www.nlm.nih.gov/medlineplus/druginfo/uspdi/202760.html›.
5. Parisi, A.F. "Diet-Drug Debacle." Annals of Internal Medicine Editorial. 1998. 01 Dec 1998 ‹http://www.annals.org/cgi/content/full/129/11_Part_1/903›. Wee, C.C, et al. "Risk for valvular heart disease among users of fenfluramine and dexfenfluramine who underwent echocardiography before use of medication." Annals of Internal Medicine. 1998. 01 Dec 1998 ‹http://www.annals.org/cgi/content/abstract/129/11_Part_1/870#FN›.

prompted the FDA to recall the drug and resulted in a large class action lawsuit.[1] In April 2004, a $1 billion verdict against Wyeth was awarded by a Texas judge after fen-phen was shown to be linked to the death from primary pulmonary hypertension.[2]

Unfortunately, individuals afflicted by this drug may never collect on this settlement. In February 2005, a Philadelphia judge reversed a $780,000 jury verdict against Wyeth stating the patient "knowingly and voluntarily assumed the risks" associated with fen-phen before she took the drug.[3] This is a combination of med-speak and legalese for "it is your fault you have ruined your heart and lungs because you believed the FDA's, your doctor's and the drug manufacturer's assurances that the drug was relatively safe for the stated treatment." This decision sets a dangerous precedent for those injured by medical therapy. The "informed consent" that is thrust upon you by physicians and nurses is a legal statement that you agree to assume the risks of the treatment offered. The courts appear to be siding with the drug companies and hospitals that the document you hastily signed while under duress exempts them from any culpability because you "obviously knew and accepted the risks of the therapy offered by your physician." One must assume the poor patient also had extensive knowledge of pathophysiology, pharmacology, medicine, and is prescient of medical literature published after hundreds of unexplained deaths or injuries related to the offered medical therapy. Once again the lawyers win with a simple yet proven strategy, Caveat emptor; "Let the buyer beware."

Another weight loss drug, Meridia, was approved after the recall of Fen-phen. This approval came despite the FDA's own advisory vote against its approval because of its associated risks.[4] One reviewer claimed: "Since approval, there have been reports of a total of 56 cardiovascular deaths in people using Meridia, a large proportion of whom were under the age of 50."[5]

The anti-impotency drug Viagra may seem relatively safe; however, it also has risks associated with its use. One study estimated that 16 million men worldwide had taken Viagra. The authors concluded it was linked to 240 deaths during 7.5 months of availability, and to 522 reported deaths after 13 months of availability.[6] There is currently litigation against its manufacturer concerning its

1. ⟨http://adrugrecall.com/newsletter/jun04/fen-phen.html⟩. "Fen-Phen Safety Update Information." Center for rug Evaluation and Research. 2001. 27 Mar 2001 ⟨http://www.fda.gov/cder/news/feninfo.htm⟩.
2. Abelson, R., Glater, J.D. "A Texas Jury Rules Against A Diet Drug." Ney York Times: Health. 2004. 28 Apr 2004 ⟨http://query.nytimes.com/gst/full-page.html?sec=health&res=9902E4DD1F3AF93BA15757C0A9629C8B63⟩.
3. "Pa. judge reverses verdict Wyeth verdict." ABC News. 2005. 24 Feb 2005 ⟨http://abcnews.go.com/Business/wireStory?id=526685⟩.
4. "Congressional Testimony by Sidney Wolfe M.D. on Current Issues Related to Medical Liability Reform." Public Citizen. 2005. 10 Feb 2005 ⟨http://www.citizen.org/publications/release.cfm?ID=7360⟩.
5. "Petition to FDA to ban the diet drug sibutramine (MERIDIA) (HRG Publication #1613)." Public Citizen. 2002. 19 Mar 2002 ⟨http://www.citizen.org/publications/release.cfm?ID=7160⟩.

safety profile because it has been linked to a rare type of blindness called non-arteritic ischemic optic neuropathy.[1]

Sexual dysfunction is the newest entry as a disease. A government site on clinical trials reports, "Virtually all antidepressant medications are associated with a high incidence of adverse sexual side effects." In women, the side effects most commonly reported include decreased sexual arousal with decreased lubrication, delayed or inhibited orgasm, and decreased sexual desire. To date, there are no effective pharmacological antidotes for treating these sexual side effects. The real joke is that this clinical trial is recruiting applicants to determine if the herb Ginkgo biloba causes sexual dysfunction in women.[2] These same side effects are minimized for women on prescription anti-depressants. If these side effects of antidepressant therapy aren't significant enough to discourage their use, then consider that the FDA asked manufacturers to include the following warning on the label of antidepressants: "recommends close observation of adult and pediatric patients treated with these agents for worsening depression or the emergence of suicidality."[3] Their expanded use for the treatment of shyness, PMS, and other dysfunctional orders is highly questionable.

Menopause is a natural condition that was a forerunner in the medicalization of life. The advent of hormone replacement therapy with estrogen provided an enormous market for the manufacturer of Premarin.[4] Medical researchers were convinced men also would benefit from the "cardioprotective" effects attributed to estrogen. One clinical study of 16,608 women was conducted to see if the estrogen plus progestin therapy would reduce the incidence of heart disease and hip fractures.[5] It also sought to evaluate possible risks from breast cancer, endometrial cancer, and blood clots associated with estrogen supplementation. The study was terminated abruptly after 5.2 years because it was discovered that the risk for injury far outweighed and outnumbered any potential benefits.[6] The researchers concluded not only

6. Cohen, J.S. "Comparison of FDA reports of patient deaths associated with sildenafil and with injectable alprostadil." The Annals of Pharmacotherapy. 2001. Mar 2001 ⟨http://www.thean-nals.com/cgi/content/abstract/35/3/285⟩.

1. "Viagra maker sued." Defective Drugs. 2005. 08 Jun 2005 ⟨http://www.adrugrecall.com/news/viagra-sued.html⟩. "Government warns Viagra use could make you blind." Defective Drugs. 2001. 11 Jul 2005 ⟨http://www.theannals.com/cgi/content/abstract/35/3/285⟩.

2. "Ginkgo Biloba: Antidepressant-Induced Sexual Dysfunction." Clinical Trials. 2004. Sep 2004 ⟨http://clinicaltrials.gov/ct/gui/show/NCT00034021; jses-sionid=D8F053D1D71D7B6FCEC45478385C41C6?amp; order=1⟩

3. "Worsening Depression and Suicidality in Patients." Center for Drug Evaluation and Research. 2004. U.S. Food and Drug Administration. 22 Mar 2004 ⟨http://www.fda.gov/cder/drug/antide-pressants/AntidepressanstPHA.htm⟩.

4. Meyer, V.F. "Medicalization of menopause: critique and consequences." Int J Health Serv vol 31(4) 2001. p. 769-92.

5. Grady, D. et al. "Cardiovascular disease outcomes during 6.8 years of hormone therapy: Heart and Estrogen/progestin Replacement Study follow-up." JAMA vol 288 2002. p. 49-57.

6. Writing Group for the Women's Health Initiative Investigators. "Risks and Benefits of Estrogen Plus Progestin in Healthy Postmenopausal Women." JAMA. 2002. 7 Jul 2002 ⟨http://jama.ama-assn.org/cgi/content/short/288/3/321⟩.

did estrogen plus progestin therapy not protect against heart disease but actually increased the risk of heart attacks, stroke, and blood clots. It also increased the chance of breast cancer.[1] Women taking Prempro were shown to have a 29% increased risk of heart attack, 41% increased risk of stroke, and 26% higher risk of breast cancer.[2] It also was found to double the risk of dementia and Alzheimer's disease. Other side effects attributed to the use of Prempro were intense gallbladder inflammation, lupus, and uterine, vaginal or endometrial cancer.

In 1948 the Framingham Heart Study was initiated to ascertain what factors were contributory to the development of heart disease.[3] Although this study found a correlation between high cholesterol and increased incidence of heart attacks, so were 245 other factors[4] including short stature, male baldness, ear lobe creases,[5] and being married to a highly educated woman.[6] Cholesterol received a disproportionate amount of attention because many viewed it as being a potentially modifiable risk factor by either lifestyle or drugs.[7] Cholesterol lowering drugs have since been a mainstay for cardiologists. The standards for what is an acceptable value for cholesterol are continuously being revised. New standards set by the National Institute of Health's "National Cholesterol Education Program" recommend LDL cholesterol to be no more than 70 mg/dl.[8] Emphasis upon risk factors has resulted in elevated cholesterol levels being treated as though they were a disease. This emphasis has resulted in the release of six different statins from different manufacturers.

Statins have been promoted as drugs that safely lower your cholesterol levels while reducing your risk of heart attack. Their safety is currently a matter of debate because two separate agents have been shown to increase your risk of dying from liver dysfunction, kidney failure or rhabdomyolysis, a muscle-weakening disorder. Baycol was withdrawn from the market in August 2001 after it was linked to 100 deaths from kidney failure.[9] Bayer, the manufacturer,

1. Persson, I., Weiderpass, E., Bergkvist, L., Bergstrom, R., Schairer, C. "Risks of breast and endometrial cancer after estrogen and estrogen-progestin replacement." Cancer Causes Control Aug; 10(4) 1999. p. 253-60. Ross, RK et al. "Effect of Hormone Replacement Therapy on Breast Cancer Risk: Estrogen Versus Estrogen Plus Progestin." J Natl Cancer Inst Feb 16; 92(4) 2000. p. 328-332.
2. Hulley, S. "Randomized trial of estrogen plus progestin for secondary prevention of coronary heart disease in postmenopausal women." JAMA Aug 19; 280(7): 1998. p. 605-13.
3. Lenfant, C., Friedman, L., Thom, T. "Fifty Years of Death Certificates: The Framingham Heart Study." Annals of Internal Medicine. 1998. 15 Dec 1998 ‹http://www.annals.org/cgi/content/full/129/12/1066›.
4. Hopkins, P.N., Williams, R.R. "A survey of 246 suggested coronary risk factors." Atherosclerosis Aug-Sep; 40(1) 1981. p. 1-52
5. Miric, D. "Dermatological indicators of coronary risk: a case-control study.." Int J Cardiol Dec 31; 67(3) 1998. p. 251-55.
6. Frankish, C.J., Linden, W. "Spouse-pair risk factors and cardiovascular reactivity." J Psychosom Res Jan; 40(1) 1996. p. 37-51.
7. "Everything you need to know about statin drugs — Almost." Healthfacts. 2003. Nov 2003 ‹http://www.med-articles.com/med/marticles/lipitor/lipitor-article-16427.html›.
8. "Implications of Recent Clinical Trials for the National Cholesterol Education Program Adult Treatment Panel III Guidelines." Circulation. 2004. American Heart Association. 10 Aug 2004 ‹http://circ.ahajournals.org/cgi/content/full/110/2/227›.

had 9,400 Baycol lawsuits filed against them in U.S. courts.[1] Court documents showed Bayer continued to promote Baycol even after they were aware of these fatal side effects. As of May 10, 2005, Bayer had settled 3,000 cases for $1.133 billion and still had nearly 6,000 cases pending.[2]

Another statin, Crestor, may be destined to a similar fate. *Public Citizen* on August 13, 2003 claims seven people had already reported serious side effects (rhabdomyolysis and kidney failure) during the pre-approval drug trials and an additional three more after its approval.[3] There is one reported fatality linked to its use.

A class action suit has been filed against its manufacturer, AstraZeneca, stating that these side effects are not listed on the company's official web site.[4] *Public Citizen* also accuses the manufacturer of not disclosing their close financial ties to a top government researcher who was instrumental in its approval.[5] These serious and sometimes fatal side effects are a consequence of attempting to lower your cholesterol number to a sufficiently low enough number to reduce your risk of a heart attack.

MEDICAL ERRORS AND IATROGENIC INDUCED ILLNESS

> *Doctors are just the same as lawyers; the only difference is that lawyers*
> *merely rob you, whereas doctors rob you and kill you too.*
> *Anton Chekhov. Russian playwright (1860-1904)*

In November of 1999, the Institute of Medicine (IOM) released a study entitled *To Err Is Human: Building a Safer Health System*, revealing another problem associated with the actual process of medicine.[6] The IOM study suggests estimates of 44,000 to 98,000 deaths per year from medical errors. Even using the lower estimate, more people die from medical errors than from highway accidents. The increasing use of drugs and associated prescriptions increases the likelihood for adverse drug/drug interactions, adverse drug/disease interactions and errors related to handling.[7] The emergence of antibiotic-resistant strains of bacteria also

---

9. Furberg, C.D., Pitt, B. "Withdrawal of cerivastatin from the world market." Curr Control Trials Cardiovasc Med vol 2(5) 2001. p. 205-07. SoRelle, R. "Baycol withdrawn from market." Circulation Aug 21; 104(8) 2001. p. E9015-6.
1. "Baycol Side Effects." Defective Drugs. 2006. 18 Feb 2006 ⟨http://www.adrugrecall.com/baycol/effects.html⟩.
2. " Bayer settles 3,000 Baycol lawsuits worldwide." Defective Drugs. 2006. 10 May 2005 ⟨http://www.adrugrecall.com/news/baycol-bayer.html⟩.
3. "Cases of Kidney Failure, Muscle Damage Should Prompt FDA to Ban Crestor." Public Citizen. 2004. 04 Mar 2004 ⟨http://www.citizen.org/pressroom/release.cfm?ID=1657⟩.
4. "Crestor." Defective Drugs. 2006. 18 Feb 2006 ⟨http://www.adrugrecall.com/crestor/crestor.html⟩.
5. "Statement of Sidney M. Wolfe, MD before the FDA Endocrinologic and Metabolic Drugs Advisory Committee Hearing on Rosuvastatin (HRG Publication #1669)." Public Citizen. 2003. 09 Jul 2003 ⟨http://www.tradewatch.org/publications/release.cfm?ID=7262&secID=1666&catID=126⟩.
6. To err is human: building a safer health system. Kohn, L.T., Corrigan, J.M., Donaldson, M.S. The National Acadamies Press. 2000 ⟨http://fermat.nap.edu/books/0309068371/html/⟩.

threatens to further increase medical treatment related deaths. This report by the IOM was both lauded and scorned; critics stated that the data misrepresented the deaths attributable to medical therapy. The contention was so intense, a presidential commission was appointed to determine the extent to which (if any) medical errors increase in-hospital mortality. The new study by HealthGrades evaluated 45% of all Medicare patients admitted to US hospitals between the years 2000 to 2002. As previously mentioned, they concluded the original estimates had indeed been incorrect. This study reported nearly twice the rate of preventable hospital deaths reported by the IOM."[1] The HealthGrades study determined hospitals were responsible for 195,000 preventable deaths annually within the US. These deaths were not in the weakened or those who would have died anyway; they were actually in low risk patients. The majority of deaths were attributable to "failure to rescue," bedsores, and postoperative sepsis. These three lapses accounted for nearly 60% of all "safety-related incidents."[2]

Over the past 20 years the intensive care unit (ICU) has become a symbol of modern medicine. It is a true irony to realize, according to a French study, one out of ten patients in an ICU is there because of an iatrogenic (doctor induced) event. In fact, the authors conclude, "despite 25 years of experience with high-technology medicine, iatrogenic disease still has a negative impact on the health and resources of society."[3] These findings have been reiterated by other studies. Many believe that the majority of these errors are preventable and occur early within the admission process.[4] Many are from inappropriate use of drug therapy.[5]

One study reported 6.5% of hospitalized patients developed an adverse drug reaction and another 5.5% had a potential adverse drug reaction.[6] It was determined these events were caused by errors in 28% of cases. Furthermore, when trained observers who visited a general surgery unit where asked to evaluate the rate of adverse events, they reported almost 50% of patients experienced an adverse event, which was serious in 18% of cases. A 2003 study found 63% of the time physician's failed to recognize and treat medication-

7. Furrow, B.R. "The Problem of Medical Error: The Institution as Toxin." Health Law News. 2000. Mar 2000 ‹http://www.law.uh.edu/healthlaw/news/03-2000.html›.
1. "In-Hospital Deaths from Medical Errors at 195,000 per Year, HealthGrades' Study Finds." HealthGrades. 2004. 27 Jul 2004 ‹http://www.healthgrades.com/aboutus/index.cfm?fuseaction=mod&modtype=content&modact=Media_PressRelease_Detail&&press_id=135›.
2. Ibid.
3. Darchy, B. et al. "Iatrogenic Diseases as a Reason for Admission to the Intensive Care Unit." Archives of Internal Medicine. 1999. 11 Jan 1999 ‹http://archinte.ama-assn.org/cgi/content/abstract/159/1/71›. Schimmel, E.M. "The hazards of hospitalization." Qual Saf Health Care: Classic Paper. 2003. 12 Feb 2003.
4. Bates, D.W., et al. "Incidence of adverse drug events and potential adverse drug events. Implications for prevention." JAMA. 1995. 05 Jul 1995 ‹http://jama.ama-assn.org/cgi/content/abstract/274/1/29›.
5. Shelton, P.S., Fritsch, M.A., Scott, M. "Assessing medication appropriateness in the elderly: a review of available measures." Drugs and Aging vol 16 2000. p. 437-50.
6. Weingart, S.N. "Epidemiology of medical error." BMJ: Education and debate. 2000. 18 Mar 2000 ‹http://bmj.bmjjournals.com/cgi/content/full/320/7237/774›.

related symptoms.[1] Another paper suggests 50%-96% of adverse events are not even reported![2] If this data is correct, preventable deaths from errors in medical management have become endemic within the healthcare system, and the extent of injury is largely underestimated.[3]

A study of critical care patients found on average for the whole ICU, an average of two severe or potentially detrimental errors occurred each day.[4] Many of these errors are committed as the result of too great of a workload on the nurse or resident.[5] The error rates are probably even greater than reflected by most studies because healthcare workers are generally very reluctant to confess to committing errors for fear of reprisal.[6] The frequency of error rates are so high, one recent paper concluded death due to preventable adverse events in hospitalized patients is at least the 8th leading cause of mortality in the US.[7] More recent studies suggest this is a very optimistic figure, preventable hospital deaths may actually be the third leading cause of death.[8] Drug induced events are so common that two separate studies report nearly 28% of all emergency room visits are for the very drugs prescribed by physicians to "help" the patient.[9] Twenty-five percent of these admissions are considered serious to life-threatening.[10]

Almost one out of five patients who take prescription drugs experiences a treatment-related complication.[11] One study on 2,248 randomly chosen patients

1. Gandhi, T.J., et al. "Adverse drug events in ambulatory care." NEJM. 2003. 17 Apr 2003 ‹http://content.nejm.org/cgi/content/abstract/348/16/1556›.
2. Barach, P, Small, S.D. "Reporting and preventing medical mishaps: lessons from non-medical near miss reporting systems." BMJ: Clinical Review. 2000. 18 Mar 2000 ‹http://bmj.bmjjournals.com/cgi/content/full/320/7237/759›.
3. Osmon, S., et al. "Reporting of medical errors: an intensive care unit experience." Critical Care Medicine. 2004. Mar 2004 ‹http://www.ccmjournal.com/pt/re/ccm/abstract.00003246-200403000-00017.htm; jses-sionid=D3TQZACy8m6E0sfWDIkGQWodS7KfL3omvFLM4CQLlpfbYi2zsl8p!-477899252!-949856144!9001!-1›.
4. Calabrese, A.D. "Medication administration errors in adult patients in the ICU." Intensive Care Med Oct; 27(10) 2001. p. 1592-98.
5. Donchin, Y., et al. "A look into the nature and causes of human errors in the intensive care unit." Qual Saf Health Care. 2003. 12 Apr 2003 ‹http://qhc.bmjjournals.com/cgi/content/abstract/12/2/143›. Morrison, A.L., Beckmann, U., Durie, M., Carless, R., Gillies, D.M. "The effects of nursing staff inexperience (NSI) on the occurrence of adverse patient experiences in ICUs." Aust Crit Care Aug; 14(3) 2001. p. 116-21.
6. Flaatten, H., Hevroy, O. "Errors in the intensive care unit (ICU). Experiences with an anonymous registration." Acta Anaesthesiol Scand Jul; 43(6) 1999. p. 614-17.
7. Thomas, E.J., Brennan, T.A. "Incidence and types of preventable adverse events in elderly patients: population based review of medical records." BMJ. 2000. 18 Mar 2000 ‹http://bmj.bmjjour-nals.com/cgi/content/full/320/7237/741›.
8. Starfield, B. "Is US Health Really the Best in the World?" JAMA. 2000. 26 Jul 2000 ‹http://jama.ama-assn.org/cgi/content/full/284/4/483›.
9. Patel, P., Zed, P.J.,. "Drug-related visits to the emergency department: how big is the problem?" Medscape. 2002. 17 Sep 2002 ‹http://www.medscape.com/viewarticle/439814›. Tafreshi, M.J., Melby, M.J., Kaback, K.R., Nord, T.C. "Medication-related visits to the emergency department: a prospective study." The Annals of Pharmacotherapy. 1999. Dec 1999 ‹http://www.theannals.com/cgi/content/abstract/33/12/1252›.
10. McDonnell, P.J., Jacobs, M.R. "Hospital admissions resulting from preventable adverse drug reactions." The Annals of Pharmacotherapy. 2002. sep 2002 ‹http://www.theannals.com/cgi/content/abstract/36/9/1331›.
11. Gandhi, T.K. "Drug Complications in Outpatients." J Gen Intern Med Mar; 15(3) 2000. p. 149-54.

from 11 ambulatory clinics in Massachusetts found approximately 50% of patients who experienced an adverse reaction sought medical attention as a consequence of taking the drug and 5% of them were hospitalized.[1]

The problem of adverse drug reactions is even worse for the nursing home patient. A 1999 study found one out of every 6-7 nursing home residents is hospitalized for adverse drug reactions so severe that nearly half experienced a decline in their ability to take care of themselves.[2] The "higher" level of care afforded by hospitalization only increases the likelihood of medical error and adverse drug interactions, especially for the elderly.[3]

Given the frequency of adverse drug interactions, it would seem prudent to document as many adverse drug reactions as feasible.[4] Unfortunately, several studies have concluded the large majority of serious adverse drug reactions aren't even reported![5] A 2003 report found adverse drug reactions were under-reported by nearly 50-fold using traditional chart audits and voluntary reporting as compared to a newly developed low cost and low tech "trigger tool."[6] Adverse drug reaction reporting is the keystone to recognizing an unsafe drug, yet study after study reveals the failure of all levels of healthcare workers in reporting these reactions.[7]

The Leapfrog Group is a coalition of more than 150 public or private organizations that provide health care benefits. They cite studies finding more than one million serious medication errors occur annually in U.S. hospitals.[8] Approximately 20% of these are deemed life-threatening and are responsible for 7,000 deaths each year. One adverse drug reaction is estimated to add more than $2,000 to the average to the cost of hospitalization. This increases health care spending by at least $2 billion per year nationwide. The Leapfrog group suggests use of Computer Physician Order Entry (CPOE) systems (computer entry of drug orders instead of hand written scripts) in non-rural U.S. hospitals could prevent between 570,000 and 907,000 serious medication errors each year. A

1. Peyriere, H. et al. "Adverse drug events associated with hospital admission." Ann Pharmacother Jan; 37(1) 2003. p. 5-11.
2. Cooper JW. Adverse drug reaction-related hospitalizations of nursing facility patients: a 4-year study. South Med J 1999 May; 92(5):485-90.
3. Gray SL, Sager M, Lestico MR, Jalaluddin M. "Adverse drug events in hospitalized elderly." J Gerontol A Biol Sci Med Sci Jan; 53(1) 1998. p. M59-63.
4. Ahmad, S.R. "Adverse drug event monitoring at the Food and Drug Administration." J Gen Intern Med Jan; 18(1) 2003. p. 57-60. Heeley, E., Riley, J., Layton, D., Wilton, L.V., Shakir, S.A. "Prescription-event monitoring and reporting of adverse drug reactions." Lancet Dec 1; 358(9296) 2001. p. 1872-37.
5. Dean, B. "Adverse drug events: what's the truth?" Qual Saf Health Care. 2003. 12 Jun 2003 ‹http://qhc.bmjjournals.com/cgi/content/full/12/3/165›. Morrison-Griffiths, S., Walley, T.J., Park, B.K. "Reporting of adverse drug reactions by nurses." Lancet Apr 19; 361(9366) 2001. p. 1347-48.
6. Rozich, J.D., Haraden, C.R., Rezar, R.K. "Adverse drug event trigger tool: a practical methodology for measuring medication related harm." Qual Saf Health Care. 2003. Jun 2003 ‹http://qhc.bmjjournals.com/cgi/content/abstract/12/3/194›.
7. Martin, R.M., Kapoor, K.V., Wilton, L.V., Mann, R.D. "Underreporting of suspected adverse drug reactions to newly marketed ("black triangle") drugs in general practice: observational study." BMJ. 1998. 11 Jul 1998 ‹http://bmj.bmjjournals.com/cgi/content/full/317/7151/119›.
8. Hudon, P.S. "Leapfrog Standards: Implications for Nursing Practice." Medscape. 2003. 11 Nov 2003 ‹http://www.medscape.com/viewarticle/463375_print›.

1998 study suggests use of Computer Physician Order Entry systems could reduce the rate of nonintercepted serious medication errors by 55%.[1] The lead author of this study evaluated this studies recommendations over a seven to ten week period and determined non-intercepted serious medication errors (those with the potential to cause injury) fell by 86% during the study.[2] The use of Computer Physician Order Entry systems is infrequent throughout this nation. Many would cite the expense of the system or reluctance by the medical staff to use this new technology. The savings in both lives and dollars should be sufficient to quell their fears; unfortunately, the scarcity of these systems reveals the true concern of many hospitals and physicians.[3]

More people die each year from medical errors than in traffic accidents. These medical errors are in addition to the deaths related to medical neglect, hospital acquired infections, side effects of medication, hospital falls, and malpractice. One out of every ten patients in an ICU is there because modern medicine has injured them instead of helping them. The real tragedy is the likelihood of dying is greatly increased by being in an ICU. Over-monitoring often leads to excessive use of medical therapy; each medical intervention has a concomitant risk associated with its use. These risks quickly accumulate making the ICU one of the deadliest places on earth.

1. Bate, D.W. "Effect of computerized physician order entry and a team intervention on prevention of serious medication errors." JAMA. 1998. 21 Oct 1998 ‹http://jama.ama-assn.org/cgi/content/abstract/280/15/1311›.
2. "The impact of computerized physician order entry on medication error prevention." J Am Med Inform Assoc. 1999. Aug 1999 ‹http://www.j-amia.org/cgi/content/abstract/6/4/313›.
3. Bates, D.W. et al. "The costs of adverse drug events in hospitalized patients." JAMA. 1997. 22 Jan 1997 ‹http://jama.ama-assn.org/cgi/content/abstract/277/4/307›. Classes, D.C. et al. "Adverse drug events in hospitalized patients: excess length of stay, extra costs, and attributable mortality." JAMA. 1997. 22 Jan 1997 ‹http://jama.ama-assn.org/cgi/content/abstract/277/4/301›.

CHAPTER 5. MEDICAL MALFEASANCE

SLEEP DEPRIVATION: NIGHTMARE ON YOUR STREET

> *That we are not much sicker and much madder than we are is due exclu-*
> *sively to that most blessed and blessing of all natural graces, sleep.*
> *Aldous Huxley 1894-1963, English critic & novelist*

Even if you never see a physician during your hospital stay (don't laugh, it actually does happen), you are still at increased risk of injury just by being there. Anyone who has ever been to a hospital will attest to the fact they are notoriously noisy, unclean, offer little in the way of comfort and are just plain boring; and this is just from a visitor's perspective. Hospitals are anything but hospitable. Basic necessities like sleep,[1] nutrition, warmth, comfort, privacy, and freedom from unnecessary pain or injury are ignored in the pursuit of obtaining a diagnosis or treating a disease. Disturbed sleep can affect personal well being and impede the rehabilitation and recovery of older people from illness.[2] Studies on the sleep quality and sleep patterns of older people in community hospital and nursing home settings have found major disruptions of sleeping patterns.[3] These disruptions may result in health deterioration[4] and the likelihood of

---

1. Southwell, M.T. "Sleep in hospitals at night: are patients' needs being met?" J Adv Nurs Jun; 21(6) 1995. p. 1101-09. Southwell, M.T. "In-patient sleep disturbance: the views of staff and patients." Nurs Times Sep 13-19; 91(37) 1995. p. 29-31.
2. Ersser, S., et al. "The sleep of older people in hospital and nursing homes." J Clin Nurs Jul; 8(4) 1999. p. 360-68.
3. Jarman, H. et al. "Allowing the patients to sleep: flexible medication times in an acute hospital." Int J Nurs Pract Apr; 8(2) 2002. p. 75-80. Scalise, D. "Shhh, quiet please!." Hospital Connect. 17 May 2004 ⟨http://www.hhnmag.com/hhnmag/hospitalconnect/search/article.jsp?dcrpath=AHA/PubsNewsArticle/data/0405HHN_InBox_Patient_Care&domain=HHNMAG⟩. Hoffman, S. "Sleep in the older adult: implications for nurses." Medscape. 2004. 31 Oct 2003 ⟨http://www.medscape.com/viewarticle/460615⟩.
4. Honkus, V.L. "Sleep deprivation in critical care units." Crit Care Nurs Q Jul-Sep; 26(3) 2003. p.179-89.

increased mortality for geriatric residents.[1] The main causes of sleep disturbance were the need to go to the toilet, noise, pain, and discomfort.[2]

The most critically ill patients in the hospital are in the ICU. Due to intensive individualized care and monitoring, these patients often suffer from severe sleep deprivation.[3] By impairing protein synthesis, cell division, and cellular immunity, sleep deprivation can affect the healing process thereby contributing to an increased morbidity and mortality.[4] Sleep deprivation is often a direct result of the need for intensive care, continuous surveillance and monitoring which affords very little opportunity for uninterrupted sleep.[5] The patient's chronic underlying illness, pain, medications used in treatment of the primary illness, and the ICU environment are all contributory to the process of sleep deprivation.[6]

Constant exposure to 24 hour per day fluorescent lighting plays havoc with the body's biological clock. This disruption of biorhythms increases the amount of stress on an already over-stressed system and may result in a phenomenon known as ICU psychosis.[7] During ICU psychosis, the patient enters a delirious state becoming confused and agitated.[8] Several studies have shown the most disruptive environmental factors were the sound of alarms,[9] pain, lights and endotracheal intubation[10] or mechanical ventilation.[11]

1. "Sleep Patterns and Mortality among Elderly Patients in a Geriatric Hospital." Gerontology. 2000. Nov-Dec 2000 ‹http://content.karger.com/ProdukteDB/produkte.asp?Aktion=ShowPDF-&ProduktNr=224091&Ausgabe=225846&ArtikelNr=22184&filename=22184.pdf›. Newman, A.B. et al. "Sleep disturbance, psychosocial correlates, and cardiovascular disease in 5201 older adults: the Cardiovascular Health Study." J Am Geriatric Soc vol 46(6) 1998. p. 796-97.
2. Reid, E. "Factors affecting how patients sleep in the hospital environment." Br J Nurs Jul 26-Aug 8; 10(14) 2001. p. 912-15.
3. Parthasarathy, S., Tobin, M.J. "Sleep in the intensive care unit." Intensive Care Med Feb; 30(2) 2004. p. 197-206.
4. Gabor, J.Y., Cooper, A.B., Hanly, P.J. "Sleep disruption in the intensive care unit." Curr Opin Crit Care Feb; 7(1) 2001. p. 21-27.
5. Gabor, J.Y. et al. "Contribution of the Intensive Care Unit Environment to Sleep Disruption in Mechanically Ventilated Patients and Healthy Subjects." American Journal of Respiratory and Critical Care Medicine. 2003. Mar 2003 ‹http://ajrccm.atsjournals.org/cgi/content/abstract/167/5/708›. Krachman, S.L., D'Alonzo, G.E., Criner, G.J.. "Sleep in the intensive care unit." Chest. 1995. Jun 1995 ‹http://www.chestjournal.org/cgi/reprint/107/6/1713›.
6. Parthasarathy, S., Tobin, M.J. "Sleep in the intensive care unit." Intensive Care Med Feb; 30(2) 2004. p. 197-206.
7. McGuire, B.E., et al. "Intensive care unit syndrome: a dangerous misnomer." Arch Intern Med. 2000. 10 Apr 2000 ‹http://archinte.ama-assn.org/cgi/content/abstract/160/7/906›.
8. Novaes MA; Aronovich A; Ferraz MB; Knobel E Stressors in ICU: patients' evaluation. Intensive Care Med 1997 Dec; 23(12):1282-5
9. Freedman, N.S., et al. "Abnormal sleep/wake cycles and the effect of environmental noise on sleep disruption in the intensive care unit." Am. J. Respir. Crit. Care Med. 2001. Feb 2001 ‹http://ajrccm.atsjournals.org/cgi/content/abstract/163/2/451›.
10. Cooper, A.B. et al. "Sleep in critically ill patients requiring mechanical ventilation." Chest. 2000. Mar 2000 ‹http://www.chestjournal.org/cgi/reprint/117/3/809›.
11. Cooper AB, Thornley KS, Young GB, Slutsky AS, Stewart TE, Hanly PJ. Sleep in critically ill patients requiring mechanical ventilation. Chest. 2000 Mar; 117(3):809-18. Erratum in: Chest 2001 Mar; 119(3):993. Gabor, J.Y. et al. "Contribution of the Intensive Care Unit Environment to Sleep Disruption in Mechanically Ventilated Patients and Healthy Subjects." American Journal of Respiratory and Critical Care Medicine. 2003. Mar 2003. Shilo, L., et al. "Patients in the intensive care unit suffer from severe lack of sleep associated with loss of normal melatonin secretion pattern." The American Journal of the Medical Sciences. 1999. May 1999 ‹http://www.amjmedsci.com/pt/re/ajms/abstract.00000441-199905000-00002.htm; jsessionid-D4xrfFTxCtc6q7BXrk9r8RykF0lMWglw2m4FA4U2vKamUCn29Kac!-477899252!-949856144!9001!-1›.

Sleep deprivation may contribute to impaired immune function, increase the difficulty of breathing, produce disruption in the regulation of the body's temperature, cause reduced secretion of melatonin,[1] increase the stress response of the body[2] and produces delirium.[3]

Tragically, although sleep deprivation is relatively easy to treat, the only known cure is sleep. One study found in healthy volunteers exposed to simulated ICU noises, earplugs worn during exposure to the noise significantly improved the quality of sleep.[4] A recent double blinded, placebo-controlled study of eight patients in an ICU attempted to determine if sleep could be improved by the administration of melatonin.[5] It was determined a 3mg dose of melatonin given at night dramatically improved both the duration and quality of sleep in this group. This data suggests melatonin may facilitate both sleep induction and resynchronization of the "biological clock." It has been postulated treatment with melatonin may also help in the prevention of the "ICU syndrome" and accelerate the healing process.[6] A 2005 study of nursing home residents suggests using commonsense approaches to maximize opportunities for night-time sleeping increased physical activity during waking hours and social interaction.[7]

EFFECTS OF SLEEP DEPRIVATION ON HEALTH CARE WORKERS

The woods are lovely, dark, and deep,
But I have promises to keep,
And miles to go before I sleep,
And miles to go before I sleep.
                    Robert Frost. Poet (1874-1963)

Patients are not the only ones in a hospital setting affected by sleep deprivation and disruption of biological clocks. Several studies have demonstrated these same effects on those responsible for delivering care.[8]

1. Olofsson, K., et al. "Abolished circadian rhythm of melatonin secretion in sedated and artificially ventilated intensive care patients." Acta Anaesthesiol Scand. 2004. Jul 2004 ‹http://www.ingentaconnect.com/content/mksg/aas/2004/00000048/00000006/art00002›.
2. Bourne, R.S., Mills, G.H. "Sleep disruption in critically ill patients pharmacological considerations." Anaesthesia vol 59 2004. p. 374-84. Tochikubo, O., Ikeda, A., Miyajima, E., Ishii, M. "Effects of insufficient sleep on blood pressure monitored by a new multibiomedical recorder." Hypertension. 1996. Jun 1996 ‹http://hyper.ahajournals.org/cgi/content/abstract/27/6/1318›.
3. Honkus, V.L. "Sleep deprivation in critical care units." Crit Care Nurs Q Jul-Sep; 26(3) 2003. p.179-89.
4. Wallace, C.J., Robins, J., Alvord, L.S., Walker, J.M. "The effect of earplugs on sleep measures during exposure to simulated intensive care unit noise." American Journal of Critical Care. 1999. Jul 1999 ‹http://ajcc.aacnjournals.org/cgi/content/abstract/8/4/210›.
5. Shilo L; Dagan Y; Smorjik Y; Weinberg U; Dolev S; Komptel B; Shenkman L Effect of melatonin on sleep quality of COPD intensive care patients: a pilot study. Chronobiol Int 2000 Jan; 17(1):71-6
6. Leppamaki S, Partonen T, Vakkuri O, Lonnqvist J, Partinen M, Laudon M. Effect of controlled-release melatonin on sleep quality, mood, and quality of life in subjects with seasonal or weather-associated changes in mood and behaviour. Eur Neuropsychopharmacol. ; 13(3): 137-45.
7. Alessi, C.A. "Randomized, controlled trial of a nonpharmacological intervention to improve abnormal sleep/wake patterns in nursing home residents." J Am Geriatr Soc May; 53(5) 2005. p. 803-10.

Medical residents routinely function with five or fewer hours sleep.[1] Even though they are sleep deprived, they are still expected to continue to provide expert care. Under 2003 guidelines, a resident is limited only 80 hours per week. This is an improvement over previous schedules where residents averaged 98 hours each week.[2] This is one and a half times that allowed truck drivers, who are notorious for being sleep deprived.[3] Nurses are restricted to shifts of 12 hours (and that makes for a long day) because research shows their error rates rise significantly with longer working hours.[4] According to the National Highway Traffic Safety Administration, falling asleep while driving is responsible for at least 56,000 automobile crashes, 40,000 injuries, and 1550 fatalities annually.[5] Several studies have demonstrated even healthy young healthcare workers suffer from the effects of sleep deprivation in the hospital environment.[6] One study suggested sleep deprivation affects creative or divergent thinking which are essential for complex problem-solving tasks.[7] Another study indicated residents' reaction time during potentially lifesaving procedures was significantly impaired.[8] Very recent studies involving the effects of long shifts on nurses concluded those working 12.5 hours or longer were three times more likely to commit an error.[9]

The journal *Lancet* reports, "Wakefulness for 24 hours is equivalent to a blood alcohol level of 0.10%; that is, above the legal driving limit.... Surgeons awake all night made 20% more errors and took 14% longer to complete the

8. Parthasarathy, S. "Sleep and the medical profession.." Current Opinion in Pulmonary Medicine. 2005. Nov 2005 ‹http://www.co-pulmonarymedicine.com/pt/re/copulmonary/abstract.00063198-200511000-00006.htm; jsessionid=D47vF2KFH28kForOAdBIPWEAX9FfK1EnAFalDTutrz4H2ZlyLg9R!-477899252!-949856144!9001!-1›. Scott, L.D., et al. "Effects of Critical Care Nurses' Work Hours on Vigilance and Patients' Safety." American Journal of Critical Care. 2006. Jan 2006 ‹http://ajcc.aacnjournals.org/cgi/content/short/15/1/30›.
1. Baldwin DC Jr, Daugherty SR.. "Sleep deprivation and fatigue in residency training: results of a national survey of first- and second-year residents.." Sleep Mar 15; 27(2) 2004. p. 217-23.
2. Schwartz, R.J et al. "Guidelines for surgical residents' working hours. Intent vs reality." Arch Surg Jul; 127(7) 1992. p. 778-82.
3. Dracup, K., Bryan-Brown, C.W. "First, Do No Harm." American Journal of Critical Care vol 14 2005. p. 99-101.
4. Rogers, A.E. "The Working Hours of Hospital Staff Nurses and Patient Safety." Health Affairs vol 23, Issue 4 2004. p. 202-12.
5. "Traffic Safety: Drowsy & Distracted Driving." National Highway Traffic Safety Administration. 2006. Feb 2006 ‹http://www.nhtsa.dot.gov/people/injury/drowsy_driving1/Drowsy.html›.
6. Gaba, D.M., Howard, S.K.. "Fatigue among clinicians and the safety of patients." NEJM. 2002. Oct 2002 ‹http://content.nejm.org/cgi/content/extract/347/16/1249›. Leonard, C., Fanning, N., Attwood, J., Buckley, M. "The effect of fatigue, sleep deprivation and onerous working hours on the physical and mental wellbeing of pre-registration house officers." Ir J Med Sci Jan-Mar; 167(1) 1998. p. 22-25.
7. Bartel, P., Offermeier, W., Smith, F., Becker, P. "Attention and working memory in resident anaesthetists after night duty: group and individual effects." Occupational and Environmental Medicine. 2004. Feb 2004 ‹http://oem.bmjjournals.com/cgi/content/abstract/61/2/167›.
8. Eastridge, B.J. "Effect of sleep deprivation on the performance of simulated laparoscopic surgical skill." Am J Surg Aug; 186(2) 2003. p. 169-74.
9. Compas LB.. "Nurses' working hours." Health Affairs. 2004. Nov-Dec 2004 ‹http://content.healthaffairs.org/cgi/content/full/23/6/274›. Rogers, A.E., et al. "The working hours of hospital staff nurses and patient safety." Health Affairs. 2004. July/August 2004 ‹http://content.healthaffairs.org/cgi/content/abstract/23/4/202 ›.

tasks than those who had had a full night's sleep. The decline in performance remained significant after arousal was taken into account... suggesting that sleep deprivation mediates its effect via increased stress rather than decreased arousal."[1] A separate study published in the journal *Nature* reached a similar conclusion.[2] Combine this with an increase in negative mood by sleep deprivation and it is easy to see why the ER resident is so irritable and cranky when you have to see him at 3 am for chest pain which turns out to be just indigestion. Incredibly, a recent survey suggests medical students may be the only life form on earth unaffected by sleep deprivation, 66% sleep less than 6 hours each night.[3] Errors and personality issues were noted in those with less than an average of 5 hours of sleep each night, but those with 6 hours or more were considered to be functioning normally. Two studies suggest acute sleep deprivation among medical residents was not associated with any significant changes in both cognitive functioning and level of stress perceived.[4] Perhaps we should consider sending airplane pilots and truck drivers to medical school so they also may learn the secret of functioning on lack of sleep. It is probably more likely the authors of these studies may themselves be suffering from sleep deprivation associated with following the medical residents' grueling schedules.

All other studies find major declines in fine motor skills,[5] reaction time, vigilance,[6] attention,[7] cognitive functions,[8] mood,[9] and decision-making skills.[10]

On one assignment, I had a patient who required emergency abdominal surgery at 3:00 am for peritonitis. The surgical resident was notified but had to defer to a second resident because his on duty hours had exceeded the recently implemented guidelines by the AMA. These guidelines restrict residents' hours

1. Taffinder, N J, et al. "Effect of Sleep Deprivation on Surgeons' Dexterity On Laparoscopy Simulator." The Lancet 352(1998):1191.
2. Dawson, D. Reid, K. "Fatigue, alcohol and performance impairment." Nature vol 388(6639) 1995. p. 235.
3. Baldwin, D.C. Jr, Daugherty, S.R. "Sleep deprivation and fatigue in residency training: results of a national survey of first- and second-year residents." Sleep Mar 15; 27(2) 2004. p. 217-23.
4. Jakubowicz, D.M. et al. "Effects of a twenty-four hour call period on resident performance during simulated endoscopic sinus surgery in an accreditation council for graduate medical education-compliant training program." Laryngoscope Jan; 115(1) 2005. p. 143-46. Mak, S.K., Spurgeon, P. "The effects of acute sleep deprivation on performance of medical residents in a regional hospital: prospective study." Hong Kong Med J Feb; 10(1) 2004. p. 14-20.
5. Eastridge, B.J. et al. "Effect of sleep deprivation on the performance of simulated laparoscopic surgical skill." Am J Surg Aug 2003 2003. p. 169-74. Williams, M. "Tired surgical trainees. Sleep deprivation affects psychomotor function." BMJ May 11; 324(7346) 2002. p. 1154.
6. Murray, D., Dodds, C. "The effect of sleep disruption on performance of anaesthetists—a pilot study." Anaesthesia. 2003 Jun; 58(6) 2003. p. 520-25.
7. Lockley, S.W., et al. "Effect of Reducing Interns' Weekly Work Hours on Sleep and Attentional Failures." NEJM: vol 352 2005. p. 726-28.
8. Halbach, M.M., Spann, C.O., Egan, G. "Effect of sleep deprivation on medical resident and student cognitive function: A prospective study." Am J Obstet Gynecol May 2003 2003. p. 1198-201.
9. Johnson, L.C., MacLeod, W.L. "Sleep and wake behaviour during gradual sleep reduction." Perceptual and Motor Skills vol 36 1973. p. 87-97. Lewis KE, Blagrove M, Ebden P. Sleep deprivation and junior doctors' performance and confidence.Postgrad Med J. 2002 Feb; 78(916):85-7.
10. Christopher P. Landrigan et al. Effect of Reducing Interns' Work Hours on Serious Medical Errors in Intensive Care Units N Engl J Med 2005; 352:726-728. Hendey, G.W., Barth, B.E., Soliz, T. "Overnight and Postcall Errors in Medication Orders." Acad Emerg Med. 2005. Jul 2005 ‹http://www.aemj.org/cgi/content/abstract/12/7/629›.

to no more than 80 hours per week and 24 consecutive hours on-site duty. The next resident arrived during our conversation and complained of this new legislation. He volunteered he had been awake for over 50 hours but still felt competent enough to perform emergency abdominal surgery. Surgery was performed despite my complaints concerning his impairment in fine motor skills and critical judgment. Although the patient recovered without incident, their risks were greatly increased by an arrogant surgical resident who was unwilling to acknowledge his own limitations or obey rules governing this reckless behavior.

If concern for the patient is not enough to prompt a change, one would think the resident would fear for their own life. Research clearly documents 25% of residents state they have been involved in a motor vehicle accident and 40% stated the accident had occurred after they had been on-call night.[1] The authors conclude for "every extended work shift that was scheduled in a month increased the monthly risk of a motor vehicle crash by 9.1% and increased the monthly risk of a crash during the commute from work by 16.2%." Sleep deprivation may also result in chronic fatigue, anxiety, depression or situational hyposomnia.[2]

A 2004 study found the effects of sleep deprivation are so severe, the scores of 84% of those surveyed were considered abnormal "in the range for which clinical intervention is indicated."[3] Another study determined more than one-third of general surgery residents meet criteria for clinical psychological distress.[4]

HUNGER PANGS

> *It is an eternal obligation toward the human being not to let him suffer*
> *from hunger when one has a chance of coming to his assistance.*
> Simone Weil. French philosopher (1910-1943)

Another basic necessity often neglected is nutrition.[5] Hospital meals are notoriously unpalatable, lacking texture, taste, smell and general appeal; they are often left uneaten.[6] Harried nursing assistants or nurses frequently bring late

1. Barger, L.K. et al. "Extended Work Shifts and the Risk of Motor Vehicle Crashes among Interns." NEJM. 2005. 13 Jan 2005 ‹http://content.nejm.org/cgi/content/abstract/352/2/125›.
2. Costa, G. "The problem: Shiftwork." Chronobiology International vol 14(2) 1997. p. 89-98.
3. Papp, K.K. "The effects of sleep loss and fatigue on resident-physicians: a multi-institutional, mixed-method study." Acad Med May; 79(5) 2004. p. 394-406.
4. Zare, S.M. "Psychological well-being of surgery residents before the 80-hour work week: a multi-institutional study." J Am Coll Surg Apr; 198(4) 2004. p. 633-40.
5. Farre Rovira, R., Frasquet Pons, I., Ibor Pica, J.F. "In-hospital malnutrition: indications of postoperative evolution." Nutr Hosp May-Jun; 13(3): 1998. p. 130-37. Thomas, D.R. "Starving in the hospital." Nutrition Oct; 19(10) 2003. p. 907-08.
6. Kondrup, J. "Proper hospital nutrition as a human right." Clinical Nutrition. 2004. Apr 2004 ‹http://www.nutritionday.org/uploads/media/kondrup_nutrition_human_right.pdf›.

meals that are cold upon being served in a room with unpleasant smells, which makes for a less than enjoyable experience.[1] Physical hindrances like IVs, restraints and wires further complicate this process.[2] If these seem like petty complaints consider this finding; a 1994 study showed 40% of patients admitted to an acute teaching hospital were malnourished, and in 78% of them, nutritional status further deteriorated during hospital stay.[3] In addition, two thirds of all patients lost weight during hospital stay. Some had levels of malnutrition severe enough to depress their immune system. Studies have found malnutrition was present in rates from 25% to 57%[4] of all hospitalized patients.[5] Patients with malignancies, inflammatory bowel disease, chronic heart failure and benign lung diseases were the most at risk for malnutrition. Recent studies suggest use of nursing assistants to aid in feeding decreases the need for antibiotic therapy in the elderly; unfortunately, it does not decrease the length of hospitalization.[6] A recent Veterans Administration study reported feeding patients via tube feedings reduced hospital mortality by 56% compared to those not receiving nutrition or those receiving artificial nutrition through IV access (TPN).[7] A 2005 meta-analysis study concluded early feeding does not reduce mortality of hospitalized patients. They didn't ask the patient or family members their opinion on preventing the patient from eating for days while they ran diagnostic tests.[8]

Weight loss per se may or may not be undesirable; however, in the already malnourished it can have disastrous or even fatal consequences.[9] Multiple studies have demonstrated a direct connection between malnutrition and

1. Dupertuis, Y.M. et al. "Food intake in 1707 hospitalised patients: a prospective comprehensive hospital survey." Clin Nutr Apr; 22(2) 2003. p. 115-23. Stanga Z, Zurfluh Y, Roselli M, Sterchi AB, Tanner B, Knecht G. Hospital food: a survey of patients' perceptions. Clin Nutr. 2003 Jun; 22(3):241-6.
2. Holmes, S. "Undernutrition in hospital patients." Nurs Stand Jan 22-28; 17(19) 2003. p. 45-52.
3. McWhirter, J.P., Pennington, C.R. "Incidence and recognition of malnutrition in hospital." BMJ. 1994. 09 Apr ⟨http://bmj.bmjjournals.com/cgi/content/abstract/308/6934/945⟩. Thomas, D.R. "Starving in the hospital." Nutrition Oct; 19(10) 2003. p. 907-08.
4. Naber, T.H. "Prevalence of malnutrition in nonsurgical hospitalized patients and its association with disease complications." American Journal of Clinical Nutrition. 1997. Nov 1997 ⟨http://www.ajcn.org/cgi/content/abstract/66/5/1232⟩.
5. Pirlich, M., et al. "Prevalence of malnutrition in hospitalized medical patients: impact of under-lying disease." Digestive Diseases. 2003. 2003 ⟨http://content.karger.com/ProdukteDB/produkte.asp?Aktion=ShowPDF&ProduktNr=224231&Ausgabe=229586&ArtikelNr=73342&file-name=73342.pdf⟩.
6. Hickson, M., et al. "Does additional feeding support provided by health care assistants improve nutritional status and outcome in acutely ill older in-patients?—a randomised control trial." Clin Nutr Feb; 23(1) 2004. p. 69-77. Payette, H., Boutier, V., Coulombe, C., Gray-Donald, K. "Benefits of nutritional supplementation in free-living, frail, undernourished elderly people: a prospective randomized community trial." J Am Diet Assoc Aug; 102(8) 2002. p. 1088-95.
7. Barr, J., et al. "Outcomes in critically ill patients before and after the implementation of an evidence-based nutritional management protocol.." Chest Apr; 125(4) 2004. p. 1446-57. Clark, Amanda. Personal Comm.
8. Peter, J.V., Moran, J.L., Phillips-Hughes, J. "A metaanalysis of treatment outcomes of early enteral versus early parenteral nutrition in hospitalized patients." Critical Care Medicine. 2005. Jan 2005 ⟨http://www.ccmjournal.com/pt/re/ccm/abstract.00003246-200501000-00032.htm; jses-sionid=D5NEr8dFPC7iOIK98yecapvmXy0mOSIeKmW7cmGFAqJNRU39YIa1!-477899252!-949856144!9001!-1⟩.

morbidity and mortality. A 1995 study found malnutrition increased the length of hospital stay, complications and number of deaths compared to well-nourished patients. Malnourished patients with less severe illnesses had worse clinical outcomes than sicker, well-nourished patients.[1] A 2003 study evaluated both the economic and medical impact of in-hospital malnutrition. They found mortality was 12.4% in malnourished patients vs. 4.7% in the well nourished. Malnutrition also increased hospital stay from 10.1+/-11.7 days in the nourished to 16.7+/-24.5 days in the malnourished. Hospital costs in malnourished patients were increased up to 308.9%.[2]

A 1999 study of 497 elderly patients showed 21% of patients consumed less than half of their basic energy needs, due partly to the fact they were frequently ordered to eat nothing by mouth.[3] While this may be a medical necessity, unless absolutely contraindicate, the patient should receive supplemental nutrition by either tube feedings or through an IV. Another study found patients with insufficient caloric intake were eight times more likely to die during their hospitalization and three times more likely to die within 90 days, compared to those with normal energy intake.[4] Postoperative complications and mortality occurred 2-3 times more often, and hospital costs were 35% to 75% higher, in malnourished compared to well-nourished patients. They were also approximately three times more likely to be admitted to a nursing home within a year of discharge. Protein malnutrition is a greater predictor of mortality than even the diagnosis of congestive heart failure, being discharged to a health care facility, age or marital status.[5]

A Dutch survey of 600 consumers determined physicians were the preferred source for advice relating to nutrition over ten other potential sources including dietitians, the government, consumer organizations, etc.[6] This is ironical,

9. Krishnan, J.A., Parce, P.B., Martinez, A. "Caloric intake in medical ICU patients: consistency of care with guidelines and relationship to clinical outcomes." Nutrition in Clinical Practice. 2004. 2003 ‹http://ncp.aspenjournals.org/cgi/content/abstract/19/6/645›. Naber, T.H. "Prevalence of malnutrition in nonsurgical hospitalized patients and its association with disease complications." American Journal of Clinical Nutrition. 1997. Nov 1997.
1. Giner, M., Laviano, A., Meguid, M.M., Gleason, J.R. "In 1995 a correlation between malnutrition and poor outcome in critically ill patients still exists." Nutrition Jan; 12(1) 1996. p. 23-29.
2. Correia, M.I., Waitzberg, D.L. "The impact of malnutrition on morbidity, mortality, length of hospital stay and costs evaluated through a multivariate model analysis." Clin Nutr Jun; 22(3) 2003. p. 235-39.
3. Sullivan, D.H., Sun, S., Walls, R.C. "Protein-Energy Undernutrition Among Elderly Hospitalized Patients." JAMA. 1999. 02 Jun 1999 ‹http://jama.ama-assn.org/cgi/reprint/281/21/2013›.
4. Gallagher-Allred, C.R., et al. "Malnutrition and clinical outcomes: the case for medical nutrition therapy." J Am Diet Assoc Apr; 96(4) 1996. p. 361-66.
5. Covinsky KE. "The relationship between clinical assessments of nutritional status and adverse outcomes in older hospitalized medical patients." J Am Geriatr Soc May; 47(5) 1999. p. 532-38. Sullivan, D.H., Walls, R.C. "Protein-energy undernutrition and the risk of mortality within six years of hospital discharge." Journal of the American College of Nutrition. 1998. Dec 1998 ‹http://www.jacn.org/cgi/reprint/17/6/571›.
6. Greger, M. "Food for Thought." Heart Failure — Diary of a Third Year Medical Student. 1999 ‹http://upalumni.org/medschool/appendices/appendix-4.html#fnB65›. Hiddink, G.J., et al. "Consumers' Expectations about Nutritional Guidance.." American Journal of Clinical Nutrition vol 65 1997. p. 1974S-1979S.

because, according to a 1993 report to Congress; less than a 25% of US medical schools require nutrition courses.[1] Other studies found less than 25% of physicians had any knowledge of the basic nutritional values.[2] Multiple studies have determined physicians are generally unprepared[3] to even pass[4] rudimentary nutritional tests.[5] One dismal study showed intensive nutritional training increased correct responses to a nutritional exam from 39% to a mere 62%. These findings prompted the Committee on Nutrition in Medical Education to conclude, "Nutrition education programs in US medical schools is largely inadequate to meet the present and future demands of the medical profession."[6] In 1994, Congressional hearings were called to determine why there were so many barriers to nutritional education in medical schools.[7] In 1990, the federal government decreed nutrition education should become an integral component of medical education.[8] Later studies determined nutrition was still neglected by most medical schools.[9] Few medical schools have faculty trained specifically in nutrition[10], most training in nutrition has been piecemeal and selective at best.[11] Implementation of these Congressional mandates for improving the nutritional education of physicians has progressed at a snails pace. In 1962 and 1972, the American Medical Association Council on Foods and Nutrition criticized US medical schools for "not keeping abreast of the tremendous advances in nutrition knowledge," stating "nutrition received inadequate recognition, support, and attention in medical education."[12] In 1991, only 23% of all medical schools required a nutritional course.[13] By 1995 the

1. Lazarus, K., Weinsier, R.L., Boker, J.R. "Nutritional Knowledge and Practices of Physicians in a Family Practice Residency Program." Journal of Clinical Nutrition vol 58 1997. p. 319-25.
2. Deen, D., Spencer, E., Kolasa, K. "Nutrition education in family practice residency programs." Fam Med. 2003. Feb 2003 ‹http://www.stfm.org/fmhub/fm2003/feb03/re3.pdf›. Lazarus, K. "Nutrition practices of family physicians after education by a physician nutrition specialist." American Journal of Clinical Nutrition. 1997. Jun 1997 ‹http://www.ajcn.org/cgi/content/abstract/65/6/2007S›.
3. Moore, H., Adamson, A.J. "Nutrition interventions by primary care staff: a survey of involvement, knowledge and attitude." Public Health Nutr Aug; 5(4) 2002. p. 531-36. Nightingale, J.M., Reeves, J. "Knowledge about the assessment and management of undernutrition: a pilot questionnaire in a UK teaching hospital." Clin Nutr Feb; 18(1) 1999. p. 23-27.
4. Mlodinow, S.G., Barrett-Connor, E. "Physicians' and medical students' knowledge of nutrition." Acad Med Feb; 64(2) 1989. p. 105-06. Temple, N.J. "Survey of nutrition knowledge of Canadian physicians." J Am Coll Nutr Feb; 18(1) 1999. p. 26-29.
5. Parker, D., Emmett, P.M., Heaton, K.W. "Final year medical students' knowledge of practical nutrition." J R Soc Med Jun; 85(6) 1992. p. 338.
6. Ammerman, A,. et al. "Medical Students' Knowledge, Attitudes, and Behavior Concerning Diet and Heart Disease." American Journal of Preventive Medicine vol 5 1989. p. 271-78.
7. Davis, C.H. "The report to Congress on the appropriate federal role in assuring access by medical students, residents, and practicing physicians to adequate training in nutrition." Public Health Rep Nov-Dec; 109(6) 1994. p. 824-26.
8. " National Nutrition Monitoring and Related Research Act of 1990." Public law HR1608. Section 302 1990. p. 1101-445.
9. Guagnano, M.T., et al. "Clinical nutrition: inadequate teaching in medical schools." Nutr Metab Cardiovasc Dis Apr; 11(2) 2001. p. 104-07. Lo, C. "Integrating nutrition as a theme throughout the medical school curriculum." Am J Clin Nutr Sep; 72(3 Suppl) 2000. p. 882S-9S.
10. Cooksey, K., et al. "Getting nutrition education into medical schools: a computer-based approach." Am J Clin Nutr Sep; 72(3 Suppl) 2000. p. 868S-76S.
11. Jackson, A.A. "Human nutrition in medical practice: the training of doctors." Proc Nutr Soc May; 60(2) 2001. p. 257-63.

number of medical schools offering a nutritional curriculum had increased to a paltry 25%.[1] Emphasis on pharmacotherapy has left little time for more mundane but equally effective measures like basic nutrition.

NOT SO FREE FALL

> *I am not concerned that you have fallen — I am concerned that you arise.*
> Abraham Lincoln 1809-1865, Sixteenth President of the USA

Another potential risk for the hospitalized patient is they are at increased risk for falls.[2] One study of 15,000 patients found 2% experienced falls during their hospitalization.[3] Even though they are among the most common adverse events in the hospital, they are potentially preventable.[4] A fall may result in either physical or emotional injury, increased dependence, and for some may lead to admission to a long-term care facility, which reduces the overall quality of life.[5] The elderly are particularly at risk for falls for a variety of reasons.[6]

Each year approximately one third of those over the age of 65 in the general public experiences a fall, in 5% of these falls, fractures may occur. The mortality rate for falls increases dramatically with age, falls account for 70% of accidental deaths in persons 75 years of age and older.[7] The resulting injuries add billions of dollars to the nation's healthcare expenditure. One study found fall-related hospitalizations of older adults cost $53,346,191 in 1992 dollars and was responsible for discharge to a nursing home more than any other diagnosis.[8]

12. Hark, L.A., Morrison, G. "Development of a case-based integrated nutrition curriculum for medical students." American Journal of Clinical Nutrition vol 72(3) 2000. p. 890S-897s.
13. Association of American Medical Colleges. 1991-92 AAMC curriculum directory. Washington, DC: The Association Of American Medical Colleges, 1991.
1. Schulman, J.A. "Nutrition education in medical schools: trends and implications for health educators." Med Ed Online. 2000. 16 June 2000 ‹http://www.med-ed-Online.org/f0000015.htm›.
2. "Intensive safety effort cuts falls, ulcers, and drug errors at once-disgraced FL hospital." Clin Resour Manag Oct; 1(10) 2000. p. 148-51.
3. Thomas, E.J., Brennan, T.A. "Incidence and types of preventable adverse events in elderly patients: population based review of medical records." BMJ. 2000. 18 Mar 2000 ‹http://bmj.bmjjournals.com/cgi/content/full/320/7237/741›.
4. "Guidance article: bed-exit alarms: A component (but only a component) of fall prevention." Health Devices. 2004. May 2004 ‹http://www.ecri.org/marketingdocs/hd330505-toc.pdf›. Healey, F. et al. "Using targeted risk factor reduction to prevent falls in older in-patients: a randomised controlled trial." Age and Ageing. 2004. Jul 2004 ‹http://ageing.oxfordjournals.org/cgi/content/abstract/33/4/390›.
5. Creditor, M.C. "Hazards of hospitalization of the elderly." Ann Intern Med. 1993. 01 Feb 1993 ‹http://www.annals.org/cgi/content/full/118/3/219›.
6. Hitcho, E.B. et al. "Characteristics and circumstances of falls in a hospital setting." J Gen Intern Med Jul; 19(7) 2004. p. 732-39. Kallin, K. et al. "Why the elderly fall in residential care facilities, and suggested remedies." J Fam Pract. 2004. Jan 2004 ‹http://www.looksmartcolds.com/p/articles/mi_m0689/is_1_53/ai_112592267›.
7. Fuller, G.F. "Falls in the elderly." American Family Physician. 2000. Apr 2000 ‹http://www.aafp.org/afp/20000401/2159.html›.
8. Alexander, B.H., Rivara, F.P., Wolf, M.E. "The cost and frequency of hospitalization for fall-related injuries in older adults." Am J Public Health Jul; 82(7) 1992. p. 1020-23.

Although decreased physiological reserves are an important factor, they are by no means the only reason for increased rates of falls in the elderly.[1] Disease, malnutrition,[2] and increased use of drugs are all significant contributors to this risk.[3]

Prescribed medications are clearly responsible for many falls.[4] Many drugs used to treat depression; anxiety or other mental health conditions significantly increase the risk of falling.[5] Multiple studies have documented the increased risk of falling associated with the use of heart medications,[6] antidepressants[7] or drugs used to treat anxiety.[8] Studies have found mind altering agents increase the risk of falling from two to nearly ten times that of those not using these drugs.[9] The judicious use of these behavior-modifying drugs is highly recommended and in some cases should be strongly discouraged.[10] However, the shortage of qualified healthcare workers nearly guarantees these medications will be used as a method of control for the "difficult" patient.[11]

Polypharmacy, or use of many drugs, increases the risk of injury and falls even more than use of single agents.[12] A 2004 Swedish study found two-thirds of residents living in nursing homes are treated with 10 or more different drugs.[13] The drug Ativan or lorazepam is especially prone to increasing the likelihood of

1. Von Renteln-Kruse, W., Krause, T. "When do elderly in-hospital patients fall?" Age Ageing Jul; 33(4) 2004. p. 413.
2. Garry, P.J. "Relationship between malnutrition and falls in the elderly." Nutrition Mar-Apr; 8(2) 1992. p. 105-8.
3. Vellas, B., et al. "Preventing injuries in older people by preventing falls: a meta-analysis of individual-level data." J Am Geriatr Soc May; 50(5) 2002. p. 905-11.
4. Chutka, D.S., Takahashi, P.Y., Hoel, R.W. "Inappropriate medications for elderly patients." Mayo Clin Proc Jan; 79(1) 2004. p. 122-39. Liu, B.A. "Falls among older people: relationship to medication use and orthostatic hypotension." J Am Geriatr Soc Oct; 43(10) 1995. p. 1141-45.
5. Gales, B.J., Menard, S.M. "Relationship between the administration of selected medications and falls in hospitalized elderly patients." Ann Pharmacother Apr; 29(4) 1995. p. 354-58.
6. Leipzig, R.M., Cumming, R.G., Tinetti, M.E. "Drugs and falls in older people: a systematic review and meta-analysis: II. Cardiac and analgesic drugs.." J Am Geriatr Soc Jan; 47(1) 1999. p. 40-50.
7. Winter, R., Vetter, P., Voll, G. "Falling spells associated with antidepressant drug treatment." Eur Arch Psychiatry Clin Neurosci vol 241(5) 1992. p. 314-16.
8. Cumming, R.G. "Epidemiology of medication-related falls and fractures in the elderly." Drugs Aging Jan; 12(1) 1998. p. 43-53. Leipzig, R.M., Cumming, R.G., Tinetti, M.E. "Drugs and falls in older people: a systematic review and meta-analysis: I. Psychotropic drugs." J Am Geriatr Soc Jan; 47(1) 1999. p. 30-39.
9. Lawlor, D.A., Patel, R., Ebrahim, S. "Association between falls in elderly women and chronic diseases and drug use: cross sectional study." BMJ vol 327 2003. p. 712-17. Mustard, C.A., Mayer, T. "Case-control study of exposure to medication and the risk of injurious falls requiring hospitalization among nursing home residents." Am J Epidemiol Apr 15; 145(8) 1997. p. 738-45.
10. Frels, C., Williams, P., Narayanan, S., Gariballa, SE. "Iatrogenic causes of falls in hospitalised elderly patients: a case-control study." Postgrad Med J Aug; 78(922) 2002. p. 487-89.
11. Salgado, R.I., Lord, S.R., Ehrlich, F., Janji, N., Rahman, A. "Predictors of falling in elderly hospital patients." Arch Gerontol Geriatr May-Jun; 38(3) 2004. p. 213-19.
12. Neutel, C.I., Perry, S., Maxwell, C. "Medication use and risk of falls." Drug Saf Mar; 11(2) 2002. p. 97-104. Lord, S.R., Anstey, K.J., Williams, P., Ward, J.A. "Psychoactive medication use, sensori-motor function and falls in older women." Br J Clin Pharmacol Mar; 39(3) 1995. p. 227-34. Weiner, D.K., Hanlon, J.T., Studenski, S.A. "Effects of central nervous system polypharmacy on falls liability in community-dwelling elderly." Gerontology 44(4) 1998. p. 217-21.
13. Kragh, A. "[Two out of three persons living in nursing homes for the elderly are treated with at least ten different drugs. A survey of drug prescriptions in the northeastern part of Skane]." Lakartidningen Mar 11; 101(11) 2004. p. 994-6, 999.

falling.[1] It is also one of the most frequently prescribed behavior modifying drugs to the elderly.[2]

Ativan is poorly metabolized or broken down by the liver of the elderly and results in continuously increasing levels of the drug in their blood stream. In many, daily doses of Ativan leads to higher blood or serum levels of this drug. This correlates well with increased risk of falling with long-term use.[3] A Canadian study determined the frequency of falls was 60% greater in patients using benzodiazepines (Ativan, Xanax and similar drugs) and 120% greater in users of antidepressants as compared to non-users.[4] The overuse of drugs to treat anxiety is a primary contributing factor for the increased rates of falling among the elderly. Clinical guidelines oppose the long-term use of these agents. Their continued use among the elderly is a disgrace to the medical community.[5] A British study suggests as many as 70% of the elderly use these agents.

Sadly, this dependence on medication to control potentially harmful behavior is responsible for greater injury than the verbal assault or belligerence by the patient that prompted the initial treatment. Claims that falls are simply the result of an enfeebled or an already confused patient is not substantiated by research; they simply reflect the lack of sufficient attention by the medical or nursing staff.[6]

Reliance upon devices such as restraints, bed activated alarms and side rails are no substitute for close supervision. Patients who fall once are very likely to fall again.[7] Restraints have their own associated risks for increased morbidity and mortality[8] and studies have found an increase in the seriousness of injury by the use of bedrails,[9] and recommend for their discontinuance in the elderly.[10] Withdrawal of behavior-modifying medications significantly decreases the

1. Cumming, R.G., Le Couteur, D.G. "Benzodiazepines and risk of hip fractures in older people: a review of the evidence." CNS Drugs 17(11) 2003. p. 825-37. Ensrud, K.E., et al. "Study of Osteoporotic Fractures Research Group. Central nervous system active medications and risk for fractures in older women." Intern Med Apr 28; 163(8): 2003. p. 949-57.
2. Vinkers, D.J., et al. "Benzodiazepine use and risk of mortality in individuals aged 85 years or older." JAMA Dec 10; 290(22) 2003. p. 2942-43.
3. Trewin, V.F., Lawrence, C.J., Veitch, G.B. "An investigation of the association of benzodiazepines and other hypnotics with the incidence of falls in the elderly." J Clin Pharm Ther Apr; 17(2) 1992. p. 129-33.
4. Ebly, E.M., Hogan, D.B., Fung, T.S. "Potential adverse outcomes of psychotropic and narcotic drug use in Canadian seniors." J Clin Epidemiol Jul; 50(7) 1997. p. 857-63.
5. Taylor, S., McCracken, C.F., Wilson , K.C., Copeland, J.R. "Extent and appropriateness of benzo-diazepine use. Results from an elderly urban community." The British Journal of Psychiatry vol 173 1998. p. 433-38.
6. Reed, L., Blegen, M.A., Goode, C.S. "Adverse patient occurrences as a measure of nursing care quality." J Nurs Adm May; 28(5) 1998. p. 62-69. Ross, J.E. "Iatrogenesis in the elderly. Contribu-tors to falls." J Gerontol Nurs Sep; 17(9) 1991. p. 19-23.
7. Close, J.C., Hooper, R., Glucksman, E., Jackson, S.H., Swift, C.G. "Predictors of falls in a high risk population: results from the prevention of falls in the elderly trial (PROFET)." Emerg Med J Sep; 20(5) 2003. p. 421-25. Lane, A.J. "Evaluation of the fall prevention program in an acute care setting." Orthop Nurs Nov-Dec; 18(6) 1999. p. 37-43.
8. Dawkins, V.H. "Restraints and the elderly with mental illness: ethical issues and moral reasoning." J Psychosoc Nurs Ment Health Serv Oct; 36(10) 1998. p. 22-27.
9. Tideiksaar, R., Feiner, C.F. Maby, J. "Falls prevention: the efficacy of a bed alarm system in an acute-care setting." Mt Sinai J Med Nov; 60(6) 1993. p. 522-27.
10. Hanger, H.C., Ball, M.C., Wood, L.A. "An analysis of falls in the hospital: can we do without bedrails?" J Am Geriatr Soc May; 47(5) 1999. p. 529-31.

incidence of falls.[1] Exercise training[2] and programs encouraging balancing[3] and coordination[4] have been shown to be possibly effective[5] in reducing the incidence of falls.[6] A review of all possible measures to decrease the incidence or severity of falls may be accessed through the Cochrane Collaboration site. The authors conclude a multifactoral program involving minimizing use of drugs known to increase fall risk, exercise training, increased surveillance and identifying those at the highest risk for falls may decrease their incidence and severity.[7] The use of hip pads for those of highest risk may be of some benefit in reducing hip fractures.[8] Unfortunately, none of the above measures have proven effective in reducing the incidence of falls[9] among older people with cognitive impairment and dementia.[10]

RESTRAINING ORDERS

Captivity is the greatest of all evils that can befall one.
Miguel De Cervantes 1547-1616, Novelist, Dramatist, Poet

Always being sensitive to the possibility of litigation,[11] hospitals attempt to reduce the number of patient falls using a convoluted logic so typical of modern medicine. If drugs and malnutrition increase the likelihood of a patient falling, simply don't let the patient fall. Since inadequate staffing precludes constant

1. Campbell, A.J., et al. "Psychotropic medication withdrawal and a home-based exercise program to prevent falls: a randomized, controlled trial." J Am Geriatr Soc Jul; 47(7) 1999. p. 850-53.
2. Buchner, D.M., et al. "The effect of strength and endurance training on gait, balance, fall risk, and health services use in community-living older adults." J Gerontol A Biol Sci Med Sci 1997; 52 vol 52 1997.
3. Steadman, J., Donaldson, N., Kalra, L. "A randomized controlled trial of an enhanced balance training program to improve mobility and reduce falls in elderly patients." J Am Geriatr Soc Jun; 51(6) 2003. p. 847-52. Zwick, D., Rochelle, A., Choksi, A., Domowicz, J. "Evaluation and treatment of balance in the elderly: A review of the efficacy of the Berg Balance Test and Tai Chi." Neuro Rehabilitation vol 15(1) 2000. p. 49-56.
4. Wolfson, L., et al. "Training balance and strength in the elderly to improve function." J Am Geriatr Soc 41 1993. p. 341-43.
5. Wolf, S.L., et al. "Intense tai chi exercise training and fall occurrences in older, transitionally frail adults: a randomized, controlled trial." J Am Geriatr Soc Dec; 51(12) 2003. p. 1693-701.
6. Campbell, A.J., et al. "Randomised controlled trial of a general practice programme of home based exercise to prevent falls in elderly women." BMJ vol 315 1997. p. 1065-69. Gardner, M.M., Robertson, M.C., Campbell, A.J. "Exercise in preventing falls and fall related injuries in older people: a review of randomised controlled trials." Br J Sports Med vol 34(1) 2000. p. 07-11.
7. Gillespie, L.D., et al. "Interventions for preventing falls in the elderly." The Cochrane Library vol 2 2001.⟨http://www.cochrane.org/cochrane/revabstr/AB000340.htm⟩
8. Becker, C., et al. "Effectiveness of a multifaceted intervention on falls in nursing home residents." J Am Geriatr Soc Mar; 51(3) 2003. p. 306-13.
9. Shaw, F.E., et al. "Multifactorial intervention after a fall in older people with cognitive impairment and dementia presenting to the accident and emergency department: randomised controlled trial." BMJ vol 326 2003. p. 73.
10. Jensen, J., Nyberg, L., Gustafson, Y., Lundin-Olsson, L. "Fall and injury prevention in residential care—effects in residents with higher and lower levels of cognition." J Am Geriatr Soc May; 51(5) 2003. p. 627-35. Oliver, D., Hopper, A., Seed, P. "Do hospital fall prevention programs work? A systematic review." J Am Geriatr Soc Dec; 48(12) 2000. p. 1679-89.
11. Owens, M.F. "Patient restraints. Protection for whom?" JONAS Healthc Law Ethics Regul Jun; 2(2) 2000. p. 59-65.

monitoring; they rely upon a proven low tech, inexpensive approach to reduce the incidence of patient falls, TIE UP THE PATIENT! Unfortunately, this measure has its own associated risks. The *Hartford Courant* reported 142 patients had died during or shortly after being restrained in the nation's mental hospitals, group homes and mental retardation facilities over the past decade.[1] Some experts believe the true death count is actually many times higher.[2] An Internet site compiled by the National Alliance for the Mentally Ill lists individual cases for each occurrence mentioned.[3] These cases were so egregious they prompted Senate hearings which passed a bill forbidding their use without a signed physician's order.[4]

A FDA site estimated that in 1992, there were more than half a million people restrained daily in health care facilities, in an attempt to prevent falls or other injuries.[5] The FDA grudgingly acknowledges at least 100 deaths occur annually from their improper use in nursing homes, hospitals and private homes.[6]

Western medicine relies heavily upon the use of restraints to curtail unwanted behavior.[7] This reliance is based on the assumption that patients, who aren't able to ambulate, are at decreased risk of falling.[8] It is also believed restrained patients are less prone to remove invasive devices like catheters and tubing. Despite their extensive use,[9] there is virtually no evidence to support the efficacy of restraints.[10]

ICUs often use restraints with the mistaken notion they are needed to keep the patient from removing invasive devices.[11] Research has failed to substantiate the protective value of restraints in preventing falls. Many studies have shown

---

1. . Altimari D et al. "Deadly Restraint." Hartford Courant Oct 1998, Natl ed.: 11-15.
2. "Feds tighten regulations on client/patient restraints." Outreach 27 Jul 1999.
3. "Cries of Anguish." The Nation' Voice on Mental Illness. 2006. 18 Feb 2006 ‹http://www.nami.org/Content/ContentGroups/E-News/20013/February_20012/A_Summary_of_Reports_of_Restraints_andamp__Seclusion_Abuse_Received_Since_the_October_1998_Investiga.htm›.
4. Testimony of Senator Joseph I. Lieberman on Deaths and Injuries to Mental Health Patients Senate Appropriations Committee Subcommittee on Labor, Health and Human Services, and Education ‹http://akmhcweb.org/ncarticles/testimony_of_senator_joseph_onuseofhealthQretraints.htm›. Sklar, D.P., et al. "The Use of Physical Restraints in Medical Emergencies." NEJM vol 342 2000. p. 742-44.
5. Cruzan, S. "Restraint Devices can be Dangerous." Food and Drug Administration News vol 16 Jun 1992.
6. Take-downs that kill Outreach magazine November/December 1998 http://www.psych-health.com/hartford.htm
7. Weiner, C., Tabak, N., Bergman, R. "The use of physical restraints for patients suffering from dementia." Nurs Ethics Sep; 10(5): 2003. p. 512-25.
8. Hamers, J.P., Gulpers, M.J., Strik, W. "Use of physical restraints with cognitively impaired nursing home residents." J Adv Nurs Feb; 45(3) 2004. p. 246-51. Magee, R., et al. "Institutional policy: use of restraints in extended care and nursing homes." J Gerontol Nurs Apr; 19(4) 1993. p. 31-39.
9. Marks, W. "Physical restraints in the practice of medicine." Arch Intern Med Nov; 152(11) 1992. p. 2203-06.
10. Napierkowski, D. "Using restraints with restraint." Nursing Nov; 32(11 Pt 1) 2002. p. 58-62. Williams, M.P., et al. "No restraints allowed: legalities and realities." Nursing Jan; 34(1) 2004. p. 54-55.
11. Leith, B. "Do physical restraints prevent patients from removing invasive therapeutic devices?" Off J Can Assoc Crit Care Nurs Fall; 9(3) 1998. p. 31-34.

restraints may actually increase the number and seriousness of falls. Even more startling is the finding that restraints do not decrease the incidence of self-extubation (accidental removal of a breathing tube by a patient on a ventilator).[1] More often than not, understaffing is the primary reason for much of restraint use. In the American health care system, nurses primarily determine restraint use.[2]

A 12-month study in a general ICU of patients on ventilators found self-extubation occurred despite the use of sedation and restraints.[3] The application of restraints actually increased patient agitation, increasing the likelihood of self-extubation (self removal of the breathing tube).[4] Under-sedation is frequently the cause of many self-extubations.[5] This may be cautiously corrected for most patients by adjusting the dosage of sedative being used. Other studies of ventilated patients showed most patients who self-extubated were restrained, sedated, or both.[6] A 2001 study of 75 cases of self extubation found 80% were restrained while on the ventilator, and 59% required reintubation. Seventy-three percent of the self extubations were considered deliberate rather than accidental. The authors of this study recommended the use of a continuous drip infusion of sedative to calm patients while they are on the ventilator.

Restricting restraint usage in less acute settings like nursing homes yields similar findings to that of the ICU. One study found nursing homes with the highest use of restraints had a 50% higher rate of falls.[7] Another study showed nursing homes with a liberal use of restraints had more than twice the rate of fall-related minor injuries compared to nursing homes that limited their usage.[8] The consensus from many studies seems to be restraints do not decrease the number of patient injuries[9] but may actually increase the risk of falling.[10]

1. Kapp, M.B. "Physical restraint use in critical care: legal issues." AACN Clin Issues Nov; 7(4) 1996. p. 579-84.
2. Wilson, E.B. "Physical restraint of elderly patients in critical care: historical perspectives and new directions." Crit Care Nurs Clin North Am Mar; 8(1) 1996. p. 61-70.
3. Ortiz-Pruitt, J. "Psychosocial and Environmental Considerations in Critical Care, Physical Restraint of Critically Ill Patients." A Human Issue P. 369 vol.7, Number 2, June 1995 vol 7 No.2 1995. p. 369.
4. Rieth, K.A., Bennett, C.C. "Restraint-free care. Part 1: Legal and regulatory mandates. Part 2: Creating a restraint-free environment." Nurs Manage May; 29(5) 1998. p. 36-39.
5. Powers, J. "A sedation protocol for preventing patient self-extubation." Dimens Crit Care Nurs Mar-Apr; 18(2) 1999. p. 30-43.
6. Balon, J.A. "Common factors of spontaneous self-extubation in a critical care setting." Int J Trauma Nurs Jul-Sep; 7(3) 2001. p. 93-99. Wilson, E.B. "Critical Care Nursing Clinics of North America." Physical Restraint of Elderly Patients in Critical Care vol 8 No.1 1996. p. 65.
7. Capezuti, E., et al. "The relationship between physical restraint removal and falls and injuries among nursing home residents." J Gerontol A Biol Sci Med Sci Jan; 53(1) 1998. p. M47-52.
8. Arbesman, M.C., Wright, C. "Mechanical restraints, rehabilitation therapies, and staffing adequacy as risk factors for falls in an elderly hospitalized population." Rehabil Nurs May-Jun; 24(3) 1999. p. 122-28.
9. Shorr, R.I., et al. "Restraint use, restraint orders, and the risk of falls in hospitalized patients." J Am Geriatr Soc Mar; 50(3) 2002. p. 526-29.
10. Frank, C., Hodgetts, G., Puxty, J. "Safety and efficacy of physical restraints for the elderly. Review of the evidence." Can Fam Physician Dec; 42 1996. p. 2402-09. Ginter, S.F., Mion, L.C. "Falls in the nursing home: preventable or inevitable?" J Gerontol Nurs Nov; 18(11) 1992. p. 43-48.

The opinion to use or not to use restraints is a matter of considerable debate.[1] Often, nurses working on the same unit will disagree about the appropriateness of restraints for a given patient. It is not uncommon for the physician and nurses to conflict over the use of restraints.[2] ICU nurses with more experience usually opt for the use of restraints less frequently than less experienced nurses.[3] The preferred method of restraint by most nurses is by sedation. Unfortunately, sedation has its own associated risks that may actually be worse than physical restraints.[4]

Some facilities attempt to constrain the use of restraints by conducting daily reviews on the continued use of restraints on a patient by patient basis.[5] There is often a dramatic reduction in the usage of restraints when these reviews are enforced.[6] HCFA regulations require a one-hour assessment by a physician after applying restraints, it is hoped this will reduce the usage in hospital settings.[7] The ultimate goal is to decrease restraint usage to levels similar to Britain where they are seldom used in the clinical setting.[8] Reliance upon family members and supervision are the preferred methods for dealing with patients who are at risk for falling or pulling out invasive devices.[9]

Even if patients do not fall or are restrained from pulling out devices, they are still at great risk of injury while wearing restraints.[10] Restraint use is associated with increased rates of blood clots,[11] pneumonia, metabolic acidosis[12] (a life threatening condition), and severe bruising.[13] This does not even consider the psychological trauma associated with being restrained, not to mention

1. "The University of Texas MD Anderson Cancer Center Restraints Improvement Group: Myths and Truths about Physical Restraints; Including a Nursing Survey on Restraint Practices." The Internet Journal of Advanced Nursing Practice. 1999. 01 Jul 1999 <http://www.ispub.com/journals/IJANP/Vol3NI/myths.htm>.
2. Mion, L.C., et al. "Use of Physical Restraints in the Hospital Setting: Implications for the Nurse." Geriatric Nursing vol 15 No.3 1994. p. 128.
3. Scherer, Y.K., Janelli, L.M., Wu, Y.W., Kuhn, M.M. "Restrained patients: an important issue for critical care nursing." Heart Lung Jan-Feb; 22(1) 1993. p. 77-83.
4. Janelli, L.M., et al. "Restrained Patients: An Important Issue for Critical Care Nursing." Heart & Lung vol 22 1993. p. 81.
5. "Interview with Juanita Reigle." Critical Care Nurse Vol. 17, No 4, August 1997 17 No.4 1997. Sullivan-Marx, E.M. "Achieving restraint-free care of acutely confused older adults." J Gerontol Nurs Apr; 27(4) 2001. p. 56-61.
6. Rogers, P.D., Bocchino, N.L. "Restraint-free care: is it possible?" Am J Nurs Oct; 99(10) 1999. p. 26-33.
7. "HCFA overrules JCAHO restraint standard." Hosp Peer Rev Jul; 25(7) 2000. p. 88-89.
8. O'Keeffe, S., Jack, C.I. "Use of restraints and bedrails in a British hospital." J Am Geriatr Soc Sep; 44(9 1996. p. 1086-88.
9. Moretz, C., Dommel, A., Deluca, K. "Untied: a safe alternative to restraints." Medsurg Nurs Apr; 4(2) 1995. p. 128-32. Wise, R. "New restraint standards will change your practice." ED Manag Aug; 12(8) 2000. p. 93-95.
10. Mohr, W.K., Mohr, B.D. "Mechanisms of injury and death proximal to restraint use." Arch Psychiatr Nurs Dec; 14(6) 2000. p. 285-95.
11. Hem, E., Steen, O., Opjordsmoen, S. "Thrombosis associated with physical restraints." Acta Psychiatr Scand Jan; 103(1) 2001. p. 73-75.
12. Hick, J.L., Smith, S.W., Lynch, M.T. "Metabolic acidosis in restraint-associated cardiac arrest: a case series." Acad Emerg Med Mar; 6(3) 1999. p. 239-43.
13. Landi, F., et al. "A Physical restraint and subcutaneous hematoma in an anticoagulated patient." South Med J Feb; 94(2) 2001. p. 254-55.

legal[1] or ethical considerations about their use.[2] The process of being restrained is so debasing and frightening one study found, when offered, the option of being restrained or sedated, 64% of patients preferred medication compared to only 36% who preferred seclusion or restraints.[3]

With all these contraindications for not using restraints, one may ask why clinical settings continue in their use. The reason is quite simple: fear of litigation.[4] Courts routinely uphold judgments against nurses and hospitals that failed to prevent a patient from injury by failing to use restraints.[5] However, litigation for failure to release a patient from restraints is relatively uncommon. Our legal and health care systems encourage restraint of the elderly for their "safety," while simultaneously limiting their autonomy, independence and mobility.

Hospitals are more in fear of being sued for not using restraints than they are for their use. Surprisingly, family members of the restrained are generally supportive of the use of restraints to "protect their loved ones from injury."[6] They fail to realize the patient has the right to refuse restraints unless they have been legally determined to be incompetent. One study found of 33 families interviewed, none opposed the application of restraints, but instead relied upon the staffs' judgment for their use.[7]

The alternative to restraints is amazingly simple, UNTIE THE PATIENT! Monitoring is by far the best method to reduce the risk of injury. Protests of insufficient time and staff are not adequate excuses when confronted by a jury. Many cultures like Japan and Chile not only allow but actually insist the patient's family remains at their bedside.[8] If this is not possible, a professional sitter is readily available for hire by most health care facilities. The sitter's sole function is to remain at the beck and call of the patient, assisting them with their activities of daily living and provide the nurse early warning of a potentially injurious situation.

1. Milner N. The right to refuse treatment: four case studies of legal mobilization. Law Soc Rev. 1987; 21(3):447-85.
2. Reigle, J. "The ethics of physical restraints in critical care." AACN Clin Issues Nov; 7(4) 1996. p. 585-91. Sullivan-Marx, E.M., Strumpf, N.E. "Restraint-free care for acutely ill patients in the hospital." AACN Clin Issues Nov; 7(4) 1996. p. 572-78.
3. Sheline, Y., Nelson, T. "Patient choice: deciding between psychotropic medication and physical restraints in an emergency." Bull Am Acad Psychiatry Law vol 21 1993. p. 3.
4. Mion, L.C., Minnick, A., Palmer, R. "Physical restraint use in the hospital setting: unresolved issues and directions for research." Milbank Q vol 74(3) 1996. p. 411-33. Owens, M.F. "Patient restraints. Protection for whom?" JONAS Healthc Law Ethics Regul Jun; 2(2) 2000. p. 59-65.
5. Kapp, M.B. "Physical restraint use in critical care: legal issues." AACN Clin Issues Nov; 7(4) 1996. p. 579-84.
6. Hardin, S.B., et al. "Patient and family perceptions of restraints." J Holist Nurs Dec; 11(4) 1993. p. 383-97.
7. Barazovski, S., Rosin, A. "[Should physical restraints be used in an acute geriatric ward?]." Harefuah Sep; 133(5-6) 1997. p. 180-83, 246-47. Kanski, G.W., Janelli, L.M., Jones, H.M., Kennedy, M.C. "Family reactions to restraints in an acute care setting." J Gerontol Nurs Jun; 22(6) 1996. p. 17-22.
8. Conroy, G. "The family as restraint?" Am J Nurs Apr; 100(4) 2000. p. 21.

Sore Losers

A hospital is no place to be sick.
Samuel Goldwyn 1882-1974, Film Producer, Founder, MGM

A pressure sore (also known as a "pressure ulcer", "bedsore", or "decubitus ulcer") is an area of tissue injury that develops as the result of tissue compression between the bone and a hard surface over an extended period of time. This surface may be a mattress, a chair or wheelchair, or even other parts of the body. Its location is dependent upon the position of the patient. Common sites for pressure sore formation are the heels, hipbone, and the lower back or tailbone. However, they may also develop in a variety of other areas, including the spine, ankles, knees shoulders, and head, depending upon the position of the patient. The main factors involved in pressure sore formation are infusion of a levophed drip, APACHE II score, fecal incontinence, anemia and length of stay. One study suggests elevated cortisol levels in the response to prolonged stress may be an additional factor.[1]

Pressure sores are a recurrent problem in the debilitated and chronically weakened. The US Department of Health & Human Services estimates 11% of all hospitalized patients are afflicted with pressure sores with more than half occurring in those over the age of 70.[2] They also report a 13.2% prevalence rate in nursing homes.[3] They can cause injury ranging from mild reddening of the skin, to severe deep cratering of the tissue that may penetrate all the way to the bone. Risk factors that increase their likelihood of formation include: confinement to bed, chair, or wheelchair — in as little as 1-2 hours if the pressure is not relieved, inability to change positions without help, loss of bowel or bladder control, poor nutrition and/or dehydration and decreased mental awareness. One year long study of 30 patients found the average length of treatment for pressure sore was 116 days with an average cost of $2,731 per ulcer.[4] They cite an early study which states there were almost 1.7 million hospitalized patients had pressure ulcers.[5] Nearly 60% of these sores develop in an acute care setting while being treated.[6] This cost is in addition to the original reason for hospitalization.

1. Theaker, C., Mannan, M., Ives, N., Soni, N. "The relationship between stress and pressure sore formation. Ostomy Wound Manage." Anaesthesia Mar; 55(3) 2000. p. 221-24.
2. "Nursing Home Care Improving in Many Areas New CMS Data Show, New Steps Initiated." U.S. Department of Health & Human Services News Release. 2004. 22 Dec 2004 <http://www.hhs.gov/news/press/2004pres/20041222.html>. Meehan, M. "National pressure ulcer prevalence survey." Adv Wound Care 1994; 7:27-30,34, vol 7 1994. p. 27-30, 34, 36-38.
3. Brandeis, G.H., et al. "The epidemiology and natural history of pressure ulcers in elderly nursing home residents." JAMA vol 264 1990. p. 2905-09.
4. Xakellis, G.C., Frantz, R. "The cost of healing pressure ulcers across multiple health care settings." Adv Wound Care Nov-Dec; 9(6) 1996. p. 18-22.
5. Eckman, K.L. "The prevalence of dermal ulcers among persons in the U.S. who have died." Decubitus vol 2 1989. p. 36-40.
6. Guralnik, J.M., Harris, T.B., White, L.R., Cornoni-Huntley, J.C. "Occurrence and predictors of pressure sores in the National Health and Nutrition Examination survey follow-up." J Am Geriatr Soc vol 36 1988. p. 807-12.

There clearly is a financial incentive for hospitals to enforce policies to help reduce the incidence of pressure sores. Since 95% of all pressure ulcers are preventable, the cost savings would be substantial. It would therefore be prudent for health care facilities to enforce pressure sore prevention policies.[1]

Prevention measures should include:

A complete and thorough assessment with periodic reassessments

Appropriate hygiene with prompt treatment of incontinence

Maintain adequate nutrition and hydration

Provision of supportive cushions to provide barriers against constant unrelieved pressure.

Use of lifting devices and techniques to help reduce shearing and friction

The incidence of pressure sores is remarkably stable at about 8%. Pressure sores persist despite increased knowledge of mechanisms, enhanced regulatory oversight, and new developments in technologies to aid in prevention.[2] Although the prevention of pressure sores by frequent repositioning of patients is a widely accepted practice, one study questions its efficacy and suggests there may be more effective ways of relieving pressure damage.[3]

Nurses frequently resort to massaging to help facilitate blood flow to areas with impaired blood flow. A recent study concludes not only is this ineffective, it actually may be harmful![4] It states massaging is contraindicated for the prevention of pressure sores.

Several studies suggest that pressure relieving mattresses[5] (air beds) may reduce the incidence of pressure sores.[6] A 6-month survey of 726 nurses showed patients experienced greater comfort on electric beds while producing fewer pressure sores and increasing the mobility of the patient.[7] Foam mattresses and air beds in particular seem to help greatly reduce the risk of pressure sores in the debilitated. Currently however, the most effective surface for either prevention or treatment has yet to be determined.[8] Unfortunately, many hospitals are unwilling to pay the additional expense for these items and rely exclusively upon overworked staff to turn patients. When the inevitable occurs and pressure

1. Findlay, D. "Practical management of pressure ulcers." Am Fam Physician Oct; 54(5) 1996. p. 1533-36. Grewal, P.S., et al. "Pressure sore prevention in hospital patients: a clinical audit." J Wound Care Mar 8(3) 1999. p. 129-31.
2. Thomas, D.R. "Are all pressure ulcers avoidable?" J Am Med Dir Assoc Mar-Apr; 4(2 Suppl) 2003. p. S43-8.
3. Clark, M. "Repositioning to prevent pressure sores—what is the evidence?" Nurs Stand Oct 7-13; 13(3) 1998. p. 58-60, 62, 64.
4. Buss, I.C., Halfens, R.J., Abu-Saad, H.H. "The effectiveness of massage in preventing pressure sores: a literature review." Rehabil Nurs Sep-Oct; 22(5) 1997. p. 229-34, 242.
5. Hofman, A., et al. "Pressure sores and pressure-decreasing mattresses: controlled clinical trial." Lancet Mar 5; 343(8897) 1994. p. 568-71.
6. Brown, S.J. "Bed surfaces and pressure sore prevention: an abridged report." Orthop Nurs. 2001 Jul-Aug; 20(4) 2001. p. 38-40. Preece, J. "Total bed management: the way forward in pressure sore prevention." Br J Nurs Jan 12; 8(22): 1999. p. 1524-6, 1528-9.
7. Hampton, S. "Can electric beds aid pressure sore prevention in hospitals?" Br J Nurs Sep 24-Oct 7; 7(17) 1998. p. 1010-17.
8. Cullum, N., Deeks, J., Sheldon, T.A., Song, F., Fletcher, A.W. "Beds, mattresses and cushions for pressure sore prevention and treatment.." Cochrane Database Syst Rev vol 2 2000. p. CD001735.

sores develop, the blame game is begun because management realizes they are responsible for the increased costs of care.

The best way to prevent pressure sores is by encouraging ambulating and providing adequate nutrition and hygiene.[1] The stressors related to hospitalization or nursing home is conducive to the formation of pressure sores. However, recent studies suggest the initial injury may have occurred in the emergency room or during surgery. Pressure sores do not appear randomly during hospitalization. Instead the majority occur within the first 2 weeks of being hospitalized. Multiple studies have demonstrated this "clumping" effect. In one study of orthopedic patients, 75% of the pressure ulcers develop within the first 2 weeks of hospitalization. Thirty-four percent of the pressure sores occurred within the first week. The non-randomness of their occurrence suggests they occur early within the hospitalization process.[2] It also explains why most preventive measures have so little impact upon their formation.[3] Although the initial injury may not be resolved, aggressive measures may still reduce the incidence of the floor rate of pressure sore development by 25 -30%.[4] Unfortunately, other studies suggest these reductions may simply be an artifact related to randomness and are at best transient in nature.[5]

The only medical equipment shown to help reduce the rate of pressure sore development after hospitalization are low-air-loss and air-fluidized beds.[6] However, although they are effective at pressure reduction, they do not reduce the incidence of pressure sores more than the control support surface.[7]

Malnutrition may be a primary component for the development of pressure sores. One study found patients who were malnourished upon admission were twice as likely to develop pressure ulcers as those who had adequate nutrition.[8] Another study of nursing home residents found 59% were malnourished and 7.3% were severely malnourished. Sixty-five percent of all pressure sores occurred in the most severely malnourished patients and no sores occurred in the adequately-nourished groups.[9] A separate study found low dietary protein

1. Thomas, D.R. "Prevention and treatment of pressure ulcers:What works? What doesn't?" Cleve Clin J Med. 2001. Aug 2001 ‹http://www.ccjm.org/pdffiles/Thomas801.pdf›.
2. Versluysen, M. "Pressure sores in elderly patients: The epidemiology related to hip operations." J Bone Joint Surg 1985; 67 vol 67 1985. p. 10-13.
3. Hagisawa, S., Barbenel, J. "The limits of pressure sore prevention." J R Soc Med 1999; 92: vol 92 1999. p. 576-578.
4. Berlowitz, D.R., et al. "Are we improving the quality of nursing home care: the case of pressure ulcers." J Am Geriatr Soc vol 48 2000. p. 59-62. Hopkins, B., et al. "Reducing nosocomial pressure ulcers in an acute care facility." J Nurs Care Qual vol 14 2000. p. 28-36.
5. Richardson, G.M., Gardner, S., Frantz, R.A. "Nursing assessment: impact on type and cost of interventions to prevent pressure ulcers." J Wound Ostomy Continence Nurs vol 25 1998. p. 273-80.
6. Pase, M.N. "Pressure relief devices, risk factors, and development of pressure ulcers in elderly patients with limited mobility." Adv Wound Care vol 7 1994. p. 38-42.
7. Lazzara, D.J., Buschmann, M.T. "Prevention of pressure ulcers in elderly nursing home residents: Are special support surfaces the answer?" Decubitus 1991; 4:42-48 vol 4 1991. p. 42-48.
8. Thomas, D.R., Goode, P.S., Allman, R.A. "Pressure ulcers and risk of death." J Am Geriatr Soc vol 42 1994. p. SA3.
9. Pinchcofsky-Devin, G.D., Kaminski, M.V. Jr. "Correlation of pressure sores and nutritional status." J Am Geriatr Soc vol 34 1986. p. 435-40.

intake to be predictive of pressure sore development.[1] Another study reported poor appetite, meals held due to gastrointestinal disease, or a diet of less than 1,100 calories were also predictive of pressure ulcer formation in a nursing home.[2] Unfortunately, studies on nutritional supplementation[3] found no preventive effect against pressure sore formation.[4]

Pressure sore formation is an ominous sign because it is highly predictive of pending death. One study reported early death occurred in 67% of hospitalized patients who develop a pressure ulcer compared with 15% of at-risk patients without pressure ulcers.[5] Patients developing pressure sores 6 weeks after hospitalization are three times as likely to die as those who don't.[6] The mortality rate is even higher within the long-term care setting. Those who developed pressure ulcers within 3 months of admission had a 92% mortality rate as compared to a 4% rate for those without a pressure sore.[7] The higher level of care within a skilled nursing facility reduced the 6-month mortality rate to only 77.3% as compared to 18.3% for those without ulcers.[8] Several investigators found a threefold increase in mortality with the development of a new pressure sore; however, mortality or death did not correlate to their stage or severity. Those with stage 2 ulcers were as likely to die as those with stage 4 pressure sores. The findings within a hospital setting are equally dismal. One study found the development of a new pressure ulcer to be predicted death within a year.

HURTING FOR A FIX

> *Pain is real when you get other people to believe in it. If no one believes in it*
> *but you, your pain is madness or hysteria.*
> *Naomi Wolf 1962-, American Author*

Despite decades of studies, medicine continues to have a pitiful record concerning the management of pain.[9] According to a Texas study, the problem is

1. Bergstrom, N., Braden, B. "A prospective study of pressure sore risk among institutionalized elderly." J Am Geriatr Soc 1992; 40:747–758 vol 40 1992. p. 747-58.
2. Berlowitz, D.R., Wilking, S.V.B. "Risk factors for pressure sore: A comparison of cross-sectional and cohort-derived data." J Am Geriatr Soc 1989; 37:1043–1050 vol 37 1989. p. 1043-50.
3. Hartgrink, H.H., et al. "Pressure sores and tube feeding in patients with a fracture of the hip: a randomized clinical trial." Clin Nutr vol 17 1998. p. 287-92.
4. Bourdel-Marchasson, I., et al. "Prospective audits of quality of PEM recognition and nutritional support in critically ill elderly patients." Clin Nutr vol 18 1999. p. 233-40. Bourdel-Marchasson, I., et al. "A multi-center trial of the effects of oral nutritional supplementation in critically ill older inpatients. GAGE Group." Groupe Aquitain Geriatrique d'Evaluation. Nutrition vol 16 2000. p. 1-5.
5. Baxter, C.R. "Immunologic reactions in chronic wounds." Am J Surg vol 167 1994. p. 12S-14S.
6. Berlowitz, D.R., Wilking, S.V.B. "The short-term outcome of pressure sores." J Am Geriatr Soc 1990; 38:748–752 vol 38 1990. p. 748-52.
7. Guralnik, J.M., et al. "Occurrence and predictors of pressure ulcers in the National Health and Nutrition Examination Survey Follow-up." J Am Geriatr Soc 1988; 36:807–812 vol 36 1988. p. 807-12.
8. Thomas, D. "Existing tools: Are they meeting the challenges of pressure ulcer healing?" Adv Wound Care 1997; 10:86–90 vol 10 1997. p. 86-90.
9. Rich, B.A. "A legacy of silence: bioethics and the culture of pain." Journal of Medical Humanities vol 18 1997. p. 233-59. Rupp, T., Delaney, K.A. "Inadequate analgesia in emergency medicine." Ann Emerg Med Apr; 43(4) 2004. p. 494-03.

less the result of technology than of ignorance and prejudice about pain, opioids and addiction.[1] Physicians frequently agree with general societal attitudes against the use of opioid-based pain medications.[2] Physician prejudice[3] about the use of prescription pain medications frequently replaces evidence and commonsense.[4] Racial and ethnic bias is of particular concern in the treatment of pain, non-white populations are generally more undertreated for pain than their Caucasian counterparts.[5] Significant gender bias[6] also exists against women.[7] These problems may be further exacerbated by patients' misconception about pain management. Some actually believe pain medications "worsen their disease."[8] In addition, the government's campaign of "say no to drugs" has created a fear of addiction by both patients and their families, creating yet another barrier to the appropriate use of pain medications.[9] Legal and regulatory guidelines and fear of reprisal from federal authorities frequently intimidates physicians into prescribing narcotic with less than optimal dosages and times.[10] The consequences of this mismanagement are exemplified by a recent survey at a Chicago hospital finding 203 out of the 353 surveyed stated they had experienced "unbearable" pain during their hospitalization. More than half the patients stated they were in pain at the time of the survey and eight percent of those surveyed said the pain was "excruciating" or "horrible."[11] A massive German study involving the review of 1,104,435 patients over a 3-year period

1. Weinstein, S.M., et al. "Medical students' attitudes toward pain and the use of opioid analgesics: implications for changing medical school curriculum." South Med J May; 93(5) 2000. p. 472-78. Weinstein, S.M., et al. "Physicians' attitudes toward pain and the use of opioid analgesics: results of a survey from the Texas Cancer Pain Initiative." South Med J May; 93(5) 2000. p. 479-87.
2. Bonham, V.L. "Race, ethnicity, and pain treatment: striving to understand the causes and solutions to the disparities in pain treatment." J Law Med Ethics Spring; 29(1) 2001. p. 52-68. Miller, E.R. "Misery and myth: a connection between society and inadequate pain control?" Contemp Nurse Jun; 3(2) 1994. p. 75-79.
3. Tamayo-Sarver, J.H., et al. "Variability in emergency physician decision-making about prescribing opioid analgesics." Ann Emerg Med Apr; 43(4) 2004. p. 483-93.
4. Freeman, H.P., Payne, R. "Racial injustice in health care." NEJM Apr 6; 342(14) 2000. p. 1045-47. Ger, L.P., et al. "The effect of education and clinical practice on knowledge enlightenment to and attitudes toward the use of analgesics for cancer pain among physicians and medical students." Acta Anaesthesiol Sin Sep; 41(3) 2003. p. 105-14.
5. Green, C.R., et al. "The unequal burden of pain: confronting racial and ethnic disparities in pain." Pain Med Sep; 4(3) 2003. p. 277-94.
6. Hoffmann, D.E., Tarzian, A.J. "The girl who cried pain: a bias against women in the treatment of pain." J Law Med Ethics Spring; 29(1) 2001. p. 13-27. Hoffmann, D. "Undertreating pain in women: a risky practice." J Gend Specif Med Jan-Feb; 5(1) 2002. p. 10.
7. Rothrock, S.G., et al. "Is there gender bias in the prehospital management of patients with acute chest pain?" Prehosp Emerg Care Oct-Dec; 5(4) 2001. p. 331-34. Weisse, C.S., Sorum, P.C., Dominguez, R.E. "The influence of gender and race on physicians' pain management decisions." J Pain Nov; 4(9) 2003. p. 505-10.
8. Bressler, L.R. Geraci, M.C., Schatz, B.S. "Misperceptions and inadequate pain management in cancer patients." DICP Nov; 25(11) 1991. p. 1225-30.
9. Frederich, M.E., Ferranto, D.A., Marcus, B. "Regulatory and legal barriers to effective pain management in the long-term care setting." J Am Med Dir Assoc Jul-Aug; 3(4 Suppl) 2002. p. H30-3.
10. Fazeny, B., et al. "Barriers in cancer pain management." Wien Klin Wochenschr Nov 24; 112(22) 2000. p. 978-81.
11. Sullum, J. "No Relief in Sight." Reason Online. 1997. Jan 1997 ⟨http://reason.com/9701/fe.jacob.shtml⟩.

found less than 2% of all patients received the accepted standard for pain management.[1]

Another survey of over 3000 recently discharged patients found most had suffered from severe to moderate pain, with nearly a third indicating it had been continuous. A study of nursing home residents had similar findings.[2] It found approximately 25% of residents experiencing pain each day, but received no pain medications. In cancer patients, the prevalence of chronic pain is about 30-50% for those undergoing active treatment for a solid tumor and 70-90% for those with more advanced disease.[3] A survey of ICU patients found 54% complained of significant pain during their stay.[4] A British report on chronic pain within the general community found nearly half the population indicates the presence of chronic pain with 28% expressing the need for treatment.[5] The public relies upon those within the health care setting to recognize and treat their pain. A review by pharmacists on barriers to pain management found most patients indicated the nurses had not even assessed them for pain and, on average, were dispensing just one-fourth the amount of painkiller ordered by physicians.[6] Since pain cannot be measured objectively, the health care worker is dependent on the patient to quantify the extent of the pain. Therefore, pain is defined as what the patient says it is;[7] asking the patient is the most accurate method to determine its extent.[8] Unfortunately, most physicians and nurses are poorly trained to assess pain independent of the patient.[9]

According to an article in the *Journal of Medical Humanities*, there are currently no medical schools even offering a pain curriculum.[10] Many physicians are reluctant to use narcotics because they fear the patient may become addicted to the drug.[11] Several studies have shown the fear of narcotics (opiophobia) is

1. Zenz, M., Zenz, T., Tryba, M., Strumpf, M. "Severe undertreatment of cancer pain: a 3-year survey of the German situation." J Pain Symptom Manage Apr; 10(3) 1995. p. 187-91.
2. Won, A. "Correlates and management of nonmalignant pain in the nursing home. SAGE Study Group. Systematic Assessment of Geriatric drug use via Epidemiology." J Am Geriatr Soc Aug; 47(8) 1999. p. 936-42.
3. Portenoy, R.K., Lesage, P. "Management of cancer pain." Lancet May 15; 353(9165) 1999. p. 1695-700.
4. Van de Leur, J.P., et al. "Discomfort and factual recollection in intensive care unit patients." Crit Care Dec; 8(6) 2004. p. R467-73.
5. Elliott, A.M., et al. "The epidemiology of chronic pain in the community." Lancet vol 354 1999. p. 1248-52..
6. Krick, S.E. Lindley, C.M., Bennett, M. "Pharmacy-perceived barriers to cancer pain control: results of the North Carolina Cancer Pain Initiative Pharmacist Survey." Ann Pharmacother Jul-Aug; 28(7-8) 1994. p. 857-62.
7. Arber, A. "Is pain what the patient says it is? Interpreting an account of pain." Int J Palliat Nurs Oct; 10(10) 2004. p. 491-66.
8. Ang, P., et al. "Managing acute postoperative pain: is 3 hours too long?" J Perianesth Nurs Oct; 19(5) 2004. p. 312-30. McCaffery M. The patient's report of pain. Am J Nurs. 2001 Dec; 101(12):73-4.
9. Guru, V., Dubinsky, I. "The patient vs. caregiver perception of acute pain in the emergency department." J Emerg Med vol 18 2000. p. 7-12. Turk, D.C., Okifuji, A. "What factors affect physicians' decisions to prescribe opioids for chronic noncancer pain patients?" Clin J Pain Dec; 13(4) 1997. p. 330-36.
10. Rich, B.A. "A legacy of silence: bioethics and the culture of pain." Journal of Medical Humanities vol 18 1997. p. 233-59..
11. Morley-Forster, P.K., Clark, A.J., Speechley, M., Moulin, D.E. "Attitudes toward opioid use for chronic pain: a Canadian physician survey." Pain Res Manag vol Winter; 8(4) 2003. p. 189-94.

irrational. In three studies involving nearly 25,000 cancer patients, one author found only seven patients had become addicted to the prescribed narcotics.[1] An early study of 11,882 hospitalized patients who had received narcotics with no prior history of drug abuse, found only 4 cases of drug addiction. In only one case was the addiction considered serious.[2] These findings were validated by later studies of opioid in those with chronic non-cancerous pain.[3] A survey of 93 burn units was unable to find any documented cases of iatrogenic addiction in over 10,000 patients treated for pain.[4] Another survey of 2,369 patients treated for migraines identified only three potential cases of narcotic abuse.[5] A study of 550 cancer patients found only one case of drug abuse after 22,525 treatment days.[6] Chronic use of narcotics does not appear to be linked to addiction in the terminally ill.[7]

Pain is often addressed too late or not at all, which leads to much suffering and decreased quality of life. A long-term cross-over study of patients with chronic pain unrelated to cancer found patients experienced greater comfort with larger doses of narcotics. There were no reported cases of addiction or abuse.[8] These findings were reaffirmed by a later study.[9] Patients with sickle cell anemia may experience excruciating pain from their disease. A two year university-based clinic evaluated the effect of proper pain management on patient outcome. The authors reported a 67% decrease in emergency room visits and a 44% decrease in hospital admissions with no increase in opioid abuse.[10] In fact, a bone marrow transplant study determined patients who self-administered intravenous morphine received better pain control without addiction compared to those who received morphine administered by nurses.[11]

Study after study has documented how poorly health care workers evaluate and manage pain in patients.[12] The terminally ill are not even immune from

1. Portenoy, R. "The case for opioids." Australian Doctor, 28 July 2000 vol 28 Jul 2000.
2. Porter, J., Jick, H. "Addiction rare in patients treated with narcotics." NEJM 1980; 302:123. vol 302 1980. p. 123.
3. Fanciullo, G.J., Cobb, J.L. "The use of opioids for chronic non-cancer pain.." Int J Pain Med Palliative Care vol 1(2) 2001. p. 49-55.
4. Perry, S., Heidrich, G. "Management of pain during debridement: a survey of U.S. burn units." Pain vol 13 1982. p. 267-80.
5. Medina, J.L., Diamond, S. "Drug dependency in patients with chronic headaches." Headache vol 17 1977. p. 12-14.
6. Kanner, R.M., Foley, K. "Patterns of narcotic drug use in a cancer pain clinic." Ann NY Acad Science vol 362 1981. p. 161-72.
7. Schug, S.A., et al. "A long-term survey of morphine in cancer pain patients." J Pain Symptom Manage vol 7 1992. p. 259-66.
8. Zenz, M., Strumpf, M., Tryba, M. "Long-term oral opioid therapy in patients with chronic nonmalignant pain." J Pain Symptom Manage vol 7 1992. p. 69-77.
9. Moulin, D.E., et al. "Randomized trial of oral morphine for chronic noncancer pain." Lancet vol 347 1996. p. 143-47.
10. Brookoff, D., Palomano, R. "Treating sickle cell pain like cancer pain." Ann Intern Med vol 116 1992. p. 364-68.
11. Chapman, C.R., Hill, H.F. "Prolonged morphine self-administration and addiction liability: evaluation of two theories in a bone marrow transplant unit." Cancer vol 63 1989. p. 1636-44.
12. The SUPPORT Principal Investigators. "A controlled trial to improve care for seriously ill hospitalized patients: The Study to Understand Prognoses and Preferences for Outcomes and Risks of Treatments (SUPPORT)." JAMA vol 274 1995. p. 1591-98.

health care workers prejudices and biases.[1] These findings are especially tragic because pain can be adequately controlled in nearly 90% of the terminally ill without substantial sedation. Sadly, appropriate management techniques are not often employed. Relief is too often the exception rather than the rule.[2] The problem is so invasive that in 1992 the Agency for Health Care Policy Research (AHCPR) Care Policy Research (AHCPR) had to remind health care workers the "ethical obligation to manage pain and relieve the patient's suffering is at the core of a health care professional's commitment."[3]

The failure to rely upon the patient as a barometer for their pain may result in disbelief by the health care worker. They may believe "the pain can't actually be that bad" or interpret cries of agony as "drug seeking behavior." Many believe "using too much narcotic or for too long" may produce addiction to the pain medication. The medical term for the fear of use of opioid narcotics is opiophobia. The journal *Lancet* reports "Opioids are our most powerful analgesics, but politics, prejudice, and our continuing ignorance still impede optimum prescribing."[4] All too often adequate pain relief is sacrificed to personal biases. One author even suggests mismanagement of pain should be classified as a medical error[5] and the JCAHO states pain should be considered the fifth vital sign.[6]

Musculoskeletal conditions (including arthritis and back pain), renal disease, cerebrovascular/neurological conditions and gastrointestinal disorders are the primary conditions best managed by opioids.[7] Those suffering from these same disorders are expected to "get by" on non-narcotic pain medication because physicians prefer not to bother with bureaucratic red tape or have prejudices affecting their medical decisions.[8] Tragically, nearly 90% of those in pain could achieve adequate pain control using existing drug therapies. Failure to provide adequate pain relief causes many to fear pain more than death itself. Many would best to heed the words of the great physician Albert Schweitzer, "We must all die. But if I can save him from days of torture, that is what I feel is my great and ever new privilege. Pain is a more terrible lord of mankind than even death itself."

1. Tolle, S.W., Tilden, V.P., Hickman, S.E., Rosenfeld, A.G. "Family reports of pain in dying hospital-ized patients: a structured telephone survey." West J Med 2000; 172: vol 172 2000. p. 374-77.
2. Portenoy, R.K. Lesage, P. "Management of cancer pain." Lancet 1999; 353: vol 353 1999. p. 1695-700.
3. Jansen, L.A. "Deliberative decision making and the treatment of pain." J Palliat Med Spring; 4(1) 2001. p. 23-30.
4. McQuay, H. "Opioids in pain management." Lancet vol 353 1999. p. 2229-32.
5. Starck, P.L., Sherwood, G.D., Adams-McNeill, J., Thomas, E.J. "Identifying and addressing medical errors in pain mismanagement." Jt Comm J Qual Improv Apr; 27(4) 2001. p. 191-99.
6. Lanser, P., Gesell, S. "Pain management: the fifth vital sign." Healthcare Benchmarks Jun; 8(6) 2001. p. 68-70.
7. Sprangers et al. "Which chronic conditions are associated with a better or poorer quality of life?" Journal of Clinical Epidemiology vol 53 2000. p. 895-97.
8. Dilcher, A.J. "Damned if they do, damned if they don't: the need for a comprehensive public policy to address the inadequate management of pain." Ann Health Law vol Winter; 13(1) 2004. p. 81-144.

Yet, the lack of education in health care professionals, including nurses,[1] is frequently cited as a major reason for undertreatment of patients with pain.[2] One study concluded less than half of the nurses surveyed understand the patient's self report of pain is the single most reliable indicator of pain and the nurse should increase a previously safe but ineffective dose of opioid.[3] Findings from surveys on addiction reveal the longer the patient receives opioids the more concerned nurses become about causing addiction.[4]

A study of 386 physicians answering 59 questions related to narcotic use found more than half believed, incorrectly, psychological dependence on opioids (i.e., addiction) is a common result of legitimate prescription. About one third incorrectly believed increasing requests for analgesics indicates tolerance to the analgesic, rather than unrelieved pain. They also disagreed with the statements that almost all cancer patients suffer pain; and almost all cancer patients should receive opioids to relieve chronic pain. Nearly half of the physicians surveyed indicated they preferred not to treat those with pain related to a terminal illness. The authors came to the starling conclusion that, "a disturbingly high percentage of physicians showed negative psychological traits (i.e., authoritarianism, intolerance of ambiguity, reliance on technology, loss of control) regarding patients with chronic pain."[5]

Fear of using narcotics like morphine, codeine, Dilaudid and Demerol is irrational when one considers opioids are extremely safe compared to other drugs.[6] The potential of real harm using many cardiac medications, insulin, and sedatives is far greater than that of narcotics. Physicians have little qualm about using anti-anxiety medications like Ativan, even though their potential for addiction is much higher than narcotics.[7] The American Academy of Pain Medicine released a statement at its annual meeting in 2001 that states, "The public health problem represented by misuse of prescription opioids is minuscule in comparison with that of untreated and unrelenting pain."[8]

1. Ferrell, B.R., McCaffery, M., Rhiner, M. "Pain and addiction: an urgent need for change in nursing education." J Pain Symptom Manage Feb; 7(2) 1992. p. 117-24.
2. Cleeland, C.S. "Barriers to the management of cancer pain." Oncology vol 1(suppl 2):1987. p. 19-26. Vilensky, W. "Opioid "mythstakes": opioid analgesics—current clinical and regulatory perspectives." J Am Osteopath Assoc Sep; 102(9 Suppl 3) 2002. p. S11-4.
3. Aslan, F.E., Badir, A., Selimen, D. "How do intensive care nurses assess patients' pain?" Nurs Crit Care Mar-Apr; 8(2) 2003. p. 62-67.
4. Broekmans, S. et al. "Nurses' attitudes toward pain treatment with opioids: a survey in a Belgian university hospital." Int J Nurs Stud Feb; 41(2) 2004. p. 183-99.
5. Weinstein, S.M., et al. "Physicians' attitudes toward pain and the use of opioid analgesics: results of a survey from the Texas Cancer Pain InitiativePhysicians' attitudes toward pain and the use of opioid analgesics: results of a survey from the Texas Cancer Pain Initiative." South Med J May; 93(5) 2000.
6. Drayer, R.A., Henderson J., Reidenberg, M. "Barriers to better pain control in hospitalized patients." J Pain Symptom Manage Jun; 17(6) 1999. p. 434-40.
7. Michelini, S., Cassano, G.B., Frare, F., Perugi, G. "Long-term use of benzodiazepines: tolerance, dependence and clinical problems in anxiety and mood disorders." Pharmacopsychiatry Jul; 29(4) 1996. p. 127-34.
8. "AAPM's Statement on 2004 National Drug Control Strategy." American Academy of Pain Medicine. 2004. 03 Mar 2004 ⟨http://www.painmed.org/about/academy/030304DrugControl.html⟩.

The most serious side effect of long-term use of narcotics is usually constipation. In comparison, over-the-counter pain pills like aspirin[1] or Tylenol can produce stomach ulcers and even damage the kidney and liver.[2] The real problem with opioids is they are also able to produce euphoria or make a person "get high."[3] Medical workers frequently mistake satisfactory analgesia for euphoria. The consequence of this is just as the patient is receiving proper pain relief the medication is withheld for fear they "like it too much."

Physicians, fearful of attracting the attention of the Drug Enforcement Agency, shy away from prescribing narcotic pain medications unless they are absolutely compelled to do so.[4] They fear being ensnared in massive amounts of bureaucratic paper work, not to mention embarrassment or even the loss of their license.[5] This results in countless suffering by many as a result of a pathetic attempt to prevent a few cases of addiction.[6] True, some people do abuse prescription drugs to get high; however, most of those who suffer because of inadequate pain control have no recourse if their physician fails to heed their pleas for better pain management.

The psychiatrist Jerome H. Jaffe, former drug czar under Richard Nixon, in a 1966 pharmacology textbook, agreed patients using narcotics long enough do develop tolerance and physical dependence. However, he admonished "such considerations should not in any way prevent the physician from fulfilling his primary obligation to ease the patient's discomfort."[7] The physician should not wait until the pain becomes agonizing. No patient should ever wish for death because of their physician's reluctance to use adequate amounts of potent narcotics.[8] According to a paper by Richard M. Marks and Edward J. Sachar in the February 1973 *Annals of Internal Medicine*, complaints of continued pain in spite of medical treatment was not the result of drug seeking behavior. "To our surprise," they wrote, "instead of the primary issue being personality problems in the patient, in virtually every case it was found that the patient was not being adequately treated with analgesics and, further, the house staff for various

1. Lanas, A.I. "Current approaches to reducing gastrointestinal toxicity of low-dose aspirin." Am J Med Jan 8; 110(1A) 2001. p. 70S-73S.
2. Larrey, D., Pageaux, G.P. "Drug-induced acute liver failure." Eur J Gastroenterol Hepatol Feb; 17(2) 2005. p. 141-43. Wallace, J.L. "Acetaminophen hepatotoxicity: NO to the rescue." Br J Pharmacol Sep; 143(1) 2004. p. 1-2.
3. Inciardi, J.A. "The villification of euphoria: some perspectives on an elusive issue." Addict Dis vol 1(3) 1974. p. 241-67. McAuliffe, W.E., Gordon, R.A. "A test of Lindesmith's theory of addiction: the frequency of euphoria among long-term addicts." AJS Jan; 79(4) 1974. p. 795-840.
4. Joranson, D.E. "Federal and state regulation of opioids." J Pain Symptom Manage vol 5(suppl 1) 1990. p. S12-S23.
5. Siegler, K.A., Guernsey, B.G., Ingrim, ND. "Effect of a triplicate prescription law on prescribing of schedule II drugs." Am J Hosp Pharm vol 41 1984. p. 108-111.
6. Haislip, G.R. Impact of drug abuse on legitimate drug use. Advances in Pain Research and Therapy. New York: Raven Press, 1989.
7. Sullum, J. "No Relief In Sight." Reason Online. 1997. Jan 1997 ‹http://reason.com/9701/fe.jacob.shtml›.
8. Jaffe JH: Misinformation: euphoria and addiction. Advances in Pain Research and Therapy. Hill CS, Fields WS (eds). New York, Raven Press, Vol 11, 1989, pp 163-174

reasons was hesitant to prescribe more."[1] They also found "a general pattern of under-treatment of pain with narcotic analgesics, leading to widespread and significant distress." They distinguished between a patient seeking drugs for pain relief and an addict seeking drugs for their euphoric effects. Patients are able to discontinue the use of a pain medication once the pain is gone, whereas the addict requires it to deal with daily living.[2] They estimated less than 1% of patients treated with narcotics in hospitals become addicts and advocated improved education in pain management. They concluded "For many physicians these drugs may have a special emotional significance that interferes with their rational use."[3]

Despite such reassuring findings, many patients continued to suffer because of their doctors' opiophobia even though narcotic doses can be increased indefinitely to compensate for tolerance.[4]

In 1989, the National Institute on Drug Abuse acknowledged the problem of opiophobia. They issued a statement saying, "We have been so effective in warning the medical establishment and the public in general about the inappropriate use of opiates that we have endowed these drugs with a mysterious power to enslave that is overrated."[5] As recently as 1993 their newsletter said, "these drugs are rarely abused when used for medical purposes" proclaiming that "thousands of patients suffer needlessly."[6] Unfortunately, what they endorse is not the same as how they enforce. A 1987 DEA study reported reductions of 30% to 55% in the use of Schedule II drugs within two years after the adoption of multiple-copy prescription programs in various states during the 1960s and '70s. This shows how fearful most physicians are of using narcotics. Conscientious physicians may be hassled by the authorities simply because someone thought their prescriptions looked suspicious.[7] A 1991 survey of 90 physicians reported in the *Wisconsin Medical Journal* found most were concerned enough about regulatory scrutiny to prescribe lower doses, indicate smaller amounts, fewer refills, or select a different drug because of their fear of federal authorities.

Unfortunately, proponents of improved pain management are also fighting against deeply seated prejudices. Americans have a tendency to view drugs as good or bad, legal or illegal, therapeutic or recreational and are uncomfortable

1. Sullum, J. "No Relief In Sight." Reason Online. 1997. Jan 1997 ⟨http://reason.com/9701/fe.jacob.shtml⟩.
2. Marks, R.M., Sachar, E.H. "Undertreatment of medical inpatients with narcotic analgesics." Ann Intern Med vol 78 1973. p. 173- 81
3. Gajraj, N.M., Hervias-Sanz, M. "Opiate abuse or undertreatment?" Clin J Pain Mar; 14(1) 1998. p. 90-91.
4. Greger, M. "Appendix 76 — Opiophobia." Heart Failure — Diary of a Third Year Medical Student. 1999. Jan 1999 ⟨http://upalumni.org/medschool/appendices/appendix-76.html⟩.
5. Sullum, J. "The surprising truth about heroin and addiction." Reason Online. 2003. Jun 2003 ⟨http://www.reason.com/0306/fe.js.h.shtml⟩.
6. Sullum, J. "No Relief In Sight." Reason Online. 1997. Jan 1997 ⟨http://reason.com/9701/fe.jacob.shtml⟩.
7. Lister, B.J. "Dilemmas in the treatment of chronic pain." Am J Med 1996 Jul 31; 101(1A) 1996. p. 2S-5S.

with drugs that may be used for both. Frequently, physicians cite the fear of respiratory depression as a reason not to use opioids in the treatment of pain. However, they fail to realize the response to opioids is different for those in pain compared to those just seeking a high.[1] Doses in the excess to relieve pain do cause respiratory depression. However, this concern should not prevent using opioids to provide analgesia when the pain is deemed to be opioid sensitive. The drug-seeking behavior synonymous with drug addiction does not occur in patients after pain relief with opioids in childbirth, operations, or after myocardial infarction.

Terminal weaning is a medical euphemism for giving enough opioids to ease pain and suffering in terminal patients while hopefully expediting the process of dying from those recently removed from the breathing machine. No patient receives more opioids than the terminal wean because the constraints of respiratory depression are no longer feared but actually desired. Yet, several studies have concluded the terminal wean while being effective in easing end life suffering does little to hasten the process of dying.[2] These studies once again bolster the arguments against opiophobia indicating fears of respiratory depression are generally irrational and should not prevent the initiation of high dose opioid therapy for those in pain.[3]

Morphine is the gold standard used to compare all opioids with each other. Since opioids are administered until the desired effect is achieved (lack of pain); there is little reason to prefer one narcotic over another. There is little difference between various opioids in speed of onset and duration of effect. Faster onset and longer effect are achieved by changing the route of administration or formulation. Although side effects are common, they are generally not life threatening. One study reported about 40% of patients on oral morphine were constipated or nauseated. Studies have shown many physicians lack of basic knowledge in pharmacology of opioid therapy, and are even unable to convert equianalgesic dosages from one medication to another. Many are not even able to distinguish between physical dependence (withdrawal on abrupt drug discontinuance), tolerance (increasing drug dosages needed to maintain effect), and psychological dependence (addiction or a behavioral syndrome of continued drug use despite harm).[4]

---

1. Citron, M.L., et al. "Safety and efficacy of continuous intravenous morphine for severe cancer pain." Am J Med vol 77 1984. p. 199-04.
2. Cohen, M.H. et al. "Continuous intravenous infusion of morphine for severe dyspnea." Southern Medical Journal vol 84 1991. p. 229-34.
3. Campbell, M.L., Bizek, K.S., Thill, M. "Patient responses during rapid terminal weaning from mechanical ventilation: a prospective study." Crit Care Med Jan; 27(1) 1999. p. 73-77.
4. Friedman, D.P. "Perspectives on the medical use of drugs of abuse." J Pain Symptom Manage vol 5(suppl) 1990. p. 2-5. Grossman, S.A., Sheidler, V.R. "Skills of medical students and house officers in prescribing narcotic medications." J Med Educ vol 60 1985. p. 552-57.

Although procedures like hypnosis,[1] acupuncture,[2] distraction[3] and biofeedback have marginal effects on reducing the perception of pain, they should not be used as replacement for opioids. Instead, they should be used to supplement the effects of narcotic therapy. Prejudice and ignorance are responsible for the majority of unrelieved suffering due to pain in America. Sadly, high technology pain management systems would not be needed if the health care workers would just listen and believe the patient when they describe their pain. The opioid drugs are more than sufficient for controlling most pain if they are properly administered in a timely manner.[4] Physician and nursing biases continues to be the main reason for poor management of chronic pain.

Sleep deprivation, malnutrition, injury from falls or restraints, unrelenting pain and pressure sores all sound like problems that would prompt one to seek medical help. These very conditions are frequently induced by modern medicine and are responsible for death and suffering in countless numbers of the hospitalized. The medical community is poorly prepared to treat any of these conditions but is often actually responsible for causing or exacerbating these very problems. Basic needs like freedom from pain and the provision for the essentials of life are inherent rights. The pursuit of diagnoses and its accompanying treatment may require a certain amount of discomfort; however, the indifferent attitude so prevalent among healthcare workers is cause for concern. The astute client would be well advised to expect no less from modern medicine than for other technologies. Failure to hold the medical community responsible for its laxity may simply encourage additional abuses and negligence.

It is remarkable that we hold companies like Firestone responsible for their negligence while giving the healthcare system a free pass for negligence far in excess of other technologies. In a paper present by the Robert Wood Johnson Foundation called *Pursuing Perfection*,[5] the authors cite the risk of death as 91 per million for defective Firestone tires compared to 2,917 per million for hospital-inflicted death. Medicine remains impervious to regulation because it represents nearly 25% of our nation's total spending; special interests groups oppose any

1. Montgomery, G.H., Du Hamel, K.N., Redd, W.H. "A meta-analysis of hypnotically induced analgesia: how effective is hypnosis?" Int J Clin Exp Hypn Apr; 48(2) 2000. p. 138-53.
2. Ezzo, J. "Is acupuncture effective for the treatment of chronic pain? A systematic review." Pain Jun; 86(3) 2000. p. 217-25. Van Tulder, M.W. "The effectiveness of acupuncture in the management of acute and chronic low back pain. A systematic review within the framework of the Cochrane Collaboration Back Review Group." Spine Jun 1; 24(11) 1999. p. 1113-23.
3. Kleiber, C., Harper, D.C. "Effects of distraction on children's pain and distress during medical procedures: a meta-analysis." Nurs Res Jan-Feb; 48(1) 1999. p. 44-49. Morley, S., Eccleston, C., Williams, A. "Systematic review and meta-analysis of randomized controlled trials of cognitive behaviour therapy and behaviour therapy for chronic pain in adults, excluding headache." Pain vol 80(1-2) 1999. p. 1-13.
4. Brownlee, S. Schrof, J.M. "The Quality of Mercy: Effective pain treatments already exist. Why aren't doctors using them?" U.S. News and World Report vol 17 Mar 1997.
5. "Pursuing Perfection: Raising the Bar for Health Care Performance." The Robert Wood Johnson Foundation. May 2001 ‹http://www.ihi.org/NR/rdonlyres/069A9A67-8D18-4351-863D-5B79FA9FDA0F/0/Pursuing_Perfection_CFP.pdf›.

and all regulation that may adversely affect their profit margin. Meaningful change will only occur after the public has been educated to the needless risks of modern healthcare. The individual pleas of those being abused by medicine may fall on deaf ears; however, millions of voices will surely awaken a sleeping government as to the need for reform. In this public opinion conscious congress, millions of dissenters will hopefully overcome the silent influences of special interests groups and lobbyists who encourage continued deregulation of this enormously profitable industry.

CHAPTER 6. CREEPY CRAWLIES, BAD BUGS AND MALICIOUS MICROBES

MAGIC BULLETS OR JUST SHOOTING BLANKS

> *I learned why they're called wonder drugs — you wonder what they'll do to you.*
> *Harlan Miller, Writer, Humorist*

It took only four years after pharmaceutical companies started marketing penicillin in 1943 for resistant bacteria to emerge. Alexander Fleming predicted the emergence of penicillin resistant bacteria only two years after the drugs introduction as a clinical therapy.[1] His experiments showed sub-therapeutic doses resulted in the selection of partially resistant strains. He concluded long term abuse had the potential to create fully drug resistant strains for which penicillin would be ineffective. Three years after its introduction, one hospital reported a resistance rate of 14% for staph infections. By 1950, the same hospital found 59% staph strains evaluated had now become resistant. The emergence of penicillin resistant strains was accelerated by early policies which made penicillin available to the general public without prescription until the mid 1950s.[2] With each passing decade, bacterial resistance to not only single but also to multiple antibiotics became commonplace. *Staphylococcus aureus* was the first microbe to acquire penicillin resistance but was quickly followed in 1967 by *Streptococcus pneumoniae*, which causes pneumonia.[3] Penicillin-resistant gonorrhea

---

1. Levy, S.B. The Antibiotic Paradox. New York: Plenum Press, 1992.
2. "History of Antibiotics." Princeton University: Biotechnology and Its Social Impact. 2001. Fall 2001 ‹http://www.molbio.princeton.edu/courses/mb427/2001/projects/02/antibiotics.htm›.
3. Hansman, D., Glasgow, H., Stuart, J. "Increase resistance to penicillin of pneumococci isolated from man." N Engl J Med 1971; 184:175-7 vol 184 1971. p. 175-77.

from prostitutes was introduced into society by 1976.[1] Fears about the emergence of penicillin resistance were abated by the rapid discovery of many new types of antibiotics. The ever increasing number of "magic bullets" available to physicians made them complacent with their use of antibiotics. The emergence of common drug resistant bacteria during the 1970s was an ominous portent of things to come. During the early to mid 1980s, only 0.02% of pneumococcus bacteria had acquired penicillin resistance. By 1994, one group working with the Center for Disease Control reported resistance had increased to 6.6% and 13,300 hospital patients died as a result of drug resistant diseases in 1992. Another group of researchers reported nearly 90% of staph strains were resistant to penicillin. An additional 27% of all *Staph aureus* strains were resistant to methicillin, a penicillin derivative. These strains may also resist the antibiotics: cephalosporins, aminoglycosides, erythromycin, tetracycline, and clindamycin.[2]

Physicians initially believed the problem of drug resistance could be overcome by simply using more than one antibiotic. Unfortunately this simplistic view would be shattered when researchers reported in the April 28, 1994, *New England Journal of Medicine*, on the discovery of the first strain of bacteria in hospital samples resistant to all currently available antibiotic drugs.[3] Many strains of *S. aureus* are already resistant to all antibiotics except vancomycin and recently isolated reports[4] have emerged of the newly acquired vancomycin resistance strains.[5] It now joins the ranks of three other life-threatening organisms, *Enterococcus faecalis*, *Mycobacterium tuberculosis* and *Pseudomonas aeruginosa* that have acquired drug resistance to every antibiotic known to man.

In June 2002, vancomycin resistant *S. aureus* was isolated from a catheter site of a 40 year old Michigan resident with multiple medical problems.[6] A second isolate was isolated from a foot ulcer in a patient living in Pennsylvania.[7] On April 23, 2004, the Centers for Disease Control and Prevention (CDC) reported the third identified case of Vancomycin-Resistant Staphylococcus aureus

1. Gorwitz, R.J. "Sentinel surveillance for antimicrobial resistance in Neisseria gonorrhoeae-United States, 1988-1991. The gonococcal isolate surveillance project study group." MMWR CDC Surveillance Summaries 1993; 42: vol 42 1993. p. 29-39.
2. Lewis, R. "The Rise of Antibiotic-Resistant Infections." U.S. Food and Drug Administration: Consumer Magazine. 1995. Sep 1995 ⟨http://www.fda.gov/fdac/features/795_antibio.html⟩.
3. Tomasz , A. "Multiple-Antibiotic-Resistant Pathogenic Bacteria — A Report on the Rockefeller University Workshop." NEJMVolume 330: vol 330 1994. p. 1247-51.
4. "Frequently Asked Questions about VISA/VRSA." CDC. 2003. 01 Apr 2003 ⟨http://www.cdc.gov/ncidod/dhqp/ar_visavrsa_FAQ.html#4⟩.
5. Butwin, J. "Vancomycin-Resistant Staphylococcus aureus Undetected by Laboratory Using Automated Method for Antimicrobial Susceptibility Testing." ISDH Epidemiology Research Center. 2004. 23 Apr 2004 ⟨http://www.in.gov/isdh/dataandstats/epidem/2004/may/vrsa.pdf⟩.
6. "Staphylococcus aureus Resistant to Vancomycin — United States, 2002." MMWR. 2002. 05 Jul 2002 ⟨http://www.cdc.gov/mmwr/preview/mmwrhtml/mm5126a1.htm⟩.
7. "Public Health Dispatch: Vancomycin-Resistant Staphylococcus aureus — Pennsylvania, 2002." MMWR. 2002. 11 Oct 2002 ⟨http://www.cdc.gov/mmwr/preview/mmwrhtml/mm5140a3.htm⟩. Rotun, S., et al. "Staphylococcus aureus with Reduced Susceptibility to Vancomycin Isolated from a Patient with Fatal Bacteremia." Emerging Infectious Diseases. 1999. Jan-Mar 1999 ⟨http://www.cdc.gov/ncidod/eid/vol5no1/rotun.htm⟩.

(VRSA) in the United States.[1] The isolate was obtained from a urine specimen of a resident from a long-term care facility in New York on March 17, 2004. The newest isolate was susceptible to chloramphenicol, linezolid, minocycline, quinupristin-dalfopristin, rifampin, and trimethoprim-sulfamethoxazole. This Vancomycin Resistant *Staphylococcus aureus* (VRSA) isolate was unrelated to isolates previously identified in Michigan and Pennsylvania. The CDC had been using an automated method for identifying VRSA. This automated method had failed to detect the third VRSA strain. The CDC was forced to conclude that VRSA infections may have been undetected in all previous screenings and recommended future screenings be done manually.

Vancomycin resistant *S. aureus* is no longer a theoretical possibility; it is a new strain of identifiable super-bacteria. Since the initial reports of VRSA, other countries have joined the super-bug club. Vancomycin resistant isolates are now reported in Thailand[2] and Brazil.[3] Initial studies suggested the isolate of VRSA from Michigan was 4 times more resistant to vancomycin than previously isolated strains. Later studies concluded that it was actually 32 times more resistant to vancomycin than previously isolated strains. Fortunately, this particular strain of VRSA was sensitive to two new drugs, linezolid (Zyxox) and Synercid, as well as tetracycline and Bactrim. However, this treatment is at a cost of $150 and $200 a day compared to $10 a day for vancomycin and reports of linezolid resistance have already occurred.[4] Synercid resistance has also been reported in Taiwan[5], Greece[6], and Turkey.[7]

Japanese researchers report having found vancomycin-resistant staph bacteria at six hospitals treatable with drugs approved for their market only. Previous strains with intermediate levels of vancomycin resistance (VISA) were the result of a thickened cell wall. The new highly resistant VRSA occurred as a result of DNA transfer on a plasmid (circular pieces of DNA capable of carrying genes from one bacterium to another) from a vancomycin resistant strain of enterococcus to a methicillin resistant strain of *Staphylococcus aureus* (MRSA). The vancomycin-resistance gene is called *vanA*. These clinical isolates validate

1. "Brief Report: Vancomycin-Resistant Staphylococcus aureus — New York, 2004." MMWR. 2004. 23 Apr 2004 ‹http://www.cdc.gov/mmwr/preview/mmwrhtml/mm5315a6.htm›.
2. Trakulsomboon, S., et al. "Report of Methicillin-Resistant Staphylococcus aureus with Reduced Susceptibility to Vancomycin in Thailand." J Clin Microbiol February; 39(2) 2001. p. 591-95.
3. Palazzo, I., Araujo, ,M., Darini, A. "First Report of Vancomycin-Resistant Staphylococci Isolated from Healthy Carriers in Brazil." Journal of Clinical Microbiology vol 43 No.1 2005. p. 179-85.
4. Mutnick, A.H., Enne, V., Jones, R.N. "Linezolid resistance since 2001: SENTRY Antimicrobial Surveillance Program." Ann Pharmacother Jun; 37(6) 2003. p. 769-74. Tsiodras S. et al. "Linezolid resistance in a clinical isolate of Staphylococcus aureus." Lancet Jul 21; 358(9277) 2001. p. 207-08.
5. Luh, K.T., et al. "Quinupristin-dalfopristin resistance among gram-positive bacteria in Taiwan." Antimicrob Agents Chemother Dec; 44(12) 2000. p. 3374-80.
6. Petinaki, E., Spiliopoulou, I., Maniati, M., Maniatis, A.N. "Emergence of Staphylococcus hominis strains expressing low-level resistance to quinupristin/dalfopristin in Greece." J Antimicrob Chemother Mar 2005. p. 10.
7. Baysallar, M., Kilic, A., Aydogan, H., Cilli, F., Doganci, L. "Linezolid and quinupristin/dalfopristin resistance in vancomycin-resistant enterococci and methicillin-resistant Staphylococcus aureus prior to clinical use in Turkey." Int J Antimicrob Agents May; 23(5) 2004. p. 510-12.

the findings of researchers in England who were able to produce VRSA in a laboratory setting. Other researchers have shown VanA plasmids are also associated with plasmids for resistance to gentamicin, streptomycin, and erythromycin.[1] Additional elements on the plasmid encoded resistance to trimethoprim, beta-lactams, aminoglycosides, and disinfectants.[2]

If this strain becomes established in hospitals, it will be the most feared infectious agent since Type A Influenza (also known as the Spanish flu). Type A Influenza was responsible for the great worldwide epidemic which caused the death of over 40 million worldwide.[3] If the potential threat seems to be exaggerated, consider that reputable peer-review journals are using terms like "frightening",[4] "chilling",[5] "killer",[6] "urgent"[7] and "cause for alarm"[8] to describe this problem.

SUPERBUGS

> *The genie is out of the bottle... it will happen again... the only question is when and where.*
> Dr. Donald Low. Chief Microbiologist, Mount Sinai Hospital

Enterococci, which are normal gut bacteria, have been recognized as an important cause of endocarditis (an infection of the heart) for almost a century.[9] Normally, they pose little threat to humans. It is not only harmless, but also essential for our health, joining other bacteria to protect the intestines from potentially harmful microbes.[10] Administration of vancomycin over the years has changed these once friendly gut bacteria into a gene pool for vancomycin-resistance.[11] Use of vancomycin has increased 200-fold, but has been shown to

1. Noble WC, Virani Z, Cree RG. Co-transfer of vancomycin and other resistance genes from Entero-coccus faecalis NCTC 12201 to Staphylococcus aureus. FEMS Microbiol Lett 1992; 93:195-198.
2. Flannagan, S.E., et al. "Plasmid content of a vancomycin-resistant Enterococcus faecalis isolate from a patient also colonized by Staphylococcus aureus with a VanA phenotype." Antimicrob Agents Chemotherapy Dec; 47(12) 2003. p. 3954-59. Weigel, L.M., et al. "Genetic analysis of a high-level vancomycin-resistant isolate of Staphylococcus aureus." Science Nov 28; 302(5650) 2003. p. 1569-71.
3. Davis, J.L., et al. "Ground penetrating radar surveys to locate 1918 Spanish flu victims in perma-frost." J Forensic Sci (United States) vol 45(1) 2000. p. 68-76.
4. Moellering, R.C. "Vancomycin-resistant enterococci." Clin Infect Dis May; 26(5) 1998. p. 1196-99. Tarasi, A., et al. "Activity of moxifloxacin in combination with vancomycin or teicoplanin against Staphylococcus aureus isolated from device-associated infections unresponsive to glycopeptide therapy." J Chemother Jun; 15(3) 2003. p. 239-43.
5. Murray, B.E. "Vancomycin-resistant enterococci." Am J Med Mar; 102(3) 1997. p. 284-93.
6. Shnayerson, M. "The killer bug." Fortune Sep 2002, 2002 ed.: 149-50, 152, 154.
7. Michel, M., Gutmann, L. "Methicillin-resistant Staphylococcus aureus and vancomycin-resistant enterococci: therapeutic realities and possibilities." Lancet 1997. 28 Jun 1997.
8. Slaughter, S., et al. "Vancomycin-resistant enterococci." Clin Infect Dis vol 125 1998. p. 1196-99.
9. Cetinkaya, Y., Falk, P., Mayhall, C. "Vancomycin-Resistant Enterococci." Clinical Microbiology Reviews vol 13 No.4 2000. p. 686-707. Huycke, M., Sahm, D.F., Gilmore, M. "Multiple-Drug Resistant Enterococci: The Nature of the Problem and an Agenda for the Future." Emerging Infectious Diseases vol 4(2) 1998. p. 01-14.
10. Sheff, B. "VRE & MRSA. Putting bad bugs out of business." Nurs Manage Jun; 30(6) 1999. p. 44-49.
11. Van der Auwera, P., et al. "Influence of oral glycopeptide-resistant enterococci." J Infect Dis vol 173 1996. p. 1129-36.

be unnecessary in almost two-thirds of all cases.[1] Although vancomycin is given IV, some leaks into the gut, promoting the development of vancomycin-resistant enterococci (VRE).[2] VRE is not particularly pathogenic but it does have the potential to transfer its resistance genes to more pathogenic or disease causing bacteria, this has resulted in the production of "superbugs" for which we have no treatment.[3]

Vancomycin was first released for use in 1958 and is considered by many to be the antibiotic of last choice.[4] Vancomycin-resistant enterococci (VRE) isolates first appeared in Europe in 1987 and reached the United States by 1989.[5] By 1993, there was a twenty-fold increase from 1987 levels of VRE, with 14% of patients in some intensive care units being positive for VRE. A 2005 study reports that in just a decade VRE levels had increased from 28.9% to 72.4%.[6] It is now one of the most common causes of nosocomial (hospital acquired) infections in the United States[7] with the elderly, immunosuppressed, after intra-abdominal or cardiothoracic surgery and for those receiving multiple antibiotic therapies being most at risk.[8] The occurrence of VRE is associated with larger hospital size (greater than 200 beds) and university affiliation.[9]

Multi-drug resistant strains of the *S. aureus* are currently treatable only with vancomycin. Zyvox and Synercid have recently been introduced as an intermediate antibiotic for the treatment of MRSA, however these agents also have problems of emerging resistance and are very costly. In 2002, the inevitable finally occurred in the exchange of genetic information within the microbial world and resulted in the much-feared vancomycin resistant MRSA. If this strain becomes established it will be the equivalent of our reverting back to a

1. Centers for Disease Control. "Recommendations for preventing the spread of vancomycin resistance." MMWR. 1995; 44(no RR-12 vol 44 1995. p. RR-12. Drexler, M. Secret Agents: The Menace of Emerging Infections. National Academic Press. 2002 ‹http://www.nap.edu/catalog/10232.html›.
2. Edlund, C., et al. "Effect of vancomycin on intestinal flora of patients who previously received anti-microbial therapy." Clin Infect Dis 1997; 25, vol 25 1997. p. 729-32. Van der Auwera, P., et al. "Influence of oral glycopeptides on the fecal flora of human volunteers: selection of highly glyco-peptide-resistant enterococci." J Infect Dis 1996; 173, vol 173 1996. p. 1129-1136.
3. Low, D.E., Kellner, J.D., Wright, G.D. "Superbugs: How They Evolve and Minimize the Cost of Resistance." Curr Infect Dis Rep Dec; 1(5) 1999. p. 464-69. Michel, M., Gutmann, L. "Methicillin-resistant Staphylococcus aureus and vancomycin-resistant enterococci: therapeutic realities and possibilities." Lancet vol 125 1997. p. 1901-06.
4. Boneca, I.G., Chiosism, G. "Vancomycin resistance: occurrence, mechanisms and strategies to combat it." Expert Opin Ther Targets Jun; 7(3) 2003. p. 311-28.
5. Frieden, T.R., et al. "Emergence of vancomycin-resistant enterococci in New York City." Lancet vol 342 1993. p. 76-79. Schwalbe, R.S., Stapleton, J.T., Gilligan, P.H. "Emergence of vancomycin resistance in coagulase-negative staphylococci." NEJM Apr 9; 316(15) 1987. p. 927-31.
6. Treitman, A.N., et al. "Emerging incidence of Enterococcus faecium among hospital isolates (1993 to 2002)." J Clin Microbiol Jan; 43(1) 2005. p. 462-63.
7. Boyle, J.F., et al. "Epidemiologic analysis and genotypic characterization of a nosocomial outbreak of vancomycin-resistant enterococci." J Clin Microbiol vol 31 1993. p. 1280-85.
8. Gin, A.S., Zhanel, G.G. "Vancomycin-resistant enterococci." Ann Pharmacother Jun; 30(6) 1996. p. 615-24. Vergis, E.N., et al. "Determinants of vancomycin resistance and mortality rates in entero-coccal bacteremia. a prospective multicenter study." Ann Intern Med Oct 2; 135(7) 2001. p. 484-92.
9. CDC. "Nosocomial enterococci resistant to vancomycin — United States, 1989-1993." MMWR vol 42 1993. p. 597-9.9.

pre-antibiotic age for many diseases. Fears of exotic plagues like Ebola diminish in significance for most in comparison to vancomycin resistant MRSA. You would be far more likely in most western cultures to come in contact with vancomycin resistant MRSA than with Ebola. In fact, it was recently reported that 100% of hospitals surveyed in the San Francisco Bay Area were contaminated with Vancomycin-Resistant Enterococcus.[1]

VRE has been reported in at least 40 states, with patient infection rates as high as 14% in certain units.[2] At one time, enterococcal infections were easily treated with high doses of penicillin or ampicillin. After they acquired resistance to these drugs, physicians switched to aminoglycosides like gentamicin. After *Enterococcus* developed resistance to aminoglycosides, doctors used their drug of last resort, vancomycin. It is believed by many that over-reliance on vancomycin has led to the development of VRE. The epidemiology of VRE in Europe differs from that in the United States. In Europe the rate of fecal carriage of VRE in the community is much higher (e.g., 2 to 28%) than that in the United States, where VRE seem to be more or less absent outside hospitals. In Europe, VRE has been isolated from sewage, animal waste, meat and meat products, and feces of healthy persons. It has been suggested that the use of the antibiotic avoparcin, also a glycopeptide, as a feed additive in animal husbandry in numerous European countries has resulted in the selection of vancomycin resistance in strains from farm animals.[3]

ANTIBIOTIC ABUSE

> *Even diseases have lost their prestige, there aren't so many of them left. Think it over... no more syphilis, no more clap, no more typhoid... antibiotics have taken half the tragedy out of medicine.*
> Louis-Ferdinand Celine. French author (1894-1961)

The widespread abuse of antibiotics is the main reason for the rise of antibiotic resistance. More than half of all patients in hospitals receive antibiotics either as primary treatment or as a preventive treatment.[4] Many

1. "Resistant bacteria on rise in Bay hospitals — Once-benign bug has mutated into potential killer." San Francisco Examiner 14 Sep 1997. "New antibiotic-resistant bacteria worrying hospitals." Los Angeles Times 21 Feb 1996.
2. Bates, J. "Epidemiology of vancomycin-resistant enterococci in the community and the relevance of farm animals to human infection." J.Hosp.Infect vol 37 1997. p. 89-101. Wisplinghoff, H., et al. "Nosocomial bloodstream infections in US hospitals: analysis of 24,179 cases from a prospective nationwide surveillance study." Clin Infect Dis Aug 1; 39(3) 2004. p. 309-17.
3. Coque, T.M., et al. "Vancomycin-resistant enterococci from nosocomial, community, and animal sources in the United States." Antimicrob Agents Chemother Vol 40 1996. p. 2605-09. Stobberingh, E., et al. "Enterococci with Glycopeptide Resistance in Turkeys, Turkey Farmers, Turkey Slaughterers, and (Sub)Urban Residents in the South of The Netherlands: Evidence for Transmission of Vancomycin Resistance from Animals to Humans?" Antimicrob.Agents Chemother vol 43 1999. p. 2215-21.
4. Wright, S.W. Wrenn, K.D. "Working Party of the British Society for Antimicrobial Chemotherapy. Hospital antibiotic control measures in the UK." J Antimicrob Chemother 34 1994. p. 21-42.

studies have found physicians frequently prescribe antibiotics either excessively or inappropriately.[1] A 1998 study of vancomycin use by emergency departments concluded 40% of all prescriptions were inappropriate.[2] Other studies appear to validate the vancomycin abuse[3] rate of 40%.[4] A 2005 study found a staggering 72% of prolonged vancomycin therapies were malapropos.[5] A 1998 editorial in the British Medical Journal concludes that 75% of all antibiotic prescriptions are of questionable benefit.[6] This is often the result of poor knowledge of infectious diseases, insufficient use of or access to microbiological information, need for self-reassurance, or fear of litigation.[7] The emergence of vancomycin-resistant strains has prompted many hospitals to establish new guidelines to limit its use.[8] However, many feel this is the medical equivalent of closing the barn door after the horse has already left.

Human treatment accounts for approximately 50% of all antibiotics used in the US, with only half of that being deemed appropriate.[9] Excessive use of antibiotics in hospitals,[10] day care centers[11] and farms[12] contribute to the increase of antibiotic resistance.[13] Of the 150 million outpatient prescriptions for antibiotics every year, it has been concluded by the Centers for Disease Control

1. Bauchner, H., Pelton, S.I., Klein, J.O. "Parents, physicians, and antibiotic use." Pediatrics Feb; 103(2) 1999. p. 395-401. Feucht, C.L., Rice, L.B. "An interventional program to improve antibiotic use." Ann Pharmacother May; 37(5) 2003. p. 646-51.
2. Wright, S.W., Wrenn, K.D. "Appropriateness of vancomycin use in the emergency department." Ann Emerg Med Nov; 32(5) 1998. p. 531-36.
3. Stone, S., Gonzales, R., Maselli, J., Lowenstein, S.R. "Antibiotic prescribing for patients with colds, upper respiratory tract infections, and bronchitis: A national study of hospital-based emergency departments." Ann Emerg Med Oct; 36(4) 2000. p. 320-27.
4. Cieslak, P.R., Strausbaugh, L.J. "Vancomycin in Oregon: who's using it and why." Infect Control Hosp Epidemiol Aug; 20(8) 1999. p. 557-60. Roghmann, M.C., Perdue, B.E., Polish, L. "Vancomycin use in a hospital with vancomycin restriction." Infect Control Hosp Epidemiol Jan; 20(1) 1999. p. 60-3.
5. Bolon, M.K., et al. "Evaluating vancomycin use at a pediatric hospital: new approaches and insights." Infect Control Hosp Epidemiol Jan; 26(1) 2005. p. 47-55.
6. "Antimicrobial resistance." BMJ vol 317 1998. p. 609-10.
7. Working Party of the British Society of Antimicrobial Chemotherapy. "Hospital antibiotic control measures in the UK." J Antimicrob Chemother vol 34 1994. p. 21-42. Nathwani, D., Davey, P. "Antibiotic prescribing—are there lessons for physicians?" Q J Med vol 92 1999. p. 287-92.
8. Thomas, A.R., Cieslak, P.R., Strausbaugh, L.J., Fleming, D.W. "Effectiveness of pharmacy policies designed to limit inappropriate vancomycin use: a population-based assessment." Infect Control Hosp Epidemiol Nov; 23(11) 2002. p. 683-88.
9. Harrison, P.F., Lederberg, J. Antimicrobial resistance: issues and options. National Academy Press. 1998 ‹http://fermat.nap.edu/catalog/6121.html›.
10. Tenover, F.C., McGowan, J.E. "*Reasons for the Emergence of Antibiotic Resistance.*" Emerging Microbial Threats vol 311(1) 1996. p. 9-16.
11. Jacobs, M.R., Johnson, C.E. "Macrolide resistance: an increasing concern for treatment failure in children." Pediatr Infect Dis J Aug; 22(8 Suppl) 2003. p. S131-8. Mainous, A.G.3rd, et al. "Patterns of antibiotic-resistant Streptococcus pneumoniae in children in a day-care setting." J Fam Pract Feb; 46(2) 1998. p. 142-46.
12. Burgos, J.M., Ellington, B.A., Varela, M.F. "Presence of multidrug-resistant enteric bacteria in dairy farm topsoil." J Dairy Sci Apr; 88(4) 2005. p. 1391-98. Weese, J.S., et al. "Community-associated methicillin-resistant Staphylococcus aureus in horses and humans who work with horses." J Am Vet Med Assoc vol 15; 226(4) 2005. p. 580-83.
13. Bonten, M.J., Willems, R., Weinstein, R.A. "Vancomycin-resistant enterococci: why are they here, and where do they come from?" Lancet Infect Dis Dec; 1(5) 2001. p. 314-25. Hamer, D.H., Gill, C.J. "From the farm to the kitchen table: the negative impact of antimicrobial use in animals on humans." Nutr Rev. 2002 Aug; 60(8) 2002. p. 261-64.

and Prevention nearly one-third is inappropriate.[1] Further adding to the problem of resistance is the failure of many to take the full course of treatment.[2] This actually enriches for marginally resistant strains[3] thereby increasing there total numbers in a given population. Adding to the problem of inappropriate prescription and utilization of antibiotics is that in many non-industrialized nations, prescription drugs are available over the counter.[4] Veterinary usage of antibiotics contributes to the drug resistance problem by their use of more than 40% of all antibiotics used.[5]

A study in the April 28, 1994 issue of the *New England Journal of Medicine*, showed patients' with low white blood cell counts as a result of cancer treatment, received ever increasing usage of antibiotics over the decade between 1983 to 1993 rising from 1.4% to 45%.[6] Each year the researchers isolated *E. coli* bacteria from the patients, testing for resistance to five types of fluoroquinolones. Between 1983 and 1990, all 92 *E. coli* strains tested were easily killed by the antibiotics. However, from 1991 to 1993, 11 of the 40 tested strains (28%) were resistant to all five drugs.[7]

Findings like this have prompted a reexamination of the routine use of antibiotics to prevent infection in certain surgical patients. Basic infection control practices such as hand washing or disinfection need to be reviewed because the shortage of healthcare workers often impedes implementation of proper isolation precautions. Recent studies found overall hand washing compliance was only 22.1%.[8] If the patient has been isolated for MRSA, hand washing compliance increases by only 6% to only 28%.[9] Use of alcohol based hand cleaning solutions results in a mere 2% increase in hand washing compliance.[10] Even handling high risk patients does little to improve hand

1. Levy, S.B. "The challenge of antibiotic resistance." Scientific American Mar 1998.
2. Kardas, P. "Patient compliance with antibiotic treatment for respiratory tract infections." J Antimicrob Chemother Jun; 49(6) 2002. p. 897-903. Shah, M.N. et al. "Continuity of antibiotic therapy in patients admitted from the emergency department." Ann Emerg Med Jul; 42(1) 2003. p. 117-23.
3. Pechere, J.C. "Patients' interviews and misuse of antibiotics." Clin Infect Dis Sep 15; 33 Suppl 3 2001. p. S170-3.
4. Smith, R.D., Coast, J., Millar, M.R. "Over-the-counter antimicrobials: the hidden costs of resistance." J Antimicrob Chemother May; 37(5) 1996. p. 1031-32. Wood, M.J. "Over-the-counter antibiotics." Journal of Antimicrobial Chemotherapy vol 44 1999. p. 149-50.
5. Commission of the European Communities DGXXIV Scientific Steering Committee. "Opinion of the Scientific Steering Committee on Antimicrobial Resistance." European Commision. 1999. 28 May 1999 <http://europa.eu.int/comm/food/fs/sc/ssc/out50_en.pdf>. McEwen, S.A., Fedorka-Cray, P.J. "Antimicrobial Use and Resistance in Animals." Clinical Infectious Diseases 34 2002. p. S93-S106.
6. Cometta, A., Calandra, T., Bille, J., Glauser, M.P. "Escherichia coli resistant to fluoroquinolones in patients with cancer and neutropenia." NEJM Apr 28; 330(17) 1994. p. 1240-41.
7. Lewis, R. "The Rise of Antibiotic-Resistant Infections." U.S. Food and Drug Administration: Consumer Magazine. 1995. Sep 1995 <http://www.fda.gov/fdac/features/795_antibio.html>.
8. Kim, P.W., et al. "Rates of hand disinfection associated with glove use, patient isolation, and changes between exposure to various body sites." Am J Infect Control Apr; 31(2) 2003. p. 97-103.
9. Afif, W., Huor, P., Brassard, P., Loo, V.G. "Compliance with methicillin-resistant Staphylococcus aureus precautions in a teaching hospital." Am J Infect Control Nov; 30(7):430-3 2002. p. 430-33.
10. Hugonnet, S., Perneger, T.V., Pittet, D. "Alcohol-based handrub improves compliance with hand hygiene in intensive care units." Arch Intern Med May 13; 162(9) 2002. p. 1037-43.

washing by health care workers.[1] A dermatology study concluded physicians washed their hand only 31.4% of the time. They main reasons cited for poor hand hygiene were excessive work schedule (58%), lack of awareness (35.3%), reaction to disinfectants (17.7%) and lack of readily available facilities (15.7%). Even centers reporting high rates of compliance to hand washing protocols admit only 30% of hand washers wash their hands for the prescribed 20-30 seconds.[2] Their pathetic excuses do little to help curtail the spread of virulent diseases.[3] The medical community should hang their heads in shame for their disconcern for basic hygienic practices.[4]

There is now compelling evidence the use of a vancomycin-like drug, avoparacin, as a growth promoter in the European agriculture industry, provided the initial selective pressure for the emergence of vancomycin resistant enterococcus.[5] Concerns for increasing vancomycin resistance resulted in a ban on the agricultural use of this drug. Unfortunately, resistance to antibiotics continued despite the prohibition against their use.[6] The use of antibiotics in agriculture, without regard for their impact on resistance in human pathogens,[7] may help to accelerate us to the post-antibiotic era.[8]

The establishment of daycare has facilitated the transmission of antimicrobial resistant pathogens[9] among children.[10] Many child care centers have policies forbidding the attendance of children with active infections not cleared by a physician.[11] These policies pressure both parents and physicians

1. Larson, E., Kretzer, E.K. "Compliance with handwashing and barrier precautions." J Hosp Infect vol 30 1995. p. 88-106.
2. Cohen, H.A., Kitai, E., Levy, I., Ben-Amitai, D. "Handwashing patterns in two dermatology clinics." Dermatology 205(4) 2002. p. 358-61. Sharir, R., Teitler, N., Lavi, I., Raz, R. "High-level hand-washing compliance in a community teaching hospital: a challenge that can be met!" J Hosp Infect. 2001 Sep; 49(1) 2001. p. 55-58.
3. Goldmann, D.A. "Strategies to prevent and control the emergence and spread of antimicrobial-resistant microorganisms in hospitals." JAMA vol 275 1996. p. 234-40.
4. Schlaes, D.M. "Society for Healthcare Epidemiology of America and Infectious Diseases Society of America Joint Committee on the Prevention of Antimicrobial Resistance: guidelines for the prevention of antimicrobial resistance in hospitals." Clin Infect Dis vol 25 1997. p. 584-59.
5. Del Grosso, M. et al. "Detection and characterization of vancomycin-resistant enterococci in farm animals and raw meat products in Italy." Microb Drug Resist Winter; 6(4) 2000. p. 313-18.
6. Heuer, O.E., Pedersen, K., Andersen, J.S., Madsen, M. "Vancomycin-resistant enterococci (VRE) in broiler flocks 5 years after the avoparcin ban." Microb Drug Resist Summer; 8(2) 2002. p. 133-38. Sorum, M., Holstad, G., Lillehaug, A., Kruse, H. "Prevalence of vancomycin resistant enterococci on poultry farms established after the ban of avoparcin." Avian Dis Dec; 48(4) 2004. p. 823-28.
7. *Stephens, D.S., Farley, M.M. "Emerging Microbial Threats." American Journal of the Medical Sciences vol 311(1) 1996. p. 1-2.*
8. McGeer, A.J. "Agricultural antibiotics and resistance in human pathogens: Villain or scapegoat?" CMAJ vol 159 1998. p. 1119-20. Nathwani, D., Davey, P. "Antibiotic prescribing—are there lessons for physicians?" Q J Med vol 92 1999. p. 287-92.
9. Andrews, T.M. "Current concepts in antibiotic resistance." Curr Opin Otolaryngol Head Neck Surg Dec; 11(6) 2003. p. 409-152003. Dales, R.E., et al. "Respiratory illness in children attending daycare." Pediatr Pulmonol Jul; 38(1) 2004. p. 64-69.
10. Holmes, S.J., et a. "Risk factors for carriage of penicillin-resistant Streptococcus pneumoniae (S pneumoniae) in young children." Pediatr Res 1997; 41: 41 1997. p. 122A. McCracken, G.H. Jr. "Emergence of resistant Streptococcus pneumoniae: a problem in pediatrics." Pediatr Infect Dis J May; 14(5) 1995. p. 424-28.
11. Skull, S.A., et al. "Child care center staff contribute to physician visits and pressure for antibiotic prescription." Arch Pediatr Adolesc Med Feb; 154(2) 2000. p. 180-83.

into pediatric antibiotic therapy that in many cases is against established guidelines.[1] Migration and world travel have also facilitated the global dissemination of resistant pathogens including: Methicillin-resistant *Staphylococcus aureus* (MRSA), vancomycin-resistant *enterococci* (VRE), and penicillin-resistant *Streptococcus pneumoniae*.[2]

Misuse of antibiotics greatly exacerbates the problem of drug resistance[3] because they destroy the normal bacteria that protect you from being colonized by resistant strains.[4] In fact, several investigators have shown a direct relationship between antibiotic use and the emergence of drug resistant strains.[5] One researcher found as fluoroquinolone prescriptions increased from 0.8 to 5.5 per 100 persons per year between 1988 and 1997, the number of resistant pneumococci increased from 0% in 1993 to 1.7 in 1997-1998.[6]

Another example demonstrating how inappropriate antibiotic use has selected for antibiotic resistance was shown by Finish investigators. They found use of erythromycin in Finland had affected significantly the level of erythromycin resistance in group A *streptococci*.[7] Resistant strains occurred most often among children five years old and younger: the very age group where the use of erythromycin was the highest. When the use of erythromycin was curtailed by 40% between 1991 and 1994, resistant group A *streptococci* decreased from 16.5% in 1992 to 8.6% in 1996.[8] Unfortunately, other researchers found streptomycin resistance was still present in about 20% of all isolates of *Enterobacter* even though the drug had not been used for over 20 years.[9] Four years after the prohibition on the use of tetracycline as a food additive to promote growth in pigs, there was no significant reduction in percentage of pigs harboring tetracycline resistant *E. coli*.[10] These reports suggest once resistance

1. Bauchner, H., Klein, J.O. "Parental issues in selection of antimicrobial agents for infants and children." Clin Pediatr (Phila) Apr; 36(4) 1997. p. 201-5. Osterholm, M.T., et al. "Infectious diseases and child day care." Pediatr Infect Dis J Aug; 11(8 Suppl) 1992. p. S31-41.
2. Fukuda, H. Hiramatsu, K. "Primary targets of fluoroquinolones in Streptococcus pneumoniae." Antimicrob.Agents Chemother.; 43: vol 43 1999. p. 410-41. Kataja, J., et al. "Erythromycin resistance genes in group A streptococci in Finland. The Finnish Study Group for Antimicrobial Resistance." Antimicrob.Agents Chemother vol 43 1999. p. 48-52.
3. Young, V.B., Schmidt, T.M. "Antibiotic-associated diarrhea accompanied by large-scale alterations in the composition of the fecal microbiota." J Clin Microbiol Mar; 42(3) 2004. p. 1203-06.
4. Hogenauer, C., Hammer, H.F., Krejs, G.J., Reisinger, E.C. "Mechanisms and management of antibiotic-associated diarrhea." Clin Infect Dis Oct; 27(4) 1998. p. 702-10. Krause, R., Krejs, G.J., Wenisch, C., Reisinger, E.C. "Elevated fecal Candida counts in patients with antibiotic-associated diarrhea: role of soluble fecal substances." Clin Diagn Lab Immunol Jan; 10(1) 2003. p. 167-68.
5. Defez, C., et al. "Risk factors for multidrug-resistant Pseudomonas aeruginosa nosocomial infection." J Hosp Infect Jul; 57(3) 2004. p. 209-16.
6. Chen, D., et al. "Decreased susceptibility of Streptococcus pneumoniae to fluoroquinolones in Canada." NEJM vol 341 1999. p. 233-39.
7. Huovinen, P., et al. "The relationship between erythromycin consumption and resistance in Finland. Finnish Study Group for Antimicrobial Resistance." Ciba.Found.Symp vol 207 1997. p. 36-41.
8. Seppala, H., et al. "The effect of changes in the consumption of macrolide antibiotics on erythromycin resistance in group A streptococci in Finland. Finnish Study Group for Antimicrobial Resistance." NEJM vol 337 1997. p. 441-46.
9. Chiew, Y.F. "Can susceptibility to an antimicrobial be restored by halting its use?" Journal of Antimicrobial Chemotherapy vol 41 1998. p. 247-51.
10. Smith, H.W. "Persistence of tetracycline resistance in pig E. coli." Nature vol 258 1975. p. 628-30.

has developed, simply reducing the use of antibiotics may not always eradicate or reduce resistance. The bottom line is once resistance to an antibiotic appears in pathogenic (disease causing) bacteria, it is here to stay.

INCREASING RATES OF INFECTION

> *It is not the strongest of the species that survives, nor the most intelligent,*
> *but the one most responsive to change.*
> *Charles Darwin. 1809-1882, Naturalist and Author*

The abuse of antibiotics is at near epidemic proportions. The approximately six million antibiotic prescriptions for sinusitis in 1985 increased to nearly 13 million by 1992.[1] Similarly, for middle ear infections, 15 million prescriptions in 1985 increased to 23.6 million by 1992.[2] More recent studies suggest the total number of office visits for ear infections exceeds 30 million annually.[3] It is believed by many the increase of physician visits for ear infections by preschoolers from 9.9 million in 1975 to 24.5 million in 1990 greatly contributed to the rise in drug resistance.[4] Increased numbers of homeless and drug abusers further promote the spread of infection.[5] The greater use of chemotherapy and transplantation both of which greatly suppress the immune system, also increase the risk of infection.[6] The explosion in inappropriate use of antibiotics has resulted in drug resistance to at least one antibiotic in 70% of hospital-acquired infections. Thirty-five to forty percent of hospital acquired infections are resistant to the optimum therapeutic agent.[7] From 1990 to 1996, the three most common gram-positive pathogens: *S. aureus*, coagulase-negative *staphylococci*, and *enterococci* were responsible for 34% of nosocomial infections, and the four most common gram-negative pathogens-*Escherichia coli*, *P. aeruginosa*, *Enterobacter* spp., and *Klebsiella pneumoniae* accounted for 32% of all hospital infections.[8] Herpes viruses with acquired resistance to acyclovir and ganciclovir

1. Lewis, R. "The Rise of Antibiotic-Resistant Infections." U.S. Food and Drug Administration: Consumer Magazine. 1995. Sep 1995 ‹http://www.fda.gov/fdac/features/795_antibio.html›. McCaig, L.F., Hughes, J.M. "Trends in antimicrobial drug prescribing among office-based physicians in the United States." JAMA Jan 18; 273(3) 1995. p. 214-19.
2. Kaliner, M. "Medical management of sinusitis." Am J Med Sci Jul; 316(1) 1998. p. 21-28. Spector, S.L., et al. "Parameters for the diagnosis and management of sinusitis." J Allergy Clin Immunol vol 102(6:2) 1998. p. S107 S44.
3. Blaise, L. "Acute Otitis Media." Current Treatment Options in Infectious Diseases 5 2003. p. 151-57.
4. Brook, I. "Antimicrobial management of acute sinusitis: a review of therapeutic recommendations." Infect. Med vol 19 2002. p. 231-37. Schappert, S.M. "Office visits for otitis media: United States, 1975-90." Adv Data Sep 8; (214) 1992. p. 1-19.
5. Charlebois, E.D., et al. "Population-based community prevalence of methicillin-resistant Staphylococcus aureus in the urban poor of San Francisco." Clin Infect Dis Feb 15; 34(4) 2002. p. 425-33.
6. Gold, H.S., Moellering, R.C. Jr. "Antimicrobial-drug resistance." NEJM vol 335 1996. p. 1445-53.
7. Muto, C.A., et al. "SHEA guideline for preventing nosocomial transmission of multidrug-resistant strains of staphylococcus aureus and enterococcus." Infect Control Hosp Epidemiol vol 24(5) 2003. p. 362-86.
8. Weinstein, R.A. "Nosocomial Infection Update." Emerging Infectious Diseases vol 4(3) 1998.

have also emerged as problems, particularly in HIV-infected patients.[1] Twelve percent of patients who undergo moderate to high-risk surgical procedures develop nosocomial infections with mortality rates in infected patients of 14.5%, versus 1.8% in uninfected patients.[2]

Although day schools and the homeless certainly contribute their fair share to the problem of drug resistant bacteria, the real culprits are hospitals and long-term care facilities. Nosocomial infections (from the Greek word for hospital) have always been around. They're one reason why 19th-century aristocrats avoided hospitals like the plague (pun intended) and preferred to be treated at home; hospitals were for the poor and homeless. People sick enough to be in the hospital are the perfect vessels for the development of super-bacteria because they are usually weakened by their illness or wound and are particularly susceptible to infection. According to the national Centers for Disease Control and Prevention (CDC), over the past 20 years, abuse of antibiotics has resulted in a 36% increase in the rate of hospital-acquired (nosocomial) infections.[3] It has been estimated 2 million patients develop nosocomial, or hospital-acquired, infections each year,[4] with 90,000 of these dying as a result![5] The rates of infection within long term care facilities may be nearly twice as high. Some estimates suggest rates of 3.83 million per year for nursing homes.[6] These increases are associated with massive increases in the use of vancomycin, which is associated with spread of resistance plasmids and transposons (transposable genetic element or jumping genes) among many strains of *Enterococcus*. Initially, epidemics of vancomycin resistant *enterococci* were restricted primarily to the intensive care units but later spread through out the hospitals.[7] Poor hygienic practices and failure to adequately clean contaminated surfaces are primary reasons for its rapid spread. A large review of previously published studies found no differences in infection rates of facilities using routine disinfection of surfaces (mainly floors) versus cleaning with detergent only.[8]

1. Bacon, T.H., et al. "Herpes Simplex Virus Resistance to Acyclovir and Penciclovir after Two Decades of Antiviral Therapy." Clinical Microbiology Reviews vol 16(1) 2003. p. 114-28.
2. DiPiro, J.T., ET AL. "Infection in surgical patients: effects on mortality, hospitalization, and post-discharge care." Am J Health Syst Pharm Apr :15; 55(8) 1998. p. 777-81.
3. "Monitoring hospital-acquired infections to promote patient safety—United States, 1990-1999." MMWR Morb Mortal Wkly Rep Mar 3; 49(8) 2000. p. 149-53. Haley, R.W., et al. "The nationwide nosocomial infection rate: a new need for vital statistics." Am J Epidemiol vol 121 1985. p. 159-67.
4. "Public health focus: surveillance, prevention, and control of nosocomial infections." MMWR vol 41 1992. p. 783-87.
5. Bueno-Cavanillas A, et al. "Influence of nosocomial infection on mortality rate in an intensive care unit." Crit Care Med Jan; 22(1) 1994. p. 55-60.
6. Strausbaugh, L.J., Joseph, C.L. "The burden of infection in long-term care." Infect Control Hosp Epidemiol Oct; 21(10) 2000. p. 674-79..
7. Hanberger H et al. "Antibiotic susceptibility among aerobic gram-negative bacilli in intensive care units in 5 European countries." JAMA vol 281(1) 1999. p. 67-71. Karanfil, L.V., et al. "A cluster of vancomycin-resistant Enterococcus faecium in an intensive care unit." Infect Control Hosp Epidemiol 1992 vol 13 1992. p. 195-200.
8. Bonten, J.M., et al. "Epidemiology of colonisation of patients and environment with vancomycin-resistant enterococci." Lancet vol 348 1996. p. 1615-19. Dettenkofer, M., et al. "Does disinfection of environmental surfaces influence nosocomial infection rates?" Am J Infect Control Apr; 32(2) 2004. p. 84-89.

The rate of these hospital-acquired infections is ever increasing. During 1995 it was estimated nosocomial infections cost $4.5 billion to treat and contributed to more than 88,000 deaths or approximately one death every 6 minutes.[1] Frequently they make patients sicker than they were prior to admission resulting in increased length of hospital stay by several weeks and, according to the CDC, may add an additional $50,000 to the hospital bill.[2] A 2003 Johns Hopkins study concluded infection with vancomycin-resistant enterococcal bacteria increased mortality by 30.3%, hospital stay by 17 days and added an additional $77,558 in extra charges for treatment.[3] Not only does this result in an increase in hospital spending by $5 to 10 billion a year,[4] it also decreases the quality of human life resulting in: additional pain, longer recuperation period, increased emotional stress, increased side effects related to antibiotics, with the possibility of permanent health care problems.

During the pre-antibiotic era, over 80% of the community-acquired pneumonia (CAP) was attributed to *S. pneumoniae*, with mortality rates of 20 to 40%.[5] During the antibiotic era, the overall mortality rates for CAP were 10% for non-systemic infections and 30% for pneumonia with sepsis (systemic infection).[6] Mortality is closely associated with the cause of the infection; patients with *Pseudomonas aeruginosa*, *Staphylococcus aureus*, and enteric gram-negative rod pneumonia have overall mortalities of greater than 30%.[7] If Vancomycin resistant *S. aureus* becomes established, we will again experience the same appalling death rates due to infection seen in the pre-antibiotic era.

Researchers have shown the above is not just an idle speculation. They showed ineffective antimicrobial therapy was a predictor of mortality for severe community acquired pneumonia[8] and found inappropriate antibiotic therapy increased the risk of death to patients with nosocomial blood stream infections.[9]

1. Weinstein, R.A. "Nosocomial Infection Update." Emerging Infectious Diseases vol 4(3) 1998.
2. Elward, A.M., et al. "Attributable cost of nosocomial primary bloodstream infection in pediatric intensive care unit patients." Pediatrics Apr; 115(4) 2005. p. 868-72. Sculco, T.P. "The economic impact of infected total joint arthroplasty." Instructional Course Lectures vol 42 1993. p. 349-51.
3. Song, X., et al. "Effect of nosocomial vancomycin-resistant enterococcal bacteremia on mortality, length of stay, and costs." Infect Control Hosp Epidemiol Apr; 24(4) 2003. p. 251-56.
4. US Department of Health and Human Services. "Addressing emerging infectious disease threats: a prevention strategy for the United States." Washington, DC: US Government Printing Office, 1994. Public Health Initiative Research Institute. (1997) "Report from the Bacterial Antibiotic Resistance Group/Infectious Disease Center." US Government Printing Office Washington, DC.
5. Austrian, R., Gold, J. "Pneumococcal bacteremia with especial reference to bacteremic pneumococcal pneumonia." Ann.Intern.Med vol 60 1964. p. 759-70. Bartlett, J.G., Mundy, L.M. "Community-Acquired Pneumonia." NEJM vol 333 1995. p. 1618-24.
6. British Thoracic Society and the Public Health Laboratory Service. "Community-acquired pneumonia in adults in British hospitals in 1982- 1983: a survey of aetiology, mortality, prognostic factors and outcome." Q. J. Med vol 239 1987. p. 195-220. Diekema, D.J., et al. "Epidemiology and outcome of nosocomial and community-onset bloodstream infection." J Clin Microbiol Aug; 41(8) 2003. p. 3655-60.
7. Fine, M.J., et al. "Prognosis and outcomes of patients with community-acquired pneumonia. A meta-analysis." JAMA vol 275 1996. p. 134-41.
8. Leroy, O., et al. "Severe community-acquired pneumonia in ICUs: prospective validation of a prognostic score." Intensive.Care.Med vol 22 1996. p. 1307-14.
9. Jamulitrat, S., et al. "Factors affecting mortality outcome and risk of developing nosocomial bloodstream infection." Infect Control Hosp Epi vol 15 1994. p. 163-170.

Others found inadequate antibiotic therapy contributed to poorer outcome than any other type of treatment.[1] Other important contributors to infection were central venous catheter, mechanical ventilation, pleural drainage and trauma with open fractures.[2]

Over the last several decades, reported wound infections have markedly decreased and there has been little change in urinary tract infections.[3] Nosocomial pneumonia with resistant gram-negative bacteria, however, now predominates along with increased incidence of fungal infections.[4] Currently, postoperative infections are now more severe, involve critical organs, and require closer monitoring of the changing patterns of pathogens than at any other time in the antibiotic era.[5]

Pronouncements of medicine's victory over infectious disease were premature. Death from earlier infectious diseases has merely been replaced by death from antibiotic resistant diseases.[6] The conclusion of a 1996 JAMA article from the Centers for Disease Control is quoted in its entirety, "Despite historical predictions that infectious diseases would wane in the United States, these data show that infectious diseases mortality in the United States has been increasing in recent years."[7]

From 1980 to 1994, mortality rates in individuals hospitalized for infectious disease doubled, from 1.9% to 4.0%. Death due to infectious diseases increased 6.3 times in individuals aged 25 to 44 years-old.[8] The magnitude of this problem remains uncertain because recent studies indicate that the National Nosocomial Infections Surveillance (NNIS) System is not a reliable indicator of the true incidence of nosocomial infections in hospital settings.[9] This voluntary system of reporting of nosocomial infections consistently underestimates the true incidence of nosocomial infections in US hospitals. An exhaustive review published in the journal *Shock* concluded the NNIS was able to detect only 61-

1. Mosdell, D.M., et al. "Antibiotic treatment for surgical peritonitis." Ann.Surg vol 214 1991. p. 543-49.
2. Endimiani, A., et al. "A two-year analysis of risk factors and outcome in patients with bloodstream infection." Jpn J Infect Dis Feb; 56(1) 2003. p. 1-7. Leroy, O., et al. "Severe community-acquired pneumonia in ICUs: prospective validation of a prognostic score." Intensive Care Med vol 22 1996. p. 1307-14.
3. Richards, M.J., et al. "Nosocomial infections in medical intensive care units in the United States." Critical Care Medicine vol 27(5) 1999. p. 887-92. Wallace, W.C., et al. "New epidemiology for postoperative nosocomial infections." Am Surg Sep; 66(9) 2000. p. 874-78.
4. Toscano, C.M., Jarvis, W.R. "Emerging Issues in Nosocomial Fungal Infections." Current Infectious Disease Reports vol 1 1999. p. 347-61.
5. Armstrong, G.L., et al. "Trends in infectious disease mortality in the United States during the 20th century." JAMA Jan 6; 281(1) 1999. p. 61-66. Wallace, W.C., et al. "New epidemiology for postoperative nosocomial infections." Am Surg Sep; 66(9) 2000. p. 874-78.
6. Crabtree, TD., et al. "Effect of Changes in Surgical Practice on the Rate and Detection of Nosocomial Infections: A Prospective Analysis." Shock vol 17(4) 2002. p. 258-62.
7. Pinner, R.W., et al. "Trends in infectious diseases mortality in the Unites States JAMA." JAMA Jan 17; 275(3) 1996. p. 189-93.
8. Simonsen, L., et al. "Trends in infectious disease hospitalizations in the United States, 1980-1994." Arch Intern Med Sep 28; 158(17) 1998. p. 1923-8..
9. Emori, T.G., et al. "Accuracy of reporting nosocomial infections in intensive-care-unit patients to the National Nosocomial Infections Surveillance System: a pilot study." Infect Control Hosp Epidemiol May; 19(5) 1998. p. 308-16.

81% of actual infections.[1] They admit that the meticulous gold standard for monitoring infection may miss nearly 40% of all hospital infections. A large study of 181,993 patients concluded the NNIS was not even correct about predicting the frequency of primary sites of infection. Coagulase-negative staphylococci were more frequently associated with primary bloodstream infections than reported from NNIS and enterococci were a more frequent isolate from bloodstream infections than S. *aureus*. They also found fungal urinary tract infections, which are often asymptomatic and associated with catheter use, were considerably more frequent than previously reported. The frequency of infections missed by the current surveillance systems means mortality rates attributable to nosocomial infections may be significantly higher than reported. As a consequence, all studies utilizing data from the NNIS system underestimate the true extent of morbidity and mortality from hospital acquired infections.[2]

CONTAMINATED EQUIPMENT AND SURFACES

Cleanliness is indeed next to godliness.
Wesley, John 1703-1791, British Preacher, Founder of Methodism

The squalor of most hospitals makes them the perfect habitat for deadly pathogens. Feeble attempts at infection control usually take back seat for the more budget minded managed care autocrats.[3] Failure to place more value on lives than on cost savings creates a myriad of sources harboring these germs.[4] Outbreaks of hospital acquired infections have been traced to blood pressure cuffs,[5] electronic thermometers[6] and latex gloves.[7] Most stethoscopes harbor potential pathogens,[8] some of which can be transferred to human skin.[9] A study

---

1. Crabtree, T.D., et al. "Effect of Changes in Surgical Practice on the Rate and Detection of Nosocomial Infections: A Prospective Analysis." Shock vol 17(4) 2002. p. 258-62.
2. Richards, M.J., et al. "Nosocomial infections in medical intensive care units in the United States." *Critical Care Medicine vol 27(5) 1999. p. 887-92.*
3. Harbarth, S., et al. "Outbreak of Enterobacter cloacae related to understaffing, overcrowding, and poor hygiene practices." Infect Control Hosp Epidemiol Sep; 20(9) 1999. p. 598-603.
4. McFarland,.LV. "What's lurking under the bed? Persistence and predominance of particular Clostridium difficile strains in a hospital and the potential role of environmental contamination." Infect Control Hosp Epidemiol Nov; 23(11) 2002. p. 639-40.
5. Bowen, T. "Nondisposable sphygmomanometer cuffs harbor frequent bacterial colonization and significant contamination by organic and inorganic matter." AANA J Apr; 64(2) 1996. p. 141-45.
6. Jernigan, J.A., et al. "A randomized crossover study of disposable thermometers for prevention of Clostridium difficile and other nosocomial infections." Infect Control Hosp Epidemiol vol 57 1998. p. 494-99. Porwancher, R., et al. "Epidemiological study of hospital-acquired infection with vancomycin-resistant Enterococcus faecium: Possible transmission by an electronic ear-probe thermometer." Infect Control Hosp Epidemiol vol 18 1997. p. 771-74.
7. Girou, E., et al. "Misuse of gloves: the foundation for poor compliance with hand hygiene and potential for microbial transmission?" Journal of Hospital Infect Jun; 57(2) 2004. p. 162-69. Patterson, J.E., et al. "Association of contaminated gloves with transmission of Acinetobacter calcoaceticus var. anitratus in an intensive care unit." Am J Med Nov; 91(5) 1991. p. 479-83.
8. Bernard, L., et al. "Bacterial contamination of hospital physicians' stethoscopes." Infect Control Hosp Epidemiol Sep; 20(9) 1999. p. 626-28. Panhotra, B.R., Saxena, A.K., Al-Mulhim, A.S. "Contaminated physician's stethoscope — a potential source of transmission of infection in the hospital. Need of frequent disinfection after use." Saudi Med J Feb; 26(2) 2005. p. 348-50.

of 300 randomly collected stethoscopes from healthcare workers found 87% were contaminated with bacteria.[1] A separate study evaluated the cleaning habits of the Emergency Department (ED) staff and showed 45% cleaned the stethoscope annually or never.[2] These findings were reaffirmed by another study.[3] A verbal survey revealed regular cleaning of stethoscopes is not a common practice among doctors.[4] A 1997 Michigan study found physicians' stethoscopes generally had a higher bacterial load than nurses' stethoscopes.[5]

The traditional inflatable cuff on a blood pressure monitor comes in direct contact with a patient's skin.[6] This same cuff may be used on many patients and is limited only by the lifespan of the cuff.[7] They are exposed to a wide variety of bodily fluids (blood, sweat, urine, fecal matter, and vomit) and can hold a variety of pathogenic organisms.[8] The cuff can then readily transfer these pathogens to the next unsuspecting patient through direct skin contact.

In other cases, rectal thermometer probes,[9] bedrails[10] and bathroom doors[11] have all been contaminated. Capable of living for weeks on surfaces, VRE has been detected on patient gowns, bed linens, and handrails. Cleaning a bedpan may result in contamination on hopper sink, walls, floor and spray wand as well as the caregiver's gloves, clothing and shoes, even though they appear clean.[12] Instruments used in patient care, such as stethoscopes[13], pulse oximeters[14] blood glucose monitors,[15] weighing scales[16] and blood collection supplies may

9. Nunez, S., et al. "The stethoscope in the Emergency Department: a vector of infection?" Epidemiol Infect Apr; 124(2) 2000. p. 233-37. Thofern UA. Bacterial contamination of hospital physicians' stethoscopes. Infect Control Hosp Epidemiol. 2000 Sep; 21(9):558-9.
1. Zuliani Maluf ME, Maldonado AF, Bercial ME, Pedroso SA. Stethoscope: a friend or an enemy? Sao Paulo Med J. 2002 Jan 3; 120(1):13-5.
2. Zuliani Maluf, M.E., et al. "Stethoscope: a friend or an enemy?" Epidemiol Infect Apr; 124(2) 2000. p. 233-37.
3. Bernard, L., et al. "Bacterial contamination of hospital physicians' stethoscopes." Infect Control Hosp Epidemiol Sep; 20(9) 1999. p. 626-28.
4. Sengupta, S., et al. "Stethoscopes and nosocomial infection." Indian J Pediatr Mar; 67(3) 2000. p. 197-99.
5. Marinella, M.A., Pierson, C., Chenoweth, C. "The stethoscope. A potential source of nosocomial infection?" Arch Intern Med Apr 14; 157(7) 1997. p. 786-90.
6. Cormican, M.G., et al. "The microbial flora of in-use blood pressure cuffs." Ir J Med Sci Apr; 160(4) 1991. p. 112-13.
7. Base-Smith, V. "Nondisposable sphygmomanometer cuffs harbor frequent bacterial colonization and significant contamination by organic and inorganic matter." AANA J Apr; 64(2) 1996. p. 141-45.
8. Manian, F.A., et al. "Clostridium difficile contamination of blood pressure cuffs: a call for a closer look at gloving practices in the era of universal precautions." Infect Control Hosp Epidemiol Mar; 17(3) 1996. p. 180-82.
9. Livornese, L.L., et al. "Hospital-acquired infection with vancomycin-resistant Enterococcus faecium transmitted by electronic thermometers." Ann Intern Med vol 117 1992. p. 112-16.
10. Mayer, R.A., et al. "Role of fecal incontinence in contamination of the environment with vancomycin-resistant enterococci." Am J Infect Control Jun; 31(4) 2003. p. 221-25. Noskin, G.A., Stosor, V., Cooper, I., Peterson, L.R. "Recovery of vancomycin-resistant enterococci on fingertips and environmental surfaces." Infect Control Hosp Epidemiol Oct; 16(10) 1995. p. 577-81.
11. Oie, S., Kamiya, A. "Microbial contamination of antiseptics and disinfectants." Am J Infect Control Oct; 24(5) 1996. p. 389-95.
12. Chadwick, P.R., Oppenheim, B.A. "Vancomycin-resistant enterococci and bedpan washer machines." Lancet Sep 3; 344(8923) 1994. p. 685.
13. Guinto, C.H., et al. "Evaluation of dedicated stethoscopes as a potential source of nosocomial pathogens." Am J Infect Control Dec; 30(8) 2002. p. 499-502.
14. Wilkins, M.C. et al. "Residual bacterial contamination on reusable pulse oximetry sensors." Respir Care Nov; 38(11) 1993. p. 1155-60.

also be contaminated.[1] *Enterococcus* is able to survive 5-7 days on countertops and on bedrails for 24 hours without significant die-off, on telephone hand pieces for 60 minutes,[2] on the diaphragmatic surface of stethoscopes for 30 minutes, and on gloved and ungloved fingers for at least 60 minutes. Superficial disinfection does not eliminate contamination, although more thorough cleaning does.[3]

Unfortunately, these rooms seldom achieve the level of cleaning necessary to decontaminate them completely.[4] Contamination is so pervasive that even cleaning solutions have been implicated.[5] Germicidal resistance is emerging as a new threat[6] that compounds the concerns for antibiotic resistance.[7] Trash receptacles,[8] sinks,[9] toilets,[10] curtains,[11] door handles,[12] towel dispensers,[13] beds,[14] call lights[15] and virtually all surfaces in a patient room have been implicated as reservoirs for infectious agents.[16]

---

15. "Nosocomial Hepatitis B Virus Infection Associated with Reusable Fingerstick Blood Sampling Devices — Ohio and New York City, 1996." MMWR vol 46(10) 1997. p. 217-221.
16. Jones, K.A,, et al. "Infection hazards of patient lifting slings." Nurs Times Mar 11-17; 88(11) 1992. p. 46-47.
1. Golder, M., et al. "Potential risk of cross-infection during peripheral-venous access by contamination of tourniquets." Lancet Jan 1; 355(9197) 2000. p. 44. Perry. J., Jagger, J. "Don't reuse that blood tube holder." Nursing Aug; 33(8) 2003. p. 74.
2. Singh. V., et al. "Telephone mouthpiece as a possible source of hospital infection." J Assoc Physicians India Apr; 46(4) 1998. p. 372-73.
3. Ray, A.J., et al. "Nosocomial transmission of vancomycin-resistant enterococci from surfaces." JAMA Mar 20; 287(11) 2002. p. 1400-01.
4. Martinez, J.A., et al. "Role of environmental contamination as a risk factor for acquisition of vancomycin-resistant enterococci in patients treated in a medical intensive care unit." Arch Intern Med Sep 8; 163(16) 2003. p. 1905-12.
5. Gilbert, P., McBain, A.J., Bloomfield, S.F. "Biocide abuse and antimicrobial resistance: being clear about the issues." J Antimicrob Chemother Jul; 50(1) 2002. p. 137-9. Oie S, Kamiya A. Microbial contamination of antiseptics and disinfectants. Am J Infect Control. 1996 Oct; 24(5):389-95.
6. Fraise, A.P. "Biocide abuse and antimicrobial resistance—a cause for concern?" J Antimicrob Chemother Jan; 49(1) 2002. p. 11-12.
7. McDonnell, G., Russell, A.D. "Antiseptics and disinfectants: activity, action, and resistance." Clin Microbiol Rev Jan; 12(1) 1999. p. 147-79.
8. Neely, A.N., Maley, M.P., Taylor, G.L. "Investigation of single-use versus reusable infectious waste containers as potential sources of microbial contamination." Am J Infect Control Feb; 31(1) 2003. p. 13-17.
9. Reuter, S., Sigge, A., Wiedeck, H., Trautmann, M. "Analysis of transmission pathways of Pseudomonas aeruginosa between patients and tap water outlets." Crit Care Med Oct; 30(10) 2002. p. 2222-28.
10. Noble, M.A., et al. "The toilet as a transmission vector of vancomycin-resistant enterococci." J Hosp Infect Nov; 40(3) 1998. p. 237-41. Vardhan, M.S., Allen, K.D., DeRuiter, G. "Commodes: a health hazard." J Hosp Infect Apr; 44(4) 2000. p. 320-21.
11. Palmer, R. "Bacterial contamination of curtains in clinical areas." Nurs Stand Sep 29-Oct 5; 14(2) 1999. p. 33-35.
12. Oie, S., Hosokawa, I., Kamiya, A. "Contamination of room door handles by methicillin-sensitive/ methicillin-resistant Staphylococcus aureus." J Hosp Infect Jun; 51(2) 2002. p. 140-43.
13. Harrison, W.A., Griffith, C.J., Ayers, T., Michaels, B. "Bacterial transfer and cross-contamination potential associated with paper-towel dispensing." Am J Infect Control Nov; 31(7) 2003. p. 387-91.
14. Orendi, J.M. "Relation between bed occupancy and the incidence of MRSA infection." J Hosp Infect Jan; 56(1) 2004. p. 74-75. Yanaka, Y., Tusaka, N., Yamamoto, K. "More beds: more nosocomial infections." Jpn J Infect Dis Aug; 52(4) 1999. p. 180-81.
15. Young, J.M., Naqvi, M., Richards, L. "Microbial contamination of hospital bed handsets." Am J Infect Control Apr; 33(3) 2005. p. 170-74.
16. Rutala WA, Weber DJ. Surface disinfection: should we do it? J Hosp Infect. 2001 Aug; 48 Suppl A:S64-8.

A 2005 study found antibiotic and germicide resistant bacteria were actually thriving on the handles of germicidal soap dispensers.[1] An evaluation of conventional cleaning methods found 70 and 76% of cleaned sites unacceptable after cleaning even though 82% were deemed clean by visual inspection.[2] A Brazilian study reported nearly 50% of all mattresses tested remained positive for bacteria.[3] They suggested traditional cleaning methods merely displaced the bacteria on the bed's surface. The expensive ICU beds are nearly always filled; an unfortunate death of a patient with massive sepsis from MRSA does not deter the use of this room but for an hour.[4]

One study found 19% of door handles of rooms with patients with MRSA were contaminated.[5] Even computer terminals[6] are not safe;[7] a 2002[8] and 2000[9] study found 24% of all terminals tested were contaminated with MRSA.[10] The authors suggested keyboard contamination may be an effective marker for indicating handwashing compliance. Faucet handles were also implicated. An epidemiological study found bedside computer terminals were contaminated more often than any other objects in the patients' room.[11] A Veterans Administration study found that 95 out of 100 keyboards tested in a Seattle hospital were infected with disease-causing bacteria.[12]

Any exposure to medical services greatly increases your risk for nosocomial or hospital acquired infections. The very moniker, "hospital acquired," is misleading because infections have been traced to medical services prior to

1. Brooks, S.E., Walczak, M.A., Hameed, R., Coonan, P. "Chlorhexidine resistance in antibiotic-resistant bacteria isolated from the surfaces of dispensers of soap containing chlorhexidine." Infect Control Hosp Epidemiol Nov; 23(11) 2002. p. 692-95.
2. Griffith CJ, Cooper RA, Gilmore J, Davies C, Lewis M. An evaluation of hospital cleaning regimes and standards. J Hosp Infect. 2000 May; 45(1):19-28.
3. De Andrade, D., Angerami, E.L., Padovani, C.R. "A bacteriological study of hospital beds before and after disinfection with phenolic disinfectant." Rev Panam Salud Publica Mar; 7(3): 2000. p. 179-84.
4. Boyce, J.M. Potter-Bynoe, G., Chenevert, C., King, T. "Environmental contamination due to methicillin-resistant Staphylococcus aureus: possible infection control implications." Infect Control Hosp Epidemiol Sep; 18(9) 1997. p. 622-27. Palmer, R. "Bacterial contamination of curtains in clinical areas. Nurs Stand." Nurs Stand Sep 29-Oct 5; 14(2) 1999. p. 33-35.
5. Oie S, Hosokawa I, Kamiya A. Contamination of room door handles by methicillin-sensitive/methicillin-resistant Staphylococcus aureus. J Hosp Infect. 2002 Jun; 51(2):140-3.
6. Bowman, L. "Keyboards used in hospitals are havens for bacteria." Scripps Howard News Service 12 Apr 2005. Hartmann, B., et al. "Computer keyboard and mouse as a reservoir of pathogens in an intensive care unit." J Clin Monit Comput. 2004 Feb; 18(1) 2004. p. 7-12.
7. Coia, J.E., Masterton, R.G. "Computer keyboards as a risk for nosocomial infection." Am J Infect Control Oct; 29(5) 2001. p. 345. Neely, A.N., Maley, M.P. "Dealing with contaminated computer keyboards and microbial survival." Am J Infect Control Apr; 29(2) 2001. p. 131-32.
8. Devine, J., Cooke, R.P., Wright, E.P. "Is methicillin-resistant Staphylococcus aureus (MRSA) contamination of ward-based computer terminals a surrogate marker for nosocomial MRSA transmission and handwashing compliance?" J Hosp Infect Dec; 52(4) 2002. p. 314-15.
9. Bures, S., et al. "Computer keyboards and faucet handles as reservoirs of nosocomial pathogens in the intensive care unit." Am J Infect Control Dec; 28(6) 2000. p. 465-71.
10. Isaacs, D., et al. "Swabbing computers in search of nosocomial bacteria." Pediatr Infect Dis J Jun; 17(6) 1998. p. 533.
11. Neely, A.N., Sittig, D.F. "Basic microbiologic and infection control information to reduce the potential transmission of pathogens to patients via computer hardware." J Am Med Inform Assoc Sep-Oct; 9(5) 2002. p. 500-08.
12. Schultz, M., et al. "Bacterial contamination of computer keyboards in a teaching hospital." Infect Control Hosp Epidemiol Apr; 24(4): 2003. p. 302-03.

hospitalization. The phrase "health care-associated infection" is probably more descriptive since many infections originate outside of the hospital setting.[1] The home health nurse may be a portal of entry for pathogenic bacteria into your home.[2] The ambulance they summon to "help" you may be swarming with pathogenic bacteria[3], and the emergency room is frequently a cesspool of infectious organisms. Most adults realize the quickest way to make well children ill is to take them to the pediatrician's office for their routine physical or vaccinations. Many also associate their flu or cold with a prolonged stay in a doctor's waiting room packed with infectious and contagious patients. However, a reality disconnect may occur with the urgency to seek medical care for a painful or potentially life-threatening condition.

Medical personnel may be responsible for infecting patients with bacteria far worse than their presenting disease. Coats,[4] uniforms[5] and surgical boots may be contaminated with infectious and drug resistant organisms.[6] Ink pens used by the physician to write prescriptions for antibiotics have been shown to harbor pathogenic bacteria.[7] The very case notes and charts written by doctors have been implicated with bacterial infections.[8] One study found 227 out of 228 randomly selected patient case notes were contaminated with pathogenic bacteria. Another study found 14% of hospital pagers were contaminated with methicillin resistant bacteria; simple cleaning with 70% alcohol reduced the total colony count by an average of 94%.[9] A New York study found 96% of physician PDAs were contaminated with infectious bacteria, cleaning with alcohol reduced the contamination rate to only 25%.[10] Another study found 78% of nurse's scissors were colonized with bacteria. This same simple measure effectively decontaminated them. Unfortunately the authors of this and other studies report this cleaning seldom occurs.[11] The transfer of a bacterial infection

1. Smith, T.L., et al. "Environmental contamination with vancomycin-resistant enterococci in an outpatient setting." Infect Control Hosp Epidemiol vol 125 1998. p. 515-18.
2. Friedman, M.M. "Preventing and controlling the transmission of antibiotic-resistant microorganisms in the home care setting." Caring Nov; 18(11) 1999. p. 6-11.
3. Nigam, Y., Cutter, J. "A preliminary investigation into bacterial contamination of Welsh emergency ambulances." Emerg Med J Sep; 20(5) 2003. p. 479-82.
4. Wong, D., Nye, K., Hollis, P. "Microbial flora on doctors' white coats." BMJ 303(6817) 1991. p. 1602-04.
5. Callaghan, I. "Bacterial contamination of nurses' uniforms: a study." Nurs Stand Sep 23-29; 13(1) 1998. p. 37-42.
6. Agarwal, M., Hamilton-Stewart, P., Dixon, R.A. "Contaminated operating room boots: the potential for infection." Am J Infect Control May; 30(3) 2002. p. 179-83.
7. Datz, C., et al. "What's on a doctors' ball point pens?" Lancet 350 1997. p. 1824. French, G., Rayner, D., Branson, M., Walsh, M. "Contamination of doctors' and nurses' pens with nosocomial pathogens." Lancet 351(9097) 1998. p. 213.
8. Alothman, A., et al. "Contamination of patient hospital charts by bacteria." J Hosp Infect Dec; 55(4) 2003. p. 304-05. Bebbington, A., Parkin, I., James, P.A. "Patients' case-notes: look but don't touch." J Hosp Infect Dec; 55(4) 2003. p. 299-301.
9. Singh, D., et al. "Bacterial contamination of hospital pagers." Infect Control Hosp Epidemiol May; 23(5) 2002. p. 274-76.
10. Hassoun, A., Vellozzi, E.M., Smith, M.A. "Colonization of personal digital assistants carried by healthcare professionals." Infect Control Hosp Epidemiol Nov; 25(11) 2004. p. 1000-01.
11. Embil, J.M., Zhanel, G.G., Plourde, P.J., Hoban, D. "Scissors: a potential source of nosocomial infection." Infect Control Hosp Epidemiol Mar; 23(3) 2002. p. 147-51. Kelly, J., Trundle, C. "Scissors: are they an infection control risk?" Prof Nurse Oct; 16(1) 2000. p. 830-33.

from one patient to another is called cross-over transmission. Cross-transmission of microorganisms by the hands of health care workers is considered the main route of spread of nosocomial infections.[1] A 2002 study suggests a cross-over rate of transmission was at least 37.5%; however they concede the actual rate may actually be much higher.[2]

The true irony is estimates by the CDC for death rates from nosocomial infection generally agree that it is at least the fourth leading cause of death in the United States.[3] One scenario they propose has a mortality rate of 105,500 deaths annually that are directly attributable to infections related to medical therapy. A 2003 study seems to support these estimates of death from hospital acquired infections by citing 90,000 deaths annually.[4]

A four pronged approach for controlling the spread of VRE has already been proposed by the U.S. Department of Health and Human Services. Their summarization is quoted in its entirety as; "Prevention and control of the spread of vancomycin resistance will require coordinated, concerted effort from various departments of the hospital and can only be achieved if each of the following elements is addressed: 1) prudent vancomycin use by clinicians, 2) education of hospital staff regarding the problem of vancomycin resistance, 3) early detection and prompt reporting of vancomycin resistance in enterococci and other gram-positive microorganisms by the hospital microbiology laboratory, and 4) immediate implementation of appropriate infection- control measures to prevent person-to-person transmission of VRE."[5] These recommendations were initially made in 1994. The failure of the medical community to implement these recommendations speaks volumes as to the real concern for most hospital organizations.

ICU BREEDING GROUNDS FOR INFECTION

> *Cold doth increase, the sickness will not cease,*
> *And here we lie, God knows, with little ease.*
> *From winter, plague, and pestilence, good Lord, deliver us!*
> Thomas Nashe 1567-1601, British poet.

The above conditions turn hospitals, especially intensive care units, into major breeding grounds for the development and propagation of antibiotic

1. Pittet, D., et al. "Bacterial contamination of the hands of hospital staff during routine patient care." Arch Intern Med Apr 26; 159(8) 1999. p. 821-26.
2. Weist, K., et al. "How many nosocomial infections are associated with cross-transmission? A prospective cohort study in a surgical intensive care unit." Infect Control Hosp Epidemiol Mar; 23(3) 2002. p. 127-32.
3. Wenzel, R.P., Edmond, M.B. "The Impact of Hospital-Acquired Bloodstream Infections." Emerging Infectious Diseases vol 7(2) 2001.
4. Burke, J.P. "Infection control-a problem for patient safety." NEJM vol 348 2003. p. 651-656. Clark, A.P., Susan Houston, S. "Nosocomial Infections: An Issue of Patient Safety: Part 2." Clin Nurse Spec vol 18(2) 2004. p. 62-64.
5. "Recommendations for Preventing the Spread." Recommendations of the Hospital Infection Control Practices. 1994. <http://ftp.cdc.gov/pub/infectious_diseases/brochures/vancomy.txt>.

resistant microbes.[1] Each year about two million patients acquire nosocomial infections in US hospitals.[2] Nearly 60% of these infections are antibiotic resistant. Within the US, about 40% the *Staphylococcus aureus* infections are methicillin resistant. One study found the incidence of vancomycin resistant enterococci (VRE) within the ICU had increased 25-fold since 1987 (up to 16%) since 1987. Infections are so pervasive that one study suggests 30% of all ICU patients may be infected with a hospital acquired infection.[3] The narrow confines of an ICU combined with the frequent exposure to large doses of antibiotics in immune compromised patients makes them the perfect environment for the development of increasingly resistant strains of bacteria.[4] Many disciplines are involved in the care of the critically ill. Each discipline represents an additional opportunity for cross infection to occur and spread throughout the hospital being carried unwittingly by healthcare workers. Because of the frequency of medical interventions, severity of illness and immunosuppression from illness or drugs, patients within the ICU setting are 5 to 10 times more likely to acquire a nosocomial infection.[5] This has resulted in more than a 20-fold increase of vancomycin resistance in the US.[6] One study found resistance to vancomycin had increased 34-fold from 0.3% in 1989 to 7.9% by 1993.[7] Identification of carriers and adherence to proven methods of containment (e.g. hand washing and protective barriers like gowns and gloves) are essential in containing these organisms.[8] The Centers for Disease Control and Prevention and Emory University's Rollins School of Public Health states "the intensive care unit is the single most infectious place in the world when it comes to antibiotic resistant bacteria."[9]

It has been determined that:

1. Edgeworth, J.D., Treacher, D.F., Eykyn, S.J. "A 25-year study of nosocomial bacteremia in an adult intensive care unit." Crit Care Med Aug; 27(8) 1999. p. 1421-28. Fridkin, S.K., Gaynes, R.P. "Antimicrobial resistance in intensive care units." Clin Chest Med. 1999 Jun; 20(2) 1999. p. 303-16.
2. Lowy, F.D. "Staphylococcus aureus infections." NEJM vol 339 1998. p. 520-52.
3. Vincent, J.L. "Nosocomial infections in adult intensive-care units." Lancet Jun 14; 361(9374) 2003. p. 2068-77. Vincent, J.L., Chierego, M., Struelens, M., Byl, B. "Infection control in the intensive care unit." Expert Rev Anti Infect Ther Oct; 2(5) 2004. p. 795-805.
4. Flaherty, J.P., Weinstein, R.A. "Nosocomial infection caused by antibiotic-resistant organisms in the intensive-care unit." Infect Control Hosp Epidemiol Apr; 17(4) 1996. p. 236-34. Schultz, M., Sanchez, R.O., Hernandez, N.E., Hernandez, J.M. "Nosocomial infection among immunosuppressed patients in the intensive care unit." Crit Care Nurs Q Aug; 24(2) 2001. p. 55-56.
5. Weber, D.J., Raasch, R., Rutala, W.A. "Nosocomial infections in the ICU: the growing importance of antibiotic-resistant pathogens." Chest Mar; 115(3 Suppl) 1999. p. 34S-41S.
6. Gold, H.S., Moellering, R.C. "Antimicrobial-drug resistance." NEJM vol 335 1996. p. 1445-43.
7. "Nosocomial enterococci resistant to vancomycin-United States, 1989-1993." MMWR vol 42 1993. p. 597-99.
8. Rubinovitch, B., Pittet, D. "Screening for methicillin-resistant Staphylococcus aureus in the endemic hospital: what have we learned?" J Hosp Infect Jan; 47(1) 2001. p. 9-18.
9. "Hospital ICU's a breeding place for bacteria." The Augusta (GA) Chronicle 18 May 1997. Archibald, L., et al. "Antimicrobial resistance in isolates from inpatients and outpatients in the United States: increasing importance of the intensive care unit." Clin Infect Dis Feb; 24(2) 1997. p. 211-15.

- 79.7% of *Staphylococcus epidermidis* bacteria, which causes skin infections, were resistant to the drug methicillin in ICUs; double the percentage of resistant staph found in other areas of the hospital.

- 39.4% of *Staphylococcus aureus*, which causes blood infections and pneumonia, were resistant to methicillin in ICUs, compared with 31.2% elsewhere in the hospital.

- 7.7% of enterococcus bacteria, another cause of blood infections, were resistant to vancomycin in ICUs, compared with 6.1% elsewhere in the hospital.

Health care workers infect patients with these pathogens through direct contact and tubes inserted into the body like IVs, urinary catheters and central lines.[1] These drug resistant bacteria colonize the nasal passages[2] and lower airways[3] of health care workers and patients alike.[4] This translates into patients having to take more expensive drugs and longer hospital stays.[5]

Some nosocomial infections can even kill.[6] Estimates of extra costs associated with the treatment of hospital acquired infections range from $13,973[7] to $38,656 per case.[8] If the infection enters the bloodstream (becomes systemic), the mean cost of medical therapy is increased by $38,703.[9] The Centers for Disease Control gives estimates for the number of nosocomial infections from 2.5 to 10% of all hospitalizations. The average rate of hospitalized infections is 5% or 5 infections for every 1000 patient-days.[10] The annual rates of hospitalized infections range between 875,000 to 3.5 million. The consensus of most studies is over 2 million cases and 90,000 deaths annually.[11] The extrapolated annual expenditures are between $12-$135 billion to treat

1. Neely, A.N., Maley, M.P. "Survival of enterococci and staphylococci on hospital fabrics and plastic." J Clin Microbiol Feb; 38(2) 2000. p. 724-26.
2. Dupeyron, C., et al. "A clinical trial of mupirocin in the eradication of methicillin-resistant Staphylococcus aureus nasal carriage in a digestive disease unit." J Hosp Infect Dec; 52(4) 2002. p. 281-87. Frebourg, N.B., Cauliez, B., Lemeland, J.F. "Evidence for nasal carriage of methicillin-resistant staphylococci colonizing intravascular devices." J Clin Microbiol Apr; 37(4) 1999. p. 1182-85.
3. Agvald-Ohman, C., Wernerman, J., Nord, C.E., Edlund, C. "Anaerobic bacteria commonly colonize the lower airways of intubated ICU patients." Clin Microbiol Infect May; 9(5) 2003. p. 397-405.
4. Von Eiff, C., et al. "Nasal carriage as a source of Staphylococcus aureus bacteremia." NEJM Jan 4; 344(1) 2001. p. 11-16.
5. Roberts, R.R., et al. "The use of economic modeling to determine the hospital costs associated with nosocomial infections." Clin Infect Dis Jun 1; 36(11) 2003. p. 1424-32.
6. Vincent, J.L. "Nosocomial infections in adult intensive-care units." Lancet Jun 14; 361(9374) 2003. p. 2068-77.
7. Stone, P.W., Larson, E., Kawar, L.N. "A systematic audit of economic evidence linking nosocomial infections and infection control interventions: 1990-2000." Am J Infect Control 30 2002. p. 145-52.
8. Zhan, C., Miller, M.R. "Excess length of stay, charges, and mortality attributable to medical injuries during hospitalization." JAMA Oct; 290(14) 2003. p. 1868-1874.
9. Pittet, D., Tarara, D., Wenzel, R.P. "Excess length of stay, extra costs, and attributable mortality." JAMA May 25; 271(20) 1994. p. 1598-601.
10. Wenzel, R.P., Edmond, M.B. "The Impact of Hospital-Acquired Bloodstream Infections." Emerging Infectious Diseases vol 7(2) 2001.
11. Burke, J.P. "Infection control-a problem for patient safety." NEJM vol 348 2003. p. 651-56. Clark, A.P., Susan Houston, S. "Nosocomial Infections: An Issue of Patient Safety: Part 2." Clin Nurse Spec vol 18(2) 2004. p. 62-64.

these infections. A 1999 report by the Institute of Medicine suggest an additional healthcare cost of $17-$29 billion annually.[1] Studies have shown hospital acquired infections increased the average length of ICU treatment by 8 days, hospital stay by 14 days,[2] and the death rate by 35%.[3]

The authors of one study conclude that stemming it may be a matter of going back to basics like hand washing, restricting antibiotic use and isolating the sickest patients. Nosocomial infections typically affect patients, who are immunocompromised because of age, underlying diseases, or medical or surgical treatments. Nosocomial infection rates in adult and pediatric ICUs are approximately three times higher than any other location in the hospital. In the United States, more than 5% of hospital admissions and about 14% of intensive care patients acquire infections during their stay. According to some estimates by the CDC, nosocomial bloodstream infections rank as the fourth to thirteenth causes of death in the United States.[4] Antibiotic resistance increases the morbidity and mortality[5] associated with infections and substantially increases the cost of care as the result of prolonging hospital stays and requiring the need for more expensive drugs.[6]

Methods for containing the spread of resistant bacteria within the hospital setting have generally been lackluster. The percentage of nosocomial S. *aureus* infections caused by MRSA increased significantly between 1982 and 2002, despite the use of various isolation and barrier precaution policies.[7] The CDC estimates only one-third of all hospital acquired infections are preventable.[8] Hospitals commonly flag the patient's charts and notes to notify health care workers that the patient has a communicable disease. Studies have concluded flagging of medical records does little to reduce the spread of resistant bacteria.[9]

Isolating patients alone has also not been proven to be effective in reducing the spread of bacteria[10] but it does increase the patients' risk during

1. To err is human: building a safer health system. Kohn, L.T., Corrigan, J.M., Donaldson, M.S. The National Acadamies Press. 2000 ‹http://fermat.nap.edu/books/0309068371/html/›.
2. Pittet, D., Tarara, D., Wenzel, R.P. "Excess length of stay, extra costs, and attributable mortality." JAMA May 25; 271(20) 1994. p. 1598-601.
3. Hanna HA. et al. "Antibiotic-Impregnated Catheters Associated With Significant Decrease in Nosocomial and Multidrug-Resistant Bacteremias in Critically Ill Patients." Chest 124 2003. p. 1030-38.
4. Wenzel, R.P., Edmond, M.B. "The Impact of Hospital-Acquired Bloodstream Infections." Emerging Infectious Diseases vol 7(2) 2001
5. Soriano, A., et al. "Pathogenic significance of methicillin resistance for patients with Staphylococcus aureus bacteremia." Clin Infect Dis 30 2000. p. 368-73.
6. Cohen, M.L. "Epidemiology of drug resistance: implications for a post-antimicrobial era." Science 1992 vol 257 p. 1050-1055. Shay, D.K., et al. "Epidemiology and mortality risk of vancomycin-resistant enterococcal bloodstream infections." J Infect Dis vol 172 1995. p. 993-1000.
7. Boyce, J.M., et al. "Do infection control measures work for methicillin-resistant Staphylococcus aureus?" Infect Control Hosp Epidemiol May; 25(5) 2004. p. 395-401.
8. Weinstein, R.A. "Nosocomial Infection Update." Emerging Infectious Diseases vol 4(3) 1998.
9. Barakate, M.S., et al. "A prospective survey of current methicillin-resistant Staphylococcus aureus control measures." Aust N Z J Surg Oct; 69(10) 1999. p. 712-16. Boyce, J.M. "MRSA patients: proven methods to treat colonization and infection." J Hosp Infect vol 48(suppl A) 2001. p. S9-14.

hospitalization.[1] Patients in isolation often complain of social isolation,[2] anxiety and depression.[3] Gloving seems to have a marginal impact on reducing the spread of nosocomial infections by increasing the incidence of handwashing.[4] These control measures frequently fail because patients are often already colonized upon hospitalization and existing resistant strains may be amplified in the ICU by the use of by antibiotics.[5] The major successes in control of nosocomial infections[6] are through implementing basic measures of thorough handwashing, use of appropriate antibiotics, reducing the stay in an ICU to less than 3 days[7] and reducing risks of vascular access devices (IVs).[8]

A recent study evaluated the use of hydrogen peroxide vapor as a disinfectant/germicide. Seventy-four percent of 359 swabs taken before cleaning yielded MRSA, after conventional cleaning all areas remained contaminated. In contrast, after exposing six rooms to hydrogen peroxide vapor, only one of 85 (1.2%) swabs remained contaminated.[9] A 2005 study with Clostridium botulinum spores seems to confirm these findings.[10]

Of more than 40 different decolonization regimens that have been tested during the last 60 years, topical intranasal application of mupirocin ointment has proven to be the most effective.[11] However, intranasal application of mupirocin has limited effectiveness in eradicating colonization in patients who carry the organism at multiple body sites.[12]

10. Cooper, B.S., et al. "Systematic review of isolation policies in the hospital management of methi-cillin-resistant Staphylococcus aureus: a review of the literature with epidemiological and economic modelling." Health Technol Assess vol 7 2003. p. 1-194. Farrington, M., et al. "Winning the battle but losing the war: methicillin-resistant Staphylococcus aureus (MRSA) at a teaching hospital." QJM vol 91 1998. p. 539-48.
1. Evans,.HL., et al. "Contact isolation in surgical patients: a barrier to care?" Surgery Aug; 134(2) 2003. p. 180-88. Stelfox, H.T., Bates, D.W., Redelmeier, D.A. "Safety of patients isolated for infec-tion control." JAMA Oct 8; 290(14) 2003. p. 1899-905.
2. Madeo, M. "The psychological impact of isolation." Nurs Times Feb 18-24; 99(7) 2003. p. 54-55.
3. Catalano, G. "Anxiety and depression in hospitalized patients in resistant organism isolation." South Med J Feb; 96(2) 2003. p. 141-45. Newton, J.T., Constable, D., Senior, V. "Patients' percep-tions of methicillin-resistant Staphylococcus aureus and source isolation: a qualitative analysis of source-isolated patients." J Hosp Infect Aug; 48(4) 2001. p. 275-80.
4. Trick, W.E., et al. "Comparison of routine glove use and contact-isolation precautions to prevent transmission of multidrug-resistant bacteria in a long-term care facility." J Am Geriatr Soc Dec; 52(12) 2004. p. 2003-09.
5. Weinstein, R.A. "Epidemiology and control of nosocomial infections in adult intensive care units." Am J Med vol 91(suppl 3B) 1991. p. 179S-184S.
6. Edgeworth, J.D., Treacher, D.F., Eykyn, S.J. "A 25-year study of nosocomial bacteremia in an adult intensive care unit." Crit Care Med Aug; 27(8) 1999. p. 1421-28.
7. Marshall, C., et al. "Acquisition of methicillin-resistant Staphylococcus aureus in a large intensive care unit." Infect Control Hosp Epidemiol May; 24(5) 2003. p. 322-26.
8. Hall, C.S., Ost, D.E. "Effectiveness of programs to decrease antimicrobial resistance in the inten-sive care unit." Semin Respir Infect Jun; 18(2) 2003. p. 112-21. Lepape, A. "Prevention of nosoco-mial infections in ICU. What is really effective?" Med Arh vol 57(4 Suppl 1) 2003. p. 15-18.
9. French, G.L., et al. "Tackling contamination of the hospital environment by methicillin-resistant Staphylococcus aureus (MRSA): a comparison between conventional terminal cleaning and hydrogen peroxide vapour decontamination." J Hosp Infect May; 57(1) 2004. p. 31-37.
10. Johnston, M.D., Lawson, S., Otter, J.A. "Evaluation of hydrogen peroxide vapour as a method for the decontamination of surfaces contaminated with Clostridium botulinum spores." J Microbiol Methods Mar; 60(3) 2005. p. 403-11.
11. Boyce, J.M. "MRSA patients: proven methods to treat colonization and infection." J Hosp Infect Aug; 48 Suppl A 2001. p. S9-14.

Curiously, Iceland, Netherlands, Denmark and Sweden have the lowest incidences of nosocomial infections in the world. Their infection rates are less than 1% as compared to a 10% rate for the US, 41.5% for the United Kingdom and 44.4% for Greece.[1] An analysis of leading health care indicators shows Denmark spends a larger portion of their GDP for health care services and has a greater than average nurse to patient ratio.[2] Conversely, they also have higher human consumption of antibacterial drugs than other developed nations.[3]

This discrepancy may be explained by two surveys, one by the WHO and the other by Eurostat. They questioned various European residents about the state of their health. The recommended instrument by WHO for perceived health status was as follows: "How is your health in general?" and response categories are: "very good, good, fair, bad, and very bad." Countries with the highest percentage of citizens stating that they were in good health also had the lowest incidence of nosocomial infections. Counties with the lowest level of

Proportion of male and female population reporting "good" and "very good" health status in selected countries, 1991-1996.

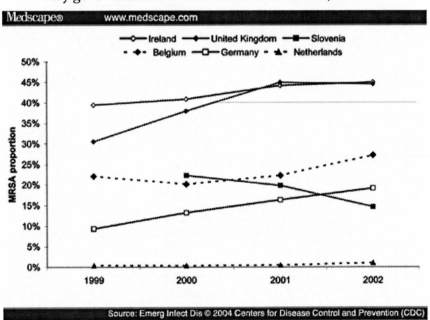

12. Ibid.
1. Tiemersma, E.W. et al. "Methicillin-resistant Staphylococcus aureus in Europe, 1999–2002." Emerging Infectious Diseases vol 10(9) 2004.
2. Vandenbroucke-Grauls, C. "Management of methicillin-resistant Staphylococcus aureus in the Netherlands." Rev Med Microbiol vol 9 1998. p. 109-116.
3. Okeke, I.N., et al. "Socioeconomic and Behavioral Factors Leading to Acquired Bacterial Resistance to Antibiotics in Developing Countries." Emerging Infectious Diseases vol 5 1999. p. 18-27.

expressed health were more likely to have higher rates of hospital acquired infections.[1]

Healthier populations are less likely to require medical services therefore are less likely to be in contact with personnel and equipment contaminated with pathogenic bacteria. Improvements in a population's general health may be the real cure for drug resistant bacteria.

Percentage of Population Satisfied With Health Status; 1991-1996

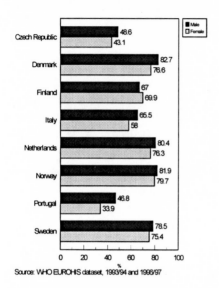

Source: WHO EUROHIS dataset, 1993/94 and 1996/97

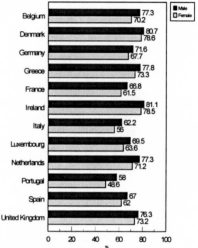

Source: EUROSTAT, European Community Household Panel Survey, Wave 1994
France: perceived health status = satisfaction with health

VISA — DON'T LEAVE THE HOSPITAL WITH IT

> "Right now, we are still in most cases able to use vancomycin. Now let's say we lose vancomycin. Where are the deaths going to go? They're going to go up. This number could double."
>
> Stuart Levy, M.D. of the Center for Adaptation Genetics and Drug Resistance at Tufts.

The majority of MRSA strains are resistant to most other antibiotics[2]; this necessitates the use of drugs, such as vancomycin.[3] Vancomycin was first introduced as a medical therapy in 1958 and is generally reserved for treatment of

1. WHO, European Region & Central Bureau of Statistics in the Netherlands (1996), Health interview surveys: towards international harmonisation of methods and instruments. Copenhagen: WHO Regional Publication European Series no. 58. EUROSTAT, European Community Household Panel Survey, Wave 1994 ⟨http://www.olis.oecd.org/OLIS/1998DOC.NSF/c16431e1b3f24c0ac12569fa005d1d99/5d888d48e9146617c12567000060ef39/$FILE/01E91615.DOC⟩
2. Zhiming, L., et al. "Comparison of Length of Hospital Stay for Patients With Known or Suspected Methicillin-Resistant Staphylococcus Species Infections Treated With Linezolid or Vancomycin: A Randomized, Multicenter Trial." Pharmacotherapy vol 21(3) 2001. p. 263-274.

life-threatening infections caused by organisms resistant to penicillin, cephalosporin, or other antibiotics. Concerns about losing this therapeutic option were heightened with the discovery of bacteria that require vancomycin in media for growth. These vancomycin-dependent enterococci (VDE) have been implicated in clinically significant infections.[1]

Until 1996, glycopeptides like vancomycin remained the standard against *S. aureus*. The emergence of glycopeptide-intermediate *S. aureus*[2] (GISA) [also called VISA[3] (vancomycin intermediate resistant *S. aureus*)][4] may herald the rise of a post-antibiotic era.[5] Two glycopeptide antibiotics, vancomycin and teicoplanin, are currently considered the drugs of "last resort" for serious drug-resistant infections. The two agents have proven remarkably versatile in many common applications.[6] A third glycopeptide antibiotic, avoparcin, is available only for agricultural/veterinary use outside of the US.[7]

The newly emerged VISA strains have intermediate levels of resistance to vancomycin related to a thickened cell wall.[8] These strains are feared by many within the scientific community because they may predate the arrival of a high level vancomycin resistant *S. aureus*. The appearance of this "superbug"[9] for which there is no known cure may have already occurred.[10] Many express concerns that we are on the threshold of a post-antibiotic[11] era that is the medical equivalent of the Dark Ages.[12]

The finding of a *S. aureus* intermediately resistant to vancomycin were first discovered in a Japanese infant's surgical wound,[13] but have also been reported

3. Livermore, D.M. "Antibiotic resistance in staphylococci." Int J Antimicrob Agents Nov; 16 Suppl 1 2000. p. S3-10.
1. Perl, T.M. "The threat of vancomycin resistance." Am J Med May 3; 106(5A) 1999. p. 26S-37S.
2. Hiramatsu, K. "The emergence of Staphylococcus aureus with reduced susceptibility to vancomycin in Japan." Am J Med May 29; 104(5A) 1998. p. 7S-10S. Menichetti, F. "Current and emerging serious Gram-positive infections." Clin Microbiol Infect May; 11 Suppl 3 2005. p. 22-28.
3. Linares, J. "The VISA/GISA problem: therapeutic implications." Clin Microbiol Infect vol 7(4) 2001. p. 8-15.
4. "Staphylococcus aureus resistant to vancomycin—United States, 2002." MMWR vl Jul 5; 51(26) 2002. p. 565-67.
5. Garrett, L. "The return of infectious disease." Glob Issues Nov; 1(17) 1996. p. 20-26. Marshall, C., et al. "Methicillin-resistant Staphylococcus aureus and beyond: what's new in the world of the golden staph?" ANZ J Surg Jun; 74(6) 2004. p. 465-69.
6. Finch, R.G., Eliopoulos, G.M. "Safety and efficacy of glycopeptide antibiotics." J Antimicrob Chemother Mar; 55 Suppl 2 2005. p. 5-13.
7. Moellering, R.C., Jr. "The specter of glycopeptide resistance: current trends and future considerations." Am J Med May 29; 104(5A) 1998. p. 3S-6S.
8. Boyle-Vavra, S., Carey, R.B., Daum, R.S. "Development of vancomycin and lysostaphin resistance in a methicillin-resistant Staphylococcus aureus isolate." J Antimicrob Chemother Nov; 48(5) 2001. p. 617-25.
9. Foster, T.J. "The Staphylococcus aureus "superbug."" J Clin Invest Dec; 114(12) 2004. p. 1693-96. Suleyman, F. "New millennium superbugs: a global nightmare." Community Nurse Dec; 5(11) 1999. p. 11-13.
10. Kmietowicz, Z. "WHO warns of threat of "superbugs."" BMJ 320(7250) 2000. p. 1624. Pirnay, J.P., De Vos, D., Zizi, M., Heyman, P. "No easy way to exterminate 'superbugs' at the dawn of the third millennium." Expert Rev Anti Infect Ther Dec; 1(4) 2003. p. 523-25.
11. Campbell, M. "Have we entered the post-antibiotic era?" J AHIMA May; 67(5) 1996. p. 46-48. Domin, M.A. "Highly virulent pathogens—a post antibiotic era?" Br J Theatre Nurs May; 8(2) 1998. p. 14-18.
12. Tomes, N. "The making of a germ panic, then and now." Am J Public Health Feb; 90(2) 2000. p. 191-18. Weinberg, J. "Superbugs: the new Dark Age?" Hosp Med Aug; 59(8) 1998. p. 662.

in Michigan, New Jersey and New York. These patients had received multiple courses of vancomycin for MRSA infections.[1]

VISA strains have been reported from Japan, the United States, Europe and the Far East[2]. Although widespread, these nosocomial infections have not yet been observed in US hospitals or in Europe, GISA strains occur with abundance in Japanese hospitals.[3] This may explain the frequent failure of vancomycin treatment for MRSA infection in this country.[4] The appearance of this isolate signals a dangerous new development.[5] That's because, since the emergence of MRSA in the 1980s, vancomycin has been the drug of choice for treating serious MRSA infections.

The emergence of VISA only briefly predated the arrival of *S. aureus* fully resistant to vancomycin (VRSA).[6] If this strain becomes established, it will leave clinicians with virtually no antibiotic to combat this microbe.[7] Whether these GISA strains will become more widespread or evolve into fully glycopeptide resistant strains is unknown at this time.[8] Fortunately, clinical infections involving *Staphylococcus aureus* with high level resistance to glycopeptide antibiotics (VRSA) are still relatively rare.[9] VRSA develops when *Staphylococcus aureus* acquires a gene for vancomycin resistance (vanA gene) from vancomycin resistant enterococci (VRE). Infections caused by *S. aureus* with intermediate resistance to glycopeptides (VISA) are more common because they do not require the transfer of genetic material.[10] Medical researchers were especially alarmed when they discovered vancomycin resistance may occur by several

13. Turco TF, Melko GP, Williams JR. Vancomycin intermediate-resistant Staphylococcus aureus. Ann Pharmacother. 1998 Jul-Aug; 32(7-8):758-60.
1. Hamilton-Miller, J.M. "Vancomycin-resistant Staphylococcus aureus: a real and present danger?" Infection Jun; 30(3) 2002. p. 118-24. Howe, R.A., et al. "Vancomycin susceptibility within methi-cillin-resistant Staphylococcus aureus lineages." Emerg Infect Dis May; 10(5) 2004. p. 855-57.
2. Rybak, M.J., et al. "Clinical isolates of Staphylococcus aureus from 1987 and 1989 demonstrating heterogeneous resistance to vancomycin and teicoplanin." Diagn Microbiol Infect Dis Feb; 51(2) 2005. p. 119-25.
3. Hiramatsu, K., et al. "Dissemination in Japanese hospitals of strains of Staphylococcus aureus heterogeneously resistant to vancomycin." Lancet 1997; 350: vol 350 1997. p. 1670-73. Tenover, F.C., Biddle, J.W., Lancaster, M.V. "Increasing resistance to vancomycin and other glycopeptides in Staphylococcus aureus." Emerg Infect Dis Mar-Apr; 7(2) 2001. p. 327-32.
4. Inaba, Y., Hiramatsu, K. "[Emergence of hetero-VRSA strains in Japanese hospitals and its coun-termeasure]." Nippon Rinsho Oct; 56(10) 1998. p. 2699-705. Tenover, F.C. "Implications of vanco-mycin-resistant Staphylococcus aureus." J Hosp Infect 43 1999. p. S3-7.
5. Howe, R.A., et al. "Vancomycin susceptibility within methicillin-resistant Staphylococcus aureus lineages." Emerg Infect Dis May; 10(5) 2004. p. 855-57. Miller, N.C., Rudoy, R.C. "Vancomycin intermediate-resistant Staphylococcus aureus (VISA)." Orthop Nurs Nov-Dec; 19(6) 2000. p. 45-48.
6. "Staphylococcus aureus with reduced susceptibility to vancomycin—Illinois, 1999." MMWR Jan 7; 48(51-52) 2000. p. 1165-7.
7. "Update: Staphylococcus aureus with reduced susceptibility to vancomycin—United States, 1997." MMWR Sep 5; 46(35) 1997. p. 813-15. Domin, M.A. "Highly virulent pathogens—a post antibiotic era?" Br J Theatre Nurs May; 8(2) 1998. p. 14-18.
8. Rybak, M.J., Akins, R.L. "Emergence of methicillin-resistant Staphylococcus aureus with interme-diate glycopeptide resistance: clinical significance and treatment options." Drugs 61(1) 2001. p. 1-7.
9. Cosgrove, S.E., Carroll, K.C., Perl, T.M. "Staphylococcus aureus with reduced susceptibility to vancomycin." Clin Infect Dis Aug 15; 39(4) 2004. p. 539-45.
10. Ruef, C. "Epidemiology and clinical impact of glycopeptide resistance in Staphylococcus aureus." Infection Dec; 32(6) 2004. p. 315-27.

mechanisms. One study found resistance to vancomycin was different in each of the vancomycin resistant strains they evaluated.[1]

Recently, new antibiotics have been released that add to the armamentarium for therapy against MRSA and include linezolid, and quinupristin/dalfopristin, but cost, side effects, and resistance may limit their long term usefulness.[2] The new emphasis has been on curbing the irrational overuse of vancomycin and teicoplanin in a hospital with high methicillin resistant S. aureus infection rates.[3] Other recent studies have focused on controlling the spread of these infectious agents. They point out that the vast majority of patients with MRSA have had frequent contact with health care providers. Failure to wash hands and disinfect equipment between patients, which has been commonly seen in studies of health care worker compliance with infection control measures, may explain much of the continuing spread. They liken the spread of drug resistant bacteria to an iceberg, with clinically obvious infections representing the tip of the iceberg and most of the spread coming from clinically unapparent colonized patients who represent most of the reservoir for transmission.[4]

The words of a leading researcher are quoted in their entirety; "The lessons of the antibiotic era are crystal clear: in the footrace between humans and microbes, the organisms' genetic repertoire and efficient response to environmental changes will win the day. New antibiotics are essential, but their shelf life will be enhanced only if used wisely and sparingly. The antibiotic era is continually threatened by inappropriate decisions regarding use, inappropriate choices, and unnecessary durations of treatment."[5]

DIRTY TALK

> *Cleanliness is indeed next to godliness.*
> *John Wesley 1703-1791, founder of the Methodist Church*

The most common means of transmission of bacteria in a hospital setting is via contact with the contaminated hands of healthcare staff.[6] Around 10% of

1. Gemmell, C.G. "Glycopeptide resistance in Staphylococcus aureus: is it a real threat?" J Infect Chemother Apr; 10(2) 2004. p. 69-75.
2. Haddadin, A.S., Fappiano, S.A., Lipsett, P.A. "Methicillin resistant Staphylococcus aureus (MRSA) in the intensive care unit." Postgrad Med J Jul; 78(921) 2002. p. 385-92.
3. Kumana, C.R., et al. "Curtailing unnecessary vancomycin usage in a hospital with high rates of methicillin resistant Staphylococcus aureus infections." Br J Clin Pharmacol Oct; 52(4) 2001. p. 427-32.
4. Farr, B.M. "Methicillin-Resistant Staphylococcus aureus Infections." Curr Infect Dis Rep Oct; 1(4) 1999. p. 328-33.
5. Wenzel, R.P., Edmond, M.B. "Vancomycin-resistant Staphylococcus aureus: infection control considerations." Clin Infect Dis Aug; 27(2) 1998. p. 245-49.
6. Barbacane, J.L. "Back to the basics: Handwashing." Geriatr Nurs Mar-Apr; 25(2) 2004. p. 90-92. Katz, J.D. "Hand washing and hand disinfection: more than your mother taught you." Anesthesiol Clin North America Sep; 22(3) 2004. p. 457-71.

hospital patients acquire a healthcare-associated infections and it has been estimated approximately one-third of these could be prevented.[1] Mathematical modeling suggests the risk of infection increases proportionately with the number of contacts with healthcare workers.[2] According to the CDC, "the appropriate use of hand washing" by hospital workers could greatly cut down on infections.[3] They report most hospital personnel, including doctors and nurses,[4] don't wash their hands as long or hard as needed to kill germs, with many not bothering to wash their hands at all![5] The Handwashing Liaison Group is emphatic: "an explicit standard [should] be set, that hands should be decontaminated before each patient contact."[6] One study using video cameras found family members and visitors had a 94% hand washing compliance rate prior to entering the ICU. ICU staff had compliance rates of only 71%.[7]

Physicians are notoriously slack[8] with compliance to handwashing policies.[9] An observational study by Johns Hopkins University Medical School on handwashing compliance found significant differences existed among healthcare workers, with MDs being the least likely to wash (15%) as compared to nurses (50%).[10] Multiple studies suggest an average handwashing compliance of less than 50%[11] for all healthcare workers.[12] Other studies find baseline handwashing rates before and after patient contact were 12.4% and 10.6%, respectively.[13] An observational study of medical school students found only an

1. Rickard, N.A. "Hand hygiene: promoting compliance among nurses and health workers." Br J Nurs Apr 8-21; 13(7) 2004. p. 404-10.
2. Cooper, B.S., Medley, G.F., Scott, G.M. "Preliminary analysis of the transmission dynamics of nosocomial infections: stochastic and management effects." J Hosp Infect vol 43 1999. p. 131-147.
3. "CDC's hand washing guidelines." Health Care Food Nutr Focus Jun; 20(6) 2003. p. 1, 3-7.
4. Gould, D. "Hand decontamination." Nurs Times Nov 12-18; 98(46) 2002. p. 48-49. McGuckin, M. "Improving handwashing in hospitals: a patient education and empowerment program." LDI Issue Brief Nov; 7(3) 2001. p. 1-4.
5. Blot, B., et al. "Hand Hygiene in the ICU." Chest vol 117 2000. p. 919-20. Serkey, J.M., Hall, G.S. "Handwashing compliance: what works?" Cleve Clin J Med Apr; 68(4) 2001. p. 325-29, 333-34, 336.
6. Handwashing Liaison Group. "Hand washing." BMJ vol 318 1999. p. 686.
7. Nishimura, S., et al. "Handwashing before entering the intensive care unit: what we learned from continuous video-camera surveillance." Am J Infect Control Aug; 27(4) 1999. p. 367-69.
8. Lipsett, P.A., Swoboda, S.M. "Handwashing compliance depends on professional status." Surg Infect (Larchmt) Fall; 2(3) 2001. p. 241-45.
9. Dorsey, S.T., Cydulka, R.K., Emerman, C'L. "Is handwashing teachable?: failure to improve handwashing behavior in an urban emergency department." Academic Emergency Medicine vol 3 1996. p. 360-65. Pittet D., et al. "Effectiveness of a hospital-wide programme to improve compliance with hand hygiene." Infection Control Programme Oct 14; 356(9238) 2000. p. 1307-12.
10. Lipsett, P.A., Swoboda, S.M. "Handwashing compliance depends on professional status." Surg Infect (Larchmt) Fall; 2(3) 2001. p. 241-45.
11. Pittet, D., Mourouga, P., Perneger, T.V. "Compliance with handwashing in a teaching hospital. Infection Control Program." Ann Intern Med vol 130 1999. p. 126- 30. Watanakunakorn, C., Wang, C. Hazy, J. "An observational study of hand washing and infection control practices by healthcare workers." Infect Control Hosp Epidemiol Nov; 19(11) 1998. p. 858-60.
12. Raboud, J. "Patterns of handwashing behavior and visits to patients on a general medical ward of healthcare workers." Infect Control Hosp Epidemiol Mar; 25(3) 2001. p. 198-02. Sen, R., Keaney, M., Trail, A., Howard, C., Chadwick, P. "Healthcare workers washed their hands on only a third of occasions." BMJ vol 319 1999. p. 518.
13. Tibballs, J. "Teaching hospital medical staff to handwash." Med J Aust Apr 1; 164(7) 1996. p. 395-98.

8.5% compliance rate; handwashing signs increased this rate to a measly 18.3%.[1] All studies have shown physicians consistently fail to wash their hands more than any other healthcare worker.[2] They seldom wash their hand more than 20% of the time after touching patients[3] and average hand-washing duration was less than recommended for all groups.[4] The choice not to wash their hands is voluntary because studies show their compliance increases if they know they are being observed.[5] Hygiene is so poor that studies have shown only a 50% handwashing rate after using the bathroom by healthcare workers.[6]

Handwashing is so simple that we teach our toddlers to do it. Unfortunately, those in a position to cause the greatest harm by omitting this practice routinely[7] choose not to practice this simple yet effective hygienic measure.[8] Various methods have been proposed to increase healthcare worker compliance with infection control policies.[9]

In one study of an electronic measuring system that measured entries and exits from rooms, electronic voice prompting increased the rate of handwashing by 41%. Increased handwashing translated into a 40% reduction in hospital acquired infections.[10]

Up to 20% of organisms may remain on the hands after a five-second wash, so health care workers who are in contact with patients with these infections should wash their hands for at least 30 seconds.[11] Failure to follow simple hygienic measures substantially increases the risk of injury to patients from medical management, and many injuries are the result of substandard care.[12]

1. Feather, A., et al. "'Now please wash your hands': the handwashing behaviour of final MBBS candidates." J Hosp Infect May; 45(1) 2000. p. 62-64.
2. Donowitz, L.G. "Handwashing technique in a pediatric intensive care unit." Am J Dis Child vol 141 1987. p. 683-85. Gould, D. "Can ward-based learning improve infection control?" Nursing Times 1996; 92: vol 92 1996. p. 42-43.
3. Kaplan, L.M., McGuckin, M. "Increasing handwashing compliance with more accessible sinks." Infect Control Aug; 7(8) 1986. p. 408-10.
4. Meengs, M.R., et al. "Hand washing frequency in an emergency department." Ann Emerg Med Jun; 23(6) 1994. p. 1307-12. Roberts, L., Bolton, P., Asman, S. "Compliance of hand washing practices: theory versus practice." Aust Health Rev vol 21(4) 1998. p. 238-44.
5. Pittet, D. et al. "Hand Hygiene among Physicians: Performance, Beliefs, and Perceptions." Annals of Internal Medicine vol 141(1) 2004. p. 1-8. Salemi, C., Canola, M.T., Eck, E.K. "Hand washing and physicians: how to get them together." Infect Control Hosp Epidemiol Jan; 23(1) 2002. p. 32-35.
6. Guinan, M.E., McGuckin-Guinan, M., Sevareid, A. "Who washes hands after using the bathroom?" Am J Infect Control Oct; 25(5) 1997. p. 424-25.
7. Daniels,.IR., Rees, B.I. "Handwashing: simple, but effective.." Ann R Coll Surg Engl Mar; 81(2) 1999. p. 117-18.
8. Fell C. "Hand washing. Simple, cost effective, evidence based... lip service!." Br J Periop Nurs Sep; 10(9) 2000. p. 461-65. Larson ,E.L. "APIC Guidelines for handwashing and hand antisepsis in health care settings." Am J Infect Control vol 23 1995. p. 251-69.
9. Bischoff, W.E., et al. "Handwashing compliance by health care workers: The impact of introducing an accessible, alcohol-based hand antiseptic." Arch Intern Med Apr 10; 160(7) 2000. p. 1017-21.
10. Swoboda, S.M., et al. "Electronic monitoring and voice prompts improve hand hygiene and decrease nosocomial infections in an intermediate care unit." Crit Care Med Feb; 32(2) 2004. p. 358-63.
11. Donoyama, N., et al. "Washing hands before and after performing massages? Changes in bacterial survival count on skin of a massage therapist and a client during massage therapy." J Altern Complement Med Aug; 10(4) 2004. p. 684-86. John, M. "Hand Hygiene: Washing and Disinfection." J Can Dent Assoc vol 66 2000. p. 546-47.

Healthcare workers who don't deal directly with patients still accumulate a load of bacteria, including bacteria that are resistant to most antibiotics. Contamination of a patient's food may occur during consumption by a variety of mechanisms, including contamination with VRE from the hands of the patient or health-care worker.[1]

This situation is remarkably similar to that of Vienna in 1846, where birthing wards had a mortality rate as high as 31%, in sharp contrast to the low mortality rate in the midwives' ward next door. Ignaz Semmelweis was the first physician to identify childbed fever as a hospital-acquired infection caused by invasive techniques and failure to wash hands before attending a birth.[2] He was ignored then, and many continue to ignore his findings.[3]

It is atrocious to acknowledge that one study found that less than 50% of doctors scrub their hands before handling patients. Another study documented hand washing in only 9% of physicians,[4] and yet another documented senior physicians washing their hands only twice during a 21-hour ward shift.[5] Studies show even if they do remember to wash their hands they wash for an average of only 9.5 seconds.[6]

Washing the hands with plain soap and water for less than 10 to 15 seconds has limited efficacy.[7] When questioned, most physicians state they think they remembered to wash hands. One study challenged this belief: physicians' average self-estimate of their own hand-washing rate was 73%, with individual responses ranging from 50% to 95%. Actual recorded observations showed they were a bit off: their actual average hand-washing rate was a pitiful 10%.[8] A similar observational study for nurses found handwashing increased 22% before to 29.9% after interventions. When questioned, nurses felt they were washing appropriately nearly 90% of the time. Another study found 86% of nurses stated

12. Brennan TA. "Incidence of adverse events and negligence in hospitalized patients." NEJM Feb 7; 324(6) 1991. p. 370-376.
1. Afif, W., Huor, P., Brassard, P., Loo, V.G. "Compliance with methicillin-resistant Staphylococcus aureus precautions in a teaching hospital." Am J Infect Control Nov; 30(7) 2002. p. 430-33. McBryde, E.S., Bradley, L.C., Whitby, M., McElwain, D.L. "An investigation of contact transmission of methicillin-resistant Staphylococcus aureus." J Hosp Infect Oct; 58(2) 2004. p. 104-08.
2. Jarvis, W.R. "Handwashing—the Semmelweis lesson forgotten?" Lancet Nov 12; 344(8933) 1994. p. 1311-12.
3. Rotter, M.L. "150 years of hand disinfection, Semmelweis' heritage." Hyg Med vol 22 1997. p. 332-39.
4. Tibballs, J. "Teaching hospital medical staff to handwash." Med J Austral vol 164 1996. p. 395-398.
5. Handwashing Liaison Group. "Hand washing. A modest measure with big effects." BMJ vol 318 1999. p. 686. Null, G. "Iatrogenic Illness: Infection." Gary Null:Your Guide to Natural Living. 2006. Feb 2006 <http://garynull.com/cms/index.php/plain/documents/iatrogenic_illness_33_nosocomial_infection_nbsp>.
6. Meengs, M.R.,et al. "Hand washing frequency in an emergency department." J Emerg Nurs vol 20 1994. p. 183-88. Quraishi, Z.A., McGuckin, M., Blais, F.X. "Duration of handwashing in intensive care units: a descriptive study." Am J Infect Control vol 12 1984. p. 83-87.
7. Boyce, J.M. "It Is Time for Action: Improving Hand Hygiene in Hospitals." Annals of Internal Medicine vol 130 1999. p. 153-55. Larson, E.L., Eke, P.I., Wilder, M.P., Laughon, B.E. "Quantity of soap as a variable in handwashing." Infect Control 8 1987. p. 37-75.
8. Tibballs, J. "Teaching Medical Staff to Handwash." Medical Journal of Australia vol 164 1996. p. 395.

they treat each patient as if they are carrying an infectious pathogen compared with 41% of doctors.[1] These findings have been reflected by other studies.[2] The apparent difference in handwashing rates between men and women may account for the differences in handwashing behavior that some observers have reported for nurses and doctors, among whom one or other sex predominates.[3]

How do you think the medical profession deals with dissenters, are they really concerned with all this fuss about hand washing? Historical facts would say otherwise. Even before Lister or Pasteur, Ignaz Semmelweis realized medical students used their "examining finger which introduces the cadaveric particles" after performing autopsies. This resulted in a surgical floor death three times that of the midwives floor.[4] Medical students were required to wash their hands with chlorine and soap solution prior to performing vaginal exams. After implementation of basic hand washing the death rate plummeted to less than that of the midwives floor, reducing mortality due to streptococcal puerperal sepsis from 22% to 3%.[5] Was he celebrated as a hero? No, his reward was that he was driven from the medical profession and forced to warn the public of the dangers of unwashed hands, by handing out pamphlets on the street corners. He was arrested, placed in a home for the insane and beaten so severely by the guards that he died only thirteen days after his commitment. According to the autopsy report, "It is obvious that these horrible injuries were... the consequences of brutal beating, tying down, trampling underfoot."[6] This is historically how medicine has dealt with dissenters.[7]

Over a century has passed since Semmelweis demonstrated the association between hand hygiene and nosocomial infections, but this simple procedure is still not recognized by many healthcare workers as one of the most important measures to prevent cross-transmission of microorganisms.[8] One author suggests some health professionals suffer from the "Omo syndrome", a belief that

1. Stein, A.D., Makarawo, T.P., Ahmad, M.F. "A survey of doctors' and nurses' knowledge, attitudes and compliance with infection control guidelines in Birmingham teaching hospitals." J Hosp Infect May; 54(1) 2003. p. 68-73.
2. Gould, D. "Nurses' hand decontamination practice; results of a local study." J Hosp Infect vol 28 1995. p. 15-20. Harris,.AD., et al. "A survey on handwashing practices and opinions of healthcare workers." J Hosp Infect Aug; 45(4) 2000. p. 318-21.
3. Dorsey, S.T., Cydulka, R.K., Emerman, C.L. "Is hand washing teachable? Failure to improve hand washing behaviour in an urban emergency department." Acad Emerg Med vol 3 1996. p. 360-65.
4. Greger, M. "Appendix 62a — Semmelweis." Heart Failure — Diary of a Third Year Medical Student. 1999 ⟨http://upalumni.org/medschool/appendices/appendix-62a.html#fn730⟩. Rotter, M.L. "150 years of hand disinfection Semmelweis' heritage." Hyg Med 22 1997. p. 332-39.
5. Elek, S.D. "Semmelweis and the Oath of Hippocrates." Proceedings of the Royal Society of Medicine vol 59 1966. p. 346-52. Jarvis, W.R. "Handwashing—the Semmelweis lesson forgotten?" Lancet Nov 12; 344(8933) 1994. p. 1311-12.
6. Carter, K.S., Abbott, S., Siebach, J.L. "Five Documents Relating to the Final Illness and Death of Ignaz Semmelweis." Bulletin of the History of Medicine vol 69 1995. p. 255-70.
7. Grossl, N.A. "The reluctant acceptance of new ideas in medicine." Pharos Alpha Omega Alpha Honor Med Soc Winter; 65(1) 2002. p. 18-22. Pritchard, R.C., Raper, R.F. "Doctors and handwashing: instilling Semmelweis' message." Medical Journal of Australia vol 164 1996. p. 389-90.
8. Hugonnet, S., Pittet, D. "Hand hygiene-beliefs or science?" Clin Microbiol Infect Jul; 6(7) 2000. p. 350-56. Pritchard, V., Hathaway, C. "Patient handwashing practice." Nursing Times vol 84 1988. p. 68-72.

they are always super clean and sterile.[1] Many are visibly upset when their poor hygiene practices are exposed and are offended when it is suggested they may be potential vectors of disease and are spreading virulent microorganisms among their patients.[2] The remark of one physician to the editors of a medical journal succinctly exemplifies the feelings of some within the medical community. They are so extraordinary that I have chosen to quote them in their entirety as follows: "EDITOR — The editorial on hand washing calls for all hospital staff to start regularly washing their hands between each patient contact. If, as the authors claim, there is such compelling evidence for the need to wash hands between each patient contact then why do I and the vast majority of my colleagues not do it? Firstly, I have never seen any convincing evidence that hand washing between each patient contact reduces infection rates. The Handwashing Liaison Group assumes that we all know that hand washing is beneficial and therefore fails to put forward any evidence for it. It seems self evident that hand washing should be beneficial before and after a person has performed any procedures, examined wounds, or dealt with specifically high risk patients, but I have never seen any evidence for it in other situations. I shake hands with patients when I see them in hospital. Should I not do this, or should I wash my hands before and after each contact? Should patients be discouraged from social contacts with each other? Where is the evidence? Secondly, I have maybe 60 "touch" contacts with patients each day, and many more with relatives. Washing hands between each contact (at 1-2 minutes per wash) would take on average 1-2 hours. Where will this time come from, and who will fund it? If hand washing is to be performed between every patient contact then it would have major resource implications. For this it needs to be shown to be effective and worth the 15% extra staffing that would be needed to cover the extra time."[3] These reactions have prompted the authors of one paper to express astonishment that "doctors can be so extraordinarily self-delusional about their behaviour."[4] This physician would probably be unwilling to reveal to his patients his penchant for poor hygiene since most cultures consider handwashing is a form of respect.

Healthcare workers routinely ignore opportunities to reduce the risk of nosocomial infections. Education programs have had little long-term impact on increasing compliance to handwashing guidelines. One study found providing feedback to staff regarding the frequency of hand washing improved compliance by 92%. However, compliance quickly returned to baseline levels when feedback was stopped.[5] Many try to use gloves as substitute for handwashing. A 2004

1. Saloojee, H., Steenhoff, A. "The health professional's role in preventing nosocomial infections." Postgrad Med vol 77 2001. p. 16-19.
2. Ibid.
3. "Hand washing Why I don't wash my hands between each patient contact." BMJ vol 319 1999. p. 518.
4. Pritchard, R.C., Raper, R.F. "Doctors and handwashing: instilling Semmelweis' message." Med J Austral vol 164 1996. p. 389-90.
5. Larson, E.L., et al. "A multifaceted approach to changing handwashing behaviour." Am J Infect Control vol 25 1997. p. 3-10.

study found glove use reduced compliance with handwashing protocols by as much as 25%. They also agreed with other studies that showed increased accessibility to sinks did not improve healthcare workers' handwashing compliance.[1] Other studies found some healthcare workers did not change their gloves between each patient contact increasing the risk of cross-infection.[2] Efforts as diverse as automated sinks[3], asking patients to remind staff to wash their hands[4], increasing the number of sinks, moving to a new facility and relying upon peer pressure[5] have all had little lasting impact on increasing handwashing compliance. Basic hygienic principles must not only be taught but enforced by physician role models.[6] Studies of heavy workload may partially vindicate some non-compliance by nursing staff;[7] unfortunately, they have other voluntary behaviors that exacerbate the spread of nosocomial infections. Healthcare staff horrified by lice on a patient may use every means at their disposal to avoid infection, yet may ignore the potentially far more serious consequences of bacteria present on their hands.

Artificial nails are a known health hazard.[8] Their use has been implicated in the spread of infections[9] and contributes to increases in hospital mortality.[10] There have been calls for their discontinuance[11] and an out right ban.[12] Yet, their

1. Vernon, M.O., et al. "Adherence with hand hygiene: does number of sinks matter?" Infect Control Hosp Epidemiol Mar; 24(3) 2003. p. 224-25. Whitby, M., McLaws, M.L. "Handwashing in health-care workers: accessibility of sink location does not improve compliance." J Hosp Infect Dec; 58(4) 2004. p. 247-53.
2. Girou, E., et al. "Misuse of gloves: the foundation for poor compliance with hand hygiene and potential for microbial transmission?" J Hosp Infect Jun; 57(2) 2004. p. 162-69. Hampton, S. "Nurses' inappropriate use of gloves in caring for patients." Br J Nurs Sep 25-Oct 8; 12(17) 2003. p. 1024-27.
3. Naikoba, S., Hayward, A. "The effectiveness of interventions aimed at increasing handwashing in healthcare workers — a systematic review." J Hosp Infect Mar; 47(3) 2001. p. 173-80. Wurtz, R., Moye, G., Jovanovic, B. "Handwashing machines, handwashing compliance, and potential for cross-contamination.." Am J Infect Control Aug; 22(4) 1994. p. 228-30.
4. Boodman, S.G. "Medicine's dirty little secret." Washington Post 30 Sep 1997.
5. Muto, C.A., Sistrom, M.G., Farr, B.M. "Hand hygiene rates unaffected by installation of dispensers of a rapidly acting hand antiseptic." Am J Infect Control Jun; 28(3) 2000. p. 273-76.
6. Emmerson, A.M., Ridgway, G.L. "Teaching asepsis to medical students." J Hosp Infection 1 1980. p. 289-92. Larson, E., et al. "Physiological, microbiologic and seasonal effects of handwashing on the skin of health care personnel." Am J Infection Control vol 14 1986. p. 51-59.
7. Al-Damouk, M., Pudney, E., Bleetman, A. "Hand hygiene and aseptic technique in the emergency department." J Hosp Infect Feb; 56(2) 2004. p. 137-41. Gould, D., Wilson, B., Ream, E. "Nurses' infection-control practice: hand decontamination, the use of gloves and sharp instruments." Int J Nurs Stud vol 33 1996. p. 143-60.
8. McNeil, S.A., Foster, C.L., Hedderwick, S.A., Kauffman, C.A. "Effect of hand cleansing with anti-microbial soap or alcohol-based gel on microbial colonization of artificial fingernails worn by health care workers." Clin Infect Dis Feb 1; 32(3) 2001. p. 367-72. Porteous, J. "Artificial nails... very real risks." Can Oper Room Nurs J Sep; 20(3):1 2002. p. 6-7, 20-21.
9. Hedderwick, S.A., McNeil, S.A., Lyons, M.J., Kauffman, C.A. "Pathogenic organisms associated with artificial fingernails worn by healthcare workers." Infect Control Hosp Epidemiol Aug; 21(8) 2000. p. 505-09. Toles, A. "Artificial nails: are they putting patients at risk? A review of the research." J Pediatr Oncol Nurs Sep-Oct; 19(5) 2002. p. 164-71.
10. Gupta, A., et al. "Outbreak of extended-spectrum beta-lactamase-producing Klebsiella pneumoniae in a neonatal intensive care unit linked to artificial nails." Infect Control Hosp Epidemiol Mar; 25(3) 2004. p. 210-15. Winslow, E.H., Jacobson, A.F. "Can a fashion statement harm the patient? Long and artificial nails may cause nosocomial infections." Am J Nurs Sep; 100(9 2000. p. 63-65.
11. Sullivan, E,E. "Off with her nails." J Perianesth Nurs Dec; 18(6) 2003. p. 417-18.

prevalence among nursing staff shows their basic disregard for patient safety. Rings have also been show to reduce the effectiveness of hand washing and pose substantial risks especially for the surgical patient.[1]

In one chilling study, healthcare workers were surveyed to determine what measure would be most effective in improving compliance. The authors reported 76% of those surveyed stated rewards for handwashing would have no effect and 73% stated punishment would have no effect. Eighty percent believed easy access to sinks and washing facilities would lead to increased compliance; however other studies found no benefit with increased access.[2] This survey suggests healthcare workers understand the importance of handwashing, but willfully choose not to comply.[3]

A study on dermatitis found hand washing more than 35 times per shift was strongly associated with occupational hand dermatitis[4]. Concerns about hand-washing associated dermatitis may be valid for nursing staff; however most physicians' poor hygienic habits make them low risk. Even these concerns may be abated by using alcohol-based hand-rubs. Recent studies have found these alcohol based systems are superior to handwashing with soap and water. It also requires less time, acts faster, irritates hands less often, and recently proved significantly to contribute to sustained improvement in compliance associated with decreased infection rates.[5] Alcohol hand rubs are quick to use (10-20 instead of 90-120 seconds) and can be used while walking and talking. Thus they may overcome objections to hand washing, including lack of time, lack of sinks, and skin damage.[6]

12. Church, N. "Ban on artificial nails recommended for anyone having direct patient contact." Oreg Nurse Feb; 68(1) 2003. p. 5. Saiman L, et al. "Banning artificial nails from health care settings." Am J Infect Control Jun; 30(4) 2002. p. 252-54.
1. Bernthal, E. "Wedding rings and hospital-acquired infection." Nurs Stand Jul 16; 11(43) 1997. p. 44-46. Salisbury DM, et al. "The effect of rings on microbial load of health care workers' hands." Am J Infect Control vol 25 1997. p. 24-27.
2. Vernon, M.O., et al. "Adherence with hand hygiene: does number of sinks matter? " Infect Control Hosp Epidemiol Mar; 24(3) 2003. p. 224-25. Whitby, M., McLaws, M.L. "Handwashing in health-care workers: accessibility of sink location does not improve compliance." J Hosp Infect Dec; 58(4) 2004. p. 247-53.
3. Harris, A.D., et al. "A survey on handwashing practices and opinions of healthcare workers." J Hosp Infect Aug; 45(4) 2000. p. 318-21.
4. Forrester, B.G., Roth, V.S. "Hand dermatitis in intensive care units." J Occup Environ Med vol 40 1998. p. 881-85.
5. Boyce, J.M., Kelliher, S., Vallande, N. "Skin irritation and dryness associated with two hand-hygiene regimens: soap-and-water hand washing versus hand antisepsis with an alcoholic hand gel." Infect Control Hosp Epidemiol Jul; 21(7) 2000. p. 442-48. Girou, E., et al. "Efficacy of handrubbing with alcohol based solution versus standard handwashing with antiseptic soap: randomised clinical trial." BMJ Aug 17; 325(7360) 2002. p. 362.
6. Boyce, J.M., Kelliher, S., Vallande, N. "Skin irritation and dryness associated with two hand-hygiene regimens: soap-and-water handwashing versus hand antisepsis with an alcoholic hand gel." Infect Control Hosp Epidemiol vol 21 2000. p. 442-48. Stone, S.P., Teare, L., Cookson, B.D. "The evidence for hand-hygiene." Lancet vol 357 2001. p. 479-80.

BAD BLOOD

For the life of the flesh is in the blood
Leviticus 17:11

It has been estimated that over 4.7 million Americans are anemic.[1] The causes of their anemia may be either chronic (for example those with kidney disease) or acute (trauma or bleeding ulcers). The consequences of anemia can be debilitating or even life threatening, therefore, transfusion may be a medical necessity. Thousands of lives are saved every year by prompt resuscitation with blood products.[2] However, a transfusion with blood or blood products has its own associated risk.[3] Physicians and researchers know each unit transfused places the recipient in some degree of peril.[4] The Red Cross and other transfusion services work diligently to minimize any hazard associated the receipt of blood products. Unfortunately, they are not able to remove all the hazards associated with transfusion.[5] The medical system attempts to limit their liability of complications associated with transfusion by obtaining informed consent prior to all but emergent transfusions.[6] About 0.5% to 3% of all transfusions result in some adverse events, but the majority of them are minor reactions with no significant consequences. In general, transfusion-related adverse events are categorized as infectious and noninfectious.[7]

Most are familiar with the threats of contacting AIDS[8] or hepatitis.[9] Although rare, infections associated with blood transfusions are a real risk[10] and have been associated with increased mortality.[11] Bacterial contamination of blood transfusions has been a problem since its inception and is probably the most common cause for concern. Transfusion-associated blood infections are

1. Brill, J.R., Baumgardner, D.J. "Normocytic Anemia." American Academy of Family Physicians. 2000. 15 Nov 2000 ‹www.aafp.org/afp/20001115/2255.html›.
2. US. American Association Of Blood Banks. Facts About Blood and Blood Banking. Bethesda, MD, 1998. Wilkinson, J., Wilkinson, C. "Administration of blood transfusions to adults in general hospital settings: a review of the literature." J Clin Nurs Mar; 10(2) 2001. p. 161-70.
3. Higgins, C. "Blood transfusion: risks and benefits." Br J Nurs Oct 27-Nov 9; 3(19) 1994. p. 986-91.
4. Atterbury, C., Wilkinson, J. "Blood transfusion." Nurs Stand May 10-16; 14(34) 2000. p. 47-52. Sloop, G.D., Friedberg, R.C. "Complications of blood transfusion: How to recognize and respond to noninfectious reactions." Postgrad Med vol 98 1995. p. 159-72.
5. Murphy, W.G. "Disease Transmission by Blood Products: Past, Present and Future." Pathophysiology of Haemostasis and Thrombosis vol 32 2002. p. 1-4.
6. Kolins, K.J. "Informed consent, risk, and blood transfusion." J Thorac Cardiovasc Surg Jul; 100(1) 1990. p. 88-91.
7. US. American Association Of Blood Banks. Standards for Blood Banks and transfusion Services. ed 18.. Bethesda, MD, 1997
8. Carson, J.L., et al. "The risks of blood transfusion: the relative influence of acquired immunodeficiency syndrome and non-A, non-B hepatitis.." Am J Med vol 92 1992. p. 45-52. Uhl, L. "Infectious risks of blood transfusion." Curr Hematol Rep Nov; 1(2) 2002. p. 156-62.
9. Faust, R.J., Warner, M.A. "Transfusion risks." Int Anesthesiol Clin Fall; 28(4) 1990. p. 184-89. Murphy, E.L., Busch, M.P., Tong, M., Cornett, P., Vyas, G.N. "A prospective study of the risk of transfusion-acquired viral infections." Transfus Med Sep; 8(3) 1998. p. 173-78.
10. Pomper, G.J., Wu, Y., Snyder, E.L. "Risks of transfusion-transmitted infections." Curr Opin Hematol Nov; 10(6) 2003. p. 412-18.
11. Dodd, R.Y. "The risk of transfusion-transmitted infection." NEJM vol 327 1992. p. 419-21. Labovich, T.M. "Transfusion therapy." Clin J Oncol vol 1 1997. p. 61-72.

more common from contaminated platelets than from red cells.[1] A Johns Hopkins study showed complications associated with bacterial contamination were reduced from 1 in 5000 to 1 in 15 000 transfusions using platelets purified to remove red blood cells.[2] A 2002 study concluded approximately one in 3000 blood products has bacterial contamination.[3] A 2000 British study found no incidence of transmitted infections in 21,923 units of transfused blood.[4] The few bacteria contaminating blood generally does little harm. However, transfusion of contaminated products may have a major impact to those weakened by disease or if it is contaminated by a particularly virulent strain of bacteria or virus.[5] Rarely, a unit may contain large numbers of virulent bacteria and their associated endotoxins. Transfusion of grossly contaminated products may significantly increase morbidity and even result in death of the recipient.[6] Fortunately, these grossly contaminated products are extremely rare. One study suggests they occur in only one in 50,000 units of platelets and one in 500,000 units of red cell.[7]

Pseudomonas, Citrobacter freundii, Escherichia coli, and *Yersinia enterocolitica* are the most common causes of bacteria contaminated blood.[8] However, reports of transfusion acquired human immunodeficiency virus (HIV), hepatitis,[9] malaria,[10] babesiosis,[11] Chagas' disease,[12] Cytomegalovirus,[13] West Nile Virus,[14] variant Creutzfeldt-Jakob Disease (vCJD),[15] and *Leishmaniasis*[16] have been documented.

1. Klein, H.G., et al. "Current status of microbial contamination of blood components: summary of a conference." Transfusion vol 37 1997. p. 95-101.
2. Ness, P.M., et al. "Single donor platelets reduce the risk of septic transfusion reactions." Transfusion vol 39 1999. p. 89S.
3. Blajchman, M.A. "Incidence and significance of the bacterial contamination of blood components." Dev Biol (Basel) vol 108 2002. p. 59-67.
4. Regan, F.A., et al.. "Prospective investigation of transfusion transmitted infection in recipients of over 20 000 units of blood." BMJ vol 320 2000. p. 403-406.
5. Depcik-Smith, N.D., Hay, S.N., Brecher, M.E. "Bacterial contamination of blood products: factors, options, and insights." J Clin Apheresis vol 16(4) 2001. p. 192-201. Vasconcelos, E., Seghatchian, J. "Bacterial contamination in blood components and preventative strategies: an overview." Transfus Apheresis Sci Oct; 31(2) 2004. p. 155-63.
6. Wagner, S.J., Friedman, L.I., Dodd, R.Y. "Transfusion-associated bacterial sepsis." Clin Microbiol Rev Jul; 7(3) 1994. p. 290-302.
7. Blajchman, M.A. "Reducing the risk of bacterial contamination of cellular blood components." Advances in Transfusion Safety, Dev Biol vol 102 1999. p. 183-93.
8. Sloop, G.D., Friedberg, R.C. "Complications of blood transfusion: How to recognize and respond to noninfectious reactions." Postgrad Med vol 98 1995. p. 159-72.
9. Alter, M.J., et al. "The prevalence of hepatitis C virus infection in the United States, 1988 through 1994." NEJM vol 341 1999. p. 556-62.
10. "Transfusion-Transmitted Malaria." CDC, Division of Media Relations. 02 Apr 1999 ⟨http://www.cdc.gov/malaria/faq.htm⟩.
11. L. Pantanowitz, L., Telford, S.R., III Cannon, M.E. "Tick-borne diseases in transfusion medicine." Transfusion Medicine vol 12(2) 2002. p. 85.
12. Schmunis, G.A. "Trypanosoma cruzi, the etiologic agent of Chagas' disease: Status in the blood supply in endemic and nonendemic countries." Transfusion vol 31 1991. p. 547-57.
13. Nichols, W.G., et al. "Transfusion-transmitted cytomegalovirus infection after receipt of leukoreduced blood products." Blood May 15; 101(10) 2003. p. 4195-200.
14. Kleinman, S., et al. "The 2003 West Nile virus United States epidemic: the America's Blood Centers experience.." Transfusion Apr 1; 45(4) 2005. p. 469-79.
15. Sibbald, B. "UK patient first to contract vCJD via blood transfusion." CMAJ Mar 30; 170(7) 2004. p. 1087.

HIV and hepatitis are the most significant viral infections associated with blood transfusions. Hepatitis C is of special concern because it is transmitted primarily through contaminated blood.[1] It is a leading cause of chronic liver disease worldwide. However, one study concluded nearly 50% of all Hepatitis C infections have no identifiable means of transmission or route.[2] Although the risk of receiving a bacterially contaminated blood product is greater than that of viral infected blood, viral infections may have more devastating consequences. HIV contaminated blood products in France[3] and Canada[4] resulted in thousand of hemophiliacs being diagnosed with AIDS in these countries. The ensuing trials of bureaucrats exposed the weaknesses within the system and resulted in many improvements with the collection and storage of blood.[5] The failings of the world's transfusion services were tragically exposed during the late 1980s and early 1990s. Many supposedly advanced nations were shocked when they discovered thousands of otherwise healthy people were now infected with HIV or Hepatitis as the result of "routine" blood transfusions.[6] Governments tried to blame pharmaceutical firms who were trying to blame blood collection agencies. This debacle left tens of thousands infected with either HIV or hepatitis worldwide. The survivors of this fiasco were left with little recourse other than the courts.[7]

Although the system has been greatly improved over the past two decades, risks still remain. One paper by hematologists at Emory University states bacterial contamination is still responsible for death rates of 1:20000 to 1:85000 per donor exposures.[8] Although these rates may initially seem low, these numbers don't stress the fact that most recipients of blood receive products from multiple donors. It is uncommon for an individual to receive only one unit of blood. Products like platelets or clotting factors may be derived from 6 or more donors. Patients with chronic anemia require transfusion more than once. The repeated exposure to blood products from multiple donors on multiple

16. Mathur, P., Samantaray, J.C. "The first probable case of platelet transfusion-transmitted visceral leishmaniasis." Transfus Med Aug; 14(4) 2004. p. 319-21.
1. Memon, M.I., Memon, M,A. "Hepatitis C: an epidemiological review." J Viral Hepat Mar; 9(2) 2002. p. 84-100..
2. Sharara, A.I. "Chronic hepatitis C." South Med J Sep; 90(9) 1997. p. 872-77.
3. Courouce AM. "A prospective study of HIV-2 prevalence in France." AIDS Aug; 2(4) 1988. p. 261-65.
4. Allaire SL. "Traceback of a case of acquired immune deficiency syndrome related to a blood transfusion." CMAJ Apr 1; 138(7) 1988. p. 630-32.
5. "Alex Lefebvre France: Court dismisses charges in tainted blood scandal." WSWS. Jun 2003 ⟨http://www.wsws.org/articles/2003/jun2003/fran-j28.shtml⟩. "Former French ministers go on trial in AIDS blood scandal." CNN. ⟨ http://www.cnn.com/WORLD/europe/9902/07/france.blood/⟩.
6. Tempest, R. "Transfusions AIDS-Tainted; Doctors on Trial France: Hemophiliacs say they were given bad blood after U.S. perfected treatment processes. A political cover-up is charged. Rone Tempest; Times Staff Writer." Los Angeles Times 21 Jul 1992.
7. "Canadian inquiry assesses blame for tainted blood supply." AIDS Policy Law Dec 26; 12(22) 1997. p. 16. Coles, P. "French haemophiliacs awarded damages." Nature Jul 27; 340(6231) 1989. p. 253.
8. Hillyer, C.D., et al. "Bacterial contamination of blood components: risks, strategies, and regulation: joint ASH and AABB educational session in transfusion medicine." Hematology (Am Soc Hematol Educ Program) 2003. p. 575-89.

occasions will quickly inflate your risks to an appreciable level. Prompt refrigeration has decreased the incidence of bacterial infections from blood products[1] and newer more reliable screening methods have improved the detection of donors positive for hepatitis and AIDS. However, detection of newer strains of hepatitis remains problematic[2] and the risk of AIDS, although extremely rare, is still ever present.[3] One study concluded the risk of transfusion-transmitted HIV is 1 in 450,000 to 660,000 cases. Another study determined AIDS contaminated blood may occur in people who are just recently infected by HIV. They recommend against soliciting blood from high risk groups.[4]

The emergence of more exotic diseases has further challenged the safety of the world's blood supplies.[5] These "emerging diseases" may be even more frightening than HIV or hepatitis. More than 18 million people in Mexico, Central and South America are infected with a parasitic disease called Chagas' disease.[6] Medical authorities estimate 50,000 deaths per year as a result of this infection.[7] A 1992 paper revealed that 20,000 cases of Chagas' disease had been contracted via blood transfusion in Brazil alone.[8] Public health experts are especially concerned because a test was not available until 2004 and widespread screening has yet to be implemented.[9] Increasing rates of immigration from Latin America certainly makes older estimates of 25,000–100,000 Chagas-infected Latin American immigrants living in the United States outdated.[10] A 2002 study of over a million donors from Los Angeles and Miami found 7.3 and 14.3% were considered high risk donors, respectively. Laboratory tests confirm that 1 in 7,500 Los Angeles and 1 in 9,000 Miami donors tested positive for antibodies for Chagas disease.[11] Although, only nine cases are KNOWN to have

1. Gibb, A.P., et al. "Rate of growth of Pseudomonas fluorescens in donated blood." J Clin Pathol Aug; 48(8) 1995. p. 717-18.
2. Kelly, D., Skidmore, S. "Hepatitis C-Z: recent advances." Arch Dis Child May; 86(5) 2002. p. 339-43.
3. Litvak, E., et al. "Whose blood is safer? The effect of the stage of the epidemic on screening for HIV." Med Decis Making Oct-Dec; 17(4) 1997. p. 455-63.
4. "Blood Products Advisory Committee 57th Meeting." FDA. 1997 <http://www.fda.gov/ohrms/dockets/ac/97/transcpt/3361t1.pdf>. AABB Advocates Change for Policy Regarding Men Who Have Sex with Another Man Even One Time Since 1977. <http://www.aabb.org/Pressroom/Press_Releases/pr091400.htm>.
5. Chamberland, et al.. "Blood Safety Emerging Infectious Diseases." CDC. 1998. Jul-Sep 1998 <http://www.cdc.gov/ncidod/EID/vol4no3/chambrln.htm>.
6. Tostes. S., Jr, et al. "Myocardiocyte apoptosis in heart failure in chronic Chagas' disease." Int J Cardiol Mar 18; 99(2) 2005. p. 233-37. Williams-Blangero, S., et al. "Genetic epidemiology of Trypanosoma cruzi infection and Chagas' disease." Front Biosci May 1; 8:e 2003. p. 337-45.
7. Eickhoff, C.S., Eckmann, L., Hoft, D.F. "Differential Interleukin-8 and Nitric Oxide Production in Epithelial Cells Induced by Mucosally Invasive and Noninvasive Trypanosoma cruzi Trypomastigotes." Infect Immun September; 71(9) 2003. p. 5394-97. Goiânia, G.O. "Sudden Death in Chagas' Disease." Arq. Bras. Cardiol. vol 76(1) 2001.
8. Wendel, S., Brener, Z. "Chagas Disease (American Trypanosomiasis): its Impact on Transfusion and Clinical Medicine." ISBT
9. McNiel, D.G. "Rare Infection Threatens To Spread in Blood Supply." New York Times 18 Nov 2003, Natl ed. Oelemann, W.M.R., Teixeira, M.G.M., Peralta, J.M. "Screening and Confirmation in Chagas Disease Serology." Inst Oswaldo Cruz, vol 94 Suppl. I 1999. p. 307-08.
10. Kirchhoff, L.V., Gam, A.A., Gilliam, F.C. "American trypanosomiasis (Chagas' disease) in Central American immigrants." Am J Med vol 82 1987. p. 915-920.

been transmitted by transfusion or transplant in the United States and Canada in the last 20 years, authorities fear there may be hundreds of blood recipients who are silently infected.[1] There is no known treatment for Chagas disease.[2] Medical researchers warn that symptoms don't appear for a decade or longer. They estimate 10—30% of those infected will die as a consequence of this parasitic infection. Death is generally a result of heart or organ failure.[3] The FDA worries about the influx of immigrants from Latino nations where this disease is relatively common. Its incidence may be as high as 25% of the total population in some South American countries. They consider it "one of the top threats to the blood supply."[4]

The blood supply is also under assault from the Middle East. In 2003, medical authorities implemented a policy to refuse blood donations from the military or those who had recently been to Iraq.[5] They fear these donors may carry a parasitic disease called Leishmaniasis that is spread through the bite of the sand fly. Military donors are told they must wait one year before their blood is no longer considered a risk. Leishmaniasis causes sores or lesions on the skin and at its severest may result in death. Cases of transfusion relayed infection have already been reported from several locations.[6] Health-care providers at Walter Reed Army Medical Center have treated almost 400 patients infected with leishmaniasis since the beginning of Operation Iraqi Freedom.[7]

You would have to be a hermit living in a cave not to know about the newest threat to public health. The medical community is advising the consumer how to protect themselves from West Nile virus. This virus is transmitted through the bite of a mosquito. We are cautioned to stay away from mosquito infested areas, wear mosquito repellant and taught the signs of an infected bite. Nothing is ever said about those living in high risk areas being potential carriers and their risks as donors to our nation's blood supplies.[8]

This concern became more than a theoretical consideration during the summer of 2002 when two different states reported newly diagnosed cases of West Nile virus in blood recipients.[9] The author of one study concluded nearly

11. Leiby DA, et al. "Trypanosoma cruzi in Los Angeles and Miami blood donors: impact of evolving donor demographics on seroprevalence and implications for transfusion transmission." Transfusion May; 42(5) 2002. p. 549-55.
1. McNiel, D.G. "Rare Infection Threatens To Spread in Blood Supply." New York Times 18 Nov 2003, Natl ed.
2. Urbina, J.A., et al. "In vitro and in vivo activities of E5700 and ER-119884, two novel orally active squalene synthase inhibitors, against Trypanosoma cruzi." Antimicrob Agents Chemother Jul; 48(7) 2004. p. 2379-87.
3. Rassi, A. et al. "Sudden Death in Chagas' Disease." FAC. <http://www.fac.org.ar/scvc/llave/chagas/rassi/rassii.htm>.
4. McIlroy, A. "Parasite may pose a risk to blood supply." The Globe and Mail. <http://www.theglobeandmail.com/servlet/ArticleNews/freeheadlines/LAC/20031119/BLOOD19/health/Health>.
5. Sample, D. "Officials halt certain blood donations." Armed Forces Military News. <http://www.af.mil/news/story_print.asp?storyID=123005845>.
6. Mathur, P., Samantaray, J.C. "The first probable case of platelet transfusion-transmitted visceral leishmaniasis." Transfusion Medicine vol 14(4) 2004. p. 319.
7. Army News Service, 10 Mar 2004.
8. Pealer LN et al — 2000 www.nejm.org September 18, 2003. "Transmission of West Nile Virus through Blood Transfusion in the United States." NEJM vol 18 Sep 2003 2003.

500 blood donors were infected by enough virus that they could potentially infect those receiving their blood. A study by the CDC at Fort Collins concluded that in 2002, at least 23 people were infected with West Nile as the result of a blood transfusion. The authors suggest "The 23 is a big underestimate." They believe the number of actual cases may be much higher because "Cases could have gone unrecognized because recipients remained asymptomatic, had West Nile virus-related illnesses that were indistinguishable from their underlying illnesses, or died ... before West Nile virus-related illness developed." First identified in the United States in 1999, West Nile virus caused approximately 3,500 infections in the late summer and fall of 2002.[1] Although the incidence was still low at 1.46 to 12.33 per 10,000 donations the risk is still real.[2] One paper reports 1000 potentially infectious donations were identified and removed from the blood supply during the 2003 season.[3]

An even more chilling threat to the nation's blood supply is a relative of mad cow disease. This infectious particle (medically known as a prion) is called variant Creutzfeldt-Jakob disease (vCJD). Research studies concluded blood products could actually transmit this fatal neurological disorder from infected donors to the hapless recipient.[4] Scientists believe it enters the body of the victim after the eating of products from cows infected with a similar disease, bovine spongiform encephalopathy, also known as mad cow disease. British studies identified 9 donors who developed vCJD after having given blood.[5]

Two studies in the medical journal *The Lancet* explored the implications of blood transfusion as a means of transmitting vCJD and the degree of infectivity of these infectious particles. A French researcher determined the infectivity of the disease remained the same no matter how the prion entered the body. They were especially concerned about the risk of transmission through infected blood donors and recommended "precautionary measures" should be implemented to protect the world's blood supply. One commentator found these results "shocking" but not surprising. As of 2005, 166 cases of vCJD had been reported worldwide.[6] The authors of one study expressed grave concerns about the safety

9. Tobler, L.H. "Detection of West Nile virus RNA and antibody in frozen plasma components from a voluntary market withdrawal during the 2002 peak epidemic." Transfusion Apr; 45(4) 2005. p. 480-86.
1. Armstrong, W.S. "A case of fatal West Nile virus meningoencephalitis associated with receipt of blood transfusions after open heart surgery." Ann Thorac Surg Aug; 76(2) 2003. p. 605-07. Harrington, T. et al. "West Nile virus infection transmitted by blood transfusion." Transfusion Aug; 43(8) 2003. p. 1018-22.
2. Biggerstaff, B.J., Petersen, L.R. "Estimated risk of transmission of the West Nile virus through blood transfusion in the US, 2002." Transfusion Aug; 43(8) 2003. p. 1007-17. Warner, J. "West Nile Virus-Tainted Blood Poses Small but Real Risk to Blood Supply." WebMD Medical News. <http://my.webmd.com/content/article/74/89064.htm>.
3. Dodd, R.Y. "Current safety of the blood supply in the United States." Int J Hematol Nov; 80(4) 2004. p. 301-15.
4. Fernandez Lopez, M.J., et al. "Creutzfeldt-Jakob disease and blood transfusion." Acta Neurol Belg Sep; 98(3) 1998. p. 247-51.
5. Naughton, P. "Thousands warned of vCJD risk." Times Online. 2004. 21 Sep 2004 <http://www.timesonline.co.uk/article/0,,2-1272734,00.html>.
6. <http://www.bseinfo.org/FAQ.aspx>.

of the world's blood supply because they feared there may be many "subclinical vCJD carriers" who may donate infected blood to others.[1] There are even calls to prevent past blood recipients from donating blood to others even if this does reduce the supply of available blood.[2] These findings may have disastrous ramifications for hemophiliacs who were already devastated by HIV and hepatitis.[3] They are now at increased risk for acquiring vCJD. The plasma from vCJD-infected donors may be mixed with the plasma from thousands of other non-infected donors to produce clotting factors.[4] There are currently no reported cases of vCJD in hemophiliacs. A 2004 British study evaluated all known cases of vCJD and concluded that at least one case was almost certainly due to receiving a blood transfusion from an infected donor.[5] A second confirmed case prompted a health department spokesman to state, "After the first person to person transmission of vCJD was identified it was expected that further cases may follow."[6] It is already known two Scottish donors have died from the human form of mad cow disease (vCJD). The recipients of their blood products have to live with the uncertainty that they too may die from this prion scourge. The BBC reports 300 Scottish hemophiliacs may have been infected by vCJD through blood plasma products.[7] Although authorities are reluctant to state this evidence as conclusive, they urge for "further precautionary measures" to prevent its spread.[8] Those infected with variant Creutzfeldt-Jakob disease (vCJD) may show no symptoms of their infection for years. This long term latency further increases the risk of infection being spread by blood donation.[9] This places those in need at a very difficult position, they must choose between very small possible risks of infection in the future versus dying today. The blood supply within the US is presumed free of variant Creutzfeldt-Jakob disease; therefore, all blood products used in operations in Britain are imported from the United States. There is currently no known blood test to screen for variant CJD.[10] There is considerable debate whether it is the ethical duty of clinicians to

1. Ramasamy, I. "The risk of accidental transmission of transmissible spongiform encephalopathy: identification of emerging issues." Public Health Sep; 118(6) 2004. p. 409-20.
2. "Blood Donation Eligibility Guidelines." American Red Cross. 2005. 21 Mar 2005 ‹http://www.redcross.org/services/biomed/0,1082,0_557_,00.html#vcjd›. Orfinger, B. "Unraveling the Cause of a Complex Disease." American Red Cross. 2001. 24 May 2001 ‹http://www.redcross.org/news/bm/tse/010524cjd.html›.
3. "Thousands of UK hemophiliacs may be infected with vCJD." Clinical Infectious Diseases. 2001. 23 Sep 2001 ‹http://www.journals.uchicago.edu/CID/journal/news/091604-1.text.html›.
4. "Protecting the Nation's blood supply from infectious agents: the need for new standards to meet new threats." BloodBook. 1996. 02 Aug 1996 ‹http://www.bloodbook.com/FDA-congres.html›.
5. Llewelyn, C.A., et al. "Possible transmission of variant Creutzfeldt-Jakob disease by blood transfusion." Lancet Feb 7; 363(9407) 2004. p. 417-21.
6. Pincock, S. "Government confirms second case of vCJD transmitted by blood transfusion." BMJ Jul 31; 329(7460) 2004. p. 251.
7. "Scottish Hemophiliacs Took Infected Blood Products Until 1987." Bloomberg News Service 06 Aug 1999.
8. "VCJD: Further precautionary measures announced." UK Department of Health. 2004. 21 Sep 2004 ‹http://www.dh.gov.uk/PublicationsAndStatistics/PressReleases/PressReleasesNotices/fs/en?CONTENT_ID=4089689&chk=JKk6V6›.
9. Aguzzi, A., Glatzel, M. "VCJD tissue distribution and transmission by transfusion—a worst-case scenario coming true?" Lancet Feb 7; 363(9407) 2004. p. 411-12. Meikle, J. "Transfusion may have given vCJD victim the disease." The Guardian 18 Dec 2003.

inform patients of theoretical risks prior to obtaining consent for blood transfusions.[1]

The risks associated with blood transfusions are not limited to infection.[2] Your body is unique even at the cellular level. The body has a system which recognizes its own cells while targeting "non-self" cells as invaders. The Histocompatibility complex is an immune response that labels your cells as being unique to you.[3] Any cell not appropriately labeled will be rejected and attacked by white blood cells. Transfusion technology was developed to minimize the risk of rejecting foreign cells. It however does not eliminate this risk entirely. The body's response to foreign cells guarantees a deleterious response to transfusion of blood products other than your own. These responses are known as transfusion reactions. They are surprising common and may cause a myriad of difficulties. One author reports adverse reactions occur in 20% of all transfusions.[4]

Transfusion reactions may occur immediately as life-threatening events, or be delayed and insidious. An acute hemolytic transfusion reaction is a rare, severe, life-threatening condition occurring once in every 25,000 units of infused erythrocytes.[5] It is usually caused by a mistyping of either the donor or recipient blood resulting in the recipient receiving an incompatible blood type.[6]

Severe transfusion reactions usually occur as a result of errors in patient identification and/or administration of incompatible blood. A ten year New York study determined transfusion errors were observed for 1 of 19,000 RBC units administered. Half of these events occurred outside the blood bank (administration to the wrong recipient, 38%; phlebotomy errors, 13%). Isolated blood bank errors, including testing of the wrong specimen, transcription errors, and issuance of the wrong unit, were responsible for 29% of events. The primary symptoms of fever and low blood pressure may occur with as little as 0.7 mL of blood product infused. Fatal transfusion reactions have been reported with as little as 30 mL (approx. 1 ounce) of the transfusion.

Rarely, the transfusion reaction may be a delayed hemolytic transfusion reaction. This reaction has been reported as once in every 2,500 units of red blood cells and frequently is not even noticed. The delayed transfusion reaction

10. Brown, P., Cervenakova ,L. "The modern landscape of transfusion-related iatrogenic Creutzfeldt-Jakob disease and blood screening tests." Curr Opin Hematol Sep; 11(5) 2004. p. 351-56. Dabaghian, R.H., Mortimer, P.P., Clewley, J.P. "Prospects for the development of pre-mortem laboratory diagnostic tests for Creutzfeldt-Jakob disease." Rev Med Virol Nov-Dec; 14(6) 2004. p. 345-61.
1. Boixiere, A., et al. " [Informing the transfused patient of the possible transmission of variant Creutzfeldt-Jakob disease by blood transfusion]." Presse Med Dec 4; 33(21) 2004. p. 1533-37.
2. Goodnough, L.T. "Risks of blood transfusion." Crit Care Med Dec; 31(12 Suppl) 2003. p. S678-86.
3. Blum A. et al.. "The Major Histocompatibility Complex and Inflammation." South Med J vol 93(2) 2000.
4. Labovich, T.M. "Transfusion therapy." Clin J Oncol vol 1 1997. p. 61-72.
5. Davenport, R.D. Hemolytic transfusion reactions. In Transfusion Reactions. Bethesda: American Association Of Blood Banks Press, 2001.
6. Sloop GD, Friedberg RC. Complications of blood transfusion: How to recognize and respond to noninfectious reactions. Postgrad Med 1995; 98:159–172

may not occur for 2-14 days.[1] It frequently results in fever, jaundice, and anemia.[2] In an even rarer reaction, the antibodies in the donor blood may cause acute lung injury.[3] This has been estimated to occur once in every 10,000 units. The rarest type of transfusion reaction is an anaphylactic reactions which occurs only once in 150,000 units. This is a hyperimmune response that may result in sudden death.[4] If a transfusion reaction is suspected the blood product should be immediately discontinued and the patient treated with epinephrine and steroids. Special care should be taken with all future transfusions and the patient should only receive only "washed" red blood cells.

A more common type of transfusion reaction is the febrile non-hemolytic transfusion reaction.[5] This may occur once in every five transfusions of platelets and once in 100 units of red blood cells. This mild reaction generally consists of the blood recipient having a mild fever within 2 hours of transfusion; it is usually treated by giving the recipient Tylenol or other drugs to reduce a fever. The transfusion is generally discontinued and future transfusions are with leukocyte-reduced products (blood products that have fewer donor white blood cells). The patient may also be premedicated with a drug to reduce their risk of developing a fever. Urticarial reactions are considered partial anaphylaxis reactions; they require close monitoring for signs of anaphylaxis. They occur about once for every 1,000 units transfused.[6] The primary symptom is itching. Alloimmunization is the development of antibodies after transfusion. It may also occur in approximately 1% of all red blood cell transfusions.[7]

Some complications are attributable to the preservation of blood. The preservation process may be of special concern for trauma patients. Blood that has been improperly stored may harbor large numbers of bacteria and endotoxins. Nearly expired blood may cause its own unique set of problems for the blood recipient. Trauma patients frequently receive large volumes of blood from multiple donors. One study documented a patient who received 25 units of blood from 80 different donors.[8]

1. Diamond et al. "Delayed hemolytic transfusion reaction presenting as sickle-cell crisis." Ann. Intern. Med vol 93 1980. p. 231. Syed, S.K. "Delayed Hemolytic Transfusion Reaction in Sickle Cell Disease." American Journal of the Medical Sciences vol 312(4) 1996. p. 175-81.
2. "Delayed transfusion reaction associated with multiple antibodies." Cleve Clin Q Fall; 41(3) 1974. p. 135-41.
3. "Transfusion Related Acute Lung Injury." FDA / Center for Biologics Evaluation and Research. 2001. 19 Oct 2001 ‹http://www.fda.gov/cber/ltr/trali101901.htm›. "TRALI: Transfusion Related Acute Lung Injury." Transfusion Medicine Bulletin vol 3(1) 2000.
4. Sloop, G.D., Friedberg, R.C. "Complications of blood transfusion: How to recognize and respond to noninfectious reactions.." Postgrad Med vol 98 1995. p. 159-72.
5. Coffland FI, Shelton DM. "Blood component replacement therapy." Crit Care Clin vol 5 1993. p. 543-56.
6. Sloop, G.D., Friedberg, R.C. "Complications of blood transfusion: How to recognize and respond to noninfectious reactions." Postgrad Med vol 98 1995. p. 159-72.
7. Klein, H.G. "Allogenic transfusion risks in the surgical patient." Am J Surg vol 170 1995. p. 21S-26S.
8. Crosson, J.T. "Massive transfusion." Clin Lab Med vol 16 1996. p. 873-82.

Transfusion of large volumes of blood has its own inherent risks.[1] Several studies have shown massive blood transfusions are an independent risk factor for multiple organ failure.[2] The risk of death is directly proportional to the volume of blood transfused.[3] Early studies suggested hypovolemia (low blood volume) may have had a negative effect on the immune system (immunosuppression).[4] This immunosuppression resulted in the body not mobilizing an attack against foreign tissue or bacteria. In fact, immunosuppression was first recognized in kidney transplant patients. Researchers determined kidney transplant recipients who received transfusions survived longer than those who did not receive blood products.[5]

Later studies attributed immunosuppression of the immune system to the donor white blood cells that remain in the blood product being transfused. One researcher states "the transfusion of blood with viable white cells may cause lifelong immunosuppression." He also reported "blood transfusion in unselected ICU patients increases mortality 37%."[6] One large multiple center study of 284 ICUs in 213 hospitals evaluated the effects of transfusion on 4,892 patients.[7] They concluded the more units of red blood cells a patient receives the longer are their ICU and hospital stays.[8] The authors of this study also found the number of red blood cell units transfused is an independent predictor of worse clinical outcome. These findings are confirmed by other researchers.[9] Those transfused with red blood cells had more total complications and transfusion with more than six units of red blood cells produced an early state of hyper-inflammation

1. Dellinger, E.P., Anaya, D.A. "Infectious and immunologic consequences of blood transfusion." Crit Care vol 8 Suppl 2 2004. p. S18-23.
2. Kooby, D.A., et al. "Influence of transfusions on perioperative and long-term outcome in patients following hepatic resection for colorectal metastases." Ann Surg Jun; 237(6) 2003. p. 869-70. Moore, F.A., Moore, E.E., Sauaia, A. "Blood transfusion. An independent risk factor for postinjury multiple organ failure." Arch Surg vol 132 1997. p. 620-24.
3. Houbiers, J.G., et al. "Randomised controlled trial comparing transfusion of leucocyte-depleted or buffy-coat-depleted blood in surgery for colorectal cancer." Lancet vol 344 1994. p. 573-78. Van de Watering, L.M., et al. "Beneficial effects of leukocyte depletion of transfused blood on postoperative complications in patients undergoing cardiac surgery: a randomized clinical trial." Circulation 1998, 97: vol 97 1998. p. 562-68.
4. Cue, J.I., Peyton, J.C., Malangoni, M.A. "Does blood transfusion or hemorrhagic shock induce immunosuppression?" J Trauma vol 32 1992. p. 613-17. Dennis, J.W. "Blood replacement, massive transfusion, and hemostasis in hemorrhagic shock." Trauma Q vol 8 1992. p. 62-68.
5. Higgins, R.M., et al. "Acute rejection after renal transplantation is reduced by approximately 50% by prior therapeutic blood transfusions, even in tacrolimus-treated patients." Transplantation Feb 15; 77(3) 2004. p. 469-71.
6. Marik, P.E. "Early goal-directed therapy for septic shock." CHEST 2002: annual meeting of. American College of Chest Physicians. San Diego, Cal. 06 Nov 2002. Zucker, M. "Bad blood: battling anemia in the ICU." Pulmonary Reviews. 2003. Feb 2003 ⟨http://www.pulmonaryreviews.com/feb03/pr_feb03_anemia.html⟩.
7. Corwin, H.L., et al. "The CRIT Study: Anemia and blood transfusion in the critically ill-Current clinical practice in the United States*." Critical Care Medicine vol 32(1) 2004. p. 39-52.
8. Ahmed, S., Kupfer, Y., Tessler, S. "Blood transfusions and mortality among critically ill patients." JAMA Mar 12; 289(10) 2003. p. 1242-43. Blajchman, M.A.. "Immunomodulation and blood transfusion." Am J Ther Sep-Oct; 9(5) 2002. p. 389-95.
9. Rathore, S.S., Krumholz, H.M. "Blood transfusions and mortality among critically ill patients." JAMA Mar 12; 289(10) 2003. p. 1242. Shorr, A.F., Duh, M.S., Kelly, K.M., Kollef, M.H. "Red blood cell transfusion and ventilator-associated pneumonia: A potential link?" Crit Care Med Mar; 32(3) 2004. p. 666-74.

that was a strong, independent predictor of multiple organ failure.[1] A 2002 randomized control study investigated the effect of reducing the number of white blood cells in transfused red blood cells had on morbidity or mortality.[2] This study was unable to demonstrate any reduction in rates of either infection or death by using leukocyte poor blood (red blood cells with most white blood cells removed).

A 2004 study evaluated both survival and mortality in a general population of 6779 transfused patients.[3] Only 4658 (69%) patients were alive one year after transfusion, 4056 (60%) were alive at 2 years, and 3092 (46%) were alive 5 years after transfusion. One year mortality rate after one year was 31%. After five years, mortality was more than half for those who had been transfused.

Another study in JAMA evaluated transfusions of more than 3,500 patients in 146 intensive care units. The death rate for patients who received transfusions was 29%, compared to 14.9% for those who did not get blood. The authors concluded "We currently believe that blood transfusions result in immunosuppressive effects, with increased risk of infections."[4]

Studies have reported transfusion with red blood cells not only causes immunosuppression, it also increases the risk of recurrence of cancers currently in remission.[5] Some studies have shown transfusion with red blood cells may more than double your risk of cancer reoccurrence and death.[6] They also documented an increase in postoperative bacterial infections for those transfused with red blood cells.[7] These researchers recommend the use of homologous transfusions (receiving your own previously stored blood) whenever possible.[8] Animal studies suggest an unknown blood factor is able to stimulate the growth of solid tumors.[9]

---

1. Silliman, C.C., et al. "Transfusion of the injured patient: proceed with caution." Shock Apr; 21(4) 2004. p. 291-99.
2. Dzik, W.H., et al. "A prospective, randomized clinical trial of universal WBC reduction." Transfusion Sep; 42(9) 2002. p. 1114-22.
3. Kleinman, S., Marshall, D., AuBuchon, J., Patton, M. "Survival after transfusion as assessed in a large multistate US cohort." Transfusion Mar; 44(3) 2004. p. 386-90.
4. Edelson, E. "Blood Transfusions Raise Death Risk in Very Ill." Health on the Net Foundation. 2002. 24 Sep 2002 ‹http://www.hon.ch/News/HSN/509290.html›. Vincent, J.L., et al. "Anemia and blood transfusion in critically ill patients." JAMA Sep 25; 288(12) 2002. p. 1499-507.
5. Hill, G.E., et al. "Allogeneic blood transfusion increases the risk of postoperative bacterial infection: a meta-analysis." J Trauma May; 54(5) 2003. p. 908-14. Nosotti, M., et al. "Correlation between perioperative blood transfusion and prognosis of patients subjected to surgery for stage I lung cancer." Chest Jul; 124(1) 2003. p. 102-07.
6. Nilsson, K.R., et al. "Preoperative predictors of blood transfusion in colorectal cancer surgery.." J Gastrointest Surg Sep-Oct; 6(5) 2002. p. 753-62.
7. Hughes, M.G., et al. "Does prior transfusion worsen outcomes from infection in surgical patients?" Surg Infect (Larchmt) Winter; 4(4) 2003. p. 335-43. Leal, Noval, S.R., Jara Lopez, I. "Do multiple blood transfusions predispose for a higher rate of non-blood-related infection complications?" Clin Microbiol Infect Jul; 8(7) 2002. p. 383-87.
8. Bortul, M., Calligaris, L., Roseano, M., Leggeri, A. "Blood transfusions and results after curative resection for gastric cancer." Suppl Tumori Sep-Oct; 2(5) 2003. p. S27-30.
9. Okuyama, M., et al. "Soluble and Cell-Associated Forms of Some Yet to be Identified Factor in Transfused Blood Which Promotes Solid Tumor Growth in Mice." Surg Today vol 34(8) 2004. p. 673-77.

A study of 1,915 patients receiving coronary artery bypass operations compared those receiving red blood cells to those who had not been transfused.[1] The authors of this study concluded transfused patients were twice as likely to die in five years compared to those not receiving blood (15% vs 7%). Even after correction for other factors, they determined transfusion was still associated with a 70% increase in death after a coronary artery bypass graph operation. A separate study suggests the increased mortality may be related to how long the transfused red blood cells had been stored prior to administration.[2]

Studies have shown transfusion with red blood cells increases the risk of hospital acquired infections six fold compared with to those not being transfused.[3] This association continued even after adjusting for probability of survival and age. There is a clear dose-dependent correlation between transfusions of red blood cells and the development of infection in trauma patients.[4] Another study concluded transfusion with red blood cells increased the risk of infection by 7-10 times in patients having hip operations.[5] The authors of this study estimated the death rates from transfusion-related postoperative infections and cancer recurrence may exceed the death rate due to all other transfusion risks combined. Concerns about the safety of transfusion of donated blood products have prompted calls for "unprecedented global initiatives to minimize the use of allogeneic blood."[6] Opponents of donated blood products believe emphasis should be placed on the use of "blood substitutes" and reducing the amount of wasted blood from needless labs to conserve the patient's own blood supply.

Some researchers believe there is a correlation between the age of the transfused red blood cells and rates of bacterial infections.[7] They call for the use of white blood cell depleted blood or blood substitutes in trauma patients requiring massive blood transfusions.[8]

The US has been criticized for using "old blood."[9] The average age of European blood is 16 days, compared to 24 days in the US.[10] Unfortunately, much of the blood reserves within the US are near the recommended 42-day

1. Engoren, M.C.,et al. "Effect of blood transfusion on long-term survival after cardiac operation." Ann Thorac Surg Oct; 74(4) 2002. p. 1180-86.
2. Vamvakas, E.C., Carven, J.H. "Transfusion and postoperative pneumonia in coronary artery bypass graft surgery: effect of the length of storage of transfused red cells." Transfusion Jul; 39(7) 1999. p. 701-10.
3. Taylor, R.W., et al. "Impact of allogenic packed red blood cell transfusion on nosocomial infection rates in the critically ill patient." Crit Care Med 30 2002. p. 2249-54.
4. Claridge, J.A., et al. "Blood transfusions correlate with infections in trauma patients in a dose-dependent manner." Am Surg Jul; 68(7) 2002. p. 566-72.
5. Blumberg, N.. "Allogeneic transfusion and infection: economic and clinical implications." Semin Hematol Jul; 34(3 Suppl 2) 1997. p. 34-40.
6. Shander, A. "Emerging risks and outcomes of blood transfusion in surgery." Semin Hematol Jan; 41(1 Suppl 1) 2004. p. 117-24.
7. Offner, P.J., et al. "Increased rate of infection associated with transfusion of old blood after severe injury." Arch Surg Jun; 137(6):711-16 2002. p. 716-17. Weil, M.H. "Does the storage time of transfused red blood cells influence critically ill patients?" Crit Care Med Jun; 32(6) 2004. p. 1443-14.
8. Shapiro, M.J., et al. "Anemia and blood transfusion in trauma patients admitted to the intensive care unit." J Trauma Aug; 55(2):269-73 2003. p. 273-74.
9. Offner, P.J. "Age of blood: does it make a difference?" Crit Care vol 8 Suppl 2 2004. p. S24-6.

expiration period.[1] One researcher complained "the cells that we transfuse are really surprisingly old: As much as 40% of the cells we transfuse are more than a month old."[2]

Before planned surgery, patients may choose to save their own blood for their pending surgery. Receiving your own blood is called an autologous transfusion. One study suggests autologous donation removes many of the hazards associated with transfusion but increases the cost of therapy by $664 for each unit received.[3] Most patients will prefer to receive their own blood for elective therapy when presented with the risks of transfusion.

Some researchers believe physicians are responsible for the very anemia they are treating.[4] They point out that severe anemia is a multifactorial condition caused by too much phlebotomy, ongoing bleeding, and inadequate production of red blood cells.[5] The limits that trigger the need for transfusion remain very controversial.[6] Physicians are reminded to reduce their numbers of blood draws needed to evaluate labs, using pediatric collection tubes[7] to reduce the volume of blood drawn for labs, and considering alternatives to transfusion.[8] A Dartmouth researcher stated "If you look at critically ill patients, you find that almost everybody is anemic by 48 hours in the ICU . . . "we're also partly responsible for the anemia in the critically ill: We phlebotomize 60 to 70 mL/d from our critically ill patients."[9]

Depletions of blood stores within the US could easily be offset by narrowing the criteria for transfusion.[10] Research shows most physicians are way too liberal in there orders to transfuse. A large multi-center study in 1999 compared outcomes for patients transfused to maintain a hemoglobin level between 10 and

10. Offner, P.J., et al. "Increased rate of infection associated with transfusion of old blood after severe injury." Arch Surg Jun; 137(6) 2002. p. 711-16.
1. Owens, W., Tokessy, M., Rock, G. "Age of blood in inventory at a large tertiary care hospital." Vox Sang Jul; 81(1) 2001. p. 21-23.
2. Zucker, M. "Bad blood: battling anemia in the ICU." Pulmonary Reviews. 2003. Feb 2003 ‹http://www.pulmonaryreviews.com/feb03/pr_feb03_anemia.html›.
3. Moxey, A.J., et al. "Blood transfusion and autologous donation: a survey of post-surgical patients, interest group members and the public." Transfus Med Feb; 15(1) 2005. p. 19-32.
4. Hebert, P.C., Tinmouth, A., Corwin, H. "Anemia and red cell transfusion in critically ill patients." Crit Care Med Dec; 31(12 Suppl) 2003. p. S672-77. Hebert, P.C., McDonald, B.J., Tinmouth, A. "Clinical consequences of anemia and red cell transfusion in the critically ill." Crit Care Clin Apr; 20(2) 2004. p. 225-35.
5. Fowler, R.A., Rizoli, S.B., Levin, P.D., Smith, T. "Blood conservation for critically ill patients." Crit Care Clin Apr; 20(2) 2004. p. 313-24. Rudis, M.I., et al. "Managing anemia in the critically ill patient." Pharmacotherapy Feb; 24(2) 2004. p. 229-47.
6. Carson, J.L., et al. "Transfusion triggers: a systematic review of the literature." Transfus Med Rev Jul; 16(3) 2002. p. 187-99. Yowler, C. "Transfusion and Autotransfusion." emedicine. 2002. 29 Mar 2002 ‹http://www.emedicine.com/med/topic3215.htm›.
7. Spahn, D.R., Marcucci, C. "Blood management in intensive care medicine: CRIT and ABC — what can we learn?" Crit Care Apr; 8(2) 2004. p. 89-90.
8. Fowler, R.A., Berenson, M. "Blood conservation in the intensive care unit." Crit Care Med Dec; 31(12 Suppl) 2003. p. S715-20.
9. Corwin, H.L. "Anemia in the critically ill." American College of Chest Physicians. 2002. 06 Nov 2002 ‹http://www.pulmonaryreviews.com/feb03/pr_feb03_anemia.html›.
10. Chohan, S.S., et al. "Red cell transfusion practice following the transfusion requirements in critical care (TRICC) study: prospective observational cohort study in a large UK intensive care unit." Vox Sang Apr; 84(3) 2003. p. 211-18.

12 g/dL to a more restrictive strategy to keep hemoglobin levels between 7 and 9 g/dL.[1] The authors report "By using the more restrictive strategy, they were able to reduce blood transfusion by 50%." Additionally, he said, "In all clinical outcomes measured, the restrictive group did better—be it 30-day mortality, hospital mortality, ICU mortality, or organ failure." Those in favor of restricting transfusion limits point out that the blood supply is a limited resource and should not be used indiscriminately. They argue most patients who are not actively bleeding and have adequate fluid volume probably get little to no benefit from blood transfusions if their hemoglobin is greater than 7 g/dL. However, if they are inappropriately transfused they are still exposed to all the risks associated with blood transfusions. Studies have shown between 40% and 50% of all patients admitted to ICUs receive at least one unit of red blood cells. If the length of stay increases to more than one week in the ICU the rate of transfusion is more than 80% with an average of five units for the length of their stay.[2] This is alarming because there is little evidence that "routine" transfusion of red blood cells is beneficial for the critically ill.[3]

Many studies have shown even critically ill patients can tolerate hemoglobin levels as low as 7 mg/dL.[4] Transfusion is rarely indicated when the hemoglobin concentration is greater than 10 g/dL and is almost always indicated when it falls below a threshold of 6 g/dL.[5] Most recent studies suggest an arbitrary trigger for transfusion (the '10/30 rule') is "ill advised."[6] Many laboratory and clinical studies have established that transfusing to normal hemoglobin concentrations does not improve organ failure and mortality in the critically ill patient.[7] Another multi-center study evaluated the appropriateness of blood transfusions against established guidelines. Thirty-five percent of those transfused were within normal guidelines of 9.5-10.0 g/dL and 80% of the orders were for two packed cell units. Although 35% of the physicians stated the patient was being transfused for acute bleeding, they opted to administer multiple units despite published guidelines to the contrary.[8] Eighty percent of those transfused received two units packed cells, guidelines recommend patients

1. Hebert, P.C., et al. "A multicenter, randomized, controlled clinical trial of transfusion requirements in critical care." NEJM vol 340 1999. p. 409-17.
2. Blomqvist, H., Sondell, K. "[Intensive care patients need blood transfusion—with limits. Risks must be weighed against potential benefit]." Lakartidningen Oct 16; 100(42) 2003. p. 3307-10.
3. Corwin, H.L., Surgenor, S.D., Gettinger, A. "Transfusion practice in the critically ill." Crit Care Med Dec; 31(12 Suppl) 2003. p. S668-71.
4. McLellan, S.A., McClelland, D.B., Walsh, T.S. "Anaemia and red blood cell transfusion in the critically ill patient." Blood Rev Dec; 17(4) 2003. p. 195-208.
5. Hardy, J.F. "Should we reconsider triggers for red blood cell transfusion?" Acta Anaesthesiol Belg 54(4) 2003. p. 287-95.
6. Fakhry, S.M., Fata, P. "How low is too low? Cardiac risks with anemia." Crit Care vol 8 Suppl 2 2004. p. S11-14.
7. Alvarez, G., Hebert, P.C., Szick, S. "Debate: transfusing to normal haemoglobin levels will not improve outcome." Crit Care vol 5(2) 2001. p. 56-63. McIntyre L, et al. "Is a restrictive transfusion strategy safe for resuscitated and critically ill trauma patients?" J Trauma Sep; 57(3) 2004. p. 563-68.
8. Hebert, P.C., et al.. "Variation in red cell transfusion practice in the intensive care unit: a multicentre cohort study." Crit Care (Lond) vol 3(2) 1999. p. 57-63.

receive only one unit at a time and only as required. A 2004 study reminded physicians that transfusion with red blood cells has not been consistently shown to improve clinical outcomes in the critically ill and may actually result in worse outcomes in some patients.[1]

Heart specialists frequently opt to transfuse cardiac patients if their hemoglobin level falls below 10 g/dL. There remains considerable controversy about the benefit of blood transfusion in elderly patients after a heart attack. A large study suggests heart attack patients may obtain benefit with a hematocrit as high as 33.0% on admission.[2] Several studies concluded cardiac patients are more intolerant of anemia and recommend a more liberal transfusion trigger of 9-10 g/dL in patients with active cardiac disease.[3] However, other studies suggest a hemoglobin level of 8.0 is well tolerated by most cardiac patients.[4]

A 1996 American Society of Anesthesiology report indicated red cell transfusion is rarely needed if the hemoglobin concentration is greater than 10g/dL, and almost always needed when the level is less than 6g/dL.[5] Weakness doesn't generally occur until hemoglobin levels drop to 6g/dL, shortness of breath while resting occurs at 3g/dL, and congestive heart failure at 2 to 2.5g/dL.[6]

Injections of a genetically engineered hormone, erythropoietin,[7] may decrease the need for transfusion in the critically ill.[8] One study suggests it reduces the need for transfusion with blood by 50%. A separate study found it to be at least as safe as conventional blood transfusions without the associated risks.[9] Unfortunately, this hormone is very expensive and may not be a cost effective alternative to blood transfusions.[10] A study of erythropoietin use from 1989-1998 estimated an average cost per recipient of $6,245 per year.[11]

---

1. Napolitano, L.M., Corwin, H.L. "Efficacy of red blood cell transfusion in the critically ill." Crit Care Clin Apr; 20(2) 2004. p. 255-68.
2. Wu, W.C., et al. "Blood transfusion in elderly patients with acute myocardial infarction." NEJM Oct 25; 345(17) 2001. p. 1230-36.
3. Freudenberger, R.S., Carson, J.L. "Is there an optimal hemoglobin value in the cardiac intensive care unit?" Curr Opin Crit Care Oct; 9(5) 2003. p. 356-61.
4. Bracey, A.W., et al. "Lowering the hemoglobin threshold for transfusion in coronary artery bypass procedures: effect on patient outcome." Transfusion Oct; 39(10) 1999. p. 1070-77. Johnson, R.G., et al.. "Comparison of two transfusion strategies after elective operations for myocardial revascularization." J Thorac Cardiovasc Surg vol 104 1992. p. 307-14.
5. American Society of Anesthesiologists. "Task Force on Blood Component Therapy. Practice guidelines for blood component therapy." Anesthesiology vol 84 1996. p. 732-47.
6. Simon, T.J., et al. "Practice parameter for the use of red blood cell transfusion.." Arch Pathol Lab Med vol 122 1998. p. 130-38.
7. Corwin, H.L., et al. "Efficacy of recombinant human erythropoietin in critically ill patients." JAMA vol 288 2002. p. 2827-35.
8. Pajoumand, M., Erstad, B.L., Camamo, J.M. "Use of epoetin alfa in critically ill patients." Ann Pharmacother Apr; 38(4) 2004. p. 641-48. Spence, R.K. "Emerging trends in surgical blood transfusion." Semin Hematol vol 34 1997. p. 48-53.
9. Corwin, H.L. "Anemia in the critically ill: the role of erythropoietin." Semin Hematol Jul; 38(3 Suppl 7) 2001. p. 24-32.
10. Tonelli, M., et al. "The cost-effectiveness of maintaining higher hemoglobin targets with erythropoietin in hemodialysis patients." Kidney Int Jul; 64(1) 2003. p. 295-304.
11. Greer, J.W., Milam, R.A., Eggers, P.W. "Trends in Use, Cost, and Outcomes of Human Recombinant Erythropoietin, 1989-98." Health Care Financing Review. 1999. Spring 1999 ‹http://www.cms.hhs.gov/review/99Spring/99Springpg55.pdf›.

Drug companies have been searching for an effective blood substitute for decades. Although there are many clinical trials of blood substitutes under way, they are reaching a consensus that blood is not an easy product to replicate. Blood's ability to carry oxygen to tissues while removing carbon dioxide has been the primary focus of these potential blood substitutes. Substitutes with long shelf life not requiring refrigeration are preferred. A study published in 1997 identified five hemoglobin-based oxygen carrier solutions in human clinical trials.[1] Three blood substitutes[2] appear to show some promise in clinical trials.[3] One substitute called Polyheme was found to be safe and effective in infusions up to six units. Fifty-nine percent of those receiving Polyheme[4] required no extra transfusions by red blood cells.[5] Clinical trials of these products are in progress. There is insufficient data to determine the long term safety profile of any blood substitute. These factors are unlikely to deter pharmaceutical firms looking for their niche in an estimated $5 billion a year market.

The above findings beg an answer to a very interesting question; do patients with anemia even need transfusions? This may seem blatantly obvious; however, there is one group of Americans who are willing to risk their very lives by answering no. Devote Jehovah's Witnesses routinely refuse to allow blood transfusions either for themselves or their loved ones. Jehovah's Witnesses often refuse blood transfusions because of their beliefs.

Many health care workers believe these patients are jeopardizing their lives by this refusal.[6] However, multiple studies have shown, generally, they fair no worse than those receiving blood products. One early study on outcomes of patients refusing red cell transfusions on religious grounds found very few deaths attributable to anemia if the hemoglobin concentrations remained above 5g/dL. These findings were reaffirmed by a 2002 study of 300 Jehovah's Witness patients.[7] The researchers found no deaths for those with hemoglobin levels of 7.1 to 8.0; however, 9.4% did have a serious medical event. Even critically low hemoglobin levels of 4.1 to 5.0 are no guarantee of death; 67.3% survived but more than half of those surviving had a serious medical event. Thirty day mortality was 33% for Jehovah's Witness cardiac patients with hemoglobin concentrations less than 6g/dL.[8]

1. Nucci, M.L., Abuchowski, A. "The search for blood substitutes." Sci Am vol 278 1997. p. 72-77.
2. Greenburg, A.G., Kim, H.W. "Hemoglobin-based oxygen carriers." Crit Care vol 8 Suppl 2 2004. p. S61-4.
3. Baxter Healthcare Corporation. "Baxter ends U.S. trauma study of HemAssist (DCLHb)." PR Newswire 1998. p. 1-2. Przybelsk, R.J., Dailey, E.K. "The pressor effect of diaspirin cross-linked hemoglobin (DCLHb). " Yearbook of Intensive and Emergency Care Medicine 1994. p. 252-63.
4. Gould SA, et al. "The first randomized trial of human polymerized hemoglobin as a blood substitute in acute trauma and emergent surgery." J Am Coll Surg Aug; 187(2) 1998. p. 113-20.
5. "Human haemoglobin." BioDrugs vol 17(4) 2003. p. 296-98. Waldspurger, R., Wendy, J. "Massive Transfusion in Trauma. AACN Clinical Issues: Advanced Practice in Acute & Critical Care." Controversies in Trauma Resuscitation vol 10(1) 1999. p. 69-84.
6. Elder, L. "Why some Jehovah's Witnesses accept blood and conscientiously reject official Watchtower Society blood policy." J Med Ethics vol 26 2000. p. 375-380. Hall, D.E., Curlin, F., Koenig, H.G. "When clinical medicine collides with religion." Lancet vol 362 2003. p. 28-29.
7. Carson, J.L., et al. "Mortality and morbidity in patients with very low postoperative Hb levels who decline blood transfusion." Transfusion Jul; 42(7) 2002. p. 812-18.

Although Jehovah's Witnesses may present a challenge to the surgeon, they do surprising well for operations as diverse as organ transplantation[1], heart surgery[2], high risk surgery[3] and even neurosurgery[4]. Refusal of blood transfusion in the severely anemic may significantly impact on the patient's health, but it is not the guaranteed death sentence many once believed.[5] A 2003 study on death from trauma evaluated the mortality rates of various religions after major trauma. Of the 556 patients studied, the death rate for 82 Jehovah's Witnesses was no different than the majority of patients belonging to other religious groups (321 patients). The study did show those expressing a religious belief as a Baptist (52) or Catholic (101) were 6% and 20% less likely to die after major trauma.[6]

Providing the best medical therapy possible in order to save lives clashes with the belief system of Jehovah's Witnesses[7] who may adamantly refuse this life saving therapy.[8] This quandary may have a paradoxical benefit. Initially, the beliefs of the Jehovah's Witnesses may be deemed selfish[9] or foolish by medical workers.[10] They cite the unnecessary loss of both life[11] and revenue from this religious belief.[12] A 1991 European survey, 63% of physicians surveyed said they

8. Carson, J.L., et al. "Effect of anaemia and cardiovascular disease on surgical mortality and morbidity." Lancet vol 348 1996. p. 1055-60.
1. Grande, A.M. "Lung transplantation in a Jehovah's witness. Case report in a twinning procedure." J Cardiovasc Surg (Torino) Feb; 44(1) 2003. p. 131-34. Jabbour, N., et al. "Live donor liver transplantation without blood products: strategies developed for Jehovah's Witnesses offer broad application." Ann Surg Aug; 240(2) 2004. p. 350-57.
2. Frimpong-Boateng, K., et al. "Cardiopulmonary bypass in Jehovah's Witnesses." West Afr J Med Jan-Mar; 22(1) 2003. p. 92-94. Spence, R.K., et al. "Transfusion guidelines for cardiovascular surgery: lessons learned from operations in Jehovah's Witnesses." Vasc Surg Dec; 16(6) 1992. p. 825-29.
3. Hachiro, Y., et al. "Endovascular Stent Grafting for Thoracic Aneurysms in Jehovah's Witnesses: Report of Three Cases." Surg Today vol 35(4) 2005. p. 317-19.
4. Suess, S., Suess, O., Brock, M. "Neurosurgical procedures in Jehovah's Witnesses: an increased risk?" Neurosurgery Aug; 49(2) 2001. p. 266-72.
5. Gannon, C.J., Napolitano, L.M. "Severe anemia after gastrointestinal hemorrhage in a Jehovah's Witness: new treatment strategies." Crit Care Med Aug; 30(8) 2002. p. 1893-95. Kitchens, C.S. "Are transfusions overrated? Surgical outcome of Jehovah's Witnesses." Am J Med Feb; 94(2) 1993. p. 117-19.
6. Varela, J.E., et al. "The risk of death for Jehovah's Witnesses after major trauma." J Trauma May; 54(5) 2003. p. 967-72.
7. Doyle, D.J. "Blood transfusions and the Jehovah's Witness patient." Am J Ther Sep-Oct; 9(5) 2002. p. 417-24.
8. Sacks, D.A., Koppes, R.H. "Caring for the female Jehovah's Witness: balancing medicine, ethics, and the First Amendment." Am J Obstet Gynecol Feb; 170(2) 1994. p. 452-55. Wiecha, J.M. "Ethics in medicine: are we blind? In support of teaching medical ethics at the bedside." J Med Humanit Fall; 12(3) 1991. p. 111-17.
9. Elger, B.S., Harding, T.W. "Compliance with the wishes of competent patients among future physicians and lawyers: is paternalism a predictable individual or group-specific trait?" Med Teach Aug; 26(5) 2004. p. 458-62. McNeil, S.B. "Johnny's story: transfusing a Jehovah's Witness." Pediatr Nurs May-Jun; 23(3) 1997. p. 287-88.
10. Catlin, A. "The dilemma of Jehovah's Witness children who need blood to survive." HEC Forum Jul; 8(4) 1996. p. 195-207. Kristine, A, et al. "Faith, Identity, and Leukemia: When Blood Products are Not an Option." The Oncologist vol 7(4) 2002. p. 371-380.
11. Beauchamp, T.L. "Methods and principles in biomedical ethics." J Med Ethics Oct; 29(5) 2003. p. 269-74.
12. Wooding, N. "Costs incurred by one severely ill Jehovah's Witness could run one unit in Africa for one year." BMJ Mar 27; 318(7187) 1999. p. 873.

would knowingly transfuse a Jehovah's Witness patient who was actively bleeding.[1] An astounding 26% said they would withhold this information from the patient.

However, the Jehovah's Witnesses may ultimately be responsible for saving more lives by the potential sacrifice of their own life. Their uncompromising beliefs have forced medical researchers to develop alternate technologies besides blood products to treat the severely anemic.[2] Their beliefs have forced surgeons to refine their technical skills and become adept at performing bloodless or near bloodless surgeries.[3]

Their faith has challenged physicians all around the world both legally and medically.[4] Those of all faiths have directly benefited by their sacrifice and yet we are all too willing use courts in an attempt usurp their autonomy.[5]

PRIMUM NON NOCERE: FIRST, DO NO HARM

Every doctor will allow a colleague to decimate a whole countryside sooner than violate the bond of professional etiquette by giving him away.
George Bernard Shaw 1856-1950, Irish-born Physician and Dramatist

Medical malpractice is even worse than adverse drug reactions, medical errors, iatrogenic induced illnesses or nosocomial infections. It is so detestable because it is so easily preventable; yet, medical malpractice has been estimated to be between the 3rd to 8th leading causes of preventable death[6] in the United States.[7] The Institute of Medicine defines medical error as "the failure to complete a planned action as intended or the use of a wrong plan to achieve an

1. Vincent, J.L. "Transfusion in the exsanguinating Jehovah's Witness patient—the attitude of intensive-care doctors." Eur J Anaesthesiol Jul; 8(4) 1991. p. 297-300.
2. Sarteschi, L.M. "Jehovah's witnesses, blood transfusions and transplantations." Transplant Proc Apr; 36(3) 2004. p. 499-501. Viele, M.K., Weiskopf, R.B. "What can we learn about the need for transfusion from patients who refuse blood? The experience with Jehovah's Witnesses." Transfusion vol 34 1994. p. 396-401.
3. Dohmen, P.M., Liu, J., Lembcke, A., Konertz, W. "Reoperation in a Jehovah's Witness 22 years after aortic allograft reconstruction of the right ventricular outflow tract." Tex Heart Inst J 30(2) 2003. p. 146-48. Jabbour, N., et al. "Live donor liver transplantation: staging hepatectomy in a Jehovah's Witness recipient.." J Hepatobiliary Pancreat Surg 11(3) 2004. p. 211-14.
4. Nash, M.J., Cohen, H. "Management of Jehovah's Witness patients with haematological problems." Blood Rev Sep; 18(3) 2004. p. 211-17. Schonholz, D.H. "Blood transfusion and the pregnant Jehovah's witness patient: avoiding a dilemma." Mt Sinai J Med Sep; 66(4) 1999. p. 277-79.
5. Dyer C. "Court says doctors were right to treat Jehovah's Witness." BMJ Aug 1; 305(6848) 1992. p. 272. Hershey, N. "Battery claim of Jehovah's Witness rejected by Michigan court." Hosp Law Newsl May; 9(7) 1992. p. 4-7.
6. Hyman, D.A., Silver, C. "Speak not of error." CATO Institute: Regulation. 2005. Spring 2005 ⟨http://www.cato.org/pubs/regulation/regv28n1/v28n1-1.pdf⟩. Lazarou, J., Pomeranz, B.M., Corey, P.N. "Incidence of adverse drug reactions in hospitalized patients: A meta-analysis of prospective studies." JAMA vol 279 1998. p. 1200-05.
7. "Adverse Drug Reactions." Bandolier: Evidence based thinking about health care. 1998. 1998 ⟨http://www.jr2.ox.ac.uk/bandolier/band52/b52-3.html⟩. Monica, B., et al. "Improving Adverse-Drug-Reaction Reporting in Ambulatory Care Clinics at a Veterans Affairs Hospital." Am J Health-Syst Pharm vol 59(9) 2002. p. 841-845.

aim." Medical errors are not medical malpractice. Medical malpractice is a legal standard that must be proven. Generally speaking, medical malpractice is an act or omission by a health care provider which deviates from accepted standards of practice in the medical community causing injury to the patient.[1] The standard of care is what the medical industry as a whole has determined to be acceptable protocols and procedures for treatment of patients, conducting tests and analyzing the results of those tests.[2] An iatrogenic event is an illness or injury resulting from a procedure, therapy, or other element of care.[3] The medical malpractice situation in many countries is reaching epidemic proportions.[4] In 1994, malpractice was estimated to be responsible for the deaths of 80,000 Americans annually; this did not include iatrogenic injury.[5] This is about the same number of those killed in combat during the Vietnam and Korean Wars combined.[6] You are over four times more likely to die at the hands of physician than you are an armed gunman[7] or twice that of an automobile accident, but guess which one gets the most coverage in the media. One report suggests 180,000 people die each year in part as a result of iatrogenic inflected injury.[8] This has been compared to the equivalent of three jumbo jet crashes every 2 days. Lucian Leape reported in *JAMA* that 64% of cardiac arrests at a teaching hospital were preventable.[9] He states most were due to use of medications and 36% of those admitted to a teaching hospital suffered an iatrogenic event, 25% of which were serious or life threatening.

In a study of 1,047 patients, adverse events (a euphemism for therapy induced side effects) 45% of patients suffered inappropriate care resulting in complications or medical injury caused by medical workers. Of the 1,047 patients, 17.7% had at least one serious adverse event. The likelihood of experiencing an adverse event increased nearly 6% for each day of hospitalization. Adverse events nearly doubled the risk of dying from hospitalization. These findings were reiterated by a 2004 English study of 18,820 patients, the authors found a 6.5% adverse drug reaction rate with the ADR directly leading to the admission in 80% of cases.[10] A 2003 study concluded

1. "Medical Malpractice." Wikipedia. 2006. 23 Feb 2006 ‹http://en.wikipedia.org/wiki/ Medical_malpractice›.
2. "Medical Malpractice." Sheller Ludwig & Badey. 2006. ‹http://www.sheller.com/Practice-Group.asp?PracticeGroupID=6›.
3. "Iatrogenic." JCAHO: Sentinel Event Glossary of Terms. 2005. 2005 ‹http://www.jcaho.org/ accredited+organizations/sentinel+event/glossary.htm›.
4. Donn, S.M. "Medical liability, risk management, and the quality of health care." Semin Fetal Neonatal Med Feb; 10(1) 2005. p. 3-9.
5. Public Citizen Magazine (A Ralph Nader Publication) 1994; May/June
6. "America's Wars." Department of Veterans Affairs. 2001. May 2001 ‹http://www.va.gov/pressrel/ amwars01.htm›.
7. Kochanek, K.D., Murphy, S.L. "Deaths: Final Data for 2002 National Vital Statistics Report." CDC. 12 Oct 2004 ‹http://www.cdc.gov/nchs/data/nvsr/nvsr53/nvsr53_05.pdf›.
8. Bates, D.W., et al. "Incidence of adverse drug events and potential adverse drug events. Implications for prevention." JAMA vol 274 1995. p. 29-34. Holland, E.G., Degruy, F.V. "Drug-Induced Disorders." American Academy of Family Physician vol 56(7) 1997. p. 1781-90.
9. Leape, L.L. "Error in medicine." JAMA vol 272(23) 1994. p. 1851-57.

infection due to medical care increased hospital stay by nearly 10 days at a cost of $38,656 in extra charges while increasing mortality by 4.31%.[1]

A 1995 estimate of costs associated with preventable drug-related morbidity and mortality was $76.6 billion.[2] A 2003 study concluded costs of adverse drug reactions had soared to $177 billion for the year 2000.[3] Individual hospital costs of adverse drug events have been estimated to be $5.6 million a year for a 700 bed hospital.[4]

A national study found from 1983 to 1993, deaths due to medication errors rose more than twofold, with 7,391 deaths attributed to medication errors in 1993 alone.[5]

Many studies have sought to determine the reasons for increases in medical errors. In one survey, 33% of respondents stated they believed the main cause of medication errors was nurses' tiredness or exhaustion, another 30% indicated the main cause was the poor legibility of doctors orders.[6] A 2003 observational study seems to validate their beliefs.[7] Another observational study concluded medication errors occurred in nearly 1 of every 5 doses in the typical hospital; 10% were deemed as being potentially life-threatening.[8]

Although recent studies suggest most medical errors result from poorly designed health care systems rather than negligence, nursing math errors still have a major impact on the rates of medical errors.[9] Hospital pharmacies providing patient medications in pre-calculated doses further reduces the frequency which these calculations are performed in the clinical setting.[10] Many studies have confirmed drug calculation skills are very poor[11] for nurses.[12] A 1997

10. Pirmohamed, M. "Adverse drug reactions as cause of admission to hospital: prospective analysis of 18 820 patients." BMJ Jul 3; 329(7456) 2004. p. 15-19.
1. Zhan, C., Miller, M.R. "Excess length of stay, charges, and mortality attributable to medical injuries during hospitalization." JAMA Oct 8; 290(14) 2003. p. 1868-74.
2. Johnson, J.A., Bootman, J.L. "Drug-related morbidity and mortality. A cost-of-illness model." Arch Intern Med vol 155(18) 1995. p. 1949-56.
3. Ernst, F.R., Grizzle, A.J. "Drug-related morbidity and mortality: updating the cost-of-illness model." J Am Pharm Assoc (Wash) Mar-Apr; 41(2) 2001. p. 192-99.
4. Bates, D.W., et al. "The costs of adverse drug events in hospitalized patients. Adverse Drug Events Prevention Study Group." JAMA vol 277(4) 1997. p. 307-11.
5. Phillips, D.P., Christenfeld, N., Glynn, L.M. "Increase in US medication-error deaths between 1983 and 1993." Lancet vol 351(9103) 1998. p. 643-44.
6. Karadeniz, G., Cakmakci, A. "Nurses' perceptions of medication errors." Int J Clin Pharmacol Res vol 22(3-4) 2002. p. 111-16.
7. Tissot, E., et al. "Observational study of potential risk factors of medication administration errors." Pharm World Sci Dec; 25(6) 2003. p. 264-68.
8. Barker, K.N., et al. "Medication errors observed in 36 health care facilities." Arch Intern Med Sep 9; 162(16) 2002. p. 1897-903.
9. Anderson, J.G. "A systems approach to preventing adverse drug events." Stud Health Technol Inform vol 92 2003. p. 95-102.
10. Cartwright, M. "Numeracy needs of the beginning registered nurse." Nurse Educ Today Apr; 16(2) 1996. p. 137-43.
11. Bindler, R., Bayne, T. "Medication calculation ability of registered nurses." Image J Nurs Sch Winter; 23(4) 1991. p. 221-24. Wright, K. "An investigation to find strategies to improve student nurses' maths skills." Br J Nurs Nov 25-Dec 8; 13(21) 2004. p. 1280-87.
12. Bayne, T., Bindler, R. "Effectiveness of medication calculation enhancement methods with nurses." J Nurs Staff Dev Nov-Dec; 13(6) 1997. p. 293-301. Laverty, D. "Drug administration: accuracy of nurses' calculations." Nurs Stand Jun 24; 3(39) 1989. p. 34-37.

study of medical surgical nurses found 56.4% were unable to solve 90% of the questions on drug exams.[1] A Canadian study replicated these findings by showing 58% of the 220 applicants were not able to accurately calculate all 11 drug dosages on a basic drug exam.[2] Scandinavian studies have shown their nurses have similar math weaknesses.[3] Misplaced decimal points are of particular concern when dispensing medications.[4] One university study detected 200 cases of tenfold prescribing error over an 18-month period. Overdoses were prescribed in 61% of the cases and underdoses in 39% of the cases. Forty-five percent of the errors were rated as potentially serious or severe.[5]

These findings are not just restricted to nurses; a study on paramedics found the mean score was 51.4% on basic drug exams. The paramedics failed to calculate IV flow rates and medication boluses in 68.8% of the cases. They also had difficulty solving both non-weight-based medication infusions and weight-based medication infusions. Scores were lower among paramedics with more years of EMS experience.[6]

A statistical analysis found nurses who failed the medication test were more likely to make medication errors than those who passed.[7] Hospitals may attempt to reduce the need for math by using "dedicated" medication nurses who are solely responsible for dispensing all patient medications. Unfortunately, a 2003 randomized clinical study found no reduction in medication error rates using this approach.[8]

The incidence of errors may actually be higher than studies suggest because many nurses may not report these errors for fear of reprisal.[9] In one study, only 45.6% of the nurses evaluated believed all drug errors are reported. Most stated they failed to report these errors for fear of manager and peer reactions.[10]

1. Ashby, D.A. "Medication calculation skills of the medical-surgical nurse." Medsurg Nurs Apr; 6(2) 1997. p. 90-94.
2. Santamaria, N., Norris, H., Clayton, L., Scott, D. "Drug calculation competencies of graduate nurses." Collegian Jul; 4(3) 1997. p. 18-21.
3. Grandell-Niemi, H., Hupli, M., Leino-Kilpi, H. "Medication calculation skills of graduating nursing students in Finland." Adv Health Sci Educ Theory Pract vol 6(1) 2001. p. 15-24. Kapborg, I.D. "Calculation and administration of drug dosage by Swedish nurses, student nurses and physicians." Int J Qual Health Care Dec; 6(4) 1994. p. 389-95.
4. "Zeroing in on medication errors." Lancet Feb 8; 349(9049) 1997. p. 369.
5. Lesar, T.S. "Tenfold medication dose prescribing errors." Ann Pharmacother Dec; 36(12) 2002. p. 1833-39.
6. Hubble, M.W., Paschal, K.R., Sanders, T.A. "Medication calculation skills of practicing paramedics." Prehosp Emerg Care Jul-Sep; 4(3) 2000. p. 253-60.
7. Calliari, D. "The relationship between a calculation test given in nursing orientation and medication errors." J Contin Educ Nurs Jan-Feb; 26(1) 1995. p. 11-14.
8. Greengold, N.L., et al. "The impact of dedicated medication nurses on the medication administration error rate: a randomized controlled trial." Arch Intern Med Oct 27; 163(19) 2003. p. 2359-67.
9. King, G., III, Hermodson, A. "Peer reporting of coworker wrongdoing: A qualitative analysis of observer attitudes in the decision to report versus not report unethical behavior." Journal of Applied Communication Research vol 28 2000. p. 309-329. Osborne, J., Blais, K., Hayes, J.S. "Nurses' perceptions: when is it a medication error?" J Nurs Adm Apr; 29(4) 1999. p. 33-38.
10. Mayo, A.M., Duncan, D. "Nurse perceptions of medication errors: what we need to know for patient safety." J Nurs Care Qual Jul-Sep; 19(3) 2004. p. 209-17.

However, nurses are still more conscientious than physicians in reporting medical errors. A 6-month study evaluating the rates of event reporting found nurses reported most of the medical events (59.1%). Residents were half as likely to report medical errors as nurses (27.2%). ICU attending physicians reported a paltry (2.6%) of all errors even though 3.0% of these errors may have contributed to patient deaths.[1]

Studies reveal that 75-85% of physicians have never reported an ADR to the governmental[2] or professional reporting systems.[3] This is appalling considering the frequency of ADRs in both in-hospital and outpatient settings.[4] In a Veterans Administration study of 198 outpatients, only 0.5% of all ADRs were reported.[5]

Although nurses and other non-physician personnel are responsible for many medical errors, most medication errors occur at the prescribing stage. A 2002 study of a large medical center in Chicago identified 1111 prescribing errors, 64% of these errors occurred upon admission; 30.8% were rated clinically significant.[6] Further investigations into medication errors at the ordering stage reveal their occurrence in up to 57.0 per 1,000 orders.[7]

Adverse drug reactions are especially worrisome in the elderly who receive more medications than any other sector in society. A 10-week study of 416 hospitalized elderly patients found only 8% were taking no drugs at all; the remaining 381 were receiving a total of 1,348 drugs. Forty-eight (11.5%) had been prescribed drugs which were clearly contra-indicated and 155 were on medications which were unnecessary. One hundred and three patients experienced adverse reactions to prescribed medications.[8] Studies have shown patients may average 4-5 medications to "treat" their illnesses.[9] Veteran

1. Osmon, S., et al. "Reporting of medical errors: an intensive care unit experience." Crit Care Med Mar; 32(3) 2004. p. 727-33.
2. Vincent, C., Stanhope, N., Crowley-Murphy, M. "Reasons for not reporting adverse incidents: an empirical study." J Eval Clin Pract Feb; 5(1) 1999. p. 13-21.
3. Eland, I.A., et al. "Attitudinal survey of voluntary reporting of adverse drug reactions." Br J Clin Pharmacol Oct; 48(4) 1999. p. 623-27. Hasford, J., Goettler, M., Munter, K.H., Muller-Oerling-hausen, B. "Physicians' knowledge and attitudes regarding the spontaneous reporting system for adverse drug reactions." J Clin Epidemiol Sep; 55(9) 2002. p. 945-50.
4. Bagian, J.P., et al. "Developing and deploying a patient safety program in a large health care delivery system: you can't fix what you don't know about." Jt Comm J Qual Improv vol 27(10) 2001. p. 522-532. Gandhi. T.K., et al. "Drug complications in outpatients." J GenIntern Med vol 15 2000. p. 149-54.
5. Monica, B., et al. "Improving Adverse-Drug-Reaction Reporting in Ambulatory Care Clinics at a Veterans Affairs Hospital." Am J Health-Syst Pharm vol 59(9) 2002. p. 841-45.
6. Bobb, A., et al. "The epidemiology of prescribing errors: the potential impact of computerized prescriber order entry." Arch Intern Med Apr 12; 164(7) 2004. p. 785-92.
7. Von Laue, N.C., Schwappach, D.L., Koeck, C.M. "The epidemiology of preventable adverse drug events: a review of the literature." Wien Klin Wochenschr Jul 15; 115(12) 2003. p. 407-15.
8. Lindley, C.M., et al.. "Inappropriate medication is a major cause of adverse drug reactions in elderly patients." Age Ageing Jul; 21(4) 1992. p. 294-300.
9. Giron, M.S., et al. "The appropriateness of drug use in an older nondemented and demented population." J Am Geriatr Soc vol 49 2001. p. 277-83. Hohl, C.M., et al. "Polypharmacy, adverse drug-related events, and potential adverse drug interactions in elderly patients presenting to an emergency department." Ann Emerg Med Dec; 38(6) 2001. p. 666-71.

Administration patients may be taking nine or more drugs daily.[1] A more recent study of ER admissions concluded adverse drug reactions occurred in 27% of patients on medication, and half of these reactions were due to drugs with absolute contraindications or deemed unnecessary.[2]

A panel of experts evaluated the prescribing patterns for 20 drugs they believed should never be given to the elderly.[3] Overall, 7.6% of elderly who received a prescription had at least one inappropriate medication prescribed. A 2002 study concluded 62% of all hospital admissions for adverse drug reactions were preventable.[4] A 2003 JAMA study[5] found the drugs most commonly associated with hospital admission for a preventable adverse drug reaction were:

- Cardiovascular medications — 24.5%
- Diuretics — 22.1%
- Nonopioid analgesics -15.4%
- Hypoglycemics — 10.9%
- Anticoagulants — 10.2%
- They reported the most common ADR events were:
- Electrolyte/renal — 26.6%
- Gastrointestinal tract — 21.1%
- Hemorrhagic — 15.9%
- Metabolic/endocrine — 13.8%
- Neuropsychiatric — 8.6%

This agrees with another study which found the medication classes most frequently involved in adverse drug events were selective serotonin-reuptake inhibitors (10%), beta-blockers (9%), angiotensin-converting-enzyme inhibitors (8%), and nonsteroidal anti-inflammatory agents (8%).[6]

Reviewing stroke, pneumonia, and heart attack deaths from 12 hospitals, one study concluded over a quarter of the deaths might have been prevented. One in seven heart attacks occurring in a hospital were actually caused by the physician![7] In a review of over 30,000 randomly selected patient records in the state of New York, researchers estimated 27,179 injuries; including 6895 deaths and 877 cases of permanent and total disability were the result of physician negligence annually.[8] Adverse events in uninsured patients were twice as likely

1. Monica, B., et al. "Improving Adverse-Drug-Reaction Reporting in Ambulatory Care Clinics at a Veterans Affairs Hospital." Am J Health-Syst Pharm vol 59(9) 2002. p. 841-845.
2. Tafreshi, M.J., et al. "Medication-related visits to the emergency department: a prospective study." Ann Pharmacother Dec; 33(12) 1999. p. 1252-57.
3. Aparasu, R.R., et al.. "Inappropriate medication prescribing for the elderly by office-based physicians." Ann Pharmacother Jul-Aug; 31(7-8) 1997. p. 823-29.
4. McDonnell, P.J., Jacobs, M.R. "Hospital admissions resulting from preventable adverse drug reactions." Ann Pharmacother Sep; 36(9) 2002. p. 1331-36.
5. Gurwitz, J.H., et al. "Incidence and preventability of adverse drug events among older persons in the ambulatory setting." JAMA Mar 5; 289(9) 2003. p. 1107-16.
6. Gandhi, T.K., et al. "Adverse drug events in ambulatory care." NEJM Apr 17; 348(16) 2003. p. 1556-64.
7. Bedell, S.E., et al. "Incidence and Characteristics of Preventable Iatrogenic Cardiac Arrests." JAMA vol 265 1991. p. 2815-2820. Greger, M. Malpractice. Heart Failure — Diary of a Third Year Medical Student. 1999 <http://upalumni.org/medschool/appendices/appendix-73b.html#fn883>

to be caused by negligence as for those with private insurance. A 2001 study concluded 22.7% of active-care patient deaths were probably preventable.[1] Their findings were similar to an older study which found 27% of drug related deaths were preventable.[2] The good news is the 2001 study also determined only 6% of these patients would have lived for three months or leave the hospital alive. Are we to conclude the remaining errors were less significant because they occurred on patients with a limited life expectancy?

The rate of adverse drug events increases in proportion to the number of medical interventions. Rates of preventable adverse drug events and potential adverse drug events in the ICU are nearly double that of non-ICUs.[3] A 1991 study of 208 ICU patients found 14% of cardiac arrests were directly attributable to the medical care they were receiving.[4] A French study concluded 10% of all ICU deaths were doctor induced, over half these deaths were considered preventable.[5] Tragically, physicians seldom report suspected adverse reactions to medicines.[6]

Patients expect there doctors to be more forthright concerning their errors. In one study, in which patients of primary care physicians were given hypothetical situations, 98% wanted honest acknowledgement of errors, even if minor.[7] These findings agree with another study of ophthalmologists where 92% of the patients expected disclosure of physician errors. Only 60% of the physicians in this study chose to disclose these errors to their patients.[8] These findings are similar to another study in which 97% of physicians surveyed agreed that an error had occurred but only 64% would disclose the error to the patient affected.[9] In a separate study in which physicians were given a hypothetical case where a patient dies because of a drug error by a physician, more than one third of those surveyed indicated they would provide the family with incomplete or misleading information about what transpired.[10] Standard medical

8. Brennan, T.A. "Incidence of Adverse Events and Negligence in Hospitalized Patients." NEJM vol 324 1991. p. 370-76.
1. Hayward, R.A., Hofer, T.P. "Estimating hospital deaths due to medical errors: preventability is in the eye of the reviewer." JAMA Jul 25; 286(4) 2001. p. 415-20.
2. Dubois, R.W., Brook, R.H. "Preventable Deaths." Annals of Internal Medicine vol 1 October 1988. p. 582-589.
3. Cullen, D.J., et al. "Preventable adverse drug events in hospitalized patients: a comparative study of intensive care and general care units." Crit Care Med Aug; 25(8) 1997. p. 1289-97.
4. Bedell, S.E., et al. "Incidence and Characteristics of Preventable Iatrogenic Cardiac Arrests." JAMA vol 265 1991. p. 2815-20.
5. Darchy, B., et al. "Iatrogenic Diseases as a Reason for Admission to the Intensive Care." Unit Arch Intern Med vol 159 1999. p. 71-78.
6. Moride, Y., et al. "Under-reporting of adverse drug reactions in general practice." Br J Clin Pharmacol vol 43 1997. p. 177-81. Smith, C.C., et al. "Adverse drug reactions in a hospital general medical unit meriting notification to the Committee on Safety of Medicines." Br J Clin Pharmacol vol 42 1996. p. 423-29.
7. Witman, A., Park, D., Hardin, S. "How do patients want physicians to handle mistakes? A survey of internal medicine patients in an academic setting." Arch Intern Med vol 156 1996. p. 2565-69.
8. Hingorani, M., Wong, T., Vafidis, G. "Patients' and doctors' attitudes to amount of information given after unintended injury during treatment: cross-sectional, questionnaire survey." BMJ vol 318 1999. p. 640-41.
9. Cook, A.F., et al. "An error by any other name." Am J Nurs Jun; 104(6) 2004. p. 32-43.

pharmacology texts admit relatively few doctors ever report adverse drug reactions to the FDA.[1] The reasons stated range from not knowing such a reporting system exists to fear of being sued because they prescribed a drug that caused harm.[2] It may be hard to accept, but not difficult to understand, why only one in twenty side effects is reported to either hospital administrators[3] or the FDA.[4]

Nondisclosure may be rationalized by concerns for increasing patient anxiety or confusing the patient with complicated information.[5] The archaic concept of therapeutic privilege,[6] that is, protecting the "child-like patient from "harmful" information, has now been generally discredited.[7] Physicians underestimate patients' desire for medical information: both good and bad.[8] Iatrogenic (doctor induced) deaths are frequently hidden from the patient's families. A survey of physicians reported twice as many would attempt to resuscitate a patient with a living will if they felt they were directly responsible for the patient's death.[9] A 1996 study found 68% of patients with iatrogenic induced congestive heart failure died within one year compared to 39% in non-iatrogenic patients.[10] Studies of outpatients found similar rates of iatrogenic injury as those within a hospital setting.[11] A 2003 survey of 114 internal medicine house officers came to a chilling conclusion. Patients had serious adverse outcomes in 90% of reported errors with 31% resulting in death. Incredibly, only 54% of the house officers mentioned their mistake to their attending physicians and only 24% told the patients or families.[12]

10. Novack, D., et al. "Physicians' attitudes towards using deception to resolve difficult ethical problems." JAMA vol 261 1989. p. 2980-85.
1. Gilman, A.G., et al. Goodman And Gilman's: The Pharmacological Basis Of Therapeutics. New York: Pergamon Press, 1996.
2. Kolata, G. "Who cares when our drugs fail?" San Diego Union-Tribune 1997, Natl ed.: E-1,5. Vincent C, Stanhope N, Crowley-Murphy M. Reasons for not reporting adverse incidents: an empirical study. J Eval Clin Pract. 1999 Feb; 5(1):13-21.
3. Moore, T.J., Psaty, B.M., Furberg, C.D. "Time to act on drug safety." JAMA vol 279 (19) 1998. p. 1571-73.
4. Cullen, D.J., et al. "The incident reporting system does not detect adverse drug events: a problem for quality improvement." Joint Commission Journal on Quality Improvement vol 21 (10) 1995. p. 541-48.
5. Lantos J. Do we still need doctors? New York: Routledge; 1997. p. 116-32.
6. Van Oosten, F.F. "The so-called 'therapeutic privilege' or 'contra-indication': its nature and role in non-disclosure cases." Med Law vol 10(1) 1991. p. 31-41. Wynia, M.K. "Invoking Therapeutic Privilege." AMA. 2005. 17 May 2005 <http://www.ama-assn.org/ama/pub/category/11937.html>.
7. President's Commission for the Study of Ethical Problems in Medicine and Biomedical and Behavioral Research: Making Health Care Decisions [Vol. 1, report]. Washington: US Government Printing Office, 1982. Hébert, P.C., Levin, A.V., Robertson, G. "Bioethics for clinicians: 23. Disclosure of medical error." CMAJ. 2001. 20 Feb 2001 <http://www.cmaj.ca/cgi/content/full/164/4/509>.
8. Beard, M., Midgley, J.R. "Therapeutic privilege and informed consent : a justified erosion of patient autonomy?" THRHR vol 68(1) 2005. p. 51.
9. Casarett, D.J., Stocking, C.B., Siegler, M. "Would physicians override a do-not-resuscitate order when a cardiac arrest is iatrogenic?" J Gen Intern Med Jan; 14(1) 1999. p. 35-38.
10. Rich, M.W., et al. "Iatrogenic congestive heart failure in older adults: clinical course and prognosis." J Am Geriatr Soc Jun; 44(6) 1996. p. 638-43.
11. Elder, N.C., Vonder Meulen, M., Cassedy, A. "The identification of medical errors by family physicians during outpatient visits." Ann Fam Med Mar-Apr; 2(2) 2004. p. 125-29.
12. Wu, A.W., Folkman, S., McPhee, S.J., Lo, B. "Do house officers learn from their mistakes?" Qual Saf Health Care Jun; 12(3) 2003. p. 221-26.

Hospital administrators fear admission of the actual number of errors and mistakes would lead to greater scrutiny.[1] The associate director of the Office of Post Marketing Drug Risk Assessment at the FDA stated, "In the broader area of adverse drug reaction data, the 250,000 reports received annually probably represent only 5% of the actual reactions that occur."[2] Hospitals routinely fail to implement or enforce policies regarding medical error reporting. A 2003 survey of medical residents found only half were aware the hospital had a medical error-reporting system, and the vast majority didn't use it at all.[3] One prospective study in the outpatient setting, using voluntary incidence reporting detected only about 3.7 events per 100,000 clinic visits.[4] In a study of 20,695 consecutive acute general medical admissions there were 1420 reports of suspected adverse drug reactions; only 6.3% of these errors were reported.[5] A 2004 British study of 18,820 admissions concluded 6.5% of all hospital admissions were the result of adverse drug reactions, 72% of these ADRs were deemed avoidable.[6]

These data do not reflect the injuries inflicted by non-physician personnel. Often times these injuries are directly the results of implemented guidelines that have been established to decrease worker error. However, workers in healthcare fields are working under ever-increasing stress as medicine shifts from a philosophy of altruism to one of for profit. The need to improve profit margins drives the system to a frenetic pace and often results in the implementation of a "make do" or "get by" mentality. The growing shortage of non-physician healthcare workers further stresses those remaining. Autocratic managers and administrators often add to the burdens by demanding improvements in patient care.

Unfortunately, their idea of improvement is the implementation of more unproven technologies and even more reliance on paper work. The paperwork mentality is particularly frustrating for healthcare workers because they find more and more of their time being taken away from direct patient care and being dedicated to complete forms to help "insure and improve" patient care. This paper work is often an endless array of standards of safety and clinical care paths whose intent is to focus and integrate patient care. Although well meaning, it simply adds to the burden of duties of those who are already over worked and over stressed. This pressure frequently results in out right falsification of medical

1. Null, G., et al. "Death by Medicine." Mercola. 2003. 26 Nov 2003 ‹http://mercola.com/2003/nov/26/death_by_medicine.htm›. Bates, D.W. "Drugs and adverse drug reactions: how worried should we be?" JAMA vol 279 (15) 1998. p. 1216-17.
2. Dickinson JG. Dickinson's FDA Review vol 7 (3) 2000. p. 13-14.
3. Stenson, J. "Few Residents Report Medical Errors, Survey Finds." Reuters Health 21 Feb 2003, Natl ed.
4. Von Laue, N.C., Schwappach, D.L., Koeck, C.M. "The epidemiology of medical errors: a review of the literature." Wien Klin Wochenschr May 30; 115(10) 2003. p. 318-25.
5. Smith, C.C., et al. "Adverse drug reactions in a hospital general medical unit meriting notification to the Committee on Safety of Medicines." Br J Clin Pharmacol Oct; 42(4) 1996. p. 423-92..
6. Pirmohamed, M., et al. "Adverse drug reactions as cause of admission to hospital: prospective analysis of 18 820 patients." BMJ vol 329 2004. p. 15-19.

records, forms are completed and signed without actually being read or implemented.

This reliance upon a "paper trail" to insure all standards have been met is particularly dangerous because now instead of assuming the standard has been met, it results in those relying upon the paperwork to believe as a matter of fact that the standard has been met. People usually question assumptions they seldom question facts. By relying upon "factual data" that is either flawed or even worse blatantly false, horrific errors of judgment may occur at all levels of care. It should then come as no surprise to see rationalization is common when one of these unfortunate events occur.[1]

Despite multiple studies by the Institute of Medicine, there remains a persistent refusal by medical workers to address the disclosure of medical errors. These silences distort public policy and delay change, resulting in thousands of patient deaths.[2] Practitioners choose not to disclose or report error for variety of reasons, including ignorance related to reporting requirements, uncertainty about filing error reports, a wish not to upset patients and concerns for the consequences of disclosure.[3] However, these concerns are generally exaggerated and misplaced.[4] Frank disclosure of errors may be very difficult, but it is still required to maintain the trust between physicians and patients.[5] An effort to cover up iatrogenic errors breaks this bond. Failure to honestly report adverse events on death certificates may be deceitful but it is still lawful. A death certificate might list a stomach hemorrhage as the cause of death, without mentioning the use of the drug that brought it on.[6] Some hospitals have decided honesty is the best policy and are now actively enforcing full disclosure of medical errors. These policies have resulted in a decline in malpractice claims.[7]

Many physicians are unconcerned by all this piffle on medical errors. A mail survey of physicians found doctors were much less likely than the public to believe quality of care is a problem (29.1% vs 67.6%).[8] A national telephone survey by the National Patient Safety Foundation found 42% of respondents did not believe hospitals were providing adequate safety for patients. Forty-two

1. McDonald, C.J., Weiner, M., Hui, S.L. "Deaths due to medical errors are exaggerated in Institute of Medicine report." JAMA vol 284 2000. p. 93-95. Sox, H.C. Jr., Woloshin, S. "How many deaths are due to medical error? Getting the number right." Eff Clin Pract Nov-Dec; 3(6) 2000. p. 277-83.
2. Millenson, M.L. "The silence." Health Aff (Millwood) Mar-Apr; 22(2) 2003. p. 103-12.
3. Victoroff, M. "The right intentions: errors and accountability." J Fam Pract vol 45 1997. p. 38-39. Vincent, C., Stanhope, N., Crowley-Murphy, M. "Reasons for not reporting adverse events: an empirical study." J Eval Clin Pract vol 5 1999. p. 13-21.
4. Studdert, D., et al. "Negligent care and malpractice claiming behavior in Utah and Colorado." Med Care vol 38 2000. p. 250-60.
5. Finkelstein, D., et al. "When a physician harms a patient by medical error: ethical, legal, and risk-management considerations." J Clin Ethic vol 8 1997. p. 330-35. Newman, M.C. "The emotional impact of mistakes on family physicians." Arch Fam Med vol 5 1996. p. 71-75.
6. Lazarou, J., Pomeranz, B.H., Corey, P.N. "Incidence of adverse drug reactions in hospitalized patients: a meta-analysis of prospective studies." JAMA Apr 15; 279(15) 1998. p. 1200-05.
7. Kraman, S., Hamm, G. "Risk management: Extreme honesty may be the best policy." Ann Intern Med vol 131 1999. p. 963-67.
8. Robinson, A.R., et al. "Physician and public opinions on quality of health care and the problem of medical errors." Arch Intern Med Oct 28; 162(19) 2002. p. 2186-90.

percent indicated they or their close friends and relatives had experienced a medical mistake.[1] A 2002 survey found medical errors were reported by physicians (35%) and members of the public (42%) in their own or a family member's care. Neither group viewed medical errors as one of the most important problems in health care today. A majority of both groups believed that the number of in-hospital deaths due to preventable errors is lower than that reported by the Institute of Medicine.[2] The public's lack of knowledge related to medical errors explains their indifference, physician unconcern is inexcusable.

Although many physicians ultimately do disclose adverse events, they often avoided stating that an error occurred, why the error happened, or how recurrences would be prevented. Patients also desired emotional support from physicians following errors,[3] including an apology. However, physicians may feel an apology could create a legal liability.[4] They are very cautious and "choose their words carefully" when telling patients about errors. When physicians disclose adverse events, they often avoid stating that an error occurred, why the error happened, or how recurrences would be prevented.[5] Policymakers attempt to circumvent physician reluctance to disclose medical errors by the creation of a system for medical error reporting. Unfortunately, healthcare providers fearful that reported error information may increase their risk for litigation have been reluctant to participate in such reporting systems.[6]

A study of 31,429 patients hospitalized in New York State in 1984 revealed their fears are unwarranted. This study reported that of the 280 patients who had adverse events caused by medical negligence, only 8 filed malpractice claims. These findings are typical throughout the medical community. Medical-malpractice litigation infrequently compensates patients injured by medical negligence and rarely identifies, and holds providers accountable for substandard care.[7] Incredibly, 70.5% of the adverse events in the New York study resulted in disability lasting less than 6 months, 2.6% caused permanently disabling injuries and 13.6% led to death.[8] A Florida health care report found only 3,177 medical malpractice claims were filed from 1996-1999. There were 19,885 reports of medical errors during this same period. The authors conclude

1. "Public Opinion of Patient Safety Issues: Research Findings." National Patient Safety Foundation. 1997. Sep 1997 ⟨http://www.npsf.org/download/1997survey.pdf⟩.
2. Blendon, R.J., et al. "Views of practicing physicians and the public on medical errors." NEJM Dec 12; 347(24) 2002. p. 1933-40.
3. Firth-Cozens, J. "Anxiety as a barrier to risk management." Qual Saf Health Care vol 11 2002. p. 115.
4. Davidoff, F. "Shame: the elephant in the room." Qual Saf Health Care vol 11 2002. p. 2-3.
5. Gallagher, T.H. "Patients' and Physicians' Attitudes Regarding the Disclosure of Medical Errors." JAMA vol 289 2003. p. 1001-1007.
6. Zivin, J.G., Pfaff, A.S. "To err on humans is not benign. Incentives for adoption of medical error-reporting systems." J Health Econ Sep; 23(5) 2004. p. 935-49.
7. Localio, A.R., et al. "Relation Between Malpractice Claims and Adverse Events Due to Negligence." NEJM vol 325 1991. p. 245-251.
8. Brennan, T.A., et al. "Harvard Medical Practice Study I. Incidence of adverse events and negligence in hospitalized patients: results of the Harvard Medical Practice Study I. 1991.." Qual Saf Health Care Apr; 13(2) 2004. p. 145-51.

only one claim is filed for every six reports of adverse events.[1] Physicians generally fail to mention that 97% of those injured by medical care do not sue for reimbursement.

For the specialties included in PIAA data collected from 1985 through 2000, 31% of malpractice claims resulted in an indemnity payout, and the average amount paid was $167,466.

A study of malpractice claims published in *Medical Economics* compared the rates of malpractice in thirteen medical specialties.[2] Their results are shown in the following table.

Malpractice Claims by Area of Practice

Area of Practice	No. of Claims Closed	% Closed with Payout	Average Payout
Cardiovascular diseases (non surgical)	2,402	19	$199,378
Dermatology	1,854	31	94,347
Emergency medicine	2,337	29	144,092
Family and general practice	19,043	36	132,356
Gastroenterology	1,286	21	147,234
General surgery	17,974	35	151,810
Gynecology	1,904	32	117,343
Internal medicine	21,591	27	169,381
Neurology	2,607	22	266,881
Ob/gyn (surgical)	22,980	36	235,059
Orthopedic surgery	16,440	30	138,799
Otorhinolaryngology	2,654	32	167,855
Pediatrics	5,022	29	232,499

They also gave the top ten reasons for malpractice claims, the ten conditions most often resulting in a claim, and the ten medical procedures most often resulting in a claim.

Top 10 Reasons for Malpractice Claims
Against Primary Care Physicians

Jan. 1, 1985 through Dec. 31, 2000

	No. of Claims Closed	% Closed with Payout	Average Payout
Errors in diagnosis	12,602	37	$171,501
No medical misadventure[1]	8,254	5	109,212
Improper performance	5,370	36	118,256
Failure to supervise or monitor case	3,637	39	157,984
Medication errors	3,127	41	112,861
Not performed[2]	1,278	42	180,425
Failure/delay in referral or consultation	1,146	46	177,388
Performed when not indicated or contraindicated	1,128	37	119,983
Failure to recognize a complication of treatment	1,056	36	115,915
Delay in performance	785	46	179,463

[1] The doctor was named in a lawsuit, but there was no allegation of inappropriate medical conduct on his part.

[2] The physician allegedly failed to perform an indicated treatment or procedure, and that failure was the main reason for the malpractice action.

1. "Risk Management Reporting Summary, 24 Hour Reports and Code 15 Reports 2001." Florida Agency for Health Care Administration Mar 2002.
2. Weiss, G. "Malpractice: Don't wait for a lawsuit to strike." Medical Economics vol 342 2000. p. 1207-1210.

Top 10 Medical Conditions
for which Primary Care Doctors are Sued
Jan. 1 1985 through Dec. 31, 2000

	No. of Claims Closed	% Closed with Payout	Average Payout
Acute myocardial infarction	1,432	39	$193,439
Cancer of bronchus and lung	894	36	171,565
Breast cancer	829	43	190,252
Colon and rectal cancer	707	43	222,335
Diabetes	613	33	120,087
Abdominal and pelvic symptoms	521	23	201,818
Pneumonia	531	28	141,734
Chest pain (not further defined)	476	29	197,101
Appendicitis	500	37	65,040
Hypertension	457	30	180,922

Closed in 2000

Acute myocardial infarction	34	38	$265,173
Chest pain (not further defined)	30	37	304,727
Abdominal and pelvic symptoms	29	17	124,250
Obesity	26	0	0
Back disorders*	19	37	152,143
Pneumonia	19	37	43,333
Disorders of soft tissue	18	28	265,000
Colon and rectal cancer	18	50	338,519
Diabetes	17	53	397,500
Injury to multiple body parts	17	35	67,961

Including lumbago and sciatica

Top 10 Procedures for which Primary Care Doctors are Sued
Jan. 1, 1985 through Dec. 31, 2000

	No. of Claims Closed	% Closed with Payout	Average Payout
Diagnostic interview evaluation, or consultation	15,159	27	$167,370
Prescription of medication	6,012	39	118,699
General physical exam	3,096	30	182,294
No care rendered	1,644	10	95,895
Injections and vaccinations	1,506	38	139,253
Diagnostic radiologic procedures excluding CT scan and contrast material	1,135	44	158,551
Diagnostic procedures involving cardiac and circulatory functions	997	37	218,300
Misc. manual exams and nonoperative procedures	906	43	181,616
Diagnostic procedures of the large intestine	489	37	160,529
Misc. nonoperative procedures	459	31	63,262
Closed in 2000			
Diagnostic interview, evaluation, or consultation	339	30	$276,053
General physical exam	183	26	370,413
Prescription of medication	162	28	215,996
Injections and vaccinations	47	40	405,377
Misc. manual exams and nonoperative procedures	44	48	234,568
No care rendered	34	3	130,000
Diagnostic radiologic procedures excluding CT scan and contrast material	30	33	130,450
Diagnostic procedures involving cardiac and circulatory functions	28	54	336,283
Diagnostic procedures of the large intestine	20	50	190,500
CT scan	17	47	163,422

A sequel to the Institute of Medicine's report "To Err is Human" calls for improvements in six dimensions of health care performance: safety, effectiveness, patient-centeredness, timeliness, efficiency, and equity; it asserts those improvements cannot be achieved within the constraints of the existing system of care.[1] Few hospitals have reached the IOM's goal of halving mistakes by 2004.[2]

Most malpractice claims are directed against a small number of physicians. Studies have shown unsolicited patient complaints are predictive of who will be sued.[3] One study compared a physician's malpractice litigation record during 1980-1984, to their records during 1985-1989. Previous malpractice suits were predictive of future claims. Physicians trained at lower ranked medical schools or who went through lower-ranked residency programs faced higher odds of developing adverse malpractice records.[4] Most malpractice claims do not actually involve a negligent injury[5]; however, a patient who suffers a negligent injury is more than 20 times more likely to file a claim.[6] The patient's disability was a positive indicator of payment to the plaintiff.[7] Intense advertising by local medical law firms increases the number of medical malpractice suits.[8]

The authors of one study found male physicians were three times as likely as female physicians to be sued, they conclude female physicians have more effective communication skills that enable them to interact more effectively with patients.[9] Empathy and honest communication are the best defenses against malpractice suits,[10] unfortunately, they are woefully lacking among many physicians.[11] Many malpractice suits occur as an expression of anger[12] about some aspect of patient-doctor relationships and communications.[13] Communicating with patients,

1. "Crossing the Quality Chasm: The IOM Health Care Quality Initiative." Institute of Medicine. 2005. 20 Dec 2001 <http://www.iom.edu/CMS/8089.aspx>. Berwick, D.M. "A user's manual for the IOM's 'Quality Chasm' report." Health Aff (Millwood) May-Jun; 21(3) 2001. p. 80-90.
2. Morrissey, J. "Patient safety proves elusive. Five years after publication of the IOM's 'To Err is Human,' there's plenty of activity on patient safety, but progress is another matter." Mod Healthc Nov 1; 34(44):6-7 2004. p. 24-55, 28-32.
3. Crane, M. "Why burned-out doctors get sued more often." Med Econ May 26; 75(10):210-2 1998. p. 215-18. Hickson, G.B., et al. "Patient complaints and malpractice risk." JAMA Jun 12; 287(22) 2002. p. 2951-57.
4. Weycker, D.A., Jensen, G.A. "Medical malpractice among physicians: who will be sued and who will pay?" Health Care Manag Sci Sep; 3(4) 2000. p. 269-77.
5. Localio, A.R., et al.. "Relation between malpractice claims and adverse events due to negligence. Results of the Harvard Medical Practice Study III." NEJM vol 325 1991. p. 245-51.
6. Mello, M.M., Hemenway, D. "Medical malpractice as an epidemiological problem." Soc Sci Med Jul; 59(1) 2004. p. 39-46.
7. Brennan, T.A., et al. "Relation between Negligent Adverse Events and the Outcomes of Medical-Malpractice Litigation." NEJM vol 335(26) 1996. p. 1963-1967.
8. Vukmir, R.B. "Medical malpractice: managing the risk." Med Law vol 23(3) 2004. p. 495-513.
9. Taragin, M.I., et al. "Physician demographics and the risk of medical malpractice." Am J Med Nov; 93(5) 1992. p. 537-42.
10. Eastaugh, S.R. "Reducing litigation costs through better patient communication." Physician Exec May-Jun; 30(3) 2004. p. 36-38. Nye, L.G. "Office staff savvy: quality staff-patient communications as a loss prevention strategy." J Med Pract Manage Jul-Aug; 17(1) 2001. p. 21-24.
11. Correia, N.G. "Adverse events: reducing the risk of litigation." Cleve Clin J Med Jan; 69(1) 2002. p. 15-17, 23-24. Weintraub, M.I. "Medicolegal aspects of iatrogenic injuries." Neurol Clin Feb; 16(1) 1998. p. 217-27.

keeping accurate records and actually taking time to examine patients are three of the top 10 ways to avoid a lawsuit.[1] Patients who view their physicians as caring tend not to sue[2] even if an adverse outcome occurs.[3] A study of 128 obstetric patients showed positive physician communication behaviors increased patients' perceptions of physician competence and decreased malpractice claim intentions toward both the physician and the hospital.[4]

Individually and collectively, physicians can and should ensure that "doing no harm" comes first in the malpractice debate.[5] A former proponent of managed care describes how his group has let marketplace forces and greed jeopardize patients.[6] Patients' now realize their interests do not always come first, what was once thought to be satisfactory care and service will be deemed insufficient for themselves and their families.[7] They no longer trust the medical profession unreservedly.[8] A 2003 editorial in the British Medical Journal may be an ominous portent of things to come. The authors discuss how there is now a change in societal views about "accidents." They state that the new social intolerance of medical mistakes has resulted in them being viewed as crimes. The perpetrators of these crimes may now face incarceration instead of the customary rebuke behind closed doors.[9]

12. Pfifferling, J.H. "Ounces of malpractice prevention." Physician Exec Feb; 20(2) 1994. p. 36-38. Roberts, J. "Doctors sued for uninterest, say researchers in US." BMJ Dec 3; 309(6967) 1994. p. 1461.
13. Panting, G. "How to avoid being sued in clinical practice." Postgraduate Medical Journal vol 80 2004. p. 165-168. Virshup, B.B., Oppenberg, A.A., Coleman, M.M. "Strategic risk management: reducing malpractice claims through more effective patient-doctor communication." Am J Med Qual Jul-Aug; 14(4) 1999. p. 153-59.
1. Colon, V.F. "10 ways to reduce medical malpractice exposure." Physician Exec Mar-Apr; 28(2) 2002. p. 16-18.
2. "Physician bedside manner linked to malpractice suit." Patient Focus Care May; 5(5) 1997. p. 58-59.
3. Lichtstein, D.M., Materson, B.J., Spicer, D.W. "Reducing the risk of malpractice claims." Hosp Pract Jul 15; 34(7) 1999. p. 69-72, 75-6, 79. Woods, D. "Good communication: the best defense against litigation." Pa Med May; 98(5) 1995. p. 46.
4. Moore, P.J., Adler, N.E., Robertson, P.A. "Medical malpractice: the effect of doctor-patient relations on medical patient perceptions and malpractice intentions." West J Med Oct; 173(4) 2000. p. 244-50.
5. Schoenbaum, S.C., Bovbjerg, R.R. "Malpractice reform must include steps to prevent medical injury." Ann Intern Med Jan 6; 140(1) 2004. p. 51-53.
6. "Are we selling out our patients?" Med Econ Oct 28; 73(20) 1996. p. 125-27.
7. Montaglione, C.J. "The physician-patient relationship: cornerstone of patient trust, satisfaction, and loyalty." Manag Care Q Summer; 7(3) 1999. p. 5-21.
8. Rachagan, S.S., Sharon, K. "The patient's view." Med J Malaysia Mar; 58 Suppl A 2003. p. 86-101.
9. "The criminalisation of fatal medical mistakes." BMJ vol 327 2003. p. 1118-19.

CHAPTER 7. BEDPAN BLUES

CRITICAL CONDITION

> *Constant attention by a good nurse may be just as important as a major operation by a surgeon.*
> Dag Hammarskjold, Swedish statesman and United Nations official, 1905-1961

Several studies published by leading nursing journals all report there is a critical nursing shortage.[1] Nursing shortages have generally been cyclical in nature, most lasting only 12-18 months and have been resolved simply by raising salaries.[2] However, the current shortage of 126,000 nurses, which began in 1998, is viewed as different from those of the past.[3] One author compared the current shortage to the movie 'The Perfect Storm' which portrayed how three separate storms merged to create the worst storm recorded by meteorologists. The three "storms" in the current nursing shortage are (a) an increased demand for nurses, (b) a decreased supply of nurses, and (c) unfavorable work conditions. The analogy to this apocalyptic event may be appropriate because these conditions

---

1. "White paper. Health care at the crossroads: Strategies for addressing the evolving nursing crisis." Joint Commission on Accreditation of Healthcare Organizations. 27 May 2005 ‹ http://www.jcaho.org/NR/rdonlyres/5C138711-ED76-4D6F-909F-B06E0309F36D/0/health_care_at_the_crossroads.pdf› Bleich, M.R., et al. "Analysis of the nursing workforce crisis: A call to action." American Journal of Nursing vol 103(4) 2003. p. 66-74.
2. Budd, K., Warino, L., Patton, M. "Traditional and Non-traditional Collective Bargaining: Strategies to Improve the Patient Care Environment." Online Journal of Issues in Nursing. 31 Jan 2004 ‹www.nursingworld.org/ojin/topic23/tpc23_5.htm›.
3. Jaklevic, M.C., Lovern, E. "A Nursing Code Blue: Few Easy Solutions Seen for a National RN Shortage That's Different from Prior Undersupplies." Modern Healthcare December 11 2000. p. 42-46. Phillips, K. "Nursing shortage redux: Everything old is new again." AMN Healthcare. 2003. 01 Dec 2003 ‹http://amnhealthcare.com/Features.asp?articleID=11322&page= AMN%5FHealthcare+News&Profile=AMN%5FFeatures&Headine=Nursing+Shortage+Redux%3A+Everything+Old+is+New+Again›.

have converged to produce an event with potentially disastrous consequences.[1] Unlike the movie, this 'storm' is not the result on random acts of nature; it has been created by greed, bureaucracies and mismanagement.[2]

A 2002 study concluded the number of employed nurses was only 6% less than recommended by the National Center for Health Workforce Analysis, yet it was already having devastating consequences.[3] This shortfall occurred primarily in 30 states. The authors of this study believe these shortages will extend to 44 states and the District Columbia by the year 2020 and deficits may reach 400,000 to 1.5 million[4] nursing vacancies.[5]

The healthcare industry in this nation has long failed to appreciate the main healthcare commodity being provided is nursing care, not medical care. Most patients are hospitalized for the need of nursing care; medical services, although important, are usually transient in nature. The healthcare industry has chosen to tackle problems of managed care, cost cutting, changes in reimbursement, onerous regulations, increasing demands of technology, and burdensome documentation while ignoring the need for adequate nursing care.[6] One bureaucrat expressed this view rather succinctly by stating, "Why should I care about what staff think? If they don't like it, I can replace them all tomorrow."[7] Myopic managers have simply "corrected" past "shortages" by throwing the beleaguered nurses a bone or two but have made no attempt to address the fundamental causes of nursing shortages.[8] The use of sign-on bonuses or wage increases was generally sufficient to entice new graduates into hospital positions.[9]

Medical administrators placed more emphasis upon profits than patient safety.[10] The increasing shortage of nurses in the 1990s coincided with hospital expansions and incorporating newly developed technology. Maximizing profits

1. Bleich, M., Hewlett, P. "Dissipating the 'Perfect Storm' — Responses from Nursing and the Health Care Industry to Protect the Public's Health." Online Journal of Issues in Nursing. 2004. 31 May 2004 ‹www.nursingworld.org/ojin/topic24/tpc24_4.htm›.
2. Unruh, L.Y., Fottler, M.D. "Projections and trends in RN supply: what do they tell us about the nursing shortage?" Policy Polit Nurs Pract Aug; 6(3) 2005. p. 171-82.
3. "Projected supply, demand and shortages of registered nurses: 2000-2002." National Center for Health Workforce Analysis, HRSA Bureau of Health Professions. 2002. ‹http://bhpr.hrsa.gov/healthworkforce/rnproject/default.htm›.
4. Bleich, M.R., et al. "Analysis of the Nursing Workforce Crisis: A Call to Action." Nursing Center. 2003. Apr 2003 ‹http://www.nursingcenter.com//library/JournalArticle.asp?Article_ID=408576#120›.
5. Murray, M. "The nursing shortage: Past, present and future." Journal of Nursing Administration vol 32 2002. p. 79-84.
6. Gordon, S., McCall, T. "Healing in a Hurry: Hospitals in the Managed Care Age." The Nation vol 268 1999. p. 11-16.
7. Hess, R.G. "From Bedside to Boardroom — Nursing Shared Governance." Online Journal of Issues in Nursing. 2004. 31 Jan 2004 ‹http://www.ana.org/ojin/topic23/tpc23_1.htm›.
8. Takase, M., Maude, P., Manias, E. "Nurses' job dissatisfaction and turnover intention: methodological myths and an alternative approach." Nurs Health Sci Sep; 7(3) 2005. p. 209-17.
9. Spetz, J., Given, R. "The Future of the Nurse Shortage: Will Wage Increases Close the Gap?" Health Affairs vol 22(6) 2003. p. 199-207. Spetz, J. "Hospital nurse wages and staffing, 1977 to 2002: cycles of shortage and surplus." J Nurs Adm Sep; 34(9) 2004. p. 415-22.
10. Hugonnet, S., et al. "Nursing resources: a major determinant of nosocomial infection?" Curr Opin Infect Dis Aug; 17(4) 2004. p. 329-33.

required curtailing medical costs. Salaries account for about 60% of a hospital's costs, with nursing salaries alone representing 35% of that amount.[1] The lure for potential increases in profit by restricting wages, downsizing and utilizing less skilled (less expensive) nursing staff proved too much for most administrators. Many routinely attempted to fill RN positions with lower-wage workers, such as LPNs or nurse aides, and only as a last resort would raise RN wages.[2] Administrators justified the poor wages and flat earnings of nurses by claiming they were simply trying to comply with Balanced Budget requirements mandated by Congress.[3] Since nursing salaries make up the largest single element in hospital costs,[4] containment of their wages was viewed as a potential source for enhancing revenues. Orientation programs for newly hired nurses and continuing education programs were slashed, even though surveys indicate many new graduates were ill prepared to provide safe patient care.[5] Cost-driven downsizing and staff reductions continued despite concerns for patient safety.[6] Many nurses used striking and collective bargaining[7] in an attempt to force hospitals to provide safer environments for both patients and staff.[8]

Although salaries are often cited as a primary factor for many leaving the nursing profession, they are not the only factor.[9] One paper predicted salaries inflation-adjusted wages must increase 3.2–3.8% per year between 2002 and 2016, with wages cumulatively rising up to 69%, to offset the other negatives of nursing. Total RN expenditures would more than double by 2016.[10]

The following graph shows recent trends in nurses' salaries. The real inflation adjusted salary has remained flat since 1990. The average actual annual earnings of RNs employed full-time in March 2000 was $46,782[11].

1. Carter, G.S. "Assistive Personnel Allow Nurses to Focus Their Expertise." New Jersey Hospital Association. 1996. Mar 1996 ⟨http://www.njha.com/paprepresadvertorials/papresadvertorials96/papresadvmar96.html⟩.
2. Ibid. Phillips, K. "Nursing shortage redux: Everything old is new again." AMN Healthcare. 2003. 01 Dec 2003 ⟨http://amnhealthcare.com/Features.asp?articleID=11322&page=AMN%5FHealthcare+News&Profile=AMN%5FFeatures&Headline=Nursing+Shortage+Redux%3A+Everything+Old+is+New+Again⟩.
3. Phillips, R.L. Jr, et al. "The Balanced Budget Act of 1997 and the financial health of teaching hospitals." Ann Fam Med Jan-Feb; 2(1) 2004. p. 71-78.
4. "Cost Analysis and Efficiency Indicators for Health Care." Harvard School of Public Health Department of Population and International Health. 1997. Jan 1997 ⟨http://www.hsph.harvard.edu/ihsg/publications/pdf/No-57.PDF⟩. Sitompul, D., Randhawa, S.U. "Nurse scheduling models: a state-of-the-art review." J Soc Health Syst Spring; 2(1) 1990. p. 62-72.
5. Berens, M.J. "Training often takes a backseat." Chicago Tribune September 11 2000. p. 7.
6. Seago, J.A., Ash, M. "Registered nurse unions and patient outcomes." Journal of Nursing Administration vol 32 2002. p. 143-51. Stone, P.W. "Nurses' working conditions: implications for infectious disease." Emerg Infect Dis Nov; 10(11) 2004. p. 1984-89.
7. Steltzer. (2001). Collective bargaining: A wake-up call. Nursing Management, 32(4), 35-39.
8. Darr, K., Schraeder, M., Friedman, L.H. "Collective bargaining in the nursing profession: Salient issues and recent developments in healthcare reform." Hospital Topics vol 80(3) 2002. p. 21-25. McGrath, K. "Shared governance works in the union setting." Washington Nurse vol 26(5) 1996. p. 28-29.
9. "Nurses Say Health and Safety Concerns Play Major Role in Employment Decisions." American Nurses Association. 2001. 07 Sep 2001 ⟨http://www.ana.org/pressrel/2001/pr0907b.htm⟩.
10. Spetz, J. Given, R. "The Future Of The Nurse Shortage: Will Wage Increases Close The Gap?" Health Affairs vol 22(6) 2003. p. 199-206.
11. Spratley, E., et al. "The Registered Nurse Population: Findings from the National Sample Survey Of Registered Nurses." National Center for Health Workforce Analysis Reports. 2000. Mar 2000 ⟨http://bhpr.hrsa.gov/healthworkforce/reports/rnsurvey/rnss1.htm⟩.

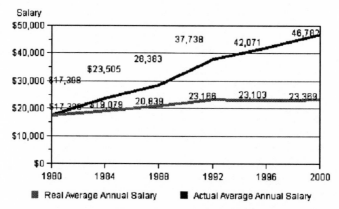

Actual and "Real" Average Income of Full-Time Registered Nurses, 1980-2000

Although pay is a consideration, it is not the only reason for discontent.[1] Work schedules frustrated and angered many nurses who turned to unions to represent them in their arguments with their employers.[2] Many stated they felt disrespected, frustrated, and disillusioned and believed unions were the only means left to "attain professional as well as personal and economic goals."[3] Nurses often express a desire to work in a more nurturing environment more appreciative of their skills. Several states, most notably California, responded by mandating staffing ratios in hospitals.[4]

The use of extended work shifts and overtime escalated as hospitals attempted to cope with a shortage of nurses. One study of logbooks completed by 393 hospital staff nurses revealed nurses usually worked longer than scheduled and approximately 40% of the 5,317 work shifts logged exceeded twelve hours.[5]

Nurses were simply asking state regulatory bodies to prohibit nursing staff from working longer than 12 hours a day and more than 60 hours per week.[6] They were generally ignored even though they cited numerous studies about mandated overtime[7] and patient safety.[8]

1. Holmas, T.H. "Keeping nurses at work: a duration analysis." Health Econ Sep; 11(6) 2002. p. 493-503.
2. "Shortage spurs more nurses to strike and unionize." The Associated Press 13 Aug 2001.
3. Breda, K.L. "Professional nurses in unions: Working together pays off." Journal of Professional Nursing vol 13 1997. p. 99-109.
4. Costello, M.A. "California seen as nurse-patient ratio testing ground." American Hospital Association News vol 38 2002. p. 3.
5. Rogers, A.E., et al. "The Working Hours Of Hospital Staff Nurses And Patient Safety." Health Affairs vol 23(4) 2004. p. 202-212.
6. "Study shows 12-hour shifts increase errors." Healthcare Benchmarks Qual Improv Sep; 11(9) 2004. p. 105-06. Fitzpatrick, J.M., et al. "Shift work and its impact upon nurse performance: current knowledge and research issues." J Adv Nurs Jan; 29(1) 1999. p. 18-27.

Nursing administration often wishes to blame the nursing shortage on smaller enrollment in nursing schools, but fails to question the reasons for decreased enrollment. Over the past decade, many of the barriers to women have been shattered. There is no longer a glass ceiling which prevents the advancement of intelligent hard working women.[1] Many now opt for more professional or lucrative careers, whether as physicians, lawyers, anesthesiologists, midwives, or other less stressful but equally fulfilling areas of employment. They are looking for positions more conducive to a healthy home environment without 12-hour shifts, forced overtime, night, weekend and holiday shifts. Nurses routinely receive benefits far less than the average teacher. The demands to maintain continued education credits, expensive licensure and the stress of dealing with people while they are at their worst (not to mention care of the dead and dying) has eroded the loyalty many once felt for this profession. In addition to these stressors, they are forced to work with physicians who are equally harried and often short-tempered at best. Managed care attempted to turn an altruistic paternal system into a for profit business. Nurses were an easy target for cost containment. Unfortunately, administrators failed to consider many nurses had already been giving far more than should be expected. This resulted in a mass exodus by many out of the nursing field.[2]

Recruitment and retention of nurses are persistent problems associated with job satisfaction.[3] A 2000 national survey determined staff nurses report lower levels of job satisfaction when compared to those in the same settings who are not staff nurses.[4] The survey found only 69.5% report being satisfied in their current position. This is much lower than that reported by the general population. Data from the General Social Survey of the National Opinion Research Center indicate that, from 1986 through 1996, 85% of workers in general and 90% of professional workers expressed satisfaction with their job. In another survey by the American Nurses Association, 75% of 7,299 respondents stated inadequate staffing had caused declines in the nursing care quality over the past two years. Nearly half reported they felt "exhausted and discouraged"

7. Cho, S.H., et al. "The effects of nurse staffing on adverse events, morbidity, mortality, and medical costs." Nurs Res Mar-Apr; 52(2) 2003. p. 71-79. Weissman, N.W. "Nurse staffing and mortality for Medicare patients with acute myocardial infarction." Med. Care Jan; 42(1) 2004. p. 4-12.

8. Aiken, L.H., et al. "Hospital nurse staffing and patient mortality, nurse burnout, and job dissatisfaction." JAMA 288(16) 2002. p. 1987-93. Morrissey, J. "Quality vs. quantity. IOM report: hospitals must cut back workload and hours of nurses to maintain patient safety." Mod Healthc Nov 10; 33(45) 2003. p. 8, 11.

1. Staiger, D., Auerback, D., Buerhaus, P. "Expanding career opportunities for women and the declining interest in nursing as a career." Nursing Economics vol 18(5) 2000. p. 230-236.

2. Erickson, J.I., Holm, L.J., Chelminiak, L. "Keeping the nursing shortage from becoming a nursing crisis." J Nurs Adm Feb; 34(2) 2004. p. 83-87.

3. Flynn, L. "The importance of work environment: evidence-based strategies for enhancing nurse retention." Home Healthc Nurse Jun; 23(6) 2005. p. 366-71. Lu H, While AE, Barriball KL. Job satisfaction among nurses: a literature review. Int J Nurs Stud. 2005 Feb; 42(2):211-27.

4. Spratley, E., et al. "The Registered Nurse Population: Findings from the National Sample Survey Of Registered Nurses." National Center for Health Workforce Analysis Reports. 2000. Mar 2000 ‹http://bhpr.hrsa.gov/healthworkforce/reports/rnsurvey/rnss1.htm›.

when they left work and 2,928 felt they were "powerless to affect change necessary for safe, quality patient care."[1]

Improvements in staffing ratios were the most important change mentioned to prevent them from leaving their jobs. In a separate study of nurses who had stayed longer than five years on their current job, the primary reasons stated were having a collegial environment, satisfactory pay and benefits, and flexible scheduling.[2] Their discontent and resulting medical errors have been the subject of many newspaper articles.[3] The *Chicago Tribune* published a series of articles blaming nurses for tragic events or portrayed nurses being under siege and unable to change their destinies or protect their patients.[4]

The baby boomers will begin retiring by 2010, less than 10% of registered nurses are under the age of 30 and aging nurses will be retiring at the same time we enter the greatest need. Nurses' salaries remain significantly lower than other professions.[5] Nursing schools have insufficient faculty to meet this growing need.[6] These factors exacerbate the pending crisis in healthcare and will have a greater impact on health than any other factor in medicine.[7] Development of new drugs or technologies will have little impact if there are no nurses to provide care. In fact, a study by researchers at the Harvard School of Public Health and Vanderbilt University cautioned staffing shortages actually increases patients' risk[8] and may result in prolonged hospital stays[9] or other complications.[10] One study by the University of Pennsylvania concluded record numbers of nurses are burned out from overwork and suggests under-staffing may result in the otherwise preventable deaths from heart attacks, pneumonia and other serious problems.[11] A Vanderbilt University study found increasing the numbers of nurses involved in patient care reduced risks of hospital acquired infection by 12% and death after surgery by 6%.[12]

1. "Analysis of American Nurses Association staffing survey." Cornerstone Communications Group. 2001. ‹www.nursingworld.org/staffing/ana_pdf.pdf›.
2. Lacey, L.M. "Called into question: What nurses want." Nursing Management vol 34(2) 2003. p. 15-17.
3. Fackelmann, K. "Working conditions send nurses walking. USA Today." USA Today. 2001. ‹www.usatoday.com/news/healthscience/health/2001-06-07-nursing-shortage.htm›.
4. Berens, M.J. "Training often takes a backseat." Chicago Tribune. Sep 11, 2000. p: 7.
5. McKinley, A. "Health care providers and facilities issue brief: nursing shortages: year end report-2004." Issue Brief Health Policy Track Serv Dec 31 2004. p. 1-8.
6. Parsons, L.C. "Who will educate the next generation of nurses? A looming faculty shortage." SCI Nurs. Summer; 21(2) 2004. p. 60-62. Thrall, T.H. "Workforce. Teachers wanted. The nursing shortage may worsen in years to come as faculty positions go unfilled." Hosp Health Netw May; 79(5) 2005. p. 28.
7. "Registered Nurses." US Department of Labor. 2005. 20 Dec 2005 ‹http://www.bls.gov/oco/ocos083.htm›.
8. Blegen, M.A., Goode, C.J., Reed, L. "Nurse staffing and patient outcomes." Nurs Res vol 47 1998. p. 43-50. Needleman, J., et al. "Nursing Staffing and patient Outcomes in Hospitals." Human Resources and Services Administration Bureau of Health Professions. 2001. 28 Feb 2001 ‹ftp://ftp.hrsa.gov/bhpr/nursing/staffstudy/part1.pdf›.
9. Kovner, C., Gergen, P.J. "Nurse staffing levels and adverse events following surgery in U.S. hospitals." Image J Nurs Sch vol 30 1998. p. 315-21.
10. Robert, J., et al. "The influence of the composition of the nursing staff on primary bloodstream infection rates in a surgical intensive care unit." Infect Control Hosp Epidemiol vol 21 2000. p. 12-7.

Job dissatisfaction is so high among American nurses that one survey found 23% stated they planned to quit within a year.[1] Another study reported one out of every 3 hospital nurses under the age of 30 is planning to leave the current job in the next year.[2] A 2001 survey of 700 nurses found 21% expected to leave direct patient care within five years for reasons other than retirement.[3] These shortages may have disastrous consequences. A JAMA study found patients in hospitals with the worst nurse staffing levels face a 31% greater chance of dying and surgical patient's odds of dying rose 7% for each additional patient added to a nurse's workload.[4] Another study concluded there was a 3% increase in cardiac mortality in poorer staffed units than in more adequately staffed cardiac units.[5] Multiple studies have shown more frequent contact with nurses is associated with better patient outcomes.[6]

Fewer nurses means there will be fewer experienced nurses to intercede for patients when physicians prescribe treatments that are unsafe or even worse, lethal. A recent survey of 800 registered nurses found 54% stating most errors they have witnessed are the result of inadequate staffing.[7] Thirty-four percent said nurses frequently missed or delayed giving patients their medication because they were so busy doing non-nursing jobs. These accusations follow the recent release of a report published in *Health Affairs* that found increasing job dissatisfaction among hospital nurses.[8]

A 2000 Health Resources and Services Administration Survey found the average age of registered nurses has increased substantially. In 1980, 52.9% were younger than age 40; in 2000, 31.7% were younger than 40. In 1980, 26% of RNs were under 30, but by 2000, less than 10% were under age 30.[9]

11. Aiken, L.H., et al. "Hospital nurse staffing and patient mortality, nurse burnout, and job dissatisfaction." JAMA Oct 23-30; 288(16) 2002. p. 1987-93. Hansen, B. "Nursing Shortage: Are Bad Working Conditions Causing Deaths?" Congressional Quarterly Researcher vol 12(32) 2002. p. 745-768.
12. Needleman. J., et al. "Nurse-staffing levels and the quality of care in hospitals." NEJM May 30; 346(22) 2002. p. 1715-22.
1. Holmas, T.H. "Keeping nurses at work: A duration analysis." Health Economics vol 11 2002. p. 493-503.
2. Crow, S.M., Hartman, S.J. "Nurse attrition as a process." Health Care Manag Jul-Sep; 24(3) 2005. p. 276-83.
3. Peter, D. Hart Research Associates, "The nurse shortage: Perspectives from current direct care nurses and former direct care nurses." 2001. ‹www.aft.org/healthcare/downloadfiles/Hart_Report.pdf›
4. Aiken, L.H., et al. "Hospital nurse staffing and patient mortality, nurse burnout, and job dissatisfaction." JAMA Oct 23-30; 288(16) 2002. p. 1987-93.
5. Person, S.D., et al. "Nurse staffing and mortality for Medicare patients with acute myocardial infarction." Med Care Jan; 42(1) 2004. p. 4-12.
6. Aiken, L., et al. "Lower Medicare Mortality among a Set of Hospitals Known for Good Nursing Care." Medical Care vol 32 1994. p. 771-87. Unruh, L. "Licensed nurse staffing and adverse events in hospitals." Medical Care vol 41 2003. p. 142-52.
7. Risher, P., Applebaum, S. "NurseWeek/American Organization of Nurse Executives National Survey of Registered Nurses." Nurseweek. 13 Mar 2002 ‹http://www.nurseweek.com/survey/part1_print.html›.
8. Fackelmann, K. "Nurses calling for safe staffing standards demonstrate on the steps of the U.S." USA Today 13 Aug 2001.
9. Maes, S. "Where have all the nurses gone?" Oncology Nursing Society News vol 15(5) 2000. p. 1, 4-5.

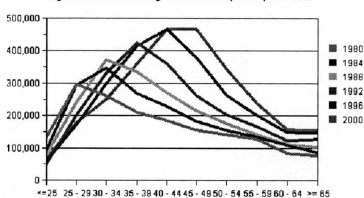

Age Distribution of the Registered Nurse Population, 1980-2000

Although, hospital nursing employment and earnings increased sharply in 2002, two-thirds of this increase was the result of employment of older nurses; the remaining one-third was by foreign-born nurses.[1] A 2004 study by Health Affairs found many of the "new" hires are simply returning to the workforce. The percentage of nurses over fifty rose 15.8% in 2002.[2] During 2003, nurses aged 50–64 accounted for 63% of the total growth in new nurses;[3] employment of nurse ages 35–49 declined.

A 2000 study concluded approximately one third of the nursing workforce was over 50 and predicted 40% will be 50 years or older by 2010.[4] One-half of the current nursing workforce is expected to retire within the next 10-15 years.[5] The US Department of Labor ranks nursing as the number one growth occupation of all occupations through 2012.[6]

Fortunately, there has recently been an influx of younger nurses into the market. One study estimated there were 66,000 young nurses entering the market since 2001. In 2003, employment of younger nurses grew by nearly 90,000, reaching the highest level observed since 1987.[7] Most of these new nurses

1. Buerhaus, P.I., et al. "Is The Current Shortage Of Hospital Nurses Ending?" Health Affairs vol 22(6) 2002. p. 191-98. Nichols, B., Kritek, P. "Globalization of the nursing profession: Negotiation diversity." American Organization of Nurse Executives 37th Annual Meeting and Exposition. Phoenix, AZ. 18 April 2004.
2. Buerhaus, P.I., Staiger, D.O., Auerbach, D.I. "New Signs Of A Strengthening U.S. Nurse Labor Market?" Health Affairs. 2004. 17 Nov 2004 ‹http://content.healthaffairs.org/cgi/content/full/hlthaff.w4.526/DC1›.
3. Buerhaus, P. "Implications of an aging registered nurse workforce." JAMA vol 283(22) 2000. p. 2948-54.
4. Ibid.
5. Maes, S. "Where have all the nurses gone?" Oncology Nursing Society News vol 15(5) 2000. p. 1, 4-5.
6. "Registered nurses. Occupational Outlook Handbook, 2004-05 Edition." U.S. Department of Labor Bureau of Labor Statistics. 2004. 30 Apr 2004 ‹www.bls.gov/oco/ocos083.htm›.
7. Ibid.

Percentage Of The Registered Nurse (RN) Workforce Under Age 35, 1983-2003

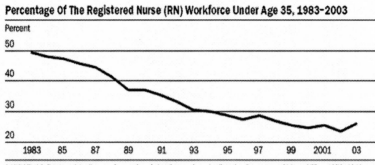

SOURCE: U.S, Bureau of the Census, Current Population Survey, Outgoing Rotation Group Annual Merged Files, 1983-2003.

are graduates of two year nursing programs. Despite increases of nearly 185,000 hospital nurses since 2001, a 2004 national survey of nurses and physicians found 82% of nurses and 81% of doctors stated they were still experiencing significant nurse shortages.[1] In a survey of Chief Nursing Officers, 84% reported a having a significant nursing shortage.[2] Attempts to supplement the number of hospital nurses using foreign-born nurses and men have generally been unsuccessful.[3]

National Supply and Demand Projections for FTE Registered Nurses: 2000 to 2020

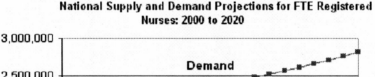
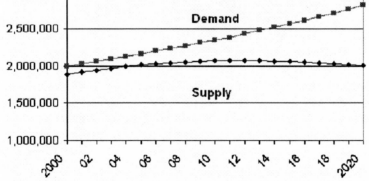

Source: Bureau of Health Professions, RN Supply and Demand Projections

1. Buerhaus P. et al. "Physicians Assess the Nursing Shortage (Unpublished paper, institution?
2. Kimball, B. "Health Care's Human Crisis — Rx for an Evolving Profession." Online Journal of Issues in Nursing. 2004. 31 May 2004 ‹www.nursingworld.org/ojin/topic24/tpc24_1.htm›.

Regrettably, the recent growth in younger nurses will be insufficient to meet the growing need for hospital nurses. Projections for nursing workforce show it will peak at 2.3 million in 2012 before shrinking to 2.2 million by 2020. This is 600,000 fewer nurses than required by US government estimates. According to projections from the Bureau of Labor Statistics, there will be more than one million vacant positions for registered nurses by 2010.[1]

Three-fourths of new graduates are from two-year associate degree programs.[2] Between 1980 and 2000 the percentage of nurses who received their basic education in diploma programs decreased from 60% to 30% while graduates of associate degree programs increased from 19% to 40%. The percentage nurses receiving basic nursing education in baccalaureate programs increased from 17% to 29%. The following graph from the U.S. Department of Health and Human Services shows the changes in education levels of nurses since 1980.

Recent studies show hospitals relying heavily upon nurses with less than

Distribution of RNs According to Basic Nursing Education, 1980-2000

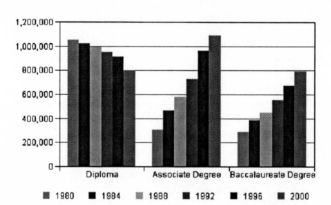

baccalaureate degrees have higher inpatient mortality.[3] Unfortunately, the shortage of nursing faculty members parallels that of hospital nurses; there is insufficient nursing faculty available to train the needed number of nurses. Nursing enrollments in entry-level baccalaureate programs in nursing increased

3. Aiken, L. et al. "Trends in International Nurse Migration." Health Affairs vol 23(3) 2004. p. 69-77. Brush, B., Sochalski, J., Berger, A. "Imported Care: Recruiting Foreign Nurses to U.S. Health Care Facilities." Health Affairs vol 23(3) 2004. p. 78-87.
1. Hecker, D.E. "Occupational employment projections to 2010." Monthly Labor Review vol 124 (11) 2001. p. 57-84.
2. Spratley, E., et al. "The Registered Nurse Population: Findings from the National Sample Survey Of Registered Nurses." National Center for Health Workforce Analysis Reports. 2000. Mar 2000 <http://bhpr.hrsa.gov/healthworkforce/reports/rnsurvey/rnss1.htm>.
3. Aiken, L., et al. "Educational Levels of Hospital Nurses and Surgical Patient Mortality." JAMA vol 290(12) 2003. p. 1617-23.

by 14.1% in fall 2004 over the previous year. Despite this significant gain, more than 32,000 qualified applications were turned away from baccalaureate and graduate nursing programs in 2002, including almost 3,000 students who could potentially fill faculty roles.[1] Over forty percent of responding schools cited insufficient number of faculty[2] as a reason for not accepting all qualified applicants.[3]

Resolution of this crisis must begin with systems-level change of the environment in which health care is provided.[4] The American College of Healthcare Executives has a Code of Ethics. The Preamble states *"Since every management decision affects the health and well-being of both individuals and communities, healthcare executives must evaluate the possible outcomes of their decisions and accept full responsibility for the consequences."*[5]

Rhetoric will do little to solve the problems associated with insufficient nurse staffing. Issues like mandated overtime have to be resolved by means other than forcing the remaining staff into providing unsafe care. Some states have already implemented bans on mandatory overtime.[6] In 1999 California became the first state to mandate minimum nurse-to-patient ratios[7] in hospitals.[8]

The government is keenly aware of the problem and is providing funds to address the nursing shortage[9]. Unfortunately, the same bureaucrats who created this mess are responsible for finding solutions to prevent rationed healthcare. If their previous efforts are any indication of future progress, the nursing crisis is here to stay.

---

1. "White paper. Faculty shortages in baccalaureate and graduate nursing programs: Scope of the problem and strategies for expanding the supply." American Association of Colleges of Nursing. 2003 ‹www.aacn.nche.edu/Publications/WhitePapers/FacultyShortages.htm›. "Press release. NLN 2002-2003 survey of RN nursing programs indicates positive upward trends in the nursing workforce supply." National League for Nursing. 2004. 05 May 2004 ‹www.nln.org/newsreleases/prelimdata12.16.03.pdf›.
2. "SREB study indicates serious shortage of nursing faculty." Council on Colligiate Education for Nursing. 2003. 02 Nov 2003 ‹http://www.sreb.org/programs/nursing/publications/02N03-Nursing_Faculty.pdf›. Hinshaw, A. "A continuing challenge: the shortage of educationally prepared nursing faculty." Online Journal of Issues in Nursing. 2001. 31 Jan 2001 ‹http://www.nursingworld.org/ojin/topic14/tpc14_3.htm›.
3. Berlin, L.E., Sechrist, K.R. "The shortage of doctorally prepared nursing faculty: a dire situation." Nursing Outlook vol 50 (2) 2002. p. 50-56. Brendtro, M., Hegge, M. "Nursing faculty: one generation away from extinction?" Journal of Professional Nursing vol 16 2000. p. 97-103.
4. Needleman, J., Buerhaus, P. "Nurse staffing and patient safety: Current knowledge and implications for action." International Journal for Quality in Health Care vol 15 2003. p. 275-77.
5. Darr, K. Ethics in health services management (2nd ed.). Baltimore, MD: Health Professions Press, 1991. Peterson, C. "Nursing Shortage: Not a Simple Problem — No Easy Answers." Online Journal of Issues in Nursing. 2001. 31 Jan 2001 ‹http://www.nursingworld.org/ojin/topic14/tpc14_1.htm›.
6. Nelson, R.R., Fitzpatrick J.J. "State labor legislation enacted in 2003." Monthly Labor Review vol 127(1) 2004. p. 4.
7. "ANA applauds introduction of mandatory overtime legislation." American Nurses Association. 2003. 12 Feb 2003 ‹http://www.nursingworld.org/pressrel/2003/pr0212.htm›.
8. Coffman, J.M., Seago, J.A., Spetz, J. "Minimum nurse-to-patient ratios in acute care hospitals in California." Health Affairs vol 21(5) 2002. p. 53-64. Jackson, S. "Nurse-patient ratios and the future of the nursing profession." CSA Bulletin vol 53(1) 2004. p. 65-72.
9. Dickerson, J.L. "The nursing shortage and its impact on retention and recruitment." SCI Nurs Fall; 21(3) 2004. p. 175-77.

CHAPTER 8. COVER YOUR ASSETS

> *The first thing we do, let's kill all the lawyers.*
> *William Shakespeare, Henry VI Part 2, Act IV, Scene 2,line 72,*
> *circa 1590*

A recent HealthGrades study estimated approximately 195,000 Americans die annually as a result of medical errors.[1] According to studies in California and New York, approximately 1% of patients admitted to hospitals are victims of medical malpractice.[2] These findings concur with a nationwide poll in which 42% of those surveyed said they had been involved in an incident where "a medical mistake was made" either personally or through a friend or relative.[3] These estimates do not include the 20-30% of malpractice claims reported to occur from physicians' offices.[4]

One physician gave testimony before the Senate estimating hospital injuries caused by medical practice cost $60 billion annually in lost earnings and medical expenses (1993 dollars). His estimate did not include malpractice occurring in physicians' offices or compensation for pain and suffering resulting from disfigurement, a lost limb, or loss of reproductive ability.[5] Even given its limited

---

1. "HealthGrades Quality Study Patient Safety in American Hospitals." Healthgrades. 2004. 28 Jul 2004 ‹http://www.healthgrades.com/media/english/pdf/HG_Patient_Safety_Study_Final.pdf›.
2. Bovbjerg, R.R. "Medical Malpractice: Folklore, Facts and the Future." Annals of Internal Medicine vol 117(9) 1992. p. 788. Brennan TA et. al. "Incidence of Adverse Events and Negligence in Hospitalized Patients: Results of the Harvard Medical Practice Study I." NEJM vol 324(6) 1991. p. 370-76.
3. "100 Million Americans See Medical Mistakes Directly Touching Them as Patients, Friends, Relatives. Public Opinion Study on Patient Safety Issues." National Patient Safety Foundation at the AMA vol 9 Oct 1997.
4. "Medical Malpractice: Problems and Reforms: A Policy-Maker's Guide to Issues and Information." The Urban Institute and Intergovernmental Health Policy Project Sep 1995. p. 6.

impact upon compensation to those unjustly injured by malpractice, the malpractice insurance/liability system is still one of the few deterrents to increased medical negligence.[1] Physicians are extremely sensitive to the threat of malpractice suits and make every attempt to modify their practices to minimize their risks of litigation. In addition, malpractice concerns may be credited with providing incentive to develop standards and guidelines to better improve patient care.[2]

A British study found general practitioners stated they are now significantly more likely to undertake diagnostic testing, refer patients, and avoid the treatment of certain conditions.[3] A separate study of 300 general practitioners found 294 (98%) claimed to have made some practice changes as a result of the possibility of a patient complaining.[4] The changes made primarily concerned increased diagnostic testing, increased referrals, increased follow up,[5] and more detailed patient explanations and note taking.[6] However, physicians generally overestimate their legal peril.[7] In an attempt insulate themselves from litigation they often adopt defensive practices.[8] Although most of these practices are benign, many alter patient care and increase costs in ways that are ethically suspect.[9] Some testing preferred by the physician may actually be detrimental to the patient, while improving the clinical outcome for some patients it may actually worsen it for others. One author provided evidence that defensive testing worsens the expected outcomes of all patients whose clinical strategies are changed and reduces the overall quality of patient care.[10]

Physicians purchase medical malpractice insurance in an attempt to avoid the financial liability associated with medical mistakes. Although this may protect the physician's personal assets, it does not come cheap. Some politicians blame the skyrocketing cost of malpractice insurance on "frivolous" lawsuits. They belittle the claims of the injured with euphemisms like "jackpot justice"[11]

5. Testimony of Dr. Troyen A. Brennan on Medical Malpractice and Health Care Reform Before the Senate Finance Committee, May 12, 1994.
1. "Myths and Realities: The District of Columbia Medical Malpractice System." Public Citizen. 2005. ‹https://www.citizen.org/congress/civjus/medmal/articles.cfm?ID=694›.
2. Bell, P.A. "Legislative Intrusions into the Common Law of Medical Malpractice: Thoughts About the Deterrent Effect of Tort Liability." Syracuse Law Review vol 35(3) 1984. p. 939-93.
3. Summerton, N. "Trends in negative defensive medicine within general practice." Br J Gen Pract Jul; 50(456) 2000. p. 565-66.
4. Summerton, N. "Positive and negative factors in defensive medicine: a questionnaire study of general practitioners." BMJ Jan 7; 310(6971) 1995. p. 27-29.
5. Anderson, R.E. "Billions for defense: the pervasive nature of defensive medicine." Arch Intern Med Nov 8; 159(20) 1999. p. 2399-402.
6. Brachfeld, J. "'Defensive Medicine' and malpractice suits." Arch Intern Med Dec 9-23; 162(22) 2002. p. 2631. Coates, J. "Defensive medicine." N Z Med J Aug 23; 115(1160) 2002. p. U144.
7. De Ville, K. "Act first and look up the law afterward?: medical malpractice and the ethics of defensive medicine." Theor Med Bioeth Dec; 19(6) 1998. p. 569-89.
8. Benbassat, J., Pilpel, D., Schor, R. "Physicians' attitudes toward litigation and defensive practice: development of a scale." Behav Med Summer; 27(2) 2001. p. 52-60.
9. Lichtstein, D.M., Materson, B.J., Spicerm, D.W. "Reducing the risk of malpractice claims." Hosp Pract Jul 15; 34(7) 1999. p. 69-72, 75-6, 79.
10. De Kay, M.L., Asch, D.A. "Is the defensive use of diagnostic tests good for patients, or bad?" Med Decis Making Jan-Mar; 18(1) 1998. p. 19-28.

or "out of control legal system."[1] These same critics fail to mention that health-care related interests have contributed $162.3 million to political campaigns or federal committees.[2] Closer scrutiny reveals escalating costs of malpractice premiums are associated with many causes, the least being the cost of compensation to the injured. A 2001 analysis concluded doctors spent $6.3 billion in the year 2000 to obtain coverage.[3] The following graph shows the trends in insurance premiums against claims payouts from 1975 to 2004:

Inflation-adjusted medical malpractice premiums had declined by one-third from 1990 until 2000. The average medical malpractice premium per doctor barely climbed from $7,701 in 1991 to $7,843 in 2000, an increase of 1.9%. If the rates are adjusted for inflation the 2000 rates have actually declined by 32.5%. It would take a rate increase of 48% to bring premium rates in 2000 back to the 1991 price level.[4]

Listening to physicians, one would believe they are nearly bankrupted by these exorbitant premium hikes. However, according to experts at the federal government's Medicare Payment Advisory Commission, liability insurance premiums represent only a small fraction of physician's expenses and have increased by only 4.4% over the last year.[5] Even though insurance premiums are at record levels, they are only a miniscule portion of total health care spending. Rising costs of medical treatments is the real culprit responsible for the increased federal spending on Medicare. A federal analysis of health care spending concluded medical costs rose 13 times faster than malpractice premiums from 1988-1998. An analysis of medical costs from 1988-1998 found medical costs had increased by 113% since 1987, while the total amount spent on medical malpractice insurance had increased by only 52%.[6]

This is displayed in the following graph.[7]

11. Greenwood, J.C. "Federal tort reform initiatives. Congressman James C. Greenwood discusses jackpot justice. Interview by Patricia A. Costante, Robert B. Goley, Janet Spicer Puro." N J Med Nov; 100(11) 2003. p. 14-20. Scarborough, C. "Jackpot justice: tort reform revisited." Healthc Ala Sep-Oct; 8(5) 1995. p. 4-7, 19-20.
1. "America's out-of-control legal system." Whistleblower Magazine. 2003. 20 Aug 2003 ‹http://www.worldnetdaily.com/news/article.asp?ARTICLE_ID=33824›. Creasy, E. "Meeting Tomorrow's Challenges." International Insurance Society, New York City. Jul 2003.
2. "Paybacks: How the White House and Congress Are Neglecting Our Health Care Because of Their Corporate Contributors." Common Dreams. 2004. 18 Aug 2004 ‹http://www.commondreams.org/news2004/0818-06.htm›.
3. A.M. Best, Statistical Study, July 16, 2001.
4. Plunket, T. "Harming Patient Access to Care: The Impact of Excessive Litigation." The Committee on Energy and Commerce. 2002. 17 Jul 2002 ‹http://energycommerce.house.gov/107/hearings/07172002Hearing648/Plunket1121print.htm›.
5. "Medical Misdiagnosis: Challenging the Malpractice Claims of the Doctors' Lobby." Public Citizen. 2003. Jan 2003 ‹http://www.misko.com/library/PublicCitizen.pdf›.
6. Office of the West Virginia Insurance Commissioner, Medical Malpractice: Report on Insurers with over 5% Market Share Nov 2002.
7. "Medical Malpractice Situation Analysis." The Georgia Trial Lawyers Association. 2004. 2004 ‹http://www.us7thamendment.com/tabl2.htm›.

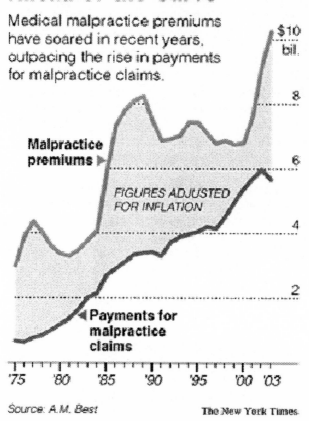

Ahead of the Curve

Medical malpractice premiums
have soared in recent years,
outpacing the rise in payments
for malpractice claims.

Malpractice
premiums ▶

*FIGURES ADJUSTED
FOR INFLATION*

◀ Payments for
malpractice
claims

'75   '80   '85   '90   '95   '00 '03

Source: A.M. Best   The New York Times

A later report by experts before the *Medicare Payment Advisory Commission* concluded malpractice insurance costs amount to only 3.2% of the average physician's revenues[1] and had increased by only 4.4% from 2000 to 2001.[2] Their data showed medical malpractice awards had increased at a slower pace than either malpractice premiums for doctors or health insurance premiums for consumers. According to the federal government's National Practitioner Data Bank, the median medical malpractice claim rose 35% from 1997 to 2000, from $100,000 to $135,000.[3]

---

1. "Medical Misdiagnosis: Challenging the Malpractice Claims of the Doctors' Lobby." Public Citizen. 2003. Jan 2003 ‹http://www.misko.com/library/PublicCitizen.pdf›.
2. Official Transcript, Medicare Payment Advisory Commission, Public Meeting, December 12, 2002. "Quick Facts on Medical Malpractice Issues." Public Citizen. 2006. ‹http://www.citizen.org/congress/civjus/medmal/articles.cfm?ID=9125›.

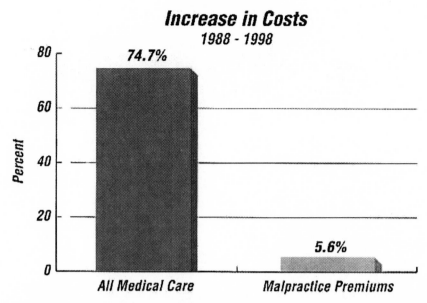

Increase in Costs
1988 - 1998

Physician's gripe about their high premiums but fail to realize the consumer is also being hammered by these usurious increases. All insurance rates, including premiums for automobile, homeowner's, health, and legal and medical malpractice insurance have been increasing.[1] Auto insurance premiums increased 8.4% from 2000 to 2001.[2] Homeowner's insurance premiums increased 8% from 2000 to 2001. Health insurance premiums also increased 11% during that same time period.

Claims that these onerous premiums are driving physicians out of medical practice have not been substantiated. A review of two separate Office of Technology Assessment studies failed to confirm the existence of a linkage between high malpractice premiums and doctors leaving the profession.[3] A later study of physician hiring found no evidence of purported shortages, some areas were actually experiencing hefty increases in the number of physicians.[4] These changes are graphically shown on the following map obtained from the Association of Trial Lawyers of America website; note that no state has reported losses in the numbers of practicing physicians.

3. Ibid.
1. "2002/2003 Outlook for Auto and Homeowners Insurance Rates." Brooks Insurance Group. 2006. ⟨http://www.brooksinsuranceagency.com/auto_home_outlook.html⟩.
2. Ibid.
3. Galanter, M. "World Torts: An Antidote to Anecdote." The Roscoe Pound Institute. 1996. ⟨http://www.roscoepound.org/new/digest/9703/cd97agal.htm⟩. Pathman,D., Tropman, S. "Obstetrical Practice Among New Rural Family Physicians." Journal of Family Practice vol 40(5) 1995. p. 457, 463.
4. "Medical Malpractice: Factsheets & Resources." Association of Trial Lawyers of America. 2005. Nov 2005 ⟨http://www.atlanet.org/pressroom/FACTS/medmal/AMAResponse/Map.aspx⟩.

Calls for "tort reform" conveniently overlook statements like those from the

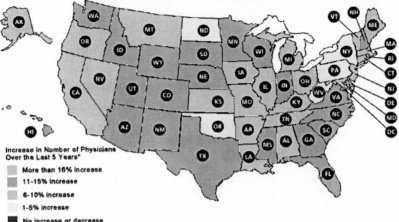

Increase in Number of Physicians
Over the Last 5 Years*

More than 16% increase

11-15% increase

6-10% increase

1-5% increase

No increase or decrease

*Based on various editions of the AMA's Physician Characteristics and Distribution (1999-2003), except in CT which
had more recent data from the CT Department of Public Health (2000-2004).

American Insurance Association reminding bureaucrats not to expect "tort reforms" to produce decreases in insurance premiums. One announcement by the AIA proclaimed on March 13, 2002: "[T]he insurance industry never promised that tort reform would achieve specific premium savings."[1] The insurance industry has consistently refuted claims that tort reform will decreases malpractice premiums. A representative of the Ohio Health Insurance Company testifying before the Wyoming Legislature stated "Tort reform will not lower rates."[2] This statement was basically reiterated by another representative for a Mississippi firm when he stated "[T]ort reform does not provide a magical 'silver-bullet' that will immediately affect medical malpractice insurance rates."[3] In 1999 the president of the American Tort Reform Association told a legal journal that: "we wouldn't tell you or anyone that the reason to pass tort reform would be to reduce insurance rates."[4] Another official stated: "many tort reform advocates do not contend that restricting litigation will lower insurance rates, and I've never said that in 30 years."[5] An exhaustive study of

1. "House Judiciary Committee — Commercial & Administrative Law Subcommittee — HEALTH CARE AND LITIGATION BILL-NO: H.R. 4600." The Foundation for Taxpayer and Consumer Rights. 2002. 12 Jun 2002 <http://www.consumerwatchdog.org/healthcare/nw/?postId=542&pageTitle=House+Judiciary+Committee+-+Commercial+%26+Administrative+Law+Subcommittee+-+HEALTH+CARE+AND+LITIGATION+BILL-NO%3A+H.R.+4600>. "Insurers And The Medical Community Admit Tort Reform Doesn't Reduce Premiums." Georgia Trial Lawyers Association. 2002. <http://www.gtla.org/public/justice-preservation/legpacket/tab3.html>.
2. "Industry Insiders Admit — And History Shows: Tort Reform Will Not Lower Insurance Rates." Americans for Insurance Reform. 2003. 02 Jun 2003 <http://www.centerjd.org/air/pr/Quotes.pdf>.
3. Ibid.
4. "Study Finds No Link Between Tort Reforms And Insurance Rates." Liability Week vol 19 Jul 1999.

"tort reform" and malpractice premiums found tort reform has historically had no impact on insurance rates.[1] No state has ever achieved a decrease in medical malpractice premiums because of passage of tort reform. One New Jersey politician asked an insurance CEO if tort reform would decrease insurance premiums. She responded by saying: "No, we're not telling them that."[2]

A 2002 study funded by the Robert Wood Johnson Foundation found "[t]he move toward more restrictive tort reform does not address the complexity of the problem. Previous rounds of tort reform that followed the malpractice insurance crisis of the 1970s and 1980s have not succeeded in preventing periodic and dramatic rises in insurance premiums."[3] This study refers to the cyclical nature of insurance premiums. In the mid-1970s and mid-1980s state legislatures attempted to pass tort reforms restricting the rights of the injured. During years of high interest rates and/or excellent insurer profits, insurance companies engage in fierce competition for premiums dollars to invest for maximum return.[4] Policies were under-priced and very poor risks were insured by companies just to obtain premium dollars for investment. Malpractice insurers slashed premiums throughout the 1990s and used questionable accounting and business practices to justify their profitability.[5] An article published in Consumer Reports states, "[a] more objective analysis suggests the "crisis" is of the insurance companies own making." They concluded high premiums of the past were the result "mostly of poor management practices by the [insurance] companies." The highly-conservative *Wall St. Journal* confirmed this analysis in its investigation of the malpractice premium crisis. It concluded in a front-page June 24, 2002 article:

"A price war that began in the early 1990s led insurers to sell malpractice coverage to obstetrician-gynecologists at rates that proved inadequate to cover claims...An accounting practice widely used in the industry made the area seem more profitable in the early 1990s than it really was. A decade of short-sighted price slashing led to industry losses of $3 billion last year."[6]

The insurance companies collaborated with politicians by proposing legislation to place arbitrary limits on our seventh amendment rights.[7] One newspaper editor summarized these events succinctly stating, "It doesn't make

5. "Groundbreaking Report Forces Business Lobbyists to Admit Publicly that "Tort Reform" Won't Reduce Insurance Rates." Center for Justice and Democracy. 2002. 12 Feb 2002 ⟨http://www.centerjd.org/press/release/990729.htm⟩.
1. Hunter, J.R., Doroshow, J. "Premium Deceit: the Failure of "Tort Reform" to Cut Insurance Rates." Center for Justice & Democracy. 2002. ⟨http://www.centerjd.org/air/PremiumDeceit.pdf⟩.
2. "Insurance companies will not promise to reduce rates even if jury awards are capped." Lewiston Sun Journal, Maine. 2003. 03 May 2003 ⟨http://www.njccj.org/medicalmalpractice/cjd-supporters.htm⟩.
3. Marchev, M. "The Medical Malpractice Insurance Crisis: Opportunity for State Action." National Academy for State Health Policy. 2002. Jul 2002 ⟨http://www.nashp.org/Files/gnl48_medical_malpractice.PDF⟩.
4. Ibid.
5. Wall Street Journal, June 24, 2002.
6. Zimmerman, R., Oster, C. "Insurers Missteps Helped Provoke Malpractice Crisis." Wall Street Journal vol 24 Jun 2002. p. 1.

sense to further harm people who have already been hurt in an effort to restrict the earnings of trial lawyers."[1] Insurers were banking on good times and easy money to sustain their obscene profits; they were totally unprepared for the events of September 11, 2001.[2]

The national tragedy of September 11, 2001 cost re-insurers billions of dollars with Lloyd's of London alone losing approximately $8 billion.[3] Re-insurers unwilling to relinquish any of their vast holdings instead opted to raise premiums on all insurance policies.[4] A consulting actuary with Tillinghast-Towers Perrin said, "[T]here is clearly an opportunity now for companies to price gouge — and it's happening... I think companies are overreacting, because they see a window in which they can do it."[5] It took less than a year for insurers to realize "Sept. 11, 2001, was a bad day for insurers; but every day since has been cause for celebration. As the one-year anniversary of the destruction of the World Trade Center approaches, insurers are looking back on 12 months of solid price increases in nearly every line of business — and they can expect more."[6] Lloyd's of London told its members in a newsletter that the September 11th terrorist attacks were a "historic opportunity" to make money, adding that premiums "had shot up to a level where very large profits are possible."[7]

The truth is most patients don't sue their physician, even if they are injured by negligence. The Harvard Medical Practice Study found only 1.53% of those injured by the medical system actually ever filed a claim.[8] This means 98.47% of those injured by negligence choose not to seek legal means to make a physician accountable for their negligence. These percentages are astounding when you consider that one out of every 200 people admitted to a hospital actually dies because of a hospital mistake.[9]

7. In Suits at common law, where the value in controversy shall exceed twenty dollars, the right of trial by jury shall be preserved, and no fact tried by a jury, shall be otherwise re-examined in any Court of the United States, than according to the rules of the common law.
1. *"What America's Opinion Pages Are Saying About Medical Malpractice."* Public Citizen. 2003. 16 Apr 2003 ‹http://www.publiccitizen.org/congress/civjus/medmal/articles.cfm?ID=9165›.
2. Hillman, R.J., Allen, K.G. "Medical Malpractice Insurance: Multiple Factors Have Contributed to Premium Increases." United States General Accounting Office. 2003. 1 Oct 2003 ‹http://www.gao.gov/new.items/d04128t.pdf›.
3. Treaster, J.B. "Lloyd's Plans To Alter How It Finances Insurance." New York Times 19 Jul 2002.
4. Insurers And The Medical Community Admit Tort Reform Doesn't Reduce Premiums." Georgia Trial Lawyers Association. 2002. ‹http://www.gtla.org/public/justice-preservation/legpacket/tab3.html›.
5. "Avoid Price Gouging, Consultant Warns." National Underwriter Avoid Price Gouging, Consultant Warns," National Underwriter, January 14, 2002. Plunket, T. "Harming Patient Access to Care: The Impact of Excessive Litigation." The Committee on Energy and Commerce. 2002. 17 Jul 2002 ‹http://energycommerce.house.gov/107/hearings/07172002Hearing648/Plunket1121.htm›.
6. Oster, C. "Insurance Companies Benefit From Sept. 11, Still Seek Federal Aid." Wall Street Journal 15 Nov 2001.
7. "Lloyd's slammed for 'national disgrace'." BBC News. 2001. 29 Oct 2001 ‹http://news.bbc.co.uk/1/hi/business/1626414.stm›.
8. "Relation between malpractice claims and adverse events due to negligence. Results of the Harvard Medical Practice Study III." NEJM vol 325 1991. p. 245-251.
9. Harvard Medical Practice Study, Patients, Doctors and Lawyers: Medical Injury, Malpractice Litigation, and Patient Compensation in New York. Washington, DC: National Academy Press, 1999.

Physicians should be glad they are not held accountable for all those injured by the medical system. Reimbursement of the remaining 98.5% of potential health care claims would have a far greater impact on medical spending.[1] The Harvard study further reported more than one third of practicing physicians and 40% of the public have experienced a medical error they defined as a mistake that resulted in death, disability or requiring additional treatment.[2] Eighteen percent of physicians and 24% of the public believed the mistake caused "serious health consequences."

It is appalling to note that 57-70% of those actually filing receive no compensation.[3] The insurance industry spins theses low levels of compensation to represent meritless claims. Another study found only 8-13% of cases filed actually went to trial with only 1.2-1.9% resulting in a decision for the patient or their family.[4] Are we to assume 98% of all malpractice claims are fallacious. Proponents of tort reform argue that most claims did not involve negligence.[5] They quote an author of one study as saying, "The evidence is growing that there is a poor correlation between injuries caused by negligent medical treatment and malpractice litigation."[6]

Cries for caps on pain and suffering awards ignore the fact that most injured patients receive no compensation.

Insurers neglect to mention that the Harvard University Medical Malpractice Study showed only 3% of victims ever file claims with the poor, elderly and uninsured least likely to sue.[7]

The US Congress Office of Technology Assessment (OTA) found the main flaw of the medical malpractice system is not related to defensive medicine but instead to the failure to receive adequate compensation to the majority of persons injured by negligence. This failure for compensation places the burden on the innocent parties (e.g. the consumers, employers and taxpayers) instead of on those who are responsible for the injury.[8] A senior editor concluded "Medical

---

1. Ibid.
2. Blendon, R.J., et al. "Views of Practicing Physicians and the Public on Medical Errors." NEJM vol 347(24) 2002. p. 1933-1940.
3. "Confronting the New Health Care Crisis: Improving Health Care Quality and Lowering Costs By Fixing Our Medical Liability System." U.S. Department of Health and Human Services. 2002. 25 Jul 2002 ⟨http://aspe.hhs.gov/daltcp/reports/litrefm.htm⟩. "Physician Insurers Association of America." Physician Insurers Association of America. 2003. 29 Jan 2003 ⟨http://www.thepiaa.org/publications/pdf_files/January_29_Piaa_Statement.pdf⟩.
4. Subcommittee on Commercial and Administrative Law before the House Judiciary Committee, testimony presented by PIAA, June 12, 2002
5. Localio, A.R., et. al. "Relation between malpractice claims and adverse events due to negligence. Results of the Harvard Medical Practice Study III." NEJM vol 325 1991. p. 245-251.
6. "Confronting the New Health Care Crisis: Improving Health Care Quality and Lowering Costs By Fixing Our Medical Liability System." U.S. Department of Health and Human Services. 2002. 24 Jul 2002 ⟨http://aspe.hhs.gov/daltcp/reports/litrefm.pdf⟩. A Review of Vidmar, Neil, "Medical Malpractice and the American Jury: Confronting the Myths About Jury Incompetence, Deep Pockets, and Outrageous Damage Awards," University of Michigan Press, 1995.
7. Brennan, T.A. "Improving the Quality of Medical Care: A Critical Evaluation of the Major Proposals." Yale Law and Policy Review vol 10 1993. p. 431.
8. "Defensive Medicine and Medical Malpractice." US Congress, Office of Technology Assessment July 1994. p. 1-8.

malpractice reform is bad medicine...Yet despite this epidemic of [medical] errors, fewer than 2% of the victims of medical malpractice ever sue their doctors ... verdicts of $1 million occur in only 4% of medical malpractice cases, and they are usually reduced to a median of $235,000 upon final judgment."[1]

The tort system allows injured parties the opportunity to recover compensation for injuries sustained as a result of negligence or malpractice. It also punishes those who harm others, and, where feasible, to force them to pay restitution to their victims. Capping doctors' malpractice liability for non-economic damages at $250,000, which is less than one year's salary for most physicians, effectively removes the deterrent the tort system is meant to create.[2] Capping payments for pain and suffering has also been shown to be ineffective.[3] States without caps on damages have 4.4% more physicians per capita than those states that do have caps on damages.[4] Also, the average malpractice premium for doctors of internal medicine is 2.2% higher in states that cap damages than in states that do not cap damages.[5] The median payout in states without caps surged 127.9% from 1991 to 2002. In contrast, the median payout grew by 83.3% in states with caps.[6] Capping awards effectively minimizes the value of human life. If you are a 20-year-old who ends up confined to a bed by medical malpractice, and you live out an average life expectancy (to 76 years old), $250,000 translates to $12.20 a day (or less than two weeks' salary for the CEO of a medical malpractice insurer).[7]

According to the U.S. Department of Labor's most recent report, obstetricians and gynecologists are the second highest-paid occupation, behind surgeons. "The seven highest-paying occupations . . were all doctors," out-ranking both corporate CEO's and lawyers.[8] The U.S. Bureau of Labor Statistics estimates that gynecologists and obstetricians earned an average income of $176,630 in 2003. Other studies found their average income may reach $261,000

1. "Med mal reform is bad medicine." Business Insurance. 2003. Feb 2003 ⟨http://www.businessin-surance.com/cgi-bin/article.pl?articleId=12379&a=a&bt=$235,000⟩.
2. "Confronting the New Health Care Crisis: Improving Health Care Quality and Lowering Costs By Fixing Our Medical Liability System." U.S. Department of Health and Human Services Office of the Assistant Secretary for Planning and Evaluation vol 25 July 2002.
3. "Medical Malpractice Caps Fail to Prevent Premium Increases, According to Weiss Ratings Study." Weiss Rating Inc. 2003. 3 Jun 2003 ⟨http://www.weissratings.com/News/Ins_General/20030602pc.htm⟩.
4. Physician Characteristics and Distribution in the US, 2001 Edition. American Medical Association, 2001.
5. "The Reason Insurers And The Medical Community Admit Tort Reform Doesn't Reduce Premiums is Because History and The Hard Data Prove It." Georgia Trial Lawyers Association. 2002. ⟨http://gtla.org/public/justice-preservation/legpacket/tab4.html#⟩. "Medical Malpractice Caps Fail to Prevent Premium Increases, According to Weiss Ratings Study." Weiss Rating Inc. 2003. 3 Jun 2003 ⟨http://www.weissratings.com/News/Ins_General/20030602pc.htm⟩.
6. "Medical Malpractice Caps Fail to Prevent Premium Increases, According to Weiss Ratings Study." Weiss Rating Inc. 2003. 3 Jun 2003 ⟨http://www.weissratings.com/News/Ins_General/20030602pc.htm⟩.
7. "The Bush Administration's Malpractice Misdiagnosis." Public Citizen. 2006 ⟨http://www.citizen.org/congress/civjus/medmal/articles.cfm?ID=8820⟩.
8. "Feds say you're well paid." American Medical Association News. 2003. 17 Nov 2003 ⟨http://www.ama-assn.org/amednews/2003/11/17/prca1117.htm⟩.

annually.[1] They are also considered a high risk profession for malpractice claims. They vehemently complain of premiums that average only 12.4% of their gross income,[2] yet seek to impose a lifetime cap on victims of medical malpractice to restitution that is less than a physicians' annual salary.

The 2003 Weiss Report on the effects of insurance caps found "most insurers continued to increase premiums at a rapid pace, regardless of caps."[3] Ironically, this study found premiums were actually higher in states with caps than in those without. The average malpractice premium in states without caps was $35,016 and $40,381 in those with caps.[4] These findings have failed to deter supporters of tort reform. At least 40 states have enacted some type of "tort reform." Immediately after these states implemented caps, insurers attempted to raise rates by 20% to 93%.[5]

Even though most cases do not actually go to trial, it still costs an average of $87,720 in legal fees to investigate these charges.[6] Proponents of tort reform assert the shear numbers of "frivolous" lawsuits are bilking billions of dollars from the health care system.[7] They also assert the numbers of multimillion dollar verdicts are increasing with the average award rising by 76% just from 1996-1999.[8] However, according to the National Center for State Courts and other studies, there has been very little change in the average number of filed malpractice claims.[9] The number of medical malpractice jury trials and plaintiff winners since 1992 has also remained stable.[10] A Florida study of medical

1. "Data shows relationship between education, income." The Associated Press 18 Apr 2005. "U.S. Physician Salaries — Ongoing Salary Survey." Allied Physicians, Nurses and Pharmacists Promoting Healthcare Excellence and Education. 2004. Jan 2004 ⟨http://207.21.203.96/sal/health-care.html⟩.
2. "Doctors Seeking Special Liability Privileges are the Highest-Paid Occupations in the United States." Center for Justice & Democracy. 2004. ⟨http://www.centerjd.org/Special-ists%20Income.pdf⟩.
3. "The Impact of Non-Economic Damage Caps on Physician Premiums, Claims Payout Levels, and Availability of Coverage." Weiss Ratings Inc. 2003. 2 Jun 2003 ⟨http://www.weissratings.com/malpractice.asp⟩.
4. "The Truth about Medical Malpractice in America." Association of Trial Lawyers of America. 2005. Jan 2005 ⟨http://www.atlanet.org/ActivistCenter/Tier3/TalkingPoints/MedMal.aspx⟩
5. "Deceptive Rhetoric vs. Documented Truth on Civil Justice." The Wisconsin Acadamy of Trial Lawyers. 2005. Mar 2005 ⟨http://www.watl.org/BRIEFING%20PAPER%20March%202005.pdf⟩.
6. "Response to Public Citizen's Medical Liability Payout Trends Report." Californians Allied for Patient Protection. 2005. 20 Apr 2005 ⟨http://www.micra.org/AMAPublicCitizenresponse.pdf⟩.
7. George Priest, G. "Punitive Damages: Tort Reform and FDA Defenses." Hearings before the Committee on the Judiciary of the United States Senate Serial No. J-104016, April 4 1995. p. 85. Silva, M. "Bush's tort reform efforts to start at 'judicial hellhole'." Chicago Tribune Online. 2005. 1 Mar 2005 ⟨http://www.jobsillinois.us/news/contentview.asp?c=137907⟩.
8. "Confronting the New Health Care Crisis: Improving Health Care Quality and Lowering Costs By Fixing Our Medical Liability System." U.S. Department of Health and Human Services. 2002. 25 Jul 2002 ⟨http://aspe.hhs.gov/daltcp/reports/litrefm.htm#note40⟩. "Medical Malpractice, III." Insurance Issues Update Mar, 2002.
9. Examining the Work of State Courts, 2001; A National Perspective from the Court Statistics Project (2001), p. 31. This finding is based on medical malpractice data from 14 states. Thorpe, K.E. "The medical malpractice 'crisis': recent trends and the impact of state tort reforms." Health Aff (Millwood) Jan-Jun; Suppl 2004. p. W4-20-30.
10. Cohen, T.H. "Medical Malpractice Trials and Verdicts in Large Counties, 2001." Bureau of Justice Statistics: Civil Justice Data Brief. 2004. Apr 2004 ⟨http://www.ojp.usdoj.gov/bjs/pub/pdf/mmtvlc01.pdf⟩.

malpractice claims confirms that only one claim is filed for every six medical errors.[1] An earlier study concluded only 1 of 8 patients who suffered injury due to medical negligence ever file claims and a 1991 analysis of phone calls found only 3.3% of medical malpractice-related calls initially received were filed as lawsuits.[2]

Trends in plaintiff winners and awards for medical malpractice jury trials in State courts in the Nation's 75 largest counties, 1992-2001

| | Medical malpractice jury trials | | Final amount awarded to plaintiff winners (in 2001 dollars) | | Percent of plaintiff winner cases with final awards — | |
Year	Total	With plaintiff award winner	Total	Median	Over $250,000	$1 million or more
1992	1,356	403	$753,667,000	$253,000	53.4%	25.3%
1996	1,118	249	371,262,000	287,000	52.2	25.1
2001	1,112	292*	596,329,000	431,000*	67.6*	31.5*

Note: Medical malpractice award data were available for plaintiff winners in 97.6% of jury trials in 1992, 97.3% of jury trials in 1996, and 98.9% of jury trials in 2001. Since the 1992 dataset does not contain award information for bench trials, the trend table only examines jury trial cases. Award amounts are rounded up to the nearest thousand.
1992 and 1996 award amounts are adjusted for inflation and presented in 2001 dollars. The inflation adjustment was calculated by utilizing the CPI inflation calculator on the U.S. Department of Labor's web page at <http://www.bls.gov/cpi/home.htm>.
Data Sources: *Civil Justice Survey of State Courts, 1992* (ICPSR 6587), *Civil Justice Survey of State Courts, 1996* (ICPSR 2883), and *Civil Justice Survey of State Courts, 2001* (ICPSR 3957).
*The 2001 estimate differs significantly (with a 95%-confidence interval) from the estimate for 1992.

Physicians and insurers inflate the number of "jack pot jury mega-awards" to vilify plaintiffs.[3] Contrary to the claims of "runaway juries" and "frivolous" suits, the number of suits in 2002 actually dropped from 1,776 to 1,656 with doctors winning most of the time.[4] Of 205 cases that went to jury verdict, the doctors won 151. They instead focus upon the increase in average awards by 6.7% from $750,000 in 1998 to $800,000 in 1999. A 43% increase in awards was reported between 1999 and 2000.[5] They intentionally use statistics to distort malpractice awards. They chose to present increases as average instead of median because average awards is the average of all awards including rare mega-awards. The

1. "Medical Misdiagnosis: Challenging the Malpractice Claims of the Doctors' Lobby." Public Citizen. 2003. 09 Jan 2003 <http://www.citizen.org/documents/PDF%20of%20Report.pdf>.
2. Huycke, L.I and Mark M. Huycke, M. "Characteristics of Potential Plaintiffs in Malpractice Ligitation." Medicine and Public Issues May 1994. p. 792-798.
3. Medical Malpractice. III Insurance Issues Update, 2002. "Symposium Starting Over?: Redesigning the Medical Malpractice System." DePaul Law Review. 2005. Winter 2005 <http://law.wustl.edu/igls/tokyo/norwood/depaul_and_uncovering_and_in.pdf>.
4. "Doctors have put a cap on the truth." Consumer for Civil Justice. 2003. 18 Feb 2003 <http://www.njccj.org/medicalmalpractice/doctors.htm>.
5. "Confronting the New Health Care Crisis: Improving Health Care Quality and Lowering Costs By Fixing Our Medical Liability System." U.S. Department of Health and Human Services. 2002. 25 Jul 2002 <http://aspe.hhs.gov/daltcp/reports/litrefm.htm>.

following table shows median awards for 2001 were $431,000 which is significantly less than the average of $800,000 reported for 1999.

The 43% increase from 1999-2000 can be attributed mainly to extremely large verdicts,[1] some as high as $100,000,000.[2] Although plaintiffs were awarded $1 million or more in approximately a third of medical malpractice trials brought against non-surgeon and surgeon defendants,[3] verdicts are generally settled for much smaller sums. According to court documents, one $55 million case was settled for $7.5 million and another $49.6 million case was settled for $8.4 million.[4] A New York state jury awarded the parents of a severely brain-damaged daughter $112 million; the family actually settled for only $6 million.

Advocates of capping awards estimate limiting unreasonable" awards for non-economic damages could reduce health care costs by 5-9% without adversely affecting quality of care. They argue the $60-108 billion in annual healthcare costs savings justifies abridgement of our seventh amendment Constitutional rights. They rationalize these "savings" would lower the cost of health insurance and permit an additional 2.4-4.3 million Americans to obtain insurance.[5] In 1994, the Office of Technology Assessment determined only "a relatively small proportion of all diagnostic procedures — certainly less than 8% — are likely to be caused primarily by CONSCIOUS concern about malpractice liability risk."[6] They found most physicians who order "aggressive diagnostic procedures ... do so primarily because they believe such procedures are medically indicated, not primarily because of concerns about liability." The effects of caps on defensive medicine "are likely to be small." It seems incredible the OTA is not appalled by the squandering of 8% of our health care budget to avoid payments of 0.55% for this same budget.[7]

An elimination of all medical malpractice claims would reduce total health care spending by only 0.5%.[8] A reduction of 25% to 30% in malpractice costs would lower health care costs by only about 0.4% to 0.5%, and the likely effect on health insurance premiums would be virtually nonexistent. Allegations that defensive medicine practices add 8% to total healthcare expenditures of $1.6

1. Physician Insurers Association of America (PIAA), Trend Analysis of Claims by Close Year, 2000.
2. ASPE Review of Media Reports from The Advocate, Las Vegas Review, and North Carolina Lawyers Weekly. McElroy, W. "Lawsuits Fueling Health Care Crisis." Fox News. 2002. 14 May 2002 ‹http://www.foxnews.com/story/0,2933,52684,00.html›.
3. Ibid.
4. "Juries Rarely Have the Last Word." The Wall Street Journal. 2005. 30 Nov 2004 ‹http://www.wsjclassroomedition.com/archive/05jan/related_05jan_teacher_malpractice.htm›.
5. Kessler, D., McClellan, M. "Do Doctors Practice Defensive Medicine." Quarterly Journal of Economics vol 111(2) 1996. p. 353-390.
6. Defensive Medicine and Medical Malpractice U.S. Congress, Office Of Technology Assessment OTA-H-602, July 1994.
7. Institute of Medicine, National Academy Press: Washington, DC, 1999 "Deceptive Rhetoric vs. Documented Truth on Civil Justice." The Wisconsin Acadamy of Trial Lawyers. 2005. Mar 2005 ‹http://www.watl.org/BRIEFING%20PAPER%20March%202005.pdf›.
8. "Setting the Record Straight: It's a Malpractice Insurance Cycle Not A Tort Crisis." Georgia Trial Lawyers Association. 2002. ‹http://www.gtla.org/public/justice-preservation/Printable-Legisla-tive-Packet.html#_ftnref68›.

trillion means $128 billion are squandered each year by physicians. In 2001, malpractice payments by physicians accounted for only $4.5 billion or 0.3% of national health expenditures. The government soft peddles the $128 billion dollar costs of defensive medicine while it lambastes lawyers for ripping off $4.5 billion from the health care budget. The real joke is, according to a 2001 study, doctors alone spent $6.3 billion in 2000 to obtain malpractice insurance coverage.[1] The $6.3 billion dollar payments were to "protect" them from the $4.5 billion awarded to patients for injuries sustained under medical care. It appears lawyers and insurers are the only ones benefiting from current regulations.

When unwarranted tests fail to protect a patient from negligence or malpractice some may opt for litigation to recover losses from improper medical care. However, victims of medical malpractice seldom sue their doctors, and, when they do, fewer than 10% of the suits make it to a jury. Even then, awards rarely come close to the magnitude of the harm that's been done. In fact, the median payment to a victim of medical malpractice in 2000 was just $125,000, according to the National Practitioner Data Bank,[2] not $1 million as reported by Jury Verdict Research,[3] the source that advocates of medical malpractice liability reform cite most often.

In fact, verdicts of $1 million occur in only 4% of medical malpractice cases, and they are usually reduced to a median of $235,000 upon final judgment.[4] The JVR collects only jury verdict information while the NPDB includes both verdicts and settlements. Since 96% of all medical malpractice cases are settled, the NPDB values are better indicators of medical malpractice payouts.[5] A 2003 study of 184,506 claim payments found 96% of malpractice cases were settled out of court for an average of $257,000.[6] Average payouts have stayed virtually flat for the last decade.[7] A 2001 study found insurance companies are paying victims of medical negligence on average only $42,607.03. This is only slightly more than the average payout was a decade earlier. Punitive damages remained rare in medical malpractice jury trials. A 1994 Rand study presented to the US Senate concluded only 13% of all financial injury verdicts received punitive

---

1. U.S. Department of Health and Human Services, 7/24/02. A.M. Best, Statistical Study, July 16, 2001.
2. "National Practitioner Data Bank 2000 Annual Report." National Practitioner Data Bank. 2000. ⟨http://63.240.212.200//pubs/stats/2000_NPDB_Annual_Report.pdf⟩.
3. "Jury Verdict Research® Releases Verdict Survey: Medical-Malpractice Jury-Award Median Up Slightly Overall Median Compensatory Award Down 30%." Jury Verdict Research. 2004. 1 Apr 2004 ⟨http://www.juryverdictresearch.com/Press_Room/Press_releases/Verdict_study/verdict_study8.html⟩.
4. Crane, M. "Could a malpractice suit wipe out your assets?" Med Econ vol 69 1992. p. 146-53. DeKay, M., Asch, D. "Is the Defensive Use of Diagnostic Tests Good for Patients, or Bad?" Medical Decision Making. 1998. Jan-Mar 1998 ⟨http://umg.umdnj.edu/smdm/pdf/18-01-019.pdf⟩.
5. Medical Malpractice and Access to Health Care. Government Accounting Office. Gao-03-836, 2003.
6. Girion, L. "Malpractice Payouts Have Not Soared, Reports Say." LATimes. 1 Jun 2005 ⟨http://www.saynotocaps.org/newsarticles/malpractice_payouts_have_not_soa.htm⟩.
7. "New Study Shows Average Medical Mal Practice Payouts Only $43,000 Virtually Unchanged in 10 Years." Common Dreams. 2001. 16 Oct 2001 ⟨http://www.commondreams.org/news2001/1016-02.htm⟩.

damages.[1] even though 90% of all claims involve permanent injury or death.[2] A study from 1992 to 2001 found only 1% to 4% of plaintiff winners in medical malpractice jury trials received punitive damages with an average award of only $250,000.[3] Injured patients generally fair poorly in the judicial system, studies have shown they win only about a quarter of trials against non-surgeon (23%) or surgeon (27%) defendants.[4]

Multimillion verdicts for malpractice are very rare. In 2001, only about 5% (895 out of 16,676 payouts), exceeded $1 million.[5] An insurance industry report found the average indemnity paid for the least severe category of injury was only $49,947. This increased to $454,454 for grave injuries that included quadriplegia, severe brain damage, lifelong care or fatal prognosis.[6] A government database found median payments for medical malpractice ranged from $100,000 in 1997 to $135,000 in 2001.[7]

Even a verdict in favor of the injured does not necessarily mean "hitting the jackpot." Insurers attempt to persuade jurists that those filing claims are merely motivated by greed. Studies have shown simple measures like showing videos of insurance fraud often persuades jurors to decide against the plaintiffs.[8] Jurors tend to be "generally favorable toward business, skeptical more about the profit motives of individual plaintiffs than of business defendants, and committed to holding down awards."[9]

A Duke University study of 105 malpractice verdicts from 1985 to 1997 in the New York City area found 44% of jury awards were further reduced after the verdict with final payments averaging only 62% of the awards. The lead author of this study concluded the larger the award, the more it was reduced by the presiding judge. One case with a total award of $90.3 million was settled for $7 million. Another award, for $65.1 million, was reduced to $3.2 million.[10] In 2000, a jury awarded $269 million to a family of a 15-year-old Texas girl who died from

1. Carroll, S. "Punitive Damages in Financial Injury Jury Verdicts." Rand Corporation. 1997. 24 Jun 1997 ‹http://www.rand.org/pubs/testimonies/CT143/index2.html#fnB9›.
2. National Practitioner Data Bank 2003 http://www.npdb-hipdb.com/pubs/stats/2003_NPDB_Annual_Report.pdf Medical Malpractice Verdicts and Trials in Large Counties, 2001 U.S. Department of Justice Office of Justice Programs Bureau of Justice Statistics Civil Justice Data Brief April 2004, NCJ 203098 http://www.medicalmalpractice.com/medical-malpractice-verdicts.cfm
3. Ibid.
4. Ibid. Bureau of Justice Statistics, Medical Malpractice Trials and Verdicts in Large Counties, 2001, April 2004.
5. National Practitioner Data Bank, as quoted in Business Week, March 3, 2003
6. "A Pocket Guide to Issues and Allegations: Medical Malpractice." The American Voice 2004. 2004. 26 Feb 2004 ‹http://www.americanvoice2004.org/health/malpractice.html›.
7. "Medical Malpractice Insurance Crisis in Pennsylvania a Result of Economic Cycle, Doctors Who Err; Bush Administration Study Flawed." Public Citizen vol 16 Jan 2003 2003.
8. Vidmar, N. Medical Malpractice and the American Jury: Confronting the Myths about Jury Incompetence, Deep Pockets, and Outrageous Damage Awards. The University Of Michigan Press, 1996.
9. Hans, V., Lofquist, W. "Jurors' Judgments of Business Liability in Tort Cases: Implications for the Litigation Explosion Debate." Law and Society Review vol 85 1992. p. 94-95.
10. Hallinan, J.T. "In Malpractice Trials, Juries Rarely Have the Last Word." Wall St. Journal 30 Nov 2004.

botched surgery to fix a narrowed trachea; the final settlement was just $3 million.

Physicians may blame the injured parties, juries or insurance companies for their inflated malpractice premiums, however, they seldom consider their own responsibility. Few mention government studies showing just 5.2% doctors with two or more claims were responsible for 55% of all payouts between 1990 and 2002.[1] Only 1.1% of all doctors with three or more malpractice payouts are responsible for 30% of all malpractice payouts. The American Medical Association (AMA) has the power to discipline the few but dangerous physicians responsible for the majority of malpractice claim yet consistently refuse to exercise this option. A 2002 government study found only 10.7% (1,401 of 13,182) of all doctors who had three or more malpractice payouts have ever been disciplined. Incredibly, only 16.9% (488 of 2,896) of doctors who made five or more malpractice payouts have been disciplined.[2] A 2003 study of Florida physicians found only 6% of their doctors were responsible for half of the states malpractice claims and their associated costs.[3] The *Saint Louis Post-Dispatch* maintains, "If states' medical boards did a better job of disciplining doctors, there likely would be fewer malpractice cases."[4] Another editor for the Public Citizen Health Research Group summarized these finds by stating, "Is it any coincidence that the states least likely to discipline doctors are among those with insurance crises?...The problem is not the compensation paid to injured patients, but an epidemic of medical errors."[5] Other commentators seem equally appalled by the AMA's indifference to bad doctors.[6] "Crack down on the few lousy doctors, and this crisis might be cured"[7] In its book *20,125 Questionable Doctors*, Public Citizen's Health Research Group found that out of 770,320 licensed medical doctors, the care or conduct of only 2.6% was considered substandard enough to be cited to a disciplinary board. Less than one-half of 1% will receive any serious state sanctions each year. The report stated that "Too little discipline is still being done," and "2,696 total serious disciplinary actions a year, the number state medical boards took in 1999, is a pittance compared to the

1. "Medical Misdiagnosis: Challenging the Malpractice Claims of the Doctors' Lobby." Public Citizen. 2003. 9 Jan 2003 ‹http://www.publiccitizen.org/congress/civjus/medmal/articles.cfm?ID=8778›. "New 2002 Government Data Dispute Malpractice Lawsuit "Crisis."" Consumers for Civil Justice. 2003. 7 Jul 2003 ‹http://www.njccj.org/medicalmalpractice/crisis.htm›.
2. Ibid.
3. "Medical Misdiagnosis: Challenging the Malpractice Claims of the Doctors' Lobby." Public Citizen. 2003. Jan 2003 ‹http://www.misko.com/library/PublicCitizen.pdf›.
4. "The Wrong Prescription." Saint Louis Post-Dispatch [St Louis] 19 Jan 2003.
5. New York Times Guest Editorial, Sidney M. Wolf, *Director, Public Citizen Health Research Group*, 3/4/03.
6. "What America's Opinion Pages Are Saying About Medical Malpractice." Illinois Trial Lawyers Association. 2003. 7 Mar 2003 ‹http://www.iltla.com/Medical%20Malpractice/OpinionExcerptsandTextSpecialReport.pdf›.
7. McLaughlin, J. "*Crack down on the few lousy doctors, and this crisis might be cured.*" The Star-Ledger. 2003. 9 Feb 2003 ‹http://www.icnj.org/Symposium2005/SiteDocuments/News/2-9-2003/malpracticecolumncrackdownonthelousydoctorssl_2-9-2003.htm›.

volume of injury and death of patients caused by negligence of doctors... Though it has improved during the past 15 years, the nation's system for protecting the public from medical incompetence and malfeasance is still far from adequate."[1] Until the AMA decides to expunge their profession of these repeat offenders, the public has no choice but to use legal intimidation to enforce safer practices.[2]

Facts, however, may not be the same as beliefs. In a 2002 physician survey, one-third stated they avoided high risk specialties for fear of litigation and 79% believed it prompted them to order more tests than medically needed, and 91% believed other physicians followed suit (pun intended). The survey also found 74% stating they referred patients to specialists more often than medically necessary, increased invasive procedures by 51% and prescriptions for medications by 41%.[3] Physicians' fear of "missing something" and being liable to litigation is the driving factor behind most of these tests. Realizing medical malpractice claims add only about 0.55% to the nation's health care costs exposes the inappropriateness of these unnecessary tests.

Medical researchers routinely overlook the obvious; many doctors just don't know how to practice good medicine. Many believe over-reliance on medical procedures and tests is an adequate substitute for a thorough history and physical exam.[4] Harried physicians have little time to establish meaningful rapport with all their patients. Some simply opt for more diagnostic studies as an alternative to social interaction. Several studies have demonstrated dependence on diagnostic studies[5] is unwarranted.[6]

Physicians order excessive tests for defensive reasons[7] or because they cannot manage the fear of uncertainty.[8] Although there are large variations in the estimates of inappropriate laboratory use (4.5%-95%)[9] most studies generally agree "routine" laboratory tests before surgery have limited clinical value[10] and

1. "Questionable Doctors." Public Citizen. 2000. 8 Aug 2000 ‹http://www.citizen.org/hrg/qdsite/introduction.htm›.
2. Meghan Mulligan and Emily Gottlieb, Lifesavers: CJ&D's Guide to Lawsuits that Protect Us All, Center for Justice & Democracy (2002).
3. "Fear of Litigation Study." Common Good. 2002. 11 Apr 2002 ‹http://cgood.org/healthcare-reading-cgpubs-polls-6.html›.
4. Alsumait, B.M., et al. "A prospective evaluation of preoperative screening laboratory tests in general surgery patients." Med Princ Pract Jan-Mar; 11(1) 2002. p. 42-45. Smetana, G.W., Macphersonn, D.S. "The case against routine preoperative laboratory testing." Med Clin North Am Jan; 87(1) 2003. p. 7-40.
5. Johnson, R.K., Mortimer, A.J. "Routine pre-operative blood testing: is it necessary?" Anaesthesia Sep; 57(9) 2002. p. 914-17.
6. Gluck, R., Munoz, E., Wise, L. "Preoperative and postoperative medical evaluation of surgical patients." Am J Surg Jun; 155(6) 1988. p. 730-34. Macpherson, D.S. "Preoperative laboratory testing: should any tests be 'routine' before surgery?" Med Clin North Am Mar; 77(2) 1993. p. 289-308.
7. Birbeck, G.L., et al. "Do malpractice concerns, payment mechanisms, and attitudes influence test-ordering decisions?" Neurology Jan 13; 62(1) 2004. p. 119-21. DeKay, M.L., Asch, D.A. "Is the defensive use of diagnostic tests good for patients, or bad?" Med Decis Making vol 18 1998. p. 19-28.
8. Sonnenberg, A. "A medical uncertainty principle." Am J Gastroenterol vol 96 2001. p. 3247-50.
9. Robinson, A. "Rationale for cost-effective laboratory medicine." Clin Microbiol Rev Apr; 7(2) 1994. p. 185-99. Van Walraven, C., Naylor, C.D. "Do we know what inappropriate laboratory utilization is? A systematic review of laboratory clinical audits." JAMA Aug 12; 280(6) 1998. p. 550-58.

recommend that physicians should order tests only if the outcome of an abnormal test will affect patient care.[1] This overuse does not improve quality of medical care, shorten hospital stay, nor reduce mortality. The primary reasons for overuse of laboratory tests are lack of incentives for patients, physicians or clinical departments to reduce costs, not fear of litigation. The fragmentation of laboratory services, conflicting interests of hospitals, as well as the multitude of personal, institutional and professional interests, also contribute to the variety and excess of superfluous laboratory tests.[2] Many strategies to control utilization of laboratory testing have been reported.[3] One physician declared to the Subcommittee on Health of the House Committee on Ways and Means that eliminating unnecessary lab and radiology tests and improved interoperability between providers and labs, and providers and radiology centers could save $87 billion annually.[4]

Researchers and managers have tried to change the test-ordering behavior of health care providers,[5] but it is not easy.[6] One study of 142 patients undergoing 155 procedures examined whether lab tests not indicated by patient history or physical examination would identify abnormalities that might affect the outcomes of surgery. The authors concluded routine or arbitrary lab tests were poor substitutes for thorough patient medical histories and physical examinations. They estimated physician failures to perform adequate physical exams and histories increased patient charges at their center by more than $400,000 annually without reducing adverse outcomes.[7] A Mayo Clinic study of 1,044 patients aged 0 to 95 years failed to show any benefit of preoperative laboratory testing. The study concluded patients who have been assessed by history and physical examination and determined to have no preoperative indication for laboratory tests can safely undergo anesthesia and operation. Tests may be obtained intra-operatively and post-operatively if clinically indicated.[8] The history should include a complete review of systems (especially

10. Smetana, G.W., Macphersonn, D.S. "The case against routine preoperative laboratory testing." Med Clin North Am Jan; 87(1) 2003. p. 7-40.
1. Johnson, R.K., Mortimer, A.J. "Routine pre-operative blood testing: is it necessary?" Anaesthesia Sep; 57(9) 2002. p. 914-17.
2. Mayer, M. "[Unnecessary laboratory tests in diagnosis and treatment]." Harefuah Jan 15; 120(2) 1991. p. 66-69.
3. "Profile trak: laboratory medicine review." Lab Industry Rep vol 5(6) 1996. Lewandrowski, K. "Managing utilization of new diagnostic tests." Clin Leadersh Manag Rev Nov-Dec; 17(6) 2003. p. 318-24.
4. Overhage, M. "Testimony Before the Subcommittee on Health of the House Committee on Ways and Means." Associate Professor of Medicine, Regenstreif Institute, Indiana University, Indianapolis, Indiana. U.S. House of Representatives: Ways and Means Committee. 2004. 17 Jun 2004 <http://waysandmeans.house.gov/hearings.asp?formmode=view&id=1655>.
5. "Altering Test-Ordering Behavior of Hospital Staff." Annals vol 141 2004. p. 1-57.
6. Marcello, P.W., Roberts, P.L. "'Routine' preoperative studies. Which studies in which patients?" Surg Clin North Am Feb; 76(1) 1996. p. 11-23. Neilson, E.G., et al. "The Impact of Peer Management on Test-Ordering Behavior." Annals vol 141 2004. p. 196-204.
7. Wattsman, T.A., Davies, R.S. "The utility of preoperative laboratory testing in general surgery patients for outpatient procedures." Am Surg Jan; 63(1) 1997. p. 81-90.
8. Narr, B.J., et al. "Outcomes of patients with no laboratory assessment before anesthesia and a surgical procedure." Mayo Clin Proc Jun; 72(6) 1997. p. 505-09.

cardiovascular and pulmonary), medication history, allergies, surgical and anesthetic history, and functional status.[1]

Cost containment demands doctors and other care givers reduce costs without compromising the quality of the care being delivered.[2] However, attempts to reduce unnecessary testing[3] have often been difficult[4] to implement[5] or sustain.[6] A Vanderbilt University study found use of computerized ordering systems utilizing "reminders" to discontinue scheduled tests decreased orders for metabolic panel component tests by 24% and electrocardiograms by 57%.[7] Unfortunately, other studies suggest physicians routinely override these prompts[8] therefore estimated annual savings in laboratory charges may be small.[9] Nationwide, approximately 10% of hospitals have implemented physician computer order entry systems to replace written orders or clerical order entry.[10] If these results were generalized across the country, up to 25% of high-volume laboratory testing,[11] electrocardiograms, and radiographs may be eliminated without affecting outcomes.[12] A 2005 study of 1395 tests performed preoperatively found only 17 (3.3%) prompted changes in patient care.[13] A large review of previous studies found no evidence to support the value of most routine preoperative tests. Most tests lead to a change of

1. Michota, F.A., Frost, S.D. "The preoperative evaluation: use the history and physical rather than routine testing." Cleve Clin J Med Jan; 71(1) 2004. p. 63-70.
2. Wu, A.H. "Improving the utilization of clinical laboratory tests." J Eval Clin Pract Aug; 4(3) 1998. p. 171-81.
3. Jamtvedt, G., et al. "Audit and feedback: effects on professional practice and health care outcomes." Cochrane Database Syst Rev vol 3 2003. p. CD000259. O'Brien, T., et al.. "Audit and feedback versus alternative strategies: effects on professional practice and health care outcomes." Cochrane Database Syst Rev vol 2 2000. p. CD000260.
4. Tierney, W.M., Miller, M.E., McDonald, C.J. "The effect on test ordering of informing physicians of the charges for outpatient diagnostic tests." NEJM vol 322 1990. p. 1499-504.
5. Emerson, J.F., Emerson, S.S. "The impact of requisition design on laboratory utilization." Am J Clin Pathol vol 116 2001. p. 879-84. Hillman, A.L., Pauly, M.V., Kerstein, J.J. "How do financial incentives affect physicians' clinical decisions and the financial performance of health maintenance organizations?" NEJM vol 321 1989. p. 86-92.
6. Boice, J.L., McGregor, M. "Effect of residents' use of laboratory tests on hospital costs." J Med Educ vol 58 1983. p. 61-64. Wang, T.J., et al. "Utilization management intervention to reduce unnecessary testing in the coronary care unit." Arch Intern Med vol 162 2002. p. 1885-90.
7. Neilson, E.G., et al. "The impact of peer management on test-ordering behavior." Ann Intern Med Aug 3; 141(3) 2004. p. 196-204.
8. Bates, D.W., et al. "A randomized trial of a computer-based intervention to reduce utilization of redundant laboratory tests." Am J Med Feb; 106(2) 1999. p. 144-50. Chueh, H., Barnett, G.O. "'Just-in-time' clinical information." Acad Med vol 72 1997. p. 512-17.
9. Sanders, D.L., Miller, R.A. "The effects on clinician ordering patterns of a computerized decision support system for neuroradiology imaging studies." Proc AMIA Symp 2001. p. 583-87. Solomon, D.H., Hashimoto, H., Daltroy, L., Liang, M.H. "Techniques to improve physicians' use of diagnostic tests: a new conceptual framework." JAMA vol 280 1998. p. 2020-27.
10. Ash, J.S., et al. "Computerized physician order entry in U.S. hospitals: results of a 2002 survey." J Am Med Inform Assoc vol 11 2004. p. 95-99.
11. Neilson, E.G., et al. "The Impact of Peer Management on Test-Ordering Behavior." Annals of Internal Medicine vol 141(3) 2004.
12. Gold, B.S., et al. "The utility of preoperative electrocardiograms in the ambulatory surgical patient." Arch Inter Med vol 152(2) 1992. Munro, J., Booth, A., Nicholl, J. "Routine preoperative testing: a systematic review of the evidence." Health Technol Assess vol 1: i-iv 1997. p. 1-62.
13. Mantha, S., et al. "Usefulness of routine preoperative testing: a prospective single-observer study." J Clin Anesth Feb; 17(1) 2005. p. 51-57.

management in only 0-2.8% of patients.[1] A separate study found perioperative management was altered in only 0.56-0.26% of patients.[2] If questioned, most physicians will state these tests are essential for the proper management or diagnosis of the disease process. Although this may be true in a small minority, the above findings demonstrate the majority are unaffected or worse, adversely affected by these interventions.

No Apology Needed

"What we've got here is ...a failya ta communicate."
Paul Newman, as quoted from the movie "Cool Hand Luke"

In this era of "instant messaging" and digital information there is paradoxically an increasing amount of miscommunication between patients and doctors. Communication failures are the root of most patient complaints and claims for malpractice.[3] Communication errors increase malpractice suits more than even acts of negligence.[4] The most common complaint of plaintiffs is that doctors do not listen to them. Several studies seem to confirm their beliefs. In one study of family doctors, patients were given, on average, just 23.1 seconds to explain their health concerns. In more than two thirds of the consultations, the physician interjected and redirected the conversation before the patient had finished talking.[5] The study showed physicians allowed patients only 18 seconds after their opening statement before interrupting them, 94% of all interruptions result in the doctor now controlling the conversation. Physicians use of closed questions and technical language may impress the patient but does little to enhance communication.[6] The authors of this and other studies recommend physicians use "patient centered" consultations allowing the patient to fully explain why they are seeking medical help.[7] A 2004 video study of 18 physicians found patients preferred positive consultations involving them in their care. Negative consultations were characterized as being more physician directed focused primarily upon the patient's history and physician beliefs. Patients may

1. Munro, J., Booth, A., Nicholl, J. "Routine preoperative testing: a systematic review of the evidence." Health Technol Assess vol 1: i-iv 1997. p. 1-62.
2. Perez, A., et al. "Value of routine preoperative tests: a multicentre study in four general hospitals." Br J Anaesth Mar; 74(3) 1995. p. 250-56.
3. Levinson, W., et al. "Physician-patient communication: the relationship with malpractice claims among primary care physicians and surgeons." JAMA vol 277 1997. p. 553-59. Ong, L.M., et al. "Doctor-patients communication: a review of the literature." Soc Sci Med vol 40 1995. p. 903-918.
4. Richards, T. "Chasms in communication." BMJ vol 301 1990. p. 1407-08.
5. Marvel, M.K., et al. "Soliciting the patients' agenda: have we improved?" JAMA vol 281 1999. p. 283-87.
6. O'Gara, P.E., Fairhurst, W. "Therapeutic communication part 1: general approaches that enhance the quality of the consultation." Accid Emerg Nurs Jul; 12(3) 2004. p. 166-72. O'gara, P.E., Fairhurst, W. "Therapeutic communication part 2: strategies that can enhance the quality of the emergency care consultation." Accid Emerg Nurs Oct; 12(4) 2004. p. 201-07.
7. Arborelius, E., Bremberg, S. "What does a human relationship with the doctor mean?" Scand J Prim Health Care Sep; 10(3) 1992. p. 163-69.

attempt to express their views but physicians may ignore these concerns.[1] In positive consultations, the doctor and patient are in agreement about the reason for the consultation and the patient is asked about their ideas and concerns or health beliefs.[2] In a Scandinavian study, patients characterized the "good doctor" as one who is caring and listens to the concerns of the patient. They act like an ordinary person while treating the patient as an equal. Conversely, the "bad doctors" appeared unreachable, unsympathetic and unwilling to communicate their viewpoints on issues raised during the consult.[3] The physicians may not be solely responsible for the patients' inability to communicate their needs effectively;[4] however, they are responsible for asking questions to provide clarification.[5] Unfortunately, physicians may be too selective about when they feel greater patient involvement is appropriate or feasible and are hesitant to implement shared decision making to the majority of consultations.[6]

Several studies have clearly shown doctors and patients have different views on what makes good and effective communication.[7] Patients desire more and better information about their problem and outcomes. They also expect more openness about the side effects of treatment, relief of pain and emotional distress, and advice on what they can do for themselves. Patients often leave doctors who failed to involve them in decisions.[8] One author stated that patients need to tell their story in their own way in their own time,[9] and physicians should try to determine how these problems are affecting the patient's life. Many doctors are reluctant to allow this open dialogue for fear that it may prolong the consultation and encroach upon the consult times of waiting patients. A physician stated in a recent editorial that the patients' hunger for attention can be almost limitless, and longer encounter times might "merely provide greater opportunities to plumb the depths of human misery."[10] Studies have shown

1. Fossum, B., Arborelius, E. "Patient-centred communication: videotaped consultations." Patient Educ Couns Aug; 54(2) 2004. p. 163-69.
2. Arborelius, E., Bremberg, S. "What can doctors do to achieve a successful consultation? Videotaped interviews analysed by the 'consultation map' method." Fam Pract Mar; 9(1) 1992. p. 61-66.
3. Arborelius, E., Timpka, T., Nyce, J.M. "Patients comment on video-recorded consultations—the "good" GP and the "bad."" Scand J Soc Med Dec; 20(4) 1992. p. 213-16.
4. Street, R.L. Jr., et al. "Patient participation in medical consultations: why some patients are more involved than others." Med Care Oct; 43(10) 2005. p. 960-69.
5. Arborelius, E., Timpka, T. "General practitioners' comments on video recorded consultations as an aid to understanding the doctor-patient relationship." Fam Pract Jun; 7(2) 1990. p. 84-90. Arborelius, E., Bremberg, S., Timpka, T. "What is going on when the general practitioner doesn't grasp the situation?" Fam Pract Mar; 8(1) 1991. p. 3-9.
6. Edwards, A., et al. "Shared decision making and risk communication in practice: a qualitative study of GPs' experiences." Br J Gen Pract Jan; 55(510) 2005. p. 6-13.
7. Sanchez-Menegay, C., Stalder, H. "Do physicians take into account patients'expectations?" J Gen Intern Med vol 9 1994. p. 404-406. Laine, C., et al. "Important elements of outpatient care: a comparison of patients' and physicians' opinions." Ann Intern Med vol 125 1996. p. 640-45.
8. Kaplan SH, Greenfield S, Gandek B, Rogers WH, Ware JE Jr. Characteristics of physicians with participatory decision-making styles. Ann Intern Med. 1996 Mar 1; 124(5):511-3.
9. Ogden, J., et al. "'I want more time with my doctor': a quantitative study of time and the consultation." Fam Pract Oct; 21(5) 2004. p. 479-83.
10. Toon, P.D. "Quality in general practice." J R Soc Med vol 90 1997. p. 241-42.

patient-perceived physician empathy significantly influences patient satisfaction and compliance.[1]

Unfortunately, managed care mandates to contain costs have resulted in doctors increasing their practice volume by decreasing the time spent per patient.[2] In 1993 family practitioners averaged one patient every 20 minutes and general internists were seeing one every 26 minutes.[3] By late 1995, 41% of U.S. physicians reported they were now spending less time with their patients.[4] The quality of consultations had also deteriorated. A 1995 study showed doctors spent just one minute out of a 20 minute consultation giving information. Physicians erroneously believed they had spent approximately half the interview giving information.[5] A London study evaluated the effects of 5, 7.5, or 10 minutes consultation times on patient outcomes.[6] Using analyses of audio taped encounters, they found physicians spent substantially more time explaining patients' problems, proposing management options, discussing prevention, and providing health education when consultations lasted 10 minutes or longer. More importantly, additional patient problems were discovered during the longer visits. The information exchange for shorter sessions becomes one sided, favoring the physicians. Incredibly, a 2004 study of emergency department visits found physicians averaged only 7 minutes 31 seconds with each patient contact.[7] The same study concluded the average time spent by the doctor providing discharge instructions was merely 76 seconds. Studies have conclusively shown demonstrated a correlation between effective physician-patient communication and improved patient health outcomes.[8] These short durations for patient/physician interaction threaten to further increase the patient's risks.

Regrettably, this results in patients receiving less information from their doctors and increases patient dissatisfaction.[9] Shorter visits provide patients less time to ask for health-related information.[10] They also may result in

1. Kim, S.S., Kaplowitz, S., Johnston, M.V. "The effects of physician empathy on patient satisfaction and compliance." Eval Health Prof Sep; 27(3) 2004. p. 237-51. Wynn, R. "Empathy in general practice consultations: a qualitative analysis." Epidemiol Psichiatr Soc Jul-Sep; 14(3) 2005. p. 163-69.
2. Davidoff, F. "Time." Ann Intern Med vol 127 1997. p. 483-85.
3. Lowes, R.L. "Are you expected to see too many patients?" Med Econ vol 72 1995. p. 52-53, 57-59.
4. Collins, K.S., Schoen, C., Sandman, D.R, et al. The Commonwealth Fund Survey Of Physician Experiences With Managed Care. New York: The Commonwealth Fund, 1997.
5. Makoul, G., Arntson, P., Schofield, T. "Health promotion in primary care: physician-patient communication and decision making about prescription medication." Soc Sci Med vol 41 1995. p. 1241-54.
6. Morrell, D.C., et al. "The "five minute" consultation: effect of time constraint on clinical content and patient satisfaction." Br Med J (Clin Res Ed) vol 292 1996. p. 870-73.
7. Rhodes, K.V., et al. "Resuscitating the physician-patient relationship: emergency department communication in an academic medical center." Ann Emerg Med Sep; 44(3) 2004. p. 262-67.
8. DiBlasi, Z., et al. "Influence of context effects on health outcomes: a systematic review." Lancet vol 357 2001. p. 757-62. Stewart, M., Brown, J.B., Donner, A., et al. "The impact of patient-centered care on outcomes." J Fam Pract 2000 vol 49 2000. p. 796-804.
9. Howie, J.G., et al. "Long to short consultation ratio: a proxy measure of quality of care for general practice." Br J Gen Pract vol 41 1991. p. 48-54. Laine C, et al. "Important elements of outpatient care: a comparison of patients' and physicians' opinions." Ann Intern Med vol 125 1996. p. 640-45.
10. Beisecker, A.E., Beisecker, T.D. "Patient information-seeking behaviors when communicating with doctors." Med Care vol 28 1990. p. 19-28.

significant lapses in the medical history.[1] Important observations about drinking patterns,[2] depression[3] and compliance with current therapies may be overlooked.[4] Many physicians believe the patient is there simply for a prescription and symbolically end the session by dispensing a script for drugs. One author states, "we should not be surprised if prescribing comes to be used more often as a "quick fix" for ending encounters as the amount of time scheduled for an office visit gets shorter."[5] Another researcher claims that a thorough "medical history is, on the whole, more powerful than the computed tomographic scan."[6] Is it any wonder physicians without claims spent longer in routine visits than their peers with claims?[7] A 2004 British study evaluated the use of leaflets encouraging patients to raise concerns and to discuss symptoms or other health related issues during the consultation. The authors of this and other studies suggest this simple reminder may be effective in increasing patient satisfaction.[8] Recent studies suggest when patients and their doctors share similar beliefs about patient participation, patient outcomes tend to be more positive.[9] Although most consultations may be imperfect,[10] they don't have to be haphazard. Simple measures like the patient compiling a list of questions and concerns has been shown to optimize the limited time of office visits.[11] Learning to like each other has also been shown to improve patient health.[12] A recent large multinational study suggests A "standard operating procedure" for an office visit should consist of 8% social behavior, 15% agreement, 4% rapport building, 10% partnership building, 11% giving directions, 28% giving information, 14% asking questions and 7% counselling.[13]

---

1. Tamblyn, R., et al. "Unnecessary prescribing of NSAIDs and the management of NSAID-related gastropathy in medical practice." Ann Intern Med vol 127 1997. p. 429-38.
2. Weller, D.P., et al. "Drug and alcohol related health problems in primary care-what do GPs think?" Med J Aust vol 156 1992. p. 43-48.
3. Marvel, M.K., Doherty, W.J., Baird, M.A. "Levels of physician involvement with psychosocial concerns of individual patients: a developmental model." Fam Med vol 25 1993. p. 337-42.
4. Levine, S.R. "Talk is cheap. Communication reduces costly medical errors." Mater Manag Health Care Jul; 13(7) 2004. p. 27-28.
5. Gilley, J. "Towards rational prescribing [Editorial]." BMJ vol 308 1994. p. 731-32.
6. Cohen-Cole, S.A. The Medical Interview: The Three-Function Approach. St. Louis, MO: Mosby-year Book, 1991.
7. Levinson, W., et al. "Physician-patient communication: the relationship with malpractice claims among primary care physicians and surgeons." JAMA vol 277 1997. p. 553-59.
8. Fleissig, A., Glasser, B., Lloyd, M. "Encouraging out-patients to make the most of their first hospital appointment: to what extent can a written prompt help patients get the information they want?" Patient Education and Counseling vol 38(1) 1999. p. 69-79. Little, P., et al. "Randomised controlled trial of effect of leaflets to empower patients in consultations in primary care." BMJ Feb 21; 328(7437) 2004. p. 441.
9. Jahng, K.H., et al. "Preferences for medical collaboration: patient-physician congruence and patient outcomes." Patient Educ Couns Jun; 57(3) 2005. p. 308-14.
10. Fallowfield, L. "The ideal consultation." Br J Hosp Med Mar 4-17; 47(5) 1992. p. 364-67.
11. Wells, T., Falk, S., Dieppe, P. "The patients' written word: a simple communication aid.." Patient Educ Couns Aug; 54(2) 2004. p. 197-200.
12. Hall, J.A., et al. "Liking in the physician—patient relationship." Patient Educ Couns Sep; 48(1) 2002. p. 69-77.
13. Deveugele, M., et al. "Consultation in general practice: a standard operating procedure?" Patient Educ Couns Aug; 54(2) 2004. p. 227-33.

Recognition of the importance of communication[1] has influenced medical schools to revise curricula and to teach communication skills in residency training and continuing medical education programs.[2] National certifying examinations also are being designed to incorporate these skills.[3] These concerns are also not being overlooked by medical insurers.[4] They are now using recorded consultations as teaching tools to show physicians how to reduce their risks of malpractice suits.[5] One study showed it only takes 10 seconds for patients to accurately predict surgeons with histories of malpractice claims.[6] In another study using video taped consultations, the use of negative communication behaviors by the physician increased litigious intentions of the 160 surveyed adults.

Paternalism,[7] or medical professional dominance as it has been called by some[8] means that the physician can override the choices of the patient if they feel it is for the patient's own good. It is assumed by the physician, that because they have expert technical knowledge, the patient grants them the authority to do whatever is needed to treat the patients condition.[9] The patient's knowledge of the situation may be discounted as being irrelevant.[10] This anachronistic presumption was first posited by the AMA *Code of Ethics* in 1848. Section 6 stated: "the obedience of a patient to the prescription of his physician should be prompt and implicit..." This dogma dominated the practice of medicine until the passage of the *Patient's Bill of Rights* in 1973 which states: "the patient has the right to refuse treatment to the extent permitted by law...."[11] Paternalists argue that "maximum patient benefit" can be achieved only by a physician's medical decision.[12] These attitudes prompted one medical ethicist to state "(Current)

1. Levinson, W., Roter, D.L. "The effects of two continuing medical education programs on communication skills of practising primary care physicians." J Gen Intern Med vol 8 1993. p. 318-24. Ong, L.M., et al. "Doctor-patients communication: a review of the literature." Soc Sci Med vol 40 1995. p. 903-18.
2. Davis, D.A., et al. "Changing physician performance. A systematic review of the effect of continuing medical education strategies." JAMA vol 274 1995. p. 700-05. Laine, C., Davidoff, F. "Patient-centered medicine: a professional evolution." JAMA vol 275 1996. p. 152-56.
3. Frymoyer, J.W., Frymoyer, N.P. "Physician-patient communication: a lost art?" J Am Acad Orthop Surg Mar-Apr; 10(2) 2002. p. 95-105.
4. Levinson, W. "In context: physician-patient communication and managed care." J Med Pract Manage Mar-Apr; 14(5) 1999. p. 226-30.
5. Gavin Lloyd, G., et al. "Communication skills training for emergency department senior house officers-a qualitative study." J Accid Emerg Med vol 17 2000. p. 246-50. Levinson. W., et al. "Physician-patient communication. The relationship with malpractice claims among primary care physicians and surgeons." JAMA Feb 19; 277(7) 1997. p. 553-59.
6. Ambady, N., et al. "Surgeons' tone of voice: a clue to malpractice history." Surgery Jul; 132(1) 2002. p. 5-9.
7. "Paternalism or partnership?" BMJ vol 319 1999. p. 719-20.
8. Phillips, D. "Medical professional dominance and client dissatisfaction. A study of doctor-patient interaction and reported dissatisfaction with medical care among female patients at four hospitals in Trinidad and Tobago." Soc Sci Med May; 42(10) 1996. p. 1419-25.
9. Yancy, W.S. Jr., et al. "Patient satisfaction in resident and attending ambulatory care clinics." J Gen Intern Med Nov; 16(11) 2001. p. 755-62.
10. "The Therapeutic Relationship Under Fire." Complementary and Alternative Medicine: Challenge and Change. 2000. <http://www.utoronto.ca/CAMlab/publications/kelner_thera_rel_under_fire.html>. Emanuel, E.J., Emanuel, L.L. "Four models of the physician-patient relationship." JAMA Apr 22-29; 267(16) 1992. p. 2221-26.

hospital specialists, it is said, rarely know their patient (or themselves) well enough to make this assumption without serious risk of ignorant arrogance."[1]

The paternalistic therapeutic relationship is characterized by a limited didactic style of communication.[2] Paternalists are very reluctant to provide "too much" information to the patient about their condition.[3] They may be evasive of direct questions and often use medical jargon where simple explanations should suffice.[4] Paternalism may explain a 2003 survey that found physicians felt highly esteemed by 90% of their patients.[5] Although most patients have high respect for the practice of medicine,[6] it may be more out of fear than regard of it's practitioners. The era of intentionally withholding medical information[7] or deluding patients died with public access to the Internet. [8]

Many patients now expect information so they may make choices about their own care.[9] Failures in physician-patient communication increase the risk for malpractice claims.[10] Uncertainty as to the reason for the bad outcomes may raise litigious feelings nearly as much as perceived physician fault.[11]

Most errors in medicine are actually the result of poor communication; [12] few are related to "bad docs" or personal negligence.[13] A review of malpractice claims data from 1976 to 1996 found 12% involved failures in communication.[14] A

11. Cheng-tek Tai, M., Tsung-po, T. "Decision-making at the end of life—Who makes the decision ?Patient's Autonomy vs paternalism." Public Health vol 44(5) 2003. p. 558-61. Miller, B. "Autonomy." Encyclopedia of Bioethics, Revised Edition. New York, NY: Simon and Shuster MacMillan, 1995.
12. Tan, N. "Deconstructing Paternalism — What Serves the Patient Best?" Singapore Med J 2002 Vol 43(3) : 148-151. 2002. ⟨http://www.sma.org.sg/smj/4303/4303sf2.pdf⟩.
1. Ruddick, W. "Medical Ethics." Encyclopedia of Ethics. 2006. 27 Jan 2006 ⟨http://people.umass.edu/uril/phil164-spr06/files/Medical%20Ethics%20-%20Ruddick.pdf⟩.
2. Lee, J.A. "Paternalistic? Me?" Lancet Oncol Jan; 4(1) 2003. p. 62.
3. Clark, S. "Paternalism and access to medical records.." J Infor Ethics Spring; 12(1) 2003. p. 80-91. Pope, T.M. "Counting the dragon's teeth and claws: the definition of hard paternalism." Ga State Univ Law Rev Spring; 20(3) 2004. p. 659-722.
4. Smith, R. "On not listening to patients." BMJ Feb 13; 306(6875) 1993. p. 410-11.
5. Daghio, M.M., et al. "GPs' satisfaction with the doctor–patient encounter: findings from a community-based survey." Family Practice vol 20(3) 2003. p. 283-88.
6. Tasso, K., et al. "Assessing patient satisfaction and quality of care through observation and interview." Hosp Top. 2002 Summer; 80(3) 2002. p. 4-10.
7. Coulter, A. "Paternalism or partnership? Patients have grown up-and there's no going back." BMJ Sep 18; 319(7212) 1999. p. 719-20. Wildes, K.W. "Patient no more: why did the golden age of medicine collapse?" America (NY) Jul 16; 185(2) 2001. p. 8-10.
8. "The internet and health." eurohealth. 2000. Summer 2000 ⟨http://www.euro.who.int/observatory/Publications/20020527_7⟩. Lee, S.J., et al. "Enhancing Physician-Patient Communication." Hematology 2002. p. 464-83.
9. Chin, J.J. "Doctor-patient relationship: from medical paternalism to enhanced autonomy." Singapore Med J Mar; 43(3) 2002. p. 152-55.
10. Nolin, C.E. "Malpractice claims, patient communication, and critical paths: a lawyer's perspective." Qual Manag Health Care Winter; 3(2) 1995. p. 65-70.
11. Egnew, T.R., et al. "Integrating communication training into a required family medicine clerkship." Acad Med Aug; 79(8) 2004. p. 737-43. Lester, G.W., Smith, S.G. "Listening and talking to patients. A remedy for malpractice suits?" West J Med Mar; 158(3) 1993. p. 268-72.
12. Beckman ,H.B., et al. "The doctor-patient relationship and malpractice. Lessons from plaintiff depositions." Arch Intern Med vol 154 1999. p. 1365-70. Eastaugh, S.R. "Reducing litigation costs through better patient communication." Physician Exec May-Jun; 30(3) 2004. p. 36-38.
13. Daniel, A.E., Burn, R.J., Horarik, S. "Patients' complaints about medical practice." MJA vol 170 1999. p. 598-602. Localio, A.R., et al. "Identifying adverse events caused by medical care: degree of physician agreement in a retrospective chart review." Ann Intern Med vol 125 1996. p. 457-464.

survey of families filing suit against pediatricians revealed they believed physicians would not listen (13% of sample), would not talk openly (32%), attempted to mislead them (48%), or did not warn them about long-term neuro-developmental problems (70%).[1]

Mandatory disclosure of medical errors has been advocated to improve patient safety. However, many physicians resist mandatory disclosure policies because of erroneous concerns about increasing their malpractice exposure.[2] Conversely, studies have shown that malpractice liability actually decreases when there is full disclosure of medical errors.[3] A 1996 survey reported that nearly all (98%) of the patients who responded wanted or expected their doctor to acknowledge errors, whether or not the error caused any harm.[4] The authors of this study concluded physicians who failed to disclose medical errors were more likely to be sued.[5]

Many physicians are pressuring Congress to apply caps on jury awards in a hope to reduce their malpractice premiums. They fail to realize that only about a quarter of injured patients said their primary motive was compensation.[6] The rest were evenly split between the desire for information, accountability or discipline. The above findings were reiterated a later study that concluded that litigation can only provide money, and a poultice of money does not cure all ills. "Only a few [of the complainants] want compensation; more want acknowledgement of the harm done; most want the doctor punished."[7] Failure to disclose their errors just angered the injured parties and increased the likelihood that a malpractice claim would be filed.[8] The public demands and expects a patient-physician relationship based on understanding, honesty, and trust.[9]

Several studies and reviews have clearly shown a correlation between effective communication[10] and improved health outcomes.[11] Orthopaedic surgeons recognize this when they ask patients to mark "no" on the healthy

14. Nakajima, K., Bidaillon, D. "Communication issues in the managed care environment." Forum vol 17 1996. p. 6-9.
1. Hickson, G.B., Clayton, E.W., Githens, P.B., Sloan, F.A. "Factors that prompted families to file medical malpractice claims following perinatal injuries." JAMA vol 267 1992. p. 1359-63.
2. Kessler, D.P., McClellan, M. "Do doctors practice defensive medicine?" Q J Econ vol 111 1996. p. 353-90.
3. Kachalia, A., et al. "Does full disclosure of medical errors affect malpractice liability? The jury is still out." Jt Comm J Qual Saf Oct; 29(10) 2003. p. 503-11.
4. Ibid.
5. Witman, A.B., Park, D.M., Hardin, S.B. "How do patients want physicians to handle mistakes?" Arch Intern Med vol 156 1996. p. 2565-69.
6. Vincent, C., Young, M., Phillips, A. "Why do people sue doctors? A study of patients and relatives taking legal action." Lancet vol 343 1994. p. 1609-1613.
7. Daniel, A.E., Burn, R.J., Horarik, S. "Patients' complaints about medical practice." Med J Aust vol 170 1999. p. 598-601.
8. Mazor, K.M., et al. "Health plan members' views about disclosure of medical errors." Ann Intern Med vol 140 2004. p. 409-18.
9. Bonds, D.E., et al. "Poor Underserved: An exploration of patients' trust in physicians in training." J Health Care May; 15(2) 2004. p. 294-306. Stock Keister, M.C., et al. "What people want from their family physician." Am Fam Physician May 15; 69(10) 2004. p. 2310.

extremity.[1] Patients are not just seeking more drugs or interventions. They desire a partnership with their physician and are seeking a forum to explain their concerns and discuss possible treatment options more congruent with their lives.[2] Patient satisfaction correlates strongly with the amount of information patients received from their physicians.[3] Patients are most satisfied when medical visits involve health education and discussions about specific therapy.[4]

In a study of 1012 women with a confirmed diagnosis of breast cancer, 22% wanted to select their own treatment and 44% wanted to select their treatment collaboratively with their doctors.[5] Fewer than half felt they had achieved the level of control over decision making that they preferred. In a 1999 study of patients with migraine, 88% of participants stated their first requirement of their medical practitioners was a willingness to answer questions.[6] They also expected their doctors to teach them about the causes, treatment options, and lifestyle management. This study found physicians had misperceptions about patients' beliefs and thought they were expected to be "experts." Physicians routinely underestimate the patients' ability to acquire information from other sources than a doctor. The Internet enables the educated consumer to research their condition and share their findings with others similarly afflicted. Many patients are simply seeking validation of their findings and the opportunity to share with another how this disease is affecting them personally. Unfortunately, a survey of 360 ambulatory patients found prevention or prognosis was seldom discussed during an office visit.[7] Another study found only four of 35 patients discussed all their issues of interest during a consultation. Nearly half of the visits had "problem outcomes" such as major misunderstandings, unwanted prescriptions, unused prescriptions, and patients not sticking to treatment.[8]

Self-imposed time constraints have decreased the patient's office visit to a fraction of what was once considered normal. These compressed evaluations

10. Fortin, A.H. 6th. "Communication skills to improve patient satisfaction and quality of care." Ethn Dis Fall; 12(4) 2002. p. S3-58-61. Stewart, M.A. "Effective physician-patient communication and health outcomes: a review." Can Med Assoc J vol 152 1995. p. 1423-33.
11. Vincent CA, Coulter A. Patient safety: what about the patient? Qual Safety Health Care 2002; 11: 76-80
1. DiGiovanni, C.W., Kang, L., Maneul, J. "Patient compliance in avoiding wrong-site surgery." J Bone Joint Surg vol 85A 2003. p. 815-19.
2. Laine, C., et al. "Important elements of outpatient care: a comparison of patients' and physicians' opinions." Ann Intern Med Oct 15; 125(8) 1996. p. 640-45.
3. Robbins, J.A., et al. "The influence of physician practice behaviors on patient satisfaction." Fam Med vol 25 1993. p. 17-20.
4. Bursch, B., Beezy, J., Shaw, R. "Emergency department satisfaction: what matters most?" Ann Emerg Med vol 22 1993. p. 586-91. Krishel, S., Baraff, L.J. "Effect of emergency department information on patient satisfaction." Ann Emerg Med vol 22 1993. p. 568-72.
5. Beaver, K., et al. "Treatment decision-making in women newly diagnosed with breast cancer." Cancer Nursing vol 19 1996. p. 8-19.
6. Lipton, R.B., Stewart, W.F. "Acute migraine therapy: do doctors understand what patients with migraine want from therapy?" Headache vol 39 1999. p. S20-6.
7. Sanchez-Menegay, C., Stalder, H. "Do physicians take into account patients' expectations?" J Gen Intern Med Jul; 9(7) 1994. p. 404-06.
8. "Speak up!." BMJ vol 327 2003. p. 303-304. Barry, C.A., et al. "Patients' unvoiced agendas in general practice consultations: qualitative study." BMJ vol 320 2000. p. 1246-50.

leave little time for thorough examinations let alone social amenities. A wise physician will remember to include at least one social grace into each visit: an apology for mistakes or inconveniences. This simple[1] yet inexpensive defensive medicine strategy is all too infrequently employed. Multiple studies have proven politeness[2] greatly reduces the risk for malpractice suits.[3] Patients are generally unlikely to sue their physician if they perceive them as being caring, even if they suffer adverse outcomes as the result of physician error.[4] Even if an error is admitted, the patient frequently will not receive an apology.[5] A 2003 JAMA study concluded physicians view an apology as tantamount to a confession of guilt exposing them to legal liability.[6]

THE DEVIL IN THE DOCTOR

> *There are three subjects on which the knowledge of the medical profession in general is woefully weak; they are manners, morals, and medicine.*
> Gerald F. Lieberman, American Writer, 1923- present

Many physicians cling to the outdated notion "doctor knows best." They are frequently derided for their haughtiness and arrogance, which often suppresses concerns, questions and new ideas.[7] A national survey of more than 1,600 hospital administrators found one in three had to deal with disruptive physician behavior on a daily, weekly or monthly basis.[8] The survey found 12% to 15% of doctors are chronically disruptive with more than half of respondents stating that nurses or physician assistants are the most frequent targets.[9] Angry physicians create problems for the staff, patients and administrators.[10] Although the problem is not new, it was documented in medical literature over 100 years

1. "Sometimes it might just pay to say you're sorry." Patient Care Manag May; 19(5) 2003. p. 3-4. Baggett, P. "I'm sorry: apologizing for a mistake might prevent a lawsuit." Tex Med Jan; 101(1) 2005. p. 56-59.
2. Crane, M. "What to say if you made a mistake." Med Econ Aug 20; 78(16) 2001. p. 26-8, 33-36.
3. Eastaugh, S.R. "Reducing litigation costs through better patient communication." Physician Exec May-Jun; 30(3) 2004. p. 36-38. Zimmerman, R. "Doctors' new tool to fight lawsuits: saying 'I'm sorry.' Malpractice insurers find owning up to errors soothes patient anger. 'The risks are extraordinary'." J Okla State Med Assoc Jun; 97(6) 2004. p. 245-47.
4. Leape, L. "Understanding the Power of Apology: How Saying "I'm Sorry" Helps Heal Patients and Caregivers." Focus on Patient Safety. 2005. ‹http://www.npsf.org/download/Focus2005Vol8No4.pdf›.
5. "Angered patients and the medical profession Changing from 'doctor's orders' to 'patient's choice'." MJA vol 170 1999. p. 576-77.
6. Gallagher, T.H., et al. "Patients' and physicians' attitudes regarding the disclosure of medical errors." JAMA Feb 26; 289(8) 2003. p. 1001-07.
7. Ingelfinger, F.J. "Arrogance." NEJM vol 303 1980. p. 1507-11.
8. Weber, D.O. "Poll results: doctors' disruptive behavior disturbs physician leaders; Survey reveals ongoing problems with physicians yelling at nurses, refusing to carry out tasks and showing a severe lack of respect for others." Physician Executive. 2004. Sep-Oct2004 ‹http://www.acpenet.org/MembersOnly/pejournal/2004/SeptemberOctober/Articles/WeberDavid.pdf›.
9. "Staff Less Tolerant of Rude Doctors." ARDMS Newswire. 2004. 20 Sep ‹http://www.ardms.org/newswire/09202004/09202004.htm#rude›.
10. Sotile, W.M., Sotile, M.O. "The angry physician-Part 1. The temper-tantruming physician." Physician Exec Aug; 22(8) 1996. p. 30-34.

ago; disruptive physician behavior has been an ongoing challenge to the hospital executives. If allowed to go unchecked, a physician exhibiting disruptive behavior may threaten a hospital's image, staff morale, finance, and quality of care.[1] Nearly 40% of surveyed executives said they excused this behavior in physicians generating high amounts of revenue.[2] Ignoring this disruptive behavior[3] is no longer an option in today's changing health care environment.[4]

Bad physician behavior has forced some to juggle schedules to prevent personality conflicts, and 40% of hospitals report it is a consideration in staff retention.[5] The severe nursing shortage has prompted some organizations to finally confront this behavior.[6] Studies of female and male nurses have reported disrespectful treatment, criticism, attacks, tirades, and baseless accusations from physicians.[7] An analysis 1,200 responses from nurses, physicians, and hospital executives found this behavior had a strong negative impact on nurses' morale and job satisfaction.[8] It is truly ironic that in surveys of those providing care,[9] 85-94% reported incidences of verbal abuse in some form during the past year.[10] One study reported these incidences occurred nearly on a daily basis[11] and a 2004 study states their incidence may be increasing.[12]

Nurses frequently endure assaults by both patients and family members,[13] however, a director for one institute states "Most verbal abuse comes from physicians."[14] It is sad to note that a 2002 study confirmed physician-perpetrated abuse to nurses was even more common than abusive acts by

---

1. "Drunk' surgeon arrested as he demands to operate on patient." The Scotsman. 2006. 10 Mar 2006 <http://news.scotsman.com/international.cfm?id=360002006>. Piper, L.E. "Addressing the phenomenon of disruptive physician behavior." Health Care Manag Oct-Dec; 22(4) 2003. p. 335-39.
2. Ibid.
3. Barnsteiner, J.H., Madigan, C., Spray, T.L. "Instituting a disruptive conduct policy for medical staff." AACN Clin Issues Aug; 12(3) 2001. p. 378-82. Kissoon, N., Lapenta, S., Armstrong, G. "Diagnosis and therapy for the disruptive physician." Physician Exec Jan-Feb; 28(1) 2002. p. 54-58.
4. Yassi, A., et al. "Causes of staff abuse in health care facilities. Implications for prevention." AAOHN J Oct; 46(10) 1998. p. 484-91.
5. Kreitzer, M.J., et al. "Creating a healthy work environment in the midst of organizational change and transition." J Nurs Admin vol 27(6) 1997. p. 35-41.
6. Linney, B.J. "Confronting the disruptive physician." Physician Exec Sep-Oct; 23(7) 1997. p. 55-58.
7. Brooks, A., Thomas, S.P., Droppleman, P. "From frustration to red fury: A description of work-related anger in male registered nurses." Nursing Forum vol 31(3), 1996. p. 4-15. Smith, M.E., Hart, G. "Nurses' responses to patient anger: From disconnecting to connecting." Journal of Advanced Nursing vol 20 1994. p. 643-51.
8. Rosenstein, A.H. "Original research: nurse-physician relationships: impact on nurse satisfaction and retention." Am J Nurs Jun; 102(6) 2002. p. 26-34.
9. Cameron, L. "Verbal abuse: a proactive approach." Nurs Manage Aug; 29(8) 1998. p. 34-36. Cook, J. "Exploring the impact of physician verbal abuse on perioperative nurses." AORN Journal. 2001. Sep 2001 <http://www.findarticles.com/p/articles/mi_m0FSL/is_3_74/ai_80159514>.
10. Manderino, M.A., Berkey, N. "Verbal abuse of staff nurses by physicians." Image:Journal of Nursing Scholarship vol 27(3) 1995. p. 244. Sofield, L. "Verbal Abuse." Verbal abuse: Summary of online survey. 2000. May 2000 <http://www.laurasofield.com/>.
11. Henderson, A.D. "Nurses and workplace violence: nurses' experiences of verbal and physical abuse at work." Can J Nurs Leadersh vol 16(4) 2003. p. 82-98.
12. Crouch, D. "Why is verbal abuse getting worse?" Nurs Times Sep 14-20; 100(37) 2004. p. 28-29.
13. Fernandes, C.M., et al. "Violence in the emergency department: a survey of health care workers." CMAJ Nov 16; 161(10) 1999. p. 1245-48. Zernike, W., Sharpe, P. "Patient aggression in a general hospital setting: do nurses perceive it to be a problem?" Int J Nurs Pract Jun; 4(2) 1998. p. 126-33.
14. Ibid.

patients.[1] This is unconscionable considering one Internet site lists 12 pages of references related to violence and abuse against nurses.[2] This abuse can be devastating to those on the receiving end.[3] The most frequent and stressful types of verbal abuse are in the forms of abusive anger, ignoring, and condescension.[4] Many researchers[5] have shown verbal abuse by physicians is commonplace against nurses.[6]

Nurses are not the only ones suffering as the result of abuse by physicians. Studies have shown repeated incidents of verbal abuse contribute to increased incidence of error.[7] Intimidation by arrogant doctors who don't trust or respect the ideas of nurses and patients can be deadly because many potential medical errors could be averted by other healthcare workers if it weren't for fear of reprisal or condemnation by the physician.[8] In fact, physician-nurse relationships even have been related to numbers of patient injuries in the hospital.[9] Researchers found when doctors acquire a reputation for tantrums, nurses hesitate to call them about a patient or make suggestions about the patient's care.[10]

There has been considerable debate about whether doctors develop mental health problems as a result of working in medicine or because they are more likely to have psychologically vulnerable personalities before selection to medical school.[11] This childlike behavior may be so deeply rooted in physician psyche that it may actually be a motivating factor to become a doctor. A 2003 paper by Tillet describes in great detail the psychopathology of 'helping profession syndrome.'[12] His authoritative work reviews studies suggesting at

1. Anderson, C. "Workplace violence: Are some nurses more vulnerable?" Issues in Mental Health Nursing vol 23(4) 2002. p. 351-66.
2. "Nurse Abuse/Workplace Violence." College and Association of Registered Nurses of Alberta. 2006. <http://www.nurses.ab.ca/pdf/Nurse%20Abuse.pdf>.
3. Brooks, A., Thomas, S.P., Droppleman, P. "From frustration to red fury: A description of work-related anger in male registered nurses." Nursing Forum vol 31(3) 1996. p. 4-15. O'Connell, B., et al. "Nurses' perceptions of the nature and frequency of aggression in general ward settings and high dependency areas." J Clin Nurs Jul; 9(4) 2000. p. 602-10.
4. Manderino, M.A., Berkey, N. "Verbal abuse of staff nurses by physicians." J Prof Nurs Jan-Feb; 13(1) 1997. p. 48-55.
5. Alderman, C. "Bullying in the workplace: A survey." Nursing Standard vol 11(35) 1997. p. 22-24. Braun, K., et al. "Verbal abuse of nurses and non-nurses." Nursing Management vol 22(3) 1991. p. 72-76.
6. Furniss, K. "Battered nurses: New research shows those giving care may need it most." Lifelines vol 3(1), 72 1999. p. 69-71. Roberts, S. "Nurse abuse: A taboo topic." Canadian Nurse vol 87(5) 1991. p. 23-25.
7. Buback, D. "Assertiveness training to prevent verbal abuse in the OR." AORN J Jan; 79(1) 2004. p. 148-50, 153-58. Cox, H.C. "Excising verbal abuse." Todays OR Nurse Jan-Feb; 16(1) 1994. p. 38-40.
8. Berger, A.S. "Arrogance among Physicians." Acad Med Feb; 77(2) 2002. p. 145-47.
9. Davidhizar, R., Policinski, H. "Getting along with the "difficult" physician." Health Care Superv Mar; 12(3) 1994. p. 11-16.
10. Burgess-Jackson, K. "Do physicians kill patients? An essay on arrogant philosophy." J Med Humanit vol Winter; 20(4) 1999. p. 265-82. Diaz, A.L., McMillin, J.D. "A definition and description of nurse abuse." Western Journal of Nursing Research vol 13(1) 1991. p. 97-109.
11. Firth Cozens, J. "The role of early family experiences in the perception of organisational stress: Fusing clinical and organisational perspectives." J Occupational and Organisational Psychology vol 65 1992. p. 61-75. Vaillant, G., Sobowale, N., McArthur, C. "Some psychological vulnerabilities of physicians." NEJM vol 287 (8) 1972. p. 372-75.
12. Tillet, R. "The patient within — psychopathology in the helping professions." Advances in Psychiatric Treatment vol 9 2003. p. 272-79.

least a third of medical students are motivated by unconscious neurotic drives and unresolved conflicts from childhood.[1] The 1972 study suggested maladaptive personality traits and poor coping styles were already present before entering medical school. Some writers suggest the choice of a medical career may serve as a defense against feelings of anxiety[2] or impotence resulting from the experience of illness or death in family members.[3]

Dysfunctional relationships are often a result of neuroses or personality disorders. A study in the *British Journal of Medical Psychology* concluded many physicians have shaky self-esteem and require patient adulation as a crutch to function.[4] Unfortunately, this dependence on patients to achieve a sense of worth may result in feelings of anger and resentment.[5] This inordinate compulsion for prestige and power coupled with poorly controlled aggressive and hostile tendencies may inevitably result in both professional and emotional disaster.[6] It should therefore come as no surprise why so many become cynical, callous and rude toward others early in their careers.[7] Is it any wonder that doctors have significantly higher rates of insanity,[8] suicide,[9] prescription drug abuse,[10] alcoholism,[11] divorce,[12] depression,[13] and chronically dysfunctional lives[14] lacking true happiness[15]? A British study of 11,600 physicians[16] found 27%

1. Ibid.
2. Gabbard, G. "The role of compulsiveness in the normal physician." JAMA vol 254 1985. p. 2926-29.
3. Lief, H. (1971) (eds. t). , USA: Thomas.. Personality characteristics of medical students. In Psychosocial Aspects of Medical Training. Springfield, IL: Coombs & Vincent, 1971. Pfeiffer, R. "Early adult development in the medical student." Mayo Clinic Proceedings vol 58 1983. p. 127-134.
4. Johnson, W. "Predisposition to emotional distress and psychiatric illness amongst doctors: the role of conscious and experiential factors." British Journal of Medical Psychology vol 64 1991. p. 317-29.
5. Thomas, S.P. "Anger: the mismanaged emotion." Medsurg Nurs Apr; 12(2) 2003. p. 103-10.
6. Gerrity, M.S. "Interventions to improve physicians' well-being and patient care: a commentary." Soc Sci Med Jan; 52(2) 2001. p. 223-25. Sotile, W.M., Sotile, M.O. "The angry physician-Part 1. The temper-tantruming physician." Physician Exec Aug; 22(8) 1996. p. 30-34.
7. Peters, J.A. "The devil in the doctor. How to cope with problem physicians." MGMA Connex Feb; 3(2) 2003. p. 50-53.
8. Heim, E. "Job stressors and coping in health professions." Psychotherapy and Psychosomatics vol 55 1991. p. 90-99.
9. Center, C., et al. "Confronting depression and suicide in physicians: a consensus statement." JAMA Jun 18; 289(23) 2003. p. 3161-66. Lindeman, S., Laara, E., Hakko, H., Lonnqvist, J. "A systematic review on gender-specific suicide mortality in medical doctors." Br J Psychiatry Mar; 168(3) 1996. p. 274-79.
10. Bohigian, G.M., Croughan, J.L., Bondurant, R. "Substance abuse and dependence in physicians: the Missouri Physicians Health Program—an update (1995-2001)." Mo Med Apr; 99(4) 2002. p. 161-65. Fields, M. "Doctors doing drugs and drinking." Physician Exec Sep-Oct; 30(5) 2004. p. 28-31.
11. Ibid. Flaherty, J.A., Richman, J.A. "Substance use and addiction among medical students, residents, and physicians." Psychiatr Clin North Am Mar; 16(1) 1993. p. 189-97.
12. Ramirez, A., et al. "Mental health of hospital consultants: the effects of stress and satisfaction at work." Lancet vol 347 1996. p. 724-728.
13. Chambers, R., Campbell, I. "Anxiety and depression in general practitioners: associations with type of practice, fundholding, gender and other personal characteristics." Fam Pract vol 13 (2) 1996. p. 170-73.
14. Guthrie, E., Black, D. "Psychiatric disorder, stress and burnout." Advances in Psychiatric Treatment vol 3 1997. p. 275-281.
15. Tillet, R. "The patient within — psychopathology in the helping professions." Advances in Psychiatric Treatment vol 9 2003. p. 272-79.
16. Wall, T., et al. "Minor psychiatric disorder in NHS Trust staff: Occupational and gender differences." British Journal of Psychiatry vol 171 1997. p. 519-23.

were considered psychologically abnormal, compared with 18% for the general population. Multiple studies have shown high levels of psychiatric dysfunction[1] in physicians with approximately one-quarter being identified as being particularly vulnerable.[2] About half of all general practitioners have been categorized as suffering from probable borderline or more severe anxiety disorders.[3] Female physicians are especially prone to problems of depression,[4] anxiety and suicide.[5] Some studies have suggested women physicians may have four times greater risk of suicide than the general female population.[6] It is sad to note that more than half of all female physicians may experience a psychiatric illness during their lifetime.[7] A 1996 study found the risk of physician suicide may be 3 to 5 times higher than that of the general population.[8]

One early study speculated that a symbiotic relationship exists between the patient and doctor, in which the doctor has many parent-like qualities and the patient has correspondingly child-like ones. The author of this study concluded that motivating factors to become doctors may also predispose them to establish "malignant symbiotic" relationships.[9] One commentator even believes doctors develop an open contempt for the people who cannot be rehabilitated because those who are beyond healing have become "a threat to newly acquired delusions of omnipotence."[10] Reliance upon authoritative symbols like "white coats"[11] to bolster scientific claims is viewed with suspicion by some authors.[12]

1. Schernhammer, E.S., Colditz, G.A. "Suicide rates among physicians: A quantitative and gender assessment." Am J Psychiatry vol 161 2004. p. 2295-02.
2. Caplan, R. "Stress, anxiety and depression in hospital consultants, general practitioners and senior health service managers." BMJ vol 309 1994. p. 1261-63. Firth-Cozens, J. "Doctors, their wellbeing, and their stress." BMJ vol 326 2003. p. 670-71.
3. Chambers, R., Campbell, I. "Anxiety and depression in general practitioners: associations with type of practice, fundholding, gender and other personal characteristics." Fam Pract vol 13 (2) 1996. p. 170-73.
4. Frank, E., Dingle, A.D. "Self-reported depression and suicide attempts among U.S. women physicians." Am J Psychiatry Dec; 156(12) 1999. p. 1887-94. McManus, I.C. "Increased mortality in women doctors." Lancet Mar 25; 345(8952) 1995. p. 796-97.
5. Carpenter, L.M., Swerdlow, A.J., Fear, N.T. "Mortality of doctors in different specialties: findings from a cohort of 20000 NHS hospital consultants." Occup Environ Med Jun; 54(6) 1997. p. 388-95. Lindeman, S., et al. "Suicide mortality among medical doctors in Finland: are females more prone to suicide than their male colleagues?" Psychol Med Sep; 27(5) 1997. p. 1219-22.
6. Frank, E., Dingle, A.D. "Self-Reported Depression and Suicide Attempts Among U.S. Women Physicians." Am J Psychiatry vol 156(1) 1999. p. 887-94.
7. Hendrie, H.C., et al. "A study of anxiety/depressive symptoms of medical students, house staff, and their spouses/partners." J Nerv Ment Dis vol 178 1990. p. 204-07. North, C.S., Ryall, J.E. "Psychiatric illness in female physicians. Are high rates of depression an occupational hazard?" Postgrad Med May; 101(5) 1997. p. 233-6, 239-40, 242.
8. Lindeman, S., et al. "A systematic review on gender-specific suicide mortality in medical doctors." Br J Psychiatry vol 168 1996. p. 274-79.
9. Rogers, D.E. "On Entering Medicine." Bulletin of the New York Academy of Medicine vol 69 1993. p. 61-68. Zigmond, D. "Physician Heal Thyself." British Journal of Holistic Healing vol 1 1984. p. 63-71.
10. "Doctors, Torture and Abuse of the Doctor-Patient Relationship." Canadian Medical Association Journal vol 116 1977. p. 708-10. Justin, R.G. "Can a physician always be compassionate?" Hastings Cent Rep Jul-Aug; 30(4) 2000. p. 26-27.
11. Harnett, P.R. "Should doctors wear white coats?" MJA vol 174 2001. p. 343-44. Rehman, S.U., et al. "What to wear today? Effect of doctor's attire on the trust and confidence of patients." Am J Med Nov; 118(11) 2005. p. 1279-86.

Doctors cannot be solely blamed for their near messianic complexes; western culture feeds this delusion[1] by portraying the average physician in almost mythical proportions in the media.[2] The medical establishment further reinforces this delusion during the medical school process. Only the brightest and most capable are admitted to medical schools.[3] It seems only natural to conclude those chosen must be the best humanity has to offer. Tom Delbanco, chief of medicine at Beth Israel was quoted as saying, "I think doctors are socialized early on to be arrogant."[4] One of medicine's most prestigious journals unapologetically recognizes this character trait when they state "Is the doctor-patient relationship marked by authoritarianism, paternalism, and domination? My answer is not only 'yes' but also that a certain measure of these characteristics is essential to good medical care." This can delude some physicians into imagining that they are all-powerful. Seriously ill or injured patients tend to view the physician as an omnipotent parent and savior, and in this way unwittingly tempt physicians to be arrogant.[5] The author of one paper reminds his fellow physicians that "we should not exaggerate our own importance. We are but an instrument of healing and not its source."[6]

This dysfunctional behavior is the mainstay of malpractice attorneys. Patients are more likely to sue physicians who are perceived as being arrogant than they are doctors they like.[7] A physician can be guilty of gross negligence or malpractice yet remain immune from litigation simply because the patient/client perceives them as being "nice."[8] The reverse of this is also true; a physician may have done everything according to the standards of care yet may be aggressively targeted by the patient/client simply because they are not liked.[9] Physicians with arrogant attitudes are often perceived as uncaring; many times an uncaring attitude may be interpreted as a negligent attitude by the patient. Failure of physicians to talk honestly with patients puts them at high risk of being perceived as being evasive which equates to "covering up something" to many.

12. Gooden, B.R., et al. "Hospitalised patients' views on doctors and white coats." Med J Aust Aug 20; 175(4) 2001. p. 219-22. Wear, D. "On white coats and professional development: the formal and the hidden curricula." Ann Intern Med vol 129 1998. p. 734-37.
1. Diem, S.J., Lantos, J.D., Tulsky, J.A. "Cardiopulmonary resuscitation on television. Miracles and misinformation." NEJM Jun 13; 334(24) 1996. p. 1578-82.
2. Flores, G. "Mad scientists, compassionate healers, and greedy egotists: the portrayal of physicians in the movies." J Natl Med Assoc Jul; 94(7) 2002. p. 635-58. Varmus, H. "How popular TV shows shape public perceptions of medical scientists." Mt Sinai J Med Nov; 68(6) 2001. p. 346-49.
3. Ingelfinger, F.J. "Arrogance." NEJM vol 303 1980. p. 1507-11.
4. Greger, M. "MDiety" Heart Failure — Diary of a Third Year Medical Student. 1999 ‹ http://upalumni.org/medschool/appendices/appendix-58.html›.
5. Berger, A.S. "The arrogant physician—a Judaic perspective." J Relig Health Summer; 41(2) 2002. p. 127-29.
6. Berger, A.S. "Arrogance among physicians." Acad Med Feb; 77(2) 2002. p. 145-47.
7. Communication gaffes: a root cause of malpractice claims. "Huntington, B., Kuhn, N." Proc (Bayl Univ Med Cent) vol 16(2) 2003. p. 157-61. "Apologies Gain Momentum." ISMP Medication Safety Alert. 2005. 21 Sep 2005 ‹http://www.medscape.com/viewarticle/512894›.
8. Hickson, G.B., et al. "Patient complaints and malpractice risk." JAMA Jun 12; 287(22) 2002. p. 2951-57. Rice, B. "Why some doctors get sued more than others." Medical Economics. 2003. 11 Jul 2003 ‹http://www.memag.com/memag/article/articleDetail.jsp?id=111458›.
9. Gaby, A.R. "The medical malpractice crisis." Townsend Letter for Doctors and Patients. 2004. Apr 2004 ‹http://www.findarticles.com/p/articles/mi_m0ISW/is_249/ai_114820691›.

Physicians with arrogant attitudes fair very poorly in the judicial system, many jurors associate this physician with others doctors they have personally known who displayed similar socially unacceptable behavior.[1] This may be seen as an opportunity to "even the score" for the injured party. Male physicians are particularly prone to this dominating arrogant attitude and therefore are much more likely to be sued.[2] Given the high cost of malpractice insurance, one would think the majority of doctors would pre-empt lawsuits simply by being polite. Malpractice attorneys don't seem to be too concerned that this will ever happen. Physicians, particularly male physicians, just seem to have a hard time admitting their faults.[3] Creating a good doctor-patient relationship requires interpersonal skills that are all too frequently lacking in the males within the medical profession.[4]

Others have suggested it is too much too expect physicians to voluntarily report their errors.[5] Dr. Jeff Drayer states in *Salon.com* "The creation of another bureaucracy would only further encourage this secretive behavior. Even getting into medical school is a competitive process, and as a result, the field is saturated with people who don't like to admit they're wrong or discuss their shortcomings. And no matter how many times they're told their name will be kept anonymous in connection with reported clinical errors, somehow, doctors still tend not to trust outside agencies, especially the government. And who's to say that a physician who reports one too many mistakes won't lose his livelihood? He knows better than anyone that unlike any other profession, if you lose your job in medicine, you're finished. Forever."[6]

Is it any wonder the motives for being a physician are frequently suspect in literature? The prominent status of fictional surgeons within the medical profession is reflected in their arrogant and patronizing attitudes towards patients, primary care doctors and non-surgical specialists. Fictional surgeons are impatient, irascible and aggressive.[7] These traits make them poor communicators and teachers. A few are suspected of harboring sadistic tendencies. On the other hand, when the surgeon turns his aggression towards the disease process rather than his colleagues or his trainees, it enables him to achieve some spectacular therapeutic successes.[8]

---

1. Rice, B. "How doctors sabotage their own defense." Med Econ Sep 9; 79(17) 2002. p. 36-8, 41.
2. Nichols, J.D. "Lawyer's advice on physician conduct with malpractice cases.." Clin Orthop Relat Res Feb; (407) 2003. p. 14-18.
3. Bertakis, K.D., Franks, P., Azari, R. "Effects of physician gender on patient satisfaction." J Am Med Womens Assoc Spring; 58(2) 2003. p. 69-75.
4. Bylund, C.L., Makoul, G. "Empathic communication and gender in the physician-patient encounter." Patient Educ Couns Dec; 48(3) 2002. p. 207-16.
5. Walshe, K. "Litigation authority. For our eyes only." Health Serv J Feb 22; 111(5743) 2001. p. 26-27.
6. Drayer, J. "The culture of secrecy." Salon. 1999. 2 Dec 1999 ‹http://www.salon.com/health/feature/1999/12/02/meaculpa/index.html›.
7. Chandler, M.R. "Dangerous medicine: horror stories from fiction." Pharos Alpha Omega Alpha Honor Med Soc Spring; 53(2) 1990. p. 18-21. Jones, A.H. "Images of physicians in literature: medical Bildungsromans." Lancet Sep 14; 348(9029) 1996. p. 734-36.
8. Posen, S. "The portrayal of the doctor in non-medical literature. 15. The surgeon." Aust N Z J Surg Sep; 66(9) 1996. p. 630-35.

"I reckon I shall stick to medicine for good. I find it's the best of all trades because whether you do any good or not you still get your money. We never get blamed for bad workmanship.... If we blunder it isn't our look out: it's always the fault of the fellow who's dead and the best part of it is that there's a sort of decency among the dead, a remarkable discretion: you never find them making any complaint against the doctor who killed them."[1]

MEDICAL OBFUSCATION AND UNINFORMED CONSENT

The doctor should be opaque to his patients and, like a mirror, should show
them nothing but what is shown to him.
Sigmund Freud 1856-1939, Father of Psychoanalysis

If the above findings worry you enough to discuss your concerns with a physician, don't be surprised if they don't listen to you.[2] A 1984 study in the *Annals of Internal Medicine* showed doctors listened to patients for an average of eighteen seconds before interrupting.[3] In only 23% of the visits were patients were allowed to complete their opening statement.[4] A 1998 Swedish study reported one in four patients had experienced, "the doctor and medical student act[ing] as if I were not there."[5] They are very busy, as you can clearly tell by that two-hour wait for a scheduled appointment.[6] They sincerely believe they are addressing your best interests by diagnosing your ailment (labeling your condition) and then prescribing the approved therapy for that diagnosis. What a pity many have forgotten a diagnosis involves more than a physical and lab exam. The patient's mental status can greatly influence their perception of their health, understanding your mental condition may help the physician diagnose your medical condition. Unfortunately, proper examinations may require interpersonal skills woefully lacking in medical students. One author suggests that these skills not only don't improve during medical school, they may actually worsen.[7] A study comparing how well physicians communicated with their patients found "that the communication skills emphasized by academic teachers do not reflect the skills important to patients."[8]

---

1. Brody, H. The Seductions of Tyranny. New Haven: Yale University Press, 1992. Greger, M. Heart Failure — Diary of a Third Year Medical Student. 1999 ‹http://upalumni.org/medschool/›.
2. Assael, L.A. "Can you hear me now? Listening to our patients and ourselves." J Oral Maxillofac Surg Apr; 63(4) 2005. p. 425-26.
3. "The Importance of Healthy Rapport." Medical Risk Management. 2006. ‹http://www.webmedin.com/riskmanagement_healthyreport.html›.
4. Beckman, H.B., Frankel, R.M. "The effect of physician behavior on the collection of data." Ann Intern Med 101 1984. p. 692-96.
5. Lynoe, N., et al. "Informed Consent in Clinical Training — Patient Experiences and Motives for Participating." Medical Education vol 32 1998. p. 465-71.
6. Shilling, V., Jenkins, V., Fallowfield, L. "Factors affecting patient and clinician satisfaction with the clinical consultation: can communication skills training for clinicians improve satisfaction?" Psychooncology Sep; 12(6) 2003. p. 599-611.
7. Silverman, J.D., Draper, D.J Kurtz, S.M. "Letter." BMJ vol 310 1995. p. 527. Greger, M. "Communication" Heart Failure — Diary of a Third Year Medical Student. 1999 ‹http://upalumni.org/medschool/appendices/appendix-24a.html›.

In a paper written for surgeons on how to improve their communications with their patients, the surgeons were reassured they, "do not need to share their patients' feelings in order to communicate effectively.... An empathetic response is not about what you feel; it is an interviewing skill.... In fact it doesn't matter what you feel; you do not have to feel."[1] This failure in empathy by physicians undermines patient trust and satisfaction.[2] Recognition of these failures in patient-physician communication has influenced some medical schools to incorporate courses that teach communication skills.[3]

The medical interview is an essential skill for all health care providers. One author suggests the average generalist will conduct between 120,000 and 160,000 interviews during a 40-year professional career.[4] Sadly, research shows many of these one-sided interviews are frequently judged[5] to be inadequate.[6] An audiotape analysis of residents' communication related to medications and follow-up appointments confirmed the failures in effective communication skills. The study found only 31% of patients returned for their follow-up appointments despite "teaching" by the resident physician.[7] A study of junior doctors found they often lack sufficient training to fully inform patients and do not even meet the legal requirements for obtaining "informed consent."[8] However, most patients will never know their resident doctors may be unqualified to assess or treat their diseases. One author states medical schools engage in active deception to prevent patients from refusing medical treatment by doctors in training. He concludes teaching hospitals intentionally mislead patients into believing interns are actually physicians.[9] A 1995 survey of 149 medical students found all had been improperly introduced as "doctor" by hospital staff[10] even though this violates federal and professional guidelines.[11] Some try to rationalize this canard by stating; "Patients in teaching hospitals are

8. Cooper, C. Mira, M. "Who should assess medical students' communication skills: their academic teachers or their patients?" Medical Education vol 32(4) 1998. p. 419.
1. Sandrick, K. "Codified principles enhance physician/patient communication." Bulletin of the American College of Surgeons vol 83(11) 1998. p. 13-17.
2. Kim, S.S., Kaplowitz, S., Johnston, M.V. "The effects of physician empathy on patient satisfaction and compliance." Eval Health Prof Sep; 27(3) 2004. p. 237-51.
3. Beck, R.S., Daughtridge, R., Sloane, P.D. "Physician-patient communication in the primary care office: a systematic review." J Am Board Fam Pract Jan-Feb; 15(1) 2002. p. 25-38. Frymoyer, J.W., Frymoyer, N.P. "Physician-patient communication: a lost art?" J Am Acad Orthop Surg Mar-Apr; 10(2) 2002. p. 95-105.
4. Lipkin, M. Jr. The medical interview: clinical care, education, and research. New York: Springer-Verlag, 1995.
5. Marvel, M.K., et al. "Soliciting the patient's agenda: have we improved?" JAMA vol 281 1999. p. 283-87.
6. Beck, R.S. "Physician-Patient Communication in the Primary Care Office: A Systematic Review." JABFP vol 15(1) 2002. p. 25-38. Bensing, J.M., Dronkers, J. "Instrumental and affective aspects of physician behavior." Med Care vol 30 1992. p. 283-98.
7. Falvo, D., Tippy, P. "Communicating information to patients. Patient satisfaction and adherence as associated with resident skill." J Fam Pract Jun; 26(6) 1988. p. 643-47.
8. Mulcahy, D., et al. "Informed consent from whom?" J R Coll Surg Edinb Jun; 42(3) 1997. p. 161-64.
9. Duncan, D.E. Residents: The Perils and Promise of Educating Young Doctors. New York, NY: Scribner, 1996. Greger, M. "Informed Consent" Heart Failure — Diary of a Third Year Medical Student. 1999 ‹http://upalumni.org/medschool/appendices/appendix-1.html#fn1›.
10. Beatty, M.E., Lewis, J. "Inaccurate medical student introductions: frequency and motivation." Conn Med Aug; 59(8) 1995. p. 455-60. Hyman, D. "Joint FTC/Department of Justice Hearing on Health Care and Competition Law and Policy." Federal Trade Commission. 2003. 10 Jun 2003 ‹http://www.ftc.gov/ogc/healthcarehearings/030610ftctrans.pdf›.

starting to instantly reject 'medical students,' but using the term 'student doctor' can get a little leeway — I'm not being deceitful, just dynamic."[1]

The students in the 1995 survey stated they personally felt uncomfortable with this deception, but less than half corrected this misinformation. This practice is directly in violation of the Joint Committee on the Accreditation of Hospitals guidelines that state, "The patient has a right to know the identity and professional status of the individuals providing service to him.... Participation by patients in clinical training programs... should be voluntary."[2] The survey of all CEOs in primary teaching hospitals found only about a third of major teaching hospitals specifically informed patients that they were being treated by medical students and not doctors.[3] A few medical schools actually instruct their students to introduce themselves as "Doctor."[4] Studies have shown patients are confused by the student descriptors 'medical student,' 'student physician,' 'student doctor,' and 'MD student.' They generally believe the label 'medical student' indicated less experience than the other three.[5] The author suggests that the use of any other label than 'medical student' is an intentional obfuscation that is blatantly unethical.[6] Medical school faculty rationalizes that overstating medical students' status will increase their patients' willingness to accept care from interns and increase their residents' case loads and opportunities to learn. A longitudinal survey of 2,603 students concluded medical students were less concerned of informing patients of their student status than patients desire.[7] The authors determined that, as medical students advance in their training, they were less inclined to reveal their student status to their patients.[8] Claims that this deceit is benign and inflation of the student's experience to assure they have a 'proper educational experience' are refuted by studies showing patients may actually be harmed by residents and medical students.[9] Educators may justify harm to one patient if they believe it may benefit a larger group.[10]

11. Epstein, L.C., Guadagnoli, E. "Introducing Medical Students to Patients." Rhode Island Medical Journal vol 74 1991. p. 321-326.
1. Bhangu. A. "There are too many restrictions on medical students." StudentBMJ 2003; 11: vol 11 2003. p. 175-218.
2. Cohen, D.L., et al. "The Ethical Implications of Medical Student Involvement in the Care and Assessment of Patients in Teaching Hospitals: Part I." Proceedings of the Annual Conference on Research on Medical Education vol 24 1985. p. 138-45.
3. Ibid.
4. "Why Medical Students are 'Medical Students.'" Journal Of General Internal Medicine 13(1998):718-719.
5. Silver-Isenstadt, A. "Medical Student Name Tags." Journal Of General Internal Medicine 12(1997):669-671.
6. Howell, J.D. "Why Medical Students are 'Medical Students'." Journal Of General Internal Medicine vol 13 1998. p. 718-19.
7. Graber, M.A., Pierre, J., Charlton, M. "Patient Opinions and Attitudes toward Medical Student Procedures in the Emergency Department." Acad Emerg Med vol 10(12) 2003. p. 1329-33. King, D., et al. "Attitudes of elderly patients to medical students." Med Educ vol 26 1992. p. 360-63.
8. Silver-Isenstadt, A., Ubel, P.A. "Erosion in medical students' attitudes about telling patients they are students." J Gen Intern Med Aug; 14(8) 1999. p. 481-87.
9. Hicks, L.K., et al. "Understanding the ethical dilemmas that shape medical students' ethical development: questionnaire survey and focus group study." BMJ vol 322 2000. p. 709-10. Jagsi, R. "The ethics of medical education." BMJ vol 329 2004. p. 332-34.
10. Coldicott, Y., Pope, C., Roberts, C. "The ethics of intimate examinations—teaching tomorrow's doctors." BMJ vol 326 2003. p. 97-101.

Patients are frequently drawn to teaching hospitals for their purported medical expertise. They may be shocked to find that the primary mission of teaching hospitals is to "teach the next generation of health professionals" and not patient care.[1] A 1998 study found the inexpert care provided by student doctors was no bargain. The authors of this national study concluded treatment at a teaching hospital costs 83% more than care delivered in a nonteaching community hospital.[2] The belief that patients are hospitalized for the medical students learning benefit is typical of the paternalistic attitudes so common among physicians. The basic assumption is patients agree to student participation in exchange for the "advanced" care received in academic institutions.[3] One medical school dean argued "Many patients are incapable of understanding the complex, subtle and often intuitive methods by which physicians make decisions; may lack the intelligence or education, or they may be too emotionally distraught.... Informed consent, therefore, may at times be undesirable and/or undesired."[4] In a national survey of 1500 medical students, half didn't think hospitals should have to obtain consent for student involvement in pelvic exams, a quarter believed, "All patients were 'teaching patients'" and 40% didn't think patients have the right to reject student participation in all aspects of their care.[5] The authors of one paper argue "Creating a habit of betraying the fiduciary trust for reasons of self-interest is ethically dangerous."[6]

Failure to inform patients of their inexperience taints the "informed consent" obtained because the patients depend upon the doctors' "knowledge and expertise" to guide them into an informed opinion. A study of emergency department patients found 66% thought they should be informed if they were being treated by inexperienced students. Medical students revealed their inexperience to less than half of those they treated. This dishonesty is especially disheartening because 90% of the patients stated they would consent to being treated by inexperienced physicians.[7]

Some patients would prefer to be partners in their medical care and desire access to their own charts to help make better informed decisions. Unfortunately, most hospitals consider the patient's chart as their property[8]

1. "Advancing Medical Knowledge Every Day." University Health System. 2006. ‹http://www.universityhealthsystem.com/aboutuhs/advancing.html›.
2. "Costs higher at teaching hospitals, study finds." Washington Business Journal. 1998. 25 Sep 1998 ‹http://www.bizjournals.com/washington/stories/1998/09/28/newscolumn6.html›. Mechanic, R., Coleman, K., Dobson, A. "Teaching Hospital Costs." JAMA vol 280 1998. p. 1015-19.
3. Greger, M. "Informed Consent" Heart Failure — Diary of a Third Year Medical Student. 1999 ‹http://upalumni.org/medschool/appendices/appendix-1.html#fn1›. Silverman, D.R. "Narrowing the Gap between the Rhetoric and the Reality of Medical Ethics." Academic Medicine vol 71 1996. p. 227-35.
4. Greer, D.S. "To Inform or Not to Inform Patients About Students." Journal of Medical Education vol 62 1987. p. 861-62. Montgomery, C., Lydon, A., Lloyd, K. "Patients may not understand enough to give their informed consent." BMJ vol 314 1997. p. 1482.
5. Beattyu, M.E., Lewis, J. "Inaccurate Medical Student Introductions." Connecticut Medicine vol 59 1995. p. 455-40. Cohen, D.L. "A National Survey Concerning the Ethical Aspects of Informed Consent and Role of Medical Students." Journal of Medical Education vol 63 1988. p. 821-29.
6. Marracino, R.K., Orr, R.D. "Entitling the Student Doctor." Journal Of General Internal Medicine vol 13 1998. p. 266-70.
7. Santen, S.A., et al. "'Sorry, it's my first time!' Will patients consent to medical students learning procedures?" Med Educ Apr; 39(4) 2005. p. 365-69.

(very convenient) and refuse access to them without the consent of the hospitals risk management (aka lawyers) and only under their supervision.[1] Common sense and law[2] argues that every person has the right to determine what will be done to their body, and the right to decide whether or not to undergo medical treatment.[3] State Supreme Court Justice Nathan Cardozo said in 1914, "Every human being of adult years and sound mind has a right to determine what shall be done with his own body."[4] Physicians who do not view patients as partners are reluctant to allow them to read abnormal reports,[5] progress notes,[6] and care notes.[7]

Requests from patients to review their own medical records often result in litigation[8] between the patient and the healthcare providers.[9] A Japanese study found more than 70% of the physicians studied believed they only had the right to control information such as the process to reach a diagnosis, subjective patient information, uncertain information and discussion with other physicians.[10] A Hebrew study found 94% of physicians surveyed had refused to give patients access to their medical records. The authors conclude restricting information from their patients was in order to legitimate and monopolize their professional power.[11] Psychiatric records are of special concern because one study found most contained potentially offensive, alarming or upsetting entries.[12]

Physicians may argue against open disclosure stating patients may be distressed by detailed information, methods, and risks.[13] Some believe forcing

8. Mitchell, M.W. "'Legally speaking'. Re: Physician medical records—patient access." J Ark Med Soc Dec; 84(7) 1987. p. 273-74. Waller, A.A., Alcantara, O.L. "Ownership of health information in the information age." J AHIMA Mar; 69(3) 1998. p. 28-38.
1. Bernstein, R.A., Andrews, E.M., Weaver, L.A. "Physician attitudes toward patients' requests to read their hospital records." Med Care J Jan; 19(1) 1981. p. 118-21. Morrissey, J. "Whose info is it, anyway? As HIPAA provisions take effect, patients may be surprised by the level confidentiality, intent on exercising new rights." Mod Healthc Apr 14; 33(15) 2003. p. 4-5, 15.
2. Mair, J. "Access and confidentiality of medical records: a legislative response in the United States." Health Inf Manag. 1996 Mar-May; 26(1) 1996. p. 33-40.
3. Giesen, D. "The patient's right to know—a comparative law perspective." Med Law vol 12(6-8) 1993. p. 553-65. Lantos, J. "Informed consent. The whole truth for patients?" Cancer Nov 1; 72(9 Suppl) 1993. p. 2811-15.
4. Schloendorff v Society of New York Hospital, 105 NE 92, NY (1914)
5. Bachorik, L. "The public's right to know." FDA Consum Nov-Dec; 34(6) 2000. p. 40. Dorr, D.A., et al. "Physicians' attitudes regarding patient access to electronic medical records." AMIA Annu Symp Proc 2003. p. 832.
6. Patterson, E.G. "The therapeutic justification for withholding medical information: what you don't know can't hurt you, or can it?" Neb Law Rev vol 64(4) 1985. p. 721-71.
7. Siegal, G., Siegal, N., Weisman, Y. "Physicians' attitudes towards patients' rights legislation." Med Law vol 20(1) 2001. p. 63-78.
8. Davies, J. "Patients' rights of access to their health records." Med Law Int vol 2(3) 1996. p. 189-13.
9. Johnson, B., Waller, A., Cattell-Gordon, D. "Should patients have access to their medical records." Hosp Health Netw Apr; 73(4) 1999. p. 24. Kennedy, I. "Access to medical records: Breen v. Williams." Med Law Rev Spring; 5(1) 1997. p. 115-21.
10. Tanimoto, S. "[Do patients and/or physicians have a right to control medical information]." J Nippon Med Sch Dec; 67(6) 2000. p. 440-54.
11. Weiss, M. "For doctors' eyes only: medical records in two Israeli hospitals." Cult Med Psychiatry Sep; 21(3) 1997. p. 283-302.
12. Bloch, S., Riddell, C.E., Sleep, T.J. "Can patients safely read their psychiatric records? Implications of freedom of information legislation." Med J Aust Dec 5-19; 161(11-12) 1994. p. 665-66.
13. Tobias, J., Souhami, R. "Fully informed consent can be needlessly cruel." BMJ vol 307 1993. p. 1199-20.

unsolicited information is needlessly cruel and may compromise recovery. They further complain open discussion of risks may keep patients from volunteering for clinical trials in sufficient numbers to make such trials possible.[1] Apologists for the medical community defend non-disclosure of risks stating there may be circumstances in which informed consent is not required.[2] These paternal arguments fail to consider that if patients discover information has been withheld, their distress and sense of betrayal may be far greater than that engendered by learning the truth.[3] Surveys have found even the terminally ill[4] desire accurate information and are not necessarily upset by it.[5]

Communication is an exchange of information; it also allows the patient to solicit additional information to clarify what they don't understand.[6] Failure to allow patients access to all their records undermines the trust between physicians and patients[7] and interferes with doctor-patient communication.[8] In a 1997 study, 93.4% of those studied (467) preferred disclosure of risk information by the physician.[9]

Most physicians agree harmful errors should be disclosed but "choose their words carefully" when telling patients about errors. They often avoided stating an error occurred, why the error happened, or how recurrences would be prevented.[10] A random sample of 1500 adults concluded full disclosure reduced the reported likelihood of changing physicians and increased patient satisfaction, trust, and positive emotional response. The authors believe patients will probably respond more favorably to physicians who fully disclose medical errors than to those who are less candid.[11] Patients expect to be notified of even rare risks,[12] failure to be forthright breaches the "the modern clinical ritual of trust."[13]

Inflation of therapeutic benefit is another ethical concern; physicians may overstate the benefit of a therapy to obtain more volunteers for clinical trials.[14] A

1. Baum, M. "The ethics of randomised controlled trials." Eur J Surg Oncol vol 21 1995. p. 136-37.
2. "Helsinki Declaration." BMJ vol 313 1996. p. 1448.
3. Bok S. Lying. Brighton, Sussex: Harvester, 1978.
4. Fallowfield, L., Ford, S.. Lewis, S. "Information preferences of patients with cancer." Lancet vol 344 1994. p. 1576.
5. Deber, R. "Physicians in health care management. 7. The patient-physician partnership: changing roles and the desire for information." Can Med Assoc J vol 151 1994. p. 171-76. Kerrigan, D.D., et al. "Who's afraid of informed consent." BMJ vol 306 1993. p. 298-300.
6. Holland, P.V. "Consent for transfusion: is it informed?" Transfus Med Rev Oct; 11(4) 1997. p. 274-85.
7. Johnson, B., Waller, A., Cattell-Gordon, D. "Should patients have access to their medical records." Hosp Health Netw Apr. 73(4) 1999. p. 24.
8. Ross, S.E., Lin, C.T. "The Effects of Promoting Patient Access to Medical Records: A Review." J Am Med Inform Assoc Mar-Apr; 10(2) 2003. p. 129-38.
9. Mazur, D.J., Hickam, D.H. "Patients' preferences for risk disclosure and role in decision making for invasive medical procedures." J Gen Intern Med Feb; 12(2) 1997. p. 114-17.
10. Gallagher, T.H., et al. "Patients' and physicians' attitudes regarding the disclosure of medical errors." JAMA Feb 26; 289(8) 2003. p. 1001-07.
11. Mazor, K.M., et al. "Health plan members' views about disclosure of medical errors." Ann Intern Med Mar 16; 140(6) 2004. p. 409-18.
12. Newton-Howes, P.A., et al. "Informed consent: what do patients want to know?" N Z Med J Sep 11; 111(1073) 1998. p. 340-42.
13. Wolpe, P. The triumph of autonomy in American bioethics: a sociological view. In: Devries R, Subedi J, eds. Bioethics and society: sociological investigations of the enterprise of bioethics. Englewood Cliff, NJ: Prentice Hall, 1998.

study of cancer patients participating in a phase I chemotherapy trial asked why patients volunteered. All volunteers responded their prime motivation was therapeutic benefit. Tragically, these patients had entered into a clinical trial whose only goal was only to assess the toxicity of a new chemotherapeutic agent with a tumor response rates at or below 5%.[1] Some patients have been outraged to discover they were used in a trial without their knowledge.[2] Subjects in some experiments believe they are receiving standard treatment even when there is no evidence of utility.[3]

It is literally taking an act of Congress to force freedom of access to your own medical record.[4] A letter to the editor of the journal *Lancet* best exemplifies the medical establishment's position regarding unfettered access to your healthcare records; "The patient wanting to read their [case-] notes indicates their lack of trust. If so, I can only see one solution: the patient seeks another medical advisor. Reading the notes does not help to achieve the rapport, mutual confidence, or trust that is essential in the healing and reassuring process of medical care...."[5] Only recently has the medical community begun to recognize the difference between legalistically signing a form versus meaningful communication of risks. An informed consent assumes the signing party is actually legally competent, understands the situation and alternatives, and is not coerced (by family or medical professionals) in the decision-making.[6]

One study determined 47% of consents were signed by patients having significant impairment without the use of a surrogate.[7] A study of medical specialists found they had different opinions regarding mental incapacity. Correct answers on capacity to consent to or refuse medical treatment were given by 58% of the psychiatrists, 34% of the geriatricians, 20% of the general practitioners and 15% of the students. They also had problems discerning competence; 15% of all respondents actually believed a competent adult could be treated against their will.[8] Physicians have a duty not to commit battery on their patients. What keeps a physician's touching of a patient from being a battery is the patient's consent. Therefore; physicians require a legal consent from their patients or legal spokesperson to authorize their treatments.[9]

---

14. Advisory Committee on Human Radiation Experiments. The Human Radiation Experiments. New York City: Oxford University Press, 1996.
1. Daugherty, C., et al. "Perceptions of cancer patients and their physicians involved in phase I trials." J Clin Oncol vol 13(5) 1995. p. 1062-72.
2. "Research without consent continue in the UK." Bull Inst Med Ethics vol 40 1988. p. 1315.
3. Adkisson, G.H., et al. "Cerebral perfusion deficits in dysbaric illness." Lancet vol ii 1989. p. 119-22. Wilmshurst, P.T., Nunan, T.O. "Cerebral perfusion deficits in dysbaric illness." Lancet vol ii 1989. p. 674-75.
4. Jackson, J.Z. "The HIPAA privacy rule and physician responses to medical-record requests in civil litigation." N J Med Sep; 100(9) 2003. p. 21-26.
5. Blau, J.N. "Letter." Lancet vol 3 1987. p. 45. Greger, M. "Depersonalization" Heart Failure — Diary of a Third Year Medical Student. 1999 ⟨http://upalumni.org/medschool/appendices/appendix-14b.html⟩.
6. English, D.C. "Valid informed consent: a process, not a signature." Am Surg Jan; 68(1) 2002. p. 45-48.
7. Auerswald, K.B., Charpentier, P.A., Inouye, S.K. "The informed consent process in older patients who developed delirium: a clinical epidemiologic study." Am J Med Nov; 103(5) 1997. p. 410-18.
8. Jackson, E. Warner, J. "How much do doctors know about consent and capacity?" J R Soc Med vol 95 2002. p. 601-03.

Many attempt to mechanize this process by using standardized "blanket consent" forms to cover subsequent medical procedures.[1] Previous studies[2] on blanket consent have suggested patients have little understanding of such documents. Fear of severe illness may potentially create a coercive atmosphere in which requesting *carte blanche* permission for medical procedures is particularly inappropriate.[3] Moreover, even in non-emergent circumstances,[4] patient understanding of the consent process may be poor.[5] A 2002 study found 40% of all written consents were invalid.[6] These findings have prompted one author to conclude that the premise of informed consent as a rational decision-making process is probably a myth.[7]

According to a 13th-century medical code of professional ethics attributed to Arnald of Villanova when a layperson asks questions that the physician is unable to answer he states "It helps greatly to use... a term not understood."[8] This tendency to intentionally obscure the meaning of medical terminology from the layman is not restricted to early medicine. The surgeon/author Michael Crichton is quoted as saying, "I don't agree... that medical writing is inept. I argued that it was actually a highly skilled, calculated attempt to confuse the reader."[9]

Crichton was more prescient than he could ever realize; a 1998 study of 10% of all US hospital consent forms found the mean grade level required to understand these consent forms was 12.6.[10] An earlier study of consent reports for radiation imaging concluded 15 years of education was required to understand the research forms and most consent forms used in radiology practice are too complex for the average patient to understand.[11] Multiple studies have shown the use of medicalese is virtually incomprehensible[12] to the average consumer/patient.[13] This problem is exacerbated by the large percentage

9. Schneider, C. The Practice of Autonomy: Patients, Doctors and Medical Decisions. New York City: Oxford University Press, 1998.

1. DeGirolamo, A., et al. "Informed consent for invasive procedures in a community hospital medical intensive care unit." Conn Med Apr; 68(4) 2004. p. 223-29. Faunce, T.A. "Medical disclosure and consent forms: proposal for an international standard." Med Law vol 16(3) 1997. p. 581-91.

2. Boisaubin, E.V., Dresser, R. "Informed consent in emergency care: illusion and reform." Ann Emerg Med vol 16 1987. p. 62-67.

3. Akkad, A., et al. "Informed consent for elective and emergency surgery: questionnaire study." BJOG Oct; 111(10) 2004. p. 1133-38.

4. Lavelle-Jones, C., et al. "Factors affecting quality of informed consent." BMJ vol 306 1993. p. 885-95.

5. Herz, D.A., Looman, J.E., Lewis, S.K. "Informed consent: is it a myth?" Neurosurgery vol 30 1992. p. 453-58. Priluck, I.A., Robertson, D.M., Buettner, H. "What patients recall of the preoperative discussion after retinal detachment surgery." Am J Ophthalmol vol 87 1979. p. 620-23.

6. Mohamed Tahir, M.A., Mason, C., Hind ,V. "Informed consent: optimism versus reality." Br Dent J Aug 24; 193(4) 2002. p. 221-24.

7. Verheggen, F.W., van Wijmen, F.C. "Myth and reality of informed consent in clinical trials." Med Law vol 16(1) 1997. p. 53-69.

8. Crichton, M. "Medical Obfuscation." NEJM vol 293 1976. p. 1257-59. Greger, M. "Medspeak" Heart Failure — Diary of a Third Year Medical Student. 1999 ‹http://upalumni.org/medschool/appendices/appendix-25.html›.

9. Ibid.

10. Hopper, K.D., et al. "The readability of currently used surgical/procedure consent forms in the United States." Surgery May; 123(5) 1998. p. 496-503.

11. Hopper, K.D., TenHave, T.R., Hartzel, J. "Informed consent forms for clinical and research imaging procedures: how much do patients understand?" Am J Roentgenol Feb; 164(2) 1995. p. 493-96.

12. Gibbs, R.D., Gibbs, P.H., Henrich, J. "Patient understanding of commonly used medical vocabulary." Journal of Family Practice vol 25 1987. p. 176-78.

of marginally literate patients. One university study concluded that the reading level of patients was at the fifth to sixth grade level-even though these subjects reported completing tenth grade on the average.[1] But let the physician beware, use of medspeak may cause more problems[2] than frank disclosure.[3]

Even when attempts are made to obtain consent in emergency settings, a minority of patients understand what they have "agreed to."[4] Patient may feel duress believing they may have no choice but to sign a consent form for fear of the consequences of not signing.[5] Consent within the ICU is even more complicated because surrogate decision makers (family members or guardians) may not necessarily reflect the wishes of the patient.[6]

A study involving obtaining informed consent from patients having a heart attack determined it should be sought despite the emergency situation and the medical condition of the patient. The authors state patients should not be pressured into decision making.[7] Studies have shown concerns about obtaining consent under duress are valid because patients signing consents for non-emergent procedures often fail to understand or recall the purpose of their consent.[8] In one study, 100 patients were interviewed between two and five days after their operation. Although all patients knew they had received an operation, 27 were unable to name the organ requiring surgery and 44 were unaware of the exact nature of the surgical procedure.[9] In a 2000 study, neurosurgical patients were asked to list as many risks they could recall just two hours after a consent interview. The average retention rate was a measly 18%; 65% failed to recall more than two of the six 'typical major risks'.[10] In another study, evaluation of retention of information immediately after signing a consent form revealed only 43.5% understood the risks just explained. In a follow-up study approximately 6 weeks later, the score dropped to 38.4%. The authors concluded the doctrine of informed consent may very well be mythical.[11]

13. Ninchoji T, et al. "Patient's comprehension of the medical informations presented before the invasive procedures." Jpn Hosp Jul 12 1993. p. 45-49. Norman, G.R., et al. "The privileged status of prestigious terminology: impact of "medicalese" on clinical judgments." Acad Med Oct; 78(10 Suppl) 2003. p. S82-4.
1. Davis, T.C., et al. "The gap between patient reading comprehension and the readability of patient education materials." Journal of Family Practice vol 31 1990. p. 533-38.
2. Terry, K. "Telling patients more will save you time." Med Econ Jul 25; 71(14) 1994. p. 40, 43, 46.
3. Gordon, D. "MDs' failure to use plain language can lead to the courtroom." CMAJ Oct 15; 155(8) 1996. p. 1152-54. Mintz, D. "What's in a word: the distancing function of language in medicine." J Med Humanit vol Winter; 13(4) 1992. p. 223-33.
4. Boisaubin, E.V., Dresser, R. "Informed consent in emergency care: illusion and reform." Ann Emerg Med vol 16 1987. p. 62-67.
5. Akkad, A., et al. "Informed consent for elective and emergency surgery: questionnaire study." BJOG Oct; 111(10) 2004. p. 1133-38.
6. Smedira, N.G., et al. "Withholding and withdrawal of life support from the critically ill." NEJM vol 322 1990. p. 309-15.
7. Gammelgaard, A., Mortensen, O.S., Rossel, P. "DANAMI-2 Investigators. Patients' perceptions of informed consent in acute myocardial infarction research: a questionnaire based survey of the consent process in the DANAMI-2 trial." Heart Oct; 90(10) 2004. p. 1124-28.
8. Murphy, S.M., et al. "Patients' recall of clinical information following laparoscopy for acute abdominal pain." Br J Surg Apr; 91(4) 2004. p. 485-88.
9. Byrne, D.J., Napier, A., Cuschieri, A. "How informed is signed consent?" Br Med J (Clin Res Ed) Mar 19; 296(6625) 1988. p. 839-40.
10. Krupp, W., Spanehl, O., Laubach, W., Seifert, V. "Informed consent in neurosurgery: patients' recall of preoperative discussion." Acta Neurochir (Wien) vol 142(3) 2000. p. 238-39.

Attempts to circumvent physicians informing patients have generally been unsuccessful. A study of information leaflets determined 97% of patients stated they read the leaflet, but only 52% had actually read the consent form. Over half complained they were dissatisfied with the lack of sufficient information.[1] In a separate study, 69% of the patients confessed to not reading the consent form prior to signing.[2] A 2004 study concluded although 75% of the patients knew their diagnoses, 63% did not know the risks associated with their surgery and 75% did not know the complications of anesthesia.[3] Ironically, several studies have found the majority of those signing informed consent felt satisfied they had been adequately informed of risks.[4] In one study, 80% of respondents were satisfied with information provided for consent; however, over half could not list even one complication of their operation.[5] A 2004 study of 265 patients reported only 8% correctly recalled all of the elements of the general consent form, 42.3% simply trusted their doctors to perform the necessary medical procedure.[6]

11. Herz, D.A., Looman, J.E., Lewis, S.K. "Informed consent: is it a myth?" Neurosurgery Mar; 30(3) 1992. p. 453-58.
1. Bassi, A., Brown, E., Kapoor, N., Bodger, K. "Dissatisfaction with consent for diagnostic gastrointestinal endoscopy." Dig Dis vol 20(3-4) 2002. p. 275-79.
2. Lavelle-Jones, C., et al. "Factors affecting quality of informed consent." BMJ Apr 3; 306(6882) 1993. p. 885-90.
3. Jebbin, N.J., Adotey, J.M. "Informed consent: how informed are patients?" Niger J Med Apr-Jun; 13(2) 2004. p. 148-51.
4. Godwin, Y. "Do they listen? A review of information retained by patients following consent for reduction mammoplasty." Br J Plast Surg Mar; 53(2) 2000. p. 121-25. Howlader, M.H., et al. "Patients' views of the consent process for adult cardiac surgery: questionnaire survey." Scand Cardiovasc J Dec; 38(6) 2004. p. 363-68.
5. Burns, P., Keogh, I., Timon, C. "Informed consent: a patients' perspective." J Laryngol Otol Jan; 119(1) 2005. p. 19-22.
6. Thorevska, N., et al. "Informed consent for invasive medical procedures from the patient's perspective." Conn Med Feb; 68(2) 2004. p. 101-05.

Chapter 9. Medicine's Marginal Benefits

Quackery has no friend like gullibility.
Proverb

America is an aggressive society, all we do is tainted by this war like nature, hence, our use of terms like "war on cancer", "fighting bacteria", referring to antibiotics as "magic bullets", etc.. This aggressive nature greatly influences how we manage disease; however, aggressive therapy does not equate to optimum therapy, or even safe therapy.[1] For example, in one study 1,222 healthy individuals having risk factors for cardiovascular disease were randomized into a treatment and a control group.[2] Those in the intervention group were visited by physicians every fourth month and were prescribed intensive dietetic-hygienic measures, and frequently received cholesterol-lowering medications (clofibrate and/or probucol) and antihypertensive (beta-blockers and/or diuretics) drugs. The control group was untreated. The intervention trial lasted 5 years. Fifteen-year overall mortality rates increased by 45% in individuals followed and treated by physicians as compared to those who received no intervention. In particular, mortality due to cardiovascular disease increased by 2.4 times, and that due to violence by 13 times, in treated versus untreated individuals. Cancer death rates were 38% lower in the treated group.[3] Later studies explained the increased mortality from intervention as being related to the exchange of small benefit in a

---

1. Wilhelmsen, L. et al. "The multifactor primary prevention trial in Goteborg, Sweden." Eur Heart J Apr; 7(4) 1986. p. 279-88.
2. Strandberg TE, et al. "Long-term mortality after 5-year multifactorial primary prevention of cardiovascular diseases in middle-aged men." JAMA Sep 4; 266(9) 1991. p. 1225-29.

3. Oglesby, P., Hennekens, C.H. "The latest report from Finland. A lesson in expectations." JAMA vol 266 1999. p. 1267-68.

low risk population for a small risk associated with pharmacotherapy.[1] The high risk patient may indeed benefit from drug therapy. However, the low risk patient may suffer from adverse effects related to the use of a drug that far outweighs any benefit from therapy.[2] One researcher summarized the phenomena best saying "in mass prevention, each individual has usually only a small expectation of benefit, and this small benefit can easily be outweighed by a small risk."[3] A 1997 systematic review of multiple risk factor interventions concluded lifestyle changes which bring reductions in risk factors have a greater impact on reducing mortality than drug intervention in the general (low risk) population.[4]

These findings are reminiscent of the conclusions of a risk factor trial called MRFIT.[5] MRFIT is an acronym for Multiple Risk Factor Intervention Trial. This large study trial on 12,000 middle-aged men, costing over $100 million dollars, sought to prove lifestyle modification and pharmacological treatment could prevent heart disease. Trial subjects were selected because cholesterol levels, blood pressure, and/or smoking put them at very high risk of heart disease. Hypertension was managed by drugs; they received intensive counseling for smoking cessation and dietary modification. After five years, there was no difference in rates of heart disease between intervention and control groups. The subjects were reevaluated after seven years and again there were no differences. After 10.5 years, the authors concluded the study by stating medical intervention produced a 10% lower rate of coronary heart disease death. Although a 10% reduction may seem significant, they downplayed the finding that this 10% decrease was actually the difference between a death rate of 3.4% in the control group and 3.1% in the intervention group. A 10% reduction from 3.4% to 3.1% hardly seems significant, but they had to report something positive after spending $100,000,000. Even this 10% reduction is questionable, because the P value was only 0.2. Scientific convention states a result is not considered significant unless the P value is less than 0.05.[6]

If you think the above studies were a fluke, then consider the following:

A study of over 21,000 patients aged 35-49 followed for 16 years, showed blood pressure management was associated with only small reductions of blood

1. "Who benefits from medical Interventions?" BMJ Editorials. 1994. 08 Jan 1994 ⟨http://bmj.bmjjournals.com/cgi/content/full/308/6921/72⟩.
2. Oliver, M.F. "Risks of correcting risks of coronary disease and stroke with drugs." NEJM vol 306 1982. p. 297-98.
3. Rose, G. "Sick individuals and sick populations." International Journal of Epidemiology. 201. 30 Jun 2001
4. Ebrahim, S., Smith, G.D. "Systematic review of randomised controlled trials of multiple risk factor interventions for preventing coronary heart disease." BMJ. 1997. 07 Jun 1997 ⟨http://bmj.bmjjournals.com/cgi/content/abstract/314/7095/1666⟩.
5. The Multiple Risk Factor Intervention Trial Research Group. "Mortality rates after 10.5 years for participants in the Multiple Risk Factor Intervention Trial." JAMA. 1990. 04 Apr 1990 ⟨http://jama.ama-assn.org/cgi/content/abstract/263/13/1795⟩.
6. "Statistics." Pharmaceutical Journal. 2005. 09 Apr 2005 ⟨http://www.pjonline.com/Editorial/20050409/comment/lett05.html⟩.

pressure, and targeted blood pressure was rarely achieved.[1] Rates of coronary heart disease mortality were 80% higher in the treated for hypertension versus the untreated group. The highest incidence of death occurred in patients with systolic blood pressure before treatment below 184 mmHg and in those with increasing blood pressure in spite of treatment. According to the authors' own conclusions "The benefit experienced from the trials turned into an adverse effect of treatment in the population setting, particularly at low pretreatment blood pressure, and when blood pressure increased during treatment."

An even more recent study came to the same conclusion. Over 14,000 individuals aged 32-51 years were invited to screening examination in the period 1974-1992; those with identified risk factors for cardiovascular disease, diabetes and breast cancer were referred to specialists for treatment.[2] Mortality and morbidity rates of the population in the intervention group were compared to those of a control group, consisting of 10,945 individuals who were not invited to screening. Overall mortality and cardiovascular mortality rates were similar in the two groups, and so were those of nonfatal myocardial infarction and stroke, indicating that screening and treatment of cardiovascular risk factors is not associated with improved health outcomes.

Another study of 686 middle-aged, hypertensive men and 6810 non-hypertensive found treatment of hypertension over a 20-22 year period produced higher mortality rates in those treated with drugs than the control group.[3] The study found death rates for those treated with antihypertensives was 37.4% compared to 29.2% for those receiving no intervention. Hypertensive patients treated with drugs had higher mortality from cardiovascular disease, especially coronary heart disease, compared to non-hypertensive men.

Still not impressed? Perhaps an even larger study published in the flagship of all medical journals will convince you. A study in 1991 of approximately 234,000 elderly individuals from US and Canada who had a new myocardial infarction showed American patients were eight times more likely to undergo angioplasty and bypass surgery compared to Canadian patients (11.7% vs. 1.5% and 10.6% vs. 1.4%, respectively).[4] Although mortality rates one month after the heart attack were slightly lower for Americans (21.4% vs. 22.3%), one-year death rates were virtually identical (34.3% for American patients vs. 34.4% for Canadian patients). These data indicate high rates of angioplasty and bypass surgery in elderly patients do not translate into improved long-term survival. A

---

1. Thurmer, H.L., Lund-Larsen, P.G., Tverdal, A. "Is blood pressure treatment as effective in a population setting as in controlled trials?" J Hypertens Apr; 12(4) 1994. p. 481-90.
2. Berglund, G. et al. "Long-term outcome of the Malmo preventive project: mortality and cardiovascular morbidity." Journal of Internal Medicine. 2000. Jan 2000 ‹http://www.blackwell-synergy.com/links/doi/10.1046/j.1365-2796.2000.00568.x›.
3. Andersson, O.K., et al. "Survival in treated hypertension: follow up study after two decades." BMJ. 1998. 18 Jul 1998 ‹http://bmj.bmjjournals.com/cgi/content/full/317/7152/167›.
4. Tu, J.V. et al. "Use of cardiac procedures and outcomes in elderly patients with myocardial infarction in the United States and Canada." NEJM. 1997. 22 May 1997 ‹http://content.nejm.org/cgi/content/short/336/21/1500›.

later study comparing outcomes of cardiac procedures in both countries concluded current treatments in cardiac care reduce one year mortality by a mere 1.27% in the United States and 1.05% in Quebec. Patients older than 75 years of age or older did show a 50% reduction in cardiac related deaths if treated in the US; however, those age 65 to 74 years showed no measurable difference in mortality rates.[1] A study published in the journal *Health Affairs* of 1,000 randomly selected adults in each country, ranked Canada as #1 in healthcare delivery and the US as last. It is believed by many the Canadian physician is in medicine for the patient and the American physician is in medicine for the money.[2] A survey of 1000 American households showed 82% agreed with the statement "Medical care has become a big business that puts profits ahead of people."[3] However, there is little likelihood of change in the near future given the numbers of those profiting from death and suffering.[4]

As shocking as these findings may be, they are certainly not rare and isolated cases. The medical literature is replete with such findings, yet, the media for the most part seems unconcerned. Much of the inattention to medical studies may be the result of two basic human conditions: fear and ignorance. We fear most that which we do not understand. It takes some effort to become proficient in the terminology used in medicine. Although much of this terminology is there to provide a "universal language" enabling one medical researcher to effectively communicate with another; it also is adept at creating an indecipherable barrier for those who are being treated.[5]

Nobody likes to acknowledge their ignorance, especially the media. They choose instead not to risk showing their ignorance on a subject for which they obviously have little understanding. The result of this abandonment by the media is most of this literature is quietly fought over by academicians while the gullible public listens to infomercials thinly disguised as public service ads exhorting them to badger their primary physician for the newest, most costly and least tested therapy. The poor overworked primary physician certainly does not have the time to read through the morass of never-ending and seemingly contradictory literature. Many therefore rely heavily upon the not so unbiased pharmaceutical representative to help them "keep current" with the latest therapies. While the battles silently wage, hundreds of thousands needlessly die[6] and even more pay exorbitant prices for therapies of unproven benefit.

1. "Cardiac procedure use and outcomes in elderly patients with acute myocardial infarction in the United States and Quebec, Canada, 1988 to 1994." Medical Care. 2003. Center for Public Health Policy. Jul 2003 ‹http://chppcor.stanford.edu/publications/cardiac_procedure_use_and_outcomes_in_elderly_patients_with_acute_myocardial_infarction_in_the_united_states_and_quebec_canada_1988_to_1994/›.
2. Dusen, L.V. "This Business Called Medicine." Canadian Medical Association Journal vol 157 1997. p. 1724.
3. National Coalition on Health Care. "How Americans Perceive the Health Care System; A Report on a National Survey." National Coalition on Health Care 1997.
4. Ibid.
5. Shaughnessy, A.F. "It's Medspeak to us, but Greek to them.." RN Dec; 50(12) 1987. p. 28-29.

THE SMALL ROLE OF MEDICINE IN MORTALITY

> *"We are, in real life, a reasonably healthy people. Far from being ineptly put together, we are amazingly tough, durable organisms, full of health, ready for most contingencies. The new danger to our well-being, if we continue to listen to all the talk, is in becoming a nation of healthy hypochondriacs, living gingerly, worrying ourselves half to death.'*
>
> Lewis Thomas — Naturalist quoted from The Medusa and the Snail. New York: Bantam Books, 1980.

Most people are born healthy and biologically suited to remain healthy throughout the majority of their lives. We are provided with far more physiological reserves than we need to function. The examples of this are numerous; the lungs and kidneys exist as pairs, insuring that if one were lost due to trauma or injury the whole body would still function in nearly an uncompromised state. The liver is endowed with incredible powers of regeneration; clinical observations and experimental studies have determined that the upper-limit for single liver resection is approximately 70-80%[1] in humans[2] and 95% in mouse and rat.[3] Even the brain has been equipped with this built in redundancy. It exists as two hemispheres each containing trillions of synaptic connections. Massive trauma or stroke may significantly impair its function, but by no means guarantees the death of the individual, as evidenced by the survival of many stroke and trauma victims.[4] One researcher of massive hydrocephalus documented the case of a man with an IQ of 126 holding a first class honors degree in mathematics with "virtually no brain." He found subjects with ventricle expansion filling 95% of the cranium were severely disabled, but half still had IQ's greater than 100.[5]

People frequently survive drowning, electrocutions, explosions, massive trauma, toxic overdoses, infections, and a host of other assaults against the body that most would believe lethal. We spend billions of dollars each year in a gamble with the insurance companies that we will die, only to be proven wrong by both their actuarians and their accumulated wealth. Even when medical

6. "Patient Safety in American Hospitals Study Released by HealthGrades." Health Grades. 2004. July 2004 ⟨http://www.healthgrades.com/media/english/pdf/HG_Patient_Safety_Study_Final.pdf⟩.
1. Minuk, G.Y. "Hepatic regeneration: If it ain't broke, don't fix it." Can J Gastroenterol Jul; 17(7) 2003. p. 418-24.
2. Cataldegirmen, G., et al. "RAGE limits regeneration after massive liver injury by coordinated suppression of TNF-alpha and NF-kappaB." J Exp Med Feb 7; 201(3) 2005. p. 473-84. Koniaris, LG, et al. "Approaching Liver Tumors and the Phenomenon of Liver Regeneration." University of Miami School of Medicine. 2003. Oct 2003 ⟨http://www.liverandpancreas.com/liver/⟩.
3. Panis, Y., McMullan, D.M., Emond, J.C. "Progressive necrosis after hepatectomy and the pathophysiology of liver failure after massive resection." Surgery Feb; 121(2) 1997. p. 142-49.
4. Cernovsky, Z.Z. A critical look at intelligence research, In Fox, D. & Prilleltensky. Critical Psychology. London: Sage, 1997.
5. Lewin, R. "Is Your Brain Really Necessary?" Science vol 210 1980. p. 1232.

intervention is warranted, the placebo effect[1] must be considered, because our thoughts can mobilize our bodies into healing or believing that we are healed[2] of a medical condition.[3] Thanks to this biological reserve, we seldom require intervention with illnesses over most of our lives.

DETERMINANTS OF HEALTH

> *Every human being is the author of his own health or disease.*
> *Gautama Siddharta, 563-483 B.C., the founder of Buddhism*

Evidence for these claims is clearly seen by studies of the Centers for Disease Control. They determined medical intervention is the least important of the four main determinants of health.[4] In an analysis of data on the ten leading causes of death in the United States, it was determined that lifestyle was by far the most important factor (51%), followed by environment (20%), biologic inheritance (19%), and lastly medical intervention (10%).[5]

Chronic diseases, including heart disease, cancer, and diabetes account for more than 70% of all deaths in the United States, this is a dramatic change from the beginning of the 20th century where infectious diseases caused the majority of premature deaths. The Centers for Disease Control has recently radically shifted its emphasis from the treatment of disease to prevention and determination of their underlying cause. McGinnis and Foege published a controversial paper in *JAMA* that challenged the preconceived notions of causes of death.[6] Although cardiac disease is considered the number one cause of death in western cultures, their report stated cardiac disease was actually secondary to lifestyle choices and therefore preventable. Their paper determined these underlying modifiable factors were the "actual causes of death." The authors' most controversial position has been the assertion that tobacco smoke was responsible for the majority of heart disease and is highly significant for the other leading causes of death.

They reported the actual causes of death in United States during 1990 were tobacco (an estimated 400,000 deaths), diet and activity patterns (300,000),

1. Kienle, G.S., Kiene, H. "The powerful placebo effect: Fact or fiction?" J Clin Epidemiol vol 50 1997. p. 1311-18. Wampold, B.E., et al. "The placebo is powerful: Estimating placebo effects in medicine and psychotherapy from randomized clinical trials." J Clin Psychol Jul; 61(7) 2005. p. 835-54.
2. Holbrook, A., Goldsmith, C. "Placebos: our most effective therapy?" Can J Clin Pharmacol Spring; 11(1) 2004. p. e39-40.
3. Kirsch, I., Sapirstein, G. "Listening to Prozac but Hearing Placebo:A Meta-Analysis of Antidepressant Medication." Prevention & Treatment vol 1 1998. p. 0002a. Sauro, M.D., Greenberg, R.P. "Endogenous opiates and the placebo effect: a meta-analytic review." J Psychosom Res Feb; 58(2) 2005. p. 115-20.
4. McKeown T. The role of medicine: dream, mirage or nemesis? Oxford: Blackwell; 1979.
5. McGinnis, J., Foege, M., William, H. "Actual Causes of Death in the United States." Centers for Disease Control and Prevention. 1993. 10 Nov 1993 ⟨http://www.cdc.gov/nccdphp/publications/ActualCauses/pdf/acd.pdf⟩.
6. Ibid.

alcohol (100,000), microbial agents (90,000), toxic agents (60,000), firearms (35,000), sexual behavior (30,000), motor vehicles (25,000), and illicit use of drugs (20,000). Use of tobacco, poor patterns of exercise and nutrition and the excessive use of alcohol are responsible for about a third of all deaths. Sadly, they also reported 88% of all healthcare spending was related to medical intervention even though it provided only a mere 10% reduction in mortality, while the 50-70% of potentially modifiable factors received a paltry 3-5% investment.[1]

A later study validated earlier reports by concluding nearly 590,000 deaths or about a fourth of all deaths in the US are related to addictive substances: 105,000 from alcohol abuse, 446,000 from tobacco use, and 39,000 from addictive drugs in 1995.[2] The leading actual causes of death contrasts very differently to the listed causes of death as seen in the following table.

Listed Cause of Death, 2000-2001[a]	Actual Cause of Death, 2000[b]
Heart Disease (1,410,902)	Tobacco (435,000)
Cancer (1,106,859)	Diet and Activity (400,000)
Cerebrovascular Disease (331,199)	Alcohol (85,000)
COPD (245,022)	Microbial Agents (75,000)
Accidents (199,437)	Toxic Agents (55,000)
Diabetes Mellitus (140,673)	Motor Vehicles (43,000)
Pneumonia and Flu (127,347)	Firearms (29,000)
Alzheimer's Disease (103,410)	Sexual Behavior (20,000)
Nephritis (76,731)	Illicit Drug Use (17,000)
Septicemia (63,462)	

a. "10 Leading Causes of Death, United States 2000 — 2001, All Races, Both Sexes." National Center for Injury Prevention and Control. 2006. 2006 <http://webapp.cdc.gov/sasweb/ncipc/leadcaus10.html>.
b. Mokdad, A.H., et al. "Diabetes trends in the U.S.: 1990-1998." Diabetes Care 2000. p. 1278-83.

1. Centers for Disease Control and Prevention. "Effectiveness in disease and injury prevention estimated national spending on prevention — United States." Morb Mortal Wkly Rep vol 41 1992. p. 529-531. Faust, H.S. "Prevention vs Cure — Which Takes Precedence." American College of Preventive Medicine. 2005. Mar 2005 <http://www.medscape.com/viewarticle/504743?src=hp42.infocus>.
2. McGinnis, J.M., Foege, W.H. "Mortality and morbidity attributable to use of addictive substances in the United States." Proc Assoc Am Physicians Mar-Apr; 111(2) 1999. p. 109-18.

Nearly 70% of all deaths are attributable to potentially modifiable lifestyle or environmental factors, yet, received little investment by the government healthcare system. The CDC often issues press releases proclaiming that our life expectancy continues to grow. The following figure is typical of many of their releases and shows how we continue to live longer lives thanks to advances in modern medical care.[1]

Advocates of allopathic medicine claim the use of drugs, surgery and other medical procedures are responsible for the recent increases in life expectancy. The inference is modern medicine can continue to improve your health and thereby add additional years to your life. This assertion is patently wrong. The Centers for Disease Control graph below clearly shows the major reductions in death rate occurred prior to the era of modern medicine.[2] However, between 1980 and 1992 (inset within box), the death rate from infectious diseases increased 58%.[3] Infectious disease mortality increases were primarily due to the emerging pandemic of acquired immunodeficiency syndrome (AIDS) which affected 33 million people and causing an estimated 13.9 million deaths by 1999.[4] The sharp increase in infectious disease deaths in 1918 and 1919 was caused by the influenza pandemic, which killed more than 20 million people worldwide and over 500,000 people in the United States.[5]

The following graph compares mortality rates to the introduction of various vaccines, little if any benefit was obtained from vaccinations for leading causes of childhood death for the general population.

IMPROVING LIFE EXPECTANCY

> *If you ask what is the single most important key to longevity, I would have to say it is avoiding worry, stress and tension. And if you didn't ask me, I'd still have to say it.*
> George F. Burns 1896-1996, American comedian

Many allopathic practitioners continue to insist modern medical therapy is responsible for the increases seen in life expectancy. They refuse to accept mortality was falling for all major causes of death prior the development of medical therapy to treat these diseases.[6]

---

1. "Life expectancy in U.S. hits record high." The Associated Press. 2005. 28 Feb 2005 ‹http://msnbc.msn.com/id/7046630/›.
2. " Trends in Deaths Caused by Infectious Diseases in the United States, 1900-1994." National Center for Infectious Diseases. 2001. 13 Oct 2001 ‹http://www.cdc.gov/ncidod/emergplan/box01.htm›.
3. Armstrong, G.L., Conn, L.A., Pinner, R.W. "Trends in infectious disease mortality in the United States during the 20th century." JAMA Jan 6; 281(1) 1999. p. 61-66.
4. Ibid. "Control of infectious diseases." Morb Mortal Wkly Rep Jul 30; 48(29) 1999. p. 621-29.
5. Noble, R.G. Epidemiological and clinical aspects of influenza. In: Beare AS, ed. Basic and applied influenza research. Boca Raton, FL: Crc Press, 1982.

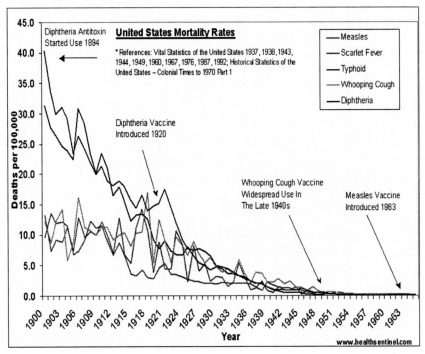

Source: United States mortality rate per age category from 1900-1970 http://www.healthsentinel.com/

Comparison of diseases and health status from 100 years ago with those of today reveals there have been major shifts in causes of death. Between 1900 and 1973, there was almost a 70% decline in overall mortality.[1] In 1900, about 44% of all deaths were accounted for by 11 major infectious diseases (typhoid, smallpox, scarlet fever, measles, whooping cough, diphtheria, influenza, tuberculosis, pneumonia, disease of the digestive system, and poliomyelitis). However, by 1936, only about 18% of deaths were caused by infectious disease. Before the advent of penicillin, mortality rates had already fallen by 40% from 1900.[2] A study by McKinlay and McKinlay concluded most of the decline in total mortality from 1900 to 1973 was the result of reductions in tuberculosis and pneumonia. They also found only influenza, whooping cough, and poliomyelitis showed substantial decreases of 25% or more in mortality after the introduction of medical therapy.[3] They believed 3.5% probably represents a reasonable upper-

6. "Achievements in Public Health, 1900-1999: Control of Infectious Diseases." MMWR. 1999. 30 Jul 1999 ⟨http://www.cdc.gov/mmwr/preview/mmwrhtml/mm4829a1.htm⟩.
1. Kronenfeld, J.J. Controversial Issues in Health Care Policy. Newbury Park, CA: Sage Publications, 1993.
2. Cutler, D. Miller, G. "The Role of Public Health Improvements in Health Advances: The 20th Century United States." Havard Univerity Economics Department. 2004. Feb 2004 ⟨http://post.economics.harvard.edu/faculty/dcutler/papers/cutler_miller_cities.pdf⟩.

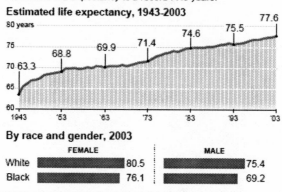

Life expectancy reaches all-time high

Declines in death rates from most major causes have pushed Americans' life expectancy to a record 77.6 years.

Estimated life expectancy, 1943-2003

By race and gender, 2003

	FEMALE	MALE
White	80.5	75.4
Black	76.1	69.2

SOURCE: Centers for Disease Control and Prevention   AP

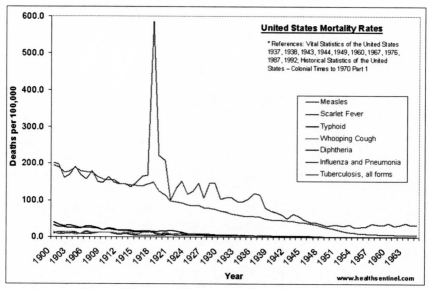

Source: "United States mortality rate per age category from 1900-1970." Health Sentinel. 2005. http://www.health-sentinel.com/graphs.php?id=11&event=graphs_print_list_item

3. McKinlay, J.B., McKinlay. S.B. "The Questionable Contribution of Medical Measures to the Decline of Mortality in the United States in the Twentieth Century." Milbank Memorial Fund Quarterly vol 53 1977. p. 405-28.

Timeline of Mortality Rates versus Antibiotic Development

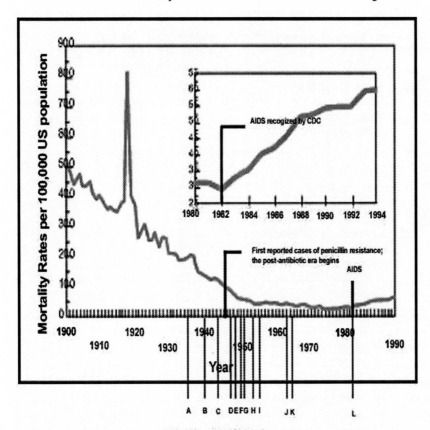

Timeline of Antibiotics*

A. 1936, Sulfanilamide, the first synthetic sulfonamide in human medicine
B. 1940, Pathologist Howard Florey and biochemist Ernest Chain produce an extract of penicillin, the first powerful antibiotic.
C. 1944, Selman A. Waksman isolated streptomycin, an effective antibiotic for TB.
D. 1947, Paul Burkholder discovers Chloramphenicol, the first broad-spectrum antibiotic.
E. 1948, Lloyd Conover discovers Chlortetracycline, the first drug of the tetracycline family.
F. 1949, Selman Waksman discovers neomycin; Krumwiede reports first appearance of penicillin resistance in children
G. 1950, Elizabeth Hazen and Rachel Brown developed the first useful fungal antibiotic, Nystatin
H. 1952, JM McGuire and coworkers discover erythromycin, the first macrolide antibiotic.
I. 1955, Cephalosporin C discovered by Giuseppe Brotzu; MH McCormick and collegues discover vancomycin
J. 1962, George Lesher dicovers Nalidixic acid, first drug of the quinolone family.
K. 1964, J Black et al. discover Gentamycin,
L. 1982, Ceftriaxone (trade name Rocephin®) is developed, a third-generation cephalosporin

* http://en.wikipedia.org/wiki/Timeline_of_antibiotics

limit estimate of the total contribution of medical measures to the decline in mortality in the United States over the last hundred years.[1]

The eminent epidemiologist Thomas McKeown,[2] former chairman of the

Trends in Causes of Death Prior to Antibiotic Therapy

	1900	1936
Major Infectious Diseases	39.3%	17.9%
Tuberculosis	11.1%	5.3%
Pneumonia	9.6%	9.3%
Diarrhea and Enteritis	7.0%	N/A
Typhoid Fever	2.4%	0.1%
Meningitis	2.4%	0.3%
Malaria	1.2%	0.1%
Smallpox	0.7%	0.0%
Influenza	0.7%	1.3%
Childhood Infectious Diseases	4.2%	0.5%
Measles	0.7%	0.0%
Scarlet Fever	0.5%	0.1%
Whooping Cough	0.6%	0.2%
Diphtheria and Croup	2.3%	0.1%

Source: United States Census Bureau's Mortality Statistics, 1900-1936.

World Health Organization Advisory Group on Health Research Strategy, concluded even though life expectancy had increased by 23 years during the first half century, medical therapy was responsible for at best one or two additional years.[3] He believed much of the decrease resulted from the decline in respiratory tuberculosis. Since the bacillus responsible for tuberculosis was not identified until 1882 and effective pharmacotherapy was not developed until 1947, he concluded medical technology accounted for only 3% of the decrease in mortality over about the last 150 years.[4]

With the exception of smallpox vaccination, medical therapy and immunization had only marginal effect before 1935.[5] Instead, the major cause of mortality decline was due to better diet. As he writes: "The death rate from

1. Ibid.
2. McKeown, T. The Role of Medicine: Dream, Mirage, or Nemesis? London: Nuffield Provincial Hospitals Trust, 1976. McKeown, T. "The Road to Health." World Health Forum vol 10 1989. p. 408-16.
3. Bunker, J.P. "The role of medical care in contributing to health improvements within societies." International Journal of Epidemiology vol 30 2001. p. 1260-63. Godber, G.E. "McKeown's 'The Role of Medicine'." Milbank Memorial Fund Quarterly Summer 1977. p. 373-78.
4. Beeson, P.B. "McKeown's 'The Role of Medicine'." Milbank Memorial Fund Quarterly Summer 1977. p. 365-71.

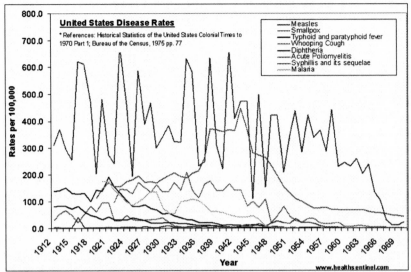

infectious diseases fell because an increase in food supplies led to better nutrition. From the second half of the 19th century this advance was strongly supported by improved hygiene and safer food and water, which reduced exposure to infection."[1] He was opposed by many within mainstream medicine[2] who viewed his conclusions as nothing more than an attack on allopathic medicine.[3] Today, McKeown's theory on the whole has, "generally been accepted by the scientific community."[4]

His work is often associated with Ivan Illich's *Medical Nemesis: The Appropriation of Health.* Illich was not content in criticizing modern medicine for its failure to improve life expectancy. He unabashedly proclaimed medical intervention was actually responsible for increasing death rates by providing ineffective, but hazardous medical therapies.[5] Illich stated patients suffered from the side-effects of prescribed drugs, hospital acquired infections, poorly performed surgery, and false positives on medical and laboratory tests. He criticized medical practitioners for being more self serving than being interested

5. Lin, K. "Health Status of the Population: Medical care Model vs Social Structural Model.." Doctorial Thesis. 1994. Sep 1994 ‹http://twrf.formosa.org/kuoming/PAPER2.htm›.
1. McKeown, T. Determinants of Health." In The Nation's Health, ed. P. R. Lee, C. L. Estes, and N. B. Ramsay. San Francisco: Boyd & Fraser Publishing Company, 1980.
2. Fairchild, A.L., Oppenheimer, G.M. "Public health nihilism vs pragmatism: history, politics, and the control of tuberculosis." Am J Public Health Jul; 88(7) 1998. p. 1105-17.
3. Colgrove, J. "The McKeown thesis: a historical controversy and its enduring influence." Am J Public Health May; 92(5) 2002. p. 725-29. Szreter, S. "Rethinking McKeown: the relationship between public health and social change." Am J Public Health May; 92(5) 2002. p. 722-25.
4. Greger, M. "Appendix 27 — The Receding Tide." Heart Failure — Diary of a Third Year Medical Student. 1999 ‹http://upalumni.org/medschool/appendices/appendix-27.html›. Mackenbach, J.P. "The Contribution of Medical Care to Mortality Decline." Clinical Epidemiology vol 49 1996. p. 1207-13.
5. Illich, I. Medical Nemesis: The Appropriation of Health. London: Calder And Boyars, 1975.

in treating patients or their conditions. He argued health care providers were often more focused upon professional ambition, corporate greed, or simply an imperative to do something.[1]

Apologists for medical therapy expound it benefits by citing studies showing every 10% increase in Medicare expenditures produces a 1–2% fall in mortality.[2] Death rates for diseases considered 'amenable to treatment' have fallen at much greater rates than have death rates for diseases that do not respond favorably to treatment. These findings lead some to believe medical care should be credited with an extension in life expectancy between 5 and 18 years.[3] However, they choose to ignore facts like:

Medical spending does not correlate to reduced death rates; countries with the greatest spending on medical therapy do not have the lowest mortalities.[4] Brief but dramatic decreases in population death rates[5] occur when physicians strike and surgery for elective (but not emergency) operations are suspended.[6]

A long-standing estimate by the Centers for Disease Control and Prevention states medical therapy reduces total mortality by only 10%.[7]

Age-adjusted death rates were reported to be greater in countries with greater numbers of doctors, and presumably with more medical care.[8]

Death rates for diseases amenable to treatment were reported to be greatest in areas with the most medical care resources.[9]

Greater access to medical care does not decrease mortality. No group has greater access to medical care than doctors and nurses. The top ten causes of death for white male physicians are essentially the same as those of the general population.[10]

A recent campaign by the Institute for Healthcare Improvement acknowledges failure to provide six basic quality improvements results in 100,000 PREVENTABLE deaths annually. They have launched the "100,000 Lives Campaign" to increase awareness of this problem.[11]

1. Illich, I. Limits to medicine. London: Marion Boyars, 1976.
2. Hadley, J. More Medical Care, Better Health? Washington DC: Urban Institute Press, 1982.
3. Mackenbach, J.P. "The contribution of medical care to mortality decline: McKeown revisited.." J Clin Epidemiology vol 49 1996. p. 1207-13.
4. Mustard, J.F., Frank, J.W. "The Determinants of Population Health: A Critical Assessment." Founders' Network. 1998. 14 Jul 1998
5. Barnoon, S., Carmel, S., Zalcman, T. "Perceived health damages during a physicians' strike in Israel." Health Serv Res Jun; 22(2) 1987. p. 141-55. Roemer, M.I. "More data on post-surgical deaths related to the 1976 Los Angeles doctor slowdown." Soc Sci Med vol 15C 1981. p. 161-63.
6. Siegel-Itzkovich, J. "Doctors' strike in Israel may be good for health." BMJ Jun 10; 320(7249) 2000. p. 1561. Steinherz, R. "Death rates and the 1983 doctors' strike in Israel." Lancet Jan 14; 1(8368) 1984. p. 107.
7. DHHS, Public Health Services. Ten Leading Causes of Death in the United States. Atlanta: Bureau Of State Services, 1980.
8. Cochrane, A.L., St Leger, A.S., Moore, F. "Health service 'input' and mortality 'output' in developed countries." J Epidemiol Community Health vol 32 1978. p. 200-05.
9. Carr-Hill, R.A., Hardman, G.F., Russell, I.T. "Variations in avoidable mortality and variations in health care resources." Lancet vol i 1987. p. 789-92.
10. Frank, E., Biola, H., Burnett, C.A. "Mortality rates and causes among U.S. physicians." Am J Prev Med Oct; 19(3) 2000. p. 155-59.

By 1973 the percentage of deaths due to infectious diseases plummeted to only 6%, while the percentage due to chronic conditions such as cancer and heart disease had skyrocketed to 58%.[1] The following table shows recent reports in the causes of death:[2]

2004 Causes of Death		
FORMAL NAME	INFORMAL NAME	% ALL DEATHS
Diseases of the heart	heart attack (mainly)	28.5%
Malignant neoplasms	cancer	22.8%
Cerebrovascular disease	stroke	6.7%
Chronic lower respiratory disease	emphysema, chronic bronchitis	5.1%
Unintentional injuries	accidents	4.4%
Diabetes mellitus	diabetes	3.0%
Influenza and pneumonia	flu & pneumonia	2.7%
Alzheimer's Disease	Alzheimer's senility	2.4%
Nephritis and Nephrosis	kidney disease	1.7%
Septicemia	systemic infection	1.4%
Intentional self-harm	suicide	1.3%
Chronic Liver/Cirrhosis	liver disease	1.1%
Essential Hypertension	high blood pressure	0.8%
Assault	homicide	0.7%
All other causes	other	17.4%

Deaths from infectious diseases were now being replaced by heart disease, cancer, and stroke.[3]

Many researchers believe our health is actually determined primarily by: genetic traits, social circumstances, environmental conditions, behavioral choices, and medical care.[4] Population studies suggest early deaths in the United States are the result of: genetic predispositions (30%), social circumstances (15%), pollution (5%), behavioral choices (40%), and problems related to medical care (10%). Infectious diseases have merely been replaced by modifiable behavioral risk factors. Recent studies suggest smoking related illnesses are now

11. "IHI Launches National Campaign to Save 100,000 Lives in U.S. Hospitals Patient Safety & Quality Healthcare." Patient Safety & Quality Healthcare. 2005. Jan/Feb 2005 ⟨http://www.psqh.com/janfeb05/100k.html⟩. Jarman, B. "Using mortality data to drive system level improvement." BMJ Publishing Group. 2005. 1 Apr 2005 ⟨http://www.bmjpg.com/Fri15/Jarman.pdf⟩.
1. McKinlay, J.B., McKinlay, S.J. "The Questionable Contribution of Medical Measures to the Decline of Mortality in the United States in the Twentieth Century." Milbank Memorial Fund Quarterly vol 53 1977. p. 405-28.
2. National Vital Statistics Report vol 53(5) 2004.
3. McKinlay, J.B., McKinlay, S.J. "The Questionable Contribution of Medical Measures to the Decline of Mortality in the United States in the Twentieth Century." Milbank Memorial Fund Quarterly vol 53 1977. p. 405-28.
4. McGinnis, J.M. 'United States', in Critical Issues in Global Health, ed. C.E. Koop. San Francisco: Jossey-bass, 2001.

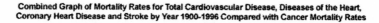

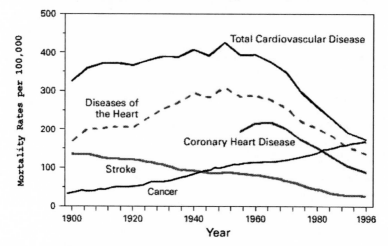

Combined Graph of Mortality Rates for Total Cardiovascular Disease, Diseases of the Heart, Coronary Heart Disease and Stroke by Year 1900-1996 Compared with Cancer Mortality Rates

Heart Disease Mortality Rates are Standardized to the 1940 US Population from Data of the National Heart, Lung and Blood Institute, NIH*
Cancer Mortality Rates are Derived from the Vital Statistics of the US 1937, 1938, 1943, 1944, 1949, 1960, 1967, 1976, 1987, 1992; Historical Statistics of the United States – Colonial Times to 1970 part I #

*Acheivements in Public Health. 1900–1999: Decline in Deaths from Heart Disease and Stroke –– United States, 1900–1999. MMWR August 6, 1999 48(30;649–656

http://www.healthsentinel.com/graphs.php?id=22&event=graphs_print_list_item

the leading cause of mortality. However, poor diet and physical inactivity may soon overtake tobacco as the leading cause of death.[1]

Poor health is usually the result of a combination of these factors. A family history of lung cancer may not affect you if you don't smoke, live in a clean rural area, have a good income and receive adequate medical care. However, if the same individual smokes cigarettes, lives in a city with poor air quality and works a low paying job without insurance they may be die as the result of poor genes, poor choices and bad circumstances. Some researchers believe 60% of diseases appearing late in life (diabetes, heart disease, and cancer) have some genetic component.[2]

1. Mokdad, A.H., et al. "Actual causes of death in the United States, 2000." JAMA Mar 10; 291(10) 2004. p. 1238-45.
2. Strohman, R.C. "The Role of Genetics in Population Health", in *Why Are Some People Healthy and Others Not?* ed. R.G. Evans, M.L. Barer, and T.R. Marmor. New York: Aldine De Gruyter, 1994.

LIFE EXTENSION

> *I see no comfort in outliving one's friends, and remaining a mere monument*
> *of the times which are past.*
> *Thomas Jefferson, third President of the US (1743-1826)*

There are those who believe medical intervention has resulted in large increases in our life expectancy. They may fail to realize the term "life expectancy" must be clarified before it has any real meaning. Life expectancy is defined as the average expected years of life remaining for an individual AT A CERTAIN AGE. Reports of increases in life expectancy by twenty-eight years are a population average of additional years from BIRTH. Infant and child mortality rates were very high during the early part of the 20th century. Improvements in hygiene and sanitation along with vaccination resulted in decreased mortality rates for the youngest sector of the population.

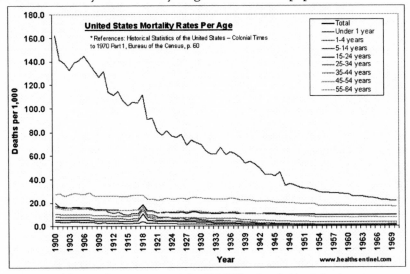

Source: United States mortality rate per age category from 1900-1970 http://www.healthsentinel.com/

graphs.php?id-11&event-graphs_print_list_item

Prolonging this sector's lives to that of the average adult simply results in an artificial increase in the average life expectancy for the WHOLE population. It is ludicrous to believe saving an infant's life adds additional years to your own. Yet, this convoluted logic is used by many to manipulate others into believing their "investment" in the future will add decades[1] more to their own lives.[2]

---

1. Manton, K., Stallard, E., Tolley, H. "Limits to Human Life Expectancy: Evidence, Prospects, and Implications." Population and Development Review December 1991. p. 603-37.

Today, life expectancy from birth for women is 78.5 years and for men, 71.8 years.[1]

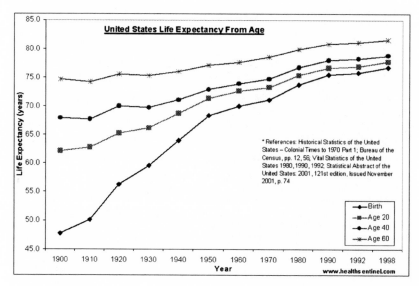

Source: United States mortality rate per age category from 1900-1970 http://www.healthsentinel.com/ graphs.php?id-11&event-graphs_print_list_item

Life expectancy FROM BIRTH did increase 30 years from 47 years to 76 years from the period of 1900 to 1999 in the United States. However, the majority of these increases are the result of improvements and advances in public health (sanitation, nutrition, expanded immunization, and safer workplaces).[2] The advances achieved from the spending of 14% of the Gross National Product ($1.6 trillion in 2003) on medical healthcare pales in contrast to those achieved by public health and preventive medicine programs.[3]

Public health programs are directly responsible for approximately 25 years of the increased life expectancy, while medicine and hospitals are able to muster only an additional 4 or 5 years.[4] Some believe a combination of preventive services and medical intervention may be credited with 5 or 5 1/2 years of the 30 years increase in life expectancy since 1900, and half of the 7 or 7 1/2 years of

2. Olshansky, S.J., Carnes, B.A., Cassel, C.K. "In Search of Methuselah: Estimating the Upper Limits to Human Longevity." Science vol 250 1990. p. 634-40. Wilmoth, J.R. "Demography of longevity: past, present, and future trends." Exp Gerontol Dec; 35(9-10) 2000. p. 1111-29.
1. "Health, United States, 1990." National Center for Health Statistics 1990. p. 67.
2. Bunker, J.P., Frazier, H.S., Mosteller, F. "Improving health: measuring effects of medical care." Milbank Quarterly vol 72 1994. p. 225-58. "Centers for Disease Control. Mortality patterns." Morb Mortal Wkly Rep vol 48 1999. p. 664-66.
3. "The Troubled Healthcare System in the U.S. The Society of Actuaries: Health Benefit Systems Practice Advancement Committee." Society of Actuaries. 2003. 13 Sep 2003 ‹http://www.soa.org/ ccm/content/research-publications/research-projects/troubled-health-care-system/›. Levit, K.R., et al. "National Health Expenditures." Health Care Financing Review Fall 1997. p. 161-200.

increase since 1950.[1] One researcher emphatically states future medical interventions may at most add only two additional years to the current life expectancy.[2] Most medical interventions provide very little benefit; one author suggests a gain of one year from a preventive intervention in high risk populations should be considered large.[3]

However, the most authoritative source on life expectancy for Americans denies even these increases. The Social Security Administration states bluntly on their website, "A related idea is to attribute the current financial pressures on Social Security to a supposed dramatic increase in life expectancy in recent years. Since average *life expectancy at birth* is now about 76, this is interpreted as implying that people collect benefits for 14 to 18 years longer than they used to...the average *life expectancy at age* 65 (i.e., the number of years a person could be expected to receive unreduced Social Security retirement benefits) has only increased a modest 5 years (on average) since 1940... So the actual increase in time that males can anticipate receiving Social Security is closer to 3 years than to 14."[4]

The claims for increased life expectancy are an exaggeration by those promoting medical and health care services.[5] Their agenda is to attribute increases in life expectancy to medical intervention; by doing so they increase their own reputations and further enrich their funding from federal and government sources.[6] The Nobel Laureate and President of Rockefeller University, Joshua Lederberg, wrote that 'by the 1960s we could celebrate the conquest of polio and the transformation of formerly lethal infections to easy targets for penicillin and other miracle drugs ... greater life expectancy—from 47 years in 1900 to 70 in 1960—can be attributed almost entirely to this mastery of infection ...'.[7]

Improvements in medical therapy have had little impact on extending the life expectancy at age 65. The following graph from The University of Michigan and National Center for Health Statistics confirms the findings of the Department of Social Security. They find medical interventions since 1970 have

4. "Ten Great Public Health Achievements — United States, 1900-1999." Morbidity and Mortality Weekly Report. 1999. 1 Apr 1999 <http://www.cdc.gov/mmwr/preview/mmwrhtml/00056796.htm>. Wright, J.C., Weinstein, M.C. "Gains in life expectancy from medical interventions—standardizing data on outcomes." NEJM vol 339(6) 1998. p. 380-86.
1. Bunker, J.P. "Medicine matters after all." J Roy Coll Physicians vol 29 1995. p. 105-12. Mackenbach, J.P. "The contribution of medical care to mortality decline: McKeown revisited." J Clin Epidemiology vol 49 1996. p. 1207-13.
2. Bunker, J.P., et al. "Improving Health: Measuring Effects of Medical Care." Milbank Quarterly vol 72(2) 1994. p. 225-58.
3. Wright, J.C., Weinstein, M.C. "Gains in Life Expectancy from Medical Interventions — Standardizing Data on Outcomes." NEJM vol 339(3) 1998. p. 380-86.
4. "Life Expectancy for Social Security." Social Security Online. 2006. <http://www.ssa.gov/history/lifeexpect.html>.
5. Ableson, P.H. "Improvements in health care." Science vol 260 1993. p. 11.
6. Lubitz, J., Cai, L., Kramarow, E., Lentzner, H. "Health, life expectancy, and health care spending among the elderly." NEJM Sep 11; 349(11) 2003. p. 1048-55.
7. Lederberg, J. "Medicine's old battle against the bugs isn't over at all." International Herald Tribune 26 Jan 1996.

increased life expectancy from age 65 by only three years in men (13 additional years was increased to 16 additional years).[1] They showed similar increases for women.

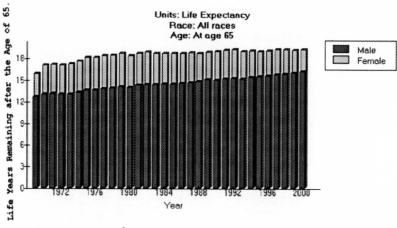

Source: American Society on Aging.[2]

Although medical science has become very adept at saving lives related to trauma, this represents only a very small component of the total medical effort, therefore adds very little to a populations average life expectancy.[3] High technology measures to improve life expectancy have generally yield poor results. International studies have shown increased medical intervention may actually worsen the patient's health.[4] The media's promotion of coronary artery bypass graft surgery (CABG) by physicians ignore studies showing on average, coronary artery bypass surgery prolongs life by only 4.26 months[5] and the six month death rates after CABG are similar to those waiting for the procedure. A 2004 study found one year survival rates AFTER a CABG were 96% compared to 98.5% for those treated with drug therapy.[6] Patients undergoing a CABG

1. "Teaching/Training Modules on Trends in Health and Aging." American Society on Aging. 2006. ‹http://www.asaging.org/nchs/module6.pdf›.
2. "Report of the New South Wales Chief Health Officer Burden of disease Life expectancy at 65 years of age." Report of the New South Wales Chief Health Officer. 2005. 2 Dec 2005 ‹http://www.health.nsw.gov.au/public-health/chorep/bod/bod_lex65.htm›.
3. Bunker, J.P. "The role of medical care in contributing to health improvements within societies." International Journal of Epidemiology vol 30 2001. p. 1260-63.
4. Cochrane AL, St Leger AS, Moore F.. "Health service 'input' and mortality 'output' in developed countries." J Epidemiol Com Health vol 32 1978. p. 200-05. Scheiber, G.J., Poulier, J.P., Greenwald, L.M. "Health spending, delivery, and outcomes in OECD countries." Health Aff Millwood vol 12 1993. p. 120-29.
5. Martin, R.M., et al. "Mortality and morbidity surrounding coronary artery bypass surgery and the public presentation of risk." J Epidemiol Community Health Jun; 56(6) 2002. p. 430-31. Yusuf, S., et al. "Effect of coronary artery bypass graft surgery on survival: overview of 10 year results from randomised controlled trials by the Coronary Artery Bypass Graft Surgery Triallists Collaboration." Lancet vol 344 1994. p. 563-70.

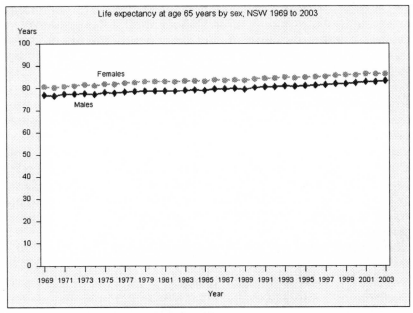

Source: Report of the New South Wales Chief Health Officer

actually increased their risk of dying by 2.5% compared to those who were managed by medical therapy. Studies of outcomes for women after CABG show they have even worse outcomes.[1] One study of 590 patients concluded patients who were free of angina prior to surgery were three times more likely to suffer a decline in physical function after a CABG than those with angina prior to surgery.[2] These findings have been replicated by foreign studies.

The primary benefit of CABG and balloon angioplasty therapy is that they help ALLIVIATE the symptoms of coronary artery disease without significantly improving all-cause mortality.[3]

A 2003 study determined medical intervention reduced cardiovascular deaths by only 40%. The authors suggested the low tech use of aspirin was the "best buy" therapy for secondary prevention of cardiovascular disease.[4] Another

6. Hueb, W., et al. "The medicine, angioplasty, or surgery study (MASS-II): a randomized, controlled clinical trial of three therapeutic strategies for multivessel coronary artery disease: one-year results." J Am Coll Cardiol May 19; 43(10) 2004. p. 1743-51.
1. Guru, V., Fremes, S.E., Tu, J.V. "Time-related mortality for women after coronary artery bypass graft surgery: a population-based study." J Thorac Cardiovasc Surg Apr; 127(4) 2004. p. 1158-65.
2. Pirraglia, P.A., et al. "Assessment of decline in health-related quality of life among angina-free patients undergoing coronary artery bypass graft surgery." Cardiology vol 99(3) 2003. p. 115-20.
3. Hannan, E.L., et al. "Long-Term Outcomes of Coronary-Artery Bypass Grafting versus Stent Implantation." NEJM vol 352 2005. p. 2174-83. Hueb, W.A., et al. "Five-year follow-op of the medicine, angioplasty, or surgery study (MASS): A prospective, randomized trial of medical therapy, balloon angioplasty, or bypass surgery for single proximal left anterior descending coronary artery stenosis." Circulation Nov 9; 100(19 Suppl):II 1999. p. 107-13.
4. Probstfield, J.L. "How cost-effective are new preventive strategies for cardiovascular disease?" Am J Cardiol May 22; 91(10A) 2003. p. 22G-27G.

study concluded low-dose diuretics ("water pills") were the most effective treatment for preventing the occurrence of cardiovascular disease morbidity and mortality.[1] An earlier study evaluated the effectiveness of different therapies on reducing cardiac related deaths. It determined aspirin and coronary artery bypass grafting surgery reduced cardiac deaths by only 2% and balloon angioplasty produced only a 0.1% reduction. Several studies have documented over half the reduction in deaths was attributable to lifestyle related [2]changes. A 2003 study of Medicare patients confirms an earlier study showing mortality from heart attacks was no longer decreasing but had achieved[3] a plateau.

A 1999 study further disputes claims life expectancy can be further increased by the reduction of cardiac related deaths. The authors remind researchers that cancer may be a competing cause of death; death from a heart attack may simply be replaced by death from cancer.[4] Elimination of all coronary heart disease deaths would only add between 5 months to 7.5 years to life expectancy at birth.[5]

Many cardiologists will quickly take credit for the decreases in cardiac related deaths.[6] However, further evaluation of the data indicates the majority of these decreases preceded the "major" advances in medical technology and drug therapy which were developed from the mid-eighties and later. This data is shown in the following graph obtained from a report called *Exceptional Returns: the Economic Value of America's Investment in Medical Research* authored in 1999 by nine of America's most distinguished economists.[7] Incredibly, these same economists estimate the average new drug saves 11,000 life-years per year (in theory it could

1. Psaty, B.M., et al. "Health outcomes associated with various antihypertensive therapies used as first-line agents: a network meta-analysis." JAMA May 21; 289(19) 2003. p. 2534-44.
2. Capewell, S., Morrison, C.E., McMurray, J.J. "Contribution of modern cardiovascular treatment and risk factor changes to the decline in coronary heart disease mortality in Scotland between 1975 and 1994." Heart Apr; 81(4) 1999. p. 380-86. Unal, B., et al. "Explaining the Decline in Coronary Heart Disease Mortality in England and Wales Between 1981 and 2000." Circulation vol 109 2004. p. 1101-07.
3. Ash, A.S., et al. "Using claims data to examine mortality trends following hospitalization for heart attack in Medicare." Health Serv Res Oct; 38(5) 2003. p. 1253-62. Wayne D. Rosamond, Ph.D., Lloyd E. Chambless, Ph.D., Aaron R. Folsom, M.D., Lawton S. Cooper, M.D., David E. Conwill, M.D., Limin Clegg, Ph.D., Chin-Hua Wang, Ph.D., and Gerardo Heiss, Ph.D.. "Trends in the Incidence of Myocardial Infarction and in Mortality Due to Coronary Heart Disease, 1987 to 1994." NEJM vol 339(13) 1998. p. 861-67.
4. Mackenbach, J.P., et al. "Competing causes of death: a death certificate study." J Clin Epidemiol Oct; 50(10) 1997. p. 1069-77. Mackenbach, J.P.,et al. "Gains in life expectancy after elimination of major causes of death: revised estimates taking into account the effect of competing causes." J Epidemiol Community Health Jan; 53(1) 1999. p. 32-37.
5. Somerville, K., Francombe, P. "Modeling disease elimination." J Insur Med vol 37(1) 2005. p. 13-19. Tsevat, J., et al. "Expected Gains in Life Expectancy from Various Coronary Heart Disease Risk Factor Modifications." Circulation Apr; 83(4) 1991. p. 1194-201.
6. Goldman, L., Cook, E.F. "The decline in ischemic heart disease mortality rates: an analysis of the comparative effects of medical interventions and changes in lifestyle." Ann Intern Med vol 101 1984. p. 825-36. Hunink, M.G.M., et al. "The recent decline in mortality from coronary heart disease, 1980-1990: the effect of secular trends in risk factors and treatment." JAMA vol 277 1997. p. 535-42.
7. Hatfield, M., et al. "Exceptional Returns: The Economic Value of America's Investment in Medical Research." Lasker Foundation. 2004. 16 Oct 2004 ‹http://www.laskerfoundation.org/reports/pdf/exceptional.pdf›.

add 10 additional years to 1,100 different patients). The medical field deserves very little credit for these lives saved. Their own table clearly shows medical therapy has not decreased mortality from many of the leading causes of death and honest medical researchers will admit the US is recovering from an epidemic of heart disease of unknown etiology.[1]

Death Rates from Coronary Artery Disease
Units: per Deaths per 100,000

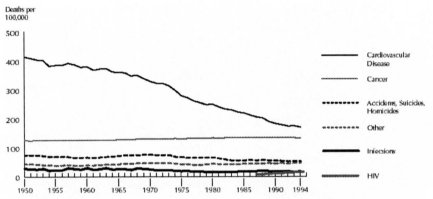

Source: *Exceptional Returns: The Economic Value of America's Investment in Medical Research.*

Nobody knows why heart disease deaths skyrocketed during the 50s and 60s let alone why they just as mysteriously plummeted long before the dawn of "modern medicine" in the 80s.[2]

Some question whether this epidemic may be related to an infectious agent[3] because the incidence of coronary heart disease appears independent of risk factor modification.[4] The recent discovery of markers for inflammation[5] and identification of bacteria[6] in coronary artery plaques may cast doubt on cholesterol as the primary cause of heart disease.[7]

1. Marmot, M.G. Coronary heart disease: rise and fall of a modern epidemic. In: Marmot M, Elliott P, eds. Coronary heart disease epidemiology. Oxford: Oxford University Press, 1992.
2. Le Fanu, J. "The case of the missing data." BMJ vol 325 2002. p. 1490-93. Reinert-Azambuja, M. "1918-19 Influenza pandemic and ischemic heart disease epidemic: cause and effect?" Atherosclerosis vol 109 1994. p. 328.
3. Ellis, R.W. "Infection and coronary heart disease." J Med Microbiol Jul; 46(7) 1997. p. 535-39. Hughes, S. "Novel risk factors for coronary heart disease: emerging connections." J Cardiovasc Nurs Jan; 14(2) 2000. p. 91-103.
4. O'Connor, S., et al. "Potential infectious etiologies of atherosclerosis: a multifactorial perspective." Emerg Infect Dis Sep-Oct; 7(5) 2001. p. 780-88. Smith, D., Gupta, S., Kaski, J.C. "Chronic infections and coronary heart disease." Int J Clin Pract Sep; 53(6) 1999. p. 460-66.
5. Ngeh, J., Gupta, S. "Inflammation, infection and antimicrobial therapy in coronary heart disease— where do we currently stand?" Fundam Clin Pharmacol Apr; 15(2) 2001. p. 85-93.
6. Franceschi, F., et al. "Helicobacter pylori infection and ischaemic heart disease: an overview of the general literature." Dig Liver Dis May; 37(5) 2005. p. 301-08.

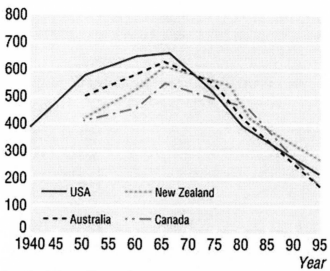

Source: Fanu JL The case of the missing data BMJ 2002; 325:1490-1493

The authors of *Exceptional Returns* acknowledge "reductions in infant mortality, presumably linked to improved diet, sanitation, housing and education and the introduction of effective pharmaceutical weapons against infectious disease, largely explains the gain prior to the middle of the 20th century." They attribute the 11 years gain in life expectancy from 1965 to 1996 to reduced death rates from chronic degenerative diseases among the elderly. They further acknowledge "Mortality from cancer, diabetes, liver and kidney diseases has hardly changed, offering opportunities for extending life expectancy from breakthroughs in research" and admit "To a large extent, then, the value of improved health is linked to the decline in cardiovascular illness, and the large returns to investment in medical research have come principally from gains against heart disease and strokes."

Their conclusions are so appalling they are nearly a joke. After billions of dollars "investing" in treating cancer and other major causes of death, one would hope for more than an "opportunity for extending life expectancy."

How much money does the public need to through down this medical rat hole before we reach the logical conclusion that our money has no impact on mortality rates for the leading causes of death? They conveniently sidestep this failure by focusing upon our supposed successes in treating heart disease. They know fully well the declines in cardiovascular deaths occurred long before the

---

7. Leinonen, M., Saikku, P. "Infections and atherosclerosis." Scand Cardiovasc J vol 34(1) 2000. p. 12-20. Lowe, G.D. "The relationship between infection, inflammation, and cardiovascular disease: an overview." Ann Periodontol Dec; 6(1) 2001. p. 1-8.

era of modern medicine and the bogus pharmaceuticals promoted as being heart healthy or efficacious. I modified their chart to include the dates of most major "advances" in heart disease. It clearly shows as the authors of this study have already stated, "improved diet, sanitation, housing and education" are responsible for the majority of decreases in heart disease deaths.

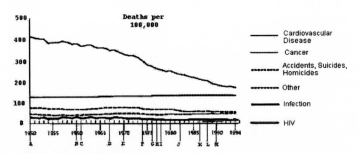

A. 1948 Start of the Framingham Heart Study
B. Cigarette smoking found to increase the risk of heart disease; CPR first demonstrated as possibly effective
C. Cholesterol level, blood pressure, and ECG arrhythmias found to increase the risk of heart disease
D. Exercise found to reduce and obesity to increase the risk of heart disease; First CABG performed in US
E. High blood pressure found to increase the risk of stroke
F. Diabetes found to increase risk of heart attack
G. Menopause found to increase the risk of heart disease
H. Effects of triglycerides and LDL and HDL cholesterol described
I. Psychosocial factors found to affect heart disease; First PTCA cases performed in America;
   TIMI (Thrombolysis in Myocardial Infarction) 1 evaluates calcium channel blocker in heart disease
J. BHAT. suggested ß-blockade may be effective for secondary prevention of MI
K. High blood cholesterol levels found to correlate directly with risk of death in young men;
   tissue plasminogen activator (TPA) approved by FDA; first use of coronary stents in humans;
   CONSENSUS-1 establishes benefit of ACEs in patients with CHF
L. High levels of HDL cholesterol found to reduce risk of death; Type "A" behavior linked to heart disease;
   Isolated systolic hypertension found to increase risk of heart disease
M. Homocysteine (an amino acid) found as possible risk factor for heart disease;
   ACC/AHA) practice guidelines advocating aspirin use in secondary prevention

They are certainly aware a correlation is not the same thing as causation. Improvements in standards of living were responsible for the majority of increased life expectancy since the turn of the century. It would not seem unreasonable to conclude they still are responsible for the majority of decreases in the rate of mortality. Heart disease is the leading cause of death in the US. The epidemic in heart disease of the 50s and 60s has receded on it's own without medical intervention. One wonders why the medical community is willing to take credit for the major cause of death when they clearly have had no impact on the other leading causes of death. Perhaps the title of the article says it all; "Exceptional Returns" is the primary focus of medicine in the US.

THE FAILURE OF MEDICAL CARE TO EXTEND LIFE EXPECTANCY

> *The doctor of the future will give no medicine, but will interest his patients
> in the care of the human frame, in diet, and in the cause and prevention of
> disease.*
>
> Thomas Edison, inventor (1847–1931)

According to Dr. Barry L. Beyerstein's article "Why Bogus Therapies Often Seem to Work" published on the QuackWatch site, even many "scientific" treatments may appear to work when in fact they may be worthless or inert.[1] He recognizes many diseases are self-limiting. "If the condition is not chronic or fatal, the body's own recuperative processes usually restore the sufferer to health." He argues "many diseases are cyclical", while others may respond to the placebo effect.

He also mentions the roles of misdiagnosis, temporary mood improvement, and psychological reasons for the apparent resolution of a disorder in response to a bogus therapy. Incredibly, he notes these effects can even occur in "new treatments in scientific medicine", yet chooses to lambaste alternative medicine for being bogus while soft peddling these same issues in allopathic medicine. Eugene Stead, Jr. recognized as one of the most important physicians in academic medicine, admits "In... 90% of your practice, you will be practicing like a quack."[2] The physician JP Baldwin seems to concur when he states, "There are more quacks in the orthodox profession than there are outside its ranks."

If the above findings still haven't convinced you, consider the following; approximately one-third of Medicare spending occurs within the last year of life with nearly 15% in the last few months.[3] In the US, the predominant philosophy is the prolongation of life no matter the cost or futility. The failure of physicians, patients, and society to accept termination of futile efforts and recognizing the limits of our technology has resulted in exorbitant amounts of spending in treating terminal conditions. This is not advocacy for euthanasia, but a basic recognition that man is mortal and will ultimately die. Some believe acknowledgment of this has the potential for generating substantial savings throughout the health care system.[4]

Even patients who have expressly stated their wishes not to have aggressive treatment to prolong their lives are not immune from this medical nonsense. A large study of seriously ill hospitalized patients showed 14% reported having

1. Beyerstein, B.L. "Why Bogus Therapies Often Seem to Work." Quack Watch. 2006. ⟨http://www.quackwatch.org/01QuackeryRelatedTopics/altbelief.html⟩.
2. Greger, M. "Shortness of Breath." Heart Failure — Diary of a Third Year Medical Student. 1999. Jan 1999 ⟨http://upalumni.org/medschool/internal-medicine.html#fn179⟩. Hughes, S.G., Wagner, G.S., Swain, M.W. "Dr. Stead on Doctoring." The Pharos Winter 1998. p. 20-22.
3. Emanuel, E.J. "Cost savings at the end of life. What do the data show?" JAMA Jun 26; 275(24) 1996. p. 1907-14.
4. Emanuel, E.J., Emanuel, L.L. "The economics of dying — the illusion of cost savings at the end of life." NEJM vol 330 1994. p. 540-44.

been provided care inconsistent with their preferences.[1] One survey found 55% of physicians felt they sometimes provided "overly burdensome" treatments to patients, whereas only 12% said they sometimes gave up too soon on patients.[2] Some departments are notorious for not honoring DNRs (do not resuscitate, or do not use heroic means to prolong life).[3] A 1998 study found 38% of the radiology departments resuscitated patients against their expressed wishes.[4] In a separate study based on a questionnaire with 248 respondents, 24% indicated they had initiated CPR for patients with DNR orders and nearly 40% indicated they had resuscitated such patients.[5] Less than 10% of all respondents stated patients were notified of the potential for revocation of their DNR status.

The practice of medicine not only may fail those who wish not to be treated, it may give false hope to those seeking a cure. A 1997 study represents a dramatic example of medicines failure to prolong life. The authors evaluated consecutive admissions to a department of internal medicine during a six-week period and found the mean life expectancy gain was only 2.25 years. Incredibly, 61% of those studied had a life expectancy gain of 0.10 years or less, while only 5% had a gain of more than 9.98 years.[6]

Although medicine may have its successes, they are generally lackluster on a population level.[7] One of its greatest successes has been reducing the death rate from stroke by 70% from 1950 to 1996.[8] However, it added little more than one year to the average life expectancy.[9] Most therapies add less than a year to the average life expectancy,[10] and generally, similar benefit may be obtained by dietary and lifestyle changes.[11] One Scottish study concluded about 60% of the

1. Teno, J.M., et al. "Medical care inconsistent with patients' treatment goals: association with 1-year Medicare resource use and survival." Journal of the American Geriatrics Society vol 50 2002. p. 496-500.
2. Solomon, M.Z., et al. "Decisions Near the End of Life: Professional Views on Life-Sustaining Treatments." American Journal of Public Health vol 83(1) 1993. p. 14-23.
3. Casarett, D., Ross, L.F. "Overriding a patient's refusal of treatment after an iatrogenic complication." NEJM Jun 26; 336(26) 1997. p. 1908-10. Clemency, M.V., Thompson, N.J. "'Do not resuscitate' (DNR) orders and the anesthesiologist: a survey." Anesth Analg Feb; 76(2) 1993. p. 394-401.
4. Heffner, J.E., Barbieri, C. "Compliance with Do-Not-Resuscitate Orders for Hospitalized Patients Transported to Radiology Departments." Annals of Internal Medicine vol 129 1998. p. 801-05.
5. Heffner, J.E. "Do-Not-Resuscitate Orders in Radiology Departments." Ann Intern Med Jul 6; 131(1) 1999. p. 73.
6. Eriksen, B.O., et al. "Does admission to a medical department improve patient life expectancy?" J Clin Epidemiol Sep; 50(9) 1997. p. 987-95.
7. Yudkin, J.S. "How can we best prolong life? Benefits of coronary risk factor reduction in non-diabetic and diabetic subjects." BMJ May 15; 306(6888) 1993. p. 1313-18.
8. Ayala, C., et al. "Sex Differences in US Mortality Rates for Stroke and Stroke Subtypes by Race/Ethnicity and Age, 1995–1998." Stroke vol 33 202. p. 1197.
9. Collins, R., et al. "Blood pressure, stroke, and coronary heart disease Part 2, short-term reductions in blood pressure: overview of randomised drug trials in their epidemiological context." Lancet vol 335 1990. p. 827-38. Drizd, T., Dannenberg, A.L., Engel, A. Blood pressure levels in persons 18-74 years of age in 1976-80, and trends in blood pressure from 1960-80 in the United States. Washington DC: US Government Printing Office, 1986.
10. Wright, J.C., Weinstein, M.C. "Gains in life expectancy from medical interventions—standardizing data on outcomes." NEJM Aug 6; 339(6) 1998. p. 380-86.
11. "Scandinavian Simvastatin Survival Study. Randomised trial of cholesterol lowering in 4444 patients with coronary heart disease: the Scandinavian Simvastatin Survival Study (4S)." Lancet vol 344 1994. p. 1383-89.

decreases in mortality was attributed to changes in major risk factors while only 40% to specific cardiac treatments.[1] Multiple studies have concluded reductions in major risk factors[2] account for over half the observed mortality declines.[3]

Medical therapy may save hundreds of thousands of lives annually, however, poor dietary and activity patterns are together accountable for at least 300,000 deaths each year. These factors increase the incidence of cardiovascular diseases (coronary artery disease, stroke, and high blood pressure), cancers (colon, breast, and prostate), and diabetes mellitus beyond the therapeutic benefit offered by medicine.[4]

The death toll is further exacerbated by addictive lifestyles;[5] more than one fourth of Americans over age 15 has a physiological dependence on at least one addictive substance.[6] Nearly a quarter of all deaths in the United States are caused by addictive substances.[7] In 1995, substance abuse accounted for some forty-three million illnesses or injuries and more than half a million deaths.[8] Combined, the effects of tobacco, alcohol, and drugs inflict a greater toll on the health and well-being of Americans than any other single preventable factor.[9] Substance abuse among older adults, including abuse of alcohol and prescription and over-the-counter drugs, has been called an invisible epidemic.[10]

1. Capewell, S., Morrison, C.E., McMurray, J.J. "Contribution of modern cardiovascular treatment and risk factor changes to the decline in coronary heart disease mortality in Scotland between 1975 and 1994." Heart Apr; 81(4) 1999. p. 380-86.
2. Beaglehole, R. "Medical management and the decline in mortality from coronary heart disease." BMJ Clin Res Ed vol 292 1986. p. 33-35.
3. Goldman, L., Cook, E.F. "The decline in ischemic heart disease mortality rates. An analysis of the comparative effects of medical interventions and changes in lifestyle." Ann Intern Med vol 101 1984. p. 825-36. Hunink, M.G., et al. "The recent decline in mortality from coronary heart disease, 1980-1990. The effect of secular trends in risk factors and treatment." JAMA vol 277 1997. p. 535-42.
4. McGinnis, J.M., Nestle, M. "The Surgeon General's Report on Nutrition and Health: policy implications and implementation strategies." Am J Clin Nutr Jan; 49(1) 1989. p. 23-28.
5. Single, E., et al. "Morbidity and mortality attributable to alcohol, tobacco, and illicit drug use in Canada." Am J Public Health May; 89(5) 1999. p. 785.
6. McGinnis, J.M., Foege, W.H. "Mortality and morbidity attributable to use of addictive substances in the United States." Proc Assoc Am Physicians Mar-Apr; 111(2) 1999. p. 109-18.
7. Schneider Institute for Health Policy and Robert Wood Johnson Foundation. Substance Abuse: The Nation's Number One Health Problem. Princeton, N.J: RWJF, 2001.
8. McGinnis, J.M., Foege, W.H. "Mortality and Morbidity Attributable to Use of Addictive Substances in the United States, Health and Economic Burdens." Proceedings of the Association of American Physicians vol 3(2) 1999. p. 109-118.
9. "Annual smoking-attributable mortality, years of potential life lost, and economic costs—United States, 1995-1999." Morb Mortal Wkly Rep Apr 12; 51(14) 2002. p. 300-03. Phillips, D.P., Christenfeld, N., Ryan, N.M. "An increase in the number of deaths in the United States in the first week of the month—an association with substance abuse and other causes of death." NEJM Jul 8; 341(2) 1999. p. 93-98.
10. Widlitz, M., Marin, D.B. "Substance abuse in older adults. An overview." Geriatrics Dec; 57(12) 2002. p. 29-34.

CHAPTER 10. DISEASE PREVENTION

PREVENTIVE MEDICINE?

> *There's no pleasure on earth that's worth sacrificing for the sake of an*
> *extra five years in the geriatric ward of the Sunset Old People's Home.*
> Horace Rumpole, fictional barrister, created by John Mortimer

For most Americans, the majority of their lives are healthy, or at worse, inflicted with rather minor or merely annoying chronic illnesses.[1] It isn't until the last few months of our lives that progressive conditions eventually result in our death. The futility of medicine to alter this course may be seen when you consider more than half of Medicare's payments is for treatments of the terminally ill. Except for cancer, we usually die within a few days or weeks of having been in reasonably good health over the last six months. Thousands live with disabling and progressive conditions such as heart disease, emphysema, stroke, dementia, and cancer.[2] Billions are spent each year to treat the terminally ill. Nonetheless, effective preventive medicine practices known to increase not only lifespan but also healthy life expectancy are consistently under-funded.[3] The special interest groups lobby hard for resources to cover the costs of research. They are not content with preventive medicine therapies that benefit

---

1. "Older Americans 2000: Key Indicators of Well-Being." Federal Interagency Forum on Aging-Related Statistics. 2004. 04 Sep 2004 ‹http://www.agingstats.gov/chartbook2000/default.htm›. "National Summit on Medical Errors and Patient Safety Research Testimony of Joanne Lynn and Sarah Myers." National Summit on Medical Errors and Patient Safety Research. 2000. 29 Aug 2000 ‹http://www.quic.gov/summit/wlynn.htm›.
2. Hogan, C., et al. "Medicare beneficiaries' costs of care in the last year of life." Health Aff (Millwood) Jul-Aug; 20(4) 2001. p. 188-95.
3. Bond, G.F. Jr, Sandele, W.L. "Public health departments: the under-funded provider of last resort." N C Med J Mar-Apr; 66(2) 2005. p. 141-43. Fleischman, C. "Preventing the preventable. Under-valued and underfunded screening is undermining primary care." Postgrad Med Jun; 103(6) 1998. p. 13-15.

millions but may take years before they manifest.[1] The lure for quick profit and easy fixes push many bureaucrats into sponsorship of high priced technology that actually provides little if any benefit. Approximately 95% of the trillion dollars spent on health goes to direct medical care services, while just 5% is allocated to population wide approaches to health improvement.[2] The same investment into public health and preventive medicine would yield returns far better than most medical therapies.[3]

Unfortunately, preventive medicine practices provide little opportunity for pharmaceutical firms and hospital organizations to increase their profits.[4] The extent for potential benefits can be seen in several international studies. Scotland has one of the highest heart disease death rates in the world. Yet, a 2003 study found lifestyle modification provided a three fold increase in life years gained over medical therapy.[5] The World Health Organization concluded simple lifestyle changes could add five to ten years to the average lifespan.[6] Modest reductions in major risk factors led to gains in life-years four times higher than did cardiological treatments. Effective policies to promote healthy diets and physical activity might achieve even greater gains.[7]

Gains are especially effective when prevention is targeted to those at the highest risks.[8] A British study concluded the simple measures of reducing smoking prevalence from 30% to 18%, decreasing mean population cholesterol from 6.2 to 5.2 mmol/l and reducing population diastolic blood pressure by 3.7 mm Hg would nearly halve their coronary heart disease mortality.[9] These reductions in blood pressure are easily achievable by non-pharmacological means by simply eating less, exercising more and abandoning harmful lifestyles like smoking and drinking alcohol.[10]

1. Lavis, J.N. "Ideas at the Margin or Marginalized Ideas? Nonmedical Determinants of Health in Canada." Health Affairs vol 21(2) 2002. p. 107-112.
2. McGinnis, J.M., Williams-Russo, P., Knickman, J.R. "The Case For More Active Policy Attention To Health Promotion." Health Affairs vol 21(2) 2002. p. 78-93.
3. Goldman, L., et al. "The effect of risk factor reductions between 1981 and 1990 on coronary heart disease incidence, prevalence, mortality and cost." J Am Coll Cardiol Oct; 38(4) 2001. p. 1012-17. Liebson, P.R., Amsterdam, E.A. "Prevention of coronary heart disease. Part I. Primary prevention." Dis Mon Dec; 45(12) 1999. p. 497-71.
4. Cutler, D.M., McClellan, M. "Is technological change in medicine worth it?" Health Aff (Millwood) Sep-Oct; 20(5) 2001. p. 11-29. Rosenberg, L.E. "Exceptional economic returns on investments in medical research." Med J Aust Oct 7; 177(7) 2002. p. 368-71.
5. Critchley, J.A., Capewell, S., Unal, B. "Life-years gained from coronary heart disease mortality reduction in Scotland: prevention or treatment?" J Clin Epidemiol Jun; 56(6) 2003. p. 583-90.
6. Dyer, O. "Simple measures could increase life expectancy by 5-10 years." BMJ Nov 2; 325(7371) 2002. p. 985.
7. Unal, B., et al. "Life-Years Gained From Modern Cardiological Treatments and Population Risk Factor Changes in England and Wales, 1981-2000." American Journal of Public Health vol 95(1) 2005. p. 103-08.
8. Wright, J.C., Weinstein, M.C. "Gains in life expectancy from medical interventions—standardizing data on outcomes." NEJM Aug 6; 339(6) 1998. p. 380-86.
9. Critchley, J.A., Capewell, S. "Substantial potential for reductions in coronary heart disease mortality in the UK through changes in risk factor levels." J Epidemiol Community Health Apr; 57(4) 2003. p. 243-47.

The Nurses' Health Study in the US confirmed the benefits of healthy living. This study found a 31% reduction of coronary disease in just 10 years by simple improvements in lifestyle. Diet and lifestyle produced a 21% decrease in the incidence of coronary disease which represents 68% of the overall decline from 1980–1994. The reduction in smoking produced a 13% decrease and improved diet explained a 16% decline. Unfortunately, they also determined an increasing prevalence of obesity caused an 8% increase in coronary disease, partially reversing this healthy trend.[1]

In 1979, the U.S. Public Health Service established goals for 1990 to reduce infant mortality by 35%, death rates among children by 20%, death rates for adolescents and young adults by 20%, adult death rates by 25%, and, for older adults, sick days by about 20%.[2] They were able to meet most of these goals by focusing on simple behavior and social interventions.[3] These goals were then broadened into the Healthy People 2010 in an attempt to further improve the quality of health and life by preventive and public health measures.[4]

HEALTHIEST NATIONS

> *The health of nations is more important than the wealth of nations.*
> Will Rogers, humorist (1879-1935)

The goals of the Healthy Nation 2010 may initially seem obtainable only by our continued research and investment in science and technology. It may come as a surprise to many that these goals have not only been achieved, they have been surpassed. Unfortunately, those already achieving these goals live in "less advanced" nations. In fact, many of these long lived countries would be considered third world by our standards. Their science and technological achievements may not be as advanced as ours; however, their lifestyles are far superior to our own. They are currently reaping the benefits of good health through moderation that our bureaucrats hope to achieve through technology and money. Our country must be content with its youthful image while others enjoy their longevity. Currently, only 13% of our population is 65 or over. We are

10. Czernichow, S., et al. "Relationships between changes in weight and changes in cardiovascular risk factors in middle-aged French subjects: effect of dieting." Int J Obes Relat Metab Disord Aug; 26(8) 2002. p. 1138-43. Walker, A.R., Walker, B.F,, Adam, F. "Nutrition, diet, physical activity, smoking, and longevity: from primitive hunter-gatherer to present passive consumer—how far can we go?" Nutrition Feb; 19(2) 2003. p. 169-73.
1. Hu, F.B., et al. "Trends in the incidence of coronary heart disease and changes in diet and lifestyle in women." NEJM Aug 24; 343(8) 2000. p. 530-37.
2. Healthy People: The Surgeon General's Report on Health Promotion and Disease Prevention. Washington: DHHS, 1979.
3. McGinnis, J.M., et al. "Healthy Progress in the United States: Results of the 1990 Objectives for the Nation." JAMA vol 11 1992. p. 2545-52.
4. "Healthy People 2010." Office of Disease Prevention and Health Promotion. 2006. 15 Sep 2005 ⟨http://www.healthypeople.gov/⟩.

considered youthful in comparison to those listed in the following graph from the National Institutes on Aging.[1]

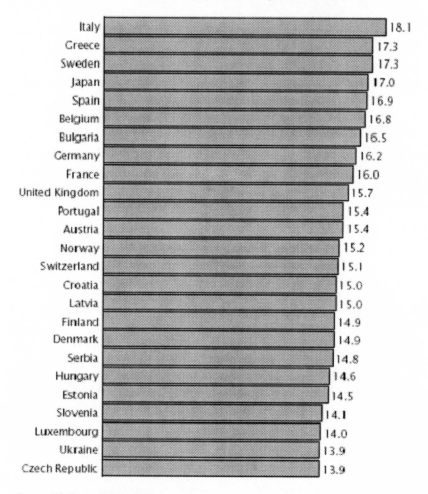

The World's 25 Oldest Countries: 2000
(Percent of population 65 years and over)

Country	Percent
Italy	18.1
Greece	17.3
Sweden	17.3
Japan	17.0
Spain	16.9
Belgium	16.8
Bulgaria	16.5
Germany	16.2
France	16.0
United Kingdom	15.7
Portugal	15.4
Austria	15.4
Norway	15.2
Switzerland	15.1
Croatia	15.0
Latvia	15.0
Finland	14.9
Denmark	14.9
Serbia	14.8
Hungary	14.6
Estonia	14.5
Slovenia	14.1
Luxembourg	14.0
Ukraine	13.9
Czech Republic	13.9

Source: U.S. Census Bureau, 2000a.

1. "An Aging World: 2001." US Census Bureau. 2001. 13 Dec 2001 ‹http://www.census.gov/prod/2001pubs/p95-01-1.pdf›.

DIETARY EFFECTS ON MORTALITY

> *Did you ever see the customers in health-food stores? They are pale, skinny*
> *people who look half dead. In a steak house, you see robust, ruddy people.*
> *They're dying, of course, but they look terrific.*
> Bill Cosby, comedian

Many believe diet is the primary component of increased life expectancy. Dietary factors have been associated with coronary heart disease, stroke, cancers of the colon, breast, and prostate and diabetes.[1] The increased life expectancy of many foreign nations may be related more to their diet than to genetics. Westernization of diets in ethnic groups[2] having low rates of heart disease[3] results in increases of risk factors leading to higher rates of cardiovascular disease and death.[4] Many of these cultures have diets rich in vegetables and low in fat or meat. Multiple studies of vegetarians confirm they have a lower risk of fatal heart disease, but it is not clear whether the absence of meat[5] or some other aspect of the vegetarian diet[6] is causal in this relationship.[7] Other studies have confirmed infrequent meat consumption[8] or vegetarianism was associated with low mortality from ischemic heart disease.[9]

A 1999 study found mortality from heart disease was 20% lower in occasional meat eaters, 34% lower in people who ate fish but not meat, 34% lower in lactoovovegetarians, and 26% lower in vegans.[10] It is unlikely meat is deleterious, instead, it appears plant derived foods may have a protective effect.[11]

1. The Surgeon General's Reporton Nutrition and Health. Washington: U.s. Department Of Health And Human Services, 1988.
2. Hatahet, W., Khosla, P., Fungwe, T.V. "Prevalence of risk factors to coronary heart disease in an Arab-American population in southeast Michigan." Int J Food Sci Nutr Jul; 53(4) 2002. p. 325-35. Kafatos, A., et al. "Heart disease risk-factor status and dietary changes in the Cretan population over the past 30 y: the Seven Countries Study." Am J Clin Nutr vol 65 1997. p. 1882-86.
3. Nakanishi, S., et al. "A comparison between Japanese-Americans living in Hawaii and Los Angeles and native Japanese: the impact of lifestyle westernization on diabetes mellitus." Biomed Pharmacother Dec; 58(10) 2004. p. 571-77.
4. Egusa, G., Yamane, K. "Lifestyle, serum lipids and coronary artery disease: comparison of Japan with the United States." J Atheroscler Thromb vol 11(6) 2004. p. 304-12. O'Dea, K. "Westernization and non-insulin-dependent diabetes in Australian Aborigines." Ethn Dis Spring; 1(2) 1991. p. 171-87.
5. Chang-Claude, J., et al. "Lifestyle determinants and mortality in German vegetarians and health-conscious persons: results of a 21-year follow-up." Cancer Epidemiol Biomarkers Prev Apr; 14(4) 2005. p. 963-68.
6. Thorogood, M. "Vegetarianism, coronary disease risk factors and coronary heart disease." Curr Opin Lipidol Feb; 5(1) 1994. p. 17-21.
7. "Fall in coronary deaths in Poland may be linked to lower meat and butter intake." BMJ Apr 4; 316(7137):b 1998. "Vegetarianism: addition by subtraction. An increasing number of studies are finding health benefits from a low- or no-meat diet." Harv Health Lett Feb; 29(4) 2004. p. 6.
8. Burr, M.L., Butlandm B.K. "Heart disease in British vegetarians." Am J Clin Nutr vol 48(suppl) 1988. p. 830-2. Chang-Claude, J., Frentzel-Beyme, R., Eilber, U. "Mortality pattern of German vegetarians after 11 years of follow-up." Epidemiology vol 3 1992. p. 395-401.
9. Key, T.J., et al. "Mortality in vegetarians and nonvegetarians: detailed findings from a collaborative analysis of 5 prospective studies." American Journal of Clinical Nutrition vol 70(3) 1999. p. 516S-524S. Thorogood, M., et al. "Risk of death from cancer and ischaemic heart disease in meat and non-meat eaters." BMJ vol 308 1994. p. 1667-71.

Epidemiological studies suggest adherence to a vegetarian diet for more than two decades can increase lifespan 3.6 years.[1] However, much of this benefit may be the result of non-dietary lifestyle factors such as a low prevalence of smoking and a generally high socio-economic status, or to aspects of the diet other than the avoidance of meat and fish.[2] Fruit consumption appears to reduce the risk of heart attack in both men and women and eating tofu more than four times per week may halve the risk of cardiac related death.[3]

The traditional Mediterranean diet may reduce heart disease mortality by 7%; [4] this benefit is similar to that achieved by pharmacotherapy. Dietary fatty fish intake of one fish meal per week[5] has been associated with a reduced risk of sudden death and total mortality.[6] Fatty fish consumption may be especially beneficial for high risk groups. A higher consumption of fish and long-chain omega-3 fatty acids decreases the rates of coronary heart disease and total mortality among diabetic women[7] and smokers.[8]

A 2004 British study recommends using a combination of known heart healthy foods as ingredients of the "Polymeal." They conclude implementation of this diet could reduce cardiovascular disease by 76%. For men, this represents a 6.6 year increase in total life expectancy with a 9.0 year reduction in cardiovascular disease. Women experienced similar benefits.[9] Regrettably, Americans are generally unmotivated by advice to protect their hearts through prudent dietary measures. They opt instead for the "easy fixes" promulgated by the pharmaceutical and medical communities. One randomized study of patients with heart disease evaluated the effects of a lifestyle intervention program that

10. Key, T.J., et al. "Mortality in vegetarians and nonvegetarians: detailed findings from a collaborative analysis of 5 prospective studies." American Journal of Clinical Nutrition vol 70(3) 1999. p. 516S-524S.
11. Sabate, J. "The contribution of vegetarian diets to human health." Forum Nutr vol 56 2003. p. 218-20.
1. Singh, P.N., Sabate, J., Fraser, G.E. "Does low meat consumption increase life expectancy in humans?" Am J Clin Nutr Sep; 78(3 Suppl) 2003. p. 526S-532S..
2. Appleby, P.N., et al. "Mortality in British vegetarians." Public Health Nutr Feb; 5(1) 2002. p. 29-36.
3. Sasazuki, S., et al. "Case-control study of nonfatal myocardial infarction in relation to selected foods in Japanese men and women." Jpn Circ J Mar; 65(3) 2001. p. 200-06.
4. Trichopoulou, A., et al. "Modified Mediterranean diet and survival: EPIC-elderly prospective cohort study." BMJ Apr 30; 330(7498) 2005. p. 991.
5. Albert CM, Hennekens CH, O'Donnell CJ, Ajani UA, Carey VJ, Willett WC, Ruskin, J.N., Manson, J.E. "Fish consumption and risk of sudden cardiac death." JAMA Jan 7; 279(1) 1998. p. 23-28. Daviglus ML, et al. "Fish consumption and the 30-year risk of fatal myocardial infarction." NEJM Apr 10; 336(15) 1997. p. 1046-53.
6. Oomen, C.M., et al. "Fish consumption and coronary heart disease mortality in Finland, Italy, and The Netherlands." Am J Epidemiol May 15; 151(10) 2000. p. 999-1006. Zhang. J., et al. "Fish consumption and mortality from all causes, ischemic heart disease, and stroke: an ecological study." Prev Med May; 28(5) 1999. p. 520-29.
7. Hu, F.B., et al. "Fish and long-chain omega-3 fatty acid intake and risk of coronary heart disease and total mortality in diabetic women." Circulation Apr 15; 107(14) 2003. p. 852-57.
8. Rodriguez, B.L., et al. "Fish intake may limit the increase in risk of coronary heart disease morbidity and mortality among heavy smokers. The Honolulu Heart Program." Circulation Sep 1; 94(5) 1996. p. 952-56.
9. Franco, O.H., et al. "The Polymeal: a more natural, safer, and probably tastier (than the Polypill) strategy to reduce cardiovascular disease by more than 75%." BMJ Dec 18; 329(7480) 2004. p. 1447-50.

emphasized a low fat diet, regular exercise, smoking cessation, psychosocial support and education delivered by nurses. The authors concluded these measures were able to reduce the five year coronary risk by 22%[1] which is similar to the benefit obtained by aspirin therapy.[2]

EXERCISE

> *To get back to my youth I would do anything in the world, except take*
> *exercise, get up early, or be respectable.*
> Oscar Wilde. *Irish novelist and critic (1854-1900)*

In addition to moderation of diet, cultures with the greatest life expectancies have large sectors of their population working in strenuous jobs involving manual labor. Agrarian societies[3] (farming based) are especially prone to this "healthy worker effect."[4] This effect was first recognized in 1976 by McMichael who reported the "HWE refers to the consistent tendency for the actively employed people to have a more favorable mortality experience than the population at large."[5] This effect is so strong, it even offsets the risks of cigarette smoking so common among farm workers.[6] Multiple studies have shown it is not only limited to farm workers but extends to many professions engaged in heavy physical labor. Truck drivers,[7] baseball players,[8] road workers,[9] electric

1. Vestfold Heartcare Study Group. "Influence on lifestyle measures and five-year coronary risk by a comprehensive lifestyle intervention programme in patients with coronary heart disease." Eur J Cardiovasc Prev Rehabil Dec; 10(6) 2003. p. 429-37.
2. Hankey, G.J., Eikelboom, J.W. "Aspirin for the primary prevention of cardiovascular events." The Medical Journal of Australia. 2002. 6 Sep 2002 ⟨http://www.mja.com.au/public/issues/177_07_071002/han10439_fm.html⟩.
3. Blair, A., et al. "Clues to cancer etiology from studies of farmers." Scand J Work Environ Health vol 18 1992. p. 209-15. Blair, A., et al. "Mortality among participants in the agricultural health study." Ann Epidemiol Apr; 15(4) 2005. p. 279-85.
4. Fleming, L.E., et al. "National Health Interview Survey mortality among US farmers and pesticide applicators." Am J Ind Med vol 43 2003. p. 227-33. Pearce, N., Reif, J.S. "Epidemiologic studies of cancer in agricultural workers." Am J Ind Med vol 18 1990. p. 133-42.
5. McMichael, A.J. "Standardized mortality ratios and the 'healthy worker effect': Scratching beneath the surface." J Occup Med Mar; 18(3) 1976. p. 165-68.
6. Blair, A., et al. "Mortality among Participants in the Agricultural Health Study." Agricultural Health Study. 2005. 02 May 2005 ⟨http://www.aghealth.org/pdfs/MortalityPaper.pdf⟩.
7. Balarajan, R., McDowall, M.E. "Professional drivers in London: A mortality study." Br J Indust Med vol 45 1988. p. 483-86. Luepker, R.V., Smith, M.L. "Mortality in unionized truck drivers." J Occup Med vol 20 1978. p. 677-82.
8. Abel, E.L., Kruger, M.L. "Longevity of Major League Baseball Players." Research in Sports Medicine: An International Journal vol 13(1) 2005. p. 1-5.
9. D'Errico, A., et al. "Mortality of a cohort of road construction and maintenance workers with work disability compensation." Med Lav Nov-Dec; 93(6) 2002. p. 519-26.

linemen,[1] firemen,[2] and fishermen[3] have all been shown to have longer lives attributed to their occupation.

Studies have shown people who state they engage in vigorous physical activity[4] are less likely to have a heart attack or other risk factors associated with heart disease.[5] Conversely, physical inactivity has been associated with increased risk for heart disease, colon cancer, diabetes, dementia, and osteoporosis.[6] The elderly may decrease their risks of death from heart disease and falls by increased physical activity and exercise training.[7] Benefits to fitness and cardiovascular risk are seen with "30-min brisk walking, 5 days a week."[8]

A separate study concluded even 1 hour/week walking reduces the risk of cardiovascular disease; [9] however, the exact duration and frequency of activity necessary to prevent heart disease remains unclear.[10] It is known that walking significantly reduces the risks associated with heart disease.[11] Two recent studies found aerobic capacity and muscular strength can be improved without causing injury even to those with a history of heart disease.[12]

1. Kelsh, M.A., Sahl, J.D. "Mortality among a cohort of electric utility workers, 1960-1991." Am J Ind Med May; 31(5) 1997. p. 534-44.
2. Deschamps, S., Momas, I., Festy, B. "Mortality amongst Paris fire-fighters." Eur J Epidemiol Dec; 11(6) 1995. p. 643-46.
3. Neutel, C.I. "Mortality in commercial fishermen of Atlantic Canada." Can J Public Health Sep-Oct; 80(5) 1989. p. 375-79.
4. Melzer, K., Kayser, B., Pichard, C. "Physical activity: the health benefits outweigh the risks." Curr Opin Clin Nutr Metab Care Nov; 7(6) 2004. p. 641-47.
5. Haapanen-Niemi, N., et al. "Body mass index, physical inactivity and low level of physical fitness as determinants of all-cause and cardiovascular disease mortality—16 y follow-up of middle-aged and elderly men and women." Int J Obes Relat Metab Disord Nov; 24(11) 2000. p. 1465-74. Hillsdon, M., et al. "Can a simple measure of vigorous physical activity predict future mortality? Results from the OXCHECK study." Public Health Nutr Jun; 7(4) 2004. p. 557-62.
6. DHHS. Physical Activity and Health: A Report of the Surgeon General. Atlanta: Centers For Disease Control And Prevention, National Center For Chronic Disease Prevention And Health Promotion, 1996. Lees, S.J., Booth, F.W. "Sedentary death syndrome." Can J Appl Physiol Aug; 29(4) 2004. p. 444-46.
7. Yanowitz, F.G., LaMonte, A.M. "Physical activity and health in the elderly." Curr Sports Med Rep Dec; 1(6) 2002. p. 354-61.
8. Tully, M.A., et al. "Brisk walking, fitness, and cardiovascular risk: A randomized controlled trial in primary care." Prev Med Aug; 41(2) 2005. p. 622-28.
9. Oguma, Y., Shinoda-Tagawa, T. "Physical activity decreases cardiovascular disease risk in women: review and meta-analysis." Am J Prev Med Jun; 26(5) 2004. p. 407-18.
10. Eaton, C.B. "Relation of physical activity and cardiovascular fitness to coronary heart disease, Part I: A meta-analysis of the independent relation of physical activity and coronary heart disease." J Am Board Fam Pract Jan-Feb; 5(1) 1992. p. 31-42.
11. Kelley, G.A., Kelley, K.S., Tran, Z.V. "Walking and Non-HDL-C in adults: a meta-analysis of randomized controlled trials." Prev Cardiol Spring; 8(2) 2005. p. 102-07. Whelton, S.P., et al. "Effect of aerobic exercise on blood pressure: a meta-analysis of randomized, controlled trials." Ann Intern Med Apr 2; 136(7) 2002. p. 493-503.
12. Kujala, U.M. "Evidence for exercise therapy in the treatment of chronic disease based on at least three randomized controlled trials—summary of published systematic reviews." Scand J Med Sci Sports Dec; 14(6) 2004. p. 339-45. Piepoli, M.F., et al. "ExTraMATCH Collaborative. Exercise training meta-analysis of trials in patients with chronic heart failure." BMJ Jan 24; 328(7433) 2004. p. 189.

OBESITY

> No diet will remove all the fat from your body because the brain is entirely
> fat. Without a brain, you might look good, but all you could do is run for
> public office.
> George Bernard Shaw, Irish critic and playwright (1856-1950)

Obesity is increasing at an alarming rate throughout the world. Today it is
estimated there are more than 300 million obese people world-wide[1] and its
prevalence within the US exceeds that of most industrialized nations.

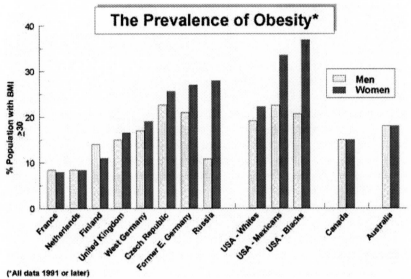

(*All data 1991 or later)

Source: The Global Challenge of Obesity and the International Obesity Task Force http://www.iuns.org/features/obesity/
obesity.htm

We also have the dubious distinction of having the highest proportion of
overweight children and adolescents with 14% of 15-year-old boys and 15% of 15-
year-old girls in the United States being overweight. This far exceeds the second
most obese nation, Greece, where 8.9% of 13-year-old boys and 8.3% of 15-year-
old boys were determined to be overweight.[2] This epidemic will further deplete
health care resources by increasing the incidence of diabetes, heart disease,
hypertension, and cancer.[3] In 1998, it was estimated 97 million adults were

---

1. "Controlling the global obesity epidemic." World Health Organization. 2003. 23 apr 2003 ‹http://
   www.who.int/nutrition/topics/obesity/en/›.
2. Lissau, I., et al. "Body mass index and overweight in adolescents in 13 European countries, Israel,
   and the United States." Arch Pediatr Adolesc Med vol 158 2004. p. 27-33.
3. Bray, G.A. "Medical consequences of obesity." J Clin Endocrinol Metab Jun; 89(6) 2004. p. 2583-
   89.

overweight or obese[1] and the CDC states the rates of obesity[2] had increased 61% in ten years and doubled in just two decades.[3]

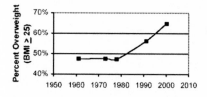 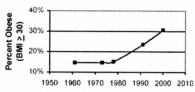

Source: Utz R. Obesity in America, 1960-2000: Is it an Age, Period, or Cohort Phenomenon? http://www.fcs.utah.edu/info/ utahdemographers/binary/?id-38

Researchers declare this epidemic is just beginning and expect the rate of obesity to again double in only 30 years.[4] The following map shows the recent increase in obesity within the US since 1991.

A 2005 report states a BMI greater than or equal to 30 (optimal BMI is approximately 23 to 25 for whites and 23 to 30 for blacks[5]) was associated with 111,909 excess deaths and underweight with 33,746 excess deaths. Thirty-four percent of adults in the US are considered overweight, and an additional 31% are obese. Some estimate, at any given time, about 45% of women and 25% of men are attempting to lose weight, but only one-fifth use the recommended combination of reducing calories while increasing exercise.[6] Although just being overweight does not appear to cause an increase in mortality,[7] obesity is a risk factor for many diseases and decreases life expectancy by about seven years. This is roughly equivalent to the combined death rates of all heart diseases and cancer.[8] Others suggest it has the same impact on health as aging 20 years.[9] It has been suggested by some that a return to a normal weight may restore 6 to 18

1. *National Institutes of Health. Clinical guidelines on the identification, evaluation, and treatment of overweight and obesity in adults. Washington DC: National Heart, Lung, And Blood Institute, 1998.*
2. Flegal, K.M., et al. "Prevalence and trends in obesity among US adults, 1999-2000." JAMA Oct 9; 288(14) 2002. p. 1723-27. Mokdad, A.H., et al. "The spread of the obesity epidemic in the United States, 1991-1998." JAMA vol 282 1999. p. 1519-22.
3. Mokdad, A.H., et al. "The continuing epidemic of obesity in the United States." JAMA vol 284 2000. p. 1650-51. Mokdad, A.H., et al. "The continuing epidemics of obesity and diabetes in the United States." JAMA vol 286 2001. p. 1195-200.
4. Freedman, D.S., et al. "Trends and correlates of class 3 obesity in the United States from 1990 through 2000." JAMA Oct 9; 288(14) 2002. p. 1758-61.
5. Fontaine, K.R., et al. "Years of life lost due to obesity." JAMA Jan 8; 289(2) 2003. p. 187-93.
6. Jousilahti, P., et al. "Body weight, cardiovascular risk factors, and coronary mortality. 15-year follow-up of middle-aged men and women in eastern Finland." Circulation Apr 1; 93(7) 1996. p. 1372-79. Mokdad, A.H.,. "Actual Causes of Death in the United States, 2000." JAMA vol 291 2004. p. 1238-1245.
7. Flegal, K.M., et al. "Excess deaths associated with underweight, overweight, and obesity." JAMA Apr 20; 293(15) 2005. p. 1861-67.
8. Mizuno, T., et al. "Obesity over the life course." Sci Aging Knowledge Environ Jun 16; 2004(24) 2004. p. re4.
9. Sturm, R. "Health Aff (Millwood)." The effects of obesity, smoking, and drinking on medical problems and costs. Obesity outranks both smoking and drinking in its deleterious effects on health and health costs Mar-Apr; 21(2) 2002. p. 245-53.

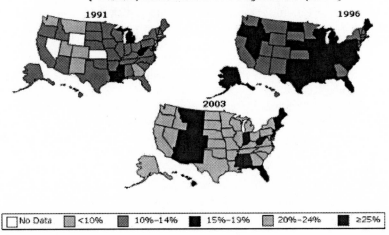

Obesity Trends* Among U.S. Adults
BRFSS, 1991, 1996, 2003
(*BMI ≥30, or about 30 lbs overweight for 5'4" person)

| No Data | <10% | 10%~14% | 15%~19% | 20%~24% | ≥25% |

Source: The worldwide obesity epidemic: a review http://www.hcgobesity.org/obesity/obreview.htm

months lifespan back to the morbidly obese. Population wide this may increase the life expectancy by 2 to 2 1/2 years.[1]

Americans are less active than in previous years[2] their continued inactivity increases the prevalence of obesity at least as much as genetics or poor dietary patterns.[3] Twenty-seven percent of US adults engage in no daily, leisure-time physical activity.[4] Lack of exercise combined with increasing caloric intake from 1826 kilocalories per day in 1978 to 2002 kcal/d by 1996[5] has resulted in two-thirds of all US adults and 20-30% of all children under age 15 being overweight.[6]

1. Bunker, J.P. Medicine Matters After All. London: Nuffield Trust, 2001.
2. Brownson, R.C., Boehmer, T.K., Luke, D.A. "Declining rates of physical activity in the United States: what are the contributors?" Annu Rev Public Health vol 26 2005. p. 421-43. Hu, F.B.,et al. "Physical activity and television watching in relation to risk for type 2 diabetes mellitus in men." Arch Intern Med Jun 25; 161(12) 2001. p. 1542-48.
3. Blair, S.N., Nichaman, M. "The public health problem of increasing prevalence rates of obesity and what should be done about it." Mayo Clin Proc Feb; 77(2) 2002. p. 109-13.
4. Mokdad, A.H., et al. "The continuing epidemics of obesity and diabetes in the United States." JAMA Sep 12; 286(10) 2001. p. 1195-200.
5. "Department of Agriculture (US). Data Tables: Results from USDA's 1994-96 Continuing Survey of Food Intakes by Individuals and 1994-96 Diet and Health Knowledge Survey." U.S Department of Agriculture, Agricultural Research Service. 2000. Jun 2000 <http://www.ars.usda.gov/SP2UserFiles/Place/12355000/pdf/Facts1.pdf>. Nestle, M., Jacobson, M.F. "Halting the Obesity Epidemic: A Public Health Policy Approach." Public Health Reports. 2000. Center for Science in the Public Interest. Feb 2000 <http://www.cspinet.org/reports/obesity.pdf>.
6. Myers, M.D. "Causes of Obesity." Weight. 2004. 28 May 2004 <http://www.weight.com/causes.asp>.

There is a chilling disconnect between the medical and public perception of obesity within the US. In a 2002 survey of nearly 1,000 Americans, most ranked obesity low on the list of serious health problems. Incredibly, only 9% believed their own weight was a problem, yet more than half of those surveyed were overweight.[1] The medical community recognizes obesity contributes more to death and disease than either smoking or alcoholism.[2] It doubles the risk of sudden death[3] and hypertension and nearly triples the incidence of Type II diabetes (8.1% vs 3.0%) while increasing the lifetime risks of coronary heart disease and stroke (41.8% vs 34.9% and 16.2% vs 13.9%, respectively).[4]

One analysis concluded that being overweight may reduce a forty-year-old female nonsmoker's life expectancy by 3.3 years and a 40-year-old male nonsmoker's by 3.1 years. Becoming obese nearly doubles the life years lost resulting in a 40-year-old female nonsmoker losing 7.1 years and a 40-year-old male nonsmoker losing 5.8 years. Life expectancy is further eroded by smoking, with obese female smokers losing 7.2 years and obese male smokers losing 6.7 years when compared with normal-weight smokers. Smoking slashes an astounding 13.3 years off the life expectancy of an obese female and 13.7 years from an obese male smoker when compared with normal-weight nonsmokers.[5] A 2005 study confirms those who are obese are also more likely to smoke.[6] Another study estimated it was responsible for an additional $11 billion in treatment costs for the year 2000 with medical spending being double that for non-obese patients.[7]

The toll from obesity in adults may pale to what awaits our children. The prevalence of overweight and obesity in children and adolescents is escalating at an alarming rate. A CDC study estimates 13-14% of children aged 6 to 19 years are considered overweight or obese[8] and rates have tripled in just 20 years.[9]

---

1. Lee, T., Oliver, J.E. "Public Opinion and the Politics of America's Obesity Epidemic." Harvard University Faculty Research Working Paper Series. 2002. 06 May 2002 ⟨http://ksgnotes1.harvard.edu/Research/wpaper.nsf/rwp/RWP02-017⟩.
2. Sturm, R., Wells, K.B. "Does obesity contribute as much to morbidity as poverty or smoking?" Public Health vol 115 2001. p. 229-35.
3. "Clinical guidelines on the identification, evaluation, and treatment of overweight and obesity in adults: the evidence report." National Heart, Lung, and Blood Institute. 2003. 19 Mar 2003 ⟨http://www.nhlbi.nih.gov/guidelines/obesity/ob_home.htm⟩.
4. Thompson, D.,et al. "Lifetime health and economic consequences of obesity." Arch Intern Med Oct 11; 159(18) 1999. p. 2177-83.
5. Peeters, A., et al. "NEDCOM, the Netherlands Epidemiology and Demography Compression of Morbidity Research Group. Obesity in adulthood and its consequences for life expectancy: a life-table analysis." Ann Intern Med Jan 7; 138(1) 2003. p. 24-32.
6. Zimlichman, E., et al. "Smoking habits and obesity in young adults." Addiction Jul; 100(7) 2005. p. 1021-25.
7. Arterburn, D.E., et al. "Impact of morbid obesity on medical expenditures in adults." Int J Obes Relat Metab Disord Mar; 29(3) 2005. p. 334-39.
8. "Prevalence of Overweight Among Children and Adolescents: United States, 1999-2002." Centers for Disease Control. 2005. 08 Feb 2005 ⟨http://www.cdc.gov/nchs/products/pubs/pubd/hestats/overwght99.htm⟩.
9. Ogden, C.L., et al. "Prevalence and trends in overweight among US children and adolescents, 1999-2000." JAMA Oct 9; 288(14) 2002. p. 1728-32.

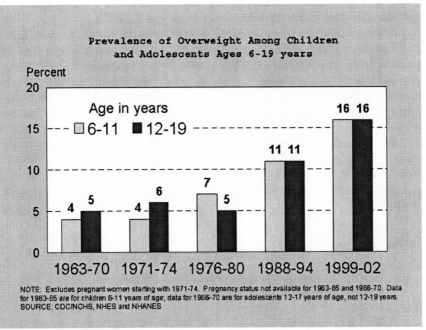

Source: Prevalence of Overweight Among Children and Adolescents: United States, 1999-2002. National Center for Health Statistics. http://www.cdc.gov/nchs/products/pubs/pubd/hestats/overwght99.htm

A major 2005 study forewarns the increase of childhood obesity has been so dramatic it will soon increase the death rate of our children when they reach middle age, thereby reversing life expectancy by mid-century.[1] They cite the sudden surge in the diagnoses of Type II diabetes among children. These increases have been so dramatic it has resulted in the renaming of adult-onset diabetes to Type II diabetes. In some areas within the US, more than 30% of all new cases of Type II diabetes are diagnosed in children, with most being attributable to obesity.[2] Childhood obesity[3] not only increases the likelihood of adult obesity,[4] it also increases the prevalence of weight-related risk factors for cardiovascular disease such as hypertension, elevated serum cholesterol, and insulin resistance.[5] Incredibly, one study found nearly 60% of overweight children between the ages

1. Olshansky, S.J., et al. "Misdirection on the road to Shangri-La." Sci Aging Knowledge Environ Jun 1; 2005(22) 2005. p. pe15. Olshansky, S.J., et al. "A potential decline in life expectancy in the United States in the 21st century." NEJM Mar 17; 352(11) 2005. p. 1138-45.
2. American Diabetes Association. "Type 2 diabetes in children and adolescents." Diabetes Care vol 23 2000. p. 381-89. Fagot-Campagna, A., et al. "Type 2 diabetes among North American children and adolescents: an epidemiologic review and a public health perspective." Pediatr vol 136 2000. p. 664-72.
3. Dietz, W.H. "Childhood weight affects adult morbidity and mortality." J Nutr vol 128 1998. p. 411S-414S.
4. McTigue, K.M., Garrett, J.M., Popkin, B.M. "The natural history of the development of obesity in a cohort of young U.S. adults between 1981 and 1998." Ann Intern Med vol 136 2002. p. 857-64.

of five and ten years have one cardiovascular risk factor (e.g., hypertension, dyslipidemia), and nearly 20% with two or more risk factors.[1]

The author of a controversial 2005 paper[2] states the rapid increase in rates of obesity in children will cause a "pulse event" of mortality[3] not seen since the Spanish influenza pandemic of 1919[4] or the Great Depression.[5] The increased rates of obesity related mortality may be so devastating one author suggests it may actually save the US Social Security.[6] The authors of the 2005 study believe obesity may shorten the average life span to a greater degree than even cancer or heart disease.[7] They ominously report data suggesting the alarming increase in childhood obesity has already shaved four to nine months off the average US life span. The real concern is, even though weight loss has been shown to lower blood pressure, cholesterol levels, and Type II diabetes,[8] no study has ever shown it reduces the risk of death[9] after considerable weight gain (> 10%) even in the obese.[10]

CIGARETTE SMOKING

> *My smoking might be bothering you, but it's killing me.*
> *Sidonie-Gabrielle Colette. French novelist (1873-1954)*

A 2003 CDC report states 22.8% of Americans regularly uses tobacco.[11] Although this is less than previous decades, it still exceeds the 12% goal for 2010.

5. Srinivasan, S.R., et al. "Adolescent overweight is associated with adult overweight and related multiple cardiovascular risk factors: the Bogalusa Heart Study." Metabolism vol 45 1996. p. 235-40. Steinberger, J., et al. "Adiposity in childhood predicts obesity and insulin resistance in young adulthood." J Pediatr vol 138 2001. p. 469-73.
1. Freedman, D.S., et al. "The relation of overweight to cardiovascular risk factors among children and adolescents: the Bogalusa Heart Study." Pediatrics Jun; 103(6 Pt 1) 1999. p. 1175-82.
2. Lang, L. "Obesity threatens u.s. Life expectancy." Gastroenterology May; 128(5) 2005. p. 1156. Olshansky, S.J., et al. "A potential decline in life expectancy in the United States in the 21st century." NEJM Mar 17; 352(11) 2005. p. 1138-45.
3. Mann, C.C. "Provocative study says obesity may reduce U.S. life expectancy." Science Mar 18; 307(5716) 2005. p. 1716-17.
4. "Obesity in children—what might be its impact on life expectancy?" Child Health Alert Apr; 23 2005. p. 1-2. Preston, S.H. "Deadweight?—The influence of obesity on longevity." NEJM Mar 17; 352(11) 2005. p. 1135-37.
5. Lalasz, R. "Will Rising Childhood Obesity Decrease U.S. Life Expectancy?" Population Reference Bureau. 2005. May 2005 <http://www.prb.org/Template.cfm?Section=PRB&template=/Content-Management/ContentDisplay.cfm&ContentID=12389>.
6. Tuljapurkar, S. "Future mortality: a bumpy road to Shangri-La?" Sci Aging Knowledge Environ Apr 6; 2005(14) 2005. p. pe9.
7. Ibid.
8. Avenell, A., et al. "Systematic review of the long-term effects and economic consequences of treatments for obesity and implications for health improvement." Health Technol Assess May; 8(21) 2004. p. iii-iv, 1-182.
9. Beasley, J.W. "Obesity and years of life lost." JAMA Apr 9; 289(14) 2003. p. 1777.
10. St-Onge MP, Heymsfield SB. "Overweight and obesity status are linked to lower life expectancy." Nutr Rev Sep; 61(9) 2003. p. 313-16. Walker, M., et al. "Weight change and risk of heart attack in middle-aged British men." Int J Epidemiol Aug; 24(4) 1995. p. 694-703.
11. "Cigarette Smoking Among Adults — United States, 2001." Morb Mortal Wkly Rep vol 52(40) 2003. p. 953-56.

Medical authorities are especially critical of tobacco usage because it extracts a far greater toll on health than even alcohol and drug abuse combined. It has been estimated to kill 2.5 times as many people each year as these addictive substances. A WHO study concluded there were 1.1 billion smokers worldwide and 10,000 tobacco-related deaths per day.[1] A 2003 CDC study reported within the US, there are approximately 440,000 deaths annually attributable to cigarette smoking. This study also estimated there were 8.6 million persons inflicted by serious tobacco related illnesses.[2] Another study found smoking has a greater impact on heart disease than high blood pressure. When hypertension is combined with smoking, it quadruples the risk of dying in men and nearly triples the rate of death for women having normal levels of cholesterol. Among persons with elevated cholesterol, the combination of high blood pressure and smoking increases the risk of all-cause death by 5.7 times in men and 4.3 in women.[3] Obesity[4] further increases the risk of dying.[5]

Multiple studies have found smoking is associated with increased all-cause mortality and morbidity. A British study lasting fifty years concluded smoking reduced the life span of smokers up to 10 years, with 50% dying from smoking related illnesses.[6] A recent WHO study suggested more than half of all non-fatal heart attacks occurring in middle age adults can be attributed to smoking.[7] A study of centenarians (people older than 100 years) found very few smokers and those who did smoke used less than 10 cigarettes daily.[8] This appears to confirm an earlier study that found smoking more than nine cigarettes daily significantly increases the risk of coronary heart disease.[9]

The life years lost due to cigarette smoking may be very substantial. A 25 year study by the Chicago Heart Association Detection Project in Industry estimated smoking reduced average life expectancies by over eight years.[10] This agrees with a recent analysis of the Framingham study that found non-smokers

1. Committee on Substance Abuse. American Academy of Pediatrics. "Tobacco's toll: implications for the pediatrician." Pediatrics Apr; 107(4) 2001. p. 794-98.
2. Centers for Disease Control and Prevention (CDC). "Cigarette smoking-attributable morbidity— United States, 2000." Morb Mortal Wkly Rep Sep 5; 52(35) 2003. p. 842-44.
3. Houterman S, Verschuren WM, Kromhout D. Smoking, blood pressure and serum cholesterol-effects on 20-year mortality. Epidemiology. 2003 Jan; 14(1):24-9.
4. Bigaard, J., et al. "Waist circumference, BMI, smoking, and mortality in middle-aged men and women." Obes Res Jul; 11(7) 2003. p. 895-03. Chyou, P.H., et al. "Obesity, alcohol consumption, smoking, and mortality." Ann Epidemiol May; 7(4) 1997. p. 311-17.
5. Krueger, P.M., et al. "Body Mass, Smoking, and Overall and Cause-Specific Mortality Among Older U.S. Adults." Research on Aging vol 26(1) 2004. p. 82-107. Meyer, H.E., et al. "Body mass index and mortality: the influence of physical activity and smoking." Med Sci Sports Exerc Jul; 34(7) 2002. p. 1065-70.
6. Doll, R., et al. "Mortality in relation to smoking: 50 years' observation on male British doctors." BMJ 328 2004. p. 1519-33.
7. Mahonen, M.S., et al. "WHO MONICA Project. Current smoking and the risk of non-fatal myocardial infarction in the WHO MONICA Project populations." Tob Control Sep; 13(3) 2004. p. 244-50.
8. Tafaro, L., et al. "Smoking and longevity: an incompatible binomial?" Arch Gerontol Geriatr Suppl vol 9 2004. p. 425-30.
9. Tervahauta, M., Pekkanen, J., Nissinen, A. "Risk factors of coronary heart disease and total mortality among elderly men with and without preexisting coronary heart disease. Finnish cohorts of the Seven Countries Study." J Am Coll Cardiol Dec; 26(7) 1995. p. 1623-29.

live 8.66 (men) and 7.59 (women) years longer than smokers. They also live more years without heart disease.[1] Multiple studies have shown smoking cessation will partially reverse these losses. The British doctor study concluded cessation at age 60, 50, 40, or 30 years gained, respectively, about 3, 6, 9, or 10 years of life expectancy.[2] A US study found similar increases associated with smoking cessation. It concluded even smokers who quit at age 65 years experienced increases in life expectancy; men gained 1.4 to 2.0 years of life, and women gained 2.7 to 3.7 years.[3] Studies have shown ex-smokers not only live longer than continued smokers,[4] they also live longer with fewer illnesses.[5]

Many worry about weight gain after smoking cessation. However, a recent preventative medicine study declared "It is unquestionably better to quit smoking and gain weight than to continue to smoke."[6] Some smokers may simply attempt to alter their route of nicotine intake from inhaling to oral by substituting snuff for cigarettes; however, there is still a modest association between the use of snuff and cardiovascular disease.[7] The best advice to reduce your risk of heart disease is to quit smoking now. The sooner you stop smoking the greater the impact you will have on your life expectancy.

SOCIAL FACTORS

> *The surest sign of age is loneliness.*
> *Amos Bronson Alcott , Social Reformer (1799-1888)*

Although genetics and lifestyle have the greatest impact on life expectancy, it may also be affected by social factors. Many studies have shown those who are socially isolated have death rates two to five times higher than those who

10. Blanco-Cedres L, Daviglus ML, Garside DB, Liu K, Pirzada, A., Stamler, J., Greenland, P. "Relation of cigarette smoking to 25-year mortality in middle-aged men with low baseline serum cholesterol: the Chicago Heart Association Detection Project in Industry." Am J Epidemiol Feb 15; 155(4) 2002. p. 354-60.
1. Mamun, A.A., et al. "NEDCOM, The Netherlands Epidermiology and Demography Compression of Morbidity Research Group. Smoking decreases the duration of life lived with and without cardiovascular disease: a life course analysis of the Framingham Heart Study." Eur Heart J Mar; 25(5) 2004. p. 409-15.
2. Doll, R., et al. "Mortality in relation to smoking: 50 years' observation on male British doctors." BMJ 328 2004. p. 1519-33.
3. Taylor, D.H. Jr, et al. "Benefits of smoking cessation for longevity." Am J Public Health Jun; 92(6) 2002. p. 990-96.
4. Twardella, D., et al. "Short-term benefit of smoking cessation in patients with coronary heart disease: estimates based on self-reported smoking data and serum cotinine measurements." Eur Heart J Dec; 25(23) 2004. p. 2101-08.
5. Critchley, J., Capewell, S. "Smoking cessation for the secondary prevention of coronary heart disease." Cochrane Database Syst Rev vol 1 2004. p. CD003041. Nusselder, W.J., et al. "Smoking and the compression of morbidity." J Epidemiol Community Health Aug; 54(8) 2000. p. 566-74.
6. Diverse Populations Collaboration. "Smoking, body weight, and CHD mortality in diverse populations." Prev Med Jun; 38(6) 2004. p. 834-40.
7. Asplund, K. "Smokeless tobacco and cardiovascular disease." Prog Cardiovasc Dis Mar-Apr; 45(5) 2003. p. 383-94. Critchley, J.A., Unal, B. "Is smokeless tobacco a risk factor for coronary heart disease? A systematic review of epidemiological studies." Eur J Cardiovasc Prev Rehabil Apr; 11(2) 2004. p. 101-12.

maintain close ties to friends, family, and community.[1] In a study of positive health practices, eight predictors (loneliness, social support, perceived health status, self-efficacy, future time perspective, self-esteem, hope, and depression) had moderate effect on health. Six other factors (stress, education, marital status, age, income, and sex) had smaller but significant impacts on health and mortality.[2] The famous Alameda County study found the more social contacts people have, the lower their mortality rates.[3] Men with the least social contacts were more than twice as likely to die as those with lots of contacts. For women, social isolation tripled their risk of dying. These findings were reaffirmed by a later study.[4]

Multiple studies have shown married people live longer than those who are unmarried. The protective effect of marriage is astounding.[5] Studies suggest the benefits of marriage are so large it may actually be equal to the benefit from giving up smoking.[6] The association between widowhood[7] and increased mortality and morbidity[8] has been well established.[9] Initially it was believed that the widows' premature deaths were the result of decreased incomes and economic factors. A 2004 British study claims to have debunked this idea. The authors concluded the death of the spouse appears to increase the surviving partner's stress to dangerous levels, resulting in their premature demise; they literally grieve themselves to death.[10] Industrialized nations have social programs in place allowing access to basic medical care, shelter and nutrition. With the implementation of these social programs, differences between high and low income appear to have little if any impact in longevity.[11]

1. Berkman, L.F., Glass, T, et al. Social Integration, Social Networks, Social Support, And Health,; In Social Epidemiology, Ed. L.f. Berkman And I. Kawachi. New York: Oxford University Press, 2000. Stek, M.L., et al. "Is depression in old age fatal only when people feel lonely?" Am J Psychiatry Jan; 162(1) 2005. p. 178-80.
2. Yarcheski, A., et al. "A meta-analysis of predictors of positive health practices." J Nurs Scholarsh vol 36(2) 2004. p. 102-08.
3. Berkman, L., Syme, S.L. "Social networks, host resistance, and mortality: A nine-year follow-up study of Alameda County residents." American Journal of Epidemiology 109(2) 1979. p. 186-204.
4. Hanson, B. Ostergren: Social network, sodal support and related concepts—Towards a model for epidemiological use. In S.O. Isacsson (Ed.), Social support in health and disease (pp. 168-78). Stockholm: Almqvist & Wiksell Int, 1986.
5. Mete, C. "Predictors of Elderly Mortality: Health Status, Socioeconomic Characteristics and Social Determinants of Health." Health Economics vol 14 2005. p. 135-148. Robles, T.F., Kiecolt-Glaser, J.K. "The physiology of marriage: pathways to health." Physiol Behav Aug; 79(3) 2003. p. 409-16.
6. Gardner, J., Oswald, A. "How is Mortality Affected by Money, Marriage and Stress?" Journal of Health Economics vol 23 2004. p. 1181-07. Wilson CM and Oswald AJ. How Does Marriage Affect Physical and Psychological Health? A Survey of the Longitudinal Evidence. http://www2.warwick.ac.uk/fac/soc/economics/research/papers/twerp728.pdf
7. Lichtenstein, P., Gatz, M., Berg, S. "A twin study of mortality after spousal bereavement." Psychol Med. 1998 May; 28(3): May; 28(3) 1998. p. 635-43. Manor, O., Eisenbach, Z. "Mortality after spousal loss: are there socio-demographic differences?" Soc Sci Med Jan; 56(2) 2003. p. 405-13.
8. Martikainen, P., Valkonen, T. "Mortality after the death of a spouse: rates and causes of death in a large Finnish cohort." Am J Public Health Aug; 86(8 Pt 1) 1996. p. 1087-93.
9. Christakis NA, Allison PD. "Mortality after the hospitalization of a spouse." NEJM Feb 16; 354(7) 2006. p. 719-30. Rees, W.P., Lutkins, S.G. "Mortality of bereavement." BMJ vol 4 1967. p. 13-16.
10. Gardner, J., Oswald, A. "How is mortality affected by money, marriage, and stress?" J Health Econ Nov; 23(6) 2004. p. 1181-207.

Studies of widowed men and divorced men found they also have nearly 50% higher than expected death rates.[1] These findings have been reaffirmed in a study of men who have never married. The authors found a 50% increased risk of death from heart disease and an 80% increase in non-heart disease deaths in men who never married. Widowed men had 2.4 times the risk of non-heart disease death. Men who divorced nearly doubled their risk of cardiac related death and quadruple the risk of non-cardiac death.[2] Incredibly, a Danish study concluded the number of years divorced was directly proportional to life years lost.[3]

11. Hattersley, L. "Trends in life expectancy by social class-an update." Health Stat Q Summer 1999. p. 16-24.
1. Ben-Shlomo, Y., et al. "Magnitude and Causes of Mortality Differences Between Married and Unmarried Men." Journal of Epidemiology and Community Health vol 47 1993. p. 200-05.
2. Ebrahim, S., et al. "Marital status, change in marital status, and mortality in middle-aged British men." Am J Epidemiol Oct 15; 142(8) 1995. p. 834-42.
3. Lund R., Holstein, B.E., Osler, M. "Marital History From Age 15 to 40 Years and Subsequent 10-Year Mortality: A Longitudinal Study of Danish Males Born in 1953." International Journal of Epidemiology vol 33 2004. p. 389-97.

Chapter 11. Stressed to Kill

Risk Factors

> *Vices are their own punishment.*
> *Aesop, Greek fabulist (620 BC-560 BC)*

Recent studies suggest heart attacks and sudden cardiac deaths do not occur randomly but are caused by daily activities and emotional stress.[1] Sudden cardiac death (SCD) is usually defined as death from a cardiac cause within one hour of the onset of symptoms in people without previously known heart disease. It is the most common cause of cardiac death and is responsible for approximately 50% of the mortality from cardiovascular disease.[2] A 2001 study of cardiac related deaths determined there were 719,456 cardiac deaths among adults over the age of 35 years in 1998; 456,076 (63%) were determined to be SCD. Nearly three-fourths of all cardiac deaths that occurred for those aged 35 to 44 were considered SCD. Autopsies revealed 62% of these sudden deaths could be attributed to undiagnosed heart disease.[3]

There is an ever growing body of literature showing psychosocial factors have the greatest influence over life expectancy.[4] Currently, it is thought psychosocial variables may exert their influence on health by regulating the immune system.[5] Intense emotions may act as triggers for acute myocardial

---

1. Kurita, A., Takase, B., Ishizuka, T. "Disaster and cardiac disease." Anadolu Kardiyol Derg Jun; 1(2) 2001. p. 101-06.
2. Zipes, D.P., Wellens, H.J. "Sudden cardiac death." Circulation vol 98 1998. p. 2334-51.
3. Zheng, Z.J., et al. "Sudden cardiac death in the United States, 1989 to 1998." Circulation Oct 30; 104(18) 2001. p. 2158-63.
4. Marmot, M. "Epidemiology of socioeconomic status and health: are determinants within countries the same as between countries?" Annals of the New York Academy of Sciences vol 896 1999. p. 16-29. Ostrove, J., Adler, N.E. "Socioeconomic status and health." Current Opinion in Psychiatry vol 11 1998. p. 649-53.

infarction. This may explain why traditional risk factors[1] account for only half of all heart attacks.[2] Some proponents of traditional risk factors (elevated cholesterol, smoking, hypertension and obesity) believe these factors are responsible for greater than 75% of all cardiac related deaths.[3] These apologists refer to a 2003 study which purportedly rebukes the long held belief that traditional risk factors accounted for only 50% of all cardiac deaths. This study concluded major risk factors were very common among those who developed heart disease.[4] Other studies reported 80% to 90% of patients with CHD had at least one of the four traditional risk factors.[5] The authors of these studies conclude only one risk factor is required to cause 90% of all cardiac related deaths.[6] These assertions are strongly refuted by others who believe each risk factor incrementally increases the likelihood of a heart attack.[7] A 2005 study concluded that those with only borderline elevations in multiple risk factors had only a small risk of having a heart attack.[8] The ten year cardiac risk assessment scale developed by the Framingham study simply adds separate risk factors together to predict the overall probability of having a cardiac event during a ten year period.[9] It is not implausible that both groups may be wrong.

The MONICA Project, a global cardiac study conducted by the World Health Organization (WHO), failed to find any correlation between heart attacks and the classic risk factors, such as smoking and high cholesterol levels.[10] Although the WHO's press release clearly emphasized the results were unexpected[11], they seemed aghast at the reception it received by the media.[12]

5. Ader, R., Cohen, N. "Psychoneuroimmunology: conditioning and stress." Annual Review of Psychology vol 44 1993. p. 53-85. Maier, S.F., Watkins, L.R. "Cytokines for psychologists: implications of bidirectional immune-to-brain communication for understanding behavior, mood, and cognition." Psychological Review vol 105 1998. p. 83-107.
1. Mosca, L. "Novel Cardiovascular Risk Factors: Do They Add Value to Your Practice?" American Family Physician Jan 15; 67(2) 2003. p. 264, 266.
2. Connelly, K.A., MacIsaac, A.I., Jelinek, V.M. "Stress, myocardial infarction, and the "tako-tsubo" phenomenon." Heart Sep; 90(9) 2004. p. e52. Oliveira, G.H. "Novel serologic markers of cardiovascular risk." Curr Atheroscler Rep Mar; 7(2) 2005. p. 148-54.
3. Beaglehole, R., Magnus, P. "The search for new risk factors for coronary heart disease: occupational therapy for epidemiologists?" Int J Epidemiol Dec; 31(6) 2002. p. 1117-22. Magnus, P., Beaglehole. R. "The real contribution of the major risk factors to the coronary epidemics: time to end the "only-50%" myth." Arch Intern Med Dec 10-24; 161(22) 2001. p. 2657-60.
4. Greenland, P., et al. "Major risk factors as antecedents of fatal and nonfatal coronary heart disease events." JAMA Aug 20; 290(7) 2003. p. 891-97.
5. Greenland, P., et al. "Major risk factors as antecedents of fatal and nonfatal coronary heart disease events." JAMA Aug 20; 290(7): 2003. p. 891-97. Khot, U.N. et al. "Prevalence of conventional risk factors in patients with coronary heart disease." JAMA Aug 20; 290(7) 2003. p. 898-904.
6. Canto JG, Iskandrian AE. Major risk factors for cardiovascular disease: debunking the "only 50%" myth. JAMA. 2003 Aug 20; 290(7):947-9. Von Eckardstein, A. "Is there a need for novel cardiovascular risk factors?" Nephrol Dial Transplant vol 19 2004. p. 761-65.
7. "Risk Assessment Tool for Estimating 10-year Risk of Developing Hard CHD (Myocardial Infarction and Coronary Death)." National Cholesterol Education Program 2006 <http://hp2010.nhlbihin.net/atpiii/calculator.asp?usertype=prof>.
8. Vasan, R.S., et al. "Relative importance of borderline and elevated levels of coronary heart disease risk factors." Ann Intern Med Mar 15; 142(6) 2005. p. 393-402.
9. Knuiman, M.W., Vu, H.T., Bartholomew, H.C. "Multivariate risk estimation for coronary heart disease: the Busselton Health Study." Aust N Z J Public Health Dec; 22(7) 1998. p. 747-53.
10. Irwin, A. "Study casts doubt on heart 'risk factors'." International News 25 Aug 1998.

Their press release stated "changing rates of coronary heart disease in different populations did not appear to relate at all well to the change in the standard risk factors, considered one by one, or in a risk factor score." Their attempts to minimize the impact or their own words resonates of double speak. They were engaging in damage control over data that conflicts with the current medical dogma.[1]

The MONICA study and subsequent reports exposes a major flaw in the treatment of the leading cause of death; its central tenet may be wrong.[2] The four major risk factors may actually have little impact on heart disease. The MONICA Project and other epidemiological studies have repeatedly shown a poor correlation between traditional risk factors[3] and the incidence of heart disease.[4] Numerous studies have shown the "correlation" between risk factors and heart disease to be fallacious even in the presence of excessive risk factors. The following graph compares mortality rates between different countries at the same cholesterol level. It shows major variations between cardiac mortality rates at all levels. The mortality of those living in Northern Europe with total cholesterol exceeding 5.2 mmol (200 mg/dl) is five times higher than those living in Mediterranean Southern Europe.[5]

A 2003 European study concluded smoking and diabetes more than doubled the risk of total, cardiovascular (CVD) and coronary heart disease (CHD) death. They failed to find any correlation between obesity, low education, hypertension, elevated total cholesterol or low HDL cholesterol and cardiac events.[6]

One provocative study of liver transplant recipients showed these patients have a high prevalence of risk factors for cardiovascular disease, exceeding that of the general population, with a predicted higher risk of developing CHD. Despite this, the investigators failed to document any deaths from CHD or stroke during their study.[7]

---

11. "World's largest and longest heart study produces some surprises." WHO MONICA Project. 1998. 28 Aug 1998 ‹http://www.ktl.fi/monica/public/vienna/press_release.htm›.
12. Tunstall-Pedoe, H. "Did MONICA really say that?" BMJ vol 317 1998. p. 1023.
1. Laurance, J. "MONICA did not deliver on task it set out to accomplish." BMJ vol 318 1999. p. 732.
2. Ravnskov, U. "A hypothesis out-of-date. the diet-heart idea." J Clin Epidemiol Nov; 55(11) 2002. p. 1057-63.
3. Ferrieres, J. "The French paradox: lessons for other countries." Heart Jan; 90(1) 2004. p. 107-11.
4. Kuulasmaa, K., et al. "Estimation of contribution of changes in classic risk factors to trends in coronary-event rates across the WHO MONICA Project populations." Lancet Feb 26; 355(9205) 2000. p. 675-87. Masiá, R., et al. "High prevalence of cardiovascular risk factors in Gerona, Spain, a province with low myocardial infarction incidence." J Epidemiol Community Health vol 52 1998. p. 707-15.
5. Kromhout, D. "On the waves of the Seven Countries Study." European Heart Journal vol 20 1999. p. 796-802.
6. De Bacquer, D., et al. "EUROASPIRE I Study Group. Predictive value of classical risk factors and their control in coronary patients: a follow-up of the EUROASPIRE I cohort." Eur J Cardiovasc Prev Rehabil Aug; 10(4) 2003. p. 289-95.
7. Neal, D.A., et al. "Is there disparity between risk and incidence of cardiovascular disease after liver transplant?" Transplantation Jan 15; 77(1) 2004. p. 93-99.

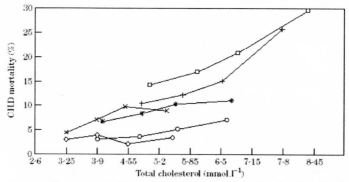

25-year coronary heart disease mortality rates to baseline cholesterol quartile, adjusted for age, smoking and blood pressure. □——□= Northern Europe; +······+ = U.S.A.; ×——× = Serbia; *——* = Inland Southern Europe; ◇——◇ = Japan; O——O = Mediterranean Southern Europe.

Source: Kromhout D. On the waves of the Seven Countries Study European Heart Journal (1999) 20, 796–802

The Framingham risk assessment scale is generally not very accurate[1] in predicting ten year cardiac outcomes.[2] Multiple studies have shown it either overestimates[3] or underestimates[4] the risks in different ethnic or economic groups.[5]

The importance of coronary heart disease risk factors may also differ among individuals, communities, and by sex or age.[6] Researchers have sought to rescue this paradigm by suggesting modifying[7] or competing factors may explain the

1. Diverse Populations Collaborative Group. "Prediction of mortality from coronary heart disease among diverse populations: is there a common predictive function?" Heart Sep; 88(3) 2002. p. 222-28. Reissigova, J., Tomeckova, M. "State of the art coronary heart disease risk estimations based on the Framingham heart study." Cent Eur J Public Health Dec; 13(4) 2005. p. 180-86.
2. Lloyd-Jones, D.M., et al. "Framingham risk score and prediction of lifetime risk for coronary heart disease." Am J Cardiol Jul 1; 94(1) 2004. p. 20-24. Phillips, G.B., Pinkernell, B.H., Jing, T.Y. "Are major risk factors for myocardial infarction the major predictors of degree of coronary artery disease in men?" Metabolism Mar; 53(3) 2004. p. 324-29.
3. Hense, H.W., et al. "Framingham risk function overestimates risk of coronary heart disease in men and women from Germany—results from the MONICA Augsburg and the PROCAM cohorts." Eur Heart J May; 24(10) 2003. p. 937-45. Masiá, R., et al. "High prevalence of cardiovascular risk factors in Gerona, Spain, a province with low myocardial infarction incidence." J Epidemiol Community Health vol 52 1998. p. 707-15.
4. Brindle, P.M., et al. "The accuracy of the Framingham risk-score in different socioeconomic groups: a prospective study." Br J Gen Pract. 2005 Nov; 55(520) 2005. p. 838-45. Michos ED, Nasir K, Braunstein JB, Rumberger JA, Budoff MJ, Post WS, Blumenthal RS.. 2005 May 19. "Framingham risk equation underestimates subclinical atherosclerosis risk in asymptomatic women." Atherosclerosis Jan; 184(1) 2005. p. 201-06.
5. Brindle, P., et al. "Predictive accuracy of the Framingham coronary risk score in British men: prospective cohort study." BMJ Nov 29; 327(7426) 2003. p. 1267. Liao, Y., et al. "How generalizable are coronary risk prediction models? Comparison of Framingham and two national cohorts." Am Heart J May; 137(5) 1999. p. 837-45.
6. Empana, J.P., et al. "Are the Framingham and PROCAM coronary heart disease risk functions applicable to different European populations? The PRIME Study.." Eur Heart J Nov; 24(21) 2003. p. 1903-11. Schnohr, P., et al. "Coronary heart disease risk factors ranked by importance for the individual and community. A 21 year follow-up of 12 000 men and women from The Copenhagen City Heart Study." Eur Heart J Apr; 23(8) 2002. p. 620-06.

perceived discrepancies.[1] Their rationalization has become an impediment to understanding the actual causes of heart disease. One esteemed critic complains their slipshod commercialized research has "sullied the scientific integrity of medicine as a whole."[2]

WORRY

> *Who of you by worrying can add a single hour to his life? Since you can not*
> *do this very little thing, why do you worry about the rest?*
> Luke 12:25-26

Many now believe stress and psychosocial factors are the real culprits behind most heart disease.[3] The direct evidence that psychosocial stressors actually cause heart disease remains inconclusive. However, there are multiple studies suggesting stress[4] plays a primary role in cardiac related death[5], especially in persons with coronary heart disease.[6] A 2003 study actually estimates the increased risk associated from psychosocial factors is at least equal to smoking, high cholesterol and hypertension.[7] These stressful emotions may act as triggers for heart attacks or sudden cardiac death, especially in susceptible individuals. Many triggers operate within one to two hours of symptom onset.[8]

Emotional stress has been well established as a trigger of sudden death[9] even in patients with apparently normal hearts.[10] Multiple studies have shown

7. Menotti, A., et al. "Comparison of multivariate predictive power of major risk factors for coronary heart diseases in different countries: results from eight nations of the Seven Countries Study, 25-year follow-up." J Cardiovasc Risk Feb; 3(1) 1996. p. 69-75.
1. Roeters van Lennep, J.E., et al. "Risk factors for coronary heart disease: implications of gender." Cardiovasc Res Feb 15; 53(3) 2002. p. 538-49. Wilson, P.W. "Assessing coronary heart disease risk with traditional and novel risk factors." Clin Cardiol Jun; 27(6 Suppl 3) 2004. p. III7-11.
2. Stehbens, W.E. "Epidemiological risk factors of coronary heart disease are not causal in athero-sclerosis." Clin Exp Hypertens May; 22(4) 2000. p. 445-53.
3. Rozanski, A., Blumenthal, J.A., Kaplan, J. "Impact of psychological factors on the pathogenesis of cardiovascular disease and implications for therapy." Circulation Apr 27; 99(16) 1999. p. 2192-217.
4. Frank, C., Smith, S. "Stress and the heart: biobehavioral aspects of sudden cardiac death." Psycho-somatics Summer; 31(3) 1990. p. 255-64.
5. Kamarck, T., Jennings, J.R. "Biobehavioral factors in sudden cardiac death." Psychol Bull Jan; 109(1) 1991. p. 42-75. Strike, P.C., Steptoe, A. "Behavioral and emotional triggers of acute coronary syndromes: a systematic review and critique." Psychosom Med Mar-Apr; 67(2) 2005. p. 179-86.
6. Owada, M., et al. "Risk factors and triggers of sudden death in the working generation: an autopsy proven case-control study." Tohoku J Exp Med Dec; 189(4) 1999. p. 245-58. Ramachandruni, S., Handberg, E., Sheps, D.S. "Acute and chronic psychological stress in coronary disease." Curr Opin Cardiol Sep; 19(5) 2004. p. 494-99.
7. Bunker, S.J., et al. "'Stress' and coronary heart disease: psychosocial risk factors." Med J Aust Mar 17; 178(6) 2003. p. 272-76.
8. Strike, P.C., Steptoe, A. "Behavioral and emotional triggers of acute coronary syndromes: a system-atic review and critique." Psychosom Med Mar-Apr; 67(2) 2005. p. 179-86.
9. Lane, R.D., et al. "Psychological stress preceding idiopathic ventricular fibrillation." Psychosom Med May-Jun; 67(3) 2005. p. 359-65.
10. Ramachandruni, S., Handberg, E., Sheps, D.S. "Acute and chronic psychological stress in coronary disease." Curr Opin Cardiol Sep; 19(5) 2004. p. 494-99. Todaro, J.F., Shen, B.J., Niaura, R., Spiro, A. 3rd, Ward, K.D. "Effect of negative emotions on frequency of coronary heart disease (The Normative Aging Study)." Am J Cardiol Oct 15; 92(8) 2003. p. 901-06.

negative emotions[1] may increase your risk of heart disease and death.[2] Fear[3], superstition[4], and anxiety[5] may actually cause you to "worry yourself to death."[6] Men appear to be more susceptible to these deleterious effects than women.[7] Research shows that stereotypical Type A personality[8] persons actually have increased cardiac risks[9] which may nearly triple their likelihood of a cardiac event or death.[10] However, the hyperactive, aggressive, overachieving Type A personality fairs better than the negative, brooding type. This personality type has been labeled as Type D (distressed). This personality trait may increase the risk for heart disease and death by as much as ninefold and is additive to traditional cardiac risk factors.[11]

Although the above findings suggest a causal connection between negative emotions and CHD, they may also suggest simply that negative emotions and CHD often coexist.[12] Recent studies, however, suggest neurohormonal changes may literally be at the heart of the matter. Excess levels of stress hormones called catecholamines may be responsible for "stunning" the heart.[13] These hormones may produce vasospasms or constrictions of coronary arteries[14] resulting in

1. Denollet, J. "Emotional distress and fatigue in coronary heart disease: the Global Mood Scale (GMS)." Psychol Med Feb; 23(1) 1993. p. 111-21. Januzzi,JL, Stern,TA, Pasternak,RC and DeSanctis, RW s of Patients With Coronary Artery Disease. "The Influence of Anxiety and Depression on Outcomes of Patients With Coronary Artery Disease." Arch Intern Med 160 2000. p. 1913-21.
2. Scheier, M.F., Bridges, M.W. "Person variables and health: personality predispositions and acute psychological states as shared determinants for disease." Psychosom Med vol 57 1995. p. 255-68. Suinn, R.M. "The terrible twos—anger and anxiety. Hazardous to your health." Am Psychol Jan; 56(1) 2001. p. 27-36.
3. Pashkow, F.J. "Is stress linked to heart disease? The evidence grows stronger." Cleve Clin J Med Feb; 66(2) 1999. p. 75-77.
4. Phillips, D.P., et al. "The Hound of the Baskervilles effect: natural experiment on the influence of psychological stress on timing of death." BMJ Dec 22-29; 323(7327) 2001. p. 1443-46.
5. Krantz, D.S., Quigley, J.F., O'Callahan, M. "Mental stress as a trigger of acute cardiac events: the role of laboratory studies." Ital Heart J Dec; 2(12) 2001. p. 895-99.
6. Watkins, L.L., Blumenthal, J.A. "Worried to death?" Circulation vol 100 1999. p. 1251.
7. Weidner, G. "Why do men get more heart disease than women? An international perspective." J Am Coll Health May; 48(6) 2000. p. 291-94.
8. Gallacher, J.E., et al. "Is type A behavior really a trigger for coronary heart disease events?" Psychosom Med May-Jun; 65(3) 2003. p. 339-46. Kawachi, I., et al. "Prospective study of a self-report type A scale and risk of coronary heart disease: test of the MMPI-2 type A scale." Circulation Aug 4; 98(5) 1998. p. 405-12.
9. Sprafka, J.M., et al. "Type A behavior and its association with cardiovascular disease prevalence in blacks and whites: the Minnesota Heart Survey." J Behav Med Feb; 13(1) 1990. p. 1-13.
10. Madigan, M.F., Jr, Dale, J.A., Cross, J.D. "No respite during sleep: heart-rate hyperreactivity to rapid eye movement sleep in angry men classified as Type A." Percept Mot Skills Dec; 85(3 Pt 2) 1997. p. 1451-54. Munakata, M., et al. "Type A behavior is associated with an increased risk of left ventricular hypertrophy in male patients with essential hypertension." J Hypertens Jan; 17(1) 1999. p. 115-20.
11. Denollet, J. "Type D personality. A potential risk factor refined." J Psychosom Res Oct; 49(4) 2000. p. 255-66. Pedersen, S.S., Denollet, J. "Type D personality, cardiac events, and impaired quality of life: a review." Eur J Cardiovasc Prev Rehabil Aug; 10(4) 2003. p. 241-48.
12. Smith, D.F. "Negative emotions and coronary heart disease: causally related or merely coexistent? A review." Scand J Psychol Feb; 42(1) 2001. p. 57-69.
13. Wittstein, I.S., et al. "Neurohumoral features of myocardial stunning due to sudden emotional stress." NEJM Feb 10; 352(6) 2005. p. 539-48.
14. Rozanski, A., Blumenthal, J.A., Kaplan, J. "Impact of psychological factors on the pathogenesis of cardiovascular disease and implications for therapy." Circulation vol 99 1999. p. 2192-217.

blockages and death.[1] Negative thoughts can more than double the risk of myocardial ischemia in the subsequent hour[2] and increase the incidence of ECG abnormalities.[3]

WORK RELATED STRESS

> *And the LORD said, I have surely seen the affliction of my people which are in Egypt, and have heard their cry by reason of their taskmasters; for I know their sorrows.*
> Exodus 3:7

Stressful conditions are often commonplace within the work environment.[4] Studies have shown even the anticipation of work[5] increases the frequency of heart attacks as much as 33%.[6] Men with high demands at work and low job control may more than double their risk of cardiovascular death.[7] Curiously, employed women with high demands-low control jobs actually have a lower risk of mortality than their homemaker counterparts.[8] However, contrary to expectation, female executives with high demands-high control jobs nearly triple their risk for cardiac disease.[9] Blue-collar men are especially at risk for cardiovascular events.[10] Multiple studies have shown blue-collar workers may increase their cardiac disease by 50% as compared to those in white-collar occupations.[11]

1. Sheps, D.S., et al. "Mental stress-induced ischemia and all-cause mortality in patients with coronary artery disease: Results from the Psychophysiological Investigations of Myocardial Ischemia study." Circulation Apr 16; 105(15) 2002. p. 1780-84. Sloan, R.P., et al. "Socioeconomic status and health: is parasympathetic nervous system activity an intervening mechanism?" Int J Epidemiol Apr; 34(2) 2005. p. 309-15.
2. Gullette, E.C. "Effects of mental stress on myocardial ischemia during daily life." JAMA May 21; 277(19) 1997. p. 1521-26.
3. Stansfeld, S.A., et al. "Psychological distress as a risk factor for coronary heart disease in the Whitehall II Study." Int J Epidemiol vol 31 2002. p. 248-55.
4. Peter, R., et al. "High effort, low reward, and cardiovascular risk factors in employed Swedish men and women: baseline results from the WOLF Study." J Epidemiol Community Health Sep; 52(9) 1998. p. 540-47.
5. Gruska, M., et al. "Increased occurrence of out-of-hospital cardiac arrest on Mondays in a community-based study." Chronobiol Int vol 22(1) 2005. p. 107-20. Jakovljevic, D. "Day of the week and ischemic stroke: is it Monday high or Sunday low?" Stroke Sep; 35(9) 2004. p. 2089-93.
6. Willich, S.N., et al. "Weekly variation of acute myocardial infarction. Increased Monday risk in the working population." Circulation Jul; 90(1) 1994. p. 87-93.
7. Kivimaki, M., et al. "Work stress and risk of cardiovascular mortality: prospective cohort study of industrial employees." BMJ Oct 19; 325(7369) 2002. p. 857. Tennant, C. "Work stress and coronary heart disease." J Cardiovasc Risk Aug; 7(4) 2000. p. 273-76.
8. Rose, K.M., et al. "Women's employment status and mortality: the atherosclerosis risk in communities study." J Womens Health (Larchmt) Dec; 13(10) 2004. p. 1108-18.
9. Eaker, E.D., et al. "Does job strain increase the risk for coronary heart disease or death in men and women? The Framingham Offspring Study." Am J Epidemiol May 15; 159(10) 2004. p. 950-58.
10. Siegrist, J. "Adverse health effects of high-effort/low-reward conditions." J Occup Health Psychol Jan; 1(1) 1996. p. 27-41.
11. Luepker, R.V., et al. "Socioeconomic status and coronary heart disease risk factor trends. The Minnesota Heart Survey." Circulation Nov; 88(5 Pt 1) 1993. p. 2172-79. Nordstrom, C.K., et al. "The association of personal and neighborhood socioeconomic indicators with subclinical cardiovascular disease in an elderly cohort. The cardiovascular health study." Soc Sci Med Nov; 59(10) 2004. p. 2139-47.

A 2004 study sought to determine if the increase in cardiac risks in high demand/low control jobs was associated with smaller family income. The authors concluded starting salary did not significantly affect the risk of mortality during the following decade. However, they did find a history of unemployment contributed to premature mortality.[1]

LACK OF EDUCATION

> *Poverty must not be a bar to learning and learning must offer an escape*
> *from poverty.*
> Lyndon B. Johnson. 36th US President (1908-1973)

Lack of education may actually be the primary factor for work related stress.[2] Patients with less than six years of schooling are at highest risk for in-hospital avoidable mortality, followed by those with middle levels of education (7-10 years of schooling).[3] Another study suggests those of higher educational status will remain healthy for a greater number of years while the poor will continue to experience fewer years of good health.[4] Those with the lowest levels of education between the ages of 45–64 have death rates 2.5 times higher than those with higher degrees.[5] Lower income workers have more than three times the risk of cardiac death.[6]

Failure to achieve a high school education more than doubles a woman's risk of coronary heart disease while increasing a man's risk by more than a half.[7] These discrepancies are so great, one study estimated those in the top 20% of earnings had a life expectancy of 4.3 years longer than those in the lower 80% of earnings. They were also found to have nearly six additional years of better health than lower income earners.[8] The authors state, "The income-associated burden of disease appears to be a leading cause of morbidity and mortality in the US."

1. Gardner, J., Oswald, A. "How is mortality affected by money, marriage, and stress?" J Health Econ Nov; 23(6) 2004. p. 1181-207.
2. Muller, A. "Education, income inequality, and mortality: a multiple regression analysis." BMJ Jan 5; 324(7328) 2002. p. 23-25.
3. Bautista, D., Alfonso, J.L., Corella, D., Saiz, C. "Influence of social factors on avoidable mortality: a hospital-based case-control study." Public Health Rep Jan-Feb; 120(1) 2005. p. 55-62.
4. Crimmins, E.M., Saito, Y. "Trends in healthy life expectancy in the United States, 1970-1990: gender, racial, and educational differences." Soc Sci Med Jun; 52(11) 2001. p. 1629-41.
5. McGinnis, M.J., Williams-Russo, P., Knickman, J.R. "The case for more active policy attention to health promotion. To succeed, we need leadership that informs and motivates, economic incentives that encourage change, and science that moves the frontiers." Health Aff (Millwood) Mar-Apr; 21(2) 2002. p. 78-93.
6. Lantz, P.M., et al. "Socioeconomic factors, health behaviors, and mortality: results from a nationally representative prospective study of US adults." JAMA Jun 3; 279(21) 1998. p. 1703-08.
7. Thurston, R.C., et al. "Is the Association between Socioeconomic Position and Coronary Heart Disease Stronger in Women than in Men?" Am J Epidemiol Jul 1; 162(1) 2005. p. 57-65.
8. Muennig, P., et al. "The income-associated burden of disease in the United States." Soc Sci Med Nov; 61(9) 2005. p. 2018-26.

These findings have been reiterated by foreign studies. A British researcher concluded there was an estimated 9½-year difference in life expectancy between men in the upper class and unskilled laborers; for women the differential was 6½ years.[1] A Canadian study of more than 500,000 males showed a clear gradient in mortality when sorted by income.[2] A separate British study found a similar gradient.[3]

The poor generally have multiple risk factors[4] and are less prone to engage in healthy lifestyle choices.[5] Those with feelings of hopelessness are at especially high risk for cancer, heart disease[6] and suicide.[7] Indeed, highly hopeless men have a more than three-fold increased risk of death from violence or injury compared with the general population.[8] Recent studies suggest the factors responsible for this health divide are worsening. It is expected future generations will see a greater burden on the poor while the affluent will experience increasing years of healthy living.[9] A major 2004 study concluded the poor health of low income earners was not related to access of care or lower use of medical procedures or drugs. The authors state increased access to medical care was unlikely to decrease coronary heart disease in this group.[10] Others caution these socially driven health patterns are learned at an early age; attempts to alter this learned behavior in adults may be unsuccessful.[11]

---

1. Hattersley, L. "Trends in life expectancy by social class: an update." Health Stat Q Summer 1999. p. 16-24.
2. Wolfson, M., et al. "Career earnings and death: a longitudinal analysis of older Canadian men." J Gerontol Jul; 48(4) 1993. p. S167-79.
3. Sturm, R., Gresenz, C.R. "Relations of income inequality and family income to chronic medical conditions and mental health disorders: national survey." BMJ Jan 5; 324(7328) 2002. p. 20-23.
4. Choiniere, R., Lafontaine, P., Edwards, A.C. "Distribution of cardiovascular disease risk factors by socioeconomic status among Canadian adults." CMAJ vol 162(9 Suppl) 2000. p. S13-24. Kaplan GA et al. "The health of poor women under welfare reform." Am J Public Health Jul; 95(7) 2005. p. 1252-58.
5. Reeves, M.J., Rafferty, A.P. "Healthy lifestyle characteristics among adults in the United States, 2000." Arch Intern Med Apr 25; 165(8) 2005. p. 854-57. Strand, B.H., Tverdal, A. "Can cardiovascular risk factors and lifestyle explain the educational inequalities in mortality from ischaemic heart disease and from other heart diseases? 26 year follow up of 50,000 Norwegian men and women." J Epidemiol Community Health Aug; 58(8) 2004. p. 705-09.
6. Anda, R., et al. "Depressed affect, hopelessness, and the risk of ischemic heart disease in a cohort of U.S. adults." Epidemiology Jul; 4(4) 1993. p. 285-94. Johnson, L.H., Roberts, S.L. "Hopelessness in the myocardial infarction patient." Prog Cardiovasc Nurs Spring; 11(2) 1996. p. 19-32.
7. Stern, S.L., Dhanda, R., Hazuda, H.P. "Hopelessness predicts mortality in older Mexican and European Americans." Psychosom Med May-Jun; 63(3) 2001. p. 344-51.
8. Everson, S.A., et al. "Hopelessness and risk of mortality and incidence of myocardial infarction and cancer." Psychosom Med Mar-Apr; 58(2) 1996. p. 113-21.
9. Wilkinson, R., Marmot, M. "Social determinants of health. The solid facts." World Health Organization. 2005. 08 Jul 2005 ⟨http://www.euro.who.int/document/e81384.pdf⟩.
10. Britton, A., et al. "Does access to cardiac investigation and treatment contribute to social and ethnic differences in coronary heart disease? Whitehall II prospective cohort study." BMJ Aug 7; 329(7461) 2004. p. 318.
11. Brunner, E., et al. "When does cardiovascular risk start? Past and present socioeconomic circumstances and risk factors in adulthood." J Epidemiol Community Health Dec; 53(12) 1999. p. 757-64. Egeland, G.M., et al. "A man's heart and a wife's education: a 12-year coronary heart disease mortality follow-up in Norwegian men." Int J Epidemiol Aug; 31(4) 2002. p. 799-805.

ENVIRONMENTAL STRESSORS

> *We live in the midst of alarms; anxiety beclouds the future; we expect some*
> *new disaster with each newspaper we read.*
> *Abraham Lincoln 1809-1865, 16th US President*

Environmental stressors may be just as hazardous to your health as social interaction.[1] Earthquakes may increase the rates of heart attacks by three[2] to five times[3] the number that would ordinarily be expected.[4] Several studies have shown an association between noise exposure and cardiovascular disease. [5] Researchers theorize loud unexpected noises may induce the release of stress hormones.[6] These noises are especially harmful during sleep. They may be perceived as danger signals[7] and trigger the release of stress hormones.[8] A 2004 study shocked many within the medical community with their findings that exposure to traffic tripled the risk of a heart attack within one hour afterward. They were able to demonstrate a consistent linkage between the amounts of time spent in cars, on public transportation, or on motorcycles with the onset of a myocardial infarction one hour later.[9]

SEASONAL & DIURNAL STRESSORS

> *Do you know the terror of he who falls asleep? To the very toes he is*
> *terrified, because the ground gives way under him, and the dream begins.*
> *Friedrich Nietzsche. German Philosopher (1844-1900)*

Medical workers are very familiar with the seasonal and diurnal (cyclical on a daily basis) nature of heart attacks.[10] Studies demonstrate more heart attacks occur nationwide during winter[11] than any other season.[12]

---

1. Kloner, R.A., Leor, J. "Natural disaster plus wake-up time: a deadly combination of triggers." Am Heart J May; 137(5) 1999. p. 779-81. Willich, S.N., Klatt, S., Arntz, H.R. "Circadian variation and triggers of acute coronary syndromes." Eur Heart J Apr; 19 Suppl C 1998. p. C12-23.
2. Kario, K., McEwen, B.S., Pickering, T.G. "Disasters and the heart: a review of the effects of earth-quake-induced stress on cardiovascular disease." Hypertens Res May; 26(5) 2003. p. 355-67.
3. Leor, J., Poole, W.K., Kloner, R.A. "Sudden cardiac death triggered by an earthquake." NEJM Feb 15; 334(7) 1996. p. 413-19. Muller, J.E., Verrier, R.L. "Triggering of sudden death: lessons from an earthquake." NEJM vol 334 1996. p. 460-61.
4. Stalnikowicz, R., Tsafrir, A. "Acute psychosocial stress and cardiovascular events." Am J Emerg Med Sep; 20(5) 2002. p. 488-91.
5. Babisch, W., et al. "Traffic noise and risk of myocardial infarction." Epidemiology Jan; 16(1) 2005. p. 33-40.
6. Bigert, C., Bluhm, G., Theorell, T. "Saliva cortisol—a new approach in noise research to study stress effects." Int J Hyg Environ Health vol 208(3) 2005. p. 227-30. Spreng, M. "Noise induced nocturnal cortisol secretion and tolerable overhead flights." Noise Health Jan-Mar; 6(22) 2004. p. 35-47.
7. Babisch, W. "The Noise/Stress Concept, Risk Assessment and Research Needs." Noise Health vol 4(16) 2002. p. 1-11. Babisch, W. "Stress hormones in the research on cardiovascular effects of noise." Noise Health Jan-Mar; 5(18) 2003. p. 1-11.
8. Ising, H., Kruppa, B. "Health effects caused by noise: evidence in the literature from the past 25 years." Noise Health Jan-Mar; 6(22) 2004. p. 5-13.
9. Peters, A., et al. "Exposure to traffic and the onset of myocardial infarction." NEJM Oct 21; 351(17) 2004. p. 1721-30.

The risk of heart attack may increase by 30%[1] or more from 6 to 9 AM than during other times of the day.[2] The increase frequency of heart attacks after awakening suggests they may be triggered by neurohormonal changes.[3] Folklore abounds with accounts of "being scared to death by a dream."[4] Recent medical research has found this may be more factual than mythical. Several studies have shown an association between vivid, frightening dreams[5] and the onset of a heart attack.[6]

The linkage between frightening dreams and sudden cardiac death suggests negative thoughts may produce a cardiac event.[7] Although short term stressors significantly increase the risk these cardiac events, they pale in comparison to the detrimental effects of chronic negative thoughts. Multiple studies have documented a near causal relationship between chronic depression and increased rates of heart attacks and cardiac events.[8]

In healthy individuals, depression increases the risk of heart disease between 1.5 and 2.0 times; whereas, in those with existing heart disease the risk may be increased 2.5[9] to 4.5[10] times. Depression is commonly seen in those with heart disease. Estimates suggest it may occur in nearly one fifth of those with cardiovascular disease.[11] A 2003 British study concluded despite advances in medical therapy, depression is an important independent predictor of death in

10. Franklin, B.A., et al. "Snow shoveling: a trigger for acute myocardial infarction and sudden coronary death." Am J Cardiol Apr 15; 77(10) 1996. p. 855-58.
11. Arntz, H.R., Muller-Nordhorn, J., Willich, S.N. "Cold Monday mornings prove dangerous: epidemiology of sudden cardiac death." Curr Opin Crit Care Jun; 7(3) 2001. p. 139-44.
12. Spencer, F.A., et al. "Seasonal distribution of acute myocardial infarction in the Second National Registry of Myocardial Infarction." J Am Coll Cardiol vol 31 1998. p. 1226-33. Zipes, D. "Warning: The short days of winter may be hazardous to your health." Circulation vol 100 1999. p. 1590-1592.
1. Cohen, M.C., et al. "Meta-analysis of the morning excess of acute myocardial infarction and sudden cardiac death." Am J Cardiol Jun 1; 79(11) 1997. p. 1512-16.
2. D'Avila, A., et al. "At what time are implantable defibrillator shocks delivered? Evidence for individual circadian variance in sudden cardiac death." Eur Heart J Sep; 16(9) 1995. p. 1231-33. Elliott, W.J. "Cyclic and circadian variations in cardiovascular events." Am J Hypertens vol 14 2001. p. 291-95.
3. Willich, S.N., et al. "Sudden cardiac death. Support for a role of triggering in causation." Circulation May; 87(5) 1993. p. 1442-50.
4. Cheng, T.O. "Scared to Death." Circulation vol 102 2000. p. e98. Watkins, L.L., Blumenthal, J.A. "Worried to death?" Circulation vol 100 1999. p. 1251.
5. Lavery, C.E., et al. "Nonuniform Nighttime Distribution of Acute Cardiac Events." Circulation vol 96 1997. p. 3321-27. Lecomte, D., Fornes, P., Nicolas, G. "Stressful events as a trigger of sudden death: a study of 43 medico-legal autopsy cases." Forensic Sci Int May 17; 79(1) 1996. p. 1-10.
6. Parmar, M.S., Luque-Coqui, A.F. "Killer dreams." Can J Cardiol Nov; 14(11) 1998. p. 1389-91.
7. Asplund, R., Aberg, H.E. "Nightmares, cardiac symptoms and the menopause." Climacteric Dec; 6(4) 2003. p. 314-20. Verrier, R.L., Muller, J.E., Hobson, J.A. "Sleep, dreams, and sudden death: the case for sleep as an autonomic stress test for the heart." Cardiovasc Res Feb; 31(2) 1996. p. 181-211.
8. Frasure-Smith N, Lespérance F, Talajic M. Depression and 18 month prognosis after myocardial infarction. Circulation 1995; 91:999-1005 Ladwig, K.H., et al. "Post-infarction depression and incomplete recovery 6 months after acute myocardial infarction." Lancet vol 343 1994. p. 20-23.
9. Lett, H.S., et al. "Depression as a risk factor for coronary artery disease: evidence, mechanisms, and treatment." Psychosom Med May-Jun; 66(3) 2004. p. 305-15.
10. Sheps, D.S., Sheffield, D. "Depression, anxiety, and the cardiovascular system: the cardiologist's perspective." J Clin Psychiatry vol 62 Suppl 8 2001. p. 12-16.
11. Ibid.

patients receiving coronary bypass surgery.[1] Simply treating heart disease patients with antidepressants fails to reduce cardiac event events or mortality.[2]

GRIEF

No one ever told me that grief felt so like fear.
C.S. Lewis. British novelist (1898-1963)

Researchers at Johns Hopkins discovered sudden emotional stress may produce a severe but reversible heart muscle weakness mimicking the classic heart attack.[3] They called this "broken heart" syndrome, stress cardiomyopathy. They attribute this condition to a chronic surge in adrenalin and other stress hormones. Other cultures report similar syndromes[4] but the 2005 Johns Hopkins study was the first to link it to elevated catecholamine levels. The death of a loved one may increase the risk of cardiac death by nearly one third.[5] Women, in particular, are more likely to report emotional stress prior to a heart attack.[6] These acute stressors associated with loss[7] greatly increase the risk of cardiac death[8] and the subsequent social isolation[9] further compounds these risks.[10] Several studies have shown major biochemical changes that are

1. Blumenthal, J.A., et al. "Depression as a risk factor for mortality after coronary artery bypass surgery." Lancet Aug 23; 362(9384) 2003. p. 604-09.
2. Carney, R.M.,et al. "Can treating depression reduce mortality after an acute myocardial infarction?" Psychosom Med Sep-Oct; 61(5) 1999. p. 666-75.
3. Sharkey, S.W., et al. "Acute and reversible cardiomyopathy provoked by stress in women from the United States." Circulation Feb 1; 111(4) 2005. p. 472-79. Wittstein, I.S., et al. "Neurohumoral features of myocardial stunning due to sudden emotional stress." NEJM Feb 10; 352(6) 2005. p. 539-48.
4. Lee, S.Y., et al. "Stress-induced cardiomyopathy presenting as acute myocardial infarction." Yonsei Med J Oct; 43(5) 2002. p. 670-74. Tsuchihashi, K., et al. "Transient left ventricular apical ballooning without coronary artery stenosis: a novel heart syndrome mimicking acute myocardial infarction. Angina Pectoris-Myocardial Infarction Investigations in Japan." J Am Coll Cardiol Jul; 38(1) 2001. p. 11-18.
5. Li, J., et al. "Myocardial infarction in parents who lost a child: a nationwide prospective cohort study in Denmark." Circulation Sep 24; 106(13) 2002. p. 1634-39. Martikainen, P., Valkonen, T. "Mortality after the death of a spouse: rates and causes of death in a large Finnish cohort." Am J Public Health Aug; 86(8 Pt 1) 1996. p. 1087-93.
6. Culic, V., Eterovic, D., Miric, D. "Meta-analysis of possible external triggers of acute myocardial infarction." Int J Cardiol Mar 10; 99(1) 2005. p. 1-8. Gueffet, J.P., et al. "[Can one die of sorrow?]." Arch Mal Coeur Vaiss Dec; 94(12) 2001. p. 1413-17.
7. Hemingway, H., Malik, M., Marmot, M. "Social and psychosocial influences on sudden cardiac death, ventricular arrhythmia and cardiac autonomic function." Eur Heart J vol 22 2001. p. 1082-101.
8. Rozanski, A., Blumenthal, J.A., Kaplan, J. "Impact of psychological factors on the pathogenesis of cardiovascular disease and implications for therapy." Circulation 99 1999. p. 2192-17. Tennant, C. "Life stress, social support and coronary heart disease." Aust N Z J Psychiatry vol 33 1999. p. 636-41.
9. Case, R.B., et al. "Living alone after myocardial infarction: impact on progress." JAMA vol 267 1992. p. 515-19. Jenkinson, C.M., et al. "The influence of psychosocial factors on survival after myocardial infarction." Public Health vol 107 1993. p. 305-17.
10. Lespérance, F., Frasure-Smith, N., Talajic, M. "Depression and beyond: affect, arteriosclerosis and death." European Neuropsychopharmacology vol 3 1995. p. 219-220. Sorkin, D., Rook, K.S., Lu, J.L. "Loneliness, lack of emotional support, lack of companionship, and the likelihood of having a heart condition in an elderly sample." Ann Behav Med Fall; 24(4) 2002. p. 290-98.

detrimental to health occur during prolonged episodes of social isolation.[1] A 2005 study found those who suffered from both depression and feelings of loneliness more than doubled their risk of dying.[2]

Several studies have reported conflicting results using psychosocial interventions[3] to reduce cardiac mortality among depressed patients.[4] Those bereaving often further increase their isolation from friends and family. This self-destructive behavior impedes recovery using traditional support groups.[5] Studies have also shown they are three times more likely to be noncompliant with medical treatment recommendations than those who are not depressed.[6]

Cardiac rehabilitation programs may achieve a four fold reduction in future cardiac events.[7] Several studies suggest practices as diverse as transcendental,[8] yoga,[9] regular consumption of breakfast cereal,[10] aerobics[11] and herbal supplements may also reduce the risk of cardiac death associated with depression. However, an in depth analysis of non-pharmacologic treatments for depression concluded social programs like cognitive behavior therapy and interpersonal therapy were superior to other measures in reducing depression but still had no effect on cardiac mortality.[12] A separate study suggests social support, altruism, faith and optimism have the greatest effect on reducing cardiac risks.[13] Social isolation greatly increases morbidity and mortality from

1. Cacioppo, J.T., et al. "Loneliness and health: potential mechanisms." Psychosom Med May-Jun; 64(3) 2002. p. 407-17. Steptoe, A., et al. "Loneliness and neuroendocrine, cardiovascular, and inflammatory stress responses in middle-aged men and women." Psychoneuroendocrinology Jun; 29(5) 2004. p. 593-611.
2. Stek, M.L., et al. "Is depression in old age fatal only when people feel lonely?" Am J Psychiatry Jan; 162(1) 2005. p. 178-80.
3. Frasure-Smith N, Lespérance, Prince RH, et al. 1771; 350:. "Randomised trial of home-based psychosocial nursing intervention for patients recovering from myocardial infarction." Lancet vol 350 1997. p. 473-79.
4. Jones, D.A., West, R.R. "Psychological rehabilitation after myocardial infarction. Multicentre randomised controlled trial." BMJ vol 313 1996. p. 1517-21. Linden, W., Stossel, C., Maurice, J. "Psychosocial interventions for patients with coronary artery disease: a meta-analysis." Arch Intern Med Apr 8; 156(7) 1996. p. 745-52.
5. Van Baarsen, B. "Theories on coping with loss: the impact of social support and self-esteem on adjustment to emotional and social loneliness following a partner's death in later life." J Gerontol B Psychol Sci Soc Sci Jan; 57(1) 2002. p. S33-42.
6. DiMatteo, M.R., Lepper, H.S., Croghan, T.W. "Depression is a risk factor for noncompliance with medical treatment: meta-analysis of the effects of anxiety and depression on patient adherence." Arch Intern Med Jul 24; 160(14) 2000. p. 2101-07.
7. Denollet, J., Brutsaert, D.L. "Reducing emotional distress improves prognosis in coronary heart disease: 9-year mortality in a clinical trial of rehabilitation." Circulation Oct 23; 104(17) 2001. p. 2018-23.
8. King, M.S., Carr, T., D'Cruz, C. "Transcendental meditation, hypertension and heart disease." Aust Fam Physician Feb; 31(2) 2002. p. 164-68. Zamarra, J.W., et al. "Usefulness of the transcendental meditation program in the treatment of patients with coronary artery disease." Am J Cardiol vol 77 1996. p. 867-70.
9. Mamtani, R., Mamtani, R. "Ayurveda and yoga in cardiovascular diseases." Cardiol Rev May-Jun; 13(3) 2005. p. 155-62.
10. Smith, A.P. "Breakfast and mental health." Int J Food Sci Nutr Sep; 49(5) 1998. p. 397-402. Smith, A.P. "Stress, breakfast cereal consumption and cortisol." Nutr Neurosci Apr; 5(2) 2002. p. 141-44.
11. Lett, H.S., Davidson, J., Blumenthal, J.A. "Nonpharmacologic treatments for depression in patients with coronary heart disease." Psychosom Med May-Jun; 67 Suppl 1 2005. p. S58-62.
12. Rees, K., et al. "Psychological interventions for coronary heart disease." Cochrane Database Syst Rev vol 2 2004. p. CD002902.

cancer,[1] cardiovascular disease,[2] and a host of other diseases; [3] however, little is known about the mechanisms for these increases.[4]

13. O'Keefe, J.H. Jr, et al. "Psychosocial stress and cardiovascular disease: how to heal a broken heart." Compr Ther Spring; 30(1) 2004. p. 37-43.
1. Launoy, G., et al. "Influence of rural environment on diagnosis, treatment, and prognosis of colorectal cancer." J Epidemiol Community Health Aug; 46(4) 1992. p. 365-67.
2. Herlitz, J., et al. "The feeling of loneliness prior to coronary artery bypass grafting might be a predictor of short-and long-term postoperative mortality." Eur J Vasc Endovasc Surg Aug; 16(2) 1998. p. 120-25.
3. Grace, S.L., et al. "Effect of depression on five-year mortality after an acute coronary syndrome." Am J Cardiol Nov 1; 96(9) 2005. p. 1179-85.
4. Hawkley, L.C., Cacioppo, J.T. "Loneliness and pathways to disease." Brain Behav Immun Feb; 17 Suppl 2003. p. S98-105.

CHAPTER 12. BROKEN HEARTED

BOONDOGGLES IN CARDIOLOGY

> *Stupidity has a knack of getting its way.*
> *Albert Camus. French novelist and playwright (1913-1960)*

Following World War II, increasing rates of cardiovascular disease prompted the United States Public Health Service to initiate a large-scale study to determine why heart disease was now the nation's number one killer.[1] They chose 5,209 healthy residents from the town of Framingham, Massachusetts to follow throughout their lives to in an attempt to determine which biological and environmental factors contributed to cardiovascular disease.[2] In 1971, this study was expanded by adding an additional 5,124 children (and their spouses) to the original participants. The investigators of this epidemiological study suggested diet, hypertension, cigarette smoking, and diabetes were among 246 risk factors[3] possibly responsible for the increasing incidence of coronary heart disease.[4] Other reported risk factors were baldness, type A personality, Jewish religion, sense of exhaustion in college, slow beard growth, and psychiatric disorders. Cardiovascular researchers recognized many "risk factors" were not causal while others were non-modifiable (sex and age) and therefore not amenable to medical or social intervention.[5] The Framingham and British Regional Heart Studies[6] placed their emphasis on alleviating the burden from cardiovascular disease by

---

1. "The Framingham Heart Study: The Town That Changed America's Heart." Framingham Heart Study. 2006. <http://www.framingham.com/heart/backgrnd.htm>.
2. Kannel, W.B., et al. "Factors of risk in the development of coronaryheart disease—six year follow-up experience: The Framingham Study." Ann Intern Med vol 55 1961. p. 33-50.
3. Hopkins, P.N., Williams, R.R. "A survey of 246 suggested coronary risk factors." Atherosclerosis Aug-Sep; 40(1) 1981. p. 1-52.
4. Dawber, T.R., Meadors, G.F., Moore, F.E., Jr. "Epidemiological approaches to heart disease: the Framingham Study." Am J Public Health Mar; 41(3) 1951. p. 279-81.

stressing the importance of reducing "major" risk factors they deemed potentially modifiable. Over time, the consensus emerged within the medical communities that serum cholesterol, smoking, hypertension, and diabetes were the major amenable risk factors predictive of heart disease.[1]

In July 1970, the National Heart, Lung, and Blood Institute, the governing body of the Framingham study, concluded sufficient data was now available to test if modification of these risk factors would reduce the incidence of heart disease.[2] They launched the Multiple Risk Factor Intervention Trial (MRFIT) to ascertain whether modification of elevated serum cholesterol levels, hypertension, and cigarette smoking would decrease the rates of cardiac death in high risk individuals.[3]

The study recruited 12,866 healthy men aged 35 to 57 years with no clinical evidence of heart disease. However, the subjects were considered to be at high risk of cardiac death because they had three or more unhealthy risk factors that placed them in a 10% risk of a cardiac event within a decade. This intervention program was in addition to usual medical care and included an intensive integrated effort to lower the three major risk factors. Blood pressure was strictly controlled by both diet and drugs.[4] Weight reduction was initiated before drug therapy. Nutritionists assisted the subjects in developing lifelong shopping, cooking, and eating patterns rather than specifying a structured diet. The goal was to reduce saturated fat intake to less than 8% of calories and dietary cholesterol intake to less than 250 mg/day, and increased polyunsaturated fat intake to 10% of calories.[5] If the subject was more than 15% overweight, weight loss was achieved through caloric reduction and increased physical activity. Cigarette smokers were urged to quit; however, no effort was made to influence the smoking habits of pipe and cigar smokers.[6]

5. "Aping Science: A Critical Analysis of Research at the Yerkes." Americans for Medical Advancement. 1995. ⟨http://www.curedisease.com/Perspectives/vol_5_1995/Researchforthefuture.html⟩. McCormick, I. "The multifactorial aetiology of coronary heart disease: A dangerous delusion." Perspectives in Biology and Medicine vol 32 1988. p. 103-108.
6. Shaper, A.G., et al. "British Regional Heart Study: cardiovascular risk factors in middle-aged men in 24 towns." BMJ Clin Res Ed vol 283 1981. p. 179-86.
1. "Estimating Coronary Heart Disease (CHD) Risk Using Framingham Heart Study Prediction Score Sheets." NHLBI Framingham Heart Study. 2002. Dec 2002 ⟨http://www.nhlbi.nih.gov/about/framingham/riskabs.htm⟩.
2. Arteriosclerosis: A Report by the National Heart and Lung Institute Task Force on Arteriosclerosis, vol 1. US Dept of Health, Education, and Welfare publication No. (NIH) 72-137. [Washington, DC] National Institutes Of Health, 1971.
3. The Multiple Risk Factor Intervention Trial Group. "The Multiple Risk Factor Intervention Trial Group: Statistical design considerations in the NHLI Multiple Risk Factor Intervention Trial." J Chronic Dis. vol 30 1977. p. 261-75. "Multiple Risk Factor Intervention Trial: Risk Factor Changes and Mortality Results." JAMA. 1997. 19 Feb 1997 ⟨http://hanson.gmu.edu/EC496/Sources/JAMA97.html⟩.
4. Cohen, J.D., Grimm, R.H. Jr, Smith, W.M. "The Multiple Risk Factor Intervention Trial (MRFIT): VI. Intervention on blood pressure." Prev Med vol 10 1981. p. 501-18.
5. Caggiula, A.W., et al. "The Multiple Risk Factor Intervention Trial (MRFIT): IV. Intervention on blood lipids." Prev Med vol 10 1981. p. 443-75.
6. Hughes, G.H., et al. "The Multiple Risk Factor Intervention Trial (MRFIT): V. Intervention on smoking." Prev Med vol 10 1981. p. 476-500.

The men received annual physical exams and were initially followed for seven years. Those receiving medical interventions had reductions in all three risk factors. After six years, 50% of smokers receiving intervention had quit compared with 29% of those receiving usual care. Diastolic blood pressure fell in the two groups by 10.5 and 7.3 respectively. Plasma cholesterol fell in the two groups by 12.1 and 7.5 mg/dl respectively. After seven years, mortality rates were 41.2 deaths per 1000 in those receiving intensive medical intervention versus 40.4/1000 for those receiving the usual care. Coronary heart disease death rates were 17.9 and 19.3/1000.

The researchers concluded intensive individual counseling with behavioral scientists, nutritionists, nurses, physicians, and general health counselors INCREASED the death rate for all causes by 2.1% compared to those receiving the usual care. Conveniently, they decided this increased mortality in those receiving medical treatment was insignificant. They also decided to blame those in the usual care group for not dying at a rate they had predicted. The cardiac risk score predicted 442 of those receiving usual care should have been dead by now; inconveniently, only 219 had died.

The researchers had to find an explanation why 50% of those not receiving intensive care refused to die. They also minimized the fact their interventions had increased the death rates from cancer in those receiving "better" treatment over those receiving "less intensive" treatment. They were forced to admit death rates from heart disease were falling without medical treatment across the nation for some unexplained reason.[1] They also confessed: "three possible explanations for these results must be considered: (1) such an intervention program is without benefit in terms of substantial decreases in mortality; (2) the intervention program does affect CHD mortality, but the benefit was not observed in this study; or (3) one or more constituents in the intervention program may have had an unfavorable effect on survival in some subgroups offsetting beneficial effects of others."

So what do we get for this $115 million experiment?[2] Perhaps the lead investigators own words say it best, "In conclusion, we have shown that it is possible to apply an intensive long-term intervention program against three coronary risk factors with considerable success in terms of risk factor changes. The overall results do not show a beneficial effect on CHD or total mortality from this multifactor intervention."

Medical researchers (and drug companies) refused to be deterred by these dismal findings. They were positive medical and pharmaceutical therapies were superior to no intervention. They had many studies and theories predicting these

1. National Institutes Of Health. Report of the Working Group on Arteriosclerosis of the National Heart, Lang, and Blood Institute: Arteriosclerosis 1981, vol 2. NIH publication 82-203. Bethesda, Md: National Institutes of Health, 1981.
2. "Memorandum Re: Multiple Risk Factor Intervention Trial." Tobacco Documents. 2001. 30 May 2001 ‹http://tobaccodocuments.org/bliley_ti/19444.html›.

therapies must reduce heart disease, therefore, the individual was somehow to blame for the MRFIT debacle. These bureaucrats were determined now to set things right. Perhaps community leaders and governmental bodies could "help" those inflicted by these scourges. This logic seems reasonable in a convoluted sort of way, after all the community and government leaders were responsible for policies proven to be detrimental to our health (remember Love Canal, Three Mile Island and thalidomide).

They reasoned we are influenced by our environment, therefore, changing individual behaviors requires changing the environment as a whole.[1] Individual interventions were now changed to community prevention programs. Governmental leaders were successful in convincing Congress to fund three new community intervention programs: the Stanford Five City Project[2], the Minnesota Heart Health Program[3] and the Pawtucket Heart Health Program.[4] These community intervention programs compared "treated" cities to similarly matched "untreated" or control cities. These studies were of a similar duration as the MRFIT study and had similar goals; however, the interventions were now adjusted to a community level.

Instead of individual counseling, the investigators ran media promos and gave handouts. They also deluged communities with school-based "health education" programs. The researchers estimated each adult in the treatment cities was exposed to 527 educational episodes over the five year period of the trial, or about 26 hours per adult.[5] Risk factor screening fairs were commonplace; it was very easy to have your blood pressure, blood sugar or cholesterol checked while shopping in the mall. It is estimated 60% of adults residing in these communities received on-site measurement, education, and counseling; while 30% participated in face-to-face intervention programs.

The message was basically the same as the MRFIT study; "you need to recognize these behaviors are bad for you and change them, or you will die." Schools, churches, social organizations, employers and city governments were all saturated with cries for behavior modification. The American Heart Association started pimping its "heart healthy" logo to manufacturers of low fat

1. Cutler, D.M. "Behavioral Health Interventions: What whorks and Why?" Harvard Department of Economics. 2002. 03 Jun 2002 ‹http://econweb.fas.harvard.edu/faculty/dcutler/papers/interventions_6-02.pdf›.
2. Farquhar, J.W., et al., "Effects of Communitywide Education on Cardiovascular Disease Risk Factors: The Stanford FiveCity Project." JAMA vol 264(3) 1990. p. 359-65.
3. Luepker, R.V.,et al. "Community Education for CardiovascularDisease Prevention: Risk Factor Changes in the Minnesota Heart Health Program." American Journalof Public Health vol 84(9) 1994. p. 1383-93. Luepker, R.V., et al. "Community Education for CardiovascularDisease Prevention: Morbidityand MortalityResults from the Minnesota Heart Health Program." American Journal of Epidemiology vol 144(4) 1996. p. 351-62.
4. Carleton, R.A., et al. "The Pawtucket Heart Health Program: Community Changes in Cardiovascular Risk Factors and Projected Disease Risk." American Journalof Public Health vol 85(6) 1995. p. 777-85.
5. Cutler, D.M. "Behavioral Health Interventions: What whorks and Why?" Harvard Department of Economics. 2002. 03 Jun 2002 ‹http://econweb.fas.harvard.edu/faculty/dcutler/papers/interventions_6-02.pdf›.

food (calories be damned). They succeeded in improving public knowledge of these unhealthy lifestyles; however, the control cities also showed similar changes. Worse, levels of cholesterol, smoking, blood pressure and obesity were generally unaffected by this media blitz. One study attempted to squeeze at least a little positive data from this massive boondoggle by combining all the data into one large pooled study[1]. The results were similar to MRFIT, a dismal failure showing no benefit to either the individual or the community.

Once again, researchers were forced to conclude medical interventions have very little impact on altering cardiac events or death from coronary artery disease.[2] The price tag for this information; the Stanford Five-City Project cost \$4.95 per person per year to achieve a measly 4% decrease in diastolic blood pressure and a 13% decrease in smoking in addition to the piddling 2% decrease in serum cholesterol.[3] One critic reports "Intriguingly, these uniformly disappointing developed-country programmes have been reported as successes."[4] Incredibly, this horrendous waste of time and effort is considered by some as being "cost-effective."[5] Regrettably, most health care research projects appear to be more focused on health care spending rather than health. One critic believes they are more concerned about discovering the nature and occurrence of various diseases than the health of its subjects.[6]

Foreign interventional studies have had equally dismal findings. The North Karelia Project in Finland studied the effects of lifestyle and medical interventions on 11,992 men and women aged 25-59 over ten years.[7] In one short decade, they succeeded in reducing the population's use of butter on bread from 90% to only 15% and more than doubled fruit consumption in two decades. Although cigarette smoking decreased dramatically among men, smoking among women increased. They compared their interventions to Kuopio, another region with similar risk factors. Although there were dramatic decreases in cardiac events, there were parallel decreases in the control region that did not receive intervention. These downward trends occurred not only in North Karelia[8] and Kuopio,[9] but throughout all counties of the country.[10]

1. Winkleby, M.A., Feldman, H.A., Murray, D.M. "Joint Analysis of Three U.S. Community Intervention Trials for Reduction of Cardiovascular DiseaseRisk." Journal of Clinical Epidemiology vol 50(6) 1997. p. 645-58.
2. Mitchell, J.R. "What do we gain by modifying risk factors for coronary disease?" Schweiz Med Wochenschr Mar 17; 120(11) 1990. p. 359-64.
3. "Economic analyses of primary prevention of coronary heart disease (CHD) and stroke." International Task Force for Prevention of Coronary Heart Disease. 2002. 21 Nov 2002 ‹http://www.chd-taskforce.de/pdf/sk_cost_03.pdf›.
4. Ebrahim, S. Smith, G.D. "Exporting failure? Coronary heart disease and stroke in developing countries." International Journal of Epidemiology vol 30 2001. p. 201-205.
5. Hoffman, K., Jackson, S. "A Review of the Evidence for the Effectiveness and Costs of Interventions: Preventing the Burden of Non-communicable Diseases: How can Health Systems Respond?" Centre for Health Promotion. 2003. Jul 2003 ‹http://www.utoronto.ca/chp/ReportsandPresentations.htm›.
6. Liberati, A., Chatziandreou, E., Miettinen, O.S. "Health care research: what is it about?" Qual Assur Health Care vol 1(4) 1989. p. 249-57.
7. Puska, P., Tuomilehto, J., Nissinen, A., Salonen, J. "Ten years of the North Karelia project." Acta Med Scand Suppl vol 701 1985. p. 66-71.

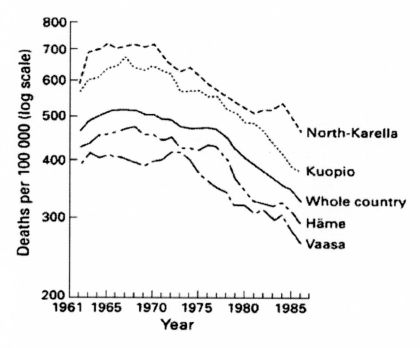

Source: Valkonen, T. Trends in regional and socioeconomic mortality differentials in Finland. Int J Health Sciences 1993; 3(3/4):157–66

Once again, medical researches were jubilant[1] with their "success"[2] in affecting changes in risk factors and proclaimed they had dramatically reduced the incidence of coronary artery disease.[3] Spurred on by these "achievements," governments opted to incorporate these interventions into Public Health Policies.[4]

8. Salonen, J.T., et al. "Contribution of risk factor changes to the decline in coronary incidence during the North Karelia project: a within-community analysis." Int J Epidemiol Sep; 18(3) 1989. p. 595-601.
9. Salonen, J.T. "Prevention of coronary heart disease in Finland—application of the population strategy." Ann Med Dec; 23(6) 1991. p. 607-12.
10. McCormick, J., Skrabanek, P. "Coronary heart disease is not preventable by population interventions." Lancet vol ii 1988. p. 839-41. Valkonen, T. "Trends in regional and socioeconomic mortality differentials in Finland." Int J Health Sciences vol 3(3/4) 1993. p. 157-66.
1. Puska, P. "Nutrition and global prevention on non-communicable diseases." Asia Pac J Clin Nutr vol 11 Suppl 9 2002. p. S755-8. Vartiainen, E., et al. "Twenty-year trends in coronary risk factors in north Karelia and in other areas of Finland." Int J Epidemiol Jun; 23(3) 1994. p. 495-504.
2. Ebrahim, S. Smith, G.D. "Exporting failure? Coronary heart disease and stroke in developing countries." International Journal of Epidemiology vol 30 2001. p. 201-205.
3. Vartiainen, E., et al. "Do changes in cardiovascular risk factors explain changes in mortality from stroke in Finland?" BMJ Apr 8; 310(6984) 1995. p. 901-04.

As previous mentioned, the World Health Organization's MONICA study was a huge embarrassment for its researchers.[1] They were unable to find any association between the major risks factors and cardiac events. The Los Angeles Veterans Administration Study of men aged 55 years and older found a significant reduction in mortality from atherosclerotic diseases, but not in total mortality.[2]

Attempts to simplify potentially confounding variables by focusing only on reductions in one risk factor have also been unsuccessful. COMMIT was a 4-year program to accelerate the rate of quitting among heavy smokers. There were no overall differences in prevalence of smoking, or in the quit rates of heavy smokers, which was the primary target. Light to moderate smokers showed only a slight decrease in their rates of smoking.[3] Most researchers would agree that voluntary attempts to alter health behavior have generally been unsuccessful.[4] Irrespective of the nature of the intervention,[5] these trials have uniformly failed[6] to produce desirable outcomes.[7]

High risks groups may benefit by measures to reduce blood pressure,[8] cholesterol[9] and smoking,[10] however, extension of these therapies to low risk populations has generally been unsuccessful. Treatment of those at low risk provides only minimal benefit that is neutralized or even reversed by the risks

4. Dunbar, J.A., et al. "Implementing the North Karelia Project in Scotland." Scott Med J Aug; 43(4) 1998. p. 99-101. Rastenyte, D. "Comparison of trends in ischaemic heart disease between North Karelia, Finland, and Kaunas, Lithuania, from 1971 to 1987." Br Heart J Nov; 68(5) 1992. p. 516-23.
1. "World's largest and longest heart study produces some surprises." WHO MONICA Project. 1998. 28 Aug 1998 ‹http://www.ktl.fi/monica/public/vienna/press_release.htm›.
2. Administration Cooperative Study Group on Antihypertensive Agents. "Effects of treatment on morbidity in hypertension: II. Results in patients with diastolic blood pressure averaging 90 through 114 mm Hg." JAMA vol 213 1970. p. 1143-52. Dayton, S., et al. "Controlled clinical trial of a diet high in unsaturated fat in preventing complications of atherosclerosis.." Circulation vol 40 1969. p. II-1.
3. Community Intervention Trial for Smoking Cessation (COMMIT): I. cohort results from a four-year community intervention Am J Public Health. 1995 Feb; 85(2):183-92.
4. Attebring, M.F., et al. "Risk indicators for recurrence among patients with coronary artery disease. Problems associated with their modification.." Scand Cardiovasc J vol 32(1) 1998. p. 9-16.
5. Haber, D., et al. "Impact of a health promotion course on inactive, overweight, or physically limited older adults." Family and Community Health vol 22 2000. p. 48-56. Miller, W.C. "How effective are traditional dietary and exercise interventions for weight loss?" Medicine and Science in Sports and Exercise vol 31 1999. p. 1129-34.
6. Tudor-Smith, C., Nutbeam, D., Moore, L., Catford, J. "Effects of the Heartbeat Wales programme over five years on behavioural risks for cardiovascular disease: quasi-experimental comparison of results from Wales and a matched reference area." BMJ vol 316 1998. p. 818-22.
7. Eakin, E.G., Glasgow, R.E., Riley, K.M. "Review of primary care-based physical activity intervention studies: effectiveness and implications for practice and future research." Journal of Family Practice vol 49 2000. p. 158-68. Ebrahim, S., Smith, G.D., Bennett, R. "Health promotion activity should be retargeted at secondary prevention." BMJ vol 320 2000. p. 185-86.
8. Collins, R., et al. "Blood pressure, stroke, and coronary heart disease.II. Short-term reductions in blood pressure: overview of randomised drug trials in their epidemiological context." Lancet vol 335 1990. p. 827-38. Collins, R., MacMahon, S. "Blood pressure, antihypertensive drug treatment and the risks of stroke and coronary heart disease." Br Med Bull vol 50 1994. p. 272-98.
9. Law, M., Wald, N., Thompson, S. "By how much and how quickly does reduction in serum cholesterol concentration lower risk of ischaemic heart disease?" BMJ vol 308 1994. p. 367-72. Smith, D.G, Song, S., Sheldon, T. "Cholesterol lowering and mortality: the importance of considering initial level of risk." BMJ vol 306 1993. p. 1367-73.
10. Mamun, A.A., et al. "Smoking decreases the duration of life lived with and without cardiovascular disease: a life course analysis of the Framingham Heart Study." Eur Heart J Mar; 25(5) 204. p. 409-15.

associated with the therapy.[1] In patients with moderately high cholesterol levels without overt heart disease, statin therapy may actually increase the risk of death. Studies have shown a small increase of around 1-2 deaths per 1000 patient-years of treatment is associated with cholesterol lowering therapy. This may be enough to neutralize the benefit of drug therapy.[2]

Some suggest more intensive interventions will produce better results. They ignore the fact that most clinical trial interventions far exceed what is feasible in routine practice.[3] Well funded studies of intensive community based health promotion have had virtually no impact on reducing cardiac morbidity[4] or mortality.[5] Apologists argue their may be a significant delay between the initiation of a treatment program and measurable reductions in disease or death rates.[6] They ignore studies showing benefits from blood pressure and cholesterol reduction are measurable in only two to four years[7] and the risk of stroke falls rapidly after smoking cessation.[8] The unfortunate consequences of cigarette smoking may be permanent for heart disease.[9]

FLAWED STUDIES

There are three kinds of lies: lies, damned lies, and statistics.
Benjamin Disraeli. British prime minister (1804-1881)

The eminent Dr. William Stehbens is a long standing critic of most research on coronary heart disease. A recent PUBMED search shows he has authored over

1. Multiple Risk Factor Intervention Trial Research Group. "Multiple risk factor intervention trial. Risk factor changes and mortality results." JAMA vol 248 1982. p. 1465-77. Miettinen, T., et al. "Multifactorial primary prevention of cardiovascular diseases in middle-aged men. Risk factor changes, incidence, and mortality." JAMA vol 254 1985. p. 2097-102.
2. Davey Smith, G., Egger, M. "Who benefits from medical interventions?" BMJ vol 308 1994. p. 72-74.
3. Hart, J.T. "Commentary: Can health outputs of routine practice approach those of clinical trials?" Int J Epidemiol Dec; 30(6) 2001. p. 1263-67. Nolte, E., McKee, M. "Does Healthcare Save Lives? Avoidable Mortality Revisited." Pro-Adess. 2004. 2004 ⟨http://www.proadess.cict.fiocruz.br/artigos/avoidablemortality.pdf⟩.
4. Luepker, R.V., et al. "Community education for cardiovascular disease prevention: risk factor changes in the Minnesota heart health program." Am J Public Health vol 84 1994. p. 1383-93. Luepker, R.V., et al. "Community education for cardiovascular disease prevention: morbidity and mortality results from the Minnesota heart health programme." Am J Epidemiol vol 144 1996. p. 351-62.
5. Ravnskov U. Cholesterol lowering trials in coronary heart disease: frequency of citation and outcome. BMJ. 1992 Jul 4; 305(6844):15-9.
6. Multiple Risk Factor Intervention Trial Research Group. "Mortality rates after 10.5 years for participants in the multiple risk factor intervention trial. Findings related to a priori hypotheses of the trial." JAMA vol 263 1990. p. 1795-801.
7. Scandinavian Simvastatin Survival Study Group. "Randomised trial of cholesterol lowering in 4444 patients with coronary heart disease: the Scandanavian simvastatin survival study (4S)." Lancet vol 344 1994. p. 1383-89. Collins, R., et al. "Blood pressure, stroke, and coronary heart disease.II. Short-term reductions in blood pressure: overview of randomised drug trials in their epidemiological context." Lancet vol 335 1990. p. 827-38.
8. Wannamethee, G., et al. "Smoking cessation and the risk of stroke in middle-aged men." JAMA vol 274 1995. p. 155-60.
9. Ben-Shlomo, Y., et al. "What determines mortality risk in male former cigarette smokers?" Am J Public Health vol 84 1994. p. 1235-42.

243 articles in science journals. His first publication nearly coincided with the founding of the Framingham Heart Study. He vehemently condemns medical researchers for their misuse of terminology,[1] use of fallacious data and methodological errors,[2] being overzealous and misrepresenting data,[3] use of fallacious vital statistics,[4] being guilty of a disservice to the tenets of their discipline,[5] failure to use rigorous and scientific standards,[6] and failure to take note of inconsistencies.[7] This is the literary equivalent of being taken to the woodshed by one of the grand old men of cardiac research. Unfortunately, most are not deterred by his admonitions. They are using the latest advances in computer technology to evaluate the benefits of lifestyle changes and medical therapy.[8] They remain blissfully unaware they are inputting bogus and distorted data. Many seem perplexed when their projections fail in the face of realty.[9]

Life expectancy and mortality curves of "less developed" nations are especially difficult to understand. Repeated studies have shown less than half the recent increases in life expectancy may be attributable to medical therapy.[10] Many developing nations exceed our average life expectancy without medical or social interventions.[11] The longevity of less technological nations conflicts with the claims of medical researchers. A Nobel Laureate and former research director of Burroughs Wellcome claimed "the increase in life expectancy over the last 50 years has been attributed to new medicines."[12]

---

1. Stehbens, W.E. "Misuse of "coronary heart disease."" Heart vol 82 1999. p. 1-2. Stehbens, W.E. "Analysis of definitions and word misusage in vascular pathology." Cardiovasc Pathol Sep-Oct; 10(5) 2001. p. 251-57.
2. Stehbens, W.E. "Hypothetical hypercholesterolaemia and atherosclerosis." Med Hypotheses vol 62(1) 2004. p. 72-78.
3. Stehbens, W.E. "Coronary heart disease, hypercholesterolemia, and atherosclerosis. II. Misrepresented data." Exp Mol Pathol Apr; 70(2) 2001. p. 120-39.
4. Stehbens, W.E. "Coronary heart disease, hypercholesterolemia, and atherosclerosis. I. False premises." Exp Mol Pathol Apr; 70(2) 2001. p. 103-19.
5. Stehbens, W.E. "Epidemiological risk factors of coronary heart disease are not causal in atherosclerosis." Clin Exp Hypertens May; 22(4) 2000. p. 445-53.
6. Stehbens, W.E. "The quality of epidemiological data in coronary heart disease and atherosclerosis." J Clin Epidemiol Dec; 46(12) 1993. p. 1337-46.
7. Stehbens, W.E. "Science, atherosclerosis and the 'age of unreason': a review." Integr Physiol Behav Sci Oct-Dec; 28(4) 1993. p. 388-95.
8. Grover, S.A., et al. "The benefits of treating hyperlipidemia to prevent coronary heart disease. Estimating changes in life expectancy and morbidity." JAMA Feb 12; 267(6) 1992. p. 816-22. Tsevat J, et al. "Expected gains in life expectancy from various coronary heart disease risk factor modifications." Circulation Apr; 83(4) 1991. p. 1194-201.
9. Yudkin, J.S. "How can we best prolong life? Benefits of coronary risk factor reduction in non-diabetic and diabetic subjects." BMJ May 15; 306(6888) 1993. p. 1313-18.
10. Goldman, L., Cook, E.F. "The decline in ischemic heart disease mortality rates. An analysis of the comparative effects of medical interventions and changes in lifestyle." Ann Intern Med Dec; 101(6) 1984. p. 825-36. Hunink, M.G., et al. "The recent decline in mortality from coronary heart disease, 1980-1990. The effect of secular trends in risk factors and treatment." JAMA vol 277 1997. p. 535-42.
11. National Center For Health Statistics. Health, United States, 1998, with Socioeconomic Status and Health Chartbook, Pub. no. (PHS)98-1232. Hyattsville, Md: National Center for Health Statistics, 1998.
12. Hitchings, G.H. "Health care and life expectancy." Science vol 262 1993. p. 1632.; Kinsella, K., Velkoff, V.A. "An Aging World: 2001." International Population Reports Nov 2001. p. 24.

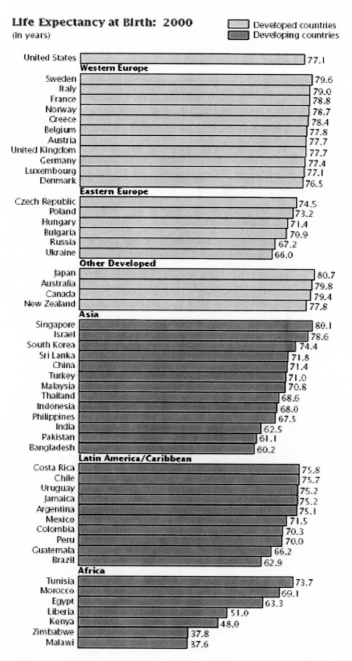

Life Expectancy at Birth: 2000
(In years)

Developed countries
Developing countries

United States 77.1

Western Europe
Sweden 79.6
Italy 79.0
France 78.8
Norway 78.7
Greece 78.4
Belgium 77.8
Austria 77.7
United Kingdom 77.7
Germany 77.4
Luxembourg 77.1
Denmark 76.5

Eastern Europe
Czech Republic 74.5
Poland 73.2
Hungary 71.4
Bulgaria 70.9
Russia 67.2
Ukraine 66.0

Other Developed
Japan 80.7
Australia 79.8
Canada 79.4
New Zealand 77.8

Asia
Singapore 80.1
Israel 78.6
South Korea 74.4
Sri Lanka 71.8
China 71.4
Turkey 71.0
Malaysia 70.8
Thailand 68.6
Indonesia 68.0
Philippines 67.5
India 62.5
Pakistan 61.1
Bangladesh 60.2

Latin America/Caribbean
Costa Rica 75.8
Chile 75.7
Uruguay 75.2
Jamaica 75.2
Argentina 75.1
Mexico 71.5
Colombia 70.3
Peru 70.0
Guatemala 66.2
Brazil 62.9

Africa
Tunisia 73.7
Morocco 69.1
Egypt 63.3
Liberia 51.0
Kenya 48.0
Zimbabwe 37.8
Malawi 37.6

Source: U.S. Census Bureau, 2000a.

CHAPTER 13. BAD MEDICINE

THE FAILURE OF SUCCESS

I have not failed. I've just found 10,000 ways that won't work.
Thomas Edison. American inventor (1847-1931)

Clinical cardiology is largely based on what Lewis Thomas presciently referred to as "halfway technologies."[1] Heart transplantation, angioplasty, coronary artery bypass, left ventricular assist devices, implantable defibrillators, and a host of non-biologically targeted therapeutic agents form the cornerstones of modern cardiovascular therapy.[2] These technologies do not cure or prevent disabilities, but keep people alive at enormous costs — both human and financial.[3] Some argue medicine's inability to provide cures for many illnesses is a "failure of success."[4] Many are skeptical about the actual contribution of medical care[5] and biomedical knowledge in improving health for the general population.[6] In 1959, Rene Dubos showed mortality falling in western nations long before the microbial theory of disease and the availability of "magic bullets."[7] As previously stated, Thomas McKeown reasoned living conditions were responsible for most of the decline of mortality.[8] He stated, "Medical practice, including such

---

1. Thomas, L. "The technology of medicine." In: The Lives of a Cell. New York, NY: Viking Press, 1974.
2. Chien, K.R. "Mentors for the New Millennium." Circulation vol 101 2000. p. 1616.
3. Brown, E. "Halfway technologies." Physician Exec Dec; 22(12) 1996. p. 44-45.
4. Gruenberg, E..M. "The Failure of Success." Milbank Memorial Fund Quarterly vol 55 1977. p. 3-24.
5. Nolte, E., McKee, M. "Does Healthcare Save Lives? Avoidable Mortality Revisited." Pro-Adess. 2004. 2004 ⟨http://www.proadess.cict.fiocruz.br/artigos/avoidablemortality.pdf⟩.
6. Evans, R.G., Barer, M.L., Marmor, T.R, et al. Why Are Some People Health And Others Not: The Determinants Of Health Of Populations. New York, NY: Aldine De Gruyter, 1994. Mackenbach, J.P. "The contribution of medical care to mortality decline." Journal of Clinical Epidemiology vol 49 1996. p. 1207-13.
7. Dubos, R. Mirage of Health: Utopias, Progress, and Biological Change. New York, NY: Harper & Row, 1959.

preventive measures as immunization, has had an almost insignificant role in the improvement of health.... In short, our medical care system has received more credit and more financial support than can be justified after critical appraisal of its effectiveness."[1]

A more recent researcher attempted to estimate the contribution of medicine to improvements in life expectancy and quality of life from 1950 to 1989. During this period, life expectancy had increased by 7.1 years; he determined 3.4 years of this increase was related to decreases in cardiac related deaths.[2] He was able to attribute only 40% (1.4 years) of the increased life expectancy to specific cardiac treatments. There are many medical researchers who feel more emphasis should be placed on prevention programs.[3] Many believe federal dollars would provide better outcomes through investing in social programs improving education, housing, and employment.[4] Bunker's extrapolated his findings to all causes of death and concluded medical therapy was responsible for only five of the 30 years of increased life expectancy in this century.[5] His beliefs have now become incorporated into the body of medicine. A RAND study of international new drug releases concluded they increased average annual life expectancy by a mere three weeks.[6] Others reaffirm these pessimistic opinions. Consider the following quotes from medical texts:

> [T]he empirical evidence indicates [that] the overall contribution of medical care to health is rather modest at the margin...education, lifestyle, the environment, and income [are] the major contributing factors.[7]

> [The] increase in life expectancy [has] been much more influenced by economic development than improvements in medical care...the most important medical advances are being brought about by improvements in information technology, not pills and scalpels.[8]

> Research on the relationship between health status and medical care frequently has found that the marginal contribution of medical care to health status is rather small...any significant improvements in health status are more likely to originate

8. McKeown, T. The Role of Medicine: Dream, Mirage, or Nemesis? Princeton, NJ: Princeton Univ Pr, 1979.
1. Godber, G.E. "'McKeown's' The Role of Medicine.." Milbank Memorial Fund Quarterly Summer 1977. p. 373-78. McKeown, T. "The Road to Health." World Health Forum vol 10 1989. p. 408-16.
2. Bunker, J.P. "Medicine matters after all." J Roy Coll Phys (Lond) vol 29 1995. p. 105-19.
3. Evans RG.. 1994; 123. "Health care as a threat to health: defence, opulaence, and the social environ-ment." Daedalus vol 123 1994. p. 21-42. Lavis, J.N., Stoddart, G.L. "Can we have too much health care?" Daedalus vol 123 1994. p. 43-60.
4. Smith, R. "Medicine's core values." BMJ vol 309 1994. p. 1247-48.
5. Bunker, J.P. "The role of medical care in contributing to health improvements within societies." International Journal of Epidemiology vol 30 2001. p. 1260-63.
6. Lichtenberg, F.R. "The impact of new drug launches on longevity: evidence from longitudinal, disease-level data from 52 countries, 1982-2001." RAND Corporation. 2003. 16 Feb 2003 ‹http://www.rand.org/labor/adp_pdfs/adp_lichtenberg.pdf›.
7. Santerre, R., Neun, S, et al. Health Economics: Theories, Insights, And Industry Studies,. Orlando, FL: Dryden Press, 2000.
8. Thomas, G. Health Economics: Fundamentals and Flow of Funds. New York, NY: John Wiley And Sons, 1997.

from factors other than medical care...Factors that determine the level of health include income and education, environmental and life-style factors, and genetics.[1]

The historical declines in population mortality rates were not due to medical interventions because effective medical interventions became available to populations largely after the mortality had declined. Instead, public health, improved environment, and improved nutrition probably played substantial roles.[2]

A 2003 study on the impact of newly released drugs on life expectancy for 52 countries concluded average life expectancy had increased by not even two years between 1986 and 2000. Annually, new drugs were responsible for less than three weeks of this increase.[3] A Harvard study suggests at best only half of the reduction in cardiac risk is the result of medication, the other half is from behavioral change.[4]

Many complain too much money is wasted on costly technology and bio-medical research producing only trivial effects. They believe more emphasis should be placed on extending quality life years instead of simply extending life expectancy in a debilitated state.[5] Longevity experts agree that it is very unlikely death can ever be entirely eliminated.[6] Prolongation of life past a certain point[7] will require exponentially increasing spending while yielding diminishing returns.[8] Many believe we have nearly reached the limits of life extension.[9] The old axiom, the last gains are the hardest[10], is probably especially true concerning health care spending.

Although much of the debate about the contribution of medical care to health status has focused on mortality, it is but one measure of health status. Its real value may not be in life extension but in improving the quality of life by relieving pain or suffering and improving and decreasing disabilities.[11] Cardiac patients are especially affected by quality of life issues. Studies have shown those

1. Henderson, J. Health Economics and Policy. Cincinnati, OH: South-western Publishing Co, 1999.
2. Folland, S., Goodman, A., Stano, M, et al. The Economics Of Health And Health Care. Upper Saddle River, NJ: Prentice Hall, 2001.
3. Lichtenberg, F.R. "The impact of new drug launches on longevity: evidence from longitudinal, disease-level data from 52 countries, 1982-2001." RAND Corporation. 2003. 16 Feb 2003 ‹http://www.rand.org/labor/adp_pdfs/adp_lichtenberg.pdf›.
4. Cutler, D.M., Kadiyala, S. "The Return to Biomedical Research: Treatment and Behavioral Effects." Harvard University Economics Department. 2001. 27 Nov 2001 ‹http://econweb.fas.harvard.edu/faculty/dcutler/papers/cutler_kadiyala_for_topel.pdf›.
5. Cassell, E.J. The nature of suffering and the goals of medicine. Oxford: Oxford University Press, 1991. Little, J.M. "Money, morals and the conquest of mortality." MJA vol 179 (8) 2003. p. 432-35.
6. Carnes, B.A., Olshansky, S.J., Grahn, D. "Biological evidence for limits to the duration of life." Biogerontology vol 4(1) 2003. p. 31-45. Hayflick, L. "'Anti-aging' is an oxymoron." J Gerontol A Biol Sci Med Sci Jun; 59(6) 2004. p. B573-8.
7. Charlton, B.G., Andras, P. "Medical research funding may have over-expanded and be due for collapse." QJM Jan; 98(1) 2005. p. 53-55. Cutler, D.M., McClellan, M. "Is technological change in medicine worth it?" Health Aff (Millwood) Sep-Oct; 20(5) 2001. p. 11-29.
8. Murphy, K., Topel, R. "Diminishing returns? The costs and benefits of improving health." Perspect Biol Med Summer; 46(3 Suppl) 2003. p. S108-28. Rice, D.P., Fineman, N. "Economic implications of increased longevity in the United States." Annu Rev Public Health vol 25 2004. p. 457-73.
9. Olshansky, S.J., Carnes, B.A., Desesquelles, A. "Demography. Prospects for human longevity." Science Feb 23; 291(5508) 2001. p. 1491-92.
10. Landes, D.S. Revolution in time: clocks and the making of the modern world. Cambridge, Mass: Belknap Press Of Harvard University Press, 1983.

having angina consistently express dissatisfaction with the quality of their lives.[1] Women with heart disease have significantly lower quality of life than their male counterparts.[2] Although quality of life may improve for 50% of those undergoing coronary artery bypasses, women again report less satisfaction about long-term quality benefits than men.[3]

Multiple studies reflect the dissatisfaction most cardiac patients have related to quality of life.[4] Cardiac patients generally place more emphasis on mental well-being than on physical functioning.[5] Women are worried about psychosocial well-being and physical competence while men state concerns related to vitality and personal resources.[6] There concerns seem justified, studies of ICU patients following discharge found 63% complained of poorer quality of life after discharge.[7] Hospitalization generally fails to provide substantial improvement in quality of life for most cardiac patients.[8]

Although life expectancy has shown recent increases, the onset of nonfatal, disabling diseases remains fairly constant.[9] If these increases continue and the onset of disabling diseases remains the same as in previous decades, the population will inevitably experience longer durations of disability.[10] Some suggest 80% (9.6 months) of each year of increased life expectancy will be spent in a disabled state.[11] Studies of longevity trends during the 80s and 90s suggest the elderly will be spending a greater time with disabilities.[12] Others suggest Americans are entering old age in a healthier state[13], therefore have fewer

11. Brenner MH, Curbow B, Javitt JC et al. Vision change and quality of life in the elderly: response to cataract surgery and treatment of other chronic ocular conditions. Arch Ophthalmol 1993; 111:680–85 Bunker, J.P. "Medicine matters after all." J Roy Coll Physicians vol 29 1995. p. 105-12.
1. Heller, R.F., et al. "Predictors of quality of life after hospital admission for heart attack or angina." Int J Cardiol Apr 18; 59(2) 1997. p. 161-66.
2. Emery, C.F., et al. "Gender differences in quality of life among cardiac patients." Psychosom Med Mar-Apr; 66(2) 2004. p. 190-97.
3. Phillips Bute, B., et al. "Female gender is associated with impaired quality of life 1 year after coronary artery bypass surgery." Psychosom Med Nov-Dec; 65(6) 2003. p. 944-51. Riedinger, M.S., et al. "Quality of life in patients with heart failure: do gender differences exist?" Heart Lung Mar-Apr; 30(2) 2001. p. 105-16.
4. Ahmed, A. "Quality and outcomes of heart failure care in older adults: role of multidisciplinary disease-management programs." J Am Geriatr Soc Sep; 50(9) 2002. p. 1590-93.
5. Smith, K.W., Avis, N.E., Assmann, S.F. "Distinguishing between quality of life and health status in quality of life research: a meta-analysis." Qual Life Res Aug; 8(5) 1999. p. 447-59.
6. Dibble, S.L., et al. "Gender differences in the dimensions of quality of life." Oncol Nurs Forum Apr; 25(3) 1998. p. 577-83.
7. Brooks, R., et al. "Quality of life outcomes after intensive care. Comparison with a community group." Intensive Care Med May; 23(5) 1997. p. 581-86.
8. Kinney, M.R., et al. "Quality of life in cardiac patient research: a meta-analysis." Nurs Res May-Jun; 45(3) 1996. p. 173-80.
9. Cassel, C.K., Rudberg, M.A., Olshansky, S.J. "The Price of Success: Health Care in an Aging Society." Health Affairs (Millwood). 2003. 04 Nov 2003 ⟨http://content.healthaffairs.org/cgi/reprint/11/2/87⟩.
10. Mathers, C.D. "Gains in health expectancy from the elimination of diseases among older people." Disabil Rehabil May-Jun; 21(5-6) 1999. p. 211-21.
11. Katz, S., et al. "Active Life Expectancy." NEJM vol 309 1983. p. 1218-24.
12. Jagger, C. "Compression or expansion of morbidity-what does the future hold?" Age and Ageing vol 29 2001. p. 93-94.
13. Wilhelmson, K., Allebeck, P., Steen, B. "Improved health among 70-year olds: comparison of health indicators in three different birth cohorts." Aging Clin Exp Res Oct; 14(5) 2002. p. 361-70.

infirmities and disabilities.[1] One provocative study suggests a dichotomy exists; the educated are living longer lives free of disability while those of lower status are living with longer periods of disability.[2] The Rand Corporation issued a report on obesity and disability trends in America. They project if obesity trends continue at their current rate through 2020, those reporting poor health will increase by 12% for men and 14% for women compared with the year 2000.[3]

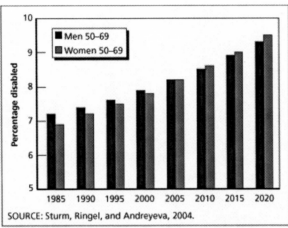

Source: Sturm, R., J. Ringel, and T. Andreyeva, "Increasing Obesity Rates and Disability Trends," *Health Affairs, Vol. 23, No. 2, March/April 2004, pp. 1-7.*

A British study suggests these upward trends in disability are more than theoretical. They found the expected time lived in poor health for males had risen from 6.5 years in 1981 to 8.7 years by 2001.[4] Time lived by females in poor health had increased from 10.1 years to 11.6 years during this same period. Researchers are especially concerned about the increased incidence in debilitating diseases like cancer and Alzheimer's disease. The incidence of prostate and breast cancer have continued to climb since 1975. Prostate cancer is the most common cancer in men and has the second highest mortality rate; it ranks among the top 10 overall causes of death.[5]

1. Hubert, H.B., et al. "Lifestyle habits and compression of morbidity." J Gerontol A Biol Sci Med Sci Jun; 57(6) 2002. p. M347-51.
2. Crimmins, E.M., Saito, Y. "Trends in healthy life expectancy in the United States, 1970-1990: gender, racial, and educational differences." Soc Sci Med Jun; 52(11) 2001. p. 1629-41. Perenboom, R.J., et al. "Life expectancy without chronic morbidity: trends in gender and socioeconomic disparities." Public Health Rep Jan-Feb; 120(1) 2005. p. 46-54.
3. "Obesity and Disability: The Shape of Things to Come." RAND Corporation. 2006. 13 Mar 2006 ⟨http://www.rand.org/pubs/research_briefs/RB9043/index1.html⟩.

4. "Health Expectancy: Living longer, more years in poor health." U⟩K⟩ National Statistics. 2006. Jan 2006 ⟨http://www.statistics.gov.uk/CCI/nugget.asp?ID=918&Pos=2&ColRank=2&Rank=1000⟩.
5. Chan, J.M., Jou, R.M., Carroll, P.R. "The relative impact and future burden of prostate cancer in the United States." J Urol Nov; 172(5 Pt 2) 2004. p. S13-16.

The rates of all other cancers have been relatively stable except for a decrease of lung cancer in men.[1]

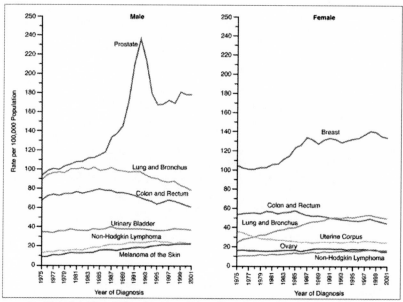

Annual Age-adjusted Cancer Incidence Rates* Among Males and Female for Selected Cancer Types, US, 1975 to 2001.
*Rates are age-adjusted to the 2000 US standard population.
Source: Surveillance, Epidemiology, and End Results (SEER) program, nine oldest registries, 1975 to 2001, Division of Cancer Control and Population Sciences, National Cancer Institute, 2004.

A total of 557,271 cancer deaths were recorded in the United States in 2002. The number of cancer deaths increased by 3,500 from 2001, predominantly because of growth and aging of the population. Deaths from cancer now rank second only to heart disease.[2] A total of 1,372,910 new cancer cases and 570,280 deaths are expected in the United States in 2005. Astonishingly, cancer has become the leading cause of death in those younger than 85 since 1999.[3]

After decades of research and billions of dollars, the combined death rate for all cancers has decreased by only 1.5% per year since 1993 among men and by 0.8% per year since 1992 among women. It is expected the total number of deaths for heart disease and cancer will increase 2.8-fold and 2.3-fold between 2000 and 2050.[4]

1. Jemal, A., Chu, K.C., Tarone, R.E. "Recent trends in lung cancer mortality in the United States." J Natl Cancer Inst Feb 21; 93(4) 2001. p. 277-83.
2. Jemal, A. et al. "Cancer Statistics, 2005." Cancer J Clin vol 55 2005. p. 10-30.
3. Twombly, R. "Cancer surpasses heart disease as leading cause of death for all but the very elderly." J Natl Cancer Inst Mar 2; 97(5) 2005. p. 330-31.
4. Sonnenschein, E., Brody, J.A. "Effect of population aging on proportionate mortality from heart disease and cancer, U.S. 2000-2050." J Gerontol B Psychol Sci Soc Sci Mar; 60(2) 2005. p. S110-12.

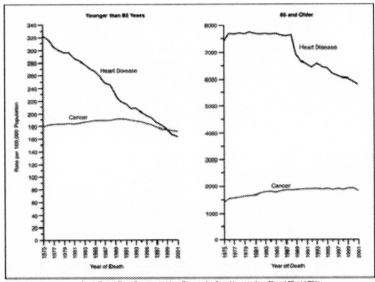

Death Rates' From Cancer and Heart Disease for Ages Younger than 85 and 85 and Older.
'Rates are age adjusted to the 2000 US standard population.
Source: US Mortality Public Use Data Tapes, 1960 to 2001, National Center for Health Statistics, Centers for Disease Control and Prevention, 2004.

Within the next 50 years the number of dementia cases is expected to rise from 7.1 million in 2000 to about 16.2 million. The annual number of new dementia cases will increase from about 1.9 million in the year 2000 to about 4.1 million by 2050.[1] Some project the prevalence will nearly quadruple in the next 50 years, with approximately 1 in 45 Americans being afflicted by this disease.[2] This burden will continue to increase[3] as the baby boomers age.[4] One researcher concluded the incidence of dementia increases ten fold from 2.8% at ages 65 to 28% at age eighty-five and older.[5] A Boston study suggests dementia will affect nearly half of those over 85 with Alzheimer's disease.[6] African Americans are expected to be particularly ravaged by these increases in dementia.[7] A 2002

1. Hebert, L.E., et al. "Alzheimer disease in the US population: prevalence estimates using the 2000 census." Arch Neurol Aug; 60(8) 2003. p. 1119-22. Wancata, J., et al. "Number of dementia sufferers in Europe between the years 2000 and 2050." Eur Psychiatry Oct; 18(6) 2003. p. 306-13.
2. Brookmeyer, R., Gray, S., Kawas, C. "Projections of Alzheimer's disease in the United States and the public health impact of delaying disease onset." Am J Public Health Sep; 88(9) 1998. p. 1337-42. Hebert, L.E., et al. "Annual incidence of Alzheimer disease in the United States projected to the years 2000 through 2050." Alzheimer Dis Assoc Disord Oct-Dec; 15(4) 2001. p. 169-73.
3. Van de Water, H.P. "Health expectancy and the problem of substitute morbidity." Philos Trans R Soc Lond B Biol Sci Dec 29; 352(1363) 1997. p. 1819-27.
4. Childers, L. "The Alzheimer's epidemic: preparing for the influx of dementia patients." Healthplan Sep-Oct; 44(5) 2003. p. 50-52. Foley, D.J., Brock, D.B., Lanska, D.J. "Trends in dementia mortality from two National Mortality Followback Surveys." Neurology Feb 25; 60(4) 2003. p. 709-11.
5. Brody, J.A. "Prospects for an Aging Society." Nature June 1985. p. 463-66.
6. Evans, D.A., et al. "Prevalence of Alzheimer's Disease in a Community Population of Older Persons." JAMA vol 262 1989. p. 2551-56.
7. Taylor, D.H. Jr., Sloan, F.A., Doraiswamy, P. "Marked increase in Alzheimer's disease identified in medicare claims records between 1991 and 1999." J Gerontol A Biol Sci Med Sci Jul; 59(7) 2004. p. 762-66.

study expects at least a threefold increase in the total number of persons with Alzheimer's disease between 2000 and 2050.[1]

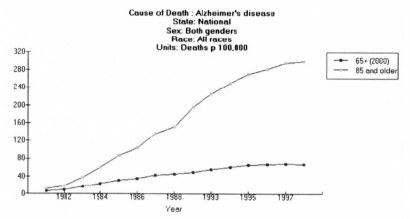

Cause of Death : Alzheimer's disease
State: National
Sex: Both genders
Race: All races
Units: Deaths p 100,000

Table: msra398[1].ivt - Death Rates by State, Sex, Race, Cause, 1981-1998 (10-Year Age Groups)
Source: SSDAN at The University of Michigan and The National Center for Health Statistics Life Expectancy and Mortality. Module #6 http://www.asaging.org/nchs/

Most people are less interested in their number of years[2] than their quality.[3] No studies have shown the onset of nonfatal, disabling diseases is occurring any later in life; therefore, increasing longevity may bring greater years of disability.[4] Studies predict men and women may live 19% and 24% of their life after age 60 in a disabled state. They may be unable to manage basic self-care activities for 10% of their lives.[5]

1. Sloane, P.D., et al. "The public health impact of Alzheimer's disease, 2000-2050: potential implication of treatment advances." Annu Rev Public Health vol 23 2002. p. 213-31.
2. Diehr, P., et al. "Survival versus years of healthy life: which is more powerful as a study outcome?" Control Clin Trials Jun; 20(3) 1999. p. 267-79.
3. Shephard, R.J., Franklin, B. "Changes in the quality of life: a major goal of cardiac rehabilitation." J Cardiopulm Rehabil Jul-Aug; 21(4) 2001. p. 189-200. Swenson, J.R., Clinch, J.J. "Assessment of quality of life in patients with cardiac disease: the role of psychosomatic medicine." J Psychosom Res Apr-May; 48(4-5) 2000. p. 405-15.
4. Cassel, C.K., Rudberg, M.A., Olshansky, S.J. "The Price of Success: Health Care in an Aging Society." Health Affairs (Millwood). 2003. 04 Nov 2003 ⟨http://content.healthaffairs.org/cgi/reprint/11/2/87⟩.
5. Jitapunkul, S., et al. "Disability-free life expectancy of elderly people in a population undergoing demographic and epidemiologic transition." Age Ageing Jul; 32(4) 2003. p. 401-05.

EPILOGUE

THE FUTURE OF HEALTH CARE IN AMERICA

We have met the enemy and he is us.
Walt Kelly, Creator of comic strip "Pogo." (1913-1973)

These dismal findings are not lost on governmental leaders. The continuing battles over the federal budget[1], Social Security[2], Medicaid/Medicare[3] spending and concerns over the safety of drugs[4] are just a portent of things to come. The medical consumer and diseases are often referred to in regards to their "market potential."[5] Pharmaceutical and biotechnology firms lobby and pressure Congress for increased funding for the drug du jour.[6] Woe to those who attempt to quash their profits.[7] A Canadian group published a paper stating pharmaceutical leaders threaten and cajole those who report findings that may affect their corporate profits. Pharmaceutical firms attempted to stop the publishing of this report.[8] Although initially unsuccessful, they finally managed to expurgate this document from nearly all sources. This report is now nearly impossible to find on the Internet. A sole link exists at Healthyscepticism.org; however, even here the report is only available in an HTML version of the

---

1. Wolf, R. "Congress bucking on budget." USA Today 16 Jun 2005.
2. "Battle Over Social Security." The Associated Press 18 Jun 2005.
3. Heckman, M. "Medicare drug plan under fire." Concord Monitor 14 Jul 2005. Schwarzen, C. "Medicare changes expected to cause confusion.." The Seattle Times 13 Jul 2005.
4. "Safety of American Drugs Is Questioned." NewsMax Wires [ ] 01 Dec 2004.
5. Francis, D.R. "Why the healthcare crisis won't go away." Christian Science Monitor 18 Jul 2005.
6. Ismail, M.A. "Drug Lobby Second to None How the pharmaceutical industry gets its way in Washington." Center for Public Integrity 17 Jul 2005.
7. Deyo, R.A., et al. "The messenger under attack: intimidation of researchers by special-interest groups." NEJM vol 336(16) 1997. p. 1176-80.
8. Skolnick, A.A. "Drug firm suit fails to halt publication of Canadian Health Technology Report." JAMA vol 280(8) 1998. p. 683-84.

original PDF file.[1] Billions are made through the sale of drugs with marginal benefit and billions more are "invested" into research to assure this cash cow never dies.[2]

Unfortunately, we may be dangerously close to milking it dry. Attempts to curtail medical spending have proven to be inadequate. State governments are now passing laws requiring pharmacists to prescribe generic drugs whenever available,[3] imported prescription drugs are further eroding pharmaceutical company profits[4] and removal of drugs from the market for safety reasons threaten to undermine the profitability of prescription medications.[5]

Tragically, most Americans remain willfully ignorant of the effects their lifestyle has on their health. They continue to demand access to the newer and least tested therapies. They fall easy prey to direct to consumer ads advising them to "check with their doctor" about a new drug to treat an invented disease. Recreational use of drugs to treat erectile dysfunction is encouraged, despite the fact these drugs should only be used for those with medical disorders. Premenopausal professional women clamoring for children are exploited by fertility specialists to promulgate research for stem cell cloning. The wealthy and elite sponsor studies for life extension in an attempt to avoid the aging process and the grave.

All the while, our children and grandchildren are being robbed of their inheritance. And what of the poor, who will speak for them? We are at a critical crossroad, do we abandon future generations for our own selfish gain or do we acknowledge we have social obligations going beyond our own self interests? The bottom line is that we are the gatekeepers to our own health and the key to wellness is moderation.

1. Barer, M.L., et al. "Tales from the Other Drug Wars." UBC Centre for Health Services and Policy Research. 2000. ⟨http://www.healthyskepticism.org/reports/chspr%2000%20barer%20drug-wars.pdf⟩.
2. "Study Shows Pharmaceutical Companies Are Price-Gouging Pennsylvania Consumers." Public Citizen. 2000. 18 Apr 2000 ⟨http://www.citizen.org/pressroom/release.cfm?ID=452⟩. Smith, J. "The U.S. must develop a new drug system." The Battalion 09 Mar 2005.
3. "Docket# 9297: In the Matter of Schering-Plough Corporation, Upsher-Smith Laboratories, and American Home Products Corporation." Federal Trade Commission. 2001. Apr 2001 ⟨http://www.ftc.gov/os/2001/04/scheringpart3cmp.pdf⟩.
4. "Would Prescription Drug Importation Reduce U.S. Drug Spending?" Congressional Budget Office. 2004. 29 Apr 2004 ⟨http://www.cbo.gov/showdoc.cfm?index=5406&sequence=0⟩. Higgins, M. "Drug makers take on imports." The Washington Times. 2005. 08 Jul 2005 ⟨http://washingtontimes.com/business/20050707-104312-2558r.htm⟩.
5. "FDA Chooses Drug Industry Health Over Public HealthGoldstein, R." Common Dreams News Center. 2005. 23 Feb 2005 ⟨http://www.commondreams.org/views05/0223-35.htm⟩. Kaufman, M. "FDA Plans New Board To Monitor Drug Safety." Washington Post 16 Feb 2005.

INDEX

Printed in the United States
74522LV00002BA/11

9 780875 864563